JUXTAPOSITIONS
Ideas for College Writers

Marlene Clark, Editor

Associate Professor
The City College Center for Worker Education
City University of New York

Cover photographs by Andrew Clark.

Printed in the United States of America

10 9 8 7 6 5 4

ISBN 0-536-96471-8

2005240172

CS/JW

Please visit our web site at *www.pearsoncustom.com*

PEARSON CUSTOM PUBLISHING
75 Arlington Street, Suite 300, Boston, MA 02116
A Pearson Education Company

CONTENTS

MORE JUXTAPOSITIONS

ACKNOWLEDGMENTS

I am deeply grateful to the colleagues and friends who helped in various ways during the composition of *Juxtapositions*:

For their invaluable support and assistance, I thank the members, past and present, of the Composition Committee at Borough of Manhattan Community College: Milton Baxter, Peter DeNegre, Joyce Harte, Nancy McClure, Ruth Misheloff, Stephanie Oppenheim, Diana Polley, Jonathan Scott, and Roger Sedarat.

For infectious enthusiasm and for generous sharing of scholarly and teaching savvy while piloting the earliest edition of *Juxtapositions,* special thanks to Danny Sexton.

For piloting early editions and offering useful and often insightful suggestions, thank you Roy Benjamin, Miriam Delgado, Lois Griffith, Louis Pogue and Roger Sedarat.

For sharing his expertise in urban literature, I thank Barney Pace and, for more of the same, as well as allowing me to include a chapter of his book, *Triple Exposure: Black, Jewish and Red in the 1950s,* thanks to Dexter Jeffries.

For their insights, I thank my teaching interns from The Graduate Center of the City University of New York: Debarati Biswas, Jessamine Buck, Louis Bury, Gary Lim, Lindsey Freer, Szidonia Haragos, Linda Mahkovec, Neil Meyer, Jaime Weida, Dan Wuebben, and Sung Hee Yook.

For the kind of friendship and generous support only the very best teacher, scholar, editor and Chair can offer, my sincere appreciation to Phil Eggers.

For the intellectual sustenance and exchange that helped to shape the thought that went into this book, I will always be grateful to the members of my long-standing reading group: Jeff Cassvan, Mikhal Dekel, William Moeck, Nickolas Pappas, and most especially, Joshua Wilner.

For the friendship and warm hospitality that sustained me during the difficult months of composition and editing in Melrose, Massachusetts, I thank Kathy Curley and Rochelle Dellacroix. For the head-clearing walks and talks, as well as crucial library assistance, special thanks to Marilyn Dean.

For the kind of deep faith found in the best and truest of friends, thank you Doris Barkin and Scott Pilarz, S.J.

And for their professional guidance in shaping this book and much, much more, a most sincere thank you to my editors: Lynn Huddon, Don Golini, Cymbeline Storey, and Delia Uherec.

Most of all, I thank my son, Andrew Clark, for everything.

READING AND WRITING WITH JUXTAPOSITIONS

jux-ta-po-si-tion: the act or an instance of placing two or more things side by side; *also*: the state of being so placed.

Juxtapositions pairs a wide variety of canonical readings in the humanities disciplines with an equally wide variety of current, diverse autobiographical essays and short stories. Essays include the disciplines of psychology, political science, women's studies, philosophy, philosophy of science, and anthropology. Autobiographical essays range from a transcript of a !Kung woman's oral narration of her weaning, to the reminiscence of an adult recalling sailing his boat in Central Park as a seven year-old in the 1950s. Short stories include standards such as Herman Melville's "Bartleby the Scrivener" and Ralph Ellison's "Battle Royal," as well as those by more current writers such as Yukio Mishima, Flannery O'Connor, Sandra Cisneros, and Toni Cade Bambara.

The three types of texts described above are clustered in groups: One disciplinary essay representing an important insight in the history of ideas is grouped with two shorter selections, one a short story, one a nonfiction essay (usually, but not always autobiographical). As such, the lead essay in each unit represents a **theory**; the following two pieces represent a social **context** for the theory. The task of the student writer is to make an argument placing the theory in each unit within a social context, thereby juxtaposing at least two texts from each cluster. These pairings of texts help student writers learn to move between the abstract and the concrete— a necessary component to successful college writing.

The main goal of this book is to help writers compose text-based critical arguments. Since there are a number of ways to structure and support a point of view on any topic, the first text in each unit demonstrates a different mode of argumentation. The note at the head of each unit tells the reader/writer about the salient feature/s of the lead essay's type of argument. In addition, a number of features designed to help student writers and readers understand both the essay's **form** and the essay's **content** follow the first essay in each unit. While the essays themselves help to expand academic horizons, the features following show students of writing the ways in which these essays express a thesis statement, sometimes explicitly and sometimes implicitly; demonstrate various approaches to structuring an essay; marshal a number of strategies in defense of an argument (e.g., extended demonstration, narrative, hypothetical situations, conventional "points"); and use specific rhetorical devices creatively and purposefully. These features include:

- **Coming to Terms with the Argument:** It is probably best for readers to acquaint themselves with unfamiliar terms *prior* to reading a theoretical essay. Therefore, a list of pertinent "technical" vocabulary words precedes each essay.
- **Thesis (and its counterargument):** Since text-based writing generally calls upon writers to have a point of view, the ability to locate the main idea of another writer's essay is a useful skill for readers *and* writers. Readers of the essays in this book will find that a thesis statement can be either explicit or implicit; can be located at the beginning, middle or even end of the argument; and can sometimes be discerned more readily by understanding the counterargument against which the writer of the essay places his or her own ideas. Student writers will see there is a variety of ways to state their own point of view.
- **Mapping the Shape of the Argument:** Outlining an argument offers a sure way to help understand even the most complexly shaped essays. In following the essay writer's train of thought, paragraph by paragraph, inconsistencies, contradictions, digressions, and the "flow" of the main idea all become more apparent. Each unit offers a step-by-step outline of the lead essay, with questions to help reading comprehension. The many different shapes of the arguments in this book also show student writers a number of ways to structure their own essays.
- **Rhetorical Moves:** Each unit highlights a particular rhetorical device used by the essay writer in the course of making his or her argument. Freud's abundantly clear analogies, Dr. King's mastery of parallelism and antithesis, Hannah Arendt's circuitous route through paradox and false premises, Darwin's rhetorical questions—all of these and more show student writers that creativity and style, as well as logic, have a place in humanities-based academic writing.

The short story and autographical essay that follow the lead essay in each cluster invite student readers and writers to approach the close reading of a piece of writing in three different ways: **summary**, the most concrete interpretation of the text; **analysis**, a "literary" reading mindful of the text's more symbolic import; and an **application** of a not always apparently related theory to the texts. While **Juxtapositions** offers several ideas in each unit for application, these suggestions represent a start rather than an end. The text encourages critical thinking; the topics available to students for their own essays are nearly limitless. The three **levels of reading** outlined in the book include:

- **Summary:** Summaries should be brief and to the point, highlighting only the most important elements of the story or essay.
- **Analysis:** When moving to analysis, readers should be more attuned to the symbolic, or what is implicit in the text. There need be no special literary "training" to discern symbols, since most are conventions built into language. Names, for instance can be highly symbolic, such as "Faith," the wife of Young Goodman Brown. Writing a brief summary offers a useful exercise in determining the **explicit**, or directly stated, in a text but much in these texts is suggested, rather than stated directly, and is therefore **implicit**. Analysis encourages student readers to dig more deeply for meaning and to pay close attention to the language of the text, both of which help to make student writing more text-based and therefore more persuasive.
- **Application:** The most challenging way of reading, this step prepares the reader for writing. Using one or more of the ideas learned in the lead essay in each cluster, student writers compose an essay making an argument that applies the theory to a social context found in the story and/or autobiographical essay. Suggestions offered for possible topics suggest only a few possibilities; creative critical thinking coupled with our diverse life experiences encourage seeing these ideas and their connection to practical, everyday life from any number of new and unique points of view.

ONE

THE FIVE-PART ESSAY

Freud's "Second Lecture" is an example of one of the most common essay forms arguing a point of view on a subject. Five-part essays generally begin with an introduction, often including or followed by a **thesis statement;** at least three points of "support" or evidence for the argument; and a conclusion.

SIGMUND FREUD

Sigmund Freud (1856–1939) is often called the "father of psychoanalysis." Born in Frieburg, Moravia (now part of the Czech Republic), to a struggling merchant and his young third wife, he excelled in school from an early age. When he was four, his parents moved to Vienna, Austria, just as work and housing restrictions against Jews lifted and new opportunities for them arose. There, his father prospered, and Sigmund was able to concentrate on study from an early age. At eighteen, he entered the University of Vienna, with the idea of taking up law, and then medicine, specifically neurology. But before long, he was immersed in a branch of "science" now known as psychology.

In 1882, he met and fell in love with his sister's German friend, Martha Bernays. Four years later, just as Freud opened his first practice devoted mainly to the treatment of female "hysterics," the couple married. They had six children, the youngest of whom became the noted child psychologist, Anna Freud. She served for many years as her father's student, secretary, scribe, and finally, voice, especially after palate cancer, diagnosed and surgically removed in April 1923, left Freud able to speak only with painful difficulty.

A scientist, and an avowed atheist, Freud believed his fame and assimilation within Viennese culture and society would protect him from the rampant persecution of Jews in Vienna after the Nazis invaded Austria in March 1938. He was, unfortunately, wrong. Only weeks after the Nazis invaded, Freud's beloved

beloved daughter Anna was summoned to Gestapo headquarters, generally a first step in the process of the deportation of Jews for "resettlement" to labor or death camps. Alarmed, Freud at last accepted the financial and political help of many in the psychoanalytic community—both practitioners and famous former patients—who had offered to protect and shelter his family should he need to leave Vienna. On June 6, 1938, Freud, preceded by his family, arrived in London after months of tense and costly "negotiations" with the Nazis. Old, sick, and disillusioned, he continued to work for more than a year, but on September 29, 1939, he asked his physician to give him a lethal dose of morphine.

The "Second Lecture" is one of five lectures given by Freud on his only trip to the United States, in 1909, barely nine years after the publication of his second important book, *The Interpretation of Dreams.* G. Stanley Hall, a psychologist and president of Clark University in Worcester, Massachusetts, invited Freud and several other founders of the European psychoanalytic movement to celebrate the twenty-year anniversary of the university by giving lectures and receiving honorary degrees. Given extempore, these five lectures were written down later, when Freud returned home to Vienna. Since many in the audience were initiates, the lectures in this volume, *Five Lectures on Psychoanalysis,* are written the same way they were spoken—in relatively simple, nontechnical language, with sufficient examples to round out the more theoretical material. In fact, several of the other honorees present, when reviewing the later written versions, remarked that Freud's incredible memory served him well once again: the written form of the lectures is virtually the same as the verbal.

The "Second Lecture" concerns Freud's work with his first patients, mainly females suffering from what was then known as "hysteria." A much-abbreviated summary of his first book, coauthored with J. Breuer, *Studies on Hysteria,* the "Second Lecture" introduces the audience to early psychoanalytic practice. But Freud's clinical experience with hysteria is only one aspect of this lecture, since his work with these patients led to other innovative and important insights into the working of the human mind. In this lecture then, we find the kernel of Freud's theory, subject to constant revision over the next thirty years, of the tripartite structure of the human mind. According to Freud, the ego, the id, and the superego work together—not always in perfect harmony—to form personality. Illness results when these three interdependent parts of the mind fail to integrate or conflict with one another. With this insight, Freud begins the debate with his predecessors regarding both the origin and nature of hysteria.

When reading and thinking about this lecture, in addition to marveling at the novelty of the content, notice also the tight form of the essay, the clear examples and analogies offered, and the relaxed writing style, all still worth emulating in expository prose. In terms of structure, Freud's essay bears more than a passing resemblance to the traditional "five-part essay," though the "points" he makes in the body of his essay to defend his argument are far from discrete. Important also is Freud's alternation between very abstract psychological theory, and accessible, concrete examples or humorous analogies, which help to make his revolutionary, but difficult, ideas understandable even to those unacquainted with his theory.

Coming to Terms with the Reading:

Before reading/rereading Freud's "Second Lecture," it is best to have a firm grasp of the meaning of the following terms:

1. ego
2. id
3. super-ego
4. pathogenic
5. hysteria
6. psychical
7. resistance
8. repression
9. cathartic
10. symptom
11. neurosis
12. sublimation

SECOND LECTURE
Sigmund Freud

1   Ladies and Gentlemen,—At about the same time at which Breuer was carrying on the 'talking cure' with his patient, the great Charcot in Paris had begun the researches into hysterical patients at the Salpêtrière which were to lead to a new understanding of the disease. There was no possibility of his findings being known in Vienna at that time. But when, some ten years later, Breuer and I published our 'Preliminary Communication' on the psychical mechanism of hysterical phenomena [1893*a*], we were completely under the spell of Charcot's researches. We regarded the pathogenic experiences of our patients as psychical traumas, and equated them with the somatic traumas whose influence on hysterical paralyses had been established by Charcot; and Breuer's hypothesis of hypnoid states was itself nothing but a reflection of the fact that Charcot had reproduced those traumatic paralyses artificially under hypnosis.

The great French observer, whose pupil I became in 1885–6, was not himself inclined to adopt a psychological outlook. It was his pupil, Pierre Janet, who first attempted a deeper approach to the peculiar psychical processes present in hysteria, and we followed his example when we took the splitting of the mind and dissociation of the personality as the centre of our position. You will find in Janet a theory of hysteria which takes into account the prevailing views in France on the part played by heredity and degeneracy. According to him, hysteria is a form of degenerate modification of the nervous system, which shows itself in an innate weakness in the power of psychical synthesis. Hysterical patients, he believes, are inherently incapable of holding together the multiplicity of mental processes into a unity, and hence arises the tendency to mental dissociation. If I may be allowed to draw a homely but clear analogy, Janet's hysterical patient reminds one of a feeble woman who has gone out shopping and is now returning home laden with a multitude of parcels and boxes. She cannot contain the whole heap of them with her two arms and ten fingers. So first of all one object slips from her grasp; and when she stoops to pick it up, another one escapes her in its place, and so on. This supposed mental weakness of hysterical patients is

Reprinted from *Five Lectures on Psychoanalysis,* translated by James Strachey, (1961), by permission of W.W. Norton & Company, Inc. Copyright © 1961 by James Strachey.

not confirmed when we find that, alongside these phenomena of diminished capacity, examples are also to be observed of a partial increase in efficiency, as though by way of compensation. At the time when Breuer's patient had forgotten her mother tongue and every other language but English, her grasp of English reached such heights that, if she was handed a German book, she was able straight away to read out a correct and fluent translation of it.

When, later on, I set about continuing on my own account the investigations that had been begun by Breuer, I soon arrived at another view of the origin of hysterical dissociation (the splitting of consciousness). A divergence of this kind, which was to be decisive for everything that followed, was inevitable, since I did not start out, like Janet, from laboratory experiments, but with therapeutic aims in mind.

I was driven forward above all by practical necessity. The cathartic procedure, as carried out by Breuer, presupposed putting the patient into a state of deep hypnosis; for it was only in a state of hypnosis that he attained a knowledge of the pathogenic connections which escaped him in his normal state. But I soon came to dislike hypnosis, for it was a temperamental and, one might almost say, a mystical ally. When I found that, in spite of all my efforts, I could not succeed in bringing more than a fraction of my patients into a hypnotic state, I determined to give up hypnosis and to make the cathartic procedure independent of it. Since I was not able at will to alter the mental state of the majority of my patients, I set about working with them in their *normal* state. At first, I must confess, this seemed a senseless and hopeless undertaking. I was set the task of learning from the patient something that I did not know and that he did not know himself. How could one hope to elicit it? But there came to my help a recollection of a most remarkable and instructive experiment which I had witnessed when I was with Bernheim at Nancy [in 1889]. Bernheim showed us that people whom he had put into a state of hypnotic somnambulism, and who had had all kinds of experiences while they were in that state, only *appeared* to have lost the memory of what they had experienced during somnambulism; it was possible to revive these memories in their normal state. It is true that, when he questioned them about their somnambulistic experiences, they began by maintaining that they knew nothing about them; but if he refused to give way, and insisted, and assured them that they *did* know about them, the forgotten experiences always reappeared.

5   So I did the same thing with my patients. When I reached a point with them at which they maintained that they knew nothing more, I assured them that they *did* know it all the same, and that they had only to say it; and I ventured to declare that the right memory would occur to them at the moment at which I laid my

hand on their forehead. In that way I succeeded, without using hypnosis, in obtaining from the patients whatever was required for establishing the connection between the pathogenic scenes they had forgotten and the symptoms left over from those scenes. But it was a laborious procedure, and in the long run an exhausting one; and it was unsuited to serve as a permanent technique.

I did not abandon it, however, before the observations I made during my use of it afforded me decisive evidence. I found confirmation of the fact that the forgotten memories were not lost. They were in the patient's possession and were ready to emerge in association to what was still known by him; but there was some force that prevented them from becoming conscious and compelled them to remain unconscious. The existence of this force could be assumed with certainty, since one became aware of an effort corresponding to it if, in opposition to it, one tried to introduce the unconscious memories into the patient's consciousness. The force which was maintaining the pathological condition became apparent in the form of *resistance* on the part of the patient.

It was on this idea of resistance, then, that I based my view of the course of psychical events in hysteria. In order to effect a recovery, it had proved necessary to remove these resistances. Starting out from the mechanism of cure, it now became possible to construct quite definite ideas of the origin of the illness. The same forces which, in the form of resistance, were now offering opposition to the forgotten material's being made conscious, must formerly have brought about the forgetting and must have pushed the pathogenic experiences in question out of consciousness. I gave the name of *'repression'* to this hypothetical process, and I considered that it was proved by the undeniable existence of resistance.

The further question could then be raised as to what these forces were and what the determinants were of the repression in which we now recognized the pathogenic mechanism of hysteria. A comparative study of the pathogenic situations which we had come to know through the cathartic procedure made it possible to answer this question. All these experiences had involved the emergence of a wishful impulse which was in sharp contrast to the subject's other wishes and which proved incompatible with the ethical and aesthetic standards of his personality. There had been a short conflict, and the end of this internal struggle was that the idea which had appeared before consciousness as the vehicle of this irreconcilable wish fell a victim to repression, was pushed out of consciousness with all its attached memories, and was forgotten. Thus the incompatibility of the wish in question with the patient's ego was the motive for the repression; the subject's ethical and other standards were the repressing forces. An acceptance of the incompatible wishful impulse or a prolongation of the conflict would have produced a high degree of unpleasure; this unpleasure was avoided by means of repression, which was thus revealed as one of the devices serving to protect the mental personality.

To take the place of a number of instances, I will relate a single one of my cases, in which the determinants and advantages of repression are sufficiently evident. For my present purpose I shall have once again to abridge the case history and omit some important underlying material. The patient was a girl, who had lost her beloved father after she had taken a share in nursing him—a situation analogous to that of Breuer's patient. Soon afterwards her elder sister married, and her new brother-in-law aroused in her a peculiar feeling of sympathy which was easily masked under a disguise of family affection. Not long afterwards her sister fell ill and died, in the absence of the patient and her mother. They were summoned in all haste without being given any definite information of the tragic event. When the girl reached the bedside of her dead sister, there came to her for a brief moment an idea that might be expressed in these words: 'Now he is free and can marry me.' We may assume with certainty that this idea, which betrayed to her consciousness the intense love for her brother-in-law of which she had not herself been conscious, was surrendered to repression a moment later, owing to the revolt of her feelings. The girl fell ill with severe hysterical symptoms; and while she was under my treatment it turned out that she had completely forgotten the scene by her sister's bedside and the odious egoistic impulse that had emerged in her. She remembered it during the treatment and reproduced the pathogenic moment with signs of the most violent emotion, and, as a result of the treatment, she became healthy once more.

10   Perhaps I may give you a more vivid picture of repression and of its necessary relation to resistance, by a rough analogy derived from our actual situation at the present moment. Let us suppose that in this lecture-room and among this audience, whose exemplary quiet and attentiveness I cannot sufficiently commend, there is nevertheless someone who is causing a disturbance and whose ill-mannered laughter, chattering and shuffling with his feet are distracting my attention from my task. I have to announce that I cannot proceed with my lecture; and thereupon three or four of you who are strong men stand up and, after a short struggle, put the interrupter outside the door. So now he is 'repressed,' and I can continue my lecture. But in order that the interruption shall not be repeated, in case the individual who has been expelled should try to enter the room once more, the gentlemen who have put my will into effect place their chairs up against the door and thus establish a 'resistance' after the repression has

been accomplished. If you will now translate the two localities concerned into psychical terms as the 'conscious' and the 'unconscious,' you will have before you a fairly good picture of the process of repression.

You will now see in what it is that the difference lies between our view and Janet's. We do not derive the psychical splitting from an innate incapacity for synthesis on the part of the mental apparatus; we explain it dynamically, from the conflict of opposing mental forces and recognize it as the outcome of an active struggling on the part of the two psychical groupings against each other. But our view gives rise to a large number of fresh problems. Situations of mental conflict are, of course, exceedingly common; efforts by the ego to ward off painful memories are quite regularly to be observed without their producing the result of a mental split. The reflection cannot be escaped that further determinants must be present if the conflict is to lead to dissociation. I will also readily grant you that the hypothesis of repression leaves us not at the end but at the beginning of a psychological theory. We can only go forward step by step however, and complete knowledge must await the results of further and deeper researches.

Nor is it advisable to attempt to explain the case of Breuer's patient from the point of view of repression. That case history is not suited to this purpose, because its findings were reached with the help of hypnotic influence. It is only if you exclude hypnosis that you can observe resistances and repressions and form an adequate idea of the truly pathogenic course of events. Hypnosis conceals the resistance and renders a certain area of the mind accessible; but, as against this, it builds up the resistance at the frontiers of this area into a wall that makes everything beyond it inaccessible.

Our most valuable lesson from Breuer's observation was what it proved concerning the relation between symptoms and pathogenic experiences or psychical traumas, and we must not omit now to consider these discoveries from the standpoint of the theory of repression. At first sight it really seems impossible to trace a path from repression to the formation of symptoms. Instead of giving a complicated theoretical account, I will return here to the analogy which I employed earlier for my explanation of repression. If you come to think of it, the removal of the interrupter and the posting of the guardians at the door may not mean the end of the story. It may very well be that the individual who has been expelled, and who has now become embittered and reckless, will cause us further trouble. It is true that he is no longer among us; we are free from his presence, from his insulting laughter and his *sotto voce* comments. But in some respects, nevertheless, the repression has been unsuccessful; for now he is making an intolerable exhibition of himself outside the room, and his shouting and banging on the door with his fists interfere with my lecture even more than his bad behaviour did before. In these circumstances we could not fail to be delighted if our respected president, Dr. Stanley Hall, should be willing to assume the role of mediator and peacemaker. He would have a talk with the unruly person outside and would then come to us with a request that he should be re-admitted after all: he himself would guarantee that the man would now behave better. On Dr. Hall's authority we decide to lift the repression, and peace and quiet are restored. This presents what is really no bad picture of the physician's task in the psychoanalytic treatment of the neuroses.

To put the matter more directly. The investigation of hysterical patients and of other neurotics leads us to the conclusion that their repression of the idea to which the intolerable wish is attached has been a *failure*. It is true that they have driven it out of consciousness and out of memory and have apparently saved themselves a large amount of unpleasure. *But the repressed wishful impulse continues to exist in the unconscious.* It is on the look-out for an opportunity of being activated, and when that happens it succeeds in sending into consciousness a disguised and unrecognizable *substitute* for what had been repressed, and to this there soon become attached the same feelings of unpleasure which it was hoped had been saved by the repression. This substitute for the repressed idea—the *symptom*—is proof against further attacks from the defensive ego; and in place of the short conflict an ailment now appears which is not brought to an end by the passage of time. Alongside the indication of distortion in the symptom, we can trace in it the remains of some kind of indirect resemblance to the idea that was originally repressed. The paths along which the substitution was effected can be traced in the course of the patient's psycho-analytic treatment; and in order to bring about recovery, the symptom must be led back along the same paths and once more turned into the repressed idea. If what was repressed is brought back again into conscious mental activity—a process which presupposes the overcoming of considerable resistances—the resulting psychical conflict, which the patient had tried to avoid, can, under the physician's guidance, reach a better outcome than was offered by repression. There are a number of such opportune solutions, which may bring the conflict and the neurosis to a happy end, and which may in certain instances be combined. The patient's personality may be convinced that it has been wrong in rejecting the pathogenic wish and may be led into accepting it wholly or in part; or the wish itself may be directed to a higher and consequently unobjectionable aim (this is what we call its 'sublimation'); or the rejection of the wish may be recognized as a justifiable one, but the automatic and therefore inefficient mechanism of repression may be replaced by a condemning judgement with the help of the highest human mental functions—conscious control of the wish is attained.

15   You must forgive me if I have not succeeded in giving you a more clearly intelligible account of these basic positions adopted by the method of treatment that is now described as 'psycho-analysis.' The difficulties have not lain only in the novelty of the subject. The nature of the incompatible wishes which, in spite of repression, succeed in making their existence in the unconscious perceptible, and the subjective and constitutional determinants which must be present in anyone before a failure of repression can occur and a substitute or symptom be formed—on all this I shall have more light to throw in some of my later observations.

READING/WRITING ASSISTS

Thesis (and its counterargument):

Readers often expect to find a clear statement of the writer's argument in a **thesis statement**, usually found in a sentence or two at the end of the first, or at the latest, second paragraph of an argumentative essay. Although Freud's argument is so subtle it is nearly invisible, his "Second Lecture" is based upon a thesis.

Read the first two paragraphs carefully and see if you can find a clearly stated thesis statement. Is it possible to underline one thesis sentence in the first two paragraphs? If not, read over the paragraphs again and, synthesizing the information given by Freud, write a clear, brief sentence encapsulating his argument. It may be easier to identify Freud's argument by working "backwards." What point of view is Freud here arguing *against*? This opposing point of view is called a **counterargument**. Who makes the counterargument? Stating Freud's point of view in opposition to his teachers' helps to identify his thesis in this essay. Note that in some essays, it is necessary to process the information given early in an essay to arrive at a clear restatement of the argument of the writer.

The Shape of the Argument:

"Mapping" the structure of an argument can help us better understand the argument itself, while also showing us new models for shaping our own arguments in essay form. In a sense, Freud's lecture could be characterized as a fairly typical "five-part essay," with additional material as background and examples. To better understand this pared-down version of the argument, it is best to start by outlining the entire essay, paragraph by paragraph:

Paragraphs 1 and 2:	Introduction and **thesis** statement, balanced by a **counterargument.**
Paragraph 3:	Background/history. Leads Freud to the most important question of his essay, which forms the basis of his entire argument. What is this important question?
Paragraph 4:	**Hypnosis:** What is hypnosis? Why does the analyst hypnotize patients?
Paragraph 5:	Does Freud need hypnosis? What does he do instead?
Paragraph 6:	**Resistance:** What is resistance?
Paragraph 7:	**Repression:** What is repression? Are resistance and repression the same thing?
Paragraph 8:	How does repression work?
Paragraph 9:	**Example:** Paraphrase Freud's example. Does his example help to explain his concepts? How so?
Paragraph 10:	**Analogy:** Does Freud's analogy help you understand his theory? Explain.
Paragraph 11:	**Return to thesis/antithesis:** Now that Freud has covered most of the important points in his argument, but before making his strongest point in his own favor, he repeats his own argument (**thesis**) and reminds the reader of the argument of his opponent, Janet (**antithesis**).
Paragraph 12:	Freud sums up what he has learned about the relationship between resistance, repression, and hypnosis. What did he learn through his inability to hypnotize patients?
Paragraph 13:	Asks the most important question of his essay. What is this question? Notice that Freud offers a continuation of his **analogy** by way of an answer. Also notice the connection between paragraphs 6, 7, and 8 and this one. How does this paragraph help to further explain and clarify the terms introduced in paragraphs 6, 7, and 8?
Paragraph 14:	Freud offers "three solutions." With the help of the following diagram, explain both the "failure of repression" and the "cure."

The "failure of repression":

      1. _____

      2. _____

The "cure":

      1. _____

      2. _____

The "three solutions":

      1. _____

      2. _____

      3. _____

Paragraph 15:   Conclusion

Now that you have "the big picture," reduce the lecture to its "five parts," assigning paragraph numbers to the categories below:

1. Introduction, counterargument, thesis
2. Body
3. Body
4. Body
5. Conclusion

What three main points would you place in the "body" of the essay?

RHETORIC MOVES:

Anal-o-gy \ e-'nal-e-je** *n, pl* **—*gies* (15c) **1**: inference that if two or more things agree with one another in some respects they will probably agree in others **2 a**: resemblance in some particulars between things otherwise unalike: SIMILARITY **b**: comparison based on such resemblance

Note the way Freud's essay moves between the abstract and the concrete. Just when Freud's theory seems to defeat or overwhelm us, he offers a **concrete example** or an **analogy**. In the long outline above, mark those paragraphs that seem mostly abstraction with an **A**, and those with a concrete example or an analogy with a **C**. Note the effect on the structure of the argument.

Freud writes some memorable analogies. Try including some analogies in lieu of examples in your own essays.

NATHANIEL HAWTHORNE

Nathaniel Hawthorne (1804–1864) spent most of his life in Massachusetts. The descendant of Puritan immigrants to the "New World," Hawthorne immersed himself in colonial American history, rather than the issues of his own time, specifically the Civil War. Drawn to themes treating the alienation of humans from one another, hypocrisy, and guilt, Hawthorne wrote most of his oeuvre early in life. Hawthorne's family, however, internalized the Puritan work ethic, even if they lived 150 years after the Puritan founding of New England, and his attempts with writing were not looked upon as serious "work" to support a family.

Later, Nathaniel Hawthorne worked both in the Boston Custom House and as an ambassador to England in the administration of President Benjamin Pierce (Pierce was a good friend). Though early freedom from responsibility and a measure of isolation gave him plenty of time for literary output early on, later work responsibilities interfered with Hawthorne's literary career, and his publications became more sporadic. Nevertheless, he died with a considerable reputation as a writer, having published short stories, children's books, and novels, including what is probably his best-known work, The Scarlet Letter.

YOUNG GOODMAN BROWN
Nathaniel Hawthorne

1   Young Goodman Brown came forth at sunset into the street of Salem village; but put his head back, after crossing the threshold, to exchange a parting kiss with his young wife. And Faith, as the wife was aptly named, thrust her own pretty head into the street, letting the wind play with the pink ribbons of her cap while she called to Goodman Brown.

"Dearest heart," whispered she, softly and rather sadly, when her lips were close to his ear, "prithee put off your journey until sunrise and sleep in your own bed to-night. A lone woman is troubled with such dreams and such thoughts that she's afeard of herself sometimes. Pray tarry with me this night, dear husband, of all nights in the year."

"My love and my Faith," replied young Goodman Brown, "of all nights in the year, this one night must I tarry away from thee. My journey, as thou callest it, forth and back again, must needs be done 'twixt now and sunrise. What, my sweet, pretty wife, dost thou doubt me already, and we but three months married?"

"Then God bless you!" said Faith, with the pink ribbons; "and may you find all well when you come back."

5   "Amen!" cried Goodman Brown. "Say thy prayers, dear Faith, and go to bed at dusk, and no harm will come to thee."

So they parted; and the young man pursued his way until, being about to turn the corner by the meeting house, he looked back and saw the head of Faith still peeping after him with a melancholy air, in spite of her pink ribbons.

"Poor little Faith!" though he, for his heart smote him. "What a wretch am I to leave her on such an errand! She talks of dreams, too. Methought as she spoke there was trouble in her face, as if a dream had warned her what work is to be done to-night. But no, no; 'twould kill her to think it. Well, she's a blessed angel on earth; and after this one night I'll cling to her skirts and follow her to heaven."

With this excellent resolve for the future, Goodman Brown felt himself justified in making more haste on his present evil purpose. He had taken a dreary road, darkened by all the gloomiest trees of the forest, which barely stood aside to let the narrow path creep through, and closed immediately behind. It was all as lonely as could be; and there is this peculiarity in such a solitude, that the traveller knows not who may be concealed by the innumerable trunks and the thick boughs overhead; so that with lonely footsteps he may yet be passing through an unseen multitude.

"There may be a devilish Indian behind every tree," said Goodman Brown to himself; and he glanced fearfully behind him as he added, "What if the devil himself should be at my very elbow!"

10   His head being turned back, he passed a crook of the road, and, looking forward again, beheld the figure of a man, in grave and decent attire, seated at the foot of an old tree. He arose at Goodman Brown's approach and walked onward side by side with him.

"You are late, Goodman Brown," said he. "The clock of the Old South was striking as I came through Boston; and that is full fifteen minutes agone."

"Faith kept me back a while," replied the young man, with a tremor in his voice, caused by the sudden appearance of his companion, though not wholly unexpected.

It was now deep dusk in the forest, and deepest in that part of it where these two were journeying. As nearly as could be discerned, the second traveller was about fifty years old, apparently in the same rank of life as Goodman Brown, and bearing a considerable resemblance to him, though perhaps more in expression than features. Still they might have been taken for father and son. And yet, though the elder person was as simply clad as the younger and as simple in manner too, he had an indescribable air of one who knew the world, and who would not have felt abashed at the governor's dinner table or in King William's court, were it possible that his affairs should call him thither. But the only thing about him that could be fixed upon as remarkable was his staff, which bore the likeness of a great black snake, so curiously wrought that it might almost be seen to twist and wriggle itself like a living serpent. This, of course, must have been an ocular deception, assisted by the uncertain light.

"Come, Goodman Brown," cried his fellow-traveller, "this is a dull pace for the beginning of a journey. Take my staff, if you are so soon weary."

15   "Friend," said the other, exchanging his slow pace for a full stop, "having kept covenant by meeting thee here, it is my purpose now to return whence I came. I have scruples touching the matter thou wot'st of."

"Sayest thou so?" replied he of the serpent, smiling apart. "Let us walk on, nevertheless, reasoning as we go; and if I convince thee not thou shalt turn back. We are but a little way in the forest yet."

"Too far! too far!" exclaimed the goodman, unconsciously resuming his walk. "My father never went into the woods on such an errand, nor his father before

him. We have been a race of honest men and good Christians since the days of
the martyrs; and shall I be the first of the name of Brown that ever took this
path and kept—"

"Such company, thou wouldst say," observed the elder person, interpreting
his pause. "Well said, Goodman Brown! I have been as well acquainted with
your family as with ever a one among the Puritans; and that's no trifle to say. I
helped your grandfather, the constable, when he lashed the Quaker woman so
smartly through the streets of Salem; and it was I that brought your father a
pitch-pine knot, kindled at my own hearth, to set fire to an Indian village, in King
Philip's war. They were my good friends, both; and many a pleasant walk have
we had along this path, and returned merrily after midnight. I would fain be
friends with you for their sake."

"If it be as thou sayest," replied Goodman Brown, "I marvel they never spoke
of these matters; or, verily, I marvel not, seeing that the least rumor of the sort
would have driven them from New England. We are a people of prayer, and
good works to boot, and abide no such wickedness."

20   "Wickedness or not," said the traveller with the twisted staff, "I have a very
general acquaintance here in New England. The deacons of many a church have
drunk the communion wine with me; the selectmen of divers towns make me
their chairman; and a majority of the Great and General Court are firm sup-
porters of my interest. The governor and I, too—But these are state secrets."

"Can this be so?" cried Goodman Brown, with a stare of amazement at his
undisturbed companion. "Howbeit, I have nothing to do with the governor and
council; they have their own ways, and are no rule for a simple husbandman
like me. But, were I to go on with thee, how should I meet the eye of that good
old man, our minister, at Salem village? O, his voice would make me tremble both
Sabbath day and lecture day."

Thus far the elder traveller had listened with due gravity; but now burst into
a fit of irrepressible mirth, shaking himself so violently that his snakelike staff
actually seemed to wriggle in sympathy.

"Ha! ha! ha!" shouted he again and again; then composing himself. "Well, go
on, Goodman Brown, go on; but, prithee, don't kill me with laughing."

"Well, then, to end the matter at once," said Goodman Brown, considerably
nettled, "there is my wife, Faith. It would break her dear little heart; and I'd
rather break my own."

25   "Nay, if that be the case," answered the other, "e'en go thy ways, Goodman
Brown. I would not for twenty old women like the one hobbling before us that
Faith should come to any harm."

As he spoke, he pointed his staff at a female figure on the path, in whom Goodman Brown recognized a very pious and exemplary dame, who had taught him his catechism in youth, and was still his moral and spiritual adviser, jointly with the minister and Deacon Gookin.

"A marvel, truly, that Goody Cloyse should be so far in the wilderness at nightfall," said he. "But, with your leave, friend, I shall take a cut through the woods until we have left this Christian woman behind. Being a stranger to you, she might ask whom I was consorting with and whither I was going."

"Be it so," said his fellow-traveller. "Betake you to the woods, and let me keep the path."

Accordingly the young man turned aside, but took care to watch his companion, who advanced softly along the road until he had come within a staff's length of the old dame. She, meanwhile, was making the best of her way, with singular speed for so aged a woman, and mumbling some indistinct words—a prayer, doubtless—as she went. The traveller put forth his staff and touched her withered neck with what seemed the serpent's tail.

30   "The devil!" screamed the pious old lady.

"Then Goody Cloyse knows her old friend?" observed the traveller, confronting her and leaning on his writhing stick.

"Ah, forsooth, and is it your worship indeed?" cried the good dame. "Yea, truly is it, and in the very image of my old gossip, Goodman Brown, the grandfather of the silly fellow that now is. But—would your worship believe it?—my broomstick hath strangely disappeared, stolen, as I suspect, by that unhanged witch, Goody Cory, and that, too, when I was all anointed with the juice of smallage, and cinquefoil, and wolf's bane—"

"Mingled with fine wheat and the fat of a new-born babe," said the shape of old Goodman Brown.

"Ah, your worship knows the recipe," cried the old lady, cackling aloud. "So, as I was saying, being all ready for the meeting, and no horse to ride on, I made up my mind to foot it; for they tell me there is a nice young man to be taken into communion to-night. But now your good worship will lend me your arm, and we shall be there in a twinkling."

35   "That can hardly be," answered her friend. "I may not spare you my arm, Goody Cloyse; but here is my staff, if you will."

So saying, he threw it down at her feet, where, perhaps, it assumed life, being one of the rods which its owner had formerly lent to the Egyptian magi. Of this fact, however, Goodman Brown could not take cognizance. He had cast up his eyes in astonishment, and, looking down again, beheld neither Goody Cloyse nor the serpentine staff, but his fellow-traveller alone, who waited for him as calmly as if nothing had happened.

"That old woman taught me my catechism," said the young man; and there was a world of meaning in this simple comment.

They continued to walk onward, while the elder traveller exhorted his companion to make good speed and persevere in the path, discoursing so aptly that his arguments seemed rather to spring up in the bosom of his auditor than to be suggested by himself. As they went, he plucked a branch of maple to serve for a walking stick, and began to strip it of the twigs and little boughs, which were wet with evening dew. The moment his fingers touched them they became strangely withered and dried up as with a week's sunshine. Thus the pair proceeded, at a good free pace, until suddenly, in a gloomy hollow of the road, Goodman Brown sat himself down on the stump of a tree and refused to go any farther.

"Friend," said he, stubbornly, "my mind is made up. Not another step will I budge on this errand. What if a wretched old woman do choose to go the devil when I thought she was going to heaven: is that any reason why I should quit my dear Faith and go after her?"

40   "You will think better of this by and by," said his acquaintance, composedly. "Sit here and rest yourself a while; and when you feel like moving again, there is my staff to help you along."

Without more words, he threw his companion the maple stick, and was as speedily out of sight as if he had vanished into the deepening gloom. The young man sat a few moments by the roadside, applauding himself greatly, and thinking with how clear a conscience he should meet the minister in his morning walk, nor shrink from the eye of good old Deacon Gookin. And what calm sleep would be his that very night, which was to have been spent so wickedly, but so purely and sweetly now, in the arms of Faith! Amidst these pleasant and praiseworthy meditations, Goodman Brown heard the tramp of horses along the road, and deemed it advisable to conceal himself within the verge of the forest, conscious of the guilty purpose that had brought him thither, though now so happily turned from it.

On came the hoof tramps and the voices of the riders, two grave old voices, conversing soberly as they drew near. These mingled sounds appeared to pass along the road, within a few yards of the young man's hiding-place; but, owing doubtless to the depth of the gloom at that particular spot, neither the travellers nor their steeds were visible. Though their figures brushed the small boughs by the wayside, it could not be seen that they intercepted, even for a moment, the faint gleam from the strip of bright sky athwart which they must have passed.

Goodman Brown alternately crouched and stood on tiptoe, pulling aside the branches and thrusting forth his head as far as he durst without discerning so much as a shadow. It vexed him the more, because he could have sworn, were such a thing possible, that he recognized the voices of the minister and Deacon Gookin, jogging along quietly, as they were wont to do, when bound to some ordination or ecclesiastical council. While yet within hearing, one of the riders stopped to pluck a switch.

"Of the two, reverend sir," said the voice like the deacon's, "I had rather miss an ordination dinner than to-night's meeting. They tell me that some of our community are to be here from Falmouth and beyond, and others from Connecticut and Rhode Island, besides several of the Indian powwows, who, after their fashion, know almost as much deviltry as the best of us. Moreover, there is a goodly young woman to be taken into communion."

"Mighty well, Deacon Gookin!" replied the solemn old tones of the minister. "Spur up, or we shall be late. Nothing can be done, you know, until I get on the ground."

45   The hoofs clattered again; and the voices, talking so strangely in the empty air, passed on through the forest, where no church had ever been gathered or solitary Christian prayed. Whither, then, could these holy men be journeying so deep into the heathen wilderness? Young Goodman Brown caught hold of a tree for support, being ready to sink down on the ground, faint and overburdened with the heavy sickness of his heart. He looked up to the sky, doubting whether there really was a heaven above him. Yet there was the blue arch, and the stars brightening in it.

"With heaven above and Faith below, I will yet stand firm against the devil!" cried Goodman Brown.

While he still gazed upward into the deep arch of the firmament and had lifted his hands to pray, a cloud, though no wind was stirring, hurried across the zenith and hid the brightening stars. The blue sky was still visible except directly overhead, where this black mass of cloud was sweeping swiftly northward. Aloft in the air, as if from the depths of the cloud, came a confused and doubtful sound of voices. Once the listener fancied that he could distinguish the accents of townspeople of his own, men and women, both pious and ungodly, many of whom he had met at the communion table, and had seen others rioting at the tavern. The next moment, so indistinct were the sounds, he doubted whether he had heard aught but the murmur of the old forest, whispering without a wind. Then came a stronger swell of those familiar tones, heard daily in the sunshine at Salem village, but never until now from a cloud of night. There was one voice, of a young woman, uttering lamentations, yet with an uncertain sorrow, and entreating for some favor, which, perhaps, it would grieve her to obtain; and all the unseen multitude, both saints and sinners, seemed to encourage her onward.

"Faith!" shouted Goodman Brown, in a voice of agony and desperation; and the echoes of the forest mocked him, crying, "Faith! Faith!" as if bewildered wretches were seeking her all through the wilderness.

The cry of grief, rage, and terror was yet piercing the night, when the unhappy husband held his breath for a response. There was a scream, drowned immediately in a louder murmur of voices, fading into far-off laughter, as the dark cloud swept away, leaving the clear and silent sky above Goodman Brown. But something fluttered lightly down through the air and caught on the branch of a tree. The young man seized it, and beheld a pink ribbon.

50   "My Faith is gone!" cried he, after one stupefied moment. "There is no good on earth; and sin is but a name. Come, devil; for to thee is this world given."

And, maddened with despair, so that he laughed loud and long, did Goodman Brown grasp his staff and set forth again, at such a rate that he seemed to fly along the forest path rather than to walk or run. The road grew wilder and drearier and more faintly traced, and vanished at length, leaving him in the heart of the dark wilderness, still rushing onward with the instinct that guides mortal man to evil. The whole forest was peopled with frightful sounds—the creaking of the trees, the howling of wild beasts, and the yell of Indians; while sometimes the wind tolled like a distant church bell, and sometimes gave a broad roar around the traveller, as if all Nature were laughing him to scorn. But he was himself the chief horror of the scene, and shrank not from its other horrors.

"Ha! ha! ha!" roared Goodman Brown when the wind laughed at him. "Let us hear which will laugh loudest. Think not to frighten me with your deviltry. Come witch, come wizard, come Indian powwow, come devil himself, and here comes Goodman Brown. You may as well fear him as he fear you."

In truth, all through the haunted forest there could be nothing more frightful than the figure of Goodman Brown. On he flew among the black pines, brandishing his staff with frenzied gestures, now giving vent to an inspiration of horrid blasphemy, and now shouting forth such laughter as set all the echoes of the forest laughing like demons around him. The fiend in his own shape is less hideous than when he rages in the breast of man. Thus sped the demoniac on his course, until, quivering among the trees, he saw a red light before him, as when the felled trunks and branches of a clearing have been set on fire, and throw up their lurid blaze against the sky, at the hour of midnight. He paused, in a lull of the tempest that had driven him onward, and heard the swell of what seemed a hymn, rolling solemnly from a distance with the weight of many voices. He knew the tune; it was a familiar one in the choir of the village meeting house. The verse died heavily away, and was lengthened by a chorus, not of human voices, but of all the sounds of the benighted wilderness pealing in awful harmony together. Goodman Brown cried out; and his cry was lost to his own ear by its unison with the cry of the desert.

In the interval of silence he stole forward until the light glared full upon his eyes. At one extremity of an open space, hemmed in by the dark wall of the forest, arose a rock, bearing some rude, natural resemblance either to an altar or a pulpit, and surrounded by four blazing pines, their tops aflame, their stems untouched, like candles at an evening meeting. The mass of foliage that had overgrown the summit of the rock was all on fire, blazing high into the night and fitfully illuminating the whole field. Each pendent twig and leafy festoon was in a blaze. As the red light arose and fell, a numerous congregation alternately shone forth, then disappeared in shadow, and again grew, as it were, out of the darkness, peopling the heart of the solitary woods at once.

55   "A grave and dark-clad company," quoth Goodman Brown.

In truth they were such. Among them, quivering to and fro between gloom and splendor, appeared faces that would be seen next day at the council board of the province, and others which, Sabbath after Sabbath, looked devoutly heavenward, and benignantly over the crowded pews, from the holiest pulpits in the land. Some affirm that the lady of the governor was there. At least there were high dames well known to her, and wives of honored husbands, and widows, a great multitude, and ancient maidens, all of excellent repute, and fair young girls, who trembled lest their mothers should espy them. Either the sudden gleams of light flashing over the obscure field bedazzled Goodman Brown, or he recognized a score of the church members of Salem village famous for their especial sanctity. Good old Deacon Gookin had arrived, and waited at the skirts of that venerable saint, his revered pastor. But, irreverently consorting with these grave, reputable, and pious people, these elders of the church, these chaste dames and dewy virgins, there were men of dissolute lives and women of spotted fame, wretches given over to all mean and filthy vice, and suspected even of horrid crimes. It was strange to see that the good shrank not from the wicked, nor were the sinners abashed by the saints. Scattered also among their palefaced enemies were the Indian priests, or powwows, who had often scared their native forest with more hideous incantations than any known to English witchcraft.

"But where is Faith?" thought Goodman Brown, and, as hope came into his heart, he trembled.

Another verse of the hymn arose, a slow and mournful strain, such as the pious love, but joined to words which expressed all that our nature can conceive of sin, and darkly hinted at far more. Unfathomable to mere mortals is the lore of fiends. Verse after verse was sung; and still the chorus of the desert swelled between like the deepest tone of a mighty organ; and with the final peal of that dreadful anthem there came a sound, as if the roaring wind, the rushing streams, the howling beasts, and every other voice of the unconverted wilderness was mingling and according with the voice of guilty man in homage to the prince of all. The four blazing pines threw up a loftier flame, and obscurely discovered shapes and visages of horror on the smoke wreaths above the impious assembly. At the same moment the fire on the rock shot redly forth and formed a glowing arch above its base, where now appeared a figure. With reverence be it spoken, the figure bore no slight similitude, both in garb and manner, to some grave divine of the New England churches.

"Bring forth the converts!" cried a voice that echoed through the field and rolled into the forest.

60   At the word, Goodman Brown stepped forth from the shadow of the trees and approached the congregation, with whom he felt a loathful brotherhood by the sympathy of all that was wicked in his heart. He could have well nigh sworn that the shape of his own dead father beckoned him to advance, looking downward from a smoke wreath, while a woman, with dim features of despair, threw out her hand to warn him back. Was it his mother? But he had no power to retreat one step, nor to resist, even in thought, when the minister and good old Deacon Gookin seized his arms and led him to the blazing rock. Thither came also the slender form of a veiled female, led between Goody Cloyse, that pious teacher of the catechism, and Martha Carrier, who had received the devil's promise to be queen of hell. A rampant hag was she. And there stood the proselytes beneath the canopy of fire.

"Welcome, my children," said the dark figure, "to the communion of your race. Ye have found thus young your nature and your destiny. My children, look behind you!"

They turned; and flashing forth, as it were, in a sheet of flame, the fiend worshippers were seen; the smile of welcome gleamed darkly on every visage.

"There," resumed the sable form, "are all whom ye have reverenced from youth. Ye deemed them holier than yourselves, and shrank from your own sin, contrasting it with their lives of righteousness and prayerful aspirations heavenward. Yet here are they all in my worshipping assembly. This night it shall be granted you to know their secret deeds; how hoary-bearded elders of the church have whispered wanton words to the young maids of their households; how many a woman, eager for widow's weeds, has given her husband a drink at bedtime and let him sleep his last sleep in her bosom; how beardless youths have made haste to inherit their fathers' wealth; and how fair damsels—blush not, sweet ones—have dug little graves in the garden, and bidden me, the sole guest, to an infant's funeral. By the sympathy of your human hearts for sin ye shall scent out all the places—whether in church, bed chamber, street, field, or forest—where crime has been committed, and shall exult to behold the whole earth one stain of guilt, one mighty blood spot. Far more than this. It shall be yours to penetrate, in every bosom, the deep mystery of sin, the fountain of all wicked arts, and which inexhaustibly supplies more evil impulses than human power—than my power at its utmost—can make manifest in deeds. And now, my children, look upon each other."

They did so; and, by the blaze of the hell-kindled torches, the wretched man beheld his Faith, and the wife her husband, trembling before that unhallowed altar.

65   "Lo, there ye stand, my children," said the figure, in a deep and solemn tone, almost sad with its despairing awfulness, as if his once angelic nature could yet mourn for our miserable race. "Depending upon one another's hearts, ye had still hoped that virtue were not all a dream. Now are ye undeceived. Evil is the nature of mankind. Evil must be your only happiness. Welcome again, my children, to the communion of your race."

"Welcome," repeated the fiend worshippers, in one cry of despair and triumph.

And there they stood, the only pair, as it seemed, who were yet hesitating on the verge of wickedness in this dark world. A basin was hollowed, naturally, in the rock. Did it contain water, reddened by the lurid light? or was it blood? or, perchance, a liquid flame? Herein did the shape of evil dip his hand and prepare to lay the mark of baptism upon their foreheads, that they might be partakers of the mystery of sin, more conscious of the secret guilt of others, both in deed and thought, than they could now be of their own. The husband cast one look at his pale wife, and Faith at him. What polluted wretches would the next glance show them to each other, shuddering alike at what they disclosed and what they saw!

"Faith! Faith!" cried the husband, "look up to heaven, and resist the wicked one."

Whether Faith obeyed, he knew not. Hardly had he spoken when he found himself amid calm night and solitude, listening to a roar of the wind which died heavily away through the forest. He staggered against the rock, and felt it chill and damp; while a hanging twig, that had been all on fire, besprinkled his cheek with the coldest dew.

70　　　The next morning young Goodman Brown came slowly into the street of Salem village, staring around him like a bewildered man. The good old minister was taking a walk along the graveyard to get an appetite for breakfast and meditate his sermon, and bestowed a blessing, as he passed, on Goodman Brown. He shrank from the venerable saint as if to avoid an anathema. Old Deacon Gookin was at domestic worship, and the holy words of his prayer were heard through the open window. "What God doth the wizard pray to?" quoth Goodman Brown. Goody Cloyse, that excellent old Christian, stood in the early sunshine at her own lattice, catechizing a little girl who had brought her a pint of morning's milk. Goodman Brown snatched away the child as from the grasp of the fiend himself. Turning the corner by the meeting house, he spied the head of Faith, with the pink ribbons, gazing anxiously forth, and bursting into such joy at sight of him that she skipped along the street and almost kissed her husband before the whole village. But Goodman Brown looked sternly and sadly into her face, and passed on without a greeting.

Had Goodman Brown fallen asleep in the forest and only dreamed a wild dream of a witch meeting?

Be it so, if you will; but, alas! it was a dream of evil omen for young Goodman Brown. A stern, a sad, a darkly meditative, a distrustful, if not a desperate, man did he become from the night of that fearful dream. On the Sabbath day, when the congregation were singing a holy psalm, he could not listen, because an anthem of sin rushed loudly upon his ear and drowned all the blessed strain. When the minister spoke from the pulpit, with power and fervid eloquence and with his hand on the open Bible, of the sacred truths of our religion, and of saintlike lives and triumphant deaths, and of future bliss or misery unutterable, then did Goodman Brown turn pale, dreading lest the roof should thunder down upon the gray blasphemer and his hearers. Often, awaking suddenly at midnight, he shrank from the bosom of Faith; and at morning or eventide, when the family knelt down at prayer, he scowled, and muttered to himself, and gazed sternly at his wife, and turned away. And when he had lived long, and was borne to his grave, a hoary corpse, followed by Faith, an aged woman, and children and grandchildren, a goodly procession, besides neighbors not a few, they carved no hopeful verse upon his tombstone; for his dying hour was gloom.

LEVELS OF READING

Summary:

Pay attention to the **literal** meaning of the text. Briefly describe the sequence of events in Nathaniel Hawthorne's "Young Goodman Brown." What story does the text tell? Concentrate on the highlights; avoid too much detail when summarizing. Drawing a simple outline of the main points or events of the story will help you better analyze the text at other levels of interpretation.

Analysis:

It is necessary to move beyond summary to properly analyze a text. In this story, there are deeper meanings embedded within the story told. In order to move from summary to analysis, begin by finding what you believe is **symbolic** in "Young Goodman Brown." Explain the meaning of these symbols. What, for instance, might Faith's "pink ribbon" symbolize? Perhaps even more important, what symbolic power do the names *Young Goodman Brown* and *Faith* carry in Puritan New England and beyond? What might the woods symbolize? With the help of the background material provided about Nathaniel Hawthorne and his world, make an argument about the story related, and include the mention of the more **figurative** or **symbolic** aspects of the text when making points in defense of your argument.

Application:

In the "Second Lecture," Freud uses the five-part essay structure to relate the "new" idea he has about "hysteria" and its causes. According to Freud, what kind of ailment is "hysteria," and how does it originate? In his examples and analogies, what roles do "repression" and "resistance" play in his "hysterical" patients? In what ways to the parts of the mind—ego, id, and super-ego—interact to produce "hysterical" symptoms? What conclusions does Freud reach about possible "solutions" for someone suffering from "hysteria"?

Apply Freud's theory of the mind to "Young Goodman Brown." Outline an argument you wish to make about this story using Freud's theory to help you explain some part of this story. The "part" of the text you choose to analyze may include any of the following: a person or character, a setting, a symbol or symbols, an important change, a motivation, a goal, a result.

The following ideas are offered as *suggestions* only. You may apply any aspect of Freud's theory to "Young Goodman Brown." Your argument may or may not take the form of a **five-part essay**:

- Freud's lecture is especially helpful in trying to explain the cause and effect of certain psychological changes, particularly **repression**. In Hawthorne's short story is something repressed? Who represses, and what are the effects of that repression?
- How does **resistance** work in "Young Goodman Brown"?
- Could the different scenes in "Young Goodman Brown" represent the different parts of the mind as sketched by Freud? Describe the mental journey that parallels Brown's physical one.
- Would any of Freud's **three solutions** work for Young Goodman Brown? How might these solutions have helped in an analysis of Young Goodman Brown? In other words, according to each solution, what might Young Goodman Brown have said or done to effect a "cure"?
- Explain how the man with the staff Young Goodman Brown meets in the woods might play the same role as the psychoanalyst.

NISA

Nisa (c.1921–?), an African !Kung woman, was interviewed by American anthropologist Marjorie Shostak in 1971. At that time Nisa was about fifty years old. By then, she had outlived all of her children. Part of a nomadic tribe that lived at subsistence level on whatever they could gather from the land, the remaining !Kung lived in the remotest regions of the Kalahari Desert in southern Africa.

Nisa's story was transmitted in the oral tradition. That is to say, Nisa, who could neither read nor write, recalled a remarkably detailed account of her life to Marjorie Shostak, who served as Nisa's scribe. As such, the entire text offered here could be placed within quotation marks. And yet, it is interesting to see how little Nisa's narration differs from written autobiographies. Having been part of the oral tradition of storytelling since infancy, it is not at all surprising that Nisa became adept at oral narration herself. Since the story is autobiographical, Nisa began with her earliest memories ("Weaning" is one example) and progressed through her story chronologically. The entire account of her life—a rare glimpse into the culture of a people seldom seen by anyone outside its circle—was published in 1981.

FROM *WEANING*
Nisa, as told to Marjorie Shostak

1   Fix my voice on the machine so that my words come out clear. I am an old person who has experienced many things and I have much to talk about. I will tell my talk, of the things I have done and the things that my parents and others have done. But don't let the people I live with hear what I say.

Our father's name was Gau and our mother's was Chuko. Of course, when my father married my mother, I wasn't there. But soon after, they gave birth to a son whom they called Dau. Then they gave birth to me, Nisa, and then my younger brother was born, their youngest child who survived, and they named him Kumsa.

I remember when my mother was pregnant with Kumsa. I was still small and I asked, "Mommy, that baby inside you . . . when that baby is born, will it come out from your belly button? Will the baby grow and grow until Daddy breaks open your stomach with a knife and takes my little sibling out?" She said, "No, it won't come out that way. When you give birth, a baby comes from here," and she pointed to her genitals. Then she said, "And after he is born, you can carry your little sibling around." I said, "Yes, I'll carry him!"

Later, I asked, "Won't you help me and let me nurse?" She said, "You can't nurse any longer. If you do, you'll die." I left her and went and played by myself for a while. When I came back, I asked to nurse again but she still wouldn't let me. She took some paste made from the dch'a root and rubbed it on her nipple. When I tasted it, I told her it was bitter.

5   When mother was pregnant with Kumsa, I was always crying. I *wanted* to nurse! Once, when we were living in the bush and away from other people, I was especially full of tears. I cried all the time. That was when my father said he was going to beat me to death; I was too full of tears and too full of crying. He had a big branch in his hand when he grabbed me, but he didn't hit me; he was only trying to frighten me. I cried out, "Mommy, come help me! Mommy! Come! Help me!" When my mother came, she said, "No, Gau, you are a man. If you hit Nisa you will put sickness into her and she will become very sick. Now, leave

Reprinted from *Nisa: The Life and Words of a !Kung Woman (Exploited Earth)* (1981), by permission of Elaine Markson Literary Agency.

her alone. I'll hit her if it's necessary. My arm doesn't have the power to make her sick; your arm, a man's arm, does."

When I finally stopped crying, my throat was full of pain. All the tears had hurt my throat.

Another time, my father took me and left me alone in the bush. We had left one village and were moving to another and had stopped along the way to sleep. As soon as night sat, I started to cry. I cried and cried and cried. My father hit me, but I kept crying. I probably would have cried the whole night, but finally, he got up and said, "I'm taking you and leaving you out in the bush for the hyenas to kill. What kind of child are you? If you nurse your sibling's milk, you'll die!" He picked me up, carried me away from camp and set me down in the bush. He shouted, "Hyenas! There's meat over here . . . Hyenas! Come and take this meat!" Then he turned and started to walk back to the village.

After he left, I was so afraid! I started to run and, crying, I ran past him. Still crying, I ran back to my mother and lay down beside her. I was afraid of the night and of the hyenas, so I lay there quietly. When my father came back, he said, "Today, I'm really going to make you shit! You can see your mother's stomach is huge, yet you still want to nurse." I started to cry again and cried and cried; then I was quiet again and lay down. My father said, "Good, lie there quietly. Tomorrow, I'll kill a guinea fowl for you to eat."

The next day, he went hunting and killed a guinea fowl. When he came back, he cooked it for me and I ate and ate and ate. But when I was finished, I said I wanted to take my mother's nipple again. My father grabbed a strap and started to hit me, "Nisa, have you no sense? Can't you understand? Leave your mother's chest alone!" And I began to cry again.

10   Another time, when we were walking together in the bush, I said, "Mommy . . . carry me!" She said yes, but my father told her not to. He said I was big enough to walk along by myself. Also, my mother was pregnant. He wanted to hit me, but my older brother Dau stopped him, "You've hit her so much, she's skinny! She's so thin, she's only bones. Stop treating her this way!" Then Dau picked me up and carried me on his shoulders.

When mother was pregnant with Kumsa, I was always crying, wasn't I? I would cry for a while, then be quiet and sit around, eating regular food: sweet nin berries and starchy chon and klaru bulbs, foods of the rainy season. One day, after I had eaten and was full, I said, "Mommy, won't you let me have just a little milk? Please, let me nurse." She cried, "Mother! My breasts are things of shit! Shit! Yes, the milk is like vomit and smells terrible. You can't drink it. If you do, you'll go, 'Whaagh . . . Whaagh . . .' and throw up." I said, "No, I won't throw up, I'll just nurse." But she refused and said, "Tomorrow, Daddy will trap a springhare, just for you to eat." When I heard that, my heart was happy again.

The next day, my father killed a springhare. When I saw him coming home with it, I shouted, "Ho, ho, Daddy! Ho, ho, Daddy's come! Daddy killed a springhare; Daddy's bringing home meat! Now I will eat and won't give any to *her*." My father cooked the meat and when it was done, I ate and ate and ate. I told her, "You stinged your milk, so I'll stinge this meat. You think your breasts are such wonderful things? They're not, they're terrible things." She said, "Nisa, please listen to me—my milk is not good for you anymore." I said, "Grand-mother! I don't want it anymore! I'll eat meat instead. I'll never have anything to do with your breasts again. I'll just eat the meat Daddy and Dau kill for me."

Mother's stomach grew very large. The first labor pains came at night and stayed with her until dawn. That morning, everyone went gathering. Mother and I stayed behind. We sat together for a while, then I went and played with the other children. Later, I came back and ate the nuts she had cracked for me. She got up and started to get ready. I said, "Mommy, let's go to the water well, I'm thirsty." She said, "Uhn, uhn, I'm going to gather some mongongo nuts." I told the children that I was going and we left; there were no other adults around.

We walked a short way, then she sat down by the base of a large nehn tree, leaned back against it, and little Kumsa was born. At first, I just stood there; then I sat down and watched. I thought, "Is that the way it's done? You just sit like that and that's where the baby comes out? Am I also like that?" Did I have any understanding of things?

15   After he was born, he lay there, crying. I greeted him, "Ho, ho, my baby brother! Ho, ho, I have a little brother! Some day we'll play together." But my mother said, "What do you think this thing is? Why are you talking to it like that? Now, get up and go back to the village and bring me my digging stick." I said, "What are you going to dig?" She said, "A hole. I'm going to dig a hole so I can bury the baby. Then you, Nisa, will be able to nurse again." I refused. "My baby brother? My little brother? Mommy, he's my *brother!* Pick him up and carry him back to the village. I don't want to nurse!" Then I said, "I'll tell Daddy when he comes home!" She said, "You won't tell him. Now, run back and bring me my digging stick. I'll bury him so you can nurse again. You're much too thin." I didn't want to go and started to cry. I sat there, my tears falling, crying and cry-ing. But she told me to go, saying she wanted my bones to be strong. So, I left and went back to the village, crying as I walked.

I was still crying when I arrived. I went to the hut and got her digging stick. My mother's younger sister had just arrived home from the nut groves. She put the mongongo nuts she had gathered into a pile near her hut and sat down. Then she began roasting them. When she saw me, she said, "Nisa, what's wrong? Where's your mother?" I said, "By the nehn tree way out there. That's where we went together and where she just now gave birth to a baby. She told me to come back and get her digging stick so she could . . . bury him! This is terrible!" and I started to cry again. Then I added, "When I greeted him and called him 'my little brother' she told me not to. What she wants to do is bad . . . that's why I'm crying. Now I have to bring this digging stick to her!"

My mother's sister said, "Oooo . . . people! This Chuko, she's certainly a bad one to be talking like that. And she's out there alone with the baby! No matter what it is—a boy or a girl—she should keep it." I said, "Yes, he's a little boy with a little penis just resting there at the bottom of his stomach." She said, "Mother! Let's go! Let's go and talk to her. When I get there I'll cut his umbilical cord and carry him back."

I left the digging stick behind and we ran to where my mother was still sitting, waiting for me. Perhaps she had already changed her mind, because, when we got there, she said, "Nisa, because you were crying like that, I'll keep the baby and carry him back with me." My aunt went over to Kumsa lying beside my mother and said, "Chuko, were you trying to split your face into pieces? You can see what a big boy you gave birth to, yet you wanted Nisa to bring back your digging stick? You wanted to bury this great big baby? Your own father worked to feed you and keep you alive. This child's father would surely have killed you if you had buried his little boy. You must have no sense, wanting to kill such a nice big baby."

My aunt cut his umbilical cord, wiped him off, put him into her kaross, and carried him back to the village. Mother soon got up and followed, shamed by her sister's talk. Finally, she said, "Can't you understand? Nisa is still a little child. My heart's not happy that she hasn't any milk to drink. Her body is weak. I want her bones to grow strong." But my aunt said, "When Gau hears about this, he'll beat you. A grown woman with one child following after another so nicely, doesn't behave like this." When we arrived back in the village, my mother took the baby and lay down.

20   Everyone was now coming back from the mongongo groves. After they put down their gatherings, they came to look at Kumsa. The women all said, "Oooh . . . this woman has no sense! She gave birth to such a big baby, yet she was going to kill it!" My mother said, "I wanted his older sister to nurse, that's

why I would have done it, and if I had been alone, I would have! I did the wrong thing by not taking my digging stick with me, but others did the wrong thing by taking him away from me. That's why I'm here with him at all." The women did not agree. They told my aunt, "You did very well. You were right to take the baby from Chuko and save him for his father. Wouldn't Chuko have had to answer to him if she had killed his baby?"

When the sun was low in the sky, my father came home from hunting. I greeted him, "Ho, ho, Daddy! Ho, ho, Daddy's home! There's Daddy!" He came and sat down beside the hut. He asked my mother, "What's wrong? Why are you lying down? Is something hurting you?" She said, "No, I'm just lying down." Then he said, "Eh-hey . . . my wife gave birth? Chuko, it's a boy?" She said, "Yes, a little boy." Then her sister said, "And a very large baby, too! But Chuko said she was going to . . ." I interrupted, "*Kill* him!" I rushed on, "She told me to come back and get her digging stick so she could kill my baby brother. I started to cry and came back to the village. But Aunt Koka went back with me and took the baby away from her." My aunt said, "Yes, I pulled the baby from his grave and carried him back." Then I said, "There he is lying over there. Mommy wanted to kill him."

My father said, "Chuko, why did you want to kill my son? If you had, I would have killed you. I would have struck you with my spear and killed you. Do you think I wouldn't do that? I surely would. What was making you feel so much pain that you would have killed such a large baby? You'll keep both children, now. Nisa will continue to grow up eating regular food."

After Kumsa was born, I sometimes just played by myself. I'd take the big kaross and lie down in it. I'd think, "Oh, I'm a child playing all alone. Where could I possibly go by myself?" Then I'd sit up and say, "Mommy, take my little brother from your kaross and let me play with him." But whenever she did, I hit him and made him cry. Even though he was still a little baby, I hit him. Then my mother would say, "You still want to nurse, but I won't let you. When Kumsa wants to, I'll let him. But whenever you want to, I'll cover my breasts with my hand and you'll feel ashamed."

I wanted the milk she had in her breasts, and when she nursed him, my eyes watched as the milk spilled out. I'd cry all night, cry and cry until dawn broke. Some mornings I just stayed around and my tears fell and I cried and refused all food. That was because I saw him nursing. I saw with my eyes the milk spilling out, the milk *I* wanted. I thought it was mine.

25   One day, my older brother came back from hunting carrying a duiker he had killed. I was sitting, playing by myself when I saw him, "Mommy! Mommy! Look! Big brother killed a duiker! Look over there, he's killed a duiker." My mother said, "Eh, didn't I tell you this morning that you should stop crying and wait for your older brother to come home? Now, see what he's brought back for you!"

When my brother started to skin it, I watched. "Oooo, a *male* duiker. Mommy . . . look, it's a male." I pointed, "There are its testicles and there's its penis." My older brother said, "Yes, those are its testicles and there's its penis."

After he skinned it, he gave me the feet. I put them in the coals to roast. Then he gave me some meat from the calf and I put that in the coals, too. When it was ready, I ate and ate and ate. Mother told me to give her some, but I refused, "Didn't you stinge your breasts? Didn't I say I wanted to nurse? I'm the only one who's going to eat this meat. I won't give any of it to you!" She said, "The milk you want belongs to your brother. What's making you still want to nurse?" I said, "My big brother killed this duiker. You won't have any of it. Not *you*. He'll cut the rest into strips and hang it to dry for me to eat. You refused to let me nurse so your son could. Now you say I should give you meat?"

Another day, my mother was lying down asleep with Kumsa, and I quietly sneaked up on them. I took Kumsa away from her, put him down on the other side of the hut, and came back and lay down beside her. While she slept, I took her nipple, put it in my mouth and began to nurse. I nursed and nursed and nursed. Maybe she thought it was my little brother. But he was still lying where I left him, while I stole his milk. I had already begun to feel wonderfully full when she woke up. She saw me and cried, "Where . . . tell me . . . what did you do with Kumsa? Where is he?" At that moment, he started to cry. I said, "He's over there."

She grabbed me and pushed me, hard, away from her. I lay there and cried. She went to Kumsa, picked him up, and laid him down beside her. She insulted me, cursing my genitals, "Have you gone crazy? Nisa-Big-Genitals, what's the matter with you? What craziness grabbed you that you took Kumsa, put him somewhere else, then lay down and nursed? Nisa-Big-Genitals! You must be crazy! I thought it was Kumsa nursing!" I lay there, crying. Then I said, "I've already nursed. I'm full. Let your baby nurse now. Go, feed him. I'm going to play." I got up and went and played. Later, I came back and stayed with my mother and her son. We stayed around together the rest of the day.

30   Later, when my father came back from the bush, she said, "Do you see what kind of mind your daughter has? Go, hit her! Hit her after you hear what she's done. Your daughter almost killed Kumsa! This tiny little baby, this tiny little thing, she took from beside me and dropped somewhere else. I was lying down,

holding him, and fell asleep. That's when she took him from me and left him by himself. She came back, lay down, and started to nurse. Now, hit your daughter!"

I lied, "What? She's lying! Me . . . Daddy, I didn't nurse. I didn't take Kumsa and leave him by himself. Truly, I didn't. She's tricking you. She's lying. I didn't nurse. I don't even want her milk anymore." My father said, "If I ever hear of this again, I'll beat you! Don't ever do something like that again!" I said, "Yes, he's my little brother, isn't he? My brother, my little baby brother, and I *love* him. I won't do that again. He can nurse all by himself. Daddy, even if you're not here, I won't steal mommy's breasts. They belong to my brother." He said, "Yes, daughter. But if you ever try to nurse your mother's breasts again, I'll hit you so that it *really* hurts." I said, "Eh, from now on, I'm going to go wherever you go. When you go to the bush, I'll go with you. The two of us will kill springhare together and you'll trap guinea fowl and you'll give them all to me."

My father slept beside me that night. When dawn broke, he and my older brother left to go hunting. I watched as they walked off. I thought, "If I stay here, mother won't let me nurse," so I got up and ran after them. But when my brother saw me, he pushed me back toward the village, "Go back and stay in the village. When the sun is hot like this, it could kill you. Why do you want to come with us, anyway?"

This was also when I used to steal food, although it only happened once in a while. Some days I wouldn't steal anything and would just stay around playing, without doing any mischief. But other times, when they left me in the village, I'd steal and ruin their things. That's what they said when they yelled at me and hit me. They said I had no sense.

It happened over all types of food: sweet nin berries or klaru bulbs, other times it was mongongo nuts. I'd think, "Uhn, uhn, they won't give me any of that. But if I steal it, they'll hit me." Sometimes, before my mother went gathering, she'd leave food inside a leather pouch and hang it high on one of the branches inside the hut. If it was klaru, she'd peel off the skins before putting them inside.

35   But as soon as she left, I'd steal whatever was left in the bag. I'd find the biggest bulbs and take them. I'd hang the bag back on the branch and go sit somewhere to eat. When my mother came back, she'd say, "Oh! Nisa was in here and stole all the bulbs!" She'd hit me and yell, "Don't steal! What's the matter with you that inside you there is so much stealing? Stop taking things! Why are you so full of something like that?"

One day, right after they left, I climbed the tree where she had hung the pouch, took out some bulbs, put the pouch back, and mashed them with water in a mortar. I put the paste in a pot and cooked it. When it was ready, I ate and finished everything I had stolen.

Another time, I took some klaru and kept the bulbs beside me, eating them very slowly. That's when mother came back and caught me. She grabbed me and hit me, "Nisa, stop stealing! Are you the only one who wants to eat klaru? Now, let me take what's left and cook them for all of us to eat. Did you really think you were the only one who was going to eat them all?" I didn't answer and started to cry. She roasted the rest of the klaru and the whole family ate. I sat there, crying. She said, "Oh, this one has no sense, finishing all those klaru like that. Those are the ones I had peeled and had left in the pouch. Has she no sense at all?" I cried, "Mommy, don't talk like that." She wanted to hit me, but my father wouldn't let her.

Another time, I was out gathering with my mother, my father, and my older brother. After a while, I said, "Mommy, give me some klaru." She said, "I still have to peel these. As soon as I do, we'll go back to the village and eat them." I had also been digging klaru to take back to the village, but I ate all I could dig. My mother said, "Are you going to eat all your klaru right now? What will you eat when you get back to the village?" I started to cry. My father told me the same, "Don't eat all your klaru here. Leave them in your pouch and soon your pouch will be full." But I didn't want that, "If I put all my klaru in my pouch, which ones am I going to eat now?"

Later, I sat down in the shade of a tree while they gathered nearby. As soon as they had moved far enough away, I climbed the tree where they had left a pouch hanging, full of klaru, and stole the bulbs. I had my little pouch, the one my father had made me, and as I took the bulbs, I put them in it. I took out more and more and put them all in together. Then I climbed down and sat, waiting for them to return.

40   They came back, "Nisa, you ate the klaru! What do you have to say for yourself?" I said, "Uhn, uhn, I didn't take them." My mother said, "So, you're afraid of your skin hurting, afraid of being hit?" I said, "Uhn, uhn, I didn't eat those klaru." She said, "You ate them. You certainly did. Now, don't do that again! What's making you keep on stealing?"

My older brother said, "Mother, don't punish her today. You've already hit her too many times. Just leave her alone. We can see. She says she didn't steal the klaru. Well then, what did eat them? Who else was here?"

I started to cry. Mother broke off a branch and hit me, "Don't steal! Can't you understand! I tell you, but you don't listen. Don't your ears hear when I talk to you?" I said, "Uhn, uhn. Mommy's been making me feel bad for too long now. I'm going to go stay with Grandma. Mommy keeps saying I steal things and hits me so that my skin hurts. I'm going to go stay with Grandma. I'll go where she goes and sleep beside her wherever she sleeps. And when she goes out digging klaru, I'll eat what she brings back."

But when I went to my grandmother, she said, "No, I can't take care of you this time. If you stay with me, you'll be hungry. I'm old and only go gathering one day in many. Most mornings I just stay around. We'll sit together and hunger will kill you. Now, go back and sit beside your mother and father." I said, "No, Daddy will hit me. Mommy will hit me. My skin hurts from being hit. I want to stay with you."

I lived with her for a while. But I was still full of tears. I just cried and cried and cried. I sat with her and no matter if the sun was setting or was high in the sky, I just cried. One month, when the nearly full moon rose just after sunset, I went back to my mother's hut. I said, "Mommy, you hate me. You always hit me. I'm going to stay on with Grandma. You hate me and hit me until I can't stand it any more. I'm tired."

45   Another time when I went to my grandmother, we lived in another village, nearby. While I was there, my father said to my mother, "Go, go bring Nisa back. Get her so she can be with me. What did she do that you chased her away from here?" When I was told they wanted me to come back I said, "No, I won't go back. I'm not going to do what he said. I don't want to live with Mother. I want to stay with Grandma; my skin still hurts. Today, yes, this very day here, I'm going to just continue to sleep beside Grandma."

So, I stayed with her. Then, one day she said, "I'm going to take you back to your mother and father." She took me to them, saying, "Today, I'm giving Nisa back to you. But isn't there someone here who will take good care of her? You don't just hit and hit a child like this one. She likes food and likes to eat. All of you are lazy. You've just left her so she hasn't grown well. If there were still plenty of food around, I'd continue to take care of her. She'd just continue to grow up beside me. Only after she had grown up, would she leave. Because all of you have killed this child with hunger. With your own fingers you've beaten her, beaten her as though she weren't a Zhun/twa. She was always crying. Look at her now, how small she still is." But my mother said, "No, listen to me. Your little granddaughter . . . whenever she saw food with her eyes, she'd just start crying."

Oh, but my heart was happy! Grandmother was scolding Mother! I held so much happiness in my heart that I laughed and laughed. But when Grandmother went home and left me there I cried and cried. My father yelled at me, but he didn't hit me. His anger usually came out only from his mouth. "You're so senseless! Don't you realize that after you left, everything felt less important? We wanted you to be with us. Yes, even your mother wanted you and missed you. Today, everything will be all right when you stay with us. Your mother will take you where she goes; the two of you will do things together and go gathering together. Why do you refuse to leave your grandmother now?"

But I cried and cried. I didn't want to leave her. "Mommy, let me go back and stay with Grandma, let me follow after her." But my father said, "That's enough. No more talk like that. There's nothing here that will hit you. Now, be quiet." And I was quiet. After that, when my father dug klaru bulbs, I ate them, and when he dug chon bulbs, I ate them. I ate everything they gave me, and I wasn't yelled at any more.

LEVELS OF READING

Summary:

Pay attention to the **literal** meaning of the text. Briefly describe the sequence of events in Nisa's description of her weaning. What story does she tell? Concentrate on the highlights; avoid too much detail when summarizing. Drawing a simple outline of the main points or events of the story will help you better analyze the text at other levels of interpretation.

Analysis:

It is necessary to move beyond summary to properly analyze a text. In this story, there are deeper meanings embedded within the story told. In order to move from summary to analysis, begin by finding what you believe is **implicit** in "Weaning." In addition to the **explicit** answer given, why does Nisa'a mother wish to bury her "big boy" after he is born? What does the baby's size signify to her? Taking into account the simple need of a child for food, for what more important reasons does Nisa begin stealing? What causes her insatiable appetite? Explain the deeper meaning in the details of Nisa's story. With the help of the background material provided about Nisa and her world, make an argument about Nisa's story and include the mention of the more **implicit** aspects of the text when making points in defense of your argument.

Application:

In the "Second Lecture," Freud uses the five-part essay structure to relate the "new" idea he has about "hysteria" and its causes. According to Freud, what kind of ailment is "hysteria," and how does it originate? In his examples and analogies, what roles do "repression" and "resistance" play in his "hysterical" patients? In what ways to the parts of the mind—ego, id, and super-ego—interact to produce "hysterical" symptoms? What conclusions does Freud reach about possible "solutions" for someone suffering from "hysteria"?

Apply Freud's theory of the mind to "Weaning." Outline an argument you wish to make about this story using Freud's theory to help you explain some part of this story. The "part" of the text you choose to analyze may include any of the following: a person, the setting, the lifestyle, an important change, a motivation, a goal, a result.

The following ideas are offered as *suggestions* only. You may apply any aspect of Freud's theory to "Weaning." Your argument may or may not take the form of a **five-part essay**:

- Freud's lecture is especially helpful in trying to explain the cause and effect of certain psychological changes, particularly **repression**. In Nisa's story, is something repressed? Who represses, and what are the effects of that repression?
- How does **resistance** work in "Weaning"?
- Could the different places Nisa is taken to in "Weaning" represent the different parts of the mind as sketched by Freud? Describe Nisa's mental journey in terms of this new topography.
- Would any of Freud's **three solutions** work for Nisa? How might these solutions have helped in an analysis of Nisa? In other words, according to each solution, what might Nisa have said or done to effect a "cure"?
- Using Freud's theory, explain why you think Nisa remembers this story of her very early childhood so vividly when she is fifty years old.

Start Your Own Argument:

Is repression ever "successful"?

ESSAY OFFERING AS EVIDENCE: AN EXTENDED EXAMPLE

Like the typical five-part essay, nearly all essays making an argument offer a clear statement of the argument, or **thesis**; evidence to support the argument, or **body**; and a **conclusion** or **conclusions**. But writers need not offer three or more points of evidence for their arguments in the bodies of their essays. Sometimes writers make an argument offering one point of "evidence" in the form of an extended example. In the case of Carl Jung's "The Personal and the Collective Unconscious," the one example offered in the body of the essay to prove the argument takes the form of a long narrative.

CARL GUSTAV JUNG

Though he traveled extensively, visiting India, Africa, and America, Carl Gustav Jung (1875–1961) was born and died in Switzerland. Jung's education began when he was just six years old, with the reading of Latin. His facility with languages prompted him to learn most modern European languages, as well as Sanskrit, which enabled him to learn much about early Hindu holy books.

As a lover of languages and literature, Jung's first career choice at the University of Basel in Switzerland was archaeology, and yet he went on to study medicine. After meeting the famous neurologist Krafft-Ebing, he chose psychiatry as his medical specialty. Once graduated from medical school, he began working at the Burghoeltzli Mental Hospital in Zurich with Eugene Bleuler, the psychiatrist who studied and named the disorder schizophrenia. Jung also taught at the University of Zurich at this time, as well as maintaining a private practice.

Jung met Freud in Vienna in 1907. A near father-son relationship between the two men soon developed. In fact, Freud, long considered "the father of psychoanalysis," came to see Jung as his "heir apparent" in the psychoanalytic community centered in Vienna. But Jung's differences of opinion with Freud soon caused the relationship to deteriorate.

One of these differences involved the nature of the unconscious and its role in the formation and treatment of neuroses. Jung took a much wider view of the unconscious, as his essay, "The Personal and the Collective Unconscious" demonstrates. Also, Jung's exposure to and interest in Eastern philosophy caused him to diverge from Freud's mostly Western viewpoint. A third point of contention between the two arose from Freud's interest in neurosis, particularly hysteria, obsessive-compulsive disorder, and paranoia, which contrasted sharply with Jung's abiding interest in psychosis, mainly dementia praecox, or schizophrenia. Freud's treatment of psychotic patients had been notably less successful than his treatment of neurotics, and he was not at all sanguine about "cures" for psychotic individuals. In contrast, Jung's hypothesis concerning the contents of the "collective unconscious" made these patients particularly interesting to him and his circle. Maintaining this early split between the "father" and "son" of the psychoanalytic community to this day, some therapists even now refer to themselves as either "Freudians" or "Jungians."

Unlike Freud, who uses a number of examples and analogies to make his argument about the operation of the personal unconscious, Jung uses one long example, a case study of one of his patients, to make his point about the "collective" contents of the unconscious. In this analysis, Jung traces the mechanism of his patient's transference (in this case, an attachment to male figures) as it progresses in the course of her treatment. By doing so, Jung is able to make an argument for what he calls the "collective unconscious," and explain how, to an extent, the collective unconscious is an important part of the mental life of us all.

In *The Spirit in Man, Art, and Literature* (1967), Jung wrote that he considered Herman Melville's *Moby Dick* "the greatest American novel," offering "the greatest opportunities for psychological elucidation." Many would add that Melville's "Bartleby the Scrivener" offers the same.

Coming to Terms with the Reading:

Before reading/rereading Jung's "The Personal and the Collective Unconscious," it is best to have a firm grasp on the meaning of the following terms:

1. personal unconscious
2. collective unconscious
3. archetype
4. father archetype
5. transference
6. God complex

In addition, it is helpful to understand the meanings of the following words, not present in this essay, but often used by Jung in his essays explaining his theories of the human psyche:

1. **Mother archetype:** the inherent ability of humans to recognize the concept of "mothering," in the sense of nature, comfort, love and protection. Typical symbols of the archetypal mother include the mythological "earth mother," and, in the western Christian tradition, Mary, the mother of Jesus. Less specific symbols of the mother archetype include the church, the nation, the ocean, and the cave (womb). In fact, any enclosed space can symbolize the safety, security, and nourishment of the maternal womb.

2. **The shadow:** The "shadow" in Jung bears a strong resemblance to Freud's "id." In Jung's theory, however, the shadow is the dark side of the ego, where the contents of our prehistoric, primitive urges are stored, including those having to do with the more animalistic sexual urges and reproduction. Shadow figures include snakes, dragons, monsters, and demons of all sorts.

3. **The persona:** "Persona" comes from the Latin word for "mask." Hence, Jung's persona describes the mask we wear before the public. In a sense, Jung's persona could be interchangeable with "personality." But we all know that in addition to presenting the world with a persona that will evoke a positive response from others, we sometimes alter our person to manipulate people. In other words, a single persona can wear a number of masks.

4. **Anima and Animus:** Most early psychologists believed that humans are essentially "bisexual." Hence, at birth, we are neither "masculine" nor "feminine" in the social sense. Our gender is socially constructed, beginning with the pink blanket or the blue blanket we are wrapped in shortly after birth. Though we are socially conditioned to take on gender characteristics considered "appropriate" to our biological sex, Jung

believed that we all maintain elements of the opposite sex in our psychical lives. Therefore, Jung coined the term **anima** to describe the female element present in men, and the term **animus** to connote the male element present in women.

5. **Original Man:** Though somewhat different, every culture seems to have a version of an "origin myth." In western Judeo-Christianity, *Genesis,* despite evolutionary theory, maintains a strong hold on the human imagination intent on visualizing its origin. In this tradition, Adam is the symbolic original man.

6. **Imago:** An idealized image of a person, sometimes a parent, formed in childhood and persisting into adulthood.

THE PERSONAL AND THE COLLECTIVE UNCONSCIOUS
Carl Jung

1   In Freud's view, as most people know, the contents of the unconscious are limited to infantile tendencies which are repressed because of their incompatible character. Repression is a process that begins in early childhood under the moral influence of the environment and lasts throughout life. Through analysis the repressions are removed and the repressed wishes made conscious.

According to this theory, the unconscious contains only those parts of the personality which could just as well be conscious and are in fact suppressed only through upbringing. Although from one point of view the infantile tendencies of the unconscious are the most conspicuous, it would nonetheless be incorrect to define or evaluate the unconscious entirely in these terms. The unconscious has still another side to it: it includes not only repressed contents, but also all psychic material that lies below the threshold of consciousness. It is impossible to explain the subliminal nature of all this material on the principle of repression; otherwise, through the removal of repressions, a man would acquire a phenomenal memory which would thenceforth forget nothing.

We therefore emphatically say that in addition to the repressed material the unconscious contains all those psychic components that have fallen below the threshold, including subliminal sense perceptions. Moreover we know, from abundant experience as well as for theoretical reasons, that the unconscious also contains components that have *not yet* reached the threshold of consciousness. These are the seeds of future conscious contents. Equally we have reason to suppose that the unconscious is never at rest in the sense of being inactive, but is continually engaged in grouping and regrouping its contents. Only in pathological cases can this activity be regarded as completely autonomous; normally it is co-ordinated with the conscious mind in a compensatory relationship.

It is to be assumed that all these contents are personal in so far as they are acquired during the individual's life. Since this life is limited, the number of acquired contents in the unconscious must also be limited. This being so, it might be thought possible to empty the unconscious either by analysis or by making a complete inventory of unconscious contents, on the ground that the unconscious cannot produce anything more than is already known and accepted in the conscious mind. We should also have to infer, as already indicated, that if one could stop the descent of conscious contents into the unconscious by doing away with repression, unconscious productivity would be paralyzed. This is possible only to a very limited extent, as we know from experience. We urge our patients to hold fast to repressed contents that have been re-associated with consciousness, and to assimilate them into their plan of life. But this procedure, as we may daily convince ourselves, makes no impression on the unconscious, since it calmly continues to produce dreams and fantasies which, according to Freud's original theory, must arise from personal repressions. If in such cases we pursue our observations systematically and without prejudice, we shall find material which, although similar in form to the previous personal contents, yet seems to contain allusions that go far beyond the personal sphere.

5   Casting about in my mind for an example to illustrate what I have just said, I have a particularly vivid memory of a woman patient with a mild hysterical neurosis which, as we expressed it in those days, had its principal cause in a "father complex." By this we wanted to denote the fact that the patient's peculiar relationship to her father stood in her way. She had been on very good terms with her father, who had since died. It was a relationship chiefly of feeling. In such cases it is usually the intellectual function that is developed, and this later becomes the bridge to the world. Accordingly our patient became a student of philosophy. Her energetic pursuit of knowledge was motivated by her need to extricate herself from the emotional entanglement with her father. This operation may succeed if her feelings can find an outlet on the new intellectual level, perhaps in the formation of an emotional tie with a suitable man, equivalent to the former tie. In this particular case, however, the transition refused to take place, because the patient's feelings remained suspended, oscillating between her father and a man who was not altogether suitable. The progress of her life was thus held up, and that inner disunity so characteristic of a neurosis promptly made its appearance. The so-called normal person would probably be able to break the emotional bond in one or the other direction by a powerful act of will, or else—and this is perhaps the more usual thing—he would come through the difficulty unconsciously, on the smooth path of instinct, without ever being aware of the sort of conflict that lay behind his headaches or other physical discomforts. But any weakness of instinct (which may have many causes) is enough to hinder a smooth unconscious transition. Then all progress is delayed by conflict, and the resulting stasis of life is equivalent to a neurosis. In consequence of the standstill, psychic energy

flows off in every conceivable direction, apparently quite uselessly. For instance, there are excessive innervations of the sympathetic system, which lead to nervous disorders of the stomach and intestines; or the vagus (and consequently the heart) is stimulated; or fantasies and memories, uninteresting enough in themselves, become over-valued and prey on the conscious mind (mountains out of mole hills). In this state a new motive is needed to put an end to the morbid suspension. Nature herself paves the way for this, unconsciously and indirectly, through the phenomenon of the transference (Freud). In the course of treatment the patient transfers the father imago to the doctor, thus making him, in a sense, the father, and in the sense that he is *not* the father, also making him a substitute for the man she cannot reach. The doctor therefore becomes both a father and a kind of lover—in other words, the object of conflict. In him the opposites are united, and for this reason he stands for a quasi-ideal solution of the conflict. Without in the least wishing it, he draws upon himself an overvaluation that is almost incredible to the outsider, for to the patient he seems like a savior or a god. This way of speaking is not altogether so laughable as it sounds. It is indeed a bit much to be a father and lover at once. Nobody could possibly stand up to it in the long run, precisely because it is too much of a good thing. One would have to be a demigod at least to sustain such a role without a break, for all the time one would have to be the giver. To the patient in the state of transference, this provisional solution naturally seems ideal, but only at first; in the end she comes to a standstill that is just as bad as the neurotic conflict was. Fundamentally, nothing has yet happened that might lead to a real solution. The conflict has merely been transferred. Nevertheless a successful transference can—at least temporarily—cause the whole neurosis to disappear, and for this reason it has been very rightly recognized by Freud as a healing factor of first-rate importance, but, at the same time, as a provisional state only, for although it holds out the possibility of a cure, it is far from being the cure itself.

This somewhat lengthy discussion seemed to me essential if my example was to be understood, for my patient had arrived at the state of transference and had already reached the upper limit where the standstill begins to make itself disagreeable. The question now arose: what next? I had of course become the complete savior, and the thought of having to give me up was not only exceedingly distasteful to the patient, but positively terrifying. In such a situation "sound common sense" generally comes out with a whole repertory of admonitions: "you simply must," "you really ought," "you just cannot," etc. So far as sound common sense is, happily, not too rare and not entirely without effect (pessimists, I know, exist), a rational motive can, in the exuberant feeling of health you get from transference, release so much enthusiasm that a painful sacrifice can be risked with a mighty effort of will. If successful—and these things sometimes are—the sacrifice bears blessed fruit, and the erstwhile patient leaps at one bound into the state of being practically cured. The doctor is generally so delighted that he fails to tackle the theoretical difficulties connected with this little miracle.

If the leap does not succeed—and it did not succeed with my patient—one is then faced with the problem of severing the transference. Here "psychoanalytic" theory shrouds itself in a thick darkness. Apparently we are to fall back on some nebulous trust in fate: somehow or other the matter will settle itself. "The transference stops automatically when the patient runs out of money," as a slightly cynical colleague once remarked to me. Or the ineluctable demands of life make it impossible for the patient to linger on in the transference—demands which compel the involuntary sacrifice, sometimes with a more or less complete relapse as a result. (One may look in vain for accounts of such cases in the books that sing the praises of psychoanalysis!)

To be sure, there are hopeless cases where nothing helps; but there are also cases that do not get stuck and do not inevitably leave the transference situation with bitter hearts and sore heads. I told myself, at this juncture with my patient, that there must be a clear and respectable way out of the impasse. My patient had long since run out of money—if indeed she ever possessed any—but I was curious to know what means nature would devise for a satisfactory way out of the transference deadlock. Since I never imagined that I was blessed with that "sound common sense" which always knows exactly what to do in every tangled situation, and since my patient knew as little as I, I suggested to her that we could at least keep an eye open for any movements coming from a sphere of the psyche uncontaminated by our superior wisdom and our conscious plannings. That meant first and foremost her dreams.

Dreams contain images and thought associations which we do not create with conscious intent. They arise spontaneously without our assistance and are representatives of a psychic activity withdrawn from our arbitrary will. Therefore the dream is, properly speaking, a highly objective, natural product of the psyche, from which we might expect indications, or at least hints, about certain basic trends in the psychic process. Now, since the psychic process, like any other life process, is not just a causal sequence, but is also a process with a teleological orientation, we might expect dreams to give us certain indicia about the objective causality as well as about the objective tendencies, because they are nothing less than self-portraits of the psychic life process.

10   On the basis of these reflections, then, we subjected the dreams to a careful examination. It would lead too far to quote word for word all the dreams that now followed. Let it suffice to sketch their main character: the majority referred to the person of the doctor, that is to say, the actors were unmistakably the dreamer herself and her doctor. The latter, however, seldom appeared in this natural shape, but was generally distorted in a remarkable way. Sometimes his figure was of supernatural size, sometimes he seemed to be extremely aged, then again he resembled her father, but was at the same time curiously woven into nature, as in the following dream: *Her father (who in reality was of small stature) was standing with her on a hill that was covered with wheat fields. She was quite tiny beside him, and he seemed to her like a giant. He lifted her up from the ground and held her in his arms like a little child. The wind swept over the wheat fields, and as the wheat swayed in the wind, he rocked her in his arms.*

From this dream and from others like it I could discern various things. Above all I got the impression that her unconscious was holding unshakably to the idea of my being the father-lover, so that the fatal tie we were trying to undo appeared to be doubly strengthened. Moreover one could hardly avoid seeing that the unconscious placed a special emphasis on the supernatural, almost "divine" nature of the father-lover, thus accentuating still further the overvaluation occasioned by the transference. I therefore asked myself whether the patient had still not understood the wholly fantastic character of her transference, or whether perhaps the unconscious could never be reached by understanding at all, but must blindly and idiotically pursue some nonsensical chimera. Freud's idea that the unconscious can "do nothing but wish," Schopenhauer's blind and aimless Will, the gnostic demi-urge who in his vanity deems himself perfect and then in the blindness of his limitation creates something lamentably imperfect—all these pessimistic suspicions of an essentially negative background to the world and the soul came threateningly near. And indeed there would be nothing to set against this except a well-meaning "you ought," reinforced by a stroke of the ax that would cut down the whole phantasmagoria for good and all.

But as I turned the dreams over and over in my mind, there dawned on me another possibility. I said to myself: it cannot be denied that the dreams continue to speak in the same old metaphors with which our conversations have made both doctor and patient sickeningly familiar. But the patient has an undoubted understanding of her transference fantasy. She knows that I appear to her as a semidivine father-lover, and she can, at least intellectually, distinguish this from my factual reality. Therefore the dreams are obviously reiterating the conscious standpoint minus the conscious criticism, which they completely ignore. They reiterate the conscious contents, not *in toto,* but insist on the fantastic standpoint as opposed to "sound common sense."

I naturally asked myself what was the source of this obstinacy and what was its purpose? That it must have some purposive meaning I was convinced, for there is no truly living thing that does not have a final meaning, that can in other words be explained as a mere leftover from antecedent facts. But the energy of the transference is so strong that it gives one the impression of a vital instinct. That being so, what is the purpose of such fantasies? A careful examination and analysis of the dreams, especially of the one just quoted, revealed a very marked tendency—in contrast to conscious criticism, which always seeks to reduce things to human proportions—to endow the person of the doctor with superhuman attributes. He had to be gigantic, primordial, huger than the father, like the wind that sweeps over the earth—was he then to be made into a god? Or, I said to myself, was it rather the case that the unconscious was trying to *create* a god out of the person of the doctor, as it were to free a vision of God from the veils of the personal, so that the transference to the person of the doctor was no more than a misunderstanding on the part of the conscious mind, a stupid trick played by "sound common sense?" Was the urge of the unconscious perhaps only apparently reaching out towards the person, but in a deeper sense towards a god? Could the longing for a god be a *passion* welling up from our darkest, instinctual nature, a passion unswayed by any outside influences, deeper and stronger perhaps than the love for a human person? Or was it perhaps the highest and truest meaning of that inappropriate love we call transference, a little bit of real *Gottesminne,* that has been lost to consciousness ever since the fifteenth century?

No one will doubt the reality of a passionate longing for a human person; but that a fragment of religious psychology, an historical anachronism, indeed something of a medieval curiosity—we are reminded of Mechtild of Magdeburg—should come to light as an immediate living reality in the middle of the consulting room, and be expressed in the prosaic figure of the doctor, seems almost too fantastic to be taken seriously.

15   A genuinely scientific attitude must be unprejudiced. The sole criterion for the validity of an hypothesis is whether or not it possesses an heuristic—i.e., explanatory—value. The question now is, can we regard the possibilities set forth above as a valid hypothesis? There is no a priori reason why it should not be just as possible that the unconscious tendencies have a goal beyond the human person, as that the unconscious can "do nothing but wish." Experience alone can decide which is the more suitable hypothesis.

This new hypothesis was not entirely plausible to my very critical patient. The earlier view that I was the father-lover, and as such presented an ideal solution of the conflict, was incomparably more attractive to her way of feeling. Nevertheless her intellect was sufficiently clear to appreciate the theoretical possibility of the new hypothesis. Meanwhile the dreams continued to disintegrate the person of the doctor and swell them to ever vaster proportions. Concurrently with this there now occurred something which at first I alone perceived, and with the utmost astonishment, namely a kind of subterranean undermining of the transference. Her relations with a certain friend deepened perceptibly, notwithstanding the fact that consciously she still clung to the transference. So that when the time came for leaving me, it was no catastrophe, but a perfectly reasonable parting. I had the privilege of being the only witness during the process of severance. I saw how the transpersonal control point developed—I cannot call it anything else—a *guiding function* and step by step gathered to itself all the former personal overvaluations; how, with this afflux of energy, it gained influence over the resisting conscious mind without the patient's consciously noticing what was happening. From this I realized that the dreams were not just fantasies, but self-representations of unconscious developments which allowed the psyche of the patient gradually to grow out of the pointless personal tie.

This change took place, as I showed, through the unconscious development of a transpersonal control point; a virtual goal, as it were, that expressed itself symbolically in a form which can only be described as a vision of God. The dreams swelled the human person of the doctor to superhuman proportions, making him a gigantic primordial father who is at the same time the wind, and in whose protecting arms the dreamer rests like an infant. If we try to make the patient's conscious, and traditionally Christian, idea of God responsible for the divine image in the dreams, we would still have to lay stress on the distortion. In religious matters the patient had a critical and agnostic attitude, and her idea of a possible deity had long since passed into the realm of the inconceivable, i.e., had dwindled into a complete abstraction. In contrast to this, the god-image of the dreams corresponded to the archaic conception of a nature demon, something like Wotan. *Theos to pneûma,* "God is spirit," is here translated back into its original form where *pneûma* means "wind:" God is the wind, stronger and mightier than man, an invisible breath-spirit. As in the Hebrew *ruach,* so in Arabic *ruh* means breath and spirit. Out of the purely personal form the dreams developed an archaic god-image that is infinitely far from the conscious idea of God. It might be objected that this is simply an infantile image, a childhood memory. I would have no quarrel with this assumption if we were dealing with an old man sitting on a golden throne in heaven. But there is no trace of any sentimentality of that kind; instead, we have a primitive conception that can correspond only to an archaic mentality. These primitive conceptions, of which I have given a large number of examples in my *Symbols of Transformation,* tempt one to make, in regard to unconscious material, a distinction very different from that between "preconscious" and "unconscious" or "subconscious" and "unconscious." The justification for these distinctions need not be discussed here. They have a definite value and are worth refining further as points of view. The fundamental distinction which experience has forced upon me merely claims the value of a further point of view. From what has been said it is clear that we have to distinguish in the unconscious a layer which we may call the *personal unconscious.* The materials contained in this layer are of a personal nature in so far as they have the character partly of acquisitions derived from the individual's life and partly of psychological factors which could just as well be conscious. It is readily understandable that incompatible psychological elements are liable to repression and therefore become unconscious; but on the other hand we also have the possibility of making and keeping the repressed contents conscious, once they have been recognized. We recognize them as personal contents because we can discover their effects, or their partial manifestation, or their specific origin in our personal past. They are the integral components of the personality, they belong to its inventory, and their loss to consciousness produces an inferiority in one or the other respect—an inferiority, moreover, that has the psychological character not so much of an organic mutilation or an inborn defect as of a want which gives rise to a feeling of moral resentment. The sense of moral inferiority always indicates that the missing element is something which, one feels, should not be missing, or which could be made conscious if only one took enough trouble. The feeling of moral inferiority does not come from a collision with the generally accepted and, in a sense, arbitrary moral law, but from the conflict with one's own self which, for reasons of psychic equilibrium, demands that the deficit be redressed. Whenever a sense of moral inferiority appears, it shows that there is not only the demand to assimilate an unconscious component, but also the possibility of assimilating it. In the last resort it is a man's moral qualities which force him, either through direct recognition of the necessity to do so, or indirectly through a painful neurosis, to assimilate his unconscious self and to keep himself fully conscious. Whoever progresses along this road of realizing the unconscious self must inevitably bring into consciousness the contents of the personal unconscious, thus widening the scope of his personality. I should add at once that this "widening" primarily concerns the moral consciousness, one's self-knowledge, for the unconscious contents that are released and brought into consciousness by analysis are usually unpleasant—which is precisely why these wishes, memories, tendencies, plans, etc. were repressed. These are the contents that are brought to light in much the same way by a thorough confession, though to a much more limited extent. The rest comes out as a rule in dream analysis. It is often very interesting to watch how the dreams fetch up the essential points, bit by bit and with the nicest choice. The total material that is added to consciousness causes a considerable widening of the horizon, a deepened self-knowledge which, more than anything else, is calculated to humanize a man and make him modest. But even self-knowledge, assumed by all wise men to be the best and most efficacious, has different effects on different characters. We make very remarkable discoveries in this respect in practical analysis, but I shall deal with this question in the next chapter.

As my example of the archaic idea of God shows, the unconscious seems to contain other things besides personal acquisitions and belongings. My patient was quite unconscious of the derivation of "spirit" from "wind," or of the parallelism between the two. This content was not the product of her thinking, nor had she ever been taught it. The critical passage in the New Testament was inaccessible to her—*to pneüma pneï hopou thelei*—since she knew no Greek. If we must take it as a wholly personal acquisition, it might be a case of so-called cryptomnesia, the unconscious recollection of a thought which the dreamer had once read somewhere. I have nothing against such a possibility in this particular case; but I have seen a sufficient number of other cases—many of them are to be found in the book mentioned above—where cryptomnesia can be excluded with certainty. Even if it were a case of cryptomnesia, which seems to me very improbable, we should still have to explain what the predisposition was that caused just this image to be retained and later, as Semon puts it, "ecphorated" (*ekphoreîn,* Latin *efferre,* "to produce"). In any case, cryptomnesia or no cryptomnesia, we are dealing with a genuine and thoroughly primitive god image that grew up in the unconscious of a civilized person and produced a living effect—an effect which might well give the psychologist of religion food for reflection. There is nothing about this image that could be called personal: it is a wholly collective image, the ethnic origin of which has long been known to us. Here is an historical image of world-wide distribution that has come into existence again through a natural psychic function. This is not so very surprising, since my patient was born into the world with a human brain which presumably still functions today much as it did of old. We are dealing with a reactivated archetype, as I have elsewhere called these primordial images. These ancient images are restored to life by the primitive, analogical mode of thinking peculiar to dreams. It is not a question of inherited ideas, but of inherited thought patterns.

In view of these facts we must assume that the unconscious contains not only personal, but also impersonal, collective components in the form of inherited categories or archetypes. I have therefore advanced the hypothesis that at its deeper levels the unconscious possesses collective contents in a relatively active state. That is why I speak of the collective unconscious.

READING/WRITING ASSISTS

Thesis (and its counterargument):

Jung's **thesis** is more explicit than Freud's. There are a number of single sentences in the first three paragraphs and beyond, all of which can be highlighted or underlined, and all of which are a statement or restatement of Jung's point of view. But once again, Jung's thesis is stated in opposition to a **counterargument**, in this case the idea of the unconscious as stated in the "Second Lecture" by Sigmund Freud, Jung's teacher and mentor.

Carefully read the first three paragraphs of Jung's essay. Can Jung's idea of the unconscious be differentiated from Freud's? What is **collective** about the nature of Jung's unconscious? In what ways are the contents of the **collective unconscious** different from the contents of Freud's **id**?

The Shape of the Argument:

"Mapping" the structure of an argument can help us better understand the argument itself, while also showing us new models for shaping our own arguments in essay form. Jung's essay differs from Freud's in structure in that it is not a typical five-part essay. Instead, Jung relies on an extended, carefully elaborated example to make his argument. To better understand Jung's argument, it is best to start by outlining the entire essay, paragraph by paragraph:

Paragraphs
1, 2 3, and 4: **Thesis/counterargument:** What exactly is Jung's thesis, and what forms the basis of the argument counter to his argument?

Paragraph 5:   Jung's case study of his patient. What does Jung mean by **father complex**? What is the meaning of **transference**, and why is transference so important in psychotherapy?

Paragraph 6:   Is it possible for therapy to conclude at this point? Why or why not? (Hint: Therapy does not end only when "the patient runs out of money.")

Paragraph 7:   **Transition:** What does Jung turn to here as another possible way to sever transference, without any harmful effects on the patient?

Paragraphs
8, 9, 10, 11:   **The dream:** Why is Jung's patient's dream so important? What important insight does Jung gain from his patient's dream? How is this insight related to his notion of **transference**?

Paragraph 12:   **Transition:** Restate in your own words the turn, or transition, this paragraph marks in Jung's argument.

Paragraphs
13, 14, 15:   By way of the **God complex**, Jung maps out his clearest route to a new hypothesis, the existence of the **collective unconscious** in the human psyche. Does the existence of a **God complex** in the mind of his patient help to prove his argument? If so, why?

Paragraph 16:   Jung questions the validity of his own argument. Does Jung have a valid argument?

Paragraph 17:   Return to antithesis, the personal unconscious.

Paragraph 18:   Return to thesis, the collective unconscious. Is it now easier to clearly state the difference between the two?

Paragraph 19:   Restatement of thesis. Note that even experienced and capable writers such as Jung recapitulate the argument of the essay at the conclusion.

Rhetorical Moves:

Like Freud's "Second Lecture," Jung's essay moves between the abstract and the concrete. But instead of offering analogies and different examples to further explain a theoretical insight, Jung instead refers us to the case study of one patient. Jung uses the extended example of one patient's analysis to unfold all the "points" of his argument. Key to the way he does so is the rhetorical strategy of the **tes-**

timonial, a process of giving evidence through a personal narrative. With reference to testimonials, three generalizations can be made:

· The testimonial comes from an expert source.
· With certain audiences, and under certain circumstances, the testimonial may be remarkably effective as a mode of argument.
· The testimonial is particularly vulnerable to refutation.

What is important is that testimonials be read carefully and critically. Through this one case study, Jung claims to have gotten important insights into transference, and hence, a glimpse into the collective unconscious. It is possible to make a forceful persuasive essay using only one example, but remember that the example must be fully elaborated and that there must be a controlling idea or set of ideas behind your use of the example. Are you persuaded by Jung's testimonial regarding his patient's psychoanalytic experience that his theory of the collective unconscious is correct? Why or why not?

HERMAN MELVILLE

Herman Melville (1819–1891) was born in New York City into a middle-class merchant family, but when he was only twelve years old his father went both bankrupt and insane, and shortly after, died. Melville's formal education came to an abrupt end at that time, but he never stopped learning, reading classical, historical, and technical literature voraciously on his own.

Though he worked as a clerk, teacher, and farmhand from the age of twelve, Melville's most formative literary experiences happened when he shipped out of New York as a cabin boy on a whaling ship in 1839. He later joined the U.S. Navy and spent many years at sea, particularly in the Atlantic and the South Seas. Both Typee *and* Omoo *are written about Melville's experiences in the South Seas.*

Melville's 1847 marriage to Elisabeth Shaw, daughter of the chief justice of the state of Massachusetts resulted three years later in the purchase of a farm, "Arrowhead," near Nathaniel Hawthorne's home at Pittsfield, Massachusetts. For years after, Hawthorne and Melville encouraged and supported one another's literary endeavors. In 1851, thanks in part to Hawthorne's relentless optimism about the work, Melville's masterpiece, Moby Dick, *was published. In fact, Melville dedicated his novel to his friend Hawthorne. Though some critics praised the work, few readers enjoyed it.*

On September 28, 1891, thirty years after the publication of his last novel, The Confidence Man, *Melville died at his residence 104 East 26th Street in New York City. He was seventy-two years old. Announcement of his death came as a surprise to most; the public thought Melville had been dead for years.*

What did Melville do during those thirty years, in fact until shortly before his death? He worked on East 18th Street in New York City, an employee of the Custom Revenue Service, as a custom inspector. A New York Times obituary dated October 2, 1891, described Melville, a common sight outside the Custom House, as "a man above ordinary stature, with a great growth of hair and beard, and a keen blue eye; and full of vigor and quickness of thought in his age. . . ." Most obituaries exhorted readers to return to Melville's novels and stories, but one published in the Springfield, Massachusetts Republican dated October 4, 1891, captured what may have been the majority Melville opinion of the time, claiming, "There were strange, dark mysterious elements in his nature, as there were in Hawthorne's, but he never learned to control them, as Hawthorne did from the beginning, and never turned their possibilities into actualities."

Today, there are many on record dissenting from this opinion, including Carl Gustav Jung.

BARTLEBY, THE SCRIVENER
A STORY OF WALL STREET
Herman Melville

1   I am a rather elderly man. The nature of my avocations, for the last thirty years, has brought me into more than ordinary contact with what would seem an interesting and somewhat singular set of men, of whom, as yet, nothing, that I know of, has ever been written—I mean, the law-copyists, or scriveners. I have known very many of them, professionally and privately, and, if I pleased, could relate divers histories, at which good-natured gentlemen might smile, and sentimental souls might weep. But I waive the biographies of all other scriveners, for a few passages in the life of Bartleby, who was a scrivener, the strangest I ever saw, or heard of. While, of other law-copyists, I might write the complete life, of Bartleby nothing of that sort can be done. I believe that no materials exist, for a full and satisfactory biography of this man. It is an irreparable loss to literature. Bartleby was one of those beings of whom nothing is ascertainable, except from the original sources, and, in his case, those are very small. What my own astonished eyes saw of Bartleby, that is all I know of him, except, indeed, one vague report, which will appear in the sequel.

Ere introducing the scrivener, as he first appeared to me, it is fit I make some mention of myself, my *employés,* my business, my chambers, and general surroundings, because some such description is indispensable to an adequate understanding of the chief character about to be presented. Imprimis: I am a man who, from his youth upwards, has been filled with a profound conviction that the easiest way of life is the best. Hence, though I belong to a profession proverbially energetic and nervous, even to turbulence, at times, yet nothing of that sort have I ever suffered to invade my peace. I am one of those unambitious lawyers who never address a jury, or in any way draw down public applause; but, in the cool tranquillity of a snug retreat, do a snug business among rich men's bonds, and mortgages, and title-deeds. All who know me, consider me an eminently *safe* man. The late John Jacob Astor, a personage little given to poetic enthusiasm, had no hesitation in pronouncing my first grand point to be prudence; my next, method. I do not speak it in vanity, but simply record the fact, that I was not unemployed in my profession by the late John Jacob Astor; a name which, I admit, I love to repeat; for it hath a rounded and orbicular sound to it, and rings like unto bullion. I will freely add, that I was not insensible to the late John Jacob Astor's good opinion.

Some time prior to the period at which this little history begins, my avocations had been largely increased. The good old office, now extinct in the State of New York, of a Master in Chancery, had been conferred upon me. It was not a very arduous office, but very pleasantly remunerative. I seldom lose my temper; much more seldom indulge in dangerous indignation at wrongs and outrages; but I must be permitted to be rash here and declare, that I consider the sudden and violent abrogation of the office of Master in Chancery, by the new Constitution, as a—premature act; inasmuch as I had counted upon a life-lease of the profits, whereas I only received those of a few short years. But this is by the way.

My chambers were up stairs, at No.__ Wall Street. At one end, they looked upon the white wall of the interior of a spacious skylight shaft, penetrating the building from top to bottom.

5   This view might have been considered rather tame than otherwise, deficient in what landscape painters call "life." But, if so, the view from the other end of my chambers offered, at least, a contrast, if nothing more. In that direction, my windows commanded an unobstructed view of a lofty brick wall, black by age and everlasting shade; which wall required no spyglass to bring but its lurking beauties, but, for the benefit of all near-sighted spectators, was pushed up to within ten feet of my window-panes. Owing to the great height of the surrounding buildings, and my chambers being on the second floor, the interval between this wall and mine not a little resembled a huge square cistern.

At the period just preceding the advent of Bartleby, I had two persons as copyists in my employment, and a promising lad as an office-boy. First, Turkey; second, Nippers; third, Ginger Nut. These may seem names, the like of which are not usually found in the Directory. In truth, they were nicknames, mutually conferred upon each other by my three clerks, and were deemed expressive of their respective persons or characters. Turkey was a short, pursy Englishman, of about my own age—that is, somewhere not far from sixty. In the morning, one might say, his face was of a fine florid hue, but after twelve o'clock, meridian—his dinner hour—it blazed like a grate full of Christmas coals; and continued blazing—but, as it were, with a gradual wane—till six o'clock, P.M., or thereabouts; after which, I saw no more of the proprietor of the face, which, gaining its meridian with the sun, seemed to set with it, to rise, culminate, and decline the following day, with the like regularity and undiminished glory. There are many singular coincidences I have known in the course of my life, not the least among which was the fact, that, exactly when Turkey displayed his fullest beams from his red and radiant countenance, just then, too, at that critical moment, began the daily period when I considered his business capacities as seriously disturbed for the remainder of the twenty-four hours. Not that he was absolutely idle, or averse to business then; far from it. The difficulty was, he was apt to be altogether too energetic. There was a strange, inflamed, flurried, flighty recklessness of activity about him. He would be incautious in dipping his pen into his ink-stand. All his blots upon my documents were dropped there after twelve o'clock, meridian. Indeed, not only would he be reckless, and sadly given to making blots in the afternoon, but, some days, he went further, and was rather noisy. At such times, too, his face flamed with augmented blazonry, as if cannel coal had been heaped on anthracite. He made an unplesant racket with his chair; spilled his sand-box; in mending his pens, impatiently split them all to pieces, and threw them on the floor in a sudden passion; stood up, and leaned over his table, boxing his papers about in a most indecorous manner, very sad to behold in an elderly man like him. Nevertheless, as he was in many ways a most valuable person to me, and all the time before twelve o'clock, meridian, was the quickest, steadiest creature, too, accomplishing a great deal of work in a style not easily to be matched—for these reasons, I was willing to overlook his eccentricities, though, indeed, occasionally, I remonstrated with him. I did this very gently, however, because, though the civilest, nay, the blandest and most reverential of men in the morning, yet, in the afternoon, he was disposed, upon provocation, to be slightly rash with his tongue—in fact, insolent. Now, valuing his morning services as I did, and resolved not to lose them—yet, at the same time, made uncomfortable by his inflamed ways after twelve o'clock—and being a man of peace, unwilling by my admonitions to call forth unseemly retorts from him, I took upon me, one Saturday noon (he was always worse on Saturdays) to hint to him, very kindly, that, perhaps, now that he was growing old, it might be well to abridge his labors; in short, he need not come to my chambers after twelve o'clock, but, dinner over, had best go home to his lodgings, and rest himself till tea-time. But no; he insisted upon his afternoon devotions. His countenance became intolerably fervid, as he oratorically assured me—gesticulating with a long ruler at the other end of the room—that if his services in the morning were useful, how indispensable, then, in the afternoon?

"With submission, sir," said Turkey, on this occasion, "I consider myself your right-hand man. In the morning I but marshal and deploy my columns; but in the afternoon I put myself at their head, and gallantly charge the foe, thus"—and he made a violent thrust with the ruler.

"But the blots, Turkey," intimated I.

"True; but, with submission, sir, behold these hairs! I am getting old. Surely, sir, a blot or two of a warm afternoon is not to be severely urged against gray hairs. Old age—even if it blot the page—is honorable. With submission, sir, we *both* are getting old."

10   This appeal to my fellow-feeling was hardly to be resisted. At all events, I saw that go he would not. So, I made up my mind to let him stay, resolving, nevertheless, to see to it that, during the afternoon, he had to do with my less important papers.

Nippers, the second on my list, was a whiskered, sallow, and, upon the whole, rather piratical-looking young man, of about five-and-twenty. I always deemed him the victim of two evil powers—ambition and indigestion. The ambition was evinced by a certain impatience of the duties of a mere copyist, an unwarrantable usurpation of strictly professional affairs such as the original drawing up of legal documents. The indigestion seemed betokened in an occasional nervous testiness and grinning irritability, causing the teeth to audibly grind together over mistakes committed in copying; unnecessary maledictions, hissed, rather than spoken, in the heat of business; and especially by a continual discontent with the height of the table where he worked. Though of a very ingenious mechanical turn, Nippers could never get this table to suit him. He put chips under it, blocks of various sorts, bits of pasteboard, and at last went so far as to attempt an exquisite adjustment, by final pieces of folded blotting-paper. But no invention would answer. If, for the sake of easing his back, he brought the table-lid at a sharp angle well up towards his chin, and wrote there like a man using the steep roof of a Dutch house for his desk, then he declared that it stopped the circulation in his arms. If now he lowered the table to his waistbands, and stooped over it in writing, then there was a sore aching in his back. In short, the truth of the matter was, Nippers knew not what he wanted. Or, if he wanted anything, it was to be rid of a scrivener's table altogether. Among the manifestations of his diseased ambition was a fondness he had for receiving visits from certain ambiguous-looking fellows in seedy coats, whom he called his clients. Indeed, I was aware that not only was he, at times, considerable of a ward-politician, but he occasionally did a little business at the justices' courts, and was not unknown on the steps of the Tombs. I have good reason to believe, however, that one individual who called upon him at my chambers, and who, with a grand air, he insisted was his client, was no other than a dun, and the alleged title-deed, a bill. But, with all his failings, and the annoyances he caused me, Nippers, like his compatriot Turkey, was a very useful man to me; wrote a neat, swift hand; and, when he chose, was not deficient in a gentlemanly sort of deportment. Added to this, he always dressed in a gentlemanly sort of way; and so, incidentally, reflected credit upon my chambers. Whereas, with respect to Turkey, I had much ado to keep him from being a reproach to me. His clothes were apt to look oily, a smell of eating-houses. He wore his pantaloons very loose and baggy in summer. His coats were execrable, his hat not to be handled. But while the hat was a thing of indifference to me, inasmuch as his natural civility and deference, as a dependent Englishman, always led him to doff it the moment he entered the loom, yet his coat was another matter. Concerning his coats, I reasoned with him; but with no effect. The truth was, I suppose, that a man with so small an income could not afford to sport such a lustrous face and a lustrous coat at one and the same time. As Nippers once observed, Turkey's money went chiefly for red ink. One winter day, I presented Turkey with a highly respectable-looking coat of my own—a padded gray coat, of a most comfortable warmth, and which buttoned straight up from the knee to the neck. I thought Turkey would appreciate the favor, and abate his rashness and obstreperousness of afternoons. But no; I verily believe that buttoning himself up in so downy and blanket-like a coat had a pernicious effect upon him—upon the same principle that too much oats are bad for horses. In fact, precisely as a rash, restive horse is said to feel his oats, so Turkey felt his coat. It made him insolent. He was a man whom prosperity harmed.

Though, concerning the self-indulgent habits of Turkey, I had my own private surmises, yet, touching Nippers, I was well persuaded that, whatever might be his faults in other respects, he was, at least, a temperate young man. But indeed, nature herself seemed to have been his vintner, and, at his birth, charged him so thoroughly with an irritable, brandy-like disposition, that all subsequent potations were needless. When I consider how, amid the stillness of my chambers, Nippers would sometimes impatiently rise from his seat, and stooping over his table, spread his arms wide apart, seize the whole desk, and move it, and jerk it, with a grim, grinding motion on the floor, as if the table were a perverse voluntary agent, intent on thwarting and vexing him, I plainly perceive that, for Nippers, brandy-and-water were altogether superfluous.

It was fortunate for me that, owing to its peculiar cause—indigestion—the irritability and consequent nervousness of Nippers were mainly observable in the morning, while in the afternoon he was comparatively mild. So that, Turkey's paroxysms only coming on about twelve o'clock, I never had to do with their eccentricities at one time. Their fits relieved each other, like guards. When

Nippers' was on, Turkey's was off; and *vice versa*. This was a good natural arrangement, under the circumstances.

Ginger Nut, the third on my list, was a lad, some twelve years old. His father was a carman, ambitious of seeing his son on the bench instead of a cart, before he died. So he sent him to my office, as student at law, errand-boy, cleaner, and sweeper, at the rate of one dollar a week. He had a little desk to himself, but he did not use it much. Upon inspection, the drawer exhibited a great array of the shells of various sorts of nuts. Indeed, to this quick-witted youth, the whole noble science of the law was contained in a nutshell. Not the least among the employments of Ginger Nut, as well as one which he discharged with the most alacrity, was his duty as cake and apple purveyor for Turkey and Nippers. Copying lawpapers being proverbially a dry, husky sort of business, my two scriveners were fain to moisten their mouths very often with Spitzenbergs, to be had at the numerous stalls nigh the Custom House and Post Office. Also, they sent Ginger Nut very frequently for that peculiar cake—small, flat, round, and very spicy—after which he had been named by them. Of a cold morning, when business was but dull, Turkey would gobble up scores of these cakes, as if they were mere wafers—indeed, they sell them at the rate of six or eight for a penny—the scrape of his pen blending with the crunching of the crisp particles in his mouth. Of all the fiery afternoon blunders and flurried rashness of Turkey, was his once moistening a ginger-cake between his lips, and clapping it on to a mortgage, for a seal. I came within an ace of dismissing him then. But he mollified me by making an oriental bow, and saying—

15   "With submission, sir, it was generous of me to find you in stationery on my own account."

Now my original business—that of a conveyancer and title hunter, and drawer-up of recondite documents of all sorts—was considerably increased by receiving the Master's office. There was now great work for scriveners. Not only must I push the clerks already with me, but I must have additional help.

In answer to my advertisement, a motionless young man one morning stood upon my office threshold, the door being open, for it was summer. I can see that figure now—pallidly neat, pitiably respectable, incurably forlorn! It was Bartleby.

After a few words touching his qualifications, I engaged him, glad to have among my corps of copyists a man of so singularly sedate an aspect, which I thought might operate beneficially upon the flighty temper of Turkey, and the fiery one of Nippers.

I should have stated before that ground-glass folding-doors divided my premises into two parts, one of which was occupied by my scriveners, the other by myself. According to my humor, I threw open these doors, or closed them. I resolved to assign Bartleby a corner by the folding-doors, but on my side of them, so as to have this quiet man within easy call, in case any trifling thing was to be done. I placed his desk close up to a small side-window in that part of the room, a window which originally had afforded a lateral view of certain grimy brickyards and bricks, but which, owing to subsequent erections, commanded at present no view at all, though it gave some light. Within three feet of the panes was a wall, and the light came down from far above, between two lofty buildings, as from a very small opening in a dome. Still further to a satisfactory arrangement, I procured a high green folding screen, which might entirely isolate Bartleby from my sight, though not remove him from my voice. And thus, in a manner, privacy and society were conjoined.

20   At first, Bartleby did an extraordinary quantity of writing. As if long famishing for something to copy, he seemed to gorge himself on my documents. There was no pause for digestion. He ran a day and night line, copying by sunlight and by candle-light. I should have been quite delighted with his application, had he been cheerfully industrious. But he wrote on silently, palely, mechanically.

It is, of course, an indispensable part of a scrivener's business to verify the accuracy of his copy, word by word. Where there are two or more scriveners in an office, they assist each other in this examination, one reading from the copy, the other holding the original. It is a very dull, wearisome, and lethargic affair. I can readily imagine that, to some sanguine temperaments, it would be altogether intolerable. For example, I cannot credit that the mettlesome poet, Byron, would have contentedly sat down with Bartleby to examine a law document of, say five hundred pages, closely written in a crimpy hand.

Now and then, in the haste of business, it had been my habit to assist in comparing some brief document myself, calling Turkey or Nippers for this purpose. One object I had, in placing Bartleby so handy to me behind the screen, was, to avail myself of his services on such trivial occasions. It was on the third day, I think, of his being with me, and before any necessity had arisen for having his own writing examined, that, being much hurried to complete a small affair I had in hand, I abruptly called to Bartleby. In my haste and natural expectancy of instant compliance, I sat with my head bent over the original on my desk, and my right hand sideways, and somewhat nervously extended with the copy, so that, immediately upon emerging from his retreat, Bartleby might snatch it and proceed to business without the least delay.

In this very attitude did I sit when I called to him, rapidly stating what it was I wanted him to do—namely, to examine a small paper with me. Imagine my surprise, nay, my consternation, when, without moving from his privacy, Bartleby, in a singularly mild, firm voice, replied, "I would prefer not to."

I sat awhile in perfect silence, rallying my stunned faculties. Immediately it occurred to me that my ears had deceived me, or Bartleby had entirely misunderstood my meaning. I repeated my request in the clearest tone I could assume; but in quite as clear a one came the previous reply, "I would prefer not to."

25 "Prefer not to," echoed I, rising in high excitement, and crossing the room with a stride. "What do you mean? Are you moonstruck? I want you to help me compare this sheet here—take it," and I thrust it towards him.

"I would prefer not to," said he.

I looked at him steadfastly. His face was leanly composed; his gray eye dimly calm. Not a wrinkle of agitation rippled him. Had there been the least uneasiness, anger, impatience, or impertinence in his manner; in other words, had there been anything ordinarily human about him, doubtless I should have violently dismissed him from the premises. But as it was, I should have as soon thought of turning my pale plaster-of-paris bust of Cicero out of doors. I stood gazing at him awhile, as he went on with his own writing, and then reseated myself at my desk. This is very strange, thought I. What had one best do? But my business hurried me. I concluded to forget the matter for the present, reserving it for my future leisure. So, calling Nippers from the other room, the paper was speedily examined.

A few days after this, Bartleby concluded four lengthy documents, being quadruplicates of a week's testimony taken before me in my High Court of Chancery. It became necessary to examine them. It was an important suit, and great accuracy was imperative. Having all things arranged, I called Turkey, Nippers, and Ginger Nut, from the next room, meaning to place the four copies in the hands of my four clerks, while I should read from the original. Accordingly, Turkey, Nippers, and Ginger Nut had taken their seats in a row, each with his document in his hand, when I called to Bartleby to join this interesting group.

"Bartleby! quick, I am waiting."

30 I heard a slow scrape of his chair legs on the uncarpeted floor, and soon he appeared standing at the entrance of his hermitage.

"What is wanted?" said he, mildly.

"The copies, the copies," said I, hurriedly. "We are going to examine them. There"—and I held towards him the fourth quadruplicate.

"I would prefer not to," he said, and gently disappeared behind the screen.

For a few moments I was turned into a pillar of salt, standing at the head of my seated column of clerks. Recovering myself, I advanced towards the screen, and demanded the reason for such extraordinary conduct.

35 "*Why* do you refuse?"

"I would prefer not to."

With any other man I should have flown outright into a dreadful passion, scorned all further words, and thrust him ignominiously from my presence: But there was something about Bartleby that not only strangely disarmed me; but, in a wonderful manner, touched and disconcerted me. I began to reason with him.

"These are your own copies we are about to examine. It is labor saving to you, because one examination will answer for your four papers. It is common usage. Every copyist is bound to help examine his copy. Is it not so? Will you not speak? Answer!"

"I prefer not to," he replied in a flute-like tone. It seemed to me that, while I had been addressing him, he carefully revolved every statement that I made; fully comprehended the meaning; could not gainsay the irresistible conclusion; but, at the same time, some paramount consideration prevailed with him to reply as he did.

40 "You are decided, then, not to comply with my request—a request made according to common usage and common sense?"

He briefly gave me to understand, that on that point my judgment was sound. Yes: his decision was irreversible.

It is not seldom the case that, when a man is browbeaten in some unprecedented and violently unreasonable way, he begins to stagger in his own plainest faith. He begins, as it were, vaguely to surmise that, wonderful as it may be, all the justice and all the reason is on the other side. Accordingly, if any disinterested persons are present, he turns to them for some reinforcement for his own faltering mind.

"Turkey," said I, "what do you think of this? Am I not right?"

"With submission, sir," said Turkey, in his blandest tone, "I think that you are."

45 "Nippers," said I, "what do *you* think of it?"

"I think I should kick him out of the office."

(The reader of nice perceptions will have perceived that, it being morning, Turkey's answer is couched in polite and tranquil terms, but Nippers replies in ill-tempered ones. Or, to repeat a previous sentence, Nippers' ugly mood was on duty, and Turkey's off.)

"Ginger Nut," said I, willing to enlist the smallest suffrage in my behalf, "what do *you* think of it?"

"I think, sir, he's a little *luny*," replied Ginger Nut, with a grin.

50   "You hear what they say," said I, turning towards the screen, "come forth and do your duty."

But he vouchsafed no reply. I pondered a moment in sore perplexity. But once more business hurried me. I determined again to postpone the consideration of this dilemma to my future leisure. With a little trouble we made out to examine the papers without Bartleby, though at every page or two Turkey deferentially dropped his opinion, that this proceeding was quite out of the common; while Nippers, twitching in his chair with a dyspeptic nervousness, ground out, between his set teeth, occasional hissing maledictions against the stubborn oaf behind the screen. And for his (Nippers') part, this was the first and the last time he would do another man's business without pay.

Meanwhile Bartleby sat in his hermitage, oblivious to everything but his own peculiar business there.

Some days passed, the scrivener being employed upon another lengthy work. His late remarkable conduct led me to regard his ways narrowly. I observed that he never went to dinner; indeed, that he never went anywhere. As yet I had never, of my personal knowledge, known him to be outside of my office. He was a perpetual sentry in the corner. At about eleven o'clock though, in the morning, I noticed that Ginger Nut would advance toward the opening in Bartleby's screen, as if silently beckoned thither by a gesture invisible to me where I sat. The boy would then leave the office, jingling a few pence, and reappear with a handful of ginger-nuts, which he delivered in the hermitage, receiving two of the cakes for his trouble.

He lives, then, on ginger-nuts, thought I; never eats a dinner, properly speaking; he must be a vegetarian, then, but no; he never eats even vegetables, he eats nothing but ginger-nuts. My mind then ran on in reveries concerning the probable effects upon the human constitution of living entirely on ginger-nuts. Ginger-nuts are so called, because they contain ginger as one of their peculiar constituents, and the final flavoring one. Now, what was ginger? A hot, spicy thing. Was Bartleby hot and spicy? Not at all. Ginger, then, had no effect upon Bartleby. Probably he preferred it should have none.

55   Nothing so aggravates an earnest person as a passive resistance. If the individual so resisted be of a not inhumane temper, and the resisting one perfectly harmless in his passivity, then, in the better moods of the former, he will endeavor charitably to construe to his imagination what proves impossible to be solved by his judgment. Even so, for the most part, I regarded Bartleby and his ways. Poor fellow! thought I, he means no mischief; it is plain he intends no insolence; his

aspect sufficiently evinces that his eccentricities are involuntary. He is useful to me. I can get along with him. If I turn him away, the chances are he will fall in with some less indulgent employer, and then he will be rudely treated, and perhaps driven forth miserably to starve. Yes. Here I can cheaply purchase a delicious self-approval. To befriend Bartleby; to humor him in his strange wilfulness, will cost me little or nothing, while I lay up in my soul what will eventually prove a sweet morsel for my conscience. But this mood was not invariable with me. The passiveness of Bartleby sometimes irritated me. I felt strangely goaded on to encounter him in new opposition—to elicit some angry spark from him answerable to my own. But, indeed, I might as well have essayed to strike fire with my knuckles against a bit of Windsor soap. But one afternoon the evil impulse in me mastered me, and the following little scene ensued:

"Bartleby," said I, "when those papers are all copied, I will compare them with you."

"I would prefer not to."

"How? Surely you do not mean to persist in that mulish vagary?"

No answer.

60   I threw open the folding-doors nearby, and turning upon Turkey and Nippers, exclaimed:

"Bartleby a second time says, he won't examine his papers. What do you think of it, Turkey?"

It was afternoon, be it remembered. Turkey sat glowing like a brass boiler; his bald head steaming; his hands reeling among his blotted papers.

"Think of it?" roared Turkey. "I think I'll just step behind his screen, and black his eyes for him!"

So saying, Turkey rose to his feet and threw his arms into a pugilistic position. He was hurrying away to make good his promise, when I detained him, alarmed at the effect of incautiously rousing Turkey's combativeness after dinner.

65   "Sit down, Turkey," said I, "and hear what Nippers has to say. What do you think of it, Nippers? Would I not be justified in immediately dismissing Bartleby?"

"Excuse me, that is for you to decide, sir. I think his conduct quite unusual, and, indeed, unjust, as regards Turkey and myself. But it may only be a passing whim."

"Ah," exclaimed I, "you have strangely changed your mind, then—you speak very gently of him now."

"All beer," cried Turkey; "gentleness is effects of beer—Nippers and I dined together to-day. You see how gentle *I* am, sir. Shall I go and black his eyes?"

"You refer to Bartleby, I suppose. No, not to-day, Turkey," I replied; "pray, put up your fists."

I closed the doors, and again advanced towards Bartleby. I felt additional incentives tempting me to my fate. I burned to be rebelled against again. I remembered that Bartleby never left the office.

"Bartleby," said I, "Ginger Nut is away; just step around to the Post Office, won't you?" (it was but a three minutes' walk) "and see if there is anything for me."

"I would prefer not to."

"You *will* not?"

"I *prefer* not."

I staggered to my desk, and sat there in a deep study. My blind inveteracy returned. Was there any other thing in which I could procure myself to be ignominiously repulsed by this lean, penniless wight?—my hired clerk? What added thing is there, perfectly reasonable, that he will be sure to refuse to do?

"Bartleby!"

No answer.

"Bartleby," in a louder tone.

No answer.

"Bartleby," I roared.

Like a very ghost, agreeably to the laws of magical invocation, at the third summons, he appeared at the entrance of his hermitage.

"Go to the next room, and tell Nippers to come to me."

"I prefer not to," he respectfully and slowly said, and mildly disappeared.

"Very good, Bartleby," said I, in a quiet sort of serenely-severe self-possessed tone, intimating the unalterable purpose of some terrible retribution very close at hand. At the moment I half intended something of the kind. But upon the whole, as it was drawing towards my dinner-hour, I thought it best to put on my hat and walk home for the day, suffering much from perplexity and distress of mind.

Shall I acknowledge it? The conclusion of this whole business was, that it soon became a fixed fact of my chambers, that a pale young scrivener, by the name of Bartleby, had a desk there; that he copied for me at the usual rate of four cents a folio (one hundred words); but he was permanently exempt from examining the work done by him, that duty being transferred to Turkey and Nippers, out of compliment, doubtless, to their superior acuteness; moreover, said Bartleby was never, on any account, to be dispatched on the most trivial errand of any sort; and that even if entreated to take upon him such a matter, it was generally understood that he would "prefer not to"—in other words, that he would refuse point-blank.

As days passed on, I became considerably reconciled to Bartleby. His steadiness, his freedom from all dissipation, his incessant industry (except when he chose to throw himself into a standing revery behind his screen), his great stillness, his unalterableness of demeanor under all circumstances, made him a valuable acquisition. One prime thing was this—*he was always there*—first in the morning, continually through the day, and the last at night. I had a singular confidence in his honesty. I felt my most precious papers perfectly safe in his hands. Sometimes, to be sure, I could not, for the very soul of me, avoid falling into sudden spasmodic passions with him. For it was exceeding difficult to bear in mind all the time those strange peculiarities, privileges, and unheard-of exemptions, forming the tacit stipulations on Bartleby's part under which he remained in my office. Now and then, in the eagerness of dispatching pressing business, I would inadvertently summon Bartleby, in a short, rapid tone, to put his finger, say, on the incipient tie of a bit of red tape with which I was about compressing some papers. Of course, from behind the screen the usual answer, "I prefer not to," was sure to come; and then, how could a human creature, with the common infirmities of our nature, refrain from bitterly exclaiming upon such perverseness—such unreasonableness? However, every added repulse of this sort which I received only tended to lessen the probability of my repeating the inadvertence.

Here it must be said, that, according to the custom of most legal gentlemen occupying chambers in densely populated law buildings, there were several keys to my door. One was kept by a woman residing in the attic, which person weekly scrubbed and daily swept and dusted my apartments. Another was kept by Turkey for convenience sake. The third I sometimes carried in my own pocket. The fourth I knew not who had.

Now, one Sunday morning I happened to go to Trinity Church, to hear a celebrated preacher, and finding myself rather early on the ground I thought I would walk round to my chambers for a while. Luckily I had my key with me, but upon applying it to the lock, I found it resisted by something inserted from the inside. Quite surprised, I called out; when to my consternation a key was turned from within; and thrusting his lean visage at me, and holding the door ajar, the apparition of Bartleby appeared, in his shirt-sleeves, and otherwise in a strangely tattered *deshabille,* saying quietly that he was sorry, but he was deeply engaged just then, and—preferred not admitting me at present. In a brief word or two, he moreover added, that perhaps I had better walk round the block two or three times, and by that time he would probably have concluded his affairs.

UNIT 2

Now, the utterly unsurmised appearance of Bartleby, tenanting my law chambers of a Sunday morning, with his cadaverously gentlemanly *nonchalance,* yet withal firm and self-possessed, had such a strange effect upon me that incontinently I slunk away from my own door, and did as desired. But not without sundry twinges of impotent rebellion against the mild effrontery of this unaccountable scrivener. Indeed, it was his wonderful mildness chiefly which not only disarmed me, but unmanned me, as it were. For I consider that one, for the time, is sort of unmanned when he tranquilly permits his hired clerk to dictate to him, and order him away from his own premises. Furthermore, I was full of uneasiness as to what Bartleby could possibly be doing in my office in his shirt-sleeves, and in an otherwise dismantled condition of a Sunday morning. Was anything amiss going on? Nay, that was out of the question. It was not to be thought of for a moment that Bartleby was an immoral person. But what could he be doing there?—copying? Nay again, whatever might be his eccentricities, Bartleby was an eminently decorous person. He would be the last man to sit down to his desk in any state approaching to nudity. Besides, it was Sunday; and there was something about Bartleby that forbade the supposition that he would by any secular occupation violate the proprieties of the day.

90   Nevertheless, my mind was not pacified; and full of a restless curiosity, at last I returned to the door. Without hindrance I inserted my key, opened it, and entered. Bartleby was not to be seen. I looked round anxiously, peeped behind his screen; but it was very plain that he was gone. Upon more closely examining the place, I surmised that for an indefinite period Bartleby must have ate, dressed, and slept in my office, and that too without plate, mirror, or bed. The cushioned seat of a rickety old sofa in one corner bore the faint impress of a lean, reclining form. Rolled away under his desk, I found a blanket; under the empty grate, a blacking box and brush; on a chair, a tin basin, with soap and a ragged towel; in a newspaper a few crumbs of ginger-nuts and a morsel of cheese. Yes, thought I, it is evident enough that Bartleby has been making his home here, keeping bachelor's hall all by himself. Immediately then the thought came sweeping across me, what miserable friendlessness and loneliness are here revealed! His poverty is great; but his solitude, how horrible! Think of it. Of a Sunday, Wall Street is deserted as Petra; and every night of every day it is an emptiness. This building, too, which of week-days hums with industry and life, at nightfall echoes with sheer vacancy, and all through Sunday is forlorn. And here Bartleby makes his home; sole spectator of a solitude which he has seen all populous—a sort of innocent and transformed Marius brooding among the ruins of Carthage?

For the first time in my life a feeling of overpowering stinging melancholy seized me. Before, I had never experienced aught but a not unpleasing sadness. The bond of a common humanity now drew me irresistibly to gloom. A fraternal melancholy! For both I and Bartleby were sons of Adam. I remembered the bright silks and sparkling faces I had seen that day, in gala trim, swan-like sailing down the Mississippi of Broadway; and I contrasted them with the pallid copyist, and thought to myself, Ah, happiness courts the light, so we deem the world is gay; but misery hides aloof, so we deem that misery there is none. These sad fancyings—chimeras, doubtless, of a sick and silly brain—led on to other and more special thoughts, concerning the eccentricities of Bartleby. Presentiments of strange discoveries hovered round me. The scrivener's pale form appeared to me laid out, among uncaring strangers, in its shivering guiding-sheet.

Suddenly I was attracted by Bartleby's closed desk, the key in open sight within the lock.

I mean no mischief, seek the gratification of no heartless curiosity, thought I; besides, the desk is mine, and its contents, too, so I will make bold to look within. Everything was methodically arranged, the papers smoothly placed. The pigeon-holes were deep, and removing the files of documents, I groped into their recesses. Presently I felt something there, and dragged it out. It was an old bandanna handkerchief, heavy and knotted. I opened it, and saw it was a saving's bank.

I now recalled all the quiet mysteries which I had noted in the man. I remembered that he never spoke but to answer; that, though at intervals he had considerable time to himself, yet I had never seen him reading—no, not even a newspaper; that for long periods he would stand looking out, at his pale window behind the screen, upon the dead brick wall; I was quite sure he never visited any refectory or eating-house; while his pale face clearly indicated that he never drank beer like Turkey; or tea and coffee even, like other men; that he never went anywhere in particular that I could learn; never went out for a walk, unless, indeed, that was the case at present; that he had declined telling who he was, or whence he came, or whether he had any relatives in the world; that though so thin and pale, he never complained of ill-health. And more than all, I remembered a certain unconscious air of pallid—how shall I call it—of pallid haughtiness, say, or rather an austere reserve about him, which had positively awed me into my tame compliance with his eccentricities, when I had feared to ask him to do the slightest incidental thing for me, even though I might know, from his long-continued motionlessness, that behind his screen he must be standing in one of those dead-wall reveries of his.

95   Revolving all these things, and coupling them with the recently discovered fact, that he made my office his constant abiding place and home, and not forgetful of his morbid moodiness; revolving all these things, a prudential feeling began to steal over me. My first emotions had been those of pure melancholy and sincerest pity; but just in proportion as the forlornness of Bartleby grew and grew to my imagination, did that same melancholy merge into fear, that pity into repulsion. So true it is, and so terrible, too, that up to a certain point the thought or sight of misery enlists our best affections; but, in certain special cases, beyond that point it does not. They err who would assert that invariably this is owing to the inherent selfishness of the human heart. It rather proceeds from a certain hopelessness of remedying excessive and organic ill. To a sensitive being, pity is not seldom pain. And when at last it is perceived that such pity cannot lead to effectual succor, common sense bids the soul be rid of it. What I saw that morning persuaded me that the scrivener was the victim of innate and incurable disorder. I might give alms to his body; but his body did not pain him; it was his soul that suffered, and his soul I could not reach.

        I did not accomplish the purpose of going to Trinity Church that morning. Somehow, the things I had seen disqualified me for the time from church-going. I walked homeward, thinking what I would do with Bartleby. Finally, I resolved upon this—I would put certain calm questions to him the next morning, touching his history, etc., and if he declined to answer them openly and unreservedly (and I supposed he would prefer not), then to give him a twenty dollar bill over and above whatever I might owe him, and tell him his services were no longer required; but that if in any other way I could assist him, I would be happy to do so, especially if he desired to return to his native place, wherever that might be, I would willingly help to defray the expenses. Moreover, if, after reaching home, he found himself at any time in want of aid, a letter from him would be sure of a reply.

        The next morning came.

        "Bartleby," said I, gently calling to him behind his screen.

        No reply.

100   "Bartleby," said I, in a still gentler tone, "come here; I am not going to ask you to do anything you would prefer not to do—I simply wish to speak to you."

        Upon this he noiselessly slid into view.

        "Will you tell me, Bartleby, where you were born?"

        "I would prefer not to."

        "Will you tell me *anything* about yourself?"

105   "I would prefer not to."

"But what reasonable objection can you have to speak to me? I feel friendly towards you."

He did not look at me while I spoke, but kept his glance fixed upon my bust of Cicero, which, as I then sat, was directly behind me, some six inches above my head.

"What is your answer, Bartleby?" said I, after waiting a considerable time for a reply, during which his countenance remained immovable, only there was the faintest conceivable tremor of the white attenuated mouth.

"At present I prefer to give no answer," he said, and retired into his hermitage.

110   It was rather weak in me I confess, but his manner, on this occasion, nettled me. Not only did there seem to lurk in it a certain calm disdain, but his perverseness seemed ungrateful, considering the undeniable good usage and indulgence he had received from me.

Again I sat ruminating what I should do. Mortified as I was at his behavior, and resolved as I had been to dismiss him when I entered my office, nevertheless I strangely felt something superstitious knocking at my heart, and forbidding me to carry out my purpose, and denouncing me for a villain if I dared to breathe one bitter word against this forlornest of mankind. At last, familiarly drawing my chair behind his screen, I sat down and said: "Bartleby, never mind, then, about revealing your history; but let me entreat you, as a friend, to comply as far as may be with the usages of this office. Say now, you will help to examine papers tomorrow or next day: in short, say now, that in a day or two you will begin to be a little reasonable:—say so, Bartleby."

"At present I would prefer not to be a little reasonable," was his mildly cadaverous reply.

Just then the folding-doors opened, and Nippers approached. He seemed suffering from an unusually bad night's rest, induced by severer indigestion than common. He overheard those final words of Bartleby.

"*Prefer not*, eh?" gritted Nippers—"I'd *prefer* him, if I were you, sir," addressing me—"I'd *prefer* him; I'd give him preferences, the stubborn mule! What is it, sir, pray, that he *prefers* not to do now?"

115   Bartleby moved not a limb.

"Mr. Nippers," said I, "I'd prefer that you would withdraw for the present."

Somehow, of late, I had got into the way of involuntarily using this word "prefer" upon all sorts of not exactly suitable occasions. And I trembled to think that my contact with the scrivener had already and seriously affected me in a mental way. And what further and deeper aberration might it not yet produce?

This apprehension had not been without efficacy in determining me to summary measures.

As Nippers, looking very sour and sulky, was departing, Turkey blandly and deferentially approached.

"With submission, sir," said he, "yesterday I was thinking about Bartleby here, and I think that if he would but prefer to take a quart of good ale every day, it would do much towards mending him, and enabling him to assist in examining his papers."

120   "So you have got the word, too," said I, slightly excited.

"With submission, what word, sir?" asked Turkey, respectfully crowding himself into the contracted space behind the screen, and by so doing, making me jostle the scrivener. "What word, sir?"

"I would prefer to be left alone here," said Bartleby, as if offended at being mobbed in his privacy.

"*That's* the word, Turkey," said I—"*that's* it."

"Oh, *prefer?* oh yes—queer word. I never use it myself. But, sir, as I was saying, if he would but prefer—"

125   "Turkey," interrupted I, "you will please withdraw."

"Oh certainly, sir, if you prefer that I should."

As he opened the folding-door to retire, Nippers at his desk caught a glimpse of me, and asked whether I would prefer to have a certain paper copied on blue paper or white. He did not in the least roguishly accent the word "prefer." It was plain that it involuntarily rolled from his tongue. I thought to myself, surely I must get rid of a demented man, who already has in some degree turned the tongues, if not the heads of myself and clerks. But I thought it prudent not to break the dismission at once.

The next day I noticed that Bartleby did nothing but stand at his window in his dead-wall revery. Upon asking him why he did not write, he said that he had decided upon doing no more writing.

"Why, how now? what next?" exclaimed I, "do no more writing?"

130   "No more."

"And what is the reason?"

"Do you not see the reason for yourself?" he indifferently replied.

I looked steadfastly at him, and perceived that his eyes looked dull and glazed. Instantly it occurred to me, that his unexampled diligence in copying by his dim window for the first few weeks of his stay with me might have temporarily impaired his vision.

I was touched. I said something in condolence with him. I hinted that of course he did wisely in abstaining from writing for a while; and urged him to embrace that opportunity of taking wholesome exercise in the open air. This, however, he did not do. A few days after this, my other clerks being absent, and being in a great hurry to dispatch certain letters by the mail, I thought that, having nothing else earthly to do, Bartleby would surely be less inflexible than usual, and carry these letters to the Post Office. But he blankly declined. So, much to my inconvenience, I went myself.

135   Still added days went by. Whether Bartleby's eyes improved or not, I could not say. To all appearance, I thought they did. But when I asked him if they did, he vouchsafed no answer. At all events, he would do no copying. At last, in replying to my urgings, he informed me that he had permanently given up copying.

"What!" exclaimed I; "suppose your eyes should get entirely well—better than ever before—would you not copy then?"

"I have given up copying," he answered, and slid aside.

He remained as ever, a fixture in my chamber. Nay—if that were possible—he became still more of a fixture than before. What was to be done? He would do nothing in the office; why should he stay there? In plain fact, he had now become a millstone to me, not only useless as a necklace, but afflictive to bear. Yet I was sorry for him. I speak less than truth when I say that, on his own account, he occasioned me uneasiness. If he would but have named a single relative or friend, I would instantly have written, and urged their taking the poor fellow away to some convenient retreat. But he seemed alone, absolutely alone in the universe. A bit of wreck in the mid-Atlantic. At length, necessities connected with my business tyrannized over all other considerations. Decently as I could, I told Bartleby that in six days' time he must unconditionally leave the office. I warned him to take measures, in the interval, for procuring some other abode. I offered to assist him in this endeavor, if he himself would but take the first step towards a removal. "And when you finally quit me, Bartleby," added I, "I shall see that you go not away entirely unprovided. Six days from this hour, remember."

At the expiration of that period, I peeped behind the screen, and lo! Bartleby was there.

140   I buttoned up my coat, balanced myself; advanced slowly towards him, touched his shoulder, and said, "The time has come; you must quit this place; I am sorry for you; here is money; but you must go."

"I would prefer not," he replied, with his back still towards me.

"You *must*."

He remained silent.

Now I had an unbounded confidence in this man's common honesty. He had frequently restored to me sixpences and shillings carelessly dropped upon the floor, for I am apt to be very reckless in such shirt-button affairs. The proceedings, then, which followed will not be deemed extraordinary.

145   "Bartleby," said I, "I owe you twelve dollars on account; here are thirty-two, the odd twenty are yours—Will you take it?" and I handed the bills towards him.

But he made no motion.

"I will leave them here, then," putting them under a weight on the table. Then taking my hat and cane and going to the door, I tranquilly turned and added—"After you have removed your things from these offices, Bartleby, you will of course lock the door—since every one is now gone for the day but you— and if you please, slip your key underneath the mat, so that I may have it in the morning. I shall not see you again; so good-bye to you. If, hereafter, in your new place of abode, I can be of any service to you, do not fail to advise me by letter. Good-bye, Bartleby, and fare you well."

But he answered not a word; like the last column of some ruined temple, he remained standing mute and solitary in the middle of the otherwise deserted room.

As I walked home in a pensive mood, my vanity got the better of my pity. I could not but highly plume myself on my masterly management in getting rid of Bartleby. Masterly I call it, and such it must appear to any dispassionate thinker. The beauty of my procedure seemed to consist in its perfect quietness. There was no vulgar bullying, no bravado of any sort, no choleric hectoring, and striding to and fro across the apartment, jerking out vehement commands for Bartleby to bundle himself off with his beggarly traps. Nothing of the kind. Without loudly bidding Bartleby depart—as an inferior genius might have done—I *assumed* the ground that depart he must; and upon that assumption built all I had to say. The more I thought over my procedure, the more I was charmed with it. Nevertheless, next morning, upon awakening, I had my doubts—I had somehow slept off the fumes of vanity. One of the coolest and wisest hours a man has, is just after he awakes in the morning. My procedure seemed as sagacious as ever—but only in theory. How it would prove in practice—there was the rub. It was truly a beautiful thought to have assumed Bartleby's departure; but, after all, that assumption was simply my own, and none of Bartleby's. The great point was, not whether I had assumed that he would quit me, but whether he would prefer to do so. He was more a man of preferences than assumptions.

150   After breakfast, I walked downtown, arguing the probabilities *pro* and *con*. One moment I thought it would prove a miserable failure, and Bartleby would be found all alive at my office as usual; the next moment it seemed certain that I should find his chair empty. And so I kept veering about. At the corner of Broadway and Canal Street, I saw quite an excited group of people standing in earnest conversation.

"I'll take odds he doesn't," said a voice as I passed.

"Doesn't go?—done!" said I, "put up your money."

I was instinctively putting my hand in my pocket to produce my own, when I remembered that this was an election day. The words I had overheard bore no reference to Bartleby, but to the success or non-success of some candidate for the mayoralty. In my intent frame of mind, I had, as it were, imagined that all Broadway shared in my excitement, and were debating the same question with me. I passed on, very thankful that the uproar of the street screened my momentary absent-mindedness.

As I had intended, I was earlier than usual at my office door. I stood listening for a moment. All was still. He must be gone. I tried the knob. The door was locked. Yes, my procedure had worked to a charm; he indeed must be vanished. Yet a certain melancholy mixed with this: I was almost sorry for my brilliant success. I was fumbling under the door mat for the key, which Bartleby was to have left there for me, when accidentally my knee knocked against a panel, producing a summoning sound, and in response a voice came to me from within— "Not yet; I am occupied."

155   It was Bartleby.

I was thunderstruck. For an instant I stood like the man who, pipe in mouth, was killed one cloudless afternoon long ago in Virginia, by summer lightning; at his own warm open window he was killed, and remained leaning out there upon the dreamy afternoon, till some one touched him, when he fell.

"Not gone!" I murmured at last. But again obeying that wondrous ascendancy which the inscrutable scrivener had over me, and from which ascendancy, for all my chafing, I could not completely escape, I slowly went downstairs and out into the street, and while walking round the block, considered what I should next do in this unheard-of perplexity. Turn the man out by an actual thrusting I could not; to drive him away by calling him hard names would not do; calling in the police was an unpleasant idea; and yet, permit him to enjoy his cadaverous triumph over me—this, too, I could not think of. What was to be done? or, if nothing could be done, was there anything further that I could *assume* in the matter? Yes, as before I had prospectively assumed that Bartleby would depart, so now I might retrospectively assume that departed he was. In the legitimate carrying out of this assumption, I might enter my office in a great hurry, and pretending not to see Bartleby at all, walk straight against him as if he were air. Such a proceeding would in a singular degree have the appearance of a home-thrust. It was hardly possible that Bartleby could withstand such an application of the doctrine of assumption. But upon second thoughts the success of the plan seemed rather dubious. I resolved to argue the matter over with him again.

"Bartleby," said I, entering the office, with a quietly severe expression, "I am seriously displeased. I am pained, Bartleby. I had thought better of you. I had imagined you of such a gentlemanly organization, that in any delicate dilemma a slight hint would suffice—in short, an assumption. But it appears I am deceived. Why," I added, unaffectedly starting, "you have not even touched that money yet," pointing to it, just where I had left it the evening previous.

He answered nothing.

160   "Will you, or will you not, quit me?" I now demanded in a sudden passion, advancing close to him.

"I would prefer *not* to quit you," he replied, gently emphasizing the *not*.

"What earthly right have you to stay here? Do you pay any rent? Do you pay my taxes? Or is this property yours?"

He answered nothing.

"Are you ready to go on and write now? Are your eyes recovered? Could you copy a small paper for me this morning? or help examine a few lines? or step round to the Post Office? In a word, will you do anything at all, to give a coloring to your refusal to depart the premises?"

165   He silently retired into his hermitage.

I was now in such a state of nervous resentment that I thought it but prudent to check myself at present from further demonstrations. Bartleby and I were alone. I remembered the tragedy of the unfortunate Adams and the still more unfortunate Colt in the solitary office of the latter; and how poor Colt, being dreadfully incensed by Adams, and imprudently permitting himself to get wildly excited, was at unawares hurried into his fatal act—an act which certainly no man could possibly deplore more than the actor himself. Often it had occurred to me in my ponderings upon the subject that had that altercation taken place in the public street, or at a private residence, it would not have terminated as it did. It was the circumstance of being alone in a solitary office, upstairs, of a building entirely unhallowed by humanizing domestic associations—an uncarpeted office, doubtless, of a dusty, haggard sort of appearance—this it must have been, which greatly helped to enhance the irritable desperation of the hapless Colt.

But when this old Adam of resentment rose in me and tempted me concerning Bartleby, I grappled him and threw him. How? Why, simply by recalling the divine injunction: "A new commandment give I unto you, that ye love one another." Yes, this it was that saved me. Aside from higher considerations, charity often operates as a vastly wise and prudent principle—a great safeguard to its possessor. Men have committed murder for jealousy's sake, and anger's sake, and hatred's sake, and selfishness' sake, and spiritual pride's sake; but no man, that ever I heard of, ever committed a diabolical murder for sweet charity's sake. Mere self-interest, then, if no better motive can be enlisted, should, especially with high-tempered men, prompt all beings to charity and philanthropy. At any rate, upon the occasion in question, I strove to drown my exasperated feelings towards the scrivener by benevolently construing his conduct. Poor fellow, poor fellow! thought I, he don't mean anything, and besides, he has seen hard times, and ought to be indulged.

I endeavored, also, immediately to occupy myself, and at the same time to comfort my despondency. I tried to fancy, that in the course of the morning, at such time as might prove agreeable to him, Bartleby, of his own free accord, would emerge from his hermitage and take up some decided line of march in the direction of the door. But no. Half-past twelve o'clock came; Turkey began to glow in the face, overturn his inkstand, and become generally obstreperous; Nippers abated down into quietude and courtesy; Ginger Nut munched his noon apple; and Bartleby remained standing at his window in one of his profoundest dead-wall reveries. Will it be credited? Ought I to acknowledge it? That afternoon I left the office without saying one further word to him.

Some days now passed, during which, at leisure intervals I looked a little into "Edwards on the Will," and "Priestley on Necessity." Under the circumstances, those books induced a salutary feeling. Gradually I slid into the persuasion that these troubles of mine, touching the scrivener, had been all predestined from eternity, and Bartleby was billeted upon me for some mysterious purpose of an all-wise Providence, which it was not for a mere mortal like me to fathom. Yes, Bartleby, stay there behind your screen, thought I; I shall persecute you no more; you are harmless and noiseless as any of these old chairs; in short, I never feel so private as when I know you are here. At last I see it, I feel it; I penetrate to the predestined purpose of my life. I am content. Others may have loftier parts to enact; but my mission in this world, Bartleby, is to furnish you with office-room for such period as you may see fit to remain.

170　　I believe that this wise and blessed frame of mind would have continued with me, had it not been for the unsolicited and uncharitable remarks obtruded upon me by my professional friends who visited the rooms. But thus it often is, that the constant friction of illiberal minds wears out at last the best resolves of the more generous. Though to be sure, when I reflected upon it, it was not strange that people entering my office should be struck by the peculiar aspect of the unaccountable Bartleby, and so be tempted to throw out some sinister observations concerning him. Sometimes an attorney, having business with me, and calling at my office, and finding no one but the scrivener there, would undertake to obtain some sort of precise information from him touching my whereabouts; but without heeding his idle talk, Bartleby would remain standing immovable in the middle of the room. So after contemplating him in that position for a time, the attorney would depart, no wiser than he came.

Also, when a reference was going on, and the room full of lawyers and witnesses, and business driving fast, some deeply-occupied legal gentleman present, seeing Bartleby wholly unemployed, would request him to run round to his (the legal gentleman's) office and fetch some papers for him. Thereupon, Bartleby would tranquilly decline, and yet remain idle as before. Then the lawyer would give a great stare, and turn to me. And what could I say? At last I was made aware that all through the circle of my professional acquaintance, a whisper of wonder was running round, having reference to the strange creature I kept at my office. This worried me very much. And as the idea came upon me of his possibly turning out a long-lived man, and keeping occupying my chambers, and denying my authority; and perplexing my visitors; and scandalizing my professional reputation; and casting a general gloom over the premises; keeping soul and body together to the last upon his savings (for doubtless he spent but half a dime a day), and in the end perhaps outlive me, and claim possession of my office by right of his perpetual occupancy: as all these dark anticipations crowded upon me more and more, and my friends continually intruded their relentless remarks upon the apparition in my room; a great change was wrought in me. I resolved to gather all my faculties together, and forever rid me of this intolerable incubus.

Ere revolving any complicated project, however, adapted to this end, I first simply suggested to Bartleby the propriety of his permanent departure. In a calm and serious tone, I commended the idea to his careful and mature consideration. But, having taken three days to meditate upon it, he apprised me, that his original determination remained the same; in short, that he still preferred to abide with me.

What shall I do? I now said to myself, buttoning up my coat to the last button. What shall I do? what ought I to do? what does conscience say I *should* do with this man, or, rather, ghost. Rid myself of him, I must; go, he shall. But how? You will not thrust him, the poor, pale, passive mortal—you will not thrust such a helpless creature out of your door? you will not dishonor yourself by such cruelty? No, I will not, I cannot do that. Rather would I let him live and die here, and then mason up his remains in the wall. What, then, will you do? For all your coaxing, he will not budge. Bribes he leaves under your own paperweight on your table; in short, it is quite plain that he prefers to cling to you.

Then something severe, something unusual must be done. What! surely you will not have him collared by a constable, and commit his innocent pallor to the common jail? And upon what ground could you procure such a thing to be done?—a vagrant, is he? What! he a vagrant, a wanderer, who refuses to budge? It is because he will *not* be a vagrant, then, that you seek to count him *as* a vagrant. That is too absurd. No visible means of support: there I have him. Wrong again: for indubitably he *does* support himself, and that is the only unanswerable proof that any man can show of his possessing the means so to do. No more, then. Since he will not quit me, I must quit him. I will change my offices; I will move elsewhere, and give him fair notice, that if I find him on my new premises I will then proceed against him as a common trespasser.

175   Acting accordingly, next day I thus addressed him: "I find these chambers too far from the City Hall; the air is unwholesome. In a word, I propose to remove my offices next week, and shall no longer require your services. I tell you this now, in order that you may seek another place."

He made no reply, and nothing more was said.

On the appointed day I engaged carts and men, proceeded to my chambers, and having but little furniture, everything was removed in a few hours. Throughout, the scrivener remained standing behind the screen, which I directed to be removed the last thing. It was withdrawn; and, being folded up like a huge folio, left him the motionless occupant of a naked room. I stood in the entry watching him a moment, while something from within me upbraided me.

I re-entered, with my hand in my pocket—and—and my heart in my mouth.

"Good-bye, Bartleby; I am going—good-bye, and God some way bless you; and take that," slipping something in his hand. But it dropped upon the floor, and then—strange to say—I tore myself from him whom I had so longed to be rid of.

UNIT 2

180   Established in my new quarters, for a day or two I kept the door locked, and started at every footfall in the passages. When I returned to my rooms, after any little absence, I would pause at the threshold for an instant, and attentively listen, ere applying my key. But these fears were needless. Bartleby never came nigh me.

I thought all was going well, when a perturbed-looking stranger visited me, inquiring whether I was the person who had recently occupied rooms at No.— Wall Street.

Full of forebodings, I replied that I was.

"Then, sir," said the stranger, who proved a lawyer, "you are responsible for the man you left there. He refuses to do any copying; he refuses to do anything; he says he prefers not to; and he refuses to quit the premises."

"I am very sorry, sir," said I, with assumed tranquillity, but an inward tremor, "but, really, the man you allude to is nothing to me—he is no relation or apprentice of mine, that you should hold me responsible for him."

185   "In mercy's name, who is he?"

"I certainly cannot inform you. I know nothing about him. Formerly I employed him as a copyist; but he has done nothing for me now for some time past."

"I shall settle him, then—good morning, sir."

Several days passed, and I heard nothing more; and, though I often felt a charitable prompting to call at the place and see poor Bartleby, yet a certain squeamishness, of I know not what, withheld me.

All is over with him, by this time, thought I, at last, when, through another week, no further intelligence reached me. But, coming to my room the day after, I found several persons waiting at my door in a high state of nervous excitement.

190   "That's the man—here he comes," cried the foremost one, whom I recognized as the lawyer who had previously called upon me alone.

"You must take him away, sir, at once," cried a portly person among them, advancing upon me, and whom I knew to be the landlord of No.—Wall Street "These gentlemen, my tenants, cannot stand it any longer; Mr. B—," pointing to the lawyer, "has turned him out of his room, and he now persists in haunting the building generally, sitting upon the banisters of the stairs by day, and sleeping in the entry by night. Everybody is concerned; clients are leaving the offices; some fears are entertained of a mob; something you must do, and that without delay."

Aghast at this torrent, I fell back before it, and would fain have locked myself in my new quarters. In vain I persisted that Bartleby was nothing to me no more than to any one else. In vain—I was the last person known to have anything to

do with him, and they held me to the terrible account. Fearful then, of being
exposed in the papers (as one person present obscurely threatened), I considered the matter, and, at length, said, that if the lawyer would give me a confi-
dential interview with the scrivener, in his (the lawyer's) own room, I would,
that afternoon, strive my best to rid them of the nuisance they complained of.

Going upstairs to my old haunt, there was Bartleby silently sitting upon the
banister at the landing.

"What are you doing here, Bartleby?" said I.

"Sitting upon the banister," he mildly replied.

I motioned him into the lawyer's room, who then left us.

"Bartleby," said I, "are you aware that you are the cause of great tribulation
to me, by persisting in occupying the entry after being dismissed from the office?"

No answer.

"Now one of two things must take place. Either you must do something or
something must be done to you. Now what sort of business would you like to
engage in? Would you like to re-engage in copying for some one?"

"No; I would prefer not to make any change."

"Would you like a clerkship in a dry-goods store?"

"There is too much confinement about that. No, I would not like a clerkship;
but I am not particular."

"Too much confinement," I cried, "why, you keep yourself confined all the
time!"

"I would prefer not to take a clerkship," he rejoined, as if to settle that little
item at once.

"How would a bartender's business suit you? There is no trying of the eyesight in that."

"I would not like it at all; though, as I said before, I am not particular."

His unwonted wordiness inspirited me. I returned to the charge.

"Well, then, would you like to travel through the country collecting bills for
the merchants? That would improve your health."

"No, I would prefer to be doing something else."

"How, then, would going as a companion to Europe, to entertain some young
gentleman with your conversation—how would that suit you?"

"Not at all. It does not strike me that there is anything definite about that. I
like to be stationary. But I am not particular."

"Stationary you shall be, then," I cried, now losing all patience, and, for the
first time in all my exasperating connection with him, fairly flying into a passion.

"If you do not go away from these premises before night, I shall feel bound—indeed, I *am* bound—to—to quit the premises myself!" I rather absurdly concluded, knowing not with what possible threat to try to frighten his immobility into compliance. Despairing of all further efforts, I was precipitately leaving him, when a final thought occurred to me—one which had not been wholly unindulged before.

"Bartleby," said I, in the kindest tone I could assume under such exciting circumstances, "will you go home with me now—not to my office, but my dwelling—and remain there till we can conclude upon some convenient arrangement for you at our leisure? Come, let us start now, right away."

"No: at present I would prefer not to make any change at all."

220   I answered nothing; but, effectually dodging every one by the suddenness and rapidity of my flight, rushed from the building, ran up Wall Street towards Broadway, and, jumping into the first omnibus, was soon removed from pursuit. As soon as tranquillity returned, I distinctly perceived that I had now done all that I possibly could, both in respect to the demands of the landlord and his tenants and with regard to my own desire and sense of duty, to benefit Bartleby, and shield him from rude persecution. I now strove to be entirely carefree and quiescent, and my conscience justified me in the attempt; though, indeed, it was not so successful as I could have wished. So fearful was I of being again hunted out by the incensed landlord and his exasperated tenants, that, surrendering my business to Nippers, for a few days, I drove about the upper part of the town and through the suburbs, in my rockaway; crossed over to Jersey City and Hoboken, and paid fugitive visits to Manhattanville and Astoria. In fact, I almost lived in my rockaway for the time.

When again I entered my office, lo, a note from the landlord lay upon the desk. I opened it with trembling hands. It informed me that the writer had sent for the police, and had Bartleby removed to the Tombs as a vagrant. Moreover, since I knew more about him than any one else, he wished me to appear at that place, and make a suitable statement of the facts. These tidings had a conflicting effect upon me. At first I was indignant; but, at last, almost approved. The landlord's energetic, summary disposition, had led him to adopt a procedure which I do not think I would have decided upon myself; and yet, as a last resort, under such peculiar circumstances, it seemed the only plan.

As I afterwards learned, the poor scrivener, when told that he must be conducted to the Tombs, offered not the slightest obstacle, but, in his pale, unmoving way, silently acquiesced.

Some of the compassionate and curious bystanders joined the party; and headed by one of the constables arm-in-arm with Bartleby, the silent procession filed its way through all the noise, and heat, and joy of the roaring thoroughfares at noon.

The same day I received the note, I went to the Tombs, or, to speak more properly, the Halls of Justice. Seeking the right officer, I stated the purpose of my call, and was informed that the individual I described was, indeed, within. I then assured the functionary that Bartleby was a perfectly honest man, and greatly to be compassionated, however unaccountably eccentric. I narrated all I knew, and closed by suggesting the idea of letting him remain in as indulgent confinement as possible, till something less harsh might be done—though, indeed, I hardly knew what. At all events, if nothing else could be decided upon, the almshouse must receive him. I then begged to have an interview.

225   Being under no disgraceful charge, and quite serene and harmless in all his ways, they had permitted him freely to wander about the prison, and, especially, in the inclosed grass-platted yards thereof. And so I found him there, standing all alone in the quietest of the yards, his face towards a high wall, while all around, from the narrow slits of the jail windows, I thought I saw peering out upon him the eyes of murderers and thieves.

"Bartleby!"

"I know you," he said, without looking round—"and I want nothing to say to you."

"It was not I that brought you here, Bartleby," said I, keenly pained at his implied suspicion. "And to you, this should not be so vile a place. Nothing reproachful attaches to you by being here. And see, it is not so sad a place as one might think. Look, there is the sky, and here is the grass."

"I know where I am," he replied, but would say nothing more, and so I left him.

230   As I entered the corridor again, a broad meatlike man, in an apron, accosted me, and, jerking his thumb over his shoulder, said—"Is that your friend?"

"Yes."

"Does he want to starve? If he does, let him live on the prison fare, that's all."

"Who are you?" asked I, not knowing what to make of such an unofficially speaking person in such a place.

"I am the grub-man. Such gentlemen as have friends here, hire me to provide them with something good to eat."

235   "Is this so?" said I, turning to the turnkey.

He said it was.

"Well, then," said I, slipping some silver into the grub-man's hands (for so they called him), "I want you to give particular attention to my friend there, let him have the best dinner you can get. And you must be as polite to him as possible."

"Introduce me, will you?" said the grub-man, looking at me with an expression which seemed to say he was all impatience for an opportunity to give a specimen of his breeding.

Thinking it would prove of benefit to the scrivener, I acquiesced; and, asking the grub-man his name, went up with him to Bartleby.

240 "Bartleby, this is a friend; you will find him very useful to you."

"Your sarvant, sir, your sarvant," said the grub-man, making a low salutation behind his apron. "Hope you find it pleasant here, sir; nice grounds—cool apartments —hope you'll stay with us some time—try to make it agreeable. What will you have for dinner today?"

"I prefer not to dine today," said Bartleby, turning away. "It would disagree with me; I am unused to dinners." So saying, he slowly moved to the other side of the inclosure, and took up a position fronting the deadwall.

"How's this?" said the grub-man, addressing me with a stare of astonishment. "He's odd, ain't he?"

"I think he is a little deranged," said I, sadly.

245 "Deranged? deranged is it? Well, now, upon my word, I thought that friend of yourn was a gentleman forger; they are always pale and genteel-like, them forgers. I can't help pity 'em—can't help it, sir. Did you know Monroe Edwards?" he added, touchingly, and paused. Then, laying his hand piteously on my shoulder, sighed, "he died of consumption at Sing-Sing. So you weren't acquainted with Monroe?"

"No, I was never socially acquainted with any forgers. But I cannot stop longer. Look to my friend yonder. You will not lose by it. I will see you again."

Some few days after this, I again obtained admission to the Tombs, and went through the corridors in quest of Bartleby; but without finding him.

"I saw him coming from his cell not long ago," said a turnkey, "may be he's gone to loiter in the yards."

So I went in that direction.

250 "Are you looking for the silent man?" said another turnkey, passing me. "Yonder he lies—sleeping in the yard there. 'Tis not twenty minutes since I saw him lie down."

The yard was entirely quiet. It was not accessible to the common prisoners. The surrounding walls, of amazing thickness, kept off all sounds behind them. The Egyptian character of the masonry weighed upon me with its gloom. But a soft imprisoned turf grew under foot. The heart of the eternal pyramids, it seemed, wherein, by some strange magic, through the clefts, grass-seed, dropped by birds, had sprung.

Strangely huddled at the base of the wall, his knees drawn up, and lying on his side, his head touching the cold stones, I saw the wasted Bartleby. But nothing stirred. I paused; then went close up to him; stooped over, and saw that his dim eyes were open; otherwise he seemed profoundly sleeping. Something prompted me to touch him. I felt his hand, when a tingling shiver ran up my arm and down my spine to my feet.

The round face of the grub-man peered upon me now. "His dinner is ready. Won't he dine today, either? Or does he live without dining?"

"Lives without dining," said I, and closed the eyes.

255 "Eh!—He's asleep, ain't he?"

"With kings and counselors," murmured I.

There would seem little need for proceeding further in this history. Imagination will readily supply the meagre recital of poor Bartleby's interment. But, ere parting with the reader, let me say, that if this little narrative has sufficiently interested him, to awaken curiosity as to who Bartleby was, and what manner of life he led prior to the present narrator's making his acquaintance, I can only reply, that in such curiosity I fully share, but am wholly unable to gratify it. Yet here I hardly know whether I should divulge one little item of rumor, which came to my ear a few months after the scrivener's decease. Upon what basis it rested, I could never ascertain; and hence, how true it is I cannot now tell. But, inasmuch as this vague report has not been without a certain suggestive interest to me, however sad, it may prove the same with some others; and so I will briefly mention it. The report was this: that Bartleby had been a subordinate clerk in the Dead Letter Office at Washington, from which he had been suddenly removed by a change in the administration. When I think over this rumor, hardly can I express the emotions which seize me. Dead letters! does it not sound like dead men? Conceive a man by nature and misfortune prone to a pallid hopelessness, can any business seem more fitted to heighten it than that of continually handling these dead letters, and assorting them for the flames? For by the cartload they are annually burned. Sometimes from out the folded paper the pale clerk takes a ring—the finger it was meant for, perhaps, moulders in the grave; a bank-note sent in swiftest charity—he whom it would relieve, nor eats nor hungers any more; pardon for those who died despairing; hope for those who died unhoping; good tidings for those who died stifled by unrelieved calamities. On errands of life, these letters speed to death.

Ah, Bartleby! Ah, humanity!

LEVELS OF READING

Summary:

Pay attention to the **literal** meaning of the text. Briefly describe the sequence of events in Herman Melville's "Bartleby, the Scrivener." Repeat the story of the text in your own words. Who tells this story? Who are the players in this little office drama? State in a few sentences the "persona" of each of the characters in this story. In the course of the story, what happens to each of them? Concentrate on the highlights; avoid too much detail when summarizing. Again, drawing a simple outline of the main points of the text will help you better analyze the text at other levels of interpretation.

Analysis:

Find what you believe is **symbolic** in the story. For instance, what do walls generally symbolize? Is it important that the story is subtitled, "A Story of Wall Street"? In the story of Nisa's weaning (Unit I), she cannot get enough food to satisfy her. Bartleby, on the other hand, eats very little before refusing food altogether. What significance does food have in "Bartleby, the Scrivener"? Find any other symbols you think are important in the story and explain the meaning of these symbols. With the help of the background material provided about Herman Melville and his world, make an argument about this text, and include the mention of the more **figurative** aspects of the text when making points in defense of your argument.

Application:

Apply Jung's theory of the mind to "Bartleby, the Scrivener." Outline an argument you wish to make about this literary text using Jung's theory to help you explain what some part of the story may mean. The "part" of the text you choose to analyze may include any of the following: a character, a setting, a symbol or symbols, an important change, a motivation, a goal, a result. Consider the following as possibilities, but explore other original interpretations too:

- Jung's essay is especially helpful in trying to explain the cause and effect of transference and its relationship to the collective unconscious. Is

Bartleby's transference as successful as Jung's patient's? In terms of the collective unconscious, what might Bartleby represent?

- Return to **Coming to Terms with the Reading,** and see if any of the terms listed help you devise an argument about the situation, setting, or any of the characters in Melville's, "Bartleby, the Scrivener." For example, is there any aspect of this story that might represent Jung's idea of the **mother archetype**? How might Jung's idea of the **shadow** apply to Bartleby?

- In terms of Jung's theory, who or what might the lawyer in this story represent? Does he have one or more than one persona? Does he wear a mask? Explain.

PAUL LAURENCE DUNBAR

Paul Laurence Dunbar (1872–1906) was born in Dayton Ohio. His parents, Matilda and Joshua Dunbar were both Kentucky natives. His mother was a former slave and his father was an escaped slave who served in the Massachusetts Regiments during the Civil War. They separated in 1874.

His mother then worked as a washerwoman in Dayton, Ohio, to support her two young sons. She worked for a time for the family of Orville and Wilbur Wright, with whom Paul attended Dayton's Central High School. Dunbar was the only African American student in his class there. Upon graduating from high school, Dunbar published an African American newsletter in Dayton, the Dayton Tattler, *with financial assistance from the Wright brothers.*

During the years 1897–1902, Dunbar was married to Alice Ruth Moore and worked for one year for the Library of Congress before leaving to write full-time. His health, like his income, became precarious, and so did his marriage, which foundered. About a year before his death of tuberculosis, Dunbar returned to his mother's home in Dayton, where he died on February 9, 1906.

Despite his personal difficulties, Dunbar wrote prolifically in his short life. Oak and Ivy, *Dunbar's first collection of poems, was published in 1892. Twelve books of poetry, four books of stories, a play, and five novels followed. Like several of the Harlem Renaissance poets who were to follow in his footsteps a few decades later, much of his poetry is personal, if not autobiographical.*

WE WEAR THE MASK
Paul Laurence Dunbar

We wear the mask that grins and lies,
It hides our cheeks and shades our eyes —
This debt we pay to human guile;
With torn and bleeding hearts we smile,
And mouth with myriad subtleties.

Why should the world be over-wise,
In counting all our tears and sighs?
Nay, let them only see us, while
   We wear the mask.

We smile, but, O great Christ, our cries
To thee from tortured souls arise.
We sing, but oh the clay is vile
Beneath our feet, and long the mile;
But let the world dream otherwise,
   We wear the mask!

LEVELS OF READING

Summary:

Pay attention to the **literal** meaning of the text. Briefly describe the story told by Paul Laurence Dunbar's poem, "We Wear the Mask." Repeat the "story" of the poem in your own words. Who tells this story? State in a few sentences the "persona" of the voice in this poem. Concentrate on the highlights; avoid too much detail when summarizing. Again, drawing a simple outline of the main points of the poem will help you better analyze the text at other levels of interpretation.

Analysis:

Find what you believe is **symbolic** in the poem. For instance, on a symbolic level, who are "we" who wear the mask? What is symbolic about the mask itself? Are there any symbolic connections between the walls in "Bartleby, the Scrivener" and Dunbar's mask? Find any other symbols you think are important in the story and explain the meaning of these symbols. With the help of the background material provided about Paul Laurence Dunbar and his world, make an argument about this text, and include the mention of the more **figurative** aspects of the text when making points in defense of your argument.

Application:

Apply Jung's theory of the mind to "We Wear the Mask." Outline an argument you wish to make about this literary text using Jung's theory to help you explain what some part of the poem could mean. Consider the following as possibilities, but explore other original interpretations too:

- What aspect of the **collective unconscious** is represented in the mask? Is the content of the collective unconscious the same for all people? In terms of the collective unconscious, who or what might those wearing the mask represent?
- How might the mask in Dunbar's poem relate to Jung's idea of **persona**? Are there signs of more than one persona in Dunbar's poem? What effect might this have on personality?
- If walls are an **archetype**, and if Dunbar's mask can be read as a type of wall, what effect does this wall have on those inside the wall? On those outside of it?
- Is there any **transference** in this poem? How does it work?

Start Your Own Argument:

Who is right about the unconscious, Freud or Jung?

THREE

THE FIVE-PART ESSAY WITHIN THE
FIVE-PART ESSAY

The "five-part essay" is so named because it generally takes the form of an introduction, which usually includes a **thesis statement;** at least three points of support; and a conclusion or conclusions. Martin Luther King, Jr.'s "Letter from Birmingham City Jail" includes a number of five-part essays *within* its overall five-part essay form. When making a point in defense of his overall viewpoint, King often begins by clearly stating his evidence in the form of another argument, or **thesis,** followed by a varying number of "points" in its defense. He then concludes each of his briefer arguments in a way that provides a bridge to the next argument within his argument. As such, King's essay provides a model for a way in which the five-part essay can be expanded and made more complex than its basic form.

DR. MARTIN LUTHER KING, JR.

Martin Luther King, Jr. (1922–1968) was born in Atlanta, Georgia. On June 18, 1953, he married Coretta Scott of Marion, Alabama. They had four children.

King graduated from Morehouse College with a B.A. in sociology. He completed a Ph.D. in theology at Boston University in 1955. During this period, he also studied at Harvard University.

Upon completion of his doctorate, Dr. King became pastor of the Dexter Avenue Baptist Church in Montgomery, Alabama. In 1959, he resigned to assume leadership of the Southern Christian Leadership Conference in Atlanta, Georgia. From 1960 until his death in 1968, he was co-pastor with his father at the Ebenezer Baptist Church in Atlanta and President of the Southern Christian Leadership Conference.

Dr. King was a pivotal figure in the civil rights movement. He was arrested for his participation in civil rights activities at least thirty times. On one such occasion, in April 1963, Dr. King composed his famous "Letter from Birmingham City Jail." Five months later, the "Four Little Girls" of the title of

Spike Lee's award-winning documentary were killed in a church bombing not far from where Dr. King had been jailed. Nevertheless, the Voting Rights Act of 1965 was passed two years later as a result of a march from Selma to Montgomery, Alabama, led by Dr. King.

On April 4, 1968, Dr. King was fatally shot while standing on the balcony of the Lorraine Hotel in Memphis, Tennessee, where he had come to encourage the union organization of underpaid African American workers. His assailant, James Earl Ray, was arrested in London on June 8, 1968. Shortly before coming to trial, Ray pleaded guilty and was sentenced to ninety-nine years in the Tennessee State Penitentiary, where he died. Dr. King's birthday is now a national holiday.

———

Dr. King makes careful use of the traditional five-part essay in his "Letter from Birmingham City Jail." Pay close attention to the ways in which Dr. King embeds brief but important arguments within his larger argument. With each new point made, Dr. King first clearly states his point in the form of a thesis statement, defends each thesis with a number of clearly delineated points, and then concludes. The transition to his next point of argument is often contained in the conclusion to the one previous. Notice also how Dr. King begins his essay with a defense of his position, addressed to the clergymen who have questioned his presence in Birmingham, and then rhetorically turns the tables on his adversaries, leaving them on the defensive. This layering of arguments helps to make Dr. King's persuasive piece one of the more intricately structured essays ever written.

Coming to Terms with the Reading:

Before reading/rereading Dr. Martin Luther King, Jr.'s, "Letter from Birmingham City Jail," it is best to have a firm grasp on the meanings of the following terms:

1. civil rights movement
2. non-violent protest
3. Birmingham, Alabama (1963)
4. Southern Christian Leadership Conference

LETTER FROM BIRMINGHAM CITY JAIL
Martin Luther King, Jr.
April 16, 1963

1   My Dear Fellow Clergymen:

While confined here in the Birmingham city jail, I came across your recent statement calling my present activities "unwise and untimely." Seldom do I pause to answer criticism of my work and ideas. If I sought to answer all the criticisms that cross my desk, my secretaries would have little time for anything other than such correspondence in the course of the day, and I would have no time for constructive work. But since I feel that you are men of genuine good will and that your criticisms are sincerely set forth, I want to try to answer your statement in what I hope will be patient and reasonable terms.

I think I should indicate why I am here in Birmingham, since you have been influenced by the view which argues against "outsiders coming in." I have the honor of serving as president of the Southern Christian Leadership Conference, an organization operating in every southern state, with headquarters in Atlanta, Georgia. We have some eighty-five affiliated organizations across the South, and one of them is the Alabama Christian Movement for Human Rights. Frequently we share staff, educational, and financial resources with our affiliates. Several months ago the affiliate here in Birmingham asked us to be on call to engage in a nonviolent direct-action program if such were deemed necessary. We readily consented, and when the hour came we lived up to our promise. So I, along with several members of my staff, am here because I was invited here. I am here because I have organizational ties here.

But more basically, I am in Birmingham because injustice is here. Just as the prophets of the eighth century B.C. left their villages and carried their "thus saith the Lord" far beyond the boundaries of their home towns, and just as the Apostle Paul left his village of Tarsus and carried the gospel of Jesus Christ to the far corners of the Greco-Roman world, so am I compelled to carry the gospel of freedom beyond my own home town. Like Paul, I must constantly respond to the Macedonian call for aid.

Moreover, I am cognizant of the interrelatedness of all communities and states. I cannot sit idly by in Atlanta and not be concerned about what happens in Birmingham. Injustice anywhere is a threat to justice everywhere. We are caught in an inescapable network of mutuality, tied in a single garment of destiny. Whatever affects one directly, affects all indirectly. Never again can we afford to live with the narrow, provincial, "outside agitator" idea. Anyone who lives inside the United States can never be considered an outsider anywhere within its bounds.

5   You deplore the demonstrations taking place in Birmingham. But your statement, I am sorry to say, fails to express a similar concern for the conditions that brought about the demonstrations. I am sure that none of you would want to rest content with the superficial kind of social analysis that deals merely with effects and does not grapple with underlying causes. It is unfortunate that demonstrations are taking place in Birmingham, but it is even more unfortunate that the city's white power structure left the Negro community with no alternative.

In any nonviolent campaign there are four basic steps: collection of the facts to determine whether injustices exist; negotiation; self-purification; and direct action. We have gone through all these steps in Birmingham. There can be no gainsaying the fact that racial injustice engulfs this community. Birmingham is probably the most thoroughly segregated city in the United States. Its ugly record of brutality is widely known. Negroes have experienced grossly unjust treatment in the courts. There have been more unsolved bombings of Negro homes and churches in Birmingham than in any other city in the nation. These are the hard brutal facts of the case. On the basis of these conditions, Negro leaders sought to negotiate with the city fathers. But the latter consistently refused to engage in good-faith negotiation.

Then, last September, came the opportunity to talk with leaders of Birmingham's economic community. In the course of the negotiations, certain promises were made by the merchants—for example, to remove the stores' humiliating racial signs. On the basis of these promises, the Reverend Fred Shuttlesworth and the leaders of the Alabama Christian Movement for Human Rights agreed to a moratorium on all demonstrations. As the weeks and months went by, we realized that we were the victims of a broken promise. A few signs, briefly removed, returned; the others remained.

As in so many past experiences, our hopes had been blasted, and the shadow of deep disappointment settled upon us. We had no alternative except to prepare for direct action, whereby we would present our very bodies as a means of laying our case before the conscience of the local and the national community. Mindful of the difficulties involved, we decided to undertake a process of self-purification. We began a series of workshops on nonviolence, and we repeatedly asked ourselves: "Are you able to accept blows without retaliating?" "Are you able to endure the ordeal of jail?" We decided to schedule our direct-action program for the Easter season, realizing that except for Christmas, this is the main shopping period of the year. Knowing that a strong economic-withdrawal program would be the by-product of direct action, we felt that this would be the best time to bring pressure to bear on the merchants for the needed change.

Then it occurred to us that Birmingham's mayoral election was coming up in March, and we speedily decided to postpone action until after election day. When we discovered that the Commissioner of Public Safety, Eugene "Bull" Connor, had piled up enough votes to be in the run-off, we decided again to postpone action until the day after the run-off so that the demonstrations could not be used to cloud the issues. Like many others, we waited to see Mr. Connor defeated, and to this end we endured postponement after postponement. Having aided in this community need, we felt that our direct-action program could be delayed no longer.

10   You may well ask, "Why direct action? Why sit-ins, marches, and so forth? Isn't negotiation a better path?" You are quite right in calling for negotiation. Indeed, this is the very purpose of direct action. Nonviolent direct action seeks to create such a crisis and foster such a tension that a community which has constantly refused to negotiate is forced to confront the issue. It seeks so to dramatize the issue that it can no longer be ignored. My citing the creation of tension as part of the work of the nonviolent resister may sound rather shocking. But I must confess that I am not afraid of the word "tension." I have earnestly opposed violent tension, but there is a type of constructive, nonviolent tension which is necessary for growth. Just as Socrates felt that it was necessary to create a tension in the mind so that individuals could rise from the bondage of myths and half truths to the unfettered realm of creative analysis and objective appraisal, so must we see the need for nonviolent gadflies to create the kind of tension in society that will help men rise from the dark depths of prejudice and racism to the majestic heights of understanding and brotherhood.

The purpose of our direct-action program is to create a situation so crisis-packed that it will inevitably open the door to negotiation. I therefore concur with you in your call for negotiation. Too long has our beloved Southland been bogged down in a tragic effort to live in monologue rather than dialogue.

One of the basic points in your statement is that the action that I and my associates have taken in Birmingham is untimely. Some have asked: "Why didn't you give the new city administration time to act?" The only answer that I can give to this query is that the new Birmingham administration must be prodded about as much as the outgoing one, before it will act. We are sadly mistaken if we feel that the election of Albert Boutwell as mayor will bring the millennium to Birmingham. While Mr. Boutwell is a much more gentle person than Mr. Connor, they are both segregationists, dedicated to maintenance of the status quo: I have hoped that Mr. Boutwell will be reasonable enough to see the futility of massive resistance to desegregation. But he will not see this without pressure from devotees of civil rights. My friends, I must say to you that we have not made a single gain in civil rights without determined legal and nonviolent pressure. Lamentably, it is an historical fact that privileged groups seldom give up their privileges voluntarily. Individuals may see the moral light and voluntarily give up their unjust posture; but, as Reinhold Niebuhr has reminded us, groups tend to be more immoral than individuals.

We know through painful experience that freedom is never voluntarily given by the oppressor; it must be demanded by the oppressed. Frankly, I have yet to engage in a direct-action campaign that was "well timed" in the view of those who have not suffered unduly from the disease of segregation. For years now I have heard the word "Wait!" It rings in the ear of every Negro with piercing familiarity. This "Wait" has almost always meant "Never." We must come to see, with one of our distinguished jurists, that "justice too long delayed is justice denied."

We have waited for more than 340 years for our constitutional and God-given rights. The nations of Asia and Africa are moving with jetlike speed toward gaining political independence, but we still creep at horse-and-buggy pace toward gaining a cup of coffee at a lunch counter. Perhaps it is easy for those who have never felt the stinging darts of segregation to say, "Wait." But when you have seen vicious mobs lynch your mothers and fathers at will and drown your sisters and brothers at whim; when you have seen hate-filled policemen curse, kick, and even kill your black brothers and sisters; when you see the vast majority of your twenty million Negro brothers smothering in an airtight cage of poverty in the midst of an affluent society; when you suddenly find your tongue twisted and your speech stammering as you seek to explain to your six-year-old daughter why she can't go to the public amusement park that has just been advertised on television, and see tears welling up in her eyes when she is told that Funtown is closed to colored children, and see ominous clouds of inferiority beginning to form in her little mental sky, and see her beginning to distort her personality by developing an unconscious bitterness toward white people; when you have to con-coct an answer for a five-year-old son who is asking, "Daddy, why do white people treat colored people so mean?;" when you take a cross-country drive and find it necessary to sleep night after night in the uncomfortable corners of your automobile because no motel will accept you; when you are humiliated day in and day out by nagging signs reading "white" and "colored;" when your first name becomes "nigger," your middle name becomes "boy" (however old you are) and your last name becomes "John," and your wife and mother are never given the respected title "Mrs."; when you are harried by day and haunted by night by the fact that you are a Negro, living constantly at tiptoe stance, never quite knowing what to expect next, and are plagued with inner fears and outer resentments; when you are forever fighting a degenerating sense of "nobodi-ness"—then you will understand why we find it difficult to wait. There comes a time when the cup of endurance runs over, and men are no longer willing to be plunged into the abyss of despair. I hope, sirs, you can understand our legit-imate and unavoidable impatience.

15   You express a great deal of anxiety over our willingness to break laws. This is certainly a legitimate concern. Since we so diligently urge people to obey the Supreme Court's decision of 1954 outlawing segregation in the public schools, at first glance it may seem rather paradoxical for us consciously to break laws. One may well ask: "How can you advocate breaking some laws and obeying others?" The answer lies in the fact that there are two types of laws; just and unjust. I would be the first to advocate obeying just laws. One has not only a legal but a moral responsibility to obey just laws. Conversely, one has a moral responsibil-ity to disobey unjust laws. I would agree with St. Augustine that "an unjust law is no law at all."

Now, what is the difference between the two? How does one determine whether a law is just or unjust? A just law is a manmade code that squares with the moral law or the law of God. An unjust law is a code that is out of harmony with the moral law. To put it in the terms of St. Thomas Aquinas: An unjust law is a human law that is not rooted in eternal law and natural law. Any law that uplifts human personality is just. Any law that degrades human personality is unjust. All segregation statutes are unjust because segregation distorts the soul and damages the personality. It gives the segregator a false sense of superiority and the segregated a false sense of inferiority. Segregation, to use the terminology of the Jewish philosopher Martin Buber, substitutes an "I-it" relationship for an "I-thou" relationship and ends up relegating persons to the status of things. Hence segregation is not only politically, economically, and sociologically unsound, it is morally wrong and sinful. Paul Tillich has said that sin is separation. Is not segregation an existential expression of man's tragic separation, his awful estrangement, his terrible sinfulness? Thus it is that I can urge men to obey the 1954 decision of the Supreme Court, for it is morally right; and I can urge them to disobey segregation ordinances, for they are morally wrong.

Let us consider a more concrete example of just and unjust laws. An unjust law is a code that a numerical or power majority group compels a minority group to obey but does not make binding on itself. This is *difference* made legal. By the same token, a just law is a code that a majority compels a minority to follow and that it is willing to follow itself. This is *sameness* made legal.

Let me give another explanation. A law is unjust if it is inflicted on a minority that, as a result of being denied the right to vote, had no part in enacting or devising the law. Who can say that the legislature of Alabama which set up that state's segregation laws was democratically elected? Throughout Alabama all sorts of devious methods are used to prevent Negroes from becoming registered voters, and there are some counties in which, even though Negroes constitute a majority of the population, not a single Negro is registered. Can any law enacted under such circumstances be considered democratically structured?

Sometimes a law is just on its face and unjust in its application. For instance, I have been arrested on a charge of parading without a permit. Now, there is nothing wrong in having an ordinance which requires a permit for a parade. But such an ordinance becomes unjust when it is used to maintain segregation and to deny citizens the First Amendment privilege of peaceful assembly and protest.

20   I hope you are able to see the distinction I am trying to point out. In no sense do I advocate evading or defying the law, as would the rabid segregationist. That would lead to anarchy. One who breaks an unjust law must do so openly, lovingly, and with a willingness to accept the penalty. I submit that an individual who breaks a law that conscience tells him is unjust, and who willingly accepts the penalty of imprisonment in order to arouse the conscience of the community over its injustice, is in reality expressing the highest respect for law.

Of course, there is nothing new about this kind of civil disobedience. It was evidenced sublimely in the refusal of Shadrach, Meshach, and Abednego to obey the laws of Nebuchadnezzar, on the ground that a higher moral law was at stake. It was practiced superbly by the early Christians, who were willing to face hungry lions and the excruciating pain of chopping blocks rather than submit to certain unjust laws of the Roman Empire. To a degree, academic freedom is a reality today because Socrates practiced civil disobedience. In our own nation, the Boston Tea Party represented a massive act of civil disobedience.

We should never forget that everything Adolf Hitler did in Germany was "legal" and everything the Hungarian freedom fighters did in Hungary was "illegal." It was "illegal" to aid and comfort a Jew in Hitler's Germany. Even so, I am sure that, had I lived in Germany at the time, I would have aided and comforted my Jewish brothers. If today I lived in a Communist country where certain principles dear to the Christian faith are suppressed, I would openly advocate disobeying that country's antireligious laws.

I must make two honest confessions to you, my Christian and Jewish brothers. First, I must confess that over the past few years I have been gravely disappointed with the white moderate. I have almost reached the regrettable conclusion that the Negro's great stumbling block in his stride toward freedom is not the White Citizen's Counciler or the Ku Klux Klanner, but the white moderate, who is more devoted to "order" than to justice; who prefers a negative peace which is the absence of tension to a positive peace which is the presence of justice; who constantly says, "I agree with you in the goal you seek, but I cannot agree with your methods of direct action;" who paternalistically believes he can set the timetable for another man's freedom; who lives by a mythical concept of time and who constantly advises the Negro to wait for a "more convenient season." Shallow understanding from people of good will is more frustrating than absolute misunderstanding from people of ill will. Lukewarm acceptance is much more bewildering than outright rejection.

I had hoped that the white moderate would understand that law and order exist for the purpose of establishing justice and that when they fail in this purpose they become the dangerously structured dams that block the flow of social progress. I had hoped that the white moderate would understand that the present tension in the South is a necessary phase of the transition from an obnoxious negative peace, in which the Negro passively accepted his unjust plight, to a substantive and positive peace, in which all men will respect the dignity and worth of human personality. Actually, we who engage in nonviolent direct action are not the creators of tension. We merely bring to the surface the hidden tension that is already alive. We bring it out in the open, where it can be seen and dealt with. Like a boil that can never be cured so long as it is covered up but must be opened with all its ugliness to the natural medicines of air and light, injustice must be exposed, with all the tension its exposure creates, to the light of human conscience and the air of national opinion, before it can be cured.

25   In your statement you assert that our actions, even though peaceful, must be condemned because they precipitate violence. But is this a logical assertion? Isn't this like condemning a robbed man because his possession of money precipitated

the evil act of robbery? Isn't this like condemning Socrates because his unswerving commitment to truth and his philosophical inquiries precipitated the act by the misguided populace in which they made him drink hemlock? Isn't this like condemning Jesus because his unique God-consciousness and never-ceasing devotion to God's will precipitated the evil act of crucifixion? We must come to see that, as the federal courts have consistently affirmed, it is wrong to urge an individual to cease his efforts to gain his basic constitutional rights because the quest may precipitate violence. Society must protect the robbed and punish the robber.

I had also hoped that the white moderate would reject the myth concerning time in relation to the struggle for freedom. I have just received a letter from a white brother in Texas. He writes: "All Christians know that the colored people will receive equal rights eventually, but it is possible that you are in too great a religious hurry. It has taken Christianity almost two thousand years to accomplish what it has. The teachings of Christ take time to come to earth." Such an attitude stems from a tragic misconception of time, from the strangely irrational notion that there is something in the very flow of time that will inevitably cure all ills. Actually, time itself is neutral; it can be used either destructively or constructively. More and more I feel that the people of ill will have used time much more effectively than have the people of good will. We will have to repent in this generation not merely for the hateful words and actions of the bad people, but for the appalling silence of the good people. Human progress never rolls in on wheels of inevitability; it comes through the tireless efforts of men willing to be co-workers with God, and without this hard work, time itself becomes an ally of the forces of social stagnation. We must use time creatively, in the knowledge that the time is always ripe to do right. Now is the time to make real the promise of democracy and transform our pending national elegy into a creative psalm of brotherhood. Now is the time to lift our national policy from the quicksand of racial injustice to the solid rock of human dignity.

You speak of our activity in Birmingham as extreme. At first I was rather disappointed that fellow clergymen would see my nonviolent efforts as those of an extremist. I began thinking about the fact that I stand in the middle of two opposing forces in the Negro community. One is a force of complacency, made up in part of Negroes who, as a result of long years of oppression, are so drained of self-respect and a sense of "somebodiness" that they have adjusted to segregation; and in part of a few middle-class Negroes who, because of a degree of academic and economic security and because in some ways they profit by segregation, have become insensitive to the problems of the masses. The other force is one of bitterness and hatred, and it comes perilously close to advocating violence. It is expressed in the various black nationalist groups that are spring-ing up across the nation, the largest and best known being Elijah Muhammad's Muslim movement. Nourished by the Negro's frustration over the continued existence of racial discrimination, this movement is made up of people who have lost faith in America, who have absolutely repudiated Christianity, and who have concluded that the white man is an incorrigible "devil."

I have tried to stand between these two forces, saying that we need emulate neither the "do-nothingism" of the complacent nor the hatred and despair of the black nationalist. For there is the more excellent way of love and nonviolent protest. I am grateful to God that, through the influence of the Negro church, the way of nonviolence became an integral part of our struggle.

If this philosophy had not emerged, by now many streets of the South would, I am convinced, be flowing with blood. And I am further convinced that if our white brothers dismiss as "rabble-rousers" and "outside agitators" those of us who employ nonviolent direct action, and if they refuse to support our nonvi-olent efforts, millions of Negroes will, out of frustration and despair, seek sol-ace and security in black nationalist ideologies—a development that would inevitably lead to a frightening racial nightmare.

30   Oppressed people cannot remain oppressed forever. The yearning for freedom eventually manifests itself, and that is what has happened to the American Negro. Something within has reminded him of his birthright of freedom, and something without has reminded him that it can be gained. Consciously or unconsciously, he has been caught up by the *Zeitgeist,* and with his black brothers of Africa and his brown and yellow brothers of Asia, South America, and the Caribbean, the United States Negro is moving with a sense of great urgency toward the prom-ised land of racial justice. If one recognizes this vital urge that has engulfed the Negro community, one should readily understand why public demonstrations are taking place. The Negro has many pent-up resentments and latent frustra-tions, and he must release them. So let him march; let him make prayer pil-grimages to the city hall; let him go on freedom rides—and try to understand why he must do so. If his repressed emotions are not released in nonviolent ways, they will seek expression through violence; this is not a threat but a fact of his-tory. So I have not said to my people, "Get rid of your discontent." Rather, I have tried to say that this normal and healthy discontent can be channeled into the creative outlet of nonviolent direct action. And now this approach is being termed extremist.

But though I was initially disappointed at being categorized as an extremist, as I continued to think about the matter I gradually gained a measure of satisfaction from the label. Was not Jesus an extremist for love: "Love your enemies, bless them that curse you, do good to them that hate you, and pray for them which despitefully use you, and persecute you." Was not Amos an extremist for justice: "Let justice roll down like waters and righteousness like an everflowing stream." Was not Paul an extremist for the Christian gospel: "I bear in my body the marks of the Lord Jesus." Was not Martin Luther an extremist: "Here I stand; I cannot do otherwise, so help me God." And John Bunyan: "I will stay in jail to the end of my days before I make a butchery of my conscience." And Abraham Lincoln: "This nation cannot survive half slave and half free." And Thomas Jefferson: "We hold these truths to be self-evident, that all men are created equal . . ." So the question is not whether we will be extremists, but what kind of extremists we will be. Will we be extremists for hate or for love? Will we be extremists for the preservation of injustice or for the extension of justice? In that dramatic scene on Calvary's hill three men were crucified. We must never forget that all three were crucified for the same crime—the crime of extremism. Two were extremists for immorality, and thus fell below their environment. The other, Jesus Christ, was an extremist for love, truth, and goodness, and thereby rose above his environment. Perhaps the South, the nation, and the world are in dire need of creative extremists.

I had hoped that the white moderate would see this need. Perhaps I was too optimistic; perhaps I expected too much. I suppose I should have realized that few members of the oppressor race can understand the deep groans and passionate yearnings of the oppressed race, and still fewer have the vision to see that injustice must be rooted out by strong, persistent, and determined action. I am thankful, however, that some of our white brothers in the South have grasped the meaning of this social revolution and committed themselves to it. They are still all too few in quantity, but they are big in quality. Some—such as Ralph McGill, Lillian Smith, Harry Golden, James McBride Dabbs, Ann Braden, and Sarah Patton Boyle—have written about our struggle in eloquent and prophetic terms. Others have marched with us down nameless streets of the South. They have languished in filthy, roach-infested jails, suffering the abuse and brutality of policemen who view them as "dirty nigger-lovers." Unlike so many of their moderate brothers and sisters, they have recognized the urgency of the moment and sensed the need for powerful "action" antidotes to combat the disease of segregation.

Let me take note of my other major disappointment. I have been so greatly disappointed with the white church and its leadership. Of course, there are some notable exceptions. I am not unmindful of the fact that each of you has taken some significant stands on this issue. I commend you, Reverend Stallings, for your Christian stand on this past Sunday, in welcoming Negroes to your worship service on a nonsegregated basis. I commend the Catholic leaders of this state for integrating Spring Hill College several years ago.

But despite these notable exceptions, I must honestly reiterate that I have been disappointed with the church. I do not say this as one of those negative critics who can always find something wrong with the church. I say this as a minister of the gospel, who loves the church; who was nurtured in its bosom; who has been sustained by its spiritual blessings and who will remain true to it as long as the cord of life shall lengthen.

35   When I was suddenly catapulted into the leadership of the bus protest in Montgomery, Alabama, a few years ago, I felt we would be supported by the white church. I felt that the white ministers priests, and rabbis of the South would be among our strongest allies. Instead, some have been outright opponents, refusing to understand the freedom movement and misrepresenting its leaders; all too many others have been more cautious than courageous and have remained silent behind the anesthetizing security of stained-glass windows.

In spite of my shattered dreams, I came to Birmingham with the hope that the white religious leadership of this community would see the justice of our cause and, with deep moral concern, would serve as the channel through which our just grievances could reach the power structure. I had hoped that each of you would understand. But again I have been disappointed . . . .

There was a time when the church was very powerful—in the time when the early Christians rejoiced at being deemed worthy to suffer for what they believed. In those days the church was not merely a thermometer that recorded the ideas and principles of popular opinion; it was a thermostat that transformed the mores of society. Whenever the early Christians entered a town, the people in power became disturbed and immediately sought to convict the Christians for being "disturbers of the peace" and "outside agitators." But the Christians pressed on, in the conviction that they were "a colony of heaven," called to obey God rather than man. Small in number, they were big in commitment. They were too God-intoxicated to be "astronomically intimidated." By their effort and example they brought an end to such ancient evils as infanticide and gladiatorial contests.

Things are different now. So often the contemporary church is a weak, ineffectual voice with an uncertain sound. So often it is an archdefender of the status quo. Far from being disturbed by the presence of the church, the powerful structure of the average community is consoled by the church's silent—and often even vocal—sanction of things as they are.

But the judgment of God is upon the church as never before. If today's church does not recapture the sacrificial spirit of the early church, it will lose its authenticity, forfeit the loyalty of millions, and be dismissed as an irrelevant social club with no meaning for the twentieth century. Every day I meet young people whose disappointment with the church has turned into outright disgust.

40   Perhaps I have once again been too optimistic. Is organized religion too inextricably bound to the status quo to save our nation and the world? Perhaps I must turn my faith to the inner spiritual church, the church within the church, as the true *ekklesia* and the hope of the world. But again I am thankful to God that some noble souls from the ranks of organized religion have broken loose from the paralyzing chains of conformity and joined us as active partners in the struggle for freedom. They have left their secure congregations and walked the streets of Albany, Georgia, with us. They have gone down the highways of the South on torturous rides for freedom. Yes, they have gone to jail with us. Some have been dismissed from their churches, have lost the support of their bishops and fellow ministers. But they have acted in the faith that right defeated is stronger than evil triumphant. Their witness has been the spiritual salt that has preserved the true meaning of the gospel in these troubled times. They have carved a tunnel of hope through the dark mountain of disappointment.

     I hope the church as a whole will meet the challenge of this decisive hour. But even if the church does not come to the aid of justice, I have no despair about the future. I have no fear about the outcome of our struggle in Birmingham, even if our motives are at present misunderstood. We will reach the goal of freedom in Birmingham and all over the nation, because the goal of America is freedom. Abused and scorned though we may be, our destiny is tied up with America's destiny. Before the pilgrims landed at Plymouth, we were here. Before the pen of Jefferson etched the majestic words of the Declaration of Independence across the pages of history, we were here. For more than two centuries our forebears labored in this country without wages; they made cotton king; they built the homes of their masters while suffering gross injustice and shameful humiliation—and yet out of a bottomless vitality they continued to thrive and develop. If the inexpressible cruelties of slavery could not stop us, the opposition we now face will surely fail. We will win our freedom because the sacred heritage of our nation and the eternal will of God are embodied in our echoing demands.

     Before closing I feel impelled to mention one other point in your statement that has troubled me profoundly. You warmly commended the Birmingham police force for keeping "order" and "preventing violence." I doubt that you would have so warmly commended the police force if you had seen its dogs sinking their teeth into unarmed, nonviolent Negroes. I doubt that you would so quickly commend the policemen if you were to observe their ugly and inhumane treatment of Negroes here in the city jail; if you were to watch them push and curse old Negro women and young Negro girls; if you were to see them slap and kick old Negro men and young boys; if you were to observe them, as they did on two occasions, refuse to give us food because we wanted to sing our grace together. I cannot join you in your praise of the Birmingham police department.

It is true that the police have exercised a degree of discipline in handling the demonstrators. In this sense they have conducted themselves rather "nonviolently" in public. But for what purpose? To preserve the evil system of segregation. Over the past few years I have consistently preached that nonviolence demands that the means we use must be as pure as the ends we seek. I have tried to make clear that it is wrong to use immoral means to attain moral ends. But now I must affirm that it is just as wrong, or perhaps even more so, to use moral means to preserve immoral ends. Perhaps Mr. Connor and his policemen have been rather nonviolent in public, as was Chief Pritchett in Albany, Georgia, but they have used the moral means of nonviolence to maintain the immoral end of racial injustice. As T. S. Eliot has said, "The last temptation is the greatest treason: To do the right deed for the wrong reason."

I wish you had commended the Negro sit-inners and demonstrators of Birmingham for their sublime courage, their willingness to suffer, and their amazing discipline in the midst of great provocation. One day the South will recognize its real heroes. They will be the James Merediths, with the noble sense of purpose that enables them to face jeering and hostile mobs, and with the agonizing loneliness that characterizes the life of the pioneer. They will be old, oppressed, battered Negro women, symbolized in a seventy-two-year-old woman in Montgomery, Alabama, who rose up with a sense of dignity and with her people decided not to ride segregated buses, and who responded with ungrammatical profundity to one who inquired about her weariness: "My feets is tired, but my soul is at rest." They will be the young high school and college students, the young ministers of the gospel and a host of their elders, courageously and nonviolently sitting in at lunch counters and willingly going to jail for conscience's sake. One day the South will know that when these disinherited children of God sat down at lunch counters, they were in reality standing up for what is best in the American dream and for the most sacred values in our Judaeo-Christian heritage, thereby bringing our nation back to those great wells of democracy which were dug deep by the founding fathers in their formulation of the Constitution and the Declaration of Independence.

45   Never before have I written so long a letter. I'm afraid it is much too long to take your precious time. I can assure you that it would have been much shorter if I had been writing from a comfortable desk, but what else can one do when he is alone in a narrow jail cell, other than write long letters, think long thoughts, and pray long prayers?

    If I have said anything in this letter that overstates the truth and indicates an unreasonable impatience, I beg you to forgive me. If I have said anything that understates the truth and indicates my having a patience that allows me to settle for anything less than brotherhood, I beg God to forgive me.

    I hope this letter finds you strong in the faith. I also hope that circumstances will soon make it possible for me to meet each of you, not as an integrationist or a civil rights leader but as a fellow clergyman and a Christian brother. Let us all hope that the dark clouds of racial prejudice will soon pass away and the deep fog of misunderstanding will be lifted from our fear-drenched communities, and in some not too distant tomorrow the radiant stars of love and brotherhood will shine over our great nation with all their scintillating beauty.

Yours in the cause of
Peace and Brotherhood,
MARTIN LUTHER KING, JR.

READING/WRITING ASSISTS

Thesis (and its counterargument):

Both Dr. King's overall **thesis statement** and its **counterargument** are clearly stated in the first two paragraphs of his "Letter." In fact, his main argument (thesis) directly counters a public statement made by eight fellow clergymen (the counterargument) published earlier. Though Dr. King's complex argument eventually branches out in a number of different directions, like a massive well-shaped tree, the "trunk," or foundation of his argument arises out of a very basic premise in response to his peers. What is that premise, and what argument of his fellow clergymen does it counter?

The Shape of the Argument:

"Mapping" the structure of an argument can help us better understand the argument itself, while also showing us new models for shaping our own arguments in essay form. Dr. King's essay returns us to the five-part essay structure, but in a much more sophisticated form. Embedded in Dr. King's argument are a series of five-part essays. But these arguments-within-argument vary in length, and the area of flexibility is generally the "body" of each mini-essay, which can be longer or shorter than three points. Using the over-all outline below as a guide, mark the paragraph numbers that detail each of the arguments contained within Dr. King's main argument, noting the thesis statement, support, and conclusions, and the paragraph numbers of each:

Paragraphs 1 and 2:	Introduction and **thesis statement**.
Paragraphs 3, 4:	What support does Dr. King offer for his thesis statement?
Paragraphs 5, 6, 7, 8 9:	Argument within the argument (1). Locate the **thesis**, **support** and **conclusion** for this argument.
Paragraphs 10, 11:	Note that the **thesis** statement for the next argument within the argument is often located at the end of the paragraph concluding the argument within the argument immediately preceding.
Paragraphs 12, 13, 14:	Argument within the argument (2)
Paragraphs 15, 16, 17, 18, 19, 20, 21 22:	Argument within the argument (3)
Paragraphs 23, 24, 25, 26:	Argument within the argument (3)
Paragraphs 27, 28, 29, 30, 31, 32:	Argument within the argument (4)
Paragraphs 33, 34, 35, 36, 37, 38, 39, 40, 41:	Argument within the argument (5)
Paragraphs 42 and 43:	Argument within the argument (6)
Paragraphs 44, 45, 46, 47:	Conclusion to overall argument

UNIT 3

Rhetorical Moves:

Par-al-lel-ism (par'e-lel-iz'em) *n.* **1:** The state or position of being parallel; a parallel relationship **2:** Likeness, correspondence, or similarity in aspect, course or tendency **3:** *Grammar.* **a.** The use of corresponding syntactical forms

An-tith-e-sis (an-tith'e-sis) *n., pl.* **–ses** (sez') **1:** Direct contrast; opposition **2:** The direct or exact opposite **3:** *Rhetoric.* **a.** The juxtaposition of sharply contrasting ideas in balanced or parallel words, phrases, or grammatical structures; for example, *"He for God only, she for God in him"* (Milton) **b.** The second and and contrasting part of such a juxtaposition

Dr. King evidently mastered the rhetorical devices of parallelism and antithesis. Study paragraph 14 of Dr. King's essay carefully. The fourth sentence of this paragraph begins a very long, single-sentence parallelism. What repeated words in this sentence keep its clauses "parallel?" Find other parallelisms in Dr. King's text.

As well, Dr. King's "Letter" contains many masterful examples of rhetorical antithesis: "harried by **day** and haunted by **night**"; "**inner** fears and **outer** resentments"; "**just** on its face and **unjust** in its application"; "from the dark **depths** . . . to the majestic **heights**." Find other examples in Dr. King's essay.

Try to incorporate both parallelisms and antitheses in your own essays.

Finally, notice too that the end of paragraph 22—the midpoint of Dr. King's forty-four paragraph essay—marks his transition from **defense** to **offense**. Strategically, why do you suppose Dr. King begins with a defense of his actions before moving to attack the position of his opponents?

RALPH WALDO ELLISON

To parents who were the children of former slaves, Ralph Waldo Ellison (1914–1994) was born in Oklahoma City, Oklahoma, where his parents had moved from the South shortly before their children were born, in the hope that the near-frontier status of this relatively new state would offer the freedom and possibility denied to them in the South.

But when Ellison was only three years old, his father died, leaving his mother the sole support of her two young sons. She worked for years as a domestic at the Avery Chapel Afro-Methodist Episcopal Church, moving her family for a short time to the rectory, which gave her son access to the library there. In later years, she brought books and magazines home for Ellison to read from the houses she cleaned. Ellison's reading life really began, however, when a black minister in Oklahoma City challenged the law barring African Americans from public libraries there and won.

Already an accomplished musician, Ellison left Oklahoma in 1933 to study music at the Tuskegee Institute in Alabama with the help of a scholarship provided by the State of Oklahoma. Financial pressures, unfortunately, forced Ellison to leave Tuskegee in 1936 without completing his degree. Ellison then moved to Harlem, which became his home for the rest of his life.

Supporting himself by playing the trumpet, Ellison began to write. With work of any kind scarce during the Depression years, Ellison was grateful for the help of his mentor, the writer Richard Wright, who helped Ellison gain a position with the Federal Writer's Project in 1938. But when Ellison began to move away from leftist politics, and when he publicly criticized Wright's protagonist, Bigger Thomas, in Wright's blockbuster novel, Native Son, *their relationship soured.*

Nevertheless, Ellison published his own novel, Invisible Man, *in 1952. "Battle Royale," first published as a short story, was later incorporated into Ellison's novel. He was named the Albert Schweitzer Professor of Humanities at New York University in 1970. At his death, he left a long-awaited unfinished novel, which was published posthumously as* Juneteenth.

BATTLE ROYALE
Ralph Waldo Ellison

1   It goes a long way back, some twenty years. All my life I had been looking for
something, and everywhere I turned someone tried to tell me what it was. I
accepted their answers too, though they were often in contradiction and even self-
contradictory. I was naïve. I was looking for myself and asking everyone except
myself questions which I, and only I, could answer. It took me a long time and
much painful boomeranging of my expectations to achieve a realization everyone else appears to have been born with: That I am nobody but myself. But first
I had to discover that I am an invisible man!

And yet I am no freak of nature, nor of history. I was in the cards, other
things having been equal (or unequal) eighty-five years ago. I am not ashamed
of my grandparents for having been slaves. I am only ashamed of myself for having at one time been ashamed. About eighty-five years ago they were told that
they were free, united with others of our country in everything pertaining to
the common good, and, in everything social, separate like the fingers of the
hand. And they believed it. They exulted in it. They stayed in their place, worked
hard, and brought up my father to do the same. But my grandfather is the one.
He was an odd old guy, my grandfather, and I am told I take after him. It was
he who caused the trouble. On his deathbed he called my father to him and
said, "Son, after I'm gone I want you to keep up the good fight. I never told
you, but our life is a war and I have been a traitor all my born days, a spy in the
enemy's country ever since I gave up my gun back in the Reconstruction. Live
with your head in the lion's mouth. I want you to overcome 'em with yeses,
undermine 'em with grins, agree 'em to death and destruction, let 'em swoller
you till they vomit or bust wide open." They thought the old man had gone out
of his mind. He had been the meekest of men. The younger children were rushed
from the room, the shades drawn and the flame of the lamp turned so low that
it sputtered on the wick like the old man's breathing. "Learn it to the young
'uns," he whispered fiercely; then he died.

Reprinted from *Invisible Man* (1995), Vintage Books, a division of Random House, Inc.

But my folks were more alarmed over his last words than over his dying. It was as though he had not died at all, his words caused so much anxiety. I was warned emphatically to forget what he had said and, indeed, this is the first time it has been mentioned outside the family circle. It had a tremendous effect upon me, however. I could never be sure of what he meant. Grandfather had been a quiet old man who never made any trouble, yet on his deathbed he had called himself a traitor and a spy, and he had spoken of his meekness as a dangerous activity. It became a constant puzzle which lay unanswered in the back of my mind. And whenever things went well for me I remembered my grandfather and felt guilty and uncomfortable. It was as though I was carrying out his advice in spite of myself. And to make it worse, everyone loved me for it. I was praised by the most lily-white men of the town. I was considered an example of desirable conduct—just as my grandfather had been. And what puzzled me was that the old man had defined it as *treachery*. When I was praised for my conduct I felt a guilt that in some way I was doing something that was really against the wishes of the white folks, that if they had understood they would have desired me to act just the opposite, that I should have been sulky and mean, and that that really would have been what they wanted, even though they were fooled and thought they wanted me to act as I did. It made me afraid that some day they would look upon me as a traitor and I would be lost. Still I was more afraid to act any other way because they didn't like that at all. The old man's words were like a curse. On my graduation day I delivered an oration in which I showed that humility was the secret, indeed, the very essence of progress. (Not that I believed this—how could I, remembering my grandfather?—I only believed that it worked.) It was a great success. Everyone praised me and I was invited to give the speech at a gathering of the town's leading white citizens. It was a triumph for our whole community.

It was in the main ballroom of the leading hotel. When I got there I discovered that it was on the occasion of a smoker, and I was told that since I was to be there anyway I might as well take part in the battle royal to be fought by some of my schoolmates as part of the entertainment. The battle royal came first.

5   All of the town's big shots were there in their tuxedoes, wolfing down the buffet foods, drinking beer and whiskey and smoking black cigars. It was a large room with a high ceiling. Chairs were arranged in neat rows around three sides of a portable boxing ring. The fourth side was clear, revealing a gleaming space of polished floor. I had some misgivings over the battle royal, by the way. Not from a distaste for fighting, but because I didn't care too much for the other fellows who were to take part. They were tough guys who seemed to have no grandfather's curse

worrying their minds. No one could mistake their toughness. And besides, I suspected that fighting a battle royal might detract from the dignity of my speech.
In those pre-invisible days I visualized myself as a potential Booker T. Washington. But the other fellows didn't care too much for me either, and there were nine
of them. I felt superior to them in my way, and I didn't like the manner in which
we were all crowded together into the servants' elevator. Nor did they like my
being there. In fact, as the warmly lighted floors flashed past the elevator we had
words over the fact that I, by taking part in the fight, had knocked one of their
friends out of a night's work.

We were led out of the elevator through a rococo hall into an anteroom and
told to get into our fighting togs. Each of us was issued a pair of boxing gloves
and ushered out into the big mirrored hall, which we entered looking cautiously
about us and whispering, lest we might accidentally be heard above the noise of
the room. It was foggy with cigar smoke. And already the whiskey was taking
effect. I was shocked to see some of the most important men of the town quite
tipsy. They were all there—bankers, lawyers, judges, doctors, fire chiefs, teachers, merchants. Even one of the more fashionable pastors. Something we could
not see was going on up front. A clarinet was vibrating sensuously and the men
were standing up and moving eagerly forward. We were a small tight group,
clustered together, our bare upper bodies touching and shining with anticipatory
sweat; while up front the big shots were becoming increasingly excited over
something we still could not see. Suddenly I heard the school superintendent,
who had told me to come, yell, "Bring up the shines, gentlemen! Bring up the
little shines!"

We were rushed up to the front of the ballroom, where it smelled even more
strongly of tobacco and whiskey. Then we were pushed into place. I almost wet
my pants. A sea of faces, some hostile, some amused, ringed around us, and in
the center, facing us, stood a magnificent blonde—stark naked. There was dead
silence. I felt a blast of cold air chill me. I tried to back away, but they were
behind me and around me. Some of the boys stood with lowered heads, trembling. I felt a wave of irrational guilt and fear. My teeth chattered, my skin turned
to goose flesh, my knees knocked. Yet I was strongly attracted and looked in
spite of myself. Had the price of looking been blindness, I would have looked.
The hair was yellow like that of a circus kewpie doll, the face heavily powdered
and rouged, as though to form an abstract mask, the eyes hollow and smeared a
cool blue, the color of a baboon's butt. I felt a desire to spit upon her as my eyes
brushed slowly over her body. Her breasts were firm and round as the domes of
East Indian temples, and I stood so close as to see the fine skin texture and beads

of pearly perspiration glistening like dew around the pink and erected buds of her nipples. I wanted at one and the same time to run from the room, to sink through the floor, or go to her and cover her from my eyes and the eyes of the others with my body; to feel the soft thighs, to caress her and destroy her, to love her and murder her, to hide from her, and yet to stroke where below the small American flag tattooed upon her belly her thighs formed a capital V. I had a notion that of all in the room she saw only me with her impersonal eyes.

And then she began to dance, a slow sensuous movement; the smoke of a hundred cigars clinging to her like the thinnest of veils. She seemed like a fair bird-girl girdled in veils calling to me from the angry surface of some gray and threatening sea. I was transported. Then I became aware of the clarinet playing and the big shots yelling at us. Some threatened us if we looked and others if we did not. On my right I saw one boy faint. And now a man grabbed a silver pitcher from a table and stepped close as he dashed ice water upon him and stood him up and forced two of us to support him as his head hung and moans issued from his thick bluish lips. Another boy began to plead to go home. He was the largest of the group, wearing dark red fighting trunks much too small to conceal the erection which projected from him as though in answer to the insinuating low-registered moaning of the clarinet. He tried to hide himself with his boxing gloves.

And all the while the blonde continued dancing, smiling faintly at the big shots who watched her with fascination, and faintly smiling at our fear. I noticed a certain merchant who followed her hungrily, his lips loose and drooling. He was a large man who wore diamond studs in a shirtfront which swelled with the ample paunch underneath, and each time the blonde swayed her undulating hips he ran his hand through the thin hair of his bald head and, with his arms upheld, his posture clumsy like that of an intoxicated panda, wound his belly in a slow and obscene grind. This creature was completely hypnotized. The music had quickened. As the dancer flung herself about with a detached expression on her face, the men began reaching out to touch her. I could see their beefy fingers sink into the soft flesh. Some of the others tried to stop them as she began to move around the floor in graceful circles, as they gave chase, slipping and sliding over the polished floor. It was mad. Chairs went crashing, drinks were spilt, as they ran laughing and howling after her. They caught her just as she reached a door, raised her from the floor, and tossed her as college boys are tossed at a hazing, and above her red, fixed-smiling lips I saw the terror and disgust in her eyes, almost like my own terror and that which I saw in some of the other boys. As I watched, they tossed her twice and her soft breasts seemed to flatten against the air and her legs flung wildly as she spun. Some of the more sober ones helped her to escape. And I started off the floor, heading for the anteroom with the rest of the boys.

10   Some were still crying in hysteria. But as we tried to leave we were stopped and ordered to get into the ring. There was nothing to do but what we were told. All ten of us climbed under the ropes and allowed ourselves to be blindfolded with broad bands of white cloth. One of the men seemed to feel a bit sympathetic and tried to cheer us up as we stood with our backs against the ropes. Some of us tried to grin. "See that boy over there?" one of the men said. "I want you to run across at the bell and give it to him right in the belly. If you don't get him, I'm going to get you. I don't like his looks." Each of us was told the same. The blindfolds were put on. Yet even then I had been going over my speech. In my mind each word was as bright as flame. I felt the cloth pressed into place, and frowned so that it would be loosened when I relaxed.

But now I felt a sudden fit of blind terror. I was unused to darkness. It was as though I had suddenly found myself in a dark room filled with poisonous cottonmouths. I could hear the bleary voices yelling insistently for the battle royal to begin.

"Get going in there!"

"Let me at that big nigger!"

I strained to pick up the school superintendent's voice, as though to squeeze some security out of that slightly more familiar sound.

15   "Let me at those black sonsabitches!" someone yelled.

"No, Jackson, no!" another voice yelled. "Here, somebody, help me hold Jack."

"I want to get at that ginger-colored nigger. Tear him limb from limb," the first voice yelled.

I stood against the ropes trembling. For in those days I was what they called ginger-colored, and he sounded as though he might crunch me between his teeth like a crisp ginger cookie.

Quite a struggle was going on. Chairs were being kicked about and I could hear voices grunting as with a terrific effort. I wanted to see, to see more desperately than ever before. But the blindfold was tight as a thick skin-puckering scab and when I raised my gloved hands to push the layers of white aside a voice yelled, "Oh, no you don't, black bastard! Leave that alone!"

20   "Ring the bell before Jackson kills him a coon!" someone boomed in the sudden silence. And I heard the bell clang and the sound of the feet scuffling forward.

A glove smacked against my head. I pivoted, striking out stiffly as someone went past, and felt the jar ripple along the length of my arm to my shoulder. Then it seemed as though all nine of the boys had turned upon me at once. Blows pounded me from all sides while I struck out as best I could. So many blows landed upon me that I wondered if I were not the only blindfolded fighter in the ring, or if the man called Jackson hadn't succeeded in getting me after all.

Blindfolded, I could no longer control my motions. I had no dignity. I stumbled about like a baby or a drunken man. The smoke had become thicker and with each new blow it seemed to sear and further restrict my lungs. My saliva became like hot bitter glue. A glove connected with my head, filling my mouth with warm blood. It was everywhere. I could not tell if the moisture I felt upon my body was sweat or blood. A blow landed hard against the nape of my neck. I felt myself going over, my head hitting the floor. Streaks of blue light filled the black world behind the blindfold. I lay prone, pretending that I was knocked out, but felt myself seized by hands and yanked to my feet. "Get going, black boy! Mix it up!" My arms were like lead, my head smarting from blows. I managed to feel my way to the ropes and held on, trying to catch my breath. A glove landed in my mid-section and I went over again, feeling as though the smoke had become a knife jabbed into my guts. Pushed this way and that by the legs milling around me, I finally pulled erect and discovered that I could see the black, sweat-washed forms weaving in the smoky-blue atmosphere like drunken dancers weaving to the rapid drumlike thuds of blows.

Everyone fought hysterically. It was complete anarchy. Everybody fought everybody else. No group fought together for long. Two, three, four, fought one, then turned to fight each other, were themselves attacked. Blows landed below the belt and in the kidney, with the gloves open as well as closed, and with my eye partly opened now there was not so much terror. I moved carefully, avoiding blows, although not too many to attract attention, fighting from group to group. The boys groped about like blind, cautious crabs crouching to protect their mid-sections, their heads pulled in short against their shoulders, their arms stretched nervously before them, with their fists testing the smokefilled air like the knobbed feelers of hypersensitive snails. In one corner I glimpsed a boy violently punching the air and heard him scream in pain as he smashed his hand against a ring post. For a second I saw him bent over holding his hand, then going down as a blow caught his unprotected head. I played one group against the other, slipping in and throwing a punch then stepping out of range while pushing the others into the melee to take the blows blindly aimed at me. The smoke was agonizing and there were no rounds, no bells at three minute intervals to relieve our exhaustion. The room spun round me, a swirl of lights, smoke, sweating bodies surrounded by tense white faces. I bled from both nose and mouth, the blood spattering upon my chest.

The men kept yelling, "Slug him, black boy! Knock his guts out!"

25 "Uppercut him! Kill that big boy!"

Taking a fake fall, I saw a boy going down heavily beside me as though we were felled by a single blow, saw a sneaker-clad foot shoot into his groin as the two who had knocked him down stumbled upon him. I rolled out of range, feeling a twinge of nausea.

The harder we fought the more threatening the men became. And yet, I had begun to worry about my speech again. How would it go? Would they recognize my ability? What would they give me?

I was fighting automatically when suddenly I noticed that one after another of the boys was leaving the ring. I was surprised, filled with panic, as though I had been left alone with an unknown danger. Then I understood. The boys had arranged it among themselves. It was the custom for the two men left in the ring to slug it out for the winner's prize. I discovered this too late. When the bell sounded two men in tuxedoes leaped into the ring and removed the blindfold. I found myself facing Tatlock, the biggest of the gang. I felt sick at my stomach. Hardly had the bell stopped ringing in my ears than it clanged again and I saw him moving swiftly toward me. Thinking of nothing else to do I hit him smash on the nose. He kept coming, bringing the rank sharp violence of stale sweat. His face was a black blank of a face, only his eyes alive—with hate of me and aglow with a feverish terror from what had happened to us all. I became anxious. I wanted to deliver my speech and he came at me as though he meant to beat it out of me. I smashed him again and again, taking his blows as they came. Then on a sudden impulse I struck him lightly and as we clinched, I whispered, "Fake like I knocked you out, you can have the prize."

"I'll break your behind," he whispered hoarsely.

30 "For *them?*"

"For *me*, sonofabitch!"

They were yelling for us to break it up and Tatlock spun me half around with a blow, and as a joggled camera sweeps in a reeling scene, I saw the howling red faces crouching tense beneath the cloud of blue-gray smoke. For a moment the world wavered, unraveled, flowed, then my head cleared and Tatlock bounced before me. That fluttering shadow before my eyes was his jabbing left hand. Then falling forward, my head against his damp shoulder, I whispered,

"I'll make it five dollars more."

"Go to hell!"

35   But his muscles relaxed a trifle beneath my pressure and I breathed, "Seven?"

"Give it to your ma," he said, ripping me beneath the heart.

And while I still held him I butted him and moved away. I felt myself bombarded with punches. I fought back with hopeless desperation. I wanted to deliver my speech more than anything else in the world, because I felt that only these men could judge truly my ability, and now this stupid clown was ruining my chances. I began fighting carefully now, moving in to punch him and out again with my greater speed. A lucky blow to his chin and I had him going too—until I heard a loud voice yell, "I got my money on the big boy."

Hearing this, I almost dropped my guard. I was confused: Should I try to win against the voice out there? Would not this go against my speech, and was not this a moment for humility, for nonresistance? A blow to my head as I danced about sent my right eye popping like a jack-in-the-box and settled my dilemma. The room went red as I fell. It was a dream fall, my body languid and fastidious as to where to land, until the floor became impatient and smashed up to meet me. A moment later I came to. An hypnotic voice said FIVE emphatically. And I lay there, hazily watching a dark red spot of my own blood shaping itself into a butterfly, glistening and soaking into the soiled gray world of the canvas.

When the voice drawled TEN I was lifted up and dragged to a chair. I sat dazed. My eye pained and swelled with each throb of my pounding heart and I wondered if now I would be allowed to speak. I was wringing wet, my mouth still bleeding. We were grouped along the wall now. The other boys ignored me as they congratulated Tatlock and speculated as to how much they would be paid. One boy whimpered over his smashed hand. Looking up front, I saw attendants in white jackets rolling the portable ring away and placing a small square rug in the vacant space surrounded by chairs. Perhaps, I thought, I will stand on the rug to deliver my speech.

40   Then the M.C. called to us, "Come on up here boys and get your money." We ran forward to where the men laughed and talked in their chairs, waiting. Everyone seemed friendly now.

"There it is on the rug," the man said. I saw the rug covered with coins of all dimensions and a few crumpled bills. But what excited me, scattered here and there, were the gold pieces.

"Boys, it's all yours," the man said. "You get all you grab."

"That's right, Sambo," a blond man said, winking at me confidentially.

I trembled with excitement, forgetting my pain. I would get the gold and the bills, I thought. I would use both hands. I would throw my body against the boys nearest me to block them from the gold.

45   "Get down around the rug now," the man commanded, "and don't anyone touch it until I give the signal."

"This ought to be good," I heard.

As told, we got around the square rug on our knees. Slowly the man raised his freckled hand as we followed it upward with our eyes.

I heard, "These niggers look like they're about to pray!"

Then, "Ready," the man said. "Go!"

50   I lunged for a yellow coin lying on the blue design of the carpet, touching it and sending a surprised shriek to join those rising around me. I tried frantically to remove my hand but could not let go. A hot, violent force tore through my body, shaking me like a wet rat. The rug was electrified. The hair bristled up on my head as I shook myself free. My muscles jumped, my nerves jangled, writhed. But I saw that this was not stopping the other boys. Laughing in fear and embarrassment, some were holding back and scooping up the coins knocked off by the painful contortions of the others. The men roared above us as we struggled.

"Pick it up, goddamnit, pick it up!" someone called like a bass-voiced parrot. "Go on, get it!"

I crawled rapidly around the floor, picking up the coins, trying to avoid the coppers and to get greenbacks and the gold. Ignoring the shock by laughing, as I brushed the coins off quickly, I discovered that I could contain the electricity— a contradiction, but it works. Then the men began to push us onto the rug. Laughing embarrassedly, we struggled out of their hands and kept after the coins. We were all wet and slippery and hard to hold. Suddenly I saw a boy lifted into the air, glistening with sweat like a circus seal, and dropped, his wet back landing flush upon the charged rug, heard him yell and saw him literally dance upon his back, his elbows beating a frenzied tattoo upon the floor, his muscles twitching like the flesh of a horse stung by many flies. When he finally rolled off, his face was gray and no one stopped him when he ran from the floor amid booming laughter.

"Get the money," the M.C. called. "That's good hard American cash!"

And we snatched and grabbed, snatched and grabbed. I was careful not to come too close to the rug now, and when I felt the hot whiskey breath descend upon me like a cloud of foul air I reached out and grabbed the leg of a chair. It was occupied and I held on desperately.

55   "Leggo, nigger! Leggo!"

The huge face wavered down to mine as he tried to push me free. But my body was slippery and he was too drunk. It was Mr. Colcord, who owned a chain of movie houses and "entertainment palaces." Each time he grabbed me I slipped out of his hands. It became a real struggle. I feared the rug more than I did the drunk, so I held on, surprising myself for a moment by trying to topple *him* upon the rug. It was such an enormous idea that I found myself actually carrying it out. I tried not to be obvious, yet when I grabbed his leg, trying to tumble him out of the chair, he raised up roaring with laughter, and, looking at me with soberness dead in the eye, kicked me viciously in the chest. The chair leg flew out of my hand and I felt myself going and rolled. It was as though I had rolled through a bed of hot coals. It seemed a whole century would pass before I would roll free, a century in which I was seared through the deepest levels of my body to the fearful breath within me and the breath seared and heated to the point of explosion. It'll all be over in a flash, I thought as I rolled clear. It'll all be over in a flash.

But not yet, the men on the other side were waiting, red faces swollen as though from apoplexy as they bent forward in their chairs. Seeing their fingers coming toward me I rolled away as a fumbled football rolls off the receiver's fingertips, back into the coals. That time I luckily sent the rug sliding out of place and heard the coins ringing against the floor and the boys scuffling to pick them up and the M.C. calling, "All right, boys, that's all. Go get dressed and get your money."

I was limp as a dish rag. My back felt as though it had been beaten with wires.

When we had dressed the M.C. came in and gave us each five dollars, except Tatlock, who got ten for being last in the ring. Then he told us to leave. I was not to get a chance to deliver my speech, I thought. I was going out into the dim alley in despair when I was stopped and told to go back. I returned to the ballroom, where the men were pushing back their chairs and gathering in groups to talk.

60   The M.C. knocked on a table for quiet. "Gentlemen," he said, "we almost forgot an important part of the program. A most serious part, gentlemen. This boy was brought here to deliver a speech which he made at his graduation yesterday . . ."

"Bravo!"

"I'm told that he is the smartest boy we've got out there in Greenwood. I'm told that he knows more big words than a pocket-sized dictionary."

Much applause and laughter.

"So now, gentlemen, I want you to give him your attention."

65   There was still laughter as I faced them, my mouth dry, my eye throbbing I began slowly, but evidently my throat was tense, because they began shouting, "Louder! Louder!"

"We of the younger generation extol the wisdom of that great leader and educator," I shouted, "who first spoke these flaming words of wisdom: 'A ship lost at sea for many days suddenly sighted a friendly vessel. From the mast of the unfortunate vessel was seen a signal: "Water, water; we die of thirst!" The answer from the friendly vessel came back: "Cast down your bucket where you are." The captain of the distressed vessel, at last heeding the injunction, cast down his bucket, and it came up full of fresh sparkling water from the mouth of the Amazon River.' And like him I say, and in his words, 'To those of my race who depend upon bettering their condition in a foreign land, or who underestimate the importance of cultivating friendly relations with the Southern white man, who is his next-door neighbor, I would say: "Cast down your bucket where you are"— cast it down in making friends in every manly way of the people of all races by whom we are surrounded . . . ' "

I spoke automatically and with such fervor that I did not realize that the men were still talking and laughing until my dry mouth, filling up with blood from the cut, almost strangled me. I coughed, wanting to stop and go to one of the tall brass, sand-filled spittoons to relieve myself, but a few of the men, especially the superintendent, were listening and I was afraid. So I gulped it down, blood, saliva, and all, and continued. (What powers of endurance I had during those days! What enthusiasm! What a belief in the rightness of things!) I spoke even louder in spite of the pain. But still they talked and still they laughed, as though deaf with cotton in dirty ears. So I spoke with greater emotional emphasis. I closed my ears and swallowed blood until I was nauseated. The speech seemed a hundred times as long as before, but I could not leave out a single word. All had to be said, each memorized nuance considered, rendered. Nor was that all. Whenever I uttered a word of three or more syllables a group of voices would yell for me to repeat it. I used the phrase "social responsibility" and they yelled:

"What's that word you say, boy?"

"Social responsibility," I said.

70   "What?"

"Social . . ."

"Louder."

". . . responsibility."

"More!"

75   "Respon—"

"Repeat!"

"—sibility."

The room filled with the uproar of laughter until, no doubt, distracted by having to gulp down my blood, I made a mistake and yelled a phrase I had often seen denounced in newspaper editorials, heard debated in private.

"Social . . ."

80   "What?" they yelled.

". . . equality—"

The laughter hung smokelike in the sudden stillness. I opened my eyes, puzzled. Sounds of displeasure filled the room. The M.C. rushed forward. They shouted hostile phrases at me. But I did not understand.

A small dry mustached man in the front row blared out, "Say that slowly, son!"

"What, sir?"

85   "What you just said!"

"Social responsibility, sir," I said.

"You weren't being smart, were you, boy?" he said, not unkindly.

"No, sir!"

"You sure that about 'equality' was a mistake?"

90   "Oh, yes, sir," I said. "I was swallowing blood."

"Well, you had better speak more slowly so we can understand. We mean to do right by you, but you've got to know your place at all times. All right, now, go on with your speech."

I was afraid. I wanted to leave but I wanted also to speak and I was afraid they'd snatch me down.

"Thank you, sir," I said, beginning where I had left off, and having them more me as before.

Yet when I finished there was a thunderous applause. I was surprised to see the superintendent come forth with a package wrapped in white tissue paper, and, gesturing for quiet, address the men.

95   "Gentlemen, you see that I did not overpraise this boy. He makes a good speech and some day he'll lead his people in the proper paths. And I don't have to tell you that that is important in these days and times. This is a good, smart boy, and so to encourage him in the right direction, in the name of the Board of Education I wish to present him a prize in the form of this . . ."

He paused, removing the tissue paper and revealing a gleaming calfskin brief case.

". . . in the form of this first-class article from Shad Whitmore's shop."

"Boy," he said, addressing me, "take this prize and keep it well. Consider it a badge of office. Prize it. Keep developing as you are and some day it will be filled with important papers that will help shape the destiny of your people."

I was so moved that I could hardly express my thanks. A rope of bloody saliva forming a shape like an undiscovered continent drooled upon the leather and I wiped it quickly away. I felt an importance that I had never dreamed.

100 "Open it and see what's inside," I was told.

My fingers a-tremble, I complied, smelling the fresh leather and finding an official-looking document inside. It was a scholarship to the state college for Negroes. My eyes filled with tears and I ran awkwardly off the floor.

I was overjoyed; I did not even mind when I discovered that the gold pieces I had scrambled for were brass pocket tokens advertising a certain make of automobile.

When I reached home everyone was excited. Next day the neighbors came to congratulate me. I even felt safe from grandfather, whose deathbed curse usually spoiled my triumphs. I stood beneath his photograph with my briefcase in hand and smiled triumphantly into his stolid black peasant's face. It was a face that fascinated me. The eyes seemed to follow everywhere I went.

That night I dreamed I was at a circus with him and that he refused to laugh at the clowns no matter what they did. Then later he told me to open my brief-case and read what was inside and I did, finding an official envelope stamped with the state seal; and inside the envelope I found another and another, endlessly, and I thought I would fall of weariness. "Them's years," he said. "Now open that one." And I did and in it I found an engraved document containing a short mes-sage in letters of gold. "Read it," my grandfather said. "Out loud!"

105 "To Whom It May Concern," I intoned. "Keep This Nigger-Boy Running."

I awoke with the old man's laughter ringing in my ears.

(It was a dream I was to remember and dream again for many years after. But at that time I had no insight into its meaning. First I had to attend college.)

LEVELS OF READING

Summary:

Pay attention to the **literal** meaning of the text. Briefly describe the story told in Ralph Ellison's "Battle Royale." Repeat the story of the text in your own words. Who tells this story? Does he have a name? Is his name or lack of name significant? Why or why not? State in a few sentences the nature of the "persona" of the narrator. Does his persona ever change in the course of the story? When, and in what way? Restate in your own words the deathbed advice of the narrator's grandfather. Why are the adults in the family so horrified by his final words? Why do they try to erase what he says? Are they successful? Concentrate on the highlights; avoid too much detail when summarizing. Again, drawing a simple outline of the main points of the text will help you better analyze the text at other levels of interpretation.

Analysis:

Find what you believe is **symbolic** in the text. For instance, is the battle itself symbolic of a larger fight within the narrator's culture? What, exactly, is the nature of that battle? What might the electrified carpet covered with coins symbolize? Return also to the family's reaction to the grandfather's final words. Might what the family does immediately following the grandfather's death be characterized as a "repression," in the Freudian sense? Is that repression accompanied by the putting up of a resistance? If so, are the repression and its resistance successful or unsuccessful? Finally, both Freud and Jung believe that dreams are highly symbolic. Reread the narrator's dream at the end of the story, and analyze any symbols in it. Find any other symbols you think are important in the story and explain the meaning of these symbols. With the help of the background material provided about Ralph Ellison, make an argument about this text, and include the mention of the more **figurative** aspects of the text when making points in defense of your argument.

Application:

Apply what you have learned about the American South in the second half of the twentieth century from Dr. Martin Luther King, Jr.'s "Letter from Birmingham Jail" to help you make an argument about Ellison's short story, "Battle Royale." Note the dates of Dr. King's "Letter from Birmingham Jail," and of the composition of Ellison's short story. Does Ellison's story give any additional insight into why Dr. King composed his angry letter more than a decade later? The "part" of the story you choose to analyze may include any of the following: a character, a setting, a symbol or symbols, an important change, a motivation, a goal, a result. Consider the following as possibilities, but explore other original interpretations too:

- State in your own words the message of the grandfather's last words at the beginning of Ellison's story. How does this message relate to King's notion of nonviolent protest?
- All the white pillars of the community are present at the smoker. What might King's response to their presence be in light of what he has to say about "white moderates"?
- Using what you have gleaned about life in Birmingham in 1963, why do the young men invited to fight feel such fear at the sight of the white dancer?
- The narrator of "Battle Royale" is given a briefcase with a scholarship to a "Negro college." Is this gift an example of the "separate but equal" opportunities for African Americans? Why or why not?
- In their setting, about twenty years before King wrote his "Letter," is it possible for the young men invited to the smoker to engage in any sort of the "direct action" King espouses? Why or why not?

ERICH FROMM

Though he was born into an orthodox German-Jewish family, as an adult Erich Fromm (1900–1980) became what he called an "atheistic mystic." An only child, his childhood was not a particularly happy one, but he excelled in school neverthe- less. In 1922, he received his Ph.D. in sociology from the University of Heidelberg; soon after, he began his psychoanalytic training and became a psychotherapist.

In 1926, Fromm married Freida Reichman, also a psychoanalyst working on schizophrenia, but the marriage ended four years later. Soon after, Fromm and his former wife were invited to join the Frankfurt Psychoanalytic Instiutute (later known as The Frankfurt School) by Max Horkheimer. The rise of Nazism in Germany forced the school to depart for New York City in 1934.

In 1944, Fromm married Henny Gurland, and in 1950 the couple relo- cated to Mexico, mainly for his wife's health. Though she died only two years after the move, Fromm remained in Mexico and founded the Mexican Institute of Psychoanalysis in Mexico City, which he directed until 1976. During these years, Fromm often spent at least three months a year in New York City, teach- ing at Columbia, New York University, and The New School.

In 1953 he married Annis Freeman, and continued until 1976 to teach and practice in New York City and Mexico. He then retired to Switzerland, where he died in 1980. Erich Fromm left behind a number of books still considered classic works in the field of social psychology, including Escape from Freedom *(1942),* The Art of Loving *(1957), and* The Anatomy of Human Destruction.

Fromm's essay, "Disobedience as a Psychological and Moral Problem" starts with some basic and commonly-held assumptions about the values implicit in the words "obedience" and "disobedience." During the course of his argument, he seems to overturn those values. And yet, Fromm's argument is much more complex than a simple restatement of the terms and their value to humans. In the course of his argument, Fromm begins by restating common assumptions as though they were his own, follows with questioning those assumptions to the point of falsifying them, and finally ends by wedding the two points of view in a new combination all his own.

DISOBEDIENCE AS A PSYCHOLOGICAL AND MORAL PROBLEM
Erich Fromm

1   For centuries kings, priests, feudal lords, industrial bosses and parents have insisted that *obedience is a virtue* and that *disobedience is a vice*. In order to introduce another point of view, let us set against this position the following statement: *human history began with an act of disobedience, and it is not unlikely that it will be terminated by an act of obedience.*

Human history was ushered in by an act of disobedience according to the Hebrew and Greek myths. Adam and Eve, living in the Garden of Eden, were part of nature; they were in harmony with it, yet did not transcend it. They were in nature as the fetus is in the womb of the mother. They were human, and at the same time not yet human. All this changed when they disobeyed an order. By breaking the ties with earth and mother, by cutting the umbilical cord, man emerged from a pre-human harmony and was able to take the first step into independence and freedom. The act of disobedience set Adam and Eve free and opened their eyes. They recognized each other as strangers and the world outside them as strange and even hostile. Their act of disobedience broke the primary bond with nature and made them individuals. "Original sin," far from corrupting man, set him free; it was the beginning of history. Man had to leave the Garden of Eden in order to learn to rely on his own powers and to become fully human.

The prophets, in their messianic concept, confirmed the idea that man had been right in disobeying; that he had not been corrupted by his "sin," but freed from the fetters of pre-human harmony. For the prophets, *history* is the place where man becomes human; during its unfolding he develops his powers of reason and of love until he creates a new harmony between himself, his fellow man and nature. This new harmony is described as "the end of days," that period of history in which there is peace between man and man, and between man and nature. It is a "new" paradise created by man himself, and one which he alone could create because he was forced to leave the "old" paradise as a result of his disobedience.

Reprinted from *On Disobedience and Other Essays* (1963), HarperCollins, Inc.

Just as the Hebrew myth of Adam and Eve, so the Greek myth of Prometheus sees all of human civilization based on an act of disobedience. Prometheus, in stealing the fire from the gods, lays the foundation for the evolution of man. There would be no human history were it not for Prometheus' "crime." He, like Adam and Eve, is punished for his disobedience. But he does not repent and ask for forgiveness. On the contrary, he proudly says: "I would rather be chained to this rock than be the obedient servant of the gods."

5   Man has continued to evolve by acts of disobedience. Not only was his spiritual development possible only because there were men who dared to say no to the powers that be in the name of their conscience or their faith, but also his intellectual development was dependent on the capacity for being disobedient—disobedient to authorities who tried to muzzle new thoughts and to the authority of long-established opinions which declared a change to be nonsense.

If the capacity for disobedience constituted the beginning of human history, obedience might very well, as I have said, cause the end of human history. I am not speaking symbolically or poetically. There is the possibility, or even the probability, that the human race will destroy civilization and even all life upon earth within the next five to ten years. There is no rationality or sense in it. But the fact is that, while we are living technically in the Atomic Age, the majority of men—including most of those who are in power—still live emotionally in the Stone Age; that while our mathematics, astronomy, and the natural sciences are of the twentieth century, most of our ideas about politics, the state, and society lag far behind the age of science. If mankind commits suicide it will be because people will obey those who command them to push the deadly buttons; because they will obey the archaic passions of fear, hate, and greed; because they will obey obsolete clichés of State sovereignty and national honor. The Soviet leaders talk much about revolutions, and we in the "free world" talk much about freedom. Yet they and we discourage disobedience—in the Soviet Union explicitly and by force, in the free world implicitly and by the more subtle methods of persuasion.

But I do not mean to say that all disobedience is a virtue and all obedience a vice. Such a view would ignore the dialectical relationship between obedience and disobedience. Whenever the principles which are obeyed and those which are disobeyed are irreconcilable, an act of obedience to one principle is necessarily an act of disobedience to its counterpart, and vice versa. Antigone is the classic example of this dichotomy. By obeying the inhuman laws of the State, Antigone necessarily would disobey the laws of humanity. By obeying the latter, she must disobey the former. All martyrs of religious faiths, of freedom and of science have had to disobey those who wanted to muzzle them in order to obey their own consciences, the laws of humanity and of reason. If a man can only obey and not disobey, he is a slave; if he can only disobey and not obey, he is a rebel (not a revolutionary); he acts out of anger, disappointment, resentment, yet not in the name of a conviction or a principle.

However, in order to prevent a confusion of terms an important qualification must be made. Obedience to a person, institution or power (heteronomous obedience) is submission; it implies the abdication of my autonomy and the acceptance of a foreign will or judgment in place of my own. Obedience to my own reason or conviction (autonomous obedience) is not an act of submission but one of affirmation. My conviction and my judgment, if authentically mine, are part of me. If I follow them rather than the judgment of others, I am being myself; hence the word *obey* can be applied only in a metaphorical sense and with a meaning which is fundamentally different from the one in the case of "heteronomous obedience."

But this distinction still needs two further qualifications, one with regard to the concept of conscience and the other with regard to the concept of authority. The word *conscience* is used to express two phenomena which are quite distinct from each other. One is the "authoritarian conscience" which is the internalized voice of an authority whom we are eager to please and afraid of displeasing. This authoritarian conscience is what most people experience when they obey their conscience. It is also the conscience which Freud speaks of, and which he called "Super-Ego." This Super-Ego represents the internalized commands and prohibitions of father, accepted by the son out of fear. Different from the authoritarian conscience is the "humanistic conscience"; this is the voice present in every human being and independent from external sanctions and rewards. Humanistic conscience is based on the fact that as human beings we have an intuitive knowledge of what is human and inhuman, what is conducive of life and what is destructive of life. This conscience serves our functioning as human beings. It is the voice which calls us back to ourselves, to our humanity.

10   Authoritarian conscience (Super-Ego) is still obedience to a power outside of myself, even though this power has been internalized. Consciously I believe that I am following my conscience; in effect, however, I have swallowed the principles of power; just because of the illusion that humanistic conscience and Super-Ego are identical, internalized authority is so much more effective than the authority which is clearly experienced as not being part of me. Obedience to the "authoritarian conscience," like all obedience to outside thoughts and power, tends to debilitate "humanistic conscience," the ability to be and to judge oneself.

The statement, on the other hand, that obedience to another person is ipso facto submission needs also to be qualified by distinguishing "irrational" from "rational" authority. An example of rational authority is to be found in the relationship between student and teacher; one of irrational authority in the relationship between slave and master. Both relationships are based on the fact that the authority of the person in command is accepted. Dynamically, however, they are of a different nature. The interests of the teacher and the student, in the ideal case, lie in the same direction. The teacher is satisfied if he succeeds in furthering the student; if he has failed to do so, the failure is his and the student's. The slave owner, on the other hand, wants to exploit the slave as much as possible. The more he gets out of him the more satisfied he is. At the same time, the slave tries to defend as best he can his claims for a minimum of happiness.

The interests of slave and master are antagonistic, because what is advantageous to the one is detrimental to the other. The superiority of the one over the other has a different function in each case; in the first it is the condition for the furtherance of the person subjected to the authority, and in the second it is the condition for his exploitation. Another distinction runs parallel to this: rational authority is rational because the authority, whether it is held by a teacher or a captain of a ship giving orders in an emergency, acts in the name of reason which, being universal, I can accept without submitting. Irrational authority has to use force or suggestion, because no one would let himself be exploited if he were free to prevent it.

Why is man so prone to obey and why is it so difficult for him to disobey? As long as I am obedient to the power of the State, the Church, or public opinion, I feel safe and protected. In fact it makes little difference what power it is that I am obedient to. It is always an institution, or men, who use force in one form or another and who fraudulently claim omniscience and omnipotence. My obedience makes me part of the power I worship, and hence I feel strong. I can make no error, since it decides for me; I cannot be alone, because it watches over me; I cannot commit a sin, because it does not let me do so, and even if I do sin, the punishment is only the way of returning to the almighty power.

In order to disobey, one must have the courage to be alone, to err and to sin. But courage is not enough. The capacity for courage depends on a person's state of development. Only if a person has emerged from mother's lap and father's commands, only if he has emerged as a fully developed individual and thus has acquired the capacity to think and feel for himself, only then can he have the courage to say "no" to power, to disobey.

15   A person can become free through acts of disobedience by learning to say no to power. But not only is the capacity for disobedience the condition for free-

dom; freedom is also the condition for disobedience. If I am afraid of freedom, I cannot dare to say "no," I cannot have the courage to be disobedient. Indeed, freedom and the capacity for disobedience are inseparable; hence any social, political, and religious system which proclaims freedom, yet stamps out disobedience, cannot speak the truth.

There is another reason why it is so difficult to dare to disobey, to say "no" to power. During most of human history obedience has been identified with virtue and disobedience with sin. The reason is simple: thus far throughout most of history a minority has ruled over the majority. This rule was made necessary by the fact that there was only enough of the good things of life for the few, and only the crumbs remained for the many. If the few wanted to enjoy the good things and, beyond that, to have the many serve them and work for them, one condition was necessary: the many had to learn obedience.

To be sure, obedience can be established by sheer force. But this method has many disadvantages. It constitutes a constant threat that one day the many might have the means to overthrow the few by force; furthermore there are many kinds of work which cannot be done properly if nothing but fear is behind the obedience. Hence the obedience which is only rooted in the fear of force must be transformed into one rooted in man's heart. Man must want and even need to obey, instead of only fearing to disobey. If this is to be achieved, power must assume the qualities of the All Good, of the All Wise; it must become All Knowing. If this happens, power can proclaim that disobedience is sin and obedience virtue; and once this has been proclaimed, the many can accept obedience because it is good and detest disobedience because it is bad, rather than to detest themselves for being cowards.

From Luther to the nineteenth century one was concerned with overt and explicit authorities. Luther, the pope, the princes, wanted to uphold it; the middle class, the workers, the philosophers, tried to uproot it. The fight against authority in the State as well as in the family was often the very basis for the development of an independent and daring person. The fight against authority was inseparable from the intellectual mood which characterized the philosophers of the enlightenment and the scientists. This "critical mood" was one of faith in reason, and at the same time of doubt in everything which is said or thought, inasmuch as it is based on tradition, superstition, custom, power. The principles *sapere aude* and *de omnibus est dubitandum*—"dare to be wise" and "of all one must doubt"—were characteristic of the attitude which permitted and furthered the capacity to say "no."

The case of Adolf Eichmann is symbolic of our situation and has a signifi-cance far beyond the one which his accusers in the courtroom in Jerusalem were concerned with. Eichmann is a symbol of the organization man, of the alienated bureaucrat for whom men, women and children have become numbers. He is a symbol of all of us. We can see ourselves in Eichmann. But the most frighten-ing thing about him is that after the entire story was told in terms of his own admissions, he was able in perfect good faith to plead his innocence. It is clear that if he were once more in the same situation he would do it again. And so would we—and so do we.

20   The organization man has lost the capacity to disobey, he is not even aware of the fact that he obeys. At this point in history the capacity to doubt, to crit-icize and to disobey may be all that stands between a future for mankind and the end of civilization.

LEVELS OF READING

Summary:

Briefly describe Erich Fromm's viewpoint in "Disobedience as a Psychological and Moral Problem." What is the basic premise of his argument?

Analysis:

Why are the Hebrew and Greek myths Fromm cites **symbolically** significant for Fromm's argument? How does Fromm's view of "original sin" differ from that of others? Why are the interpretations of these symbols important to Fromm? What does Adolf Eichmann symbolize in Fromm's essay? Find any other symbols you think are important in this essay and explain the meaning of these symbols. With the help of the background material provided about Erich Fromm, make an argu-ment about this essay, and include the mention of the more **figurative** or implicit aspects of the text when making points in defense of your argument.

Application:

Apply Fromm's theory to Martin Luther King, Jr.'s ideas in "Letter from Birm-ingham Jail." How does King's theory of "nonviolent protest" square with Fromm's ideas about obedience and disobedience? Consider the following as possibilities, but explore other original interpretations too:

- Erich Fromm distinguishes between "rational" and "irrational" authority. How might his ideas about each be applied to King's distinction between "just" and "unjust" laws?
- What important consequences do Fromm's definitions of "authoritarian conscience" and "humanistic" conscience have for Dr. King's civil rights movement?
- Is Dr. King absolutely opposed to heteronomous obedience? Why or why not?

Start Your Own Argument:

In paragraph 15, King mentions the "anxiety" of the white clergymen "over our [activists'] willingness to break laws." In paragraph 24, King outlines the consequences of a society building "dangerously structured dams that block the flow of social progress." In what ways might the idea of anxiety, along with the symbolically blocked dam and its consequences shed new light on Freud's "repression," "resistance," and "hysteria?" Fromm, meanwhile, talks about both the "super-ego" (paragraph 11) and class warfare (paragraph 16). Can a culture be psychoanalyzed in much the same way as an individual? Is there a collective, "personal" unconscious? Does it work the same way as an individual collective and/or personal unconscious?

FOUR

THE MANIFESTO, ARGUMENT DIVIDED INTO SECTIONS, ARGUMENT BY DEFINITION, ARGUMENT PROVIDING HISTORICAL BACKGROUND, ARGUMENTS WITHIN THE ARGUMENT

In terms of its form, Marx's *Manifesto of the Communist Party* has two salient features: First, it takes the form of a manifesto, in rhetoric also known as an emotional appeal, and second, it is divided into sections.

In terms of content, Marx provides evidence for his argument in the form of definitions of his terms and historical background. Marx understands that his essay cannot be effective unless his audience understands his terms, especially since the terms "communism," "bourgeois," and "proletarians" are unfamiliar to or misunderstood by most of his readers. He also knows that his readers will likely need some historical background to grasp the influence of the past on the present and the future. Rather than making conventional "points" in defense of his viewpoint, Marx defines his terms and provides an historical narrative that he hopes will persuade his readers.

KARL MARX

Karl Marx (1818–1883) was born in Trier, Germany. He studied humanities at the University of Bonn (1835), and law and philosophy at the University of Berlin (1836–41), where he first became acquainted with the writings of G.W.F. Hegel. In 1841 he received a doctorate in Jena.

Marx then worked as a writer in Cologne and Paris. He became active in leftist politics in Paris, and met his lifelong collaborator, Frederick Engels there. Banished from Paris in 1845 due to his association with leftist politics, he moved to Belgium. In 1848, he was invited to join a secret left-wing group active in London, the Communist League, for which he and Engels wrote The Manifesto of the Communist Party. *Permanently exiled from his native Germany, he moved to London in 1849 and spent the rest of his life there.*

Sporadic work as a writer kept Marx and his growing family in continual poverty, and two of his children died. His major three-volume critique of capitalism, Das Kapital, *was published from 1851–1862.*

———

Marx's *Manifesto* is, by the very nature of its genre, written to persuade. In fact, Marx envisioned his *Manifesto* as a polemical retort to all who seemed to misunderstand the Communist project in nineteenth-century Europe. Disgusted with the excesses of capitalism, the privileging of a minority at the expense of the majority, and the pernicious effects of capitalistic production on working people, Marx decided it was high time someone spoke out in favor of a more equitable distribution of human resources. It is not at all surprising then, that Marx's *Manifesto* ends in an exclamation point. In other words, in light of the form Marx chose for his argument, the reader has every right to expect the argument to come in the form of a highly charged emotional outburst. Instead, Marx's *Manifesto* is broken into three sections, which seem to be designed to explain and define, rather than to argue. In addition, much of the essay provides historical background. Ask why Marx took such an approach to the writing of this essay and decide whether you think his strategy is effective.

Coming to Terms with the Reading:

Before reading/rereading Karl Marx's *Manifesto of the Communist Party*, it is best to have a firm grasp on the meanings of the following terms:

1. communist
2. bourgeois/ie
3. proletariat
4. capital
5. class struggle
6. wage labor

THE MANIFESTO OF THE COMMUNIST PARTY
Karl Marx

1   A specter is haunting Europe—the specter of Communism. All the Powers of old Europe have entered into a holy alliance to exorcise this specter; Pope and Czar, Metternich and Guizot, French Radicals and German police-spies.

Where is the party in opposition that has not been decried as communistic by its opponents in power? Where the Opposition that has not hurled back the branding reproach of Communism against the more advanced opposition parties, as well as against its reactionary adversaries?

Two things result from this fact.

I. Communism is already acknowledged by all European Powers to be itself a Power.

5   II. It is high time that Communists should openly, in the face of the whole world, publish their views, their aims, their tendencies, and meet this nursery tale of the specter of Communism with a Manifesto of the party itself.

To this end, Communists of various nationalities have assembled in London and sketched the following Manifesto, to be published in the English, French, German, Italian, Flemish and Danish languages.

Bourgeois and Proletarians

The history of all hitherto existing society is the history of class struggles.

Freeman and slave, patrician and plebeian, lord and serf, guild-master and journeyman, in a word, oppressor and oppressed, stood in constant opposition to one another, carried on uninterrupted, now hidden, now open fight, a fight that each time ended, either in a revolutionary re-constitution of society at large, or in the common ruin of the contending classes.

In the earlier epochs of history we find almost everywhere a complicated arrangement of society into various orders, a manifold gradation of social rank. In ancient Rome we have patricians, knights, plebeians, slaves; in the Middle Ages, feudal lords, vassals, guild-masters, journeymen, apprentices, serfs; in almost all of these classes, again, subordinate gradations.

10   The modern bourgeois society that has sprouted from the ruins of feudal society, has not done away with class antagonisms. It has but established new classes, new conditions of oppression, new forms of struggle in place of the old ones.

Our epoch, the epoch of the bourgeoisie, possesses, however, this distinctive feature; it has simplified the class antagonisms. Society as a whole is more and more splitting up into two great hostile camps, into two great classes directly facing each other: Bourgeoisie and Proletariat.

From the serfs of the Middle Ages sprang the chartered burghers of the earliest towns. From these burgesses the first elements of the bourgeoisie were developed.

The discovery of America, the rounding of the Cape, opened up fresh ground for the rising bourgeoisie. The East Indian and Chinese markets, the colonization of America, trade with the colonies, the increase in the means of exchange and in commodities generally, gave to commerce, to navigation, to industry, an impulse never before known, and thereby, to the revolutionary element in the tottering feudal society, a rapid development.

The feudal system of industry, under which industrial production was monopolized by closed guilds, now no longer sufficed for the growing wants of the new market. The manufacturing system took its place. The guild-masters were pushed on one side by the manufacturing middle-class: division of labor between the different corporate guilds vanished in the face of division of labor in each single workshop.

15   Meantime the markets kept ever growing, the demand ever rising. Even manufacture no longer sufficed. Thereupon, steam and machinery revolutionized industrial production. The place of manufacture was taken by the giant, Modern Industry, the place of the industrial middle-class, by industrial millionaires, the leaders of whole industrial armies, the modern bourgeois.

Modern industry has established the world-market, for which the discovery of America paved the way. This market has given an immense development to commerce, to navigation, to communication by land. This development has, in its turn, reacted on the extension of industry; and in proportion as industry, commerce, navigation, railways extended, in the same proportion the bourgeoisie developed, increased its capital, and pushed into the background every class handed down from the Middle Ages.

We see, therefore, how the modern bourgeoisie is itself the product of a long course of development, of a series of revolutions in the modes of production and of exchange.

Each step in the development of the bourgeoisie was accompanied by a corresponding political advance of that class. An oppressed class under the sway of the feudal nobility, an armed and self-governing association in the medieval commune, here independent urban republic (as in Italy and Germany), there taxable "third estate" of the monarchy (as in France), afterwards, in the period of manufacture proper, serving either the semi-feudal or the absolute monarchy as a counterpoise against nobility, and, in fact, cornerstone of the great monarchies in general, the bourgeoisie has at last, since the establishment of Modern Industry and of the world-market, conquered for itself, in the modern representative State, exclusive political sway. The executive of the modern State is but a committee for managing the common affairs of the whole bourgeoisie.

The bourgeoisie, historically, has played a most revolutionary part.

20   The bourgeoisie, wherever it has got the upper hand, has put an end to all feudal, patriarchal, idyllic relations. It has pitilessly torn asunder the motley feudal ties that bound man to his "natural superiors," and has left no other nexus between man and man than naked self-interest, than callous "cash payment." It has drowned the most heavenly ecstasies of religious fervor, of chivalrous enthusiasm, of Philistine sentimentalism, in the icy water of egotistical calculation. It has resolved personal worth into exchange value, and in place of the numberless indefeasible chartered freedoms, has set up that single, unconscionable freedom—Free Trade. In one word, for exploitation, veiled by religious and political illusions, it has substituted naked, shameless, direct, brutal exploitation.

The bourgeoisie has stripped of its halo every occupation hitherto honored and looked up to with reverent awe. It has converted the physician, the lawyer, the priest, the poet, the man of science, into its paid wage laborers.

The bourgeoisie has torn away from the family its sentimental veil, and has reduced the family relation to a mere money relation.

The bourgeoisie has disclosed how it came to pass that the brutal display of vigor in the Middle Ages, which reactionists so much admire, found its fitting complement in the most slothful indolence. It has been the first to show what man's activity can bring about. It has accomplished wonders far surpassing Egyptian pyramids, Roman aqueducts and Gothic cathedrals; it has conducted expeditions that put in the shade all former Exoduses of nations and crusades.

The bourgeoisie cannot exist without constantly revolutionizing the instruments of production, and thereby the relations of production, and with them the whole relations of society. Conservation of the old modes of production in unaltered form was, on the contrary, the first condition of existence for all earlier industrial classes. Constant revolutionizing of production, uninterrupted disturbance of all social conditions, everlasting uncertainty and agitation distinguish the bourgeois epoch from all earlier ones. All fixed, fast frozen relations, with their train of ancient and venerable prejudices and opinions, are swept away, all new-formed ones become antiquated before they can ossify. All that is solid melts into the air, all that is holy is profaned, and man is at last compelled to face with sober senses, his real conditions of life, and his relations with his kind.

25   The need of a constantly expanding market for its products chases the bourgeoisie over the whole surface of the globe. It must nestle everywhere, settle everywhere, establish connections everywhere.

The bourgeoisie has through its exploitation of the world-market given a cosmopolitan character to production and consumption in every country. To the great chagrin of reactionists, it has drawn from under the feet of industry the national ground on which it stood. All old-established national industries have been destroyed or are daily being destroyed. They are dislodged by new industries, whose introduction becomes a life and death question for all civilized nations, by industries that no longer work up indigenous raw material, but raw material drawn from the remotest zones; industries whose products are consumed, not only at home, but in every quarter of the globe. In place of the old wants, satisfied by the productions of the country, we find new wants, requiring for their satisfaction the products of distant lands and climes. In place of the old local and national seclusion and self-sufficiency, we have intercourse in every direction, universal interdependence of nations. And as in material, so also in intellectual production. The intellectual creations of individual nations become common property. National onesidedness and narrowmindedness become more and more impossible, and from the numerous national and local literatures there arises a world-literature.

The bourgeoisie, by the rapid improvement of all instruments of production, by the immensely facilitated means of communication, draws all, even the most barbarian nations into civilization. The cheap prices of its commodities are the heavy artillery with which it batters down all Chinese walls, with which it forces the barbarians' intensely obstinate hatred of foreigners to capitulate. It compels all nations, on pain of extinction, to adopt the bourgeois mode of production; it compels them to introduce what it calls civilization into their midst, i.e., to become bourgeois themselves. In a word, it creates a world after its own image.

The bourgeoisie has subjected the country to the rule of the towns. It has created enormous cities, has greatly increased the urban population as compared with the rural and has thus rescued a considerable part of the population from the idiocy of rural life. Just as it has made the country dependent on the towns, so it has made barbarian and semi-barbarian countries dependent on civilized ones, nations of peasants on nations of bourgeois, the East on the West.

The bourgeoisie keeps more and more doing away with the scattered state of the population, of the means of production, and of property. It has agglomerated population, centralized means of production, and has concentrated property in a few hands. The necessary consequence of this was political centralization. Independent, or but loosely connected provinces, with separate interests, laws, governments and systems of taxation, became lumped together in one nation, with one government, one code of laws, one national class interest, one frontier and one customs tariff.

30   The bourgeoisie, during its rule of scarce one hundred years, has created more massive and more colossal productive forces than have all preceding generations together. Subjection of Nature's forces to man, machinery, application of chemistry to industry and agriculture, steam-navigation, railways, electric telegraphs, clearing of whole continents for cultivation, canalization of rivers, whole populations conjured out of the ground—what earlier century had even a presentiment that such productive forces slumbered in the lap of social labor?

We see then: the means of production and of exchange on whose foundation the bourgeoisie built itself up, were generated in feudal society. At a certain stage in the development of these means of production and of exchange, the conditions under which feudal society produced and exchanged, the feudal organization of agriculture and manufacturing industry, in one word, the feudal relations of property became no longer compatible with the already developed productive forces; they became so many fetters. They had to burst asunder; they were burst asunder.

Into their place stepped free competition, accompanied by a social and political constitution adapted to it, and by the economical and political sway of the bourgeois class.

A similar movement is going on before our own eyes. Modern bourgeois society with its relations of production, of exchange and of property, a society that has conjured up such gigantic means of production and of exchange, is like the sorcerer, who is no longer able to control the powers of the nether world whom he has called up by his spells. For many a decade past, the history of industry and commerce is but the history of the revolt of modern productive forces against modern conditions of production, against the property relations that are the conditions for the existence of the bourgeoisie and of its rule. It is enough to mention the commercial crises that by their periodical return put on its trial, each time more threateningly, the existence of the entire bourgeois society. In these crises a great part not only of the existing products, but also of the previously created productive forces, are periodically destroyed. In these crises there breaks out an epidemic that, in all earlier epochs, would have seemed an absurdity—the epidemic of overproduction. Society suddenly finds itself put back into a state of momentary barbarism; it appears as if a famine, a universal war of devastation, had cut off the supply of every means of subsistence; industry and commerce seem to be destroyed; and why? Because there is too much civilization, too much means of subsistence, too much industry, too much commerce. The productive forces at the disposal of society no longer tend to further the development of the conditions of the bourgeois property; on the contrary, they have become too powerful for these conditions by which they are fettered, and as soon as they overcome these fetters they bring disorder into the whole of bourgeois society, endanger the existence of bourgeois property. The conditions of bourgeois society are too narrow to comprise the wealth created by them. And how does the bourgeoisie get over these crises? On the one hand by enforced destruction of a mass of productive forces; on the other, by the conquest of new markets, and by the more thorough exploitation of the old ones. That is to say, by paving the way for more extensive and more destructive crises, and by diminishing the means whereby crises are prevented.

The weapons with which the bourgeoisie felled feudalism to the ground are now turned against the bourgeoisie itself.

35   But not only has the bourgeoisie forged the weapons that bring death to itself; it has also called into existence the men who are to wield those weapons— the modern working class—the proletarians.

In proportion as the bourgeoisie, i.e., capital, is developed, in the same proportion is the proletariat, the modern working class, developed, a class of laborers who live only so long as they find work, and who find work only so long as their labor increases capital. These laborers, who must sell themselves piecemeal, are a commodity, like every other article of commerce, and are consequently exposed to all the vicissitudes of competition, to all the fluctuations of the market.

Owing to the extensive use of machinery and to division of labor, the work of the proletarians has lost all individual character, and, consequently, all charm for the workman. He becomes an appendage of the machine, and it is only the most simple, most monotonous and most easily acquired knack that is required of him. Hence, the cost of production of a workman is restricted almost entirely to the means of subsistence that he requires for his maintenance, and for the propagation of his race. But the price of a commodity, and also of labor, is equal to its cost of production. In proportion, therefore, as the repulsiveness of the work increases the wage decreases. Nay more, in proportion as the use of machinery and division of labor increases, in the same proportion the burden of toil increases, whether by prolongation of the working hours, by increase of the work enacted in a given time, or by increased speed of the machinery, etc.

Modern industry has converted the little workshop of the patriarchal master into the great factory of the industrial capitalist. Masses of laborers, crowded into factories, are organized like soldiers. As privates of the industrial army they are placed under the command of a perfect hierarchy of officers and sergeants. Not only are they the slaves of the bourgeois class and of the bourgeois state, they are daily and hourly enslaved by the machine, by the overlooker, and, above all, by the individual bourgeois manufacturer himself. The more openly this despotism proclaims gain to be its end and aim, the more petty, the more hateful and the more embittering it is.

The less the skill and exertion or strength implied in manual labor, in other words, the more modern industry becomes developed, the more is the labor of men superseded by that of women. Differences of age and sex have no longer any distinctive social validity for the working class. All are instruments of labor, more or less expensive to use, according to their age and sex.

40 No sooner is the exploitation of the laborer by the manufacturer, so far at an end, that he receives his wages in cash, than he is set upon by the other portions of the bourgeoisie, the landlord, the shopkeeper, the pawnbroker, etc.

The lower strata of the middle class—the small trades-people, shopkeepers and retired tradesmen generally, the handicraftsmen and peasants—all these sink gradually into the proletariat, partly because their diminutive capital does not suffice for the scale on which Modern Industry is carried on, and is swamped in the competition with the large capitalists, partly because their specialized skill is rendered worthless by new methods of production. Thus the proletariat is recruited from all classes of the population.

The proletariat goes through various stages of development. With its birth begins its struggle with the bourgeoisie. At first the contest is carried on by individual laborers, then by the workpeople of a factory, then by the operatives of one trade, in one locality, against the individual bourgeois who directly exploits them. They direct their attacks not against the bourgeois conditions of production, but against the instruments of production themselves; they destroy imported wares that compete with their labor, they smash to pieces machinery, they set factories ablaze, they seek to restore by force the vanished status of the workman of the Middle Ages.

At this stage the laborers still form an incoherent mass scattered over the whole country, and broken up by their mutual competition. If anywhere they unite to form more compact bodies, this is not yet the consequence of their own active union, but of the union of the bourgeoisie, which class, in order to attain its own political ends, is compelled to set the whole proletariat in motion, and is moreover yet, for a time, able to do so. At this stage, therefore, the proletarians do not fight their enemies, but the enemies of their enemies, the remnants of absolute monarchy, the landowners, the nonindustrial bourgeois, the petty bourgeoisie. Thus the whole historical movement is concentrated in the hands of the bourgeoisie, every victory so obtained is a victory for the bourgeoisie.

But with the development of industry the proletariat not only increases in number; it becomes concentrated in greater masses, its strength grows and it feels that strength more. The various interests and conditions of life within the ranks of the proletariat are more and more equalized, in proportion as machinery obliterates all distinctions of labor, and nearly everywhere reduces wages to the same low level. The growing competition among the bourgeois, and the resulting commercial crisis, make the wages of the workers even more fluctuating. The unceasing improvement of machinery, ever more rapidly developing, makes their livelihood more and more precarious; the collisions between individual workmen and individual bourgeois take more and more the character of collisions between two classes. Thereupon the workers begin to form combinations (Trades' Unions) against the bourgeois; they club together in order to keep up the rate of wages; they found permanent associations in order to make provision beforehand for these occasional revolts. Here and there the contest breaks out into riots.

45   Now and then the workers are victorious, but only for a time. The real fruit of their battle lies not in the immediate result but in the ever-expanding union of workers. This union is helped on by the improved means of communication that are created by modern industry, and that places the workers of different localities in contact with one another. It was just this contact that was needed to centralize the numerous local struggles, all of the same character, into one national struggle between classes. But every class struggle is a political struggle. And that union, to attain which the burghers of the Middle Ages with their miserable highways, required centuries, the modern proletarians, thanks to railways, achieve in a few years.

This organization of the proletarians into a class, and consequently into a political party, is continually being upset again by the competition between the workers themselves. But it ever rises up again, stronger, firmer, mightier. It compels legislative recognition of particular interests of the workers by taking advantage of the divisions among the bourgeoisie itself. Thus the ten hours' bill in England was carried.

Altogether collisions between the classes of the old society further, in many ways, the course of development of the proletariat. The bourgeoisie finds itself involved in a constant battle. At first with the aristocracy; later on, with those portions of the bourgeoisie itself whose interests have become antagonistic to the progress of industry; at all times, with the bourgeoisie of foreign countries. In all these battles it sees itself compelled to appeal to the proletariat, to ask for its help, and thus, to drag it into the political arena. The bourgeoisie itself, therefore, supplies the proletariat with its own elements of political and general education; in other words, it furnishes the proletariat with weapons for fighting the bourgeoisie.

Further, as we have already seen, entire sections of the ruling classes are, by the advance of industry, precipitated into the proletariat, or are at least threatened in their conditions of existence. These also supply the proletariat with fresh elements of enlightenment and progress.

Finally, in times when the class struggle nears the decisive hour, the process of dissolution going on within the ruling class—in fact, within the whole range of an old society—assumes such a violent, glaring character that a small section of the ruling class cuts itself adrift and joins the revolutionary class, the class that holds the future in its hands. Just as, therefore, at an earlier period, a section of the nobility went over to the bourgeoisie, so now a portion of the bourgeoisie goes over to the proletariat, and in particular, a portion of the bourgeois ideologists, who have raised themselves to the level of comprehending theoretically the historical movements as a whole.

50   Of all the classes that stand face to face with the bourgeoisie today the proletariat alone is a really revolutionary class. The other classes decay and finally disappear in the face of Modern Industry; the proletariat is its special and essential product.

The lower middle class, the small manufacturer, the shopkeeper, the artisan, the peasant, all these fight against the bourgeoisie, to save from extinction their existence as fractions of the middle class. They are therefore not revolutionary, but conservative. Nay, more; they are reactionary, for they try to roll back the wheel of history. If by chance they are revolutionary, they are so only in view of their impending transfer into the proletariat; they thus defend not their present, but their future interests; they desert their own standpoint to place themselves at that of the proletariat.

The "dangerous class," the social scum, that passively rotting mass thrown off by the lowest layers of old society, may, here and there, be swept into the movement by a proletarian revolution; its conditions of life, however, prepare it far more for the part of a bribed tool of reactionary intrigue.

In the conditions of the proletariat, those of the old society at large are already virtually swamped. The proletarian is without property; his relation to his wife and children has no longer anything in common with the bourgeois family relations; modern industrial labor, modern subjection to capital, the same in England as in France, in America as in Germany, has stripped him of every trace of national character. Law, morality, religion, are to him so many bourgeois prejudices, behind which lurk in ambush just as many bourgeois interests.

All the preceding classes that got the upper hand sought to fortify their already acquired status by subjecting society at large to their conditions of appropriation. The proletarians cannot become masters of the productive forces of society, except by abolishing their own previous mode of appropriation, and thereby also every other previous mode of appropriation. They have nothing of their own to secure and to fortify; their mission is to destroy all previous securities for and insurances of individual property.

55   All previous historical movements were movements of minorities, or in the interest of minorities. The proletarian movement is the self-conscious, independent movement of the immense majority. The proletariat, the lowest stratum of our present society, cannot stir, cannot raise itself up without the whole superincumbent strata of official society being sprung into the air.

Though not in substance, yet in form, the struggle of the proletariat with the bourgeoisie is at first a national struggle. The proletariat of each country must, of course, first of all settle matters with its own bourgeoisie.

In depicting the most general phases of the development of the proletariat, we traced the more or less veiled civil war, raging within existing society, up to the point where that war breaks out into open revolution, and where the violent overthrow of the bourgeoisie, lays the foundations for the sway of the proletariat.

Hitherto every form of society has been based, as we have already seen, on the antagonism of oppressing and oppressed classes. But in order to oppress a class, certain conditions must be assured to it under which it can, at least, continue its slavish existence. The serf, in the period of serfdom, raised himself to membership in the commune, just as the petty bourgeois, under the yoke of feudal absolutism, managed to develop into a bourgeois. The modern laborer, on the contrary, instead of rising with the progress of industry, sinks deeper and deeper below the conditions of existence of his own class. He becomes a pauper, and pauperism develops more rapidly than population and wealth. And here it becomes evident that the bourgeoisie is unfit any longer to be the ruling class in society, and to impose its conditions of existence upon society as an over-riding law. It is unfit to rule, because it is incompetent to assure an existence to its slave within his slavery, because it cannot help letting him sink into such a state that it has to feed him, instead of being fed by him. Society can no longer live under this bourgeoisie; in other words, its existence is no longer compatible with society.

The essential condition for the existence, and for the sway of the bourgeois class, is the formation and augmentation of capital; the condition for capital is wage labor. Wage labor rests exclusively on competition between the laborers. The advance of industry, whose involuntary promoter is the bourgeoisie, replaces the isolation of the laborers, due to competition, by their involuntary combination, due to association. The development of Modern Industry, therefore, cuts from under its feet the very foundation on which the bourgeoisie produces and appropriates products. What the bourgeoisie therefore produces, above all, are its own grave diggers. Its fall and the victory of the proletariat are equally inevitable.

Proletarians and Communists

60   In what relation do the Communists stand to the proletarians as a whole?

The Communists do not form a separate party opposed to other working class parties.

They have no interests separate and apart from those of the proletariat as a whole.

They do not set up any sectarian principles of their own, by which to shape and mold the proletarian movement.

The Communists are distinguished from the other working class parties by this only: 1. In the national struggles of the proletarians of the different countries, they point out and bring to the front the common interests of the entire proletariat, independently of all nationality. 2. In the various stages of development which the struggle of the working class against the bourgeoisie has to pass through, they always and everywhere represent the interests of the movement as a whole.

65   The Communists, therefore, are on the one hand practically the most advanced and resolute section of the working class parties of every country, that section which pushes forward all others; on the other hand, theoretically, they have over the great mass of the proletariat the advantage of clearly understanding the line of march, the conditions, and the ultimate general results of the proletarian movement.

The immediate aim of the Communists is the same as that of all the other proletarian parties: formation of the proletariat into a class, overthrow of the bourgeois of supremacy, conquest of political power by the proletariat.

The theoretical conclusions of the Communists are in no way based on ideas or principles that have been invented or discovered by this or that would-be universal reformer.

They merely express, in general terms, actual relations springing from an existing class struggle, from a historical movement going on under our very eyes. The abolition of existing property relations is not at all a distinctive feature of Communism.

All property relations in the past have continually been subject to historical change consequent upon the change in historical conditions.

70   The French Revolution, for example, abolished feudal property in favor of bourgeois property.

The distinguishing feature of Communism is not the abolition of property generally, but the abolition of bourgeois property. But modern bourgeois private property is the final and most complete expression of the system of producing and appropriating products, that is based on class antagonism, on the exploitation of the many by the few.

In this sense, the theory of the Communists may be summed up in the single sentence: Abolition of private property.

We Communists have been reproached with the desire of abolishing the right of personally acquiring property as the fruit of a man's own labor, which property is alleged to be the groundwork of all personal freedom, activity and independence.

Hard won, self-acquired, self-earned property! Do you mean the property of the petty artisan and of the small peasant, a form of property that preceded the bourgeois form? There is no need to abolish that; the development of industry has to a great extent already destroyed it, and is still destroying it daily.

75   Or do you mean modern bourgeois private property?

But does wage labor create any property for the laborer? Not a bit. It creates capital, i.e., that kind of property which exploits wage labor, and which cannot increase except upon condition of getting a new supply of wage labor for fresh exploitation. Property, in its present form, is based on the antagonism of capital and wage labor. Let us examine both sides of this antagonism.

To be a capitalist is to have not only a purely personal, but a social status in production. Capital is a collective product, and only by the united action of many members, nay, in the last resort, only by the united action of all members of society, can it be set in motion.

Capital is therefore not a personal, it is a social power.

When, therefore, capital is converted into common property, into the property of all members of society, personal property is not thereby transformed into social property. It is only the social character of the property that is changed. It loses its class character.

80   Let us now take wage labor.

The average price of wage labor is the minimum wage, i.e., that quantum of the means of subsistence which is absolutely requisite to keep the laborer in bare existence as a laborer. What, therefore, the wage laborer appropriates by means of his labor, merely suffices to prolong and reproduce a bare existence. We by no means intend to abolish this personal appropriation of the products of labor, an appropriation that is made for the maintenance and reproduction of human life, and that leaves no surplus wherewith to command the labor of others. All that we want to do away with is the miserable character of this appropriation, under which the laborer lives merely to increase capital and is allowed to live only in so far as the interests of the ruling class require it.

In bourgeois society, living labor is but a means to increase accumulated labor. In Communist society accumulated labor is but a means to widen, to enrich, to promote the existence of the laborer.

In bourgeois society, therefore, the past dominates the present; in Communist society the present dominates the past. In bourgeois society, capital is independent and has individuality, while the living person is dependent and has no individuality.

And the abolition of this state of things is called by the bourgeois abolition of individuality and freedom! And rightly so. The abolition of bourgeois individuality, bourgeois independence and bourgeois freedom is undoubtedly aimed at.

85   By freedom is meant, under the present bourgeois conditions of production, free trade, free selling and buying.

But if selling and buying disappears, free selling and buying disappears also. This talk about free selling and buying, and all the other "brave words" of our bourgeoisie about freedom in general have a meaning, if any, only in contrast with

UNIT 4

restricted selling and buying, with the fettered traders of the Middle Ages, but have no meaning when opposed to the Communistic abolition of buying and selling, of the bourgeois conditions of production, and of the bourgeoisie itself.

You are horrified at our intending to do away with private property. But in your existing society private property is already done away with for nine-tenths of the population; its existence for the few is solely due to its non-existence in the hands of those nine-tenths. You reproach us, therefore, with intending to do away with a form of property, the necessary condition for whose existence is the non-existence of any property for the immense majority of society.

In one word, you reproach us with intending to do away with your property. Precisely so: that is just what we intend.

From the moment when labor can no longer be converted into capital, money, or rent, into a social power capable of being monopolized, i.e., from the moment when individual property can no longer be transformed into bourgeois property, into capital, from that moment, you say, individuality vanishes.

90   You must, therefore, confess that by "individual" you mean no other person than the bourgeois, than the middle-class owner of property. This person must, indeed, be swept out of the way and made impossible.

Communism deprives no man of the power to appropriate the products of society: all that it does is to deprive him of the power to subjugate the labor of others by means of such appropriation.

It has been objected that upon the abolition of private property all work will cease and universal laziness will overtake us.

According to this, bourgeois society ought long ago to have gone to the dogs through sheer idleness; for those of its members who work acquire nothing, and those who acquire anything do not work. The whole of this objection is but another expression of the tautology: that there can no longer be any wage labor when there is no longer any capital.

All objections urged against the Communistic mode of producing and appropriating material products have, in the same way, been urged against the Communistic modes of producing and appropriating intellectual products. Just as, to the bourgeois, the disappearance of class property is the disappearance of production itself, so the disappearance of class culture is to him identical with the disappearance of all culture.

95   That culture, the loss of which he laments, is, for the enormous majority, a mere training to act as a machine.

But don't wrangle with us so long as you apply, to our intended abolition of bourgeois property, the standard of your bourgeois notions of freedom, culture, law, etc. Your very ideas are but the outgrowth of the conditions of your bourgeois production and bourgeois property, just as your jurisprudence is but the will of your class made into a law for all, a will whose essential character and direction are determined by the economical conditions of existence of your class.

The selfish misconception that induces you to transform into eternal laws of nature and of reason the social forms springing from your present mode of production and form of property—historical relations that rise and disappear in the progress of production—this misconception you share with every ruling class that has preceded you. What you see clearly in the case of ancient property, what you admit in the case of feudal property, you are of course forbidden to admit in the case of your own bourgeois form of property.

Abolition of the family! Even the most radical flare up at this infamous proposal of the Communists.

On what foundation is the present family, the bourgeois family, based? On capital, on private gain. In its completely developed form this family exists only among the bourgeoisie. But this state of things finds its complement in the practical absence of the family among the proletarians, and in public prostitution.

100   The bourgeois family will vanish as a matter of course when its complement vanishes, and both will vanish with the vanishing of capital.

Do you charge us with wanting to stop the exploitation of children by their parents? To this crime we plead guilty.

But, you will say, we destroy the most hallowed of relations when we replace home education by social.

And your education! Is not that also social, and determined by the social conditions under which you educate; by the intervention, direct or indirect, of society by means of schools, etc.? The Communists have not invented the intervention of society in education; they do but seek to alter the character of that intervention, and to rescue education from the influence of the ruling class.

The bourgeois clap-trap about the family and education, about the hallowed correlation of parent and child, become all the more disgusting, the more, by the action of Modern Industry, all family ties among the proletarians are torn asunder and their children transformed into simple articles of commerce and instruments of labor.

105   But you Communists would introduce community of women, screams the whole bourgeoisie chorus.

The bourgeois sees in his wife a mere instrument of production. He hears that the instruments of production are to be exploited in common, and, naturally, can come to no other conclusion, than that the lot of being common to all will likewise fall to the women.

He has not even a suspicion that the real point aimed at is to do away with the status of women as mere instruments of production.

For the rest, nothing is more ridiculous than the virtuous indignation of our bourgeois at the community of women which, they pretend, is to be openly and officially established by the Communists. The Communists have no need to introduce community of women, it has existed almost from time immemorial.

Our bourgeois, not content with having the wives and daughters of their proletarians at their disposal, not to speak of common prostitutes, take the greatest pleasure in seducing each others' wives.

110   Bourgeois marriage is in reality a system of wives in common, and thus, at the most, what the Communists might possibly be reproached with, is that they desire to introduce, in substitution for a hypocritically concealed, an openly legalized community of women. For the rest, it is self-evident that the abolition of the present system of production must bring with it the abolition of the community of women springing from that system, i.e., of prostitution both public and private.

The Communists are further reproached with desiring to abolish countries and nationalities.

The working men have no country. We cannot take from them what they don't possess. Since the proletariat must first of all acquire political supremacy, must rise to be the leading class of the nation, must constitute itself the nation, it is, so far, itself national, though not in the bourgeois sense of the word.

National differences and antagonisms between peoples are daily more and more vanishing, owing to the development of the bourgeoisie, to freedom of commerce, to the world-market, to uniformity in the mode of production and in the conditions of life corresponding thereto.

The supremacy of the proletariat will cause them to vanish still faster. United action, of the leading civilized countries at least, is one of the first conditions for the emancipation of the proletariat.

115   In proportion as the exploitation of one individual by another is put an end to, the exploitation of one nation by another will also be put an end to. In proportion as the antagonism between classes within the nation vanishes, the hostility of one nation to another will come to an end.

The charges against Communism made from a religious, a philosophical, and generally, from an ideological standpoint, are not deserving of serious examination.

Does it require deep intuition to comprehend that man's ideas, views and conceptions, in one word, man's consciousness, changes with every change in the conditions of his material existence, in his social relations and in his social life?

What else does the history of ideas prove than that intellectual production changes in character in proportion as material production is changed? The ruling ideas of each age have ever been the ideas of its ruling class.

When people speak of ideas that revolutionize society they do but express the fact that within the old society the elements of a new one have been created, and that the dissolution of the old ideas keeps even pace with the dissolution of the old conditions of existence.

120   When the ancient world was in its last throes the ancient religions were overcome by Christianity. When Christian ideas succumbed in the 18th century to rationalist ideas, feudal society fought its death battle with the then revolutionary bourgeoisie. The ideas of religious liberty and freedom of conscience merely gave expression to the sway of free competition within the domain of knowledge.

"Undoubtedly," it will be said, "religious, moral, philosophical and judicial ideas have been modified in the course of historical development. But religion, morality, philosophy, political science, and law, constantly survived this change.

"There are, besides, eternal truths such as Freedom, Justice, etc., that are common to all states of society. But Communism abolishes eternal truths, it abolishes all religion and all morality, instead of constituting them on a new basis; it therefore acts in contradiction to all past historical experience."

What does this accusation reduce itself to? The history of all past society has consisted in the development of class antagonisms, antagonisms that assumed different forms at different epochs.

But whatever form they may have taken, one fact is common to all past ages, viz., the exploitation of one part of society by the other. No wonder, then, that the social consciousness of past ages, despite all the multiplicity and variety it displays, moves within certain common forms, or general ideas, which cannot completely vanish except with the total disappearance of class antagonisms.

125   The Communist revolution is the most radical rupture with traditional property relations; no wonder that its development involves the most radical rupture with traditional ideas.

But let us have done with the bourgeois objections to Communism.

We have seen above that the first step in the revolution by the working class is to raise the proletariat to the position of ruling class, to win the battle of democracy.

The proletariat will use its political supremacy to wrest, by degrees, all capital from the bourgeoisie, to centralize all instruments of production in the hands of the State, i.e., of the proletariat organized as a ruling class; and to increase the total productive forces as rapidly as possible.

Of course, in the beginning, this cannot be effected except by means of despotic inroads on the rights of property, and on the conditions of bourgeois production; by means of measures, therefore, which appear economically insufficient and untenable, but which in the course of the movement outstrip themselves, necessitate further inroads upon the old social order, and are unavoidable as a means of entirely revolutionizing the mode of production.

130 These measures will of course be different in different countries.

Nevertheless in the most advanced countries the following will be pretty generally applicable:

1. Abolition of property in land and application of all rents of land to public purposes.
2. A heavy progressive or graduated income tax.
3. Abolition of all right of inheritance.
4. Confiscation of the property of all emigrants and rebels.
5. Centralization of credit in the hands of the State, by means of a national bank with State capital and an exclusive monopoly.
6. Centralization of the means of communication and transport in the hands of the State.
7. Extension of factories and instruments of production owned by the State; the bringing into cultivation of waste lands, and the improvement of the soil generally in accordance with a common plan.
8. Equal liability of all to labor. Establishment of industrial armies, especially for agriculture.
9. Combination of agriculture with manufacturing industries; gradual abolition of the distinction between town and country by a more equable distribution of the population over the country.
10. Free education for all children in public schools. Abolition of children's factory labor in its present form. Combination of education with industrial production, etc., etc.

When, in the course of development, class distinctions have disappeared, and all production has been concentrated in the hands of a vast association of the whole nation, the public power will lose its political character. Political power, properly so called, is merely the organized power of one class for oppressing another. If the proletariat during its contest with the bourgeoisie is compelled, by the force of circumstances; to organize itself as a class, if, by means of a revolution, it makes itself the ruling class, and, as such, sweeps away by force the old conditions of production, then it will, along with these conditions, have swept away the conditions for the existence of class antagonism, and of classes generally, and will thereby have abolished its own supremacy as a class.

In place of the old bourgeois society, with its classes and class antagonisms, we shall have an association in which the free development of each is the condition for the free development of all . . . .

Position of the Communists in Relation to the Various Existing Opposition Parties

[The preceding section] has made clear the relations of the Communists to the existing working class parties, such as the Chartists in England and the Agrarian Reforms in America.

135   The Communists fight for the attainment of the immediate aims, for the enforcement of the momentary interests of the working class; but in the movement of the present they also represent and take care of the future of that movement. In France the Communists ally themselves with the Social-Democrats against the conservative and radical bourgeoisie, reserving, however, the right to take up a critical position in regard to phrases and illusions traditionally handed down from the great Revolution.

In Switzerland they support the Radicals, without losing sight of the fact that this party consists of antagonistic elements, partly of Democratic Socialists, in the French sense, partly of radical bourgeois.

In Poland they support the party that insists on an agrarian revolution, as the prime condition for national emancipation, that party which fomented the insurrection of Cracow in 1846.

In Germany they fight with the bourgeoisie whenever it acts in a revolutionary way, against the absolute monarchy, the feudal squirearchy, and the petty bourgeoisie.

But they never cease for a single instant to instill into the working class the clearest possible recognition of the hostile antagonism between bourgeoisie and proletariat, in order that the German workers may straightway use, as so many weapons against the bourgeoisie, the social and political conditions that the bourgeoisie must necessarily introduce along with its supremacy, and in order that, after the fall of the reactionary classes in Germany, the fight against the bourgeoisie itself may immediately begin.

140   The Communists turn their attention chiefly to Germany, because that country is on the eve of a bourgeois revolution, that is bound to be carried out under more advanced conditions of European civilization, and with a more developed proletariat, than that of England was in the seventeenth and of France in the eighteenth century, and because the bourgeois revolution in Germany will be but the prelude to an immediately following proletarian revolution.

In short, the Communists everywhere support every revolutionary movement against the existing social and political order of things.

In all these movements they bring to the front, as the leading question in each, the property question, no matter what its degree of development at the time.

Finally, they labor everywhere for the union and agreement of the democratic parties of all countries.

The Communists disdain to conceal their views and aims. They openly declare that their ends can be attained only by the forcible overthrow of all existing social conditions. Let the ruling classes tremble at a Communistic revolution. The proletarians have nothing to lose but their chains. They have a world to win.

145   Working men of all countries, unite!

READING/WRITING ASSISTS

Thesis (and its counterargument):

Marx's text, as indicated in his title, is a **manifesto: a public declaration of principles or intentions, especially of a political nature**. Nevertheless, his *Manifesto* does include a **thesis**, or argument. It may be necessary to read most or all of Marx's *Manifesto* in order to formulate a sentence clearly stating his thesis. What is Marx's thesis, and what is he arguing against (the **counterargument**)?

The Shape of the Argument:

"Mapping" the structure of an argument can help us better understand the argument itself, while also showing us new models for shaping our own arguments in essay form. As noted above, Marx's essay is a **manifesto**, a particular genre of argument popular with political movements. In his *Manifesto,* however, Marx does make a detailed and persuasive case for his point of view, which he counters with opposing viewpoints. Also, like Dr. King's "Letter from Birmingham City Jail," Marx sometimes places particular arguments within the more general argument. To better understand Marx's argumentative structure, it is best to outline the entire essay, paragraph by paragraph:

Paragraphs 1–6: **Introduction**: Why is it now necessary for Marx to write the *Manifesto?*

Bourgeois and Proletarians:

Paragraphs 7–17: Historical background. Read paragraph 16 carefully. In this paragraph Marx claims that the discovery of America established a "**world market**." Has America, in turn, re–created the world market Marx speaks of? In what way?

Paragraphs 18–30: History/development of the **bourgeoisie.**

Paragraph 31: What conclusion does Marx reach here?

Paragraphs 32–34: The "modern" bourgeoisie. Who are these people?

Paragraphs 35–37: The rise of **capital**. Can capital be used as a weapon? Against whom?

Paragraphs 38–45: History/development of the **proletariat**. Who are these people?

Paragraphs 46–57: **Class struggle**: Are class struggles always between two opposing classes? Why do internal conflicts arise and what shape do these conflicts take?

Paragraphs 58–59: Conclusion to first section.

Proletarians and Communists:

Paragraphs 60–65: Where do **Communists** fit in Marx's argument?

Paragraphs 66–70: What are the general aims of the Communists?

Paragraphs 71–125: Bourgeois objections to Communism:

Paragraphs 71–97: Abolition of **private property.**

Paragraphs 98–110: Abolition of the **family.**

Paragraphs 111–115: Abolition of **nationalism.**

Paragraphs 116–125: Abolition of **religion** and **morality.**

Paragraphs 126–133: What conclusions are reached here?

UNIT 4

**Position of the Communists in Relation to the
Various Existing Opposition Parties:**

Paragraphs 134–145:   Position of the Communists/Conclusion. Is this position
                             clear?

Rhetorical Moves:

Marx divides his *Manifesto* into three sections, headed by subtitles. Is this structural strategy effective, in your opinion? What is effective, i.e., what elements of this structure *work*? What is not effective, i.e., what aspects of this structure do not work? Does each section of the essay have a smooth transition to the next? Do you think this structure might be useful in your own essay writing? When might you use it?

Also, Marx writes many, many short paragraphs; when students write brief paragraphs such as these, essays are generally returned to them with advice about paragraph development for revision. Why do you think Marx used so many short paragraphs? Do you think Marx's short paragraphs could use further development? Why or why not? Are there instances in the essay where paragraphs may be combined?

TONI CADE BAMBARA

Miltona Mirkin Cade, better known in later years as Toni Cade Bambara (1939–1995), was born in Harlem and spent the first ten years of her life on 151st Street between Broadway and Amsterdam Avenue. These early years in Harlem, Bambara later claimed, had a profound influence on her work as a writer, filmmaker, activist, and political theorist.

Bambara was awarded a B.A. in English and Theater Arts by Queens College, City University of New York, in 1959. She received an M.A. in 1965 and began to teach at The City College, where she stayed until 1969.

In the late 1960s, Bambara edited and published the first anthology of fiction, nonfiction, and poetry written entirely by black feminists. In 1972, while teaching at Rutgers University, Bambara published her first book of short stories, Gorilla, My Love, *followed by another book of short fiction,* The Sea Birds Are Still Alive, *in 1977. Her first novel,* The Salt Eaters, *was published in 1980.*

In 1986, Bambara made her first film, a documentary about the MOVE organization and the bombing of its Philadelphia headquarters by the police with the full approval of Mayor Goode. All told, sixteen houses were completely destroyed by the ensuing fire. A second film, W.E.B. DuBois: An Autobiography in Four Voices, *debuted in 1995, shortly before Bambara's early death from cancer.*

THE LESSON
Toni Cade Bambara

1   **B**ack in the days when everyone was old and stupid or young and foolish and me and Sugar were the only ones just right, this lady moved on our block with nappy hair and proper speech and no makeup. And quite naturally we laughed at her, laughed the way we did at the junk man who went about his business like he was some big-time president and his sorry-ass horse his secretary. And we kinda hated her too, hated the way we did the winos who cluttered up our parks and pissed on our handball walls and stank up our hallways and stairs so you couldn't halfway play hide-and-seek without a goddamn gas mask. Miss Moore was her name. The only woman on the block with no first name. And she was black as hell, 'cept for her feet, which were fish-white and spooky. And she was always planning these boring-ass things for us to do, us being my cousin, mostly, who lived on the block cause we all moved North the same time and to the same apartment then spread out gradual to breathe. And our parents would yank our heads into some kinda shape and crisp up our clothes so we'd be presentable for travel with Miss Moore, who always looked like she was going to church, though she never did. Which is just one of the things the grownups talked about when they talked behind her back like a dog. But when she came calling with some sachet she'd sewed up or some gingerbread she'd made or some book, why then they'd all be too embarrassed to turn her down and we'd get handed over all spruced up. She'd been to college and said it was only right that she should take responsibility for the young ones' education, and she not even related by marriage or blood. So they'd go for it. Specially Aunt Gretchen. She was the main gofer in the family. You got some ole dumb shit foolishness you want somebody to go for, you send for Aunt Gretchen. She been screwed into the go-along for so long, it's a blood-deep natural thing with her. Which is how she got saddled with me and Sugar and Junior in the first place while our mothers were in a la-de-da apartment up the block having a good ole time.

So this one day Miss Moore rounds us all up at the mailbox and it's puredee hot and she's knockin herself out about arithmetic. And school suppose to let up in summer I heard, but she don't never let up. And the starch in my pinafore scratching the shit outta me and I'm really hating this nappyhead bitch and her goddamn college degree. I'd much rather go to the pool or to the show where it's cool. So me and Sugar leaning on the mailbox being surly, which is a Miss Moore word. And Flyboy checking out what everybody brought for lunch. And Fat Butt already wasting his peanut-butter-and-jelly sandwich like the pig he is. And Junebug punchin on Q.T.'s arm for potato chips. And Rosie Giraffe shifting from one hip to the other waiting for somebody to step on her foot or ask her if she from Georgia so she can kick ass, preferably Mercedes'. And Miss Moore asking us do we know what money is, like we a bunch of retards. I mean real money, she say, like it's only poker chips or monopoly papers we lay on the grocer. So right away I'm tired of this and say so. And would much rather snatch Sugar and go to the Sunset and terrorize the West Indian kids and take their hair ribbons and their money too. And Miss Moore files that remark away for next week's lesson on brotherhood, I can tell. And finally I say we oughta get to the subway cause it's cooler and besides we might meet some cute boys. Sugar done swiped her mama's lipstick, so we ready.

So we heading down the street and she's boring us silly about what things cost and what our parents make and how much goes for rent and how money ain't divided up right in this country. And then she gets to the part about we all poor and live in the slums, which I don't feature. And I'm ready to speak on that, but she steps out in the street and hails two cabs just like that. Then she hustles half the crew in with her and hands me a five-dollar bill and tells me to calculate 10 percent tip for the driver. And we're off. Me and Sugar and Junebug and Flyboy hangin out the window and hollering to everybody, putting lipstick on each other cause Flyboy a faggot anyway, and making farts with our sweaty armpits. But I'm mostly trying to figure how to spend this money. But they all fascinated with the meter ticking and Junebug starts laying bets as to how much it'll read when Flyboy can't hold his breath no more. Then Sugar lays bets as to how much it'll be when we get there. So I'm stuck. Don't nobody want to go for my plan, which is to jump out at the next light and run off to the first bar-b-que we can find. Then the driver tells us to get the hell out cause we there already. And the meter reads eighty-five cents. And I'm stalling to figure out the tip and Sugar say give him a dime. And I decide he don't need it bad as I do, so later for him. But then he tries to take off with Junebug foot still in the door so we talk about his mama something ferocious. Then we check out that we on Fifth Avenue and everybody dressed up in stockings. One lady in a fur coat, hot as it is. White folks crazy.

"This is the place," Miss Moore say, presenting it to us in the voice she uses at the museum. "Let's look in the windows before we go in."

5   "Can we steal?" Sugar asks very serious like she's getting the ground rules squared away before she plays. "I beg your pardon," say Miss Moore, and we fall out. So she leads us around the windows of the toy store and me and Sugar screamin, "This is mine, that's mine, I gotta have that, that was made for me, I was born for that," till Big Butt drowns us out.

"Hey, I'm goin to buy that there."

"That there? You don't even know what it is, stupid."

"I do so," he say punchin on Rosie Giraffe. "It's a microscope."

"Whatcha gonna do with a microscope, fool?"

10   "Look at things."

"Like what, Ronald?" ask Miss Moore. And Big Butt ain't got the first notion. So here go Miss Moore gabbing about the thousands of bacteria in a drop of water and the somethinorother in a speck of blood and the million and one living things in the air around us is invisible to the naked eye. And what she say that for? Junebug go to town on that "naked" and we rolling. Then Miss Moore ask what it cost. So we all jam into the window smudgin it up and the price tag say $300. So then she ask how long'd take for Big Butt and Junebug to save up their allowances. "Too long," I say. "Yeh," adds Sugar, "outgrown it by that time." And Miss Moore say no, you never outgrow learning instruments. "Why, even medical students and interns and," blah, blah, blah. And we ready to choke Big Butt for bringing it up in the first damn place.

"This here costs four hundred eighty dollars," says Rosie Giraffe. So we pile up all over her to see what she pointin out. My eyes tell me it's a chunk of glass cracked with something heavy, and different-color inks dripped into the splits, then the whole thing put into a oven or something. But for $480 it don't make sense.

"That's a paperweight made of semi-precious stones fused together under tremendous pressure," she explains slowly, with her hands doing the mining and all the factory work.

"So what's a paperweight?" asks Rosie Giraffe.

15   "To weigh paper with, dumbbell," say Flyboy, the wise man from the East.

"Not exactly," say Miss Moore, which is what she say when you warm or way off too. "It's to weigh paper down so it won't scatter and make your desk untidy."

So right away me and Sugar curtsy to each other and then to Mercedes who is more the tidy type.

"We don't keep paper on top of the desk in my class," say Junebug, figuring Miss Moore crazy or lyin one.

"At home, then," she say. "Don't you have a calendar and pencil case and a blotter and a letter-opener on your desk at home where you do your home-work?" And she know damn well what our homes look like cause she nosys around in them every chance she gets.

"I don't even have a desk," say Junebug. "Do we?"

20   "No. And I don't get no homework neither," says Big Butt.

"And I don't even have a home," say Flyboy like he do at school to keep the white folks off his back and sorry for him. Send this poor kid to camp posters, is his specialty.

"I do," says Mercedes. "I have a box of stationery on my desk and a picture of my cat. My godmother bought the stationery and the desk. There's a big rose on each sheet and the envelopes smell like roses."

"Who wants to know about your smelly-ass stationery," say Rosie Giraffe fore I can get my two cents in.

"It's important to have a work area all your own so that . . ."

25   "Will you look at this sailboat, please," say Flyboy, cuttin her off and pointin to the thing like it was his. So once again we tumble all over each other to gaze at this magnificent thing in the toy store which is just big enough to maybe sail two kittens across the pond if you strap them to the posts tight. We all start reciting the price tag like we in assembly. "Handcrafted sailboat of fiberglass at one thousand one hundred ninety-five dollars."

"Unbelievable," I hear myself say and am really stunned. I read it again for myself just in case the group recitation put me in a trance. Same thing. For some reason this pisses me off. We look at Miss Moore and she lookin at us, waiting for I dunno what.

"Who'd pay all that when you can buy a sailboat set for a quarter at Pop's, a tube of glue for a dime, and a ball of string for eight cents? It must have a motor and a whole lot else besides," I say. "My sailboat cost me about fifty cents."

"But will it take water?" say Mercedes with her smart ass.

"Took mine to Alley Pond Park once," say Flyboy. "String broke. Lost it. Pity."

30   "Sailed mine in Central Park and it keeled over and sank. Had to ask my father for another dollar."

"And you got the strap," laugh Big Butt. "The jerk didn't even have a string on it. My old man wailed on his behind."

Little Q.T. was staring hard at the sailboat and you could see he wanted it bad. But he too little and somebody'd just take it from him. So what the hell. "This boat for kids, Miss Moore?"

"Parents silly to buy something like that just to get all broke up," say Rosie Giraffe.

"That much money it should last forever," I figure.

35   "My father'd buy it for me if I wanted it."

"Your father, my ass," say Rosie Giraffe getting a chance to finally push Mercedes.

"Must be rich people shop here," say Q.T.

"You are a very bright boy," say Flyboy. "What was your first clue?" And he rap him on the head with the back of his knuckles, since Q.T. the only one he could get away with. Though Q.T. liable to come up behind you years later and get his licks in when you half expect it.

"What I want to know is," I says to Miss Moore though I never talk to her, I wouldn't give the bitch that satisfaction, "is how much a real boat costs? I figure a thousand'd get you a yacht any day."

40   "Why don't you check that out," she says, "and report back to the group?" Which really pains my ass. If you gonna mess up a perfectly good swim day least you could do is have some answers. "Let's go in," she say like she got something up her sleeve. Only she don't lead the way. So me and Sugar turn the corner to where the entrance is, but when we get there I kinda hang back. Not that I'm scared, what's there to be afraid of, just a toy store. But I feel funny, shame. But what I got to be shamed about? Got as much right to go in as anybody. But somehow I can't seem to get hold of the door, so I step away from Sugar to lead. But she hangs back too. And I look at her and she looks at me and this is ridiculous. I mean, damn, I have never ever been shy about doing nothing or going nowhere. But then Mercedes steps up and then Rosie Giraffe and Big Butt crowd in behind and shove, and next thing we all stuffed into the doorway with only Mercedes squeezing past us, smoothing out her jumper and walking right down the aisle. Then the rest of us tumble in like a glued-together jigsaw done all wrong. And people lookin at us. And it's like the time me and Sugar crashed into the Catholic church on a dare. But once we got in there and everything so hushed and holy and the candles and the bowin and the handkerchiefs on all the drooping heads, I just couldn't go through with the plan. Which was for me to run up to the altar and do a tap dance while Sugar played the nose flute and messed around in the holy water. And Sugar kept givin me the elbow. Then later

teased me so bad I tied her up in the shower and turned it on and locked her in. And she'd be there till this day if Aunt Gretchen hadn't finally figured I was lyin about the boarder takin a shower.

Same thing in the store. We all walkin on tiptoe and hardly touchin the games and puzzles and things. And I watched Miss Moore who is steady watchin us like she waitin for a sign. Like Mama Drewery watches the sky and sniffs the air and takes note of just how much slant is in the bird formation. Then me and Sugar bump smack into each other, so busy gazing at the toys, specially the sailboat. But we don't laugh and go into our fat-lady bumpstomach routine. We just stare at that price tag. Then Sugar run a finger over the whole boat. And I'm jealous and want to hit her. Maybe not her, but I sure want to punch somebody in the mouth.

"Watcha bring us here for, Miss Moore?"

"You sound angry, Sylvia. Are you mad about something?" Givin me one of them grins like she tellin a grown-up joke that never turns out to be funny. And she's lookin very closely at me like maybe she planning to do my portrait from memory. I'm mad, but I won't give her that satisfaction. So I slouch around the store bein very bored and say, "Let's go."

Me and Sugar at the back of the train watchin the tracks whizzin by large then small then getting gobbled up in the dark. I'm thinkin about this tricky toy I saw in the store. A clown that somersaults on a bar then does chin-ups just cause you yank lightly at his leg. Cost $35. I could see me askin my mother for a $35 birthday clown. "You wanna who that costs what?" she'd say, cocking her head to the side to get a better view of the hole in my head. Thirty-five dollars could buy new bunk beds for Junior and Gretchen's boy. Thirty-five dollars and the whole household could go visit Granddaddy Nelson in the country. Thirty-five dollars would pay for the rent and the piano bill too. Who are these people that spend that much for performing clowns and $1000 for toy sailboats? What kinda work they do and how they live and how come we ain't in on it? Where we are is who we are, Miss Moore always pointin out. But it don't necessarily have to be that way, she always adds then waits for somebody to say that poor people have to wake up and demand their share of the pie and don't none of us know what kind of pie she talking about in the first damn place. But she ain't so smart cause I still got her four dollars from the taxi and she sure ain't gettin it. Messin up my day with this shit. Sugar nudges me in my pocket and winks.

45   Miss Moore lines us up in front of the mailbox where we started from, seem like years ago, and I got a headache for thinkin so hard. And we lean all over each

other so we can hold up under the draggy-ass lecture she always finishes us off with at the end before we thank her for borin us to tears. But she just looks at us like she readin tea leaves. Finally she say, "Well, what did you think of F.A.O. Schwarz?"

Rosie Giraffe mumbles, "White folks crazy."

"I'd like to go there again when I get my birthday money," says Mercedes, and we shove her out the pack so she has to lean on the mailbox by herself.

"I'd like a shower. Tiring day," say Flyboy.

Then Sugar surprises me by sayin, "You know, Miss Moore, I don't think all of us here put together eat in a year what that sailboat costs." And Miss Moore lights up like somebody goosed her. "And?" she say, urging Sugar on. Only I'm standin on her foot so she don't continue.

50   "Imagine for a minute what kind of society it is in which some people can spend on a toy what it would cost to feed a family of six or seven. What do you think?"

"I think," say Sugar pushing me off her feet like she never done before, cause I whip her ass in a minute, "that this is not much of a democracy if you ask me. Equal chance to pursue happiness means an equal crack at the dough, don't it?" Miss Moore is beside herself and I am disgusted with Sugar's treachery. So I stand on her foot one more time to see if she'll shove me. She shuts up, and Miss Moore looks at me, sorrowfully I'm thinkin. And somethin weird is goin on, I can feel it in my chest.

"Anybody else learn anything today?" lookin dead at me. I walk away and Sugar has to run to catch up and don't even seem to notice when I shrug her arm off my shoulder.

"Well, we got four dollars anyway," she says.

"Uh hunh."

55   "We could go to Hascombs and get half a chocolate layer and then go to the Sunset and still have plenty money for potato chips and ice cream sodas."

"Un hunh."

"Race you to Hascombs," she say.

We start down the block and she gets ahead which is O.K. by me cause I'm going to the West End and then over to the Drive to think this day through. She can run if she want to and even run faster. But ain't nobody gonna beat me at nuthin.

LEVELS OF READING

Summary:

Pay attention to the **literal** meaning of the text. Briefly describe the narrative of Toni Cade Bambara's "The Lesson." Who tells the story? What happens? Concentrate on the highlights; avoid too much detail when summarizing. Again, drawing a simple outline of the main points of the text will help you better analyze the text at other levels of interpretation.

Analysis:

Find what you believe is **symbolic** in the text. Explain the meaning of these symbols. Though Bambara's story seems extremely grounded in "reality," which aspects of the text deserve closer scrutiny? What, for instance, might Miss Moore's name symbolize? What does her "nappy hair and proper speech and no make-up" as well as her lack of a first name tell us about her? (Hint: Check the date of the story's composition.) Thinking in terms of academic disciplines, name a number of lessons Miss Moore's trip teaches. Likewise, what might the sailboat itself symbolize? With the help of the background material provided about Toni Cade Bambara and her world, make an argument about this story, and include the mention of the more **figurative** aspects of the text when making points in defense of your argument.

Application:

Apply Marx's economic and political theory to Bambara's story. Outline an argument you wish to make about "The Lesson" using Marx's theory to help you explain the point of Miss Moore's lesson. To make your argument, you may analyze a character or characters, the trip itself, a setting or settings, symbols, an important change, a motivation, a goal, a result. Consider the following as possibilities, but explore other original interpretations too:

- Does Bambara's story offer us any concrete examples of Marx's notion of **class warfare**? Is there any evidence of warfare *within* classes as well as *between* them?

- What toy store does Miss Moore take the children to see? What about the location of this store is significant? In Marxist terms, what do the children learn about the political economy of New York City, circa 1972?
- By Marx's definitions, who are the **bourgeois** in this story and who are the **proletarians**? How can you tell? What outward signs of their class status are given in this story?
- Is Miss Moore's "lesson" that private property should be abolished? Do you think she would agree with Marx on this point? How about the other aims of the Communists, as listed at the end of Marx's essay? Would Miss Moore agree or disagree with Marx on these points?
- What represents **capital** in this story, and who has it?

DEXTER JEFFRIES

*Dexter Jeffries (1953–) was born in Queens, N.Y., the son of an African American
father who was adopted by his Cuban stepfather, and a mother of Russian Jewish
descent. Both parents were active members of the Communist Party.*

*The youngest of three children, Jeffries received a B.A. from Queens College,
City University of New York, an M.A. from City College, also City University
of New York, and a Ph.D. from the Graduate School and University Center of
the City University of New York, all in English. In between degrees, he served
for three years with the U.S. Army in Germany. A college professor, Jeffries currently lives and writes in Brooklyn, New York.*

————

"Sailboats in Central Park," is a chapter in Jeffries' autobiographical work,
Triple Exposure: Black, Jewish and Red in the 1950s. The lyrical quality of the
essay's title is immediately upset by the tension in the essay's opening line:
"This was the second time I saved a white man's life." From there, Jeffries gives
a brief account of the *first* time he saved a white man's life, before moving to
the main incident of the chapter's title. Not until the final paragraph, when his
standoff with the man in the park finally ends, is the most important point of
the story disclosed. Like Jung, Jeffries offers a testimonial here, one based on
the "expert opinion" of an authority: a little boy who knows more about adults
than they suspect and who finds adults more suspect than they know.

SAILBOATS IN CENTRAL PARK
Dexter Jeffries

1   This was the second time I saved a white man's life. By age ten I was pretty adept at this and prided myself at possessing such adult skills when I was really only a little kid who happened to be smart and curious and knew how to listen to everyone's words. I understood their cues, their gestures, and all variations of body language. A sigh could be separated into so many different categories. And most of all I was patient. This quality played a big role in my life and my capacity to read people and be silent as I watched. Inadvertently my father had already taught me on so many occasions how to wait, and wait, and to wait in silence. Another trait, trick, and strategy that would come in handy years later. But saving white people was also one of my fortes.

The first time I intervened I did nothing. I was just me. I was about seven and my dad had asked me, "Dex, do you want to go for a little drive, not a Sunday drive, just a little one." I ran to the car, and the rule was if you got there before my dad, you could honk the horn one time. I pushed the Ford medallion that was at the center of the horn one time. When my dad got in, he replied, "You're so fast, like Jesse Owens."

We drove from Westgate Street and headed up to Merrick Road going past the big Times Square Store. As he said, we only drove a few more blocks and made a U-turn and pulled into a small gas station. The magic bell went off when our tires hit the hose that was on the ground. This signaled the mechanic that he had a customer. A man in dirty coveralls came out, rubbing his hands with a rag that he placed in his back pocket by the time he got to our car. He came around the front of the car, leaned over and said something to my father. In just a blur, my dad's car door flew open, and he had struck the mechanic. The punch sent him into the pump. Falling next to the gas pump in another blur, the mechanic knocked over the bucket with the window wash water as he slid to the ground. My father hopped back in the car. He had never turned the Ford off. There was a screech of tires, and I turned to see that the man was holding his face; he was on the ground, sitting upright but holding his face. There was dust and gravel. I didn't say anything, and my dad spoke first. Holding the wheel tightly, he said, "If you weren't here, I would have killed that guy." We drove back onto Merrick Road, heading toward Laurelton now and another gas station.

"Pop, what did he do?"

5   "Look, what I did, never do in the South. That fella called me *boy* and that wasn't necessary. That's why I punched him." The word *South* had meaning. This was the bad place. I wasn't sure why you couldn't do what my father just did in that bad place, but I was pretty scared. We got the gas and he knew I would never tell anyone, and I never did.

This was the second time I saved a white man's life. My father had bought my brother and me two beautiful Eldon sailboats. Fine non-toys which were the only toys that he would ever purchase. A toy had to possess an educational function so this inherently placed a severe limit on all the purchases he ever made for Christmas or birthdays. A.C. Gilbert, the famous toy manufacturer that made erector sets and chemistry sets was the perfect company for my old man. All their products were functional and edifying. These sailboats were in that instructional tradition. First, there was a faithful reproduction of a Yankee Clipper ship—you could see Donald McKay beaming with joy at the attention to detail. Second, and not to be outdone in features, was an oceangoing yacht with sails that responded to the wind and a keel that kept the boat afloat under all prevailing winds.

The sailboat pond in Central Park was large; to walk around it takes a few minutes and with kids' legs you're really embarking on a journey. My old man brought us there. We had taken the classic Sunday drive from Queens to Manhattan. Belt Parkway east toward Brooklyn, the Van Wyck Expressway north toward mid-Queens, the LIE toward the Midtown Tunnel and then proceeding a few blocks over to the park. The tunnel was our favorite part of the ride since it gave us an opportunity to play a game or two. We always wanted to be able to estimate when we would see daylight again after taking that initial plunge under the East River.

"One more turn."

"No, it's around that next bend."

10   "Hey, Pop, how much longer?"

"Why do they have those green and red lights in the ceiling?"

"Hey, Pop, why is that guy sitting in that booth?"

"Hey, Pop, is that a good job?"

"Can I do that when I grow up?"

15   "That's a nice job, right, just counting the cars!"

"Hey, the light, there's the light. You see, I was right. It was right around that last bend."

And then the light of Manhattan comes smashing down on the windshield of that old Ford. Our mouths would quickly shut as we were stunned into silence by the awe and beauty of the architectural ballet that the Manhattan skyline always conjured up. We looked up and up and the Midtown Tunnel seemed pedestrian in our memory. More questions.

"Pop, how do they build buildings so high like that?"

"How do they get the girders up that high when a crane can never be that high?"

20   My father shifts the car into second as we hit a little traffic. His brown hand remains on the white knob of the shift with a Pall Mall cradled between two fingers just gently enough that it won't be crushed. His left foot hits the clutch effortlessly, and the car responds. He responds, "How would you construct something that is taller than your biggest crane? I want you guys to think about that for a while. Think. How would you use that crane to help you when the hoist can only go a certain height?"

We were silent since we knew that these types of questions were of a serious caliber, and he didn't want us to just blurt out whatever stupid answer was on the tip of our tongues. He gets to a red light and that brown hand with the cigarette comes off the white knob and he takes a nice long and relaxing drag off that butt. "Well, what's the most constructive plan to build these skyscrapers?" My brother blurts out the correct answer, "There must be a way to get the crane to higher floors after it reaches its limit." I'm glad that my brother spoke first because I was going to mumble something about a "super-duper" crane that can really reach that high and go higher and higher and higher than any crane in the universe. My father nods his head in the affirmative, and the foot comes down on the clutch, cigarette between two fingers returns to its resting place on the column shift and we're headed toward the park. "You're correct; they use the cranes to lift each other. That's how they get to the top of the, say, the Empire State Building."

Central Park strikes you as this magical place if you grow up in Queens which is the suburbs in the 1950s. Just the fact that there is this moatlike wall all around its perimeter, you know beforehand that there is something very special on the other side of it. The cobblestones that are embedded around the trees make you walk unevenly and you must watch your step. Everything about the place, even the water fountains with their sturdy little helmet-shaped steel covers are something out of *The Wizard of Oz*. We jump out of the car and run without the boats; that's how excited we are about our day in the park. My father whistles his famous recall whistle, and we run back to the car. He says quietly, "Take it easy, take it easy," as we start to run with our prized vessels.

This time, as always, my father will only participate as casual observer and instructor. He presented the initial lesson about sailboats and sailing. This involved theory, method, the antithesis and always the proscription, "Under no circumstance do the following." After that twenty-minute lecture with time for questions that are never asked, we are let loose on the pond. He sat down on a bench and took out an old copy of the *Morning Telegraph* to review the charts, the records, and the dreams. My brother and I immediately departed each other's company being that we were sworn enemies when out of my father's sight. This pond with its great distances and long radiuses meant that we could ideally practically be out of sight of each other. I can tell from the perimeter of the pond that if I engineer my position just the right way, I won't even have to see him. I don't want to see him or his stupid yacht.

I walked away from the two of them. To be out of sight and sound of both of them was heaven. My brother represented cowardice and injustice. My father stood for the future which could be bad or good. I knew that failure with the execution of boating theory that afternoon would result in another lecture in a stronger and more pronounced voice and the possible removal from the activity. For my old man, failure indicated and proved that there was a combination of incompetence and a lack of interest in the project that was at hand, or worse, stupidity. I had no desire to fall into any of these categories and would rather confront the indignity of defeat in private.

25   I walked away and found my bench. As I hoped, I was out of sight of my brother and I could see my father reading his newspaper. I launched the *Flying Cloud* under a fair sky and with a good wind in her sails. She took off, and I immediately wished I had the string I had asked my father about during the twenty-minute block of instruction.

"Don't you think it would be better to have a string attached to the boat?"

"Why a string?" he asked a bit startled.

"In case the boat goes out too far and we can't catch it."

"This won't happen; the boat will sail on its own until it reaches the other side or it returns on its own."

30   "Oh, but what if the wind dies or it just gets stuck?"

"That won't happen; that can't happen."

"But the middle is so far from the wall."

"You have to have more confidence in your equipment. That's a good thing to know in life. You have to be confident in what machines can do. This is a machine. I know it's a boat, but it's also a machine. It was designed to do certain things. It will do them."

As I watched my clipper ship sail out, I was thrilled and scared at how fast it took off once the wind filled her sails. Then, flip-flop, just like that, she had turned over. I wasn't sure if it was just a gust of wind or me not placing enough ballast in the keel; there was a small device for filling the keel with water for extra weight. I knew one thing. The *Flying Cloud* was no longer flying and Donald McKay was looking for help. The ship sank very quickly, and my heart beat rapidly as I watched her go under. I looked and looked, and because the ship was brown it blended right into the murky pond water.

35   I walked along the walk which is about a foot higher than the sidewalk. I walked only a few feet one way or the other since I wanted to be able to report this disaster with some accuracy. I scanned the water. Other boats, especially the remote-controlled ones, cruised effortlessly and adroitly up and down, across and back, all within the vicinity of the sinking. They didn't even know that a disaster had occurred. They just kept going back and forth without a care in the world.

Flip-flop and from the two-foot depth of the pond, up popped the sunken *Flying Cloud*. It was my clipper ship. Her masts and white sails poked about an inch or two above the surface of the water. I could see her brown hull. All was not lost. I rejoiced privately at my good luck. Of course, I still had to deal with the problem of rescuing the ship but at least there was something to rescue. I studied. That was the first thing to do. Just look and look at the position of the boat and study it. Immediately I went into my mathematical mode which meant I would count methodically until ten and check if the ship's position had altered or whether or not it was still capable of sinking any lower in the pond. After a few of these accountings, I was assured that she wasn't going to sink any further and all that needed to happen was for a friendly adult to come along or a good breeze or a combination of both, and the *Flying Cloud* would be retrieved.

I stepped off the wall and sat down on a bench and relaxed the best I could. Every now and then a breeze would erupt, and I would see the foundered clipper move a few feet toward the other side of the boat pond. Far enough from my brother and father, this would only be a question of time. I got up, knowing that I had the time and with confidence walked over to the hot dog and pretzel cart. Most of the carts were strategically set up a few feet from another so no one businessman was being unfairly treated when it came to the free and open trading of hot dogs and pretzels. My guy was an old man with an applejack hat tilted to the side in that cocky way. The smoke from the pretzels that were starting to burn a bit came to me and really whet my appetite. I never really knew about that chestnut smell that is supposed to inundate New York in the fall, but that blackened pretzel smell, that was unmistakably special. I counted out ten cents— two nickels—and asked for "a hot one, please." The man pulled out that metal tray where they keep the pretzels close to the flame, pulled down a sheet of wax paper wrapped up the cheap lunch and gave me a napkin. With that in hand journeyed back to my bench to wait out the salvaging of the *Flying Cloud.*

The wind picked up as the afternoon dragged on, and my ship started to come in, as I had predicted. I kept counting and predicting. It would only be a matter of minutes. The foundered ship got closer and closer to the concrete rim of the sailboat pond, and soon I knew it was just a case of reaching over and pulling her in. I got up. As I walked over to the spot on the wall where she would dock, a man—sports jacket, nice slacks, no tie, New York 1950s Sunday wear—walked in front of me. At the most he was one yard ahead of me. I could see what was happening. He had noticed the downed ship and was going to pick it up for the owner. I was more than grateful since at some point I would have to lean over the side, get wet, worry about wet clothes and explaining how that happened to me. He got to the rim, put one knee on it and reached over for the ship. Up she came letting out a ton of water. The shower from my ship sent many ripples out away from the edge of the pond that would eventually make their way to the center. I got adjacent to this Good Samaritan and had already said *Thanks* before he even acknowledged my presence. "Thanks a lot" I boomed one second after the first "thanks." He turned toward me with little or no expression. As the boat dripped dry, he said, "Thanks for what?" I quickly replied, "Oh, my mother told me that whenever someone does a favor for you, you are supposed to say Thank you."

He now turned to me and my outstretched hands. "You're not trying to say this is yours, are you?" With confidence that I possessed more than enough proof of possession, I informed him that this was my boat; it had turned over about an hour ago, and the name of the boat was the *Flying Cloud,* which he could see, if he looked on the bow. In addition, this was a model of a clipper ship, the fastest sailing ships ever designed, designed by Donald McKay for going from America to the Far East.

40   "This isn't your boat. How could a Puerto Rican ever have a nice boat like this? There is no way this is your boat." These words tumbled out of his mouth, and I understood everything except *Porto Rickan.* But those two words, *Porto*

Rickan, when repeated in my mouth after the pause of being relayed from my mouth to my brain, and then back again, had been completely rejected because there was no place to file them. They would eventually be logged into that very special cabinet drawer that existed in my consciousness, that long list of words and expressions that crushed and terrorized, but right at that moment, they meant nothing. Nothing. I looked at him, baffled, not angry, not mad, just baffled. Why wouldn't he give me my property? I had thanked him. I had given him technical proof. Why was he holding on to my boat? He did not feel obligated to hold or continue a conversation with me. After a pause, he said, "Why did you let it sink? How come you weren't at the edge of the pond waiting for it to come in? I've been watching it for fifteen minutes, and you just sat down with a pretzel. I saw you." "Mister, I've been here all afternoon. My brother is sailing his boat." I started one more sentence with the words *my old* but caught myself. I knew that from this additional information concerning myself nothing good would come of it. Futilely, I added, "If you look over there, you'll see my brother with that yachting sloop." The man had already concluded that I wasn't worth listening to and just shook his head in amazement that I would engineer such a paltry scheme in order to get something that wasn't mine. I was bereft of any other plan. I just looked at him in bafflement that someone would not return my clipper ship after I had just judiciously waited all that time.

We both sat down on the bench. He cradled the boat in his lap. It was dry. He repositioned the sails and admired the craftsmanship that went into it. I sat jealous and proud at the same time. This was not satisfactory. I was frustrated to the point of tears.

"Where are you going? I thought you said this was your boat."

"It is. I'm just going for a walk."

I headed toward my father who was sitting where I had left him. Nothing had changed.

"Little Eva—Our Kretchen by Crafty Admiral; Little Eva, ran last race, June 3rd, Santa Anita, mud, closed up, but not enough. Time, 1:09 for 6 furlongs."

45   I announced my presence.

"Hey, Pop."

"Yes."

"How's it going?"

"Studying and keeping careful records. That's the key."

50   I paused since there was no connection other than the physical. "Oh," was all I could say. He noticed that I did not have the boat with me. "Where's the *Flying Cloud?*" he said, remembering the name and sounding interested.

My prepared speech came out with genuine feeling and a bit of remorse. "It's like you said; the ship can sail itself. It doesn't need me. It's just sailing on the other side of the pond. It does everything you set it to do." A response was forthcoming since he had been vindicated. "If you follow the directions, things are always easy. Set the rudder and the sails in the same direction, and the boat will maintain an arc."

I sprang up with "That's exactly what it's doing now. I know exactly where it's going to stop."

With the paper raised back to "Morning Line and Jockey" before I even could turn back toward the new man with his strange words, I still felt better. I hadn't involved him. That was important. He would stay there, literally for hours studying and figuring. To involve him frightened me. I walked back and thought about new problems that were a bit more complicated than placating my father and having him sit with his *Morning Telegraph* for a few hours. Would this man have other reasons for keeping the boat? What if this man had a nice son whom he thought deserved a great and fine present? That was possible. Was it? Would this man just steal a boat and give it to his kid? I started to walk faster, frightened at the possibility of having the *Flying Cloud* survive her first ocean voyage and falling prey to a human being's avarice. I walked very fast now since this was a terrible possibility; it meant that everything I had just done, would be undone. The lies I had just given to my father about the clipper ship taking care of herself would be revealed if I dared to return empty-handed. I would have to tell him that a stranger had taken my boat. This could not happen.

I came around a long sweeping turn, and there he was, sitting on the bench. I increased my pace since he was an adult and an adult can get away anytime they feel like it, even at the last moment. Coming into view he looked at me with a blank face. No words were exchanged as I sat down. There was no visible triumph since my power and presence was the same in his eyes; I was still a strange entity to him, but I had exhibited the ability to keep my word. I had returned like MacArthur coming back to the Philippines. I felt good about that. I sat on his left with my arms folded. He had to look at me.

55   He coughed to initiate the contact. "Well, no one has come for this boat the whole time. I don't know how it could be yours, but I guess it is. Here." With

that disclaimer he placed the boat in my hands. He got up, brushed himself off a bit and walked away. I sat with the boat in my lap trying to understand. At least he hadn't said those two words, *Rickan something, no, Porto something Rickan.* I would remember those words since they were important. The boat felt good and cold and fresh. I picked it up by the bow and let the remaining drops of water fall from the stern. I was comfortable. The rest of the afternoon would go well. Nothing could really upset the equilibrium I had just established. My brother could wander, find true and other sorts of mischief. I had survived mine. I got a sunken boat back from the depths, an ocean. I had returned, and I had saved a white man's life. This time it wasn't just because of *me* being. I had done something. I had made plans. They had worked.

LEVELS OF READING

Summary:

Outline briefly the two narratives within "Sailboats in Central Park." What are the main events of the two incidents Dexter Jeffries relates in this essay?

Analysis:

After outlining the **explicit** events of "Sailboats in Central Park," find what you think is implied and/or symbolic. For instance, Jeffries notices that Central Park is surrounded by a "moatlike" wall. What may be significant about this wall? Is Jeffries' reaction to this wall the same as or different from Bartleby's? In what ways is solving the riddle of the crane important to the rest of Jeffries' narrative? Who has the sailboats in "Sailboats in Central Park"? Does "The Lesson" allow for this possibility? Why or why not? What do the boats the brothers take to Central Park symbolize? How is their symbolic value interpreted by the man who snatches young Dexter's? Both the children in "The Lesson" and Dexter Jeffries are outside their usual neighborhoods when the stories told occur. Is the lesson young Dexter learns from his experience outside his neighborhood the same as that learned by Miss Moore's "students"? Explain the deeper meaning in the details of Jeffries' story. With the help of the background material provided about Dexter Jeffries and his world, make an argument about his narrative and its lesson and include the mention of the more **implicit** aspects of the text when making points in defense of your argument.

Application:

Apply Marx's economic and political theory to Jeffries' essay. Outline an argument you wish to make about "Sailboats in Central Park" using Marx's theory to help you explain the main points of Jeffries' essay. To make your argument, you may analyze a person or people, the trip itself, a setting or settings, symbols, an important change, a motivation, a goal, a result. Consider the following as possibilities, but explore other original interpretations too:

- What does Jeffries' childhood experience with his sailboat say about the notion of **class warfare** as posited by Miss Moore and/or Karl Marx? Is the money to purchase sailboats the only thing necessary to transcend people's ideas concerning the boundaries of social class?
- What bearing do assumptions about Jeffries' ethnicity have on the man's conclusions about the boy's social class? What are the outward markers of social class in this story? Are they reliable indicators?
- In terms of social class, why is it significant that the story of Jeffries' essay is set in Central Park? Do issues of social class have a bearing on the way parks are used and by whom they are used in suburban as well as urban environments?

Start Your Own Argument:

"The Lesson" and "Sailboats in Central Park" both show that Marx's theory of social class has its limitations. Using either or both texts as support, explain some of those limitations.

UNIT 4

FIVE

ARGUMENT BY MEANS OF DEMONSTRATION

CHARLES DARWIN

Charles Darwin (1809–1882) was born in Shrewsbury, England, the fifth child and second son of a physician and his wife, who died when Darwin was only eight years old.

At sixteen, he entered Edinburgh University to follow in his father's footsteps as a physician, but when the sight of surgery without anesthesia revolted him, he left. He then went to Cambridge University with the intention of becoming an Anglican minister. After graduating from Cambridge, he accepted a position as an unpaid naturalist aboard the H.M.S. Beagle. The voyage set sail on December 31, 1831. Though the planned expedition was to last five years and cross the globe, the highlight of the voyage for Darwin was its cruise down the Pacific coast of South America, and its visit to the Galapagos Islands off the coast of Ecuador. There, Darwin saw many life forms unlike those on the mainland, and yet, Darwin felt, related to them in some as yet-unnamed way. He collected many specimens on this voyage and spent the rest of his life cataloguing and studying them.

The result of Darwin's experience aboard the Beagle was the publication, in 1859, of his master work, On the Origin of the Species by Means of Natural Selection. *In this work, Darwin first proposed his theory of evolution, the idea that all life on earth developed gradually, over millions of years, from a few common ancestors. This theory challenged "creationist" theories of life on earth, specifically the version of the earth's, and mankind's, creation as explained in Genesis, the first book of the Bible. Controversy swirled around Darwin's theory for decades after his death. To an extent, his theory remains the subject of heated debate to this day.*

After his enlightening voyage, Darwin settled in a suburb just outside London with his wife and children, where he wrote about botany, geology, and zoology for the rest of his life. He is buried in Westminster Abbey.

Note how Darwin's essay focuses on defining his terms. New ideas often require an explanation, and Darwin's writing tactic is to give his reader as much information about the nature and operation of natural selection—and hence, the working of evolution—as possible. Implicit in his essay, however, is the thought that previous theories about the origin and development of the many species that populate earth are incorrect. This argument is inflammatory, to say the least, since the main theory Darwin refutes is grounded in what was believed to be unassailable religious dogma. And yet, Darwin's essay, due to its patient explanation and many examples, seems far from polemic.

———

Like Marx's *Communist Manifesto,* Charles Darwin's essay "Natural Selection" is divided into sections, often defining unfamiliar terms. And like Marx and Dexter Jeffries, much of what Darwin says in support of his argument is in the form of the testimonial. Yet Darwin's essay adds another aspect to Marx's rhetorical approach, by adding a number of demonstrations of his theory.

Like Freud, Darwin's thesis statement in this essay is almost invisible. But with careful reading it is possible to discern both Darwin's argument and the counterargument to his theory on the origin of the species.

Coming to Terms with the Reading:

Before reading/rereading Charles Darwin's, "Natural Selection," it is best to have a firm grasp on the meanings of the following terms:

1. natural selection
2. sexual selection
3. extinct
4. adapt/adaptation
5. species
6. variation/variability
7. correlation
8. survival of the fittest

NATURAL SELECTION
Charles Darwin

1 How will the struggle for existence . . . act in regard to variation? Can the principle of selection, which we have seen is so potent in the hands of man, apply in nature? I think we shall see that it can act most effectually. Let it be borne in mind in what an endless number of strange peculiarities our domestic productions, and, in a lesser degree, those under nature, vary; and how strong the hereditary tendency is. Under domestication, it may be truly said that the whole organization becomes in some degree plastic. Let it be borne in mind how infinitely complex and close-fitting are the mutual relations of all organic beings to each other and to their physical conditions of life. Can it, then, be thought improbable, seeing that variations useful to man have undoubtedly occurred, that other variations useful in some way to each being in the great and complex battle of life, should sometimes occur in the course of thousands of generations? If such do occur, can we doubt (remembering that many more individuals are born than can possibly survive) that individuals having any advantage, however slight, over others, would have the best chance of surviving and or procreating their kind? On the other hand, we may feel sure that any variation in the least degree injurious would be rigidly destroyed. This preservation of favorable variations and the rejection of injurious variations, I call Natural Selection. Variations neither useful nor injurious would not be affected by natural selection, and would be left a fluctuating element, as perhaps we see in the species called polymorphic.

We shall best understand the probable course of natural selection by taking the case of a country undergoing some physical change, for instance, of climate. The proportional numbers of its inhabitants would almost immediately undergo a change, and some species might become extinct. We may conclude, from what we have seen of the intimate and complex manner in which the inhabitants of each country are bound together, that any change in the numerical proportions of some of the inhabitants, independently of the change of climate itself, would most seriously affect many of the others. If the country were open on its borders, new forms would certainly immigrate, and this also would seriously disturb the

Reprinted from *On the Origin of the Species by Means of Natural Selection*, (1859).

relations of some of the former inhabitants. Let it be remembered how powerful the influence of a single introduced tree or mammal has been shown to be. But in the case of an island, or of a country partly surrounded by barriers, into which new and better adapted forms could not freely enter, we should then have places in the economy of nature which would assuredly be better filled up, if some of the original inhabitants were in some manner modified; for, had the area been open to immigration, these same places would have been seized on by intruders. In such case, every slight modification, which in the course of ages chanced to arise, and which in any way favored the individuals of any of the species, by better adapting them to their altered conditions, would tend to be preserved; and natural selection would thus have free scope for the work of improvement.

We have reason to believe . . . that a change in the conditions of life, by specially acting on the reproductive system, causes or increases variability; and in the foregoing case the conditions of life are supposed to have undergone a change, and this would manifestly be favorable to natural selection, by giving a better chance of profitable variations occurring; and unless profitable variations do occur, natural selection can do nothing. Not that, as I believe, any extreme amount of variability is necessary; as man can certainly produce great results by adding up in any given direction mere individual differences, so could Nature, but far more easily, from having incomparably longer time at her disposal. Nor do I believe that any great physical change, as of climate, or any unusual degree of isolation to check immigration, is actually necessary to produce new and unoccupied places for natural selection to fill up by modifying and improving some of the varying inhabitants. For as all the inhabitants of each country are struggling together with nicely balanced forces, extremely slight modifications in the structure or habits of one inhabitant would often give it an advantage over others; and still further modifications of the same kind would often still further increase the advantage. No country can be named in which all the native inhabitants are now so perfectly adapted to each other and to the physical conditions under which they live, that none of them could anyhow be improved; for in all countries, the natives have been so far conquered by naturalized productions, that they have allowed foreigners to take firm possession of the land. And as foreigners have thus everywhere beaten some of the natives, we may safely conclude that the natives might have been modified with advantage, so as to have better resisted such intruders.

As man can produce and certainly has produced a great result by his methodical and unconscious means of selection, what may not nature effect? Man can act only on external and visible characters; nature cares nothing for appearances, except in so far as they may be useful to any being. She can act on every internal organ, on every shade of constitutional difference, on the whole machinery of life. Man selects only for his own good; Nature only for that of the being which she tends. Every selected character is fully exercised by her; and the being is placed under well-suited conditions of life. Man keeps the natives of many climates in the same country; he seldom exercises each selected character in some peculiar and fitting manner; he feeds a long and a short beaked pigeon on the same food; he does not exercise a long-backed or long-legged quadruped in any peculiar manner; he exposes sheep with long and short wool to the same climate. He does not allow the most vigorous males to struggle for the females. He does not rigidly destroy all inferior animals, but protects during each varying season, as far as lies in his power, all his productions. He often begins his selection by some half-monstrous form; or at least by some modification prominent enough to catch the eye, or to be plainly useful to him. Under nature, the slightest difference of structure or constitution may well turn the nicely balanced scale in the struggle for life, and so be preserved. How fleeting are the wishes and efforts of man! how short his time! and consequently how poor will his products be, compared with those accumulated by nature during whole geological periods. Can we wonder, then, that nature's productions should be far "truer" in character than man's productions; that they should be infinitely better adapted to the most complex conditions of life, and should plainly bear the stamp of far higher workmanship?

5   It may be said that natural selection is daily and hourly scrutinizing, throughout the world, every variation, even the slightest; rejecting that which is bad, preserving and adding up all that is good; silently and insensibly working, whenever and wherever opportunity offers, at the improvement of each organic being in relation to its organic and inorganic conditions of life. We see nothing of these slow changes in progress, until the hand of time has marked the long lapse of ages, and then so imperfect is our view into long past geological ages, that we only see that the forms of life are now different from what they formerly were.

Although natural selection can act only through and for the good of each being, yet characters and structures, which we are apt to consider as of very trifling importance, may thus be acted on. When we see leaf-eating insects green, and barkfeeders mottled-grey; the alpine ptarmigan white in winter, the red-grouse the color of heather, and the black-grouse that of peaty earth, we must believe that these tints are of service to these birds and insects in preserving them from danger. Grouse, if not destroyed at some period of their lives, would increase in countless numbers;

they are known to suffer largely from birds of prey; and hawks are guided by eyesight to their prey—so much so that on parts of the Continent persons are warned not to keep white pigeons, as being the most liable to destruction. Hence I can see no reason to doubt that natural selection might be most effective in giving the proper color to each kind of grouse, and in keeping that color, when once acquired, true and constant. Nor ought we to think that the occasional destruction of an animal of any particular color would produce little effect; we should remember how essential it is in a flock of white sheep to destroy every lamb with the faintest trace of black. In plants, the down on the fruit and the color of the flesh are considered by botanists as characters of the most trifling importance; yet we hear from an excellent horticulturist, Downing, that in the United States, smooth-skinned fruits suffer far more from a beetle, a curculio, than those with down; that purple plums suffer far more from a certain disease than yellow plums; whereas another disease attacks yellow-fleshed peaches far more than those with other colored flesh. If, with all the aids of art, these slight differences make a great difference in cultivating the several varieties, assuredly, in a state of nature, where the trees would have to struggle with other trees and with a host of enemies, such differences would effectually settle which variety, whether a smooth or downy, a yellow or purple fleshed fruit, should succeed.

In looking at many small points of difference between species, which, as far as our ignorance permits us to judge, seem to be quite unimportant, we must not forget that climate, food, etc., probably produce some slight and direct effect. It is, however, far more necessary to bear in mind that there are many unknown laws of correlation of growth, which, when one part of the organization is modified through variation and the modifications are accumulated by natural selection for the good of the being, will cause other modifications, often of the most unexpected nature.

As we see that those variations which under domestication appear at any particular period of life, tend to reappear in the offspring at the same period—for instance, in the seeds of the many varieties of our culinary and agricultural plants; in the caterpillar and cocoon stages of the varieties of the silkworm; in the eggs of poultry, and in the color of the down of their chickens; in the horns of our sheep and cattle when nearly adult—so in a state of nature, natural selection will be enabled to act on and modify organic beings at any age, by the accumulation of profitable variations at that age, and by their inheritance at a corresponding age. If it profit a plant to have its seeds more and more widely disseminated by the wind, I can see no greater difficulty in this being effected through natural selection than in the cotton-planter increasing and improving by selection the down in the pods on his cotton-trees. Natural selection may modify and adapt the larva of an insect to a score of contingencies, wholly different from those which concern the mature insect. These modifications will no doubt effect, through the laws of correlation, the structure of the adult; and probably in the case of those insects which live only for a few hours, and which never feed, a large part of their structure is merely the correlated result of successive changes in the structure of their larvae. So, conversely, modifications in the adult will probably often affect the structure of the larva; but in all cases natural selection will ensure that modifications consequent on other modifications at a different period of life, shall not be in the least degree injurious: for if they became so, they would cause the extinction of the species.

Natural selection will modify the structure of the young in relation to the parent, and of the parent in relation to the young. In social animals it will adapt the structure of each individual for the benefit of the community, if each in consequence profits by the selected change. What natural selection cannot do is to modify the structure of one species, without giving it any advantage, for the good of another species; and though statements to this effect may be found in works of natural history, I cannot find one case which will bear investigation. A structure used only once in an animal's whole life, if of high importance to it, might be modified to any extent by natural selection; for instance, the great jaws possessed by certain insects, and used exclusively for opening the cocoon—or the hard tip to the beak of nestling birds, used for breaking the egg. It has been asserted that of the best short-beaked tumbler-pigeons, more perish in the egg than are able to get out of it; so that fanciers assist in the act of hatching. Now, if nature had to make the beak of a full-grown pigeon very short for the bird's own advantage, the process of modification would be very slow, and there would be simultaneously the most rigorous selection of the young birds within the egg, which had the most powerful and hardest beaks, for all with weak beaks would inevitably perish; or, more delicate and more easily broken shells might be selected, the thickness of the shell being known to vary like every other structure.

SEXUAL SELECTION

10   Inasmuch as peculiarities often appear under domestication in one sex and become hereditarily attached to that sex, the same fact probably occurs under nature, and if so, natural selection will be able to modify one sex in its functional relations to the other sex, or in relation to wholly different habits of life in the two sexes, as is sometimes the case with insects. And this leads me to say

a few words on what I call Sexual Selection. This depends, not on a struggle for existence, but on a struggle between the males for possession of the females; the result is not death to the unsuccessful competitor, but few or no offspring. Sexual selection is, therefore, less rigorous than natural selection. Generally, the most vigorous males, those which are best fitted for their places in nature, will leave most progeny. But in many cases, victory will depend not on general vigor, but on having special weapons, confined to the male sex. A hornless stag or spurless cock would have a poor chance of leaving offspring. Sexual selection by always allowing the victor to breed might surely give indomitable courage, length to the spur, and strength to the wing to strike in the spurred leg, as well as the brutal cock fighter, who knows well that he can improve his breed by careful selection of the best cocks. How low in the scale of nature this law of battle descends, I know not; male alligators have been described as fighting, bellowing, and whirling round, like Indians in a wardance, for the possession of the females; male salmons have been seen fighting all day long; male stag-beetles often bear wounds from the huge mandibles of other males. The war is, perhaps, severest between the males of polygamous animals, and these seem oftenest provided with special weapons. The males of carnivorous animals are already well armed; though to them and to others, special means of defense may be given through means of sexual selection, as the mane to the lion, the shoulder-pad to the boar, and the hooked jaw to the male salmon; for the shield may be as important for victory as the sword or spear.

Among birds, the contest is often of a more peaceful character. All those who have attended to the subject believe that there is the severest rivalry between the males of many species to attract, by singing, the females. The rock-thrush of Guiana, birds of paradise, and some others, congregate; and successive males display their gorgeous plumage and perform strange antics before the females, which standing by as spectators, at last choose the most attractive partner. Those who have closely attended to birds in confinement well know that they often take individual preferences and dislikes: thus Sir R. Heron has described how one pied peacock was eminently attractive to all his hen birds. It may appear childish to attribute any effect to such apparently weak means: I cannot here enter on the details necessary to support this view; but if man can in a short time give elegant carriage and beauty to his bantams, according to his standard of beauty, I can see no good reason to doubt that female birds, by selecting, during thousands of generations, the most melodious or beautiful males, according to their standard of beauty, might produce a marked effect. I strongly suspect that some well-known laws with respect to the plumage of male and female birds, in comparison

with the plumage of the young, can be explained on the view of plumage having been chiefly modified by sexual selection, acting when the birds have come
to the breeding age or during the breeding season; the modifications thus produced being inherited at corresponding ages or seasons, either by the males alone,
or by the males and females; but I have not space here to enter on this subject.

Thus it is, as I believe, that when the males and females of any animal have
the same general habits of life, but differ in structure, color, or ornament, such
differences have been mainly caused by sexual selection; that is, individual males
have had, in successive generations, some slight advantage over other males, in
their weapons, means of defense, or charms; and have transmitted these advantages to their male offspring. Yet, I would not wish to attribute all such sexual
differences to this agency: for we see peculiarities arising and becoming attached
to the male sex in our domestic animals (as the wattle in male carriers, horn-like
protuberances in the cocks of certain fowls, etc.), which we cannot believe to be
either useful to the males in battle, or attractive to the females. We see analogous
cases under nature, for instance, the tuft of hair on the breast of the turkey-cock,
which can hardly be either useful or ornamental to this bird; indeed, had the tuft
appeared under domestication, it would have been called a monstrosity.

ILLUSTRATIONS OF THE ACTION OF NATURAL SELECTION

In order to make it clear how, as I believe, natural selection acts, I must beg permission to give one or two imaginary illustrations. Let us take the case of a wolf,
which preys on various animals, securing some by craft, some by strength, and
some by fleetness; and let us suppose that the fleetest prey, a deer for instance,
had from any change in the country increased in numbers, or that other prey had
decreased in numbers, during that season of the year when the wolf is hardest
pressed for food. I can under such circumstances see no reason to doubt that
the swiftest and slimmest wolves would have the best chance of surviving, and
so be preserved or selected, provided always that they retained strength to master their prey at this or at some other period of the year, when they might be compelled to prey on other animals. I can see no more reason to doubt this, than that
man can improve the fleetness of his greyhounds by careful and methodical selection, or by that unconscious selection which results from each man trying to
keep the best dogs without any thought of modifying the breed.

Even without any change in the proportional numbers of the animals on which
our wolf preyed, a cub might be born with an innate tendency to pursue certain
kinds of prey. Nor can this be thought very improbable; for we often observe great

differences in the natural tendencies of our domestic animals; one cat, for instance, taking to catch rats, another mice; one cat, according to Mr. St. John, bringing home winged game, another hares or rabbits, and another hunting on marshy ground and almost nightly catching woodcocks or snipes. The tendency to catch rats rather than mice is known to be inherited. Now, if any slight innate change of habit or of structure benefited an individual wolf, it would have the best chance of surviving and of leaving offspring. Some of its young would probably inherit the same habits or structure, and by the repetition of this process, a new variety might be formed which would either supplant or coexist with the parent-form of wolf. Or, again, the wolves inhabiting a mountainous district, and those frequenting the lowlands, would naturally be forced to hunt different prey; and from the continued preservation of the individuals best fitted for the two sites, two varieties might slowly be formed. These varieties would cross and blend where they met; but to this subject of inter-crossing we shall soon have to return. I may add, that, according to Mr. Pierce, there are two varieties of the wolf inhabiting the Catskill Mountains in the United States, one with a light greyhound-like form, which pursues deer, and the other more bulky, with shorter legs, which more frequently attacks the shepherd's flocks.

15   Let us now take a more complex case. Certain plants excrete a sweet juice, apparently for the sake of eliminating something injurious from their sap; this is effected by glands at the base of the stipules in some Leguminosæ, and at the back of the leaf of the common laurel. This juice, though small in quantity, is greedily sought by insects. Let us now suppose a little sweet juice or nectar to be excreted by the inner bases of the petals of a flower. In this case insects in seeking the nectar would get dusted with pollen, and would certainly often transport the pollen from one flower to the stigma of another flower. The flowers of two distinct individuals of the same species would thus get crossed; and the act of crossing, we have good reason to believe (as will hereafter be more fully alluded to), would produce very vigorous seedlings, which consequently would have the best chance of flourishing and surviving. Some of these seedlings would probably inherit the nectar-excreting power. Those individual flowers which had the largest glands or nectaries, and which excreted most nectar, would be oftenest visited by insects, and would be oftenest crossed; and so in the long-run would gain the upper hand. Those flowers, also, which had their stamens and pistils placed, in relation to the size and habits of the particular insects which visited them, so as to favor in any degree the transportal of their pollen from flower to flower, would likewise be favored or selected. We might have taken the case of insects visiting flowers for the sake of collecting pollen instead of nectar; and as

pollen is formed for the sole object of fertilization, its destruction appears a simple loss to the plant; yet if a little pollen were carried, at first occasionally and then habitually, by the pollen-devouring insects from flower to flower, and a cross thus effected, although nine-tenths of the pollen were destroyed, it might still be a great gain to the plant; and those individuals which produced more and more pollen, and had larger and larger anthers, would be selected.

When our plant, by this process of the continued preservation or natural selection of more and more attractive flowers, had been rendered highly attractive to insects, they would, unintentionally on their part, regularly carry pollen from flower to flower; and that they can most effectually do this, I could easily show by many striking instances. I will give only one—not as a very striking case, but as likewise illustrating one step in the separation of the sexes of plants, presently to be alluded to. Some holly-trees bear only male flowers, which have four stamens producing rather a small quantity of pollen, and a rudimentary pistil; other holly-trees bear only female flowers; these have a full-sized pistil, and four stamens with shrivelled anthers, in which not a grain of pollen can be detected. Having found a female tree exactly sixty yards from a male tree, I put the stigmas of twenty flowers, taken from different branches, under the microscope, and on all, without exception, there were pollen-grains, and on some a profusion of pollen. As the wind had set for several days from the female to the male tree, the pollen could not thus have been carried. The weather had been cold and boisterous, and therefore not favorable to bees; nevertheless every female flower which I examined had been effectually fertilized by the bees, accidentally dusted with pollen, having flown from tree to tree in search of nectar. But to return to our imaginary case: as soon as the plant had been rendered so highly attractive to insects that pollen was regularly carried from flower to flower, another process might commence. No naturalist doubts the advantage of what has been called the "physiological division of labor"; hence we may believe that it would be advantageous to a plant to produce stamens alone in one flower or on one whole plant, and pistils alone in another flower or on another plant. In plants under culture and placed under new conditions of life, sometimes the male organs and sometimes the female organs become more or less impotent; now if we suppose this to occur in ever so slight a degree under nature, then as pollen is already carried regularly from flower to flower, and as a more complete separation of the sexes of our plant would be advantageous on the principle of the division of labor, individuals with this tendency more and more increased, would be continually favored or selected, until at last a complete separation of the sexes would be effected.

UNIT 5

Let us now turn to the nectar-feeding insects in our imaginary case: we may suppose the plant of which we have been slowly increasing the nectar by continued selection, to be a common plant; and that certain insects depended in main part on its nectar for food. I could give many facts, showing how anxious bees are to save time; for instance, their habit of cutting holes and sucking the nectar at the bases of certain flowers, which they can, with a very little more trouble, enter by the mouth. Bearing such facts in mind, I can see no reason to doubt that an accidental deviation in the size and form of the body, or in the curvature and length of the proboscis, etc., far too slight to be appreciated by us, might profit a bee or other insect, so that an individual so characterized would be able to obtain its food more quickly, and so have a better chance of living and leaving descendants. Its descendants would probably inherit a tendency to a similar slight deviation of structure. The tubes of the corollas of the common red and incarnate clovers (Trifolium pratense and incarnatum) do not on a hasty glance appear to differ in length; yet the hive-bee can easily suck the nectar out of the incarnate clover, but not out of the common red clover, which is visited by humble-bees alone; so that whole fields of the red clover offer in vain an abundant supply of precious nectar to the hive-bee. Thus it might be a great advantage to the hive-bee to have a slightly longer or differently constructed proboscis. On the other hand, I have found by experiment that the fertility of clover greatly depends on bees visiting and moving parts of the corolla, so as to push the pollen on to the stigmatic surface. Hence, again, if humble-bees were to become rare in any country, it might be a great advantage to the red clover to have a shorter or more deeply divided tube to its corolla, so that the hive-bee could visit its flowers. Thus I can understand how a flower and a bee might slowly become, either simultaneously or one after the other, modified and adapted in the most perfect manner to each other, by the continued preservation of individuals presenting mutual and slightly favorable deviations of structure.

I am well aware that this doctrine of natural selection, exemplified in the above imaginary instances, is open to the same objections which were at first urged against Sir Charles Lyell's noble views on "the modern changes of the earth, as illustrative of geology"; but we now very seldom hear the action, for instance, of the coast-waves, called a trifling and insignificant cause, when applied to the excavation of gigantic valleys or to the formation of the longest lines of inland cliffs. Natural selection can act only by the preservation and accumulation of infinitesimally small inherited modifications, each profitable to the preserved being; and as modern geology has almost banished such views as the excavation of a great valley by a single diluvial wave, so will natural selection, if it be a true principle, banish the belief of the continued creation of new organic beings, or of any great and sudden modification in their structure.

READING/WRITING ASSISTS

Thesis (and its counterargument):

Readers often expect to find a clear statement of the writer's argument in a **thesis statement**, usually found in a sentence or two at the end of the first or, at the latest, second paragraph of an argumentative essay. Darwin's "Natural Selection," however, is mainly an essay designed to **define** his new scientific theory. Nevertheless, his essay, while mainly defining its terms, also makes an implicit argument, one that can be gleaned by careful reading of the two questions with which Darwin begins his essay, and the answer he gives in the sentence following. What is the counterargument here?

The Shape of the Argument:

20   "Mapping" the structure of an argument can help us better understand the argument itself, while also showing us new models for shaping our own arguments in essay form. As noted above, Darwin's essay strives mainly to define a number of new terms, and the theories denoted by those terms, he is introducing. But in defining the meaning of his terms, Darwin in effect offers an argument for a new way of looking at the ways in which species of living organisms are changed in the natural world over time, better known as *evolution*. In the course of his argument, he offers plenty of examples. To better understand the unusual shape of Darwin's argument, it is best to outline the entire essay, paragraph by paragraph:

Natural Selection:

Paragraph 1:	**Thesis statement:** What is Darwin's argument, and what is he arguing against?
Paragraphs 2 and 3:	First major point about his theory. How does Darwin illustrate here that one change leads to another? Is his argument logical?
Paragraph 4:	Differentiation between **acts of man** and **acts of nature**. What is the difference between man-made "selection" and "**natural selection**"?

UNIT 5

Paragraph 5:	Why is it important for Darwin to make this point about the pace of natural selection?
Paragraph 6:	Are all **adaptive changes** significant? Why?
Paragraphs 7 and 8:	Darwin here returns to the point made in paragraphs 2 and 3 with more examples. Why do you suppose Darwin circles back to this point?
Paragraph 9:	Now Darwin reiterates the point made in paragraph 4. What is the significance of this point in Darwin's argument?

Sexual Selection:

Paragraph 10:	Definition of the term **sexual selection**.
Paragraph 11:	Example: Birds.
Paragraph 12:	Anomalies. What is an **anomaly**?

Illustrations of the Action of Natural Selection:

Paragraphs 13 and 14:	The wolf.
Paragraphs 15 and 16:	Plants.
Paragraph 17:	Insects.
Paragraph 18:	Reiteration of **antithesis** and **conclusion.**

Rhetorical Moves:

Rhetorical Question: A question to which no answer is expected, or to which only one answer may be made.

Darwin often uses **rhetorical** questions in the course of making his argument. In fact, he begins the essay with two. There may, in fact, be other answers to the rhetorical questions Darwin poses, but evidently he thinks his answer is the only correct one, substantiated as it is by his research/observation. Questions are what we might ask when wishing to refute or at least undermine an argument, but **rhetorical questions**, if properly used, can strengthen an argument. Do you think Darwin's argument is strengthened or weakened by the questions he asks throughout his essay? How so? Try incorporating a rhetorical question or two into your next essay.

SHIRLEY JACKSON

Shirley Jackson (1919–1965) was born in San Francisco, where she spent the early years of her life. In 1933, her family moved to Rochester, New York. After graduation from high school, Jackson briefly attended the University of Rochester, but left after suffering from severe depression. She later resumed her studies at Syracuse University, where she wrote prolifically for the college literary magazine, and graduated with a degree in English in 1940.

That year she also married the noted American literary critic and writer, Stanley Edgar Hyman. They moved to Vermont to accommodate Hyman's position as a professor at Bennington College. The couple eventually had four children.

Despite Jackson's considerable familial responsibilities as a faculty wife and mother, she continued to write. In her short life, she authored six novels, two memoirs, and countless short stories. Her most famous short story, "The Lottery," first published in The New Yorker, *provoked a storm of controversy. It is thought to be set in North Bennington, Vermont, rife with what Jackson characterized as anti-Semitism and anti-intellectualism, directed mainly at the college, which was famous for its liberal attitudes regarding politics and education, even in the 1950s.*

Though her literary output was considerable, Jackson continued to suffer from depression, and later in her life, agoraphobia. She died at only forty-eight years old.

UNIT 5

THE LOTTERY
Shirley Jackson

1 The morning of June 27th was clear and sunny, with the fresh warmth of a full summer day; the flowers were blossoming profusely and the grass was richly green. The people of the village began to gather in the square, between the post office and the bank, around ten o'clock; in some towns there were so many people that the lottery took two days and had to be started on June 26th, but in this village, where there were only about three hundred people, the whole lottery took less than two hours, so it could begin at ten o'clock in the morning and still be through in time to allow the villagers to get home for noon dinner.

The children assembled first, of course. School was recently over for the summer, and the feeling of liberty sat uneasily on most of them; they tended to gather together quietly for a while before they broke into boisterous play, and their talk was still of the classroom and the teacher, of books and reprimands. Bobby Martin had already stuffed his pockets full of stones, and the other boys soon followed his example, selecting the smoothest and roundest stones; Bobby and Harry Jones and Dickie Delacroix—the villagers pronounced this name "Dellacroy"—eventually made a great pile of stones in one corner of the square and guarded it against the raids of the other boys. The girls stood aside, talking among themselves, looking over their shoulders at the boys, and the very small children rolled in the dust or clung to the hands of their older brothers or sisters.

Soon the men began to gather, surveying their own children, speaking of planting and rain, tractors and taxes. They stood together, away from the pile of stones in the corner, and their jokes were quiet and they smiled rather than laughed. The women, wearing faded house dresses and sweaters, came shortly after their menfolk. They greeted one another and exchanged bits of gossip as they went to join their husbands. Soon the women, standing by their husbands, began to call to their children, and the children came reluctantly, having to be called four or five times. Bobby Martin ducked under his mother's grasping hand and ran, laughing, back to the pile of stones. His father spoke up sharply, and Bobby came quickly and took his place between his father and his oldest brother.

"The Lottery," by Shirley Jackson, reprinted from *The Lottery and Other Stories* (1948), Farrar, Straus & Giroux.

The lottery was conducted—as were the square dances, the teen-age club, the Halloween program—by Mr. Summers, who had time and energy to devote to civic activities. He was a round-faced, jovial man and he ran the coal business, and people were sorry for him, because he had no children and his wife was a scold. When he arrived in the square, carrying the black wooden box, there was a murmur of conversation among the villagers, and he waved and called, "Little late today, folks." The postmaster, Mr. Graves, followed him, carrying a three-legged stool, and the stool was put in the center of the square and Mr. Summers set the black box down on it. The villagers kept their distance, leaving a space between themselves and the stool, and when Mr. Summers said, "Some of you fellows want to give me a hand?" there was a hesitation before two men, Mr. Martin and his oldest son, Baxter, came forward to hold the box steady on the stool while Mr. Summers stirred up the papers inside it.

5   The original paraphernalia for the lottery had been lost long ago, and the black box now resting on the stool had been put into use even before Old Man Warner, the oldest man in town, was born. Mr. Summers spoke frequently to the villagers about making a new box, but no one liked to upset even as much tradition as was represented by the black box. There was a story that the present box had been made with some pieces of the box that had preceded it, the one that had been constructed when the first people settled down to make a village here. Every year, after the lottery, Mr. Summers began talking again about a new box, but every year the subject was allowed to fade off without anything's being done. The black box grew shabbier each year; by now it was no longer completely black but splintered badly along one side to show the original wood color, and in some places faded or stained.

Mr. Martin and his oldest son, Baxter, held the black box securely on the stool until Mr. Summers had stirred the papers thoroughly with his hand. Because so much of the ritual had been forgotten or discarded, Mr. Summers had been successful in having slips of paper substituted for the chips of wood that had been used for generations. Chips of wood, Mr. Summers had argued, had been all very well when the village was tiny, but now that the population was more than three hundred and likely to keep on growing, it was necessary to use something that would fit more easily into the black box. The night before the lottery, Mr. Summers and Mr. Graves made up the slips of paper and put them in the box, and it was then taken to the safe of Mr. Summers' coal company and locked up until Mr. Summers was ready to take it to the square next morning. The rest of the year, the box was put away, sometimes one place, sometimes another; it had spent one year in Mr. Graves's barn and another year underfoot in the post office, and sometimes it was set on a shelf in the Martin grocery and left there.

There was a great deal of fussing to be done before Mr. Summers declared the lottery open. There were the lists to make up—of heads of families, heads of households in each family, members of each household in each family. There was the proper swearing-in of Mr. Summers by the postmaster, as the official of the lottery; at one time, some people remembered, there had been a recital of some sort, performed by the official of the lottery, a perfunctory, tuneless chant that had been rattled off duly each year; some people believed that the official of the lottery used to stand just so when he said or sang it, others believed that he was supposed to walk among the people, but years and years ago this part of the ritual had been allowed to lapse. There had been, also, a ritual salute, which the official of the lottery had had to use in addressing each person who came up to draw from the box, but this also had changed with time, until now it was felt necessary only for the official to speak to each person approaching. Mr. Summers was very good at all this; in his clean white shirt and blue jeans, with one hand resting carelessly on the black box, he seemed very proper and important as he talked interminably to Mr. Graves and the Martins.

Just as Mr. Summers finally left off talking and turned to the assembled villagers, Mrs. Hutchinson came hurriedly along the path to the square, her sweater thrown over her shoulders, and slid into place in the back of the crowd. "Clean forgot what day it was," she said to Mrs. Delacroix, who stood next to her, and they both laughed softly. "Thought my old man was out back stacking wood," Mrs. Hutchinson went on, "and then I looked out the window and the kids was gone, and then I remembered it was the twenty-seventh and came a-running." She dried her hands on her apron, and Mrs. Delacroix said, "You're in time, though. They're still talking away up there."

Mrs. Hutchinson craned her neck to see through the crowd and found her husband and children standing near the front. She tapped Mrs. Delacroix on the arm as a farewell and began to make her way through the crowd. The people separated good-humoredly to let her through; two or three people said, in voices just loud enough to be heard across the crowd, "Here comes your Missus, Hutchinson," and "Bill, she made it after all." Mrs. Hutchinson reached her husband, and Mr. Summers, who had been waiting, said cheerfully, "Thought we were going to have to get on without you, Tessie." Mrs. Hutchinson said, grinning, "Wouldn't have me leave m'dishes in the sink, now, would you, Joe?," and soft laughter ran through the crowd as the people stirred back into position after Mrs. Hutchinson's arrival.

10   "Well, now," Mr. Summers said soberly, "guess we better get started, get this over with, so's we can go back to work. Anybody ain't here?"

"Dunbar," several people said. "Dunbar, Dunbar."

Mr. Summers consulted his list. "Clyde Dunbar," he said. "That's right. He's broke his leg, hasn't he? Who's drawing for him?"

"Me, I guess," a woman said, and Mr. Summers turned to look at her. "Wife draws for her husband," Mr. Summers said. "Don't you have a grown boy to do it for you, Janey?" Although Mr. Summers and everyone else in the village knew the answer perfectly well, it was the business of the official of the lottery to ask such questions formally. Mr. Summers waited with an expression of polite interest while Mrs. Dunbar answered.

"Horace's not but sixteen yet," Mrs. Dunbar said regretfully. "Guess I gotta fill in for the old man this year."

15   "Right," Mr. Summers said. He made a note on the list he was holding. Then he asked, "Watson boy drawing this year?"

A tall boy in the crowd raised his hand. "Here," he said. "I'm drawing for m'mother and me." He blinked his eyes nervously and ducked his head as several voices in the crowd said things like "Good fellow, Jack," and "Glad to see your mother's got a man to do it."

"Well," Mr. Summers said, "guess that's everyone. Old Man Warner make it?"

"Here," a voice said, and Mr. Summers nodded.

A sudden hush fell on the crowd as Mr. Summers cleared his throat and looked at the list. "All ready?" he called. "Now, I'll read the names—heads of families first—and the men come up and take a paper out of the box. Keep the paper folded in your hand without looking at it until everyone has had a turn. Everything clear?"

20   The people had done it so many times that they only half listened to the directions; most of them were quiet, wetting their lips, not looking around. Then Mr. Summers raised one hand high and said, "Adams." A man disengaged himself from the crowd and came forward. "Hi, Steve," Mr. Summers said, and Mr. Adams said, "Hi, Joe." They grinned at one another humorlessly and nervously. Then Mr. Adams reached into the black box and took out a folded paper. He held it firmly by one corner as he turned and went hastily back to his place in the crowd, where he stood a little apart from his family, not looking down at his hand.

"Allen," Mr. Summers said. "Anderson. . . . Bentham."

"Seems like there's no time at all between lotteries any more," Mrs. Delacroix said to Mrs. Graves in the back row. "Seems like we got through with the last one only last week."

"Time sure goes fast," Mrs. Graves said.

"Clark. . . . Delacroix."

25   "There goes my old man," Mrs. Delacroix said. She held her breath while her husband went forward.

"Dunbar," Mr. Summers said, and Mrs. Dunbar went steadily to the box while one of the women said, "Go on, Janey," and another said, "There she goes."

"We're next," Mrs. Graves said. She watched while Mr. Graves came around from the side of the box, greeted Mr. Summers gravely, and selected a slip of paper from the box. By now, all through the crowd there were men holding the small folded papers in their large hands, turning them over and over nervously. Mrs. Dunbar and her two sons stood together, Mrs. Dunbar holding the slip of paper.

"Harburt. . . . Hutchinson."

"Get up there, Bill," Mrs. Hutchinson said, and the people near her laughed.

30   "Jones."

"They do say," Mr. Adams said to Old Man Warner, who stood next to him, "that over in the north village they're talking of giving up the lottery."

Old Man Warner snorted. "Pack of crazy fools," he said. "Listening to the young folks, nothing's good enough for *them*. Next thing you know, they'll be wanting to go back to living in caves, nobody work any more, live *that* way for a while. Used to be a saying about 'Lottery in June, corn be heavy soon.' First thing you know, we'd all be eating stewed chickweed and acorns. There's *always* been a lottery," he added petulantly. "Bad enough to see young Joe Summers up there joking with everybody."

"Some places have already quit lotteries," Mrs. Adams said.

"Nothing but trouble in *that*," Old Man Warner said stoutly. "Pack of young fools."

35   "Martin." And Bobby Martin watched his father go forward. "Overdyke. . . . Percy."

"I wish they'd hurry," Mrs. Dunbar said to her older son. "I wish they'd hurry."

"They're almost through," her son said.

"You get ready to run tell Dad," Mrs. Dunbar said.

Mr. Summers called his own name and then stepped forward precisely and selected a slip from the box. Then he called, "Warner."

40   "Seventy-seventh year I been in the lottery," Old Man Warner said as he went
through the crowd. "Seventy-seventh time."

"Watson." The tall boy came awkwardly through the crowd. Someone said,
"Don't be nervous, Jack," and Mr. Summers said, "Take your time, son."

"Zanini."

After that, there was a long pause, a breathless pause, until Mr. Summers,
holding his slip of paper in the air, said, "All right, fellows." For a minute, no one
moved, and then all the slips of paper were opened. Suddenly, all the women
began to speak at once, saying, "Who is it?" "Who's got it?" "Is it the Dunbars?"
"Is it the Watsons?" Then the voices began to say, "It's Hutchinson. It's Bill,"
"Bill Hutchinson's got it."

"Go tell your father," Mrs. Dunbar said to her older son.

45   People began to look around to see the Hutchinsons. Bill Hutchinson was
standing quiet, staring down at the paper in his hand. Suddenly, Tessie Hutchinson shouted to Mr. Summers, "You didn't give him time enough to take any
paper he wanted. I saw you. It wasn't fair!"

"Be a good sport, Tessie," Mrs. Delacroix called, and Mrs. Graves said, "All
of us took the same chance."

"Shut up, Tessie," Bill Hutchinson said.

"Well, everyone," Mr. Summers said, "that was done pretty fast, and now
we've got to be hurrying a little more to get done in time." He consulted his
next list. "Bill," he said, "you draw for the Hutchinson family. You got any other
households in the Hutchinsons?"

"There's Don and Eva," Mrs. Hutchinson yelled. "Make *them* take their
chance!"

50   "Daughters draw with their husbands' families, Tessie," Mr. Summers said
gently. "You know that as well as anyone else."

"It wasn't *fair*," Tessie said.

"I guess not, Joe," Bill Hutchinson said regretfully. "My daughter draws with
her husband's family, that's only fair. And I've got no other family except the
kids."

"Then, as far as drawing for families is concerned, it's you," Mr. Summers said
in explanation, "and as far as drawing for households is concerned, that's you, too.
Right?"

"Right," Bill Hutchinson said.

55   "How many kids, Bill?" Mr. Summers asked formally.

"Three," Bill Hutchinson said. "There's Bill, Jr., and Nancy, and little Dave. And Tessie and me."

"All right, then," Mr. Summers said. "Harry, you got their tickets back?"

Mr. Graves nodded and held up the slips of paper. "Put them in the box, then," Mr. Summers directed. "Take Bill's and put it in."

"I think we ought to start over," Mrs. Hutchinson said, as quietly as she could. "I tell you it wasn't *fair*. You didn't give him time enough to choose. *Everybody* saw that."

60   Mr. Graves had selected the five slips and put them in the box, and he dropped all the papers but those onto the ground, where the breeze caught them and lifted them off.

"Listen, everybody," Mrs. Hutchinson was saying to the people around her.

"Ready, Bill?" Mr. Summers asked, and Bill Hutchinson, with one quick glance around at his wife and children, nodded.

"Remember," Mr. Summers said, "take the slips and keep them folded until each person has taken one. Harry, you help little Dave." Mr. Graves took the hand of the little boy, who came willingly with him up to the box. "Take a paper out of the box, Davy," Mr. Summers said. Davy put his hand into the box and laughed. "Take just *one* paper," Mr. Summers said. "Harry, you hold it for him." Mr. Graves took the child's hand and removed the folded paper from the tight fist and held it while little Dave stood next to him and looked up at him wonderingly.

"Nancy next," Mr. Summers said. Nancy was twelve, and her school friends breathed heavily as she went forward, switching her skirt, and took a slip daintily from the box. "Bill, Jr.," Mr. Summers said, and Billy, his face red and his feet over-large, nearly knocked the box over as he got a paper out. "Tessie," Mr. Summers said. She hesitated for a minute, looking around defiantly, and then set her lips and went up to the box. She snatched a paper out and held it behind her.

65   "Bill," Mr. Summers said, and Bill Hutchinson reached into the box and felt around, bringing his hand out at last with the slip of paper in it.

The crowd was quiet. A girl whispered, "I hope it's not Nancy," and the sound of the whisper reached the edges of the crowd.

"It's not the way it used to be," Old Man Warner said clearly. "People ain't they way they used to be."

"All right," Mr. Summers said. "Open the papers. Harry, you open little Dave's."

Mr. Graves opened the slip of paper and there was a general sigh through the crowd as he held it up and everyone could see that it was blank. Nancy and

Bill, Jr., opened theirs at the same time, and both beamed and laughed, turning around to the crowd and holding their slips of paper above their heads.

70   "Tessie," Mr. Summers said. There was a pause, and then Mr. Summers looked at Bill Hutchinson, and Bill unfolded his paper and showed it. It was blank.

"It's Tessie," Mr. Summers said, and his voice was hushed. "Show us her paper, Bill."

Bill Hutchinson went over to his wife and forced the slip of paper out of her hand. It had a black spot on it, the black spot Mr. Summers had made the night before with the heavy pencil in the coal-company office. Bill Hutchinson held it up, and there was a stir in the crowd.

"All right, folks," Mr. Summers said. "Let's finish quickly."

Although the villagers had forgotten the ritual and lost the original black box, they still remembered to use stones. The pile of stones the boys had made earlier was ready; there were stones on the ground with the blowing scraps of paper that had come out of the box. Mrs. Delacroix selected a stone so large she had to pick it up with both hands and turned to Mrs. Dunbar. "Come on," she said. "Hurry up."

75   Mrs. Dunbar had small stones in both hands, and she said, gasping for breath, "I can't run at all. You'll have to go ahead and I'll catch up with you."

The children had stones already, and someone gave little Davy Hutchinson a few pebbles.

Tessie Hutchinson was in the center of a cleared space by now, and she held her hands out desperately as the villagers moved in on her. "It isn't fair," she said. A stone hit her on the side of the head.

Old Man Warner was saying, "Come on, come on, everyone." Steve Adams was in the front of the crowd of villagers with Mrs. Graves beside him.

"It isn't fair, it isn't right," Mrs. Hutchinson screamed, and then they were upon her.

LEVELS OF READING

Summary:

Pay attention to the **literal** meaning of the text. Briefly describe the narrative of Shirley Jackson "The Lottery." Who tells the story? Where is the story set? Who are the major characters? Concentrate on the highlights; avoid too much detail when summarizing. Again, drawing a simple outline of the main points of the text will help you better analyze the text at other levels of interpretation.

UNIT 5

Analysis:

Find what you believe is **symbolic** in the text. Explain the meaning of these symbols. There is a sense, from the very beginning of Jackson's story, that an unpleasant event is about to take place in this village, even though symbolically, at least, "the fresh warmth of a full-summer day," "flowers . . . blossoming profusely," and "richly green grass" indicate peace and prosperity. In fact, Shirley Jackson herself once said, "The number of people who expected Mrs. Hutchinson to win a Bendix washer would amaze you." Right from the start of the story, however, watch for symbols that serve to counteract any more benevolent reading. What might "the lottery" itself symbolize? And the "black box"? Why do most of the inhabitants of the village seem relatively blasé about the event? With the help of the background material provided about Shirley Jackson and her world, make an argument about this story, and include the mention of the more **figurative** aspects of the text when making points in defense of your argument.

Application:

Apply Darwin's theory of **natural selection** to Jackson's story. Outline an argument you wish to make about this literary text using Darwin's theory to help you explain what some part of "The Lottery" may mean. To make your argument, you may analyze a character or characters, the lottery itself, the setting, symbols, a motivation, a goal, a result. Consider the following as possibilities, but explore other original interpretations too:

- Does Darwin's theory make the uneasy approval of the villagers of this ritual more understandable? Outline an argument you wish to make about "The Lottery" using Darwin's theory to help you explain the point of the lottery itself.
- Is this selection "**natural**"? Does this town's ritual make more clear the distinctions Darwin makes between man-made "selection" and "natural selection"?
- Why do you suppose other villages, much to the disgust of Old Mr. Warner, have "given up the lottery"? Might the other villages' refusal to continue the lottery represent in some way Darwin's idea of **adaptive** changes? How so?

- Are any of Darwin's points concerning **sexual selection** germane to Jackson's story? Is it significant that a woman "wins" the lottery in Jackson's short story?
- Does Jackson's story prove or disprove Darwin's theory?

THOMAS EISNER

Thomas Eisner (1929–) was born in Uruguay, though he is now a naturalized American citizen. His father was a chemist. The family home was often filled with a variety of scents, since his father's hobby was making perfumes. Perhaps as a consequence, as a child Eisner noticed that bugs sometimes emitted smells, and he began bringing them home for further study.

Eisner earned his B.S. and Ph.D. at Harvard University. He is currently the Jacob Gould Schurman Professor of Chemical Ecology at Cornell University and the Director of the Cornell Institute for Research in Chemical Ecology (CIRCE). Among Eisner's numerous honors are the National Medal of Science, the Tyler Award for Environmental Achievement, the Harvard Centennial Medal, honorary doctorates from Switzerland, Sweden, Germany, and the United States, and membership in the National Academy of Sciences, the American Academy of Arts and Sciences, the American Philosophical Society, the Akademie der Naturforscher Leopoldina, and the Academia Europaea.

Thomas Eisner is one of the pioneers of chemical ecology, the discipline dealing with the chemical interactions of organisms. He is one of the world's experts on the chemistry of insects. Through ingenious experiments carried out in the laboratory and outdoors, in collaboration with chemists and engineers, he has shown that insects depend on special chemicals for virtually every aspect of their survival, be it the pursuit of mates, location of food, protection of young, or defense against enemies. He has also clarified various mechanisms by which insects circumvent the chemical defenses of plants and other insects.

Eisner is well-known for his photographs, which accompany most of his publications, and which have been featured in museum exhibits and countless magazines and books. He is author or coauthor of some 400 technical articles, and seven books.

Eisner has argued forcefully for the preservation of biological diversity, as an imperative for the safeguarding of the chemical and genetic resources of nature. He has played a key role in efforts to preserve wilderness areas in Florida and Texas. More recently he helped broker a contractual agreement between a pharmaceutical company (Merck, Sharp, & Dohme) and a developing nation (Costa Rica), whereby financial resources are provided for preservation of the Costa Rican rainforest. He has served on various boards of prestigious conservation organizations (Nature Conservancy, National Audubon Society, Union of Concerned Scientists), and has been active in worldwide human rights efforts.

"The Circumventers" is part of a chapter from Eisner's latest book, For Love of Insects. *In this study, Eisner details the ways in which the grasshopper mouse circumvents the protective mechanism of the* Eleode, *a beetle.*

THE CIRCUMVENTERS
Thomas Eisner

1   Fugu is Japanese for puffer fish. Valued for its exquisite taste, the fish is a cherished culinary item in Japan, sought out by thousands annually who are willing to risk consuming it. Eating puffers is dangerous indeed, and to indulge in it has been likened to playing the gastronomic equivalent of Russian roulette. The dangers are so great, in fact, that it is forbidden to serve puffer fish in any form to members of the imperial family. More than 50 people die every year from eating puffer fish, and the death is not a pleasant one.

Puffer fish contain tetrodotoxin, a lethal poison for which there is no antidote. The liver, ovaries, and to a lesser extent the skin of the fish contain the toxin, which acts by blocking cellular sodium channels, thereby preventing nerves from generating the propagated spikes that activate muscles. The consequence is paralysis and death by asphyxiation. The muscles of the puffer are devoid of tetrodotoxin and if kept uncontaminated during culinary preparation of the fish are perfectly edible. The puffer market is strictly regulated in Japan. Only special restaurants are allowed to serve fugu, and the chefs who prepare the fish must undergo extensive training before they are licensed. Yet mistakes do happen and the proof is in the statistics. The slightest cut into the tetrodotoxin-bearing organs of the fish during preparation may contaminate the edible parts, with potentially fatal consequences to the patron. Despite the risks, customers pay as much as $400 a serving for fugu. Importation of puffers into the United States is also regulated, but the rules have not prevented the occasional ill-prepared serving from ending up on someone's plate. Three cases of fugu poisoning, none lethal, were reported a few years ago from California.

In biological terms what we humans do when we partake of puffers is deal with poisonous food that has been depoisoned by special preparation. By laying open the puffer and selectively eating those parts that are harmless we are essentially circumventing the fish's natural defense. With a counterstrategy of our own, we circumvent the animal's defensive strategy, and by so doing add the species to our choice of edibles. Other animals resort to the same strategy. Prominent among these are insects, but the examples include vertebrates as well. Incredibly, there is a predator in the southern Appalachians, most likely a mammal, with the habit of dealing with a tetrodotoxin-producing newt by subjecting it, in fugu-chef fashion, to preingestive dissection.

We owe the discovery of this circumventing behavior to Donald J. Shure and his collaborators at Emory University. Working in the vicinity of Highlands, North Carolina, they found remnants of *Notophthalmus viridescens,* the red-spotted newt, strewn about on a logging trail. It had been raining and the newts had been active. The carcasses were fresh and had been mutilated. Some had been decapitated, others had been sliced open, and all were missing some of the internal organs. Whoever was feeding on these newts knew that the viscera were the harmless parts. Tetrodotoxin in the newt is stored in the skin. The spectacle of all those eviscerated corpses was pitiful—some had not quite stopped moving. Shure failed to catch the predator in the act, and to my knowledge the culprit has never been identified. Shure suggests that skunks might have been responsible.

5   I have myself come across evidence that there are predators able to deal with protected prey, and I too have been stymied at times by not being able to identify the predator. There is a wonderful site near Cornell, Taughannock State Park, which I love to visit because it includes a gorge that is a haven for millipedes. Hydrogen cyanide–producing polydesmoid millipedes abound there, as do benzoquinone-producing spiroboloids. The latter are represented by *Narceus annularis,* a large species, active at night, found in logs and leaf litter in the daytime. *Narceus* is easily provoked. Its glands are segmentally arranged along the sides of the body, and it tends to discharge even when mildly disturbed. The emission leaves the millipede virtually coated with the foul-smelling fluid.

The millipede's defense is imperfect in one respect. The segments immediately behind the head, like the head itself, lack glands. The front end of the millipede is therefore unprotected, which explains why the animal responds to disturbance by coiling its body with the head at the center of the coil.

Knowing that millipedes are best collected at night when they are active, I used to make it a point to scout around Taughannock Park after dark with my headlamp when I was in need of the animals. But there came a time when I had to be at the site in early dawn to collect insects, and it was then that I became aware of an animal I called Robespierre. Some predator at the park knew that the front end of *Narceus* was undefended and edible. At one location the evidence was all around me. Headless *Narceus,* some of them dead but others still writhing, were scattered over the leaf litter, in evidence of what must have been a feeding frenzy the night before. I suspected a rodent and set out traps at the scene, but neither the mice nor the shrews I caught proved able to deal with *Narceus*. I offered *Narceus* to each in experimental tests but none proved capable of subduing the millipede. All attacked *Narceus,* but they elicited discharges and were repelled by the secretion. To this day I remain ignorant of who Robespierre is. I still believe it is a rodent, but lack proof. I am also left wondering whether Robespierre knows from birth how to deal with *Narceus* or whether it acquires the ability through experience. I have visited the gorge again in recent years but failed to find evidence that Robespierre was still up to its tricks.

I had run into another Robespierre of sorts years earlier, in 1959, on my first trip to the Southwestern Research Station in Arizona, but on that occasion the detective work paid off and I was able to unmask the predator.

I had just made my acquaintance with the desert, and with the desert-dwelling beetles of the genus *Eleodes,* the same beetles that I was later to take to Ithaca to study in the laboratory (see Chapter 2). It wasn't long before I noticed that when these beetles were touched, they responded in a peculiar way—they assumed a head-stand. They propped themselves up on their legs and raised the rear end. *Eleodes* are flightless and nocturnal. They spend the night foraging for plant food and the day hiding, which means that at dawn and dusk they are found on the desert floor, walking about at leisure in search of food or shelter. Poke them with a finger when they are on the march, and they will halt at once and point their rears to the sky.

10   There is a passage in John Steinbeck's *Cannery Row* that alludes to the behavior.

> "I wonder why they got their asses up in the air for?"
> Hazel turned one of the stink bugs over and the shining black beetle strove madly with floundering legs to get upright again, . . .
> "Why do you think they do it?"
> "I think they're praying," said Doc.

The behavior, of course, is defensive. The animals undertake it when threatened, announcing thereby that they are ready to discharge their quinonoid spray from the abdominal tip. If further provoked, they do indeed spray, which causes them to take on a terrible stink. The glands responsible, it will be recalled, are two large sacs situated just inside the abdominal tip. Needless to say, the beetles derive advantage from the spray. But, as I was to find out, there is one enemy against which *Eleodes* has not a ghost of a chance.

There were several species of *Eleodes* at my desert site, all jet black, as is typical for the genus. The black color is part of *Eleodes*'s advertisement, since it makes the beetles extremely conspicuous against the light-colored desert soil, especially in the twilight, when they are active. Colors are barely discernible in twilight, and it is through contrast, therefore, that an animal can best achieve conspicuousness.

Eleodes were not the only black beetles at the site. Several different species also had that contrasting appearance and they were not all easy to tell apart. They differed somewhat in body shape, size, and shininess, but on the whole looked very much alike. Most belonged to the same family as *Eleodes,* the Tenebrionidae, whose members are appropriately known as darkling beetles. The family includes many desert dwellers, some from Africa, also similar in appearance to *Eleodes.*

Any insect that crawls about on the desert floor has ants to contend with, and I did experiments that showed *Eleodes* to be virtually invulnerable to ants. That was not surprising, given that the *Eleodes* secretion contains primarily benzoquinones. I released individual *Eleodes* near the entrance of ant colonies so they were sure to be attacked and watched as the secretion took effect. Whole swarms of ants sometimes materialized to take part in the assault, but the moment the beetle discharged, the swarms dispersed. Sometimes an individual ant clung to the beetle with its mandibles even as the beetle walked away. As I found out by experimenting at Cornell, ants that cling in this fashion may do so persistently until death, which indicates that they could have the ability, if engaged collectively in such behavior, to subdue even chemically protected prey. Such sacrificial behavior on the part of individual ants, if carried out close to the nest entrance, where masses of nestmates could rally to the assault, could pay off for the colony. With *Eleodes,* however, the ants did not cling in sufficient numbers for the kamikaze strategy to take effect. The beetles all managed to escape. I do have evidence, however, that the suicidal behavior occurs under natural circumstances. I have noted heads of ants, either bodiless or with the body still attached, clinging by their locked mandibles to one part or another of insects that I caught in the wild. To judge from the dried condition of the clinging parts, the ants had all died days beforehand. Among the insects that I found to be thus encumbered was an individual *Eleodes.*

15   Evidence that some predator was feasting on *Eleodes* was readily at hand. Strewn over the desert floor, and distributed with some regularity, were little piles of beetle remains that were unmistakably those of *Eleodes.* They consisted typically of the wing covers (the elytra, which in *Eleodes* are fused to form a shield over the abdomen), plus the abdominal tip (still attached to this shield), and parts of the legs. Some of the remains, particularly the elytral shields, were sometimes found by themselves, an indication that they had been dispersed by the wind. The shields

always bore jagged edges where they had become disconnected from the thorax, providing evidence that they had been chewed off, and implicating a rodent.

The station had a supply of rodent traps, and I set these out one night in an area where elytral remnants had been abundant. I was totally ignorant of rodents, but others at the station alerted me to the presence of grasshopper mice in the region, rodents with a ferocious appetite for insects and a terrifying name—*Onychomys torridus*. I did eventually trap grasshopper mice and they not only lived up to their reputation but proved unmistakably that they were the *Eleodes* eaters I was after.

I released the mice in cages containing some desert soil and they were quick to adjust to the new premises. I then fed them a variety of insects other than *Eleodes* so they would get used to me. They eagerly consumed more than a dozen mid-sized insects per feeding session, which led me to wonder where they put it all. When I finally offered them *Eleodes,* the results were quite spectacular.

The moment I introduced an *Eleodes,* the mouse grabbed it with the front feet, and while holding it upright, forced the beetle's rear into the soil. It then commenced feeding on the beetle's head, and onward into the thorax, undisturbed by the beetle's discharges, which were ineffectually ejected into the sand. I could hear the crunching sounds. Without ever releasing its grip or extricating the beetle's rear from the soil, the mouse then proceeded systematically to eat the abdomen, stopping only when it reached the abdominal tip. It seemed to know exactly what to do. When finished it retired to a corner of the cage, leaving behind a pile of remnants exactly like those I had been finding in the desert. I retrieved the elytral shield with the attached abdominal tip and by checking with a microscope was able to confirm that the mouse had stopped just short of chewing into the glands. These were almost empty, as expected, but they had not been torn open.

My camera at the time was a Leica with attached reflex housing that had kindly been lent to me by my student Ben Dane. I had the camera at the ready when I did these tests and still remember the mouse staring obligingly into the lens as I photographed it eating *Eleodes.*

20   I fed *Eleodes* to several *Onychomys* and the results were always the same. The attacks proceed so quickly that the *Eleodes* hardly ever had time to assume the headstand. I was fascinated by the headstand and had photographed a number of *Eleodes* in the field, including individuals of the largest species, *Eleodes longicollis,* while they were performing the trick. Predators other than grasshopper mice, I reasoned, must heed the warning implicit in the headstand or the headstand would not be such a standard feature of *Eleodes*'s behavior. The headstand could be deterrent to other rodents as well, even to skunks and birds. There was indirect evi-

dence that beetles benefit from pointing their rears upward. I had noted at the time that among the black beetles that roamed the desert floor with *Eleodes* there were some that assumed the headstand even though they lacked defensive glands. These beetles are evidently mimics of *Eleodes* that benefit from being misdiagnosed, when headstanding, as being chemically armed like *Eleodes*. The most spectacular of these fakers is a flightless, cactus-eating beetle of the family Cerambycidae, *Moneilema appressum,* whose headstand is uncannily imitative of that of *Eleodes*. Cerambycids all have long antennae and *Moneilema* is no exception. The long antennae could blow *Moneilema's* cover, but predators may not notice it.

LEVELS OF READING

Summary:

Pay attention to the **literal** meaning of the text. Briefly describe the steps in Eisner's discovery. Concentrate on the highlights; avoid too much detail when summarizing. Again, drawing a simple outline of the main points of the text will help you better analyze the text at other levels of interpretation.

Analysis:

Find what you believe is **implicit** in the text. The first line of his essay notes that Eisner had, in the past, "come across evidence that there are predators able to deal with protected prey." What sort of "evidence" in this regard does he encounter in "The Circumventers"? Does the outcome of his research come as a surprise? With the help of the background material provided about Thomas Eisner, make an argument about this discovery, and include the mention of the more implicit aspects of the text when making points in defense of your argument.

Application:

Apply Darwin's theory of **natural selection** to Eisner's discovery. Outline an argument you wish to make about this research text using Darwin's theory to help you explain what some part of "The Circumventers" may mean. To make your argument, you may analyze Eisner's role in his discovery, the setting, a motivation, a goal, a result. Consider the following as possibilities, but explore other original interpretations too:

- Does Darwin's theory help us to understand Eisner's discovery about the grasshopper mouse's ability to circumvent the protective mechanism of the *Eleodes*?
- Is this selection "**natural**"? Is the development of the *Eleodes'* protective mechanism a point in defense of Darwin's argument regarding **natural selection**? Is the development of the grasshopper mouse's ability to get around *Eleodes'* poison a point in defense of Darwin's argument regarding **natural selection**? Is there a way to reconcile possible apparent contradictions in this example?
- How important are the grasshopper mouse's **adaptive** changes? How important are the **adaptive** changes of the *Eleodes*? What is to be concluded based on the ability of other beetles to mimic the protective behavior of the *Eleodes* even though they lack the protective mechanism?
- What do Eisner's research discoveries add to Darwin's notion of "survival of the fittest"?
- Does Eisner's research prove or disprove Darwin's theory?

Start Your Own Argument:

In later editions of *The Origin of the Species,* from which this essay is drawn, Darwin added the subtitle "Survival of the Fittest" to this chapter. Does his essay prove that only the strong survive? Can Darwin's argument about animals, plants, and insects be extended to include human beings? Do Eisner's and Jackson's narratives relate to each other and to Darwin's theory in any way?

SIX

THE DIALOGUE

PLATO

Plato (428 BC–347 BC) was born to a prosperous and established family in Athens, Greece. He had two older brothers, one named Glaucon, and a younger sister. As a youngster, a political future for Plato was assumed, but the long-lasting Peloponnesian War drained the Athenian empire, and Plato's political prospects dried up as well. The establishment of Sparta after the final defeat of Athens, in 404 BC, marked the end of political Athens as Plato's parents had known it.

Plato turned instead to writing poetry, but eventually took up an interest in philosophy, especially what is now known as the pre-Socratic philosophers. Once he met the philosopher Socrates, he turned his attention to writing philosophy exclusively. In 399 BC, Socrates was placed on trial; the charges against him included corrupting the youth of Athens, atheism, and unusual religious practices. Though Socrates was found guilty by only a narrow margin of his judges, he was executed one month later. The events of Socrates' trial are recounted in Plato's Apology.

After 399 BC, Plato began to write in earnest. His so-called Socratic dialogues were written between 399–387 BC, and are thought to be an accurate representation of what Socrates thought and said. Socrates himself claimed to have no direct interest in politics whatsoever. Instead, he chose to engage men in random conversations, hoping to teach them something about a just and righteous lifestyle.

At forty years old, Plato founded The Academy, *located one mile outside the city walls of Athens, and named after the Attic hero Academus. Plato's* Academy *served as a model of higher learning until it was closed almost one thousand years later.*

"The Allegory of the Cave" is a section contained in Plato's Republic. *In it, Plato recounts one Socratic dialogue in which Socrates engages a young man named Glaucon as to the nature of enlightened, versus unenlightened, perception. Socrates teaches in a way that has become known as the "Socratic method." First, he asks Glaucon a question. Glaucon then gives his best answer to the question. Through further questioning, rather than direct teaching, Socrates gets Glaucon to admit that his answer might not have been the best one after all. More questions lead to*

more "answers," each in turn to be called into question once again. *Frustrating though it may be, Socrates' main objective was to help his students reach* aporia, *a state of knowing that one does not know. Many would argue that knowledge is the science of what is known, but to Socrates, knowing that we may never have the answers to some very abstract questions was in itself one of the highest forms of knowing. Some tentative answers are reached in this dialogue between Socrates and Glaucon, however. Based on the allegory Socrates offers as an example, he and Glaucon are able to reach some conclusions as to the nature of enlightenment. And though not directly political, the final lines of the dialogue do show some connection to politics, since the conclusions reached by Socrates and Glaucon have important ramifications for both the governors and those governed by them.*

Plato's dialogues are in fact arguments. This one, taken from Plato's *Republic,* concerns an argument Socrates wishes to make about the nature of enlightened perception. By questioning Glaucon about this concept, and probing Glaucon's answers most carefully, often "answering" Glaucon's response with another question, Socrates makes his own point of view apparent to the reader.

Coming to Terms with the Reading:

Before reading/rereading Plato's *The Allegory of the* Cave, it is best to have a firm grasp on the meanings of the following terms:

1. Platonic dialogue
2. figure/allegory
3. premise/conclusion
4. inference
5. philosophers/governors
6. the "good"

THE ALLEGORY OF THE CAVE
Plato

1   And now, I said, let me show in a figure how far our nature is enlightened or unenlightened:— Behold! human beings living in an underground den, which has a mouth open towards the light and reaching all along the den; here they have been from their childhood, and have their legs and necks chained so that they cannot move, and can only see before them, being prevented by the chains from turning round their heads. Above and behind them a fire is blazing at a distance, and between the fire and the prisoners there is a raised way; and you will see, if you look, a low wall built along the way, like the screen which marionette players have in front of them, over which they show the puppets.

SOCRATES, GLAUCON.
The den, the prisoners:
the light at a distance;

I see.

And do you see, I said, men passing along the wall carrying all sorts of vessels, and statues and figures of animals made of wood and stone and various materials, which appear over the wall? Some of them are talking, others silent.

the low wall, and the
moving figures of which
the shadows are seen
on the opposite wall of
the den.

You have shown me a strange image, and they are strange prisoners.

5   Like ourselves, I replied; and they see only their own shadows, or the shadows of one another, which the fire throws on the opposite wall of the cave?

True, he said; how could they see anything but the shadows if they were never allowed to move their heads?

And of the objects which are being carried in like manner they would only see the shadows?

Yes, he said.

And if they were able to converse with one another, would they not suppose that they were naming what was actually before them?

10   Very true.

"Allegory of the Cave," by Plato, reprinted from *A World of Ideas: Essential Readings for College Writers,* edited by Lee A. Jacobs and translated by Benjamin Jowett (1990), St. Martin's Press.

And suppose further that the prison had an echo which came from the other side, would they not be sure to fancy when one of the passers-by spoke that the voice which they heard came from the passing shadow?

The prisoners would mistake the shadows for realities.

No question, he replied.

To them, I said, the truth would be literally nothing but the shadows of the images.

That is certain.

15   And now look again, and see what will naturally follow if the prisoners are released and disabused of their error. At first, when any of them is liberated and compelled suddenly to stand up and turn his neck round and walk and look towards the light, he will suffer sharp pains; the glare will distress him, and he will be unable to see the realities of which in his former state he had seen the shadows; and then conceive someone saying to him, that what he saw before was an illusion, but that

And when released, they would still persist in maintaining the superior truth of the shadows.

now, when he is approaching nearer to being and his eye is turned towards more real existence, he has a clearer vision—what will be his reply? And you may further imagine that his instructor is pointing to the objects as they pass and requiring him to name them,—will he not be perplexed? Will he not fancy that the shadows which he formerly saw are truer than the objects which are now shown to him?

Far truer.

And if he is compelled to look straight at the light, will he not have a pain in his eyes which will make him turn away to take refuge in the objects of vision which he can see, and which he will conceive to be in reality clearer than the things which are now being shown to him?

True, he said.

And suppose once more, that he is reluctantly dragged up a steep and rugged ascent, and held fast until he is forced into the presence of the sun himself, is he not likely to be pained and irritated? When he approaches the light his eyes will be dazzled, and he will not be able to see anything at all of what are now called realities.

When dragged upwards, they would be dazzled by excess of light.

20   Not all in a moment, he said.

He will require to grow accustomed to the sight of the upper world. And first he will see the shadows best, next the reflections of men and other objects in the water, and then the objects themselves; then he will gaze upon the light of the moon and the stars and the spangled heaven; and he will see the sky and the stars by night better than the sun or the light of the sun by day?

Certainly.

Last of all he will be able to see the sun, and not mere reflections of him in the water, but he will see him in his own proper place, and not in another; and he will contemplate him as he is.

Certainly.

25   He will then proceed to argue that this is he who gives the season and the years, and is the guardian of

At length they will see the sun and understand his nature.

all that is in the visible world, and in a certain way the cause of all things which he and his fellows have been accustomed to behold?

Clearly, he said, he would first see the sun and then reason about him.

And when he remembered his old habitation, and the wisdom of the den and his fellow prisoners, do you not suppose that he would felicitate himself on the change, and pity them?

They would then pity their old companions of the den.

Certainly, he would.

And if they were in the habit of conferring honors among themselves on those who were quickest to observe the passing shadows and to remark which of them went before, and which followed after, and which were together; and who were therefore best able to draw conclusions as to the future, do you think that he would care for such honors and glories, or envy the possessors of them? Would he not say with Homer,

30   Better to be the poor servant of a poor master, and to endure anything, rather than think as they do and live after their manner?

Yes, he said, I think that he would rather suffer anything than entertain these false notions and live in this miserable manner.

Imagine once more, I said, such an one coming suddenly out of the sun to be replaced in his old situation; would he not be certain to have his eyes full of darkness?

To be sure, he said.

And if there were a contest, and he had to compete in measuring the shadows with the prisoners who had never moved out of the den, while his sight was still weak, and before his eyes had become steady (and the time which would be needed to acquire this new

But when they returned to the den, they would see much worse than those who had never left it.

habit of sight might be very considerable), would he not be ridiculous? Men would say of him that up he went and down he came without his eyes; and that it was better not even to think of ascending; and if any one tried to loose another and lead him up to the light, let them only catch the offender, and they would put him to death.

35   No question, he said.

The prison is the world of sight, the light of the fire is the sun.

This entire allegory, I said, you may now append, dear Glaucon, to the previous argument; the prison house is the world of sight, the light of the fire is the sun, and you will not misapprehend me if you interpret the journey upwards to be the ascent of the soul into the intellectual world according to my poor belief, which, at your desire, I have expressed—whether rightly or wrongly God knows. But, whether true or false, my opinion is that in the world of knowledge the idea of good appears last of all, and is seen only with an effort; and, when seen, is also inferred to be the universal author of all things beautiful and right, parent of light and of the lord of light in this visible world, and the immediate source of reason and truth in the intellectual; and that this is the power upon which he who would act rationally either in public or private life must have his eye fixed.

I agree, he said, as far as I am able to understand you.

Moreover, I said, you must not wonder that those who attain to this beatific vision are unwilling to descend to human affairs; for their souls are ever hastening into the upper world where they desire to dwell; which desire of theirs is very natural, if our allegory may be trusted.

Yes, very natural.

40

Nothing extraordinary in the philosopher being unable to see in the dark.

And is there anything surprising in one who passes from divine contemplations to the evil state of man, misbehaving himself in a ridiculous manner; if, while his eyes are blinking and before he has become accustomed to the surrounding darkness, he is compelled to fight in courts of law, or in other places, about the images or the shadows of images of justice, and is endeavoring to meet the conceptions of those who have never yet seen absolute justice?

Anything but surprising, he replied.

The eyes may be blinded in two ways, by excess or by defect of light.

Anyone who has common sense will remember that the bewilderments of the eyes are of two kinds, and arise from two causes, either from coming out of the light or from going into the light, which is true of the mind's eye, quite as much as of the bodily eye; and he who remembers this when he sees anyone whose vision is perplexed and weak, will not be too ready to laugh; he will first ask whether that soul of man has come out of the brighter life, and is unable to see because unaccustomed to the dark, or having turned from darkness to the day is dazzled by excess of light. And he will count the one happy in his condition and state of being, and he will pity the other; or, if he have a mind to laugh at the soul which comes from below into the light, there will be more reason in this than in the laugh which greets him who returns from above out of the light into the den.

That, he said, is a very just distinction.

But then, if I am right, certain professors of edu- *The conversion of the* cation must be wrong when they say that they can put *soul is the turning* a knowledge into the soul which was not there before, *round the eye from* like sight into blind eyes. *darkness to light.*

45   They undoubtedly say this, he replied.

Whereas, our argument shows that the power and capacity of learning exists in the soul already; and that just as the eye was unable to turn from darkness to light without the whole body, so too the instrument of knowledge can only by the movement of the whole soul be turned from the world of becoming into that of being, and learn by degrees to endure the sight of being, and of the brightest and best of being, or in other words, of the good.

Very true.

And must there not be some art which will effect conversion in the easiest and quickest manner; not implanting the faculty of sight, for that exists already, but has been turned in the wrong direction, and is looking away from the truth?

Yes, he said, such an art may be presumed.

50   And whereas the other so-called virtues of the soul seem to be akin to bodily qualities, for even when they are not originally innate they can be implanted later by habit and exercise, the virtue of wisdom more *The virtue of wisdom* than anything else contains a divine element which *has a divine power* always remains, and by this conversion is rendered use- *which may be turned* ful and profitable; or, on the other hand, hurtful and *either towards good or* useless. Did you never observe the narrow intelligence *towards evil.* flashing from the keen eye of a clever rogue—how eager he is, how clearly his paltry soul sees the way to his end; he is the reverse of blind, but his keen eyesight is forced into the service of evil, and he is mischievous in proportion to his cleverness?

Very true, he said.

But what if there had been a circumcision of such natures in the days of their youth; and they had been severed from those sensual pleasures, such as eating and drinking, which, like leaden weights, were attached to them at their birth, and which drag them down and turn the vision of their souls upon the things that are below—if, I say, they had been released from these impediments and turned in the opposite direction, the very same faculty in them would have seen the truth as keenly as they see what their eyes are turned to now.

Very likely.

Yes, I said; and there is another thing which is likely, or rather a necessary inference from what has preceded, that neither the uneducated and uninformed of the

Neither the uneducated nor the over-educated will be good servants of the State.

truth, nor yet those who never make an end of their education, will be able ministers of State; not the former, because they have no single aim of duty which is the rule of all their actions, private as well as public; nor the latter, because they will not act at all except upon compulsion, fancying that they are already dwelling apart in the islands of the blessed.

55   Very true, he replied.

Then, I said, the business of us who are the founders of the State will be to compel the best minds to attain that knowledge which we have already shown to be the greatest of all—they must continue to ascend until they arrive at the good; but when they have ascended and seen enough we must not allow them to do as they do now.

What do you mean?

Men should ascend to the upper world, but they should also return to the lower.

I mean that they remain in the upper world: but this must not be allowed; they must be made to descend again among the prisoners in the den, and partake of their labors and honors, whether they are worth having or not.

But is not this unjust? he said; ought we to give them a worse life, when they might have a better?

60   You have again forgotten, my friend, I said, the intention of the legislator, who did not aim at making any one class in the State happy above the rest; the happiness was to be in the whole State, and he held the citizens together by persuasion and necessity, making them benefactors of the State, and therefore benefactors of one another; to this end he created them, not to please themselves, but to be his instruments in binding up the State.

True, he said, I had forgotten.

Observe, Glaucon, that there will be no injustice in com- *The duties of*
pelling our philosophers to have a care and providence of oth- *philosophers.*
ers; we shall explain to them that in other States, men of their
class are not obliged to share in the toils of politics: and this is reasonable, for they
grow up at their own sweet will, and the government would rather not have
them. Being self-taught, they cannot be expected to show any gratitude for a
culture which they have never received. But we have brought you into the world
to be rulers of the hive, kings of yourselves and of the other citizens, and have
educated you far better and more perfectly than they have been educated, and
you are better able to share in the double duty. Wherefore each of you, when his
turn comes, must go down to the general underground
abode, and get the habit of seeing in the dark. When   *Their obligations to their*
you have acquired the habit, you will see ten thousand   *country will induce*
                                                         them to take part in her
times better than the inhabitants of the den, and you   *government.*
will know what the several images are, and what they
represent, because you have seen the beautiful and just and good in their truth.
And thus our State, which is also yours, will be a reality, and not a dream only,
and will be administered in a spirit unlike that of other States, in which men fight
with one another about shadows only and are distracted in the struggle for power,
which in their eyes is a great good. Whereas the truth is that the State in which
the rulers are most reluctant to govern is always the best and most quietly governed, and the State in which they are most eager, the worst.

Quite true, he replied.

And will our pupils, when they hear this, refuse to take their turn at the toils
of State, when they are allowed to spend the greater part of their time with one
another in the heavenly light?

Impossible, he answered; for they are just men, and   *They will be willing but*
the commands which we impose upon them are just;   *not anxious to rule.*
there can be no doubt that every one of them will take
office as a stern necessity, and not after the fashion of our present rulers of State.

Yes, my friend, I said; and there lies the point. You must contrive for your
future rulers another and a better life than that of a ruler, and then you may
have a well-ordered State; for only in the State which
offers this, will they rule who are truly rich, not in sil-   *The statesman must be*
                                                             provided with a better
ver and gold, but in virtue and wisdom, which are the   *life than that of a ruler;*
true blessings of life. Whereas if they go to the admin-   *and then he will not*
istration of public affairs, poor and hungering after   *covet office.*

65

their own private advantage, thinking that hence they are to snatch the chief good, order there can never be; for they will be fighting about office, and the civil and domestic broils which thus arise will be the ruin of the rulers themselves and of the whole State.

Most true, he replied.

And the only life which looks down upon the life of political ambition is that of true philosophy. Do you know of any other?

Indeed, I do not, he said.

READING/WRITING ASSISTS

Thesis (and its counterargument):

Unusually, Socrates' **thesis** and its **counterargument** are stated in the first independent clause of the first sentence in this dialogue. Though it is not yet clear what Socrates means by "enlightened" or "unenlightened," his argument, from its very beginning organizes itself around these two important words. Notice how Socrates, rather than making an overt case for humankind's nature as either "enlightened" or "unenlightened," instead leaves the question open, at least as his argument begins.

The Shape of the Argument:

"Mapping" the structure of an argument can help us better understand the argument itself, while also showing us new models for shaping our own arguments in essay form. Plato's argument is structured in a way now seldom seen for making any argument, a way that has become associated with the very name of Plato itself: the **dialogue**. A dialogue is a discussion between two or more people. In this dialogue, as in Plato's other dialogues, Socrates, Plato's teacher in ancient Greece, leads the dialogue. But his "pupil" for this lesson is not Plato; it is Glaucon. Though the speech of neither Socrates nor Glaucon is marked in the dialogue, it is easy enough to differentiate between the two speakers: Socrates speaks most often and at the greatest length; Glaucon responds. So be clear: Who is the "I" of this dialogue and who is the "he"? To better understand Socrates' argument contained within this dialogue, it best to outline the entire text, paragraph by paragraph:

Paragraph 1:   Notice the "either . . . or" structure of the first clause of
                      the first sentence in the dialogue. Why do you suppose

Socrates refuses to take a stand for either, when it is clear from the following lines in the first paragraph that he will make an argument?

Paragraphs 2–12:   Philosophic arguments, and arguments more generally, are based on **premises**, a proposition upon which an argument is based or from which a conclusion is drawn. Socrates decides to relate the most basic premise of his argument on a "figure," in this case an **allegory**. An allegory is a symbolic representation, the apparent or superficial sense of which both parallels and illustrates a deeper sense. In what ways does an allegory of a cave and its dweller's perceptions parallel and illustrate the nature of human enlightenment or lack thereof?

Paragraphs 13–14:   Conclusion drawn from the premise and Glaucon's agreement with it.

Paragraphs 15–34:   What follows from the premise:
Conclusion #1:_____
Conclusion #2:_____

Paragraphs 35–46:   The "lesson" of the figure or allegory. What lesson is learned from Socrates' figure?

Paragraphs 47–54:   How to put the lesson of the figure into practice. Socrates refers to these lessons as **inferences**, that is, conclusions based on evidence and/or **deductive reasoning**:
Inference #1:_____
Inference #2:_____

Paragraphs 55–69:   Additional inferences as to the enlightenment of governors and how this enlightenment will better serve both the governed and future generations of governors. State in your own words what is inferred at the conclusion of this dialogue.

Rhetorical Moves:

Jung used one extended case study to make his argument; Socrates uses one example too, but an example given in the form of an allegory. How does an **allegory** differ from an **analogy**? The structure of Socrates' argument in this dialogue is truly ingenuous, in that from the premise of his "figure" or allegory, Socrates goes on to draw conclusion after conclusion for the remainder of this text.

UNIT 6

Conclusion seems to lead to conclusion as Socrates guides his pupil Glaucon over the direct, but many would argue uphill, terrain of his argument. Do the conclusions of Socrates' argument follow from his premise as surely as Glaucon's responses would seem to indicate? Is Socrates' argument as airtight as it seems? Can you find any gaps in the argument?

Look up the words **imply** and **infer** in the dictionary. Socrates says that certain conclusions can be **inferred** from his premises (paragraph 53). Does his premise **imply** anything?

YUKIO MISHIMA

Born in Tokyo and originally named Hiraoka Kimitake, Yukio Mishima (1925–1970) changed his name so his demanding father would not know he wrote. Until 1937, he was raised primarily by his paternal grandmother, with whom the family was living at the time. During his early years, his mother was permitted to see him only to feed him. With his father's approval, his grandmother instilled the ancient values of samurai in her young grandson, teaching him to exercise complete control over his mind and body.

Mishima only left his grandmother when she became very ill at 62 years of age. An infirmity prevented Mishima from entering combat during World War I, so he worked during the war in an aircraft factory instead. After World War I, he studied law at the University of Tokyo. In 1949, he published Confessions of a Mask, *which chronicled the discovery of his homosexuality and his experiences with sadomasochism. Nevertheless, when his mother, who desperately wanted to see her son married with family, was incorrectly diagnosed with terminal cancer in 1958, Mishima married 19-year-old Yoko Sugiyama.*

Over the years, Mishima became ever more deeply attached to the patriotism of imperial Japan, particularly the values of samurai. He felt that modern Japan was losing touch with ancient values and becoming spiritually empty as a result. In 1968, he founded the Shield Society, a private army of 100 youths dedicated to the revival of Bushido, the samurai knightly code of honor. In 1970, in an effort to return Japan to pre-war nationalistic ideals, he and some of his followers seized control of a military headquarters in Ichigaya, demanding the resignation of Japan's prime minister. When this plot failed, Mishima committed seppuku *(ritual disembowelment), with his sword on November 25, 1970.*

On the morning of his death, Mishima delivered to his publisher the final pages of his masterpiece tetralogy, The Sea of Fertility, *the author's account of the Japanese experience in the twentieth century. Mishima was three times nominated for the Nobel Prize for Literature.*

UNIT 6

PATRIOTISM
Yukio Mishima
Translated by Geoffrey W. Sargent

I

1   On the twenty-eighth of February, 1936 (on the third day, that is, of the February 26 Incident), Lieutenant Shinji Takeyama of the Konoe Transport Battalion—profoundly disturbed by the knowledge that his closest colleagues had been with the mutineers from the beginning, and indignant at the imminent prospect of Imperial troops attacking Imperial troops—took his officer's sword and ceremoniously disemboweled himself in the eight-mat room of his private residence in the sixth block of Aoba-chō, in Yotsuya Ward. His wife, Reiko, followed him, stabbing herself to death. The lieutenant's farewell note consisted of one sentence: "Long live the Imperial Forces." His wife's, after apologies for her unfilial conduct in thus preceding her parents to the grave, concluded: "The day which, for a soldier's wife, had to come, has come. . . ." The last moments of this heroic and dedicated couple were such as to make the gods themselves weep. The lieutenant's age, it should be noted, was thirty-one, his wife's twenty-three; and it was not half a year since the celebration of their marriage.

II

Those who saw the bride and bridegroom in the commemorative photograph—perhaps no less than those actually present at the lieutenant's wedding—had exclaimed in wonder at the bearing of this handsome couple. The lieutenant, majestic in military uniform, stood protectively beside his bride, his right hand resting upon his sword, his officer's cap held at his left side. His expression was severe, and his dark brows and wide-gazing eyes well conveyed the clear integrity of youth. For the beauty of the bride in her white over-robe no comparisons

"Patriotism," by Yukio Mishima, reprinted from *Death in Midsummer* (1966), by permission of New Directions Publishing Corp.

were adequate. In the eyes, round beneath soft brows, in the slender, finely shaped nose, and in the full lips, there was both sensuousness and refinement. One hand, emerging shyly from a sleeve of the over-robe, held a fan, and the tips of the fingers, clustering delicately, were like the bud of a moonflower.

After the suicide, people would take out this photograph and examine it and sadly reflect that too often there was a curse on these seemingly flawless unions. Perhaps it was no more than imagination, but looking at the picture after the tragedy it almost seemed as if the two young people before the gold lacquered screen were gazing, each with equal clarity, at the deaths which lay before them.

Thanks to the good offices of their go-between, Lieutenant General Ozeki, they had been able to set themselves up in a new home at Aoba-chō in Yotsuya. "New home" is perhaps misleading. It was an old three-room rented house backing onto a small garden. As neither the six- nor the four-and-a-half-mat room downstairs was favored by the sun, they used the upstairs eight-mat room as both bedroom and guest room. There was no maid, so Reiko was left alone to guard the house in her husband's absence.

5   The honeymoon trip was dispensed with on the grounds that these were times of national emergency. The two of them had spent the first night of their marriage at this house. Before going to bed, Shinji, sitting erect on the floor with his sword laid before him, had bestowed upon his wife a soldierly lecture. A woman who had become the wife of a soldier should know and resolutely accept that her husband's death might come at any moment. It could be tomorrow. It could be the day after. But, no matter when it came—he asked—was she steadfast in her resolve to accept it? Reiko rose to her feet, pulled open a drawer of the cabinet, and took out what was the most prized of her new possessions, the dagger her mother had given her. Returning to her place, she laid the dagger without a word on the mat before her, just as her husband had laid his sword. A silent understanding was achieved at once, and the lieutenant never again sought to test his wife's resolve.

In the first few months of her marriage Reiko's beauty grew daily more radiant, shining serene like the moon after rain.

As both were possessed of young, vigorous bodies, their relationship was passionate. Nor was this merely a matter of the night. On more than one occasion, returning home straight from maneuvers, and begrudging even the time it took to remove his mud-splashed uniform, the lieutenant had pushed his wife to the floor almost as soon as he had entered the house. Reiko was equally ardent in her response. For a little more or a little less than a month, from the first night of their marriage Reiko knew happiness, and the lieutenant, seeing this, was happy too.

Reiko's body was white and pure, and her swelling breasts conveyed a firm and chaste refusal; but, upon consent, those breasts were lavish with their intimate, welcoming warmth. Even in bed these two were frighteningly and awe-somely serious. In the very midst of wild, intoxicating passions, their hearts were sober and serious.

By day the lieutenant would think of his wife in the brief rest periods between training; and all day long, at home, Reiko would recall the image of her husband. Even when apart, however, they had only to look at the wedding photograph for their happiness to be once more confirmed. Reiko felt not the slightest surprise that a man who had been a complete stranger until a few months ago should now have become the sun about which her whole world revolved.

10   All these things had a moral basis, and were in accordance with the Education Rescript's injunction that "husband and wife should be harmonious." Not once did Reiko contradict her husband, nor did the lieutenant ever find reason to scold his wife. On the god shelf below the stairway, alongside the tablet from the Great Ise Shrine, were set photographs of their Imperial Majesties, and regularly every morning, before leaving for duty, the lieutenant would stand with his wife at this hallowed place and together they would bow their heads low. The offering water was renewed each morning, and the sacred sprig of *sasaki* was always green and fresh. Their lives were lived beneath the solemn protection of the gods and were filled with an intense happiness, which set every fiber in their bodies trembling.

III

Although Lord Privy Seal Saitō's house was in their neighborhood, neither of them heard any noise of gunfire on the morning of February 26. It was a bugle, sounding muster in the dim, snowy dawn, when the ten-minute tragedy had already ended, which first disrupted the lieutenant's slumbers. Leaping at once from his bed, and without speaking a word, the lieutenant donned his uniform, buckled on the sword held ready for him by his wife, and hurried swiftly out into the snow-covered streets of the still darkened morning. He did not return until the evening of the twenty-eighth.

Later, from the radio news, Reiko learned the full extent of this sudden eruption of violence. Her life throughout the subsequent two days was lived alone, in complete tranquillity, and behind locked doors.

In the lieutenant's face, as he hurried silently out into the snowy morning, Reiko had read the determination to die. If her husband did not return, her own decision was made: she too would die. Quietly she attended to the disposition of her personal possessions. She chose her sets of visiting kimonos as keepsakes for friends of her schooldays, and she wrote a name and address on the stiff paper wrapping in which each was folded. Constantly admonished by her husband never to think of the morrow, Reiko had not even kept a diary and was now denied the pleasure of assiduously rereading her record of the happiness of the past few months and consigning each page to the fire as she did so. Ranged across the top of the radio were a small china dog, a rabbit, a squirrel, a bear, and a fox. There were also a small vase and a water pitcher. These comprised Reiko's one and only collection. But it would hardly do, she imagined, to give such things as keepsakes. Nor again would it be quite proper to ask specifically for them to be included in the coffin. It seemed to Reiko, as these thoughts passed through her mind, that the expression on the small animals' faces grew even more lost and forlorn.

Reiko took the squirrel in her hand and looked at it. And then, her thoughts turning to a realm far beyond these childlike affections, she gazed up into the distance at the great sunlike principle which her husband embodied. She was ready, and happy, to be hurtled along to her destruction in that gleaming sun chariot—but now, for these few moments of solitude, she allowed herself to luxuriate in this innocent attachment to trifles. The time when she had genuinely loved these things, however, was long past. Now she merely loved the memory of having once loved them, and their place in her heart had been filled by more intense passions, by a more frenzied happiness. . . . For Reiko had never, even to herself, thought of those soaring joys of the flesh as a mere pleasure. The February cold, and the icy touch of the china squirrel, had numbed Reiko's slender fingers; yet, even so, in her lower limbs, beneath the ordered repetition of the pattern which crossed the skirt of her trim *meisen* kimono, she could feel now, as she thought of the lieutenant's powerful arms reaching out toward her, a hot moistness of the flesh which defied the snows.

15   She was not in the least afraid of the death hovering in her mind. Waiting alone at home, Reiko firmly believed that everything her husband was feeling or thinking now, his anguish and distress, was leading her—just as surely as the power in his flesh—to a welcome death. She felt as if her body could melt away with ease and be transformed to the merest fraction of her husband's thought.

Listening to the frequent announcements on the radio, she heard the names of several of her husband's colleagues mentioned among those of the insurgents. This was news of death. She followed the developments closely, wondering anxiously, as the situation became daily more irrevocable, why no Imperial ordinance was sent down, and watching what had at first been taken as a movement to restore the nation's honor come gradually to be branded with the infamous name of mutiny. There was no communication from the regiment. At any moment, it seemed, fighting might commence in the city streets, where the remains of the snow still lay.

Toward sundown on the twenty-eighth Reiko was startled by a furious pounding on the front door. She hurried downstairs. As she pulled with fumbling fingers at the bolt, the shape dimly outlined beyond the frosted-glass panel made no sound, but she knew it was her husband. Reiko had never known the bolt on the sliding door to be so stiff. Still it resisted. The door just would not open.

In a moment, almost before she knew she had succeeded, the lieutenant was standing before her on the cement floor inside the porch, muffled in a khaki greatcoat, his top boots heavy with slush from the street. Closing the door behind him, he returned the bolt once more to its socket. With what significance, Reiko did not understand.

"Welcome home."

20 Reiko bowed deeply, but her husband made no response. As he had already unfastened his sword and was about to remove his greatcoat, Reiko moved around behind to assist. The coat, which was cold and damp and had lost the odor of horse dung it normally exuded when exposed to the sun, weighed heavily upon her arm. Draping it across a hanger, and cradling the sword and leather belt in her sleeves, she waited while her husband removed his top boots and then followed behind him into the "living room." This was the six-mat room downstairs.

Seen in the clear light from the lamp, her husband's face, covered with a heavy growth of bristle, was almost unrecognizably wasted and thin. The cheeks were hollow, their luster and resilience gone. In his normal good spirits he would have changed into old clothes as soon as he was home and have pressed her to get supper at once, but now he sat before the table still in his uniform, his head drooping dejectedly. Reiko refrained from asking whether she should prepare the supper.

After an interval the lieutenant spoke.

"I knew nothing. They hadn't asked me to join. Perhaps out of consideration, because I was newly married. Kanō, and Homma too, and Yamaguchi."

Reiko recalled momentarily the faces of high-spirited young officers, friends of her husband, who had come to the house occasionally as guests.

25 "There may be an Imperial ordinance sent down tomorrow. They'll be posted as rebels, I imagine. I shall be in command of a unit with orders to attack them. . . . I can't do it. It's impossible to do a thing like that."

He spoke again.

"They've taken me off guard duty, and I have permission to return home for one night. Tomorrow morning, without question, I must leave to join the attack. I can't do it, Reiko."

Reiko sat erect with lowered eyes. She understood clearly that her husband had spoken of his death. The lieutenant was resolved. Each word, being rooted in death, emerged sharply and with powerful significance against this dark, unmovable background. Although the lieutenant was speaking of his dilemma, already there was no room in his mind for vacillation.

However, there was a clarity, like the clarity of a stream fed from melting snows, in the silence which rested between them. Sitting in his own home after the long two-day ordeal, and looking across at the face of his beautiful wife, the lieutenant was for the first time experiencing true peace of mind. For he had at once known, though she said nothing, that his wife divined the resolve which lay beneath his words.

30   "Well, then . . ." The lieutenant's eyes opened wide. Despite his exhaustion they were strong and clear, and now for the first time they looked straight into the eyes of his wife. "Tonight I shall cut my stomach."

Reiko did not flinch.

Her round eyes showed tension, as taut as the clang of a bell.

"I am ready," she said. "I ask permission to accompany you."

The lieutenant felt almost mesmerized by the strength of those eyes. His words flowed swiftly and easily, like the utterances of a man in delirium, and it was beyond his understanding how permission in a matter of such weight could be expressed so casually.

35   "Good. We'll go together. But I want you as a witness, first, for my own suicide. Agreed?"

When this was said a sudden release of abundant happiness welled up in both their hearts. Reiko was deeply affected by the greatness of her husband's trust in her. It was vital for the lieutenant, whatever else might happen, that there should be no irregularity in his death. For that reason there had to be a witness. The fact that he had chosen his wife for this was the first mark of his trust. The second, and even greater mark, was that though he had pledged that they should die together he did not intend to kill his wife first—he had deferred her death to a time when he would no longer be there to verify it. If the lieutenant had been a suspicious husband, he would doubtless, as in the usual suicide pact, have chosen to kill his wife first.

When Reiko said, "I ask permission to accompany you," the lieutenant felt these words to be the final fruit of the education which he had himself given his wife, starting on the first night of their marriage, and which had schooled her, when the moment came, to say what had to be said without a shadow of hesitation. This flattered the lieutenant's opinion of himself as a self-reliant man. He was not so romantic or conceited as to imagine that the words were spoken spontaneously, out of love for her husband.

With happiness welling almost too abundantly in their hearts, they could not help smiling at each other. Reiko felt as if she had returned to her wedding night.

Before her eyes was neither pain nor death. She seemed to see only a free and limitless expanse opening out into vast distances.

40   "The water is hot. Will you take your bath now?"

"Ah yes, of course."

"And supper . . . ?"

The words were delivered in such level, domestic tones that the lieutenant came near to thinking, for the fraction of a second, that everything had been a hallucination.

"I don't think we'll need supper. But perhaps you could warm some sake?"

45   "As you wish."

As Reiko rose and took a *tanzen* gown from the cabinet for after the bath, she purposely directed her husband's attention to the opened drawer. The lieutenant rose, crossed to the cabinet, and looked inside. From the ordered array of paper wrappings he read, one by one, the addresses of the keepsakes. There was no grief in the lieutenant's response to this demonstration of heroic resolve. His heart was filled with tenderness. Like a husband who is proudly shown the childish purchases of a young wife, the lieutenant, overwhelmed by affection, lovingly embraced his wife from behind and implanted a kiss upon her neck.

Reiko felt the roughness of the lieutenant's unshaven skin against her neck. This sensation, more than being just a thing of this world, was for Reiko almost the world itself, but now—with the feeling that it was soon to be lost forever—it had freshness beyond all her experience. Each moment had its own vital strength, and the senses in every corner of her body were reawakened. Accepting her husband's caresses from behind, Reiko raised herself on the tips of her toes, letting the vitality seep through her entire body.

"First the bath, and then, after some sake . . . lay out the bedding upstairs, will you?"

The lieutenant whispered the words into his wife's ear. Reiko silently nodded.

50   Flinging off his uniform, the lieutenant went to the bath. To faint background noises of slopping water Reiko tended the charcoal brazier in the living
room and began the preparations for warming the sake.

Taking the *tanzen,* a sash, and some underclothes, she went to the bathroom
to ask how the water was. In the midst of a coiling cloud of steam the lieutenant
was sitting cross-legged on the floor, shaving, and she could dimly discern the
rippling movements of the muscles on his damp, powerful back as they responded
to the movement of his arms.

There was nothing to suggest a time of any special significance. Reiko, going
busily about her tasks, was preparing side dishes from odds and ends in stock.
Her hands did not tremble. If anything, she managed even more efficiently and
smoothly than usual. From time to time, it is true, there was a strange throbbing
deep within her breast. Like distant lightning, it had a moment of sharp intensity and then vanished without trace. Apart from that, nothing was in any way
out of the ordinary.

The lieutenant, shaving in the bathroom, felt his warmed body miraculously
healed at last of the desperate tiredness of the days of indecision and filled—in
spite of the death which lay ahead—with pleasurable anticipation. The sound of
his wife going about her work came to him faintly. A healthy physical craving,
submerged for two days, reasserted itself.

The lieutenant was confident there had been no impurity in that joy they had
experienced when resolving upon death. They had both sensed at that moment—
though not, of course, in any clear and conscious way—that those permissible
pleasures which they shared in private were once more beneath the protection of
Righteousness and Divine Power, and of a complete and unassailable morality. On
looking into each other's eyes and discovering there an honorable death, they had
felt themselves safe once more behind steel walls which none could destroy, encased
in an impenetrable armor of Beauty and Truth. Thus, so far from seeing any
inconsistency or conflict between the urges of his flesh and the sincerity of his patriotism, the lieutenant was even able to regard the two as parts of the same thing.

55   Thrusting his face close to the dark, cracked, misted wall mirror, the lieutenant
shaved himself with great care. This would be his death face. There must be no
unsightly blemishes. The clean-shaven face gleamed once more with a youthful
luster, seeming to brighten the darkness of the mirror. There was a certain elegance, he even felt, in the association of death with this radiantly healthy face.

Just as it looked now, this would become his death face! Already, in fact, it had
half departed from the lieutenant's personal possession and had become the bust

UNIT 6

above a dead soldier's memorial. As an experiment he closed his eyes tight. Every-thing was wrapped in blackness, and he was no longer a living, seeing creature.

Returning from the bath, the traces of the shave glowing faintly blue beneath his smooth cheeks, he seated himself beside the now well-kindled charcoal bra-zier. Busy though Reiko was, he noticed, she had found time lightly to touch up her face. Her cheeks were gay and her lips moist. There was no shadow of sad-ness to be seen. Truly, the lieutenant felt, as he saw this mark of his young wife's passionate nature, he had chosen the wife he ought to have chosen.

As soon as the lieutenant had drained his sake cup he offered it to Reiko. Reiko had never before tasted sake, but she accepted without hesitation and sipped timidly.

"Come here," the lieutenant said.

60   Reiko moved to her husband's side and was embraced as she leaned backward across his lap. Her breast was in violent commotion, as if sadness, joy, and the potent sake were mingling and reacting within her. The lieutenant looked down into his wife's face. It was the last face he would see in this world, the last face he would see of his wife. The lieutenant scrutinized the face minutely with the eyes of a traveler bidding farewell to splendid vistas which he will never revisit. It was a face he could not tire of looking at—the features regular yet not cold, the lips lightly closed with a soft strength. The lieutenant kissed those lips, unthinkingly. And suddenly, though there was not the slightest distortion of the face into the unsightliness of sobbing, he noticed that tears were welling slowly from beneath the long lashes of the closed eyes and brimming over into the glistening stream.

When, a little later, the lieutenant urged that they should move to the up-stairs bedroom, his wife replied that she would follow after taking a bath. Climb-ing the stairs alone to the bedroom, where the air was already warmed by the gas heater, the lieutenant lay down on the bedding with arms outstretched and legs apart. Even the time at which he lay waiting for his wife to join him was no later and no earlier than usual.

He folded his hands beneath his head and gazed at the dark boards of the ceil-ing in the dimness beyond the range of the standard lamp. Was it death he was now waiting for? Or a wild ecstasy of the senses? The two seemed to overlap, almost as if the object of this bodily desire was death itself. But, however that might be, it was certain that never before had the lieutenant tasted such total freedom.

There was the sound of a car outside the window. He could hear the screech of its tires skidding in the snow piled at the side of the street. The second of its horn reechoed from nearby walls. . . . Listening to these noises he had the feel-

ing that the house rose like a solitary island in the ocean of a society going as rest-
lessly about its business as ever. All around, vastly and untidily, stretched the
country for which he grieved. He was to give his life for it. But would that great
country, with which he was prepared to remonstrate to the extent of destroying
himself, take the slightest heed of his death? He did not know; and it did not matter. His was a battlefield without glory, a battlefield where none could display
deeds of valor: it was the front line of the spirit.

Reiko's footsteps sounded on the stairway. The steep stairs in this old house
creaked badly. There were fond memories in that creaking, and many a time,
while waiting in bed, the lieutenant had listened to its welcome sound. At the
thought that he would hear it no more he listened with intense concentration,
striving for every corner of every moment of this precious time to be filled with
the sound of those soft footfalls on the creaking stairway. The moments seemed
transformed to jewels, sparkling with inner light.

65   Reiko wore a Nagoya sash about the waist of her *yukata,* but as the lieutenant
reached toward it, its redness sobered by the dimness of the light, Reiko's hand
moved to his assistance and the sash fell away, slithering swiftly to the floor. As
she stood before him, still in her *yukata,* the lieutenant inserted his hands through
the side slits beneath each sleeve, intending to embrace her as she was; but at the
touch of his finger tips upon the warm naked flesh, and as the armpits closed
gently about his hands, his whole body was suddenly aflame.

In a few moments the two lay naked before the glowing gas heater.

Neither spoke the thought, but their hearts, their bodies, and their pounding breasts blazed with the knowledge that this was the very last time. It was as
if the words "The Last Time" were spelled out, in invisible brushstrokes, across
every inch of their bodies.

The lieutenant drew his wife close and kissed her vehemently. As their tongues
explored each other's mouths, reaching out into the smooth, moist interior, they
felt as if the still-unknown agonies of death had tempered their senses to the
keenness of red-hot steel. The agonies they could not yet feel, the distant pains
of death, had refined their awareness of pleasure.

"This is the last time I shall see your body," said the lieutenant. "Let me look
at it closely." And, tilting the shade on the lampstand to one side, he directed the
rays along the full length of Reiko's outstretched form.

70   Reiko lay still with her eyes closed. The light from the low lamp clearly revealed
the majestic sweep of her white flesh. The lieutenant, not without a touch of ego-
centricity, rejoiced that he would never see this beauty crumble in death.

At his leisure, the lieutenant allowed the unforgettable spectacle to engrave itself upon his mind. With one hand he fondled the hair, with the other he softly stroked the magnificent face, implanting kisses here and there where his eyes lingered. The quiet coldness of the high, tapering forehead, the closed eyes with their long lashes beneath faintly etched brows, the set of the finely shaped nose, the gleam of teeth glimpsed between full, regular lips, the soft cheeks and the small, wise chin . . . these things conjured up in the lieutenant's mind the vision of a truly radiant death face, and again and again he pressed his lips tight against the white throat—where Reiko's own hand was soon to strike—and the throat reddened faintly beneath his kisses. Returning to the mouth he laid his lips against it with the gentlest of pressures, and moved them rhythmically over Reiko's with the light rolling motion of a small boat. If he closed his eyes, the world became a rocking cradle.

Wherever the lieutenant's eyes moved his lips faithfully followed. The high swelling breasts, surmounted by nipples like the buds of a wild cherry, hardened as the lieutenant's lips closed about them. The arms flowed smoothly downward from each side of the breast, tapering toward the wrists, yet losing nothing of their round-ness or symmetry, and at their tips were those delicate fingers which had held the fan at the wedding ceremony. One by one, as the lieutenant kissed them, the fingers withdrew behind their neighbor as if in shame. . . . The natural hollow curving between the bosom and the stomach carried in its lines a suggestion not only of soft-ness but of resilient strength, and while it gave forewarning of the rich curves spread-ing outward from here to the hips it had, in itself, an appearance only of restraint and proper discipline. The whiteness and richness of the stomach and hips was like milk brimming in a great bowl, and the sharply shadowed dip of the navel could have been the fresh impress of a raindrop, fallen there that very moment. Where the shadows gathered more thickly, hair clustered, gentle and sensitive, and as the agi-tation mounted in the now no longer passive body there hung over this region a scent like the smoldering of fragrant blossoms, growing steadily more pervasive.

At length, in a tremendous voice, Reiko spoke.

"Show me. . . . Let me look too, for the last time."

75   Never before had he heard from his wife's lips so strong and unequivocal a request. It was as if something which her modesty had wished to keep hidden to the end had suddenly burst its bonds of constraint. The lieutenant obediently lay back and surrendered himself to his wife. Lithely she raised her white, trem-bling body, and—burning with an innocent desire to return to her husband what he had done for her—placed two white fingers on the lieutenant's eyes, which gazed fixedly up at her, and gently stroked them shut.

Suddenly overwhelmed by tenderness, her cheeks flushed by a dizzying uprush of emotion, Reiko threw her arms about the lieutenant's close-cropped head. The bristly hairs rubbed painfully against her breast, the prominent nose was cold as it dug into her flesh, and his breath was hot. Relaxing her embrace, she gazed down at her husband's masculine face. The severe brows, the closed eyes, the splendid bridge of the nose, the shapely lips drawn firmly together . . . the blue, clean-shaven cheeks reflecting the light and gleaming smoothly. Reiko kissed each of these. She kissed the broad nape of the neck, the strong erect shoulders, the powerful chest with its twin circles like shields and its russet nipples. In the armpits, deeply shadowed by the ample flesh of the shoulders and chest, a sweet and melancholy odor emanated from the growth of hair, and in the sweetness of this odor was contained, somehow, the essence of young death. The lieutenant's naked skin glowed like a field of barley, and everywhere the muscles showed in sharp relief, converging on the lower abdomen about the small, unassuming navel. Gazing at the youthful, firm stomach, modestly covered by a vigorous growth of hair, Reiko thought of it as it was soon to be, cruelly cut by the sword, and she laid her head upon it, sobbing pity, and bathed it with kisses.

At the touch of his wife's tears upon his stomach the lieutenant felt ready to endure with courage the cruelest agonies of his suicide.

What ecstasies they experienced after these tender exchanges may well be imagined. The lieutenant raised himself and enfolded his wife in a powerful embrace, her body now limp with exhaustion after her grief and tears. Passionately they held their faces close, rubbing cheek against cheek. Reiko's body was trembling. Their breasts, moist with sweat, were tightly joined, and every inch of the young and beautiful bodies had become so much one with the other that it seemed impossible there should ever again be a separation. Reiko cried out. From the heights they plunged into the abyss, and from the abyss they took wing and soared once more to dizzying heights. The lieutenant panted like the regimental standard-bearer on a route march. . . . As one cycle ended, almost immediately a new wave of passion would be generated, and together—with no trace of fatigue—they would climb again in a single breathless movement to the very summit.

IV

When the lieutenant at last turned away, it was not from weariness. For one thing, he was anxious not to undermine the considerable strength he would need in carrying out his suicide. For another, he would have been sorry to mar the sweetness of these last memories by overindulgence.

UNIT 6

80   Since the lieutenant had clearly desisted, Reiko too, with her usual compliance, followed his example. The two lay naked on their backs, with fingers interlaced, staring fixedly at the dark ceiling. The room was warm from the heater, and even when the sweat had ceased to pour from their bodies they felt no cold. Outside, in the hushed night, the sounds of passing traffic had ceased. Even the noises of the trains and streetcars around Yotsuya station did not penetrate this far. After echoing through the region bounded by the moat, they were lost in the heavily wooded park fronting the broad driveway before Akasaka Palace. It was hard to believe in the tension gripping this whole quarter, where the two factions of the bitterly divided Imperial Army now confronted each other, poised for battle.

Savoring the warmth glowing within themselves, they lay still and recalled the ecstasies they had just known. Each moment of the experience was relived. They remembered the taste of kisses which had never wearied, the touch of naked flesh, episode after episode of dizzying bliss. But already, from the dark boards of the ceiling, the face of death was peering down. These joys had been final, and their bodies would never know them again. Not that joy of this intensity—and the same thought had occurred to them both—was ever likely to be reexperienced, even it they should live on to old age.

The feel of their fingers intertwined—this too would soon be lost. Even the wood-grain patterns they now gazed at on the dark ceiling boards would be taken from them. They could feel death edging in, nearer and nearer. There could be no hesitation now. They must have the courage to reach out to death themselves, and to seize it.

"Well, let's make our preparations," said the lieutenant. The note of determination in the words was unmistakable, but at the same time Reiko had never heard her husband's voice so warm and tender.

After they had risen, a variety of tasks awaited them.

85   The lieutenant, who had never once before helped with the bedding, now cheerfully slid back the door of the closet, lifted the mattress across the room by himself, and stowed it away inside.

Reiko turned off the gas heater and put away the lamp standard. During the lieutenant's absence she had arranged this room carefully, sweeping and dusting it to a fresh cleanness, and now—if one overlooked the rosewood table drawn into one corner—the eight-mat room gave all the appearance of a reception room ready to welcome an important guest.

"We've seen some drinking here, haven't we? With Kanō and Homma and Noguchi . . ."

"Yes, they were great drinkers, all of them."

"We'll be meeting them before long, in the other world. They'll tease us, I imagine, when they find I've brought you with me."

90 Descending the stairs, the lieutenant turned to look back into this calm, clean room, now brightly illuminated by the ceiling lamp. There floated across his mind the faces of the young officers who had drunk there, and laughed, and innocently bragged. He had never dreamed then that he would one day cut open his stomach in this room.

In the two rooms downstairs husband and wife busied themselves smoothly and serenely with their respective preparations. The lieutenant went to the toilet, and then to the bathroom to wash. Meanwhile Reiko folded away her husband's padded robe, placed his uniform tunic, his trousers, and a newly cut bleached loincloth in the bathroom, and set out sheets of paper on the living-room table for the farewell notes. Then she removed the lid from the writing box and began rubbing ink from the ink tablet. She had already decided upon the wording of her own note.

Reiko's fingers pressed hard upon the cold gilt letters of the ink tablet, and the water in the shallow well at once darkened, as if a black cloud had spread across it. She stopped thinking that this repeated action, this pressure from her fingers, this rise and fall of faint sound, was all and solely for death. It was a routine domestic task, a simple paring away of time until death should finally stand before her. But somehow, in the increasingly smooth motion of the tablet rubbing on the stone, and in the scent from the thickening ink, there was unspeakable darkness.

Neat in his uniform, which he now wore next to his skin, the lieutenant emerged from the bathroom. Without as word he seated himself at the table, bolt upright, took a brush in his hand, and started undecidedly at the paper before him.

Reiko took a white silk kimono with her and entered the bathroom. When she reappeared in the living room, clad in the white kimono and with her face lightly made up, the farewell note lay completed on the table beneath the lamp. The thick black brushstrokes said simply:

95 "Long Live the Imperial Forces—Army Lieutenant Takeyama Shinji."

While Reiko sat opposite him writing her own note, the lieutenant gazed in silence, intensely serious, at the controlled movement of his wife's pale fingers as they manipulated the brush.

With their respective notes in their hands—the lieutenant's sword strapped to his side, Reiko's small dagger thrust into the sash of her white kimono—the two of them stood before the god shelf and silently prayed. Then they put out all the downstairs lights. As he mounted the stairs the lieutenant turned his head and gazed back at the striking, white-clad figure of his wife, climbing behind him, with lowered eyes, from the darkness beneath.

The farewell notes were laid side by side in the alcove of the upstairs room. They wondered whether they ought not to remove the hanging scroll, but since it had been written by their go-between, Lieutenant General Ozeki, and consisted, moreover, of two Chinese characters signifying "Sincerity," they left it where it was. Even if it were to become stained with splashes of blood, they felt that the lieutenant general would understand.

The lieutenant, sitting erect with his back to the alcove, laid his sword on the floor before him.

100   Reiko sat facing him, a mat's width away. With the rest of her so severely white the touch of rouge on her lips seemed remarkably seductive.

Across the dividing mat they gazed intently into each other's eyes. The lieutenant's sword lay before his knees. Seeing it, Reiko recalled their first night and was overwhelmed with sadness. The lieutenant spoke, in a hoarse voice:

"As I have no second to help me I shall cut deep. It may look unpleasant, but please do not panic. Death of any sort is a fearful thing to watch. You must not be discouraged by what you see. Is that all right?"

"Yes."

Reiko nodded deeply.

105   Looking at the slender white figure of his wife the lieutenant experienced a bizarre excitement. What he was about to perform was an act in his public capacity as a soldier, something he had never previously shown his wife. It called for a resolution equal to the courage to enter battle; it was a death of no less degree and quality than death in the front line. It was his conduct on the battlefield that he was now to display.

Momentarily the thought led the lieutenant to a strange fantasy. A lonely death on the battlefield, a death beneath the eyes of his beautiful wife . . . in the sensation that he was now to die in these two dimensions, realizing an impossible union of them both, there was sweetness beyond words. This must be the very pinnacle of good fortune, he thought. To have every moment of his death observed by those beautiful eyes—it was like being borne to death on a gentle, fragrant breeze. There was some special favor here. He did not understand precisely what it was, but it was a domain unknown to others: a dispensation granted to no one else had been permitted to himself. In the radiant bridelike figure of his white-robed wife the lieutenant seemed to see a vision of all those things he had loved and for which he was to lay down his life—the Imperial Household, the Nation, the Army Flag. All these, no less than the wife who sat before him, were presences observing him closely with clear and never-faltering eyes.

Reiko too was gazing intently at her husband, so soon to die, and she thought that never in this world had she seen anything so beautiful. The lieutenant always looked well in uniform, but now, as he contemplated death with severe brows and firmly closed lips, he revealed what was perhaps masculine beauty at its most superb.

"It's time to go," the lieutenant said at last.

Reiko bent her body low to the mat in a deep bow. She could not raise her face. She did not wish to spoil her makeup with tears, but the tears could not be held back.

110   When at length she looked up she saw hazily through the tears that her husband had wound a white bandage around the blade of his now unsheathed sword, leaving five or six inches of naked steel showing at the point.

Resting the sword in its cloth wrapping on the mat before him, the lieutenant rose from his knees, resettled himself cross-legged, and unfastened the hooks of his uniform collar. His eyes no longer saw his wife. Slowly, one by one, he undid the flat brass buttons. The dusky brown chest was revealed, and then the stomach. He unclasped his belt and undid the buttons of his trousers. The pure whiteness of the thickly coiled loincloth showed itself. The lieutenant pushed the cloth down with both hands, further to ease his stomach, and then reached for the white-bandaged blade of his sword. With his left hand he massaged his abdomen, glancing downward as he did so.

To reassure himself on the sharpness of his sword's cutting edge the lieutenant folded back the left trouser flap, exposing a little of his thigh, and lightly drew the blade across the skin. Blood welled up in the wound at once, and several streaks of red trickled downward, glistening in the strong light.

It was the first time Reiko had ever seen her husband's blood, and she felt a violent throbbing in her chest. She looked at her husband's face. The lieutenant was looking at the blood with calm appraisal. For a moment—though thinking at the same time that it was hollow comfort—Reiko experienced a sense of relief.

The lieutenant's eyes fixed his wife with an intense, hawklike stare. Moving the sword around to his front, he raised himself slightly on his hips and let the upper half of his body lean over the sword point. That he was mustering his whole strength was apparent from the angry tension of the uniform at his shoulders. The lieutenant aimed to strike deep into the left of his stomach. His sharp eye pierced the silence of the room.

115   Despite the effort he had himself put into the blow, the lieutenant had the impression that someone else had struck the side of his stomach agonizingly

with a thick rod of iron. For a second or so his head reeled and he had no idea what had happened. The five or six inches of naked point had vanished completely into his flesh, and the white bandage, gripped in his clenched fist, pressed directly against his stomach.

He returned to consciousness. The blade had certainly pierced the wall of the stomach, he thought. His breathing was difficult, his chest thumped violently, and in some far deep region, which he could hardly believe was a part of himself, a fearful and excruciating pain came welling up as if the ground had split open to disgorge a boiling stream of molten rock. The pain came suddenly nearer, with terrifying speed. The lieutenant bit his lower lip and stifled an instinctive moan.

Was this *seppuku?*—he was thinking. It was a sensation of utter chaos, as if the sky had fallen on his head and the world was reeling drunkenly. His will power and courage, which had seemed so robust before he made the incision, had now dwindled to something like a single hairlike thread of steel, and he was assailed by the uneasy feeling that he must advance along this thread, clinging to it with desperation. His clenched fist had grown moist. Looking down, he saw that both his hand and the cloth about the blade were drenched in blood. His loincloth too was dyed a deep red. It struck him as incredible that, amidst this terrible agony, things which could be seen could still be seen, and existing things existed still.

The moment the lieutenant thrust the sword into his left side and she saw the deathly pallor fall across his face, like an abruptly lowered curtain, Reiko had to struggle to prevent herself from rushing to his side. Whatever happened, she must watch. She must be a witness. That was the duty her husband had laid upon her. Opposite her, a mat's space away, she could clearly see her husband biting his lip to stifle the pain. The pain was there, with absolute certainty, before her eyes. And Reiko had no means of rescuing him from it.

The sweat glistened on her husband's forehead. The lieutenant closed his eyes, and then opened them again, as if experimenting. The eyes had lost their luster, and seemed innocent and empty like the eyes of a small animal.

120   The agony before Reiko's eyes burned as strong as the summer sun, utterly remote from the grief which seemed to be tearing herself apart within. The pain grew steadily in stature, stretching upward. Reiko felt that her husband had already become a man in a separate world, a man whose whole being had been resolved into pain, a prisoner in a cage of pain where no hand could reach out to him. But Reiko felt no pain at all. Her grief was not pain. As she thought about this, Reiko began to feel as if someone had raised a cruel wall of glass high between herself and her husband.

Ever since her marriage her husband's existence had been her own existence, and every breath of his had been a breath drawn by herself. But now, while her husband's existence in pain was a vivid reality, Reiko could find in this grief of hers no certain proof at all of her own existence.

With only his right hand on the sword the lieutenant began to cut sideways across his stomach. But as the blade became entangled with the entrails it was pushed constantly outward by their soft resilience; and the lieutenant realized that it would be necessary, as he cut, to use both hands to keep the point pressed deep into his stomach. He pulled the blade across. It did not cut as easily as he had expected. He directed the strength of his whole body into his right hand and pulled again. There was a cut of three or four inches.

The pain spread slowly outward from the inner depths until the whole stomach reverberated. It was like the wild clanging of a bell. Or like a thousand bells which jangled simultaneously at every breath he breathed and every throb of his pulse, rocking his whole being. The lieutenant could no longer stop himself from moaning. But by now the blade had cut its way through to below the navel, and when he noticed this he felt a sense of satisfaction, and a renewal of courage.

The volume of blood had steadily increased, and now it spurted from the wound as if propelled by the beat of the pulse. The mat before the lieutenant was drenched red with splattered blood, and more blood overflowed onto it from pools which gathered in the folds of the lieutenant's khaki trousers. A spot, like a bird, came flying across to Reiko and settled on the lap of her white kimono.

125   By the time the lieutenant had at last drawn the sword across to the right side of his stomach, the blade was already cutting shallow and had revealed its naked tip, slippery with blood and grease. But, suddenly stricken by a fit of vomiting, the lieutenant cried out hoarsely. The vomiting made the fierce pain fiercer still, and the stomach, which had thus far remained firm and compact, now abruptly heaved, opening wide its wound, and the entrails burst through as if the wound too were vomiting. Seemingly ignorant of their master's suffering, the entrails gave an impression of robust health and almost disagreeable vitality as they slipped smoothly out and spilled over into the crotch. The lieutenant's head drooped, his shoulders heaved, his eyes opened to narrow slits and a thin trickle of saliva dribbled from his mouth. The gold markings on his epaulets caught the light and glinted.

Blood was scattered everywhere. The lieutenant was soaked in it to his knees, and he sat now in a crumpled and listless posture, one hand on the floor. A raw smell filled the room. The lieutenant, his head drooping, retched repeatedly, and

UNIT 6

the movement showed vividly in his shoulders. The blade of the sword, now pushed back by the entrails and exposed to its tip, was still in the lieutenant's right hand.

It would be difficult to imagine a more heroic sight than that of the lieutenant at this moment, as he mustered his strength and flung back his head. The movement was performed with sudden violence, and the back of his head struck with a sharp crack against the alcove pillar. Reiko had been sitting until now with her face lowered, gazing in fascination at the tide of blood advancing toward her knees, but the sound took her by surprise and she looked up.

The lieutenant's face was not the face of a living man. The eyes were hollow, the skin parched, the once so lustrous cheeks and lips the color of dried mud. The right hand alone was moving. Laboriously gripping the sword, it hovered shakily in the air like the hand of a marionette and strove to direct the point at the base of the lieutenant's throat. Reiko watched her husband make this last, most heartrending, futile exertion. Glistening with blood and grease, the point was thrust at the throat again and again. And each time it missed its aim. The strength to guide it was no longer there. The straying point struck the collar and the collar badges. Although its hooks had been unfastened, the stiff military collar had closed together again and was protecting the throat.

Reiko could bear the sight no longer. She tried to go to her husband's help, but she could not stand. She moved through the blood on her knees, and her white skirts grew deep red. Moving to the rear of her husband, she helped no more than by loosening the collar. The quivering blade at last contacted the naked flesh of the throat. At that moment Reiko's impression was that she herself had propelled her husband forward; but that was not the case. It was a movement planned by the lieutenant himself, his last exertion of strength. Abruptly he threw his body at the blade, and the blade pierced his neck, emerging at the nape. There was a tremendous spurt of blood and the lieutenant lay still, cold blue-tinged steel protruding from his neck at the back.

V

130 Slowly, her socks slippery with blood, Reiko descended the stairway. The upstairs room was now completely still.

Switching on the ground-floor lights, she checked the gas jet and the main gas plug and poured water over the smoldering, half-buried charcoal in the brazier. She stood before the upright mirror in the four-and-a-half mat room and held up her skirts. The bloodstains made it seem as if a bold, vivid pattern was printed across the lower half of her white kimono. When she sat down before the mirror, she was conscious of the dampness and coldness of her husband's blood in the region of her thighs, and she shivered. Then, for a long while, she lingered over her toilet preparations. She applied the rouge generously to her cheeks, and her lips too she painted heavily. This was no longer makeup to please her husband. It was makeup for the world which she would leave behind, and there was a touch of the magnificent and the spectacular in her brushwork. When she rose, the mat before the mirror was wet with blood. Reiko was not concerned about this.

Returning from the toilet, Reiko stood finally on the cement floor of the porchway. When her husband had bolted the door here last night it had been in preparation for death. For a while she stood immersed in the consideration of a simple problem. Should she now leave the bolt drawn? If she were to lock the door, it could be that the neighbors might not notice their suicide for several days. Reiko did not relish the thought of their two corpses putrefying before discovery. After all, it seemed, it would be best to leave it open. . . . She released the bolt, and also drew open the frosted-glass door a fraction. . . . At once a chill wind blew in. There was no sign of anyone in the midnight streets, and stars glittered ice-cold through the trees in the large house opposite.

Leaving the door as it was, Reiko mounted the stairs. She had walked here and there for some time and her socks were no longer slippery. About halfway up, her nostrils were already assailed by a peculiar smell.

The lieutenant was lying on his face in a sea of blood. The point protruding from his neck seemed to have grown even more prominent than before. Reiko walked heedlessly across the blood. Sitting beside the lieutenant's corpse, she stared intently at the face, which lay on one cheek on the mat. The eyes were opened wide, as if the lieutenant's attention had been attracted by something. She raised the head, folding it in her sleeve, wiped the blood from the lips, and bestowed a last kiss.

135   Then she rose and took from the closet a new white blanket and a waist cord. To prevent any derangement of her skirts, she wrapped the blanket about her waist and bound it there firmly with the cord.

Reiko sat herself on a spot about one foot distant from the lieutenant's body. Drawing the dagger from her sash, she examined its dully gleaming blade intently, and held it to her tongue. The taste of the polished steel was slightly sweet.

Reiko did not linger. When she thought how the pain which had previously opened such a gulf between herself and her dying husband was now to become a part of her own experience, she saw before her only the joy of herself entering a realm her husband had already made his own. In her husband's agonized face there had been something inexplicable which she was seeing for the first time. Now she would solve that riddle. Reiko sensed that at last she too would be able to taste the true bitterness and sweetness of that great moral principle in which her husband believed. What had until now been tasted only faintly through her husband's example she was about to savor directly with her own tongue.

Reiko rested the point of the blade against the base of her throat. She thrust hard. The wound was only shallow. Her head blazed, and her hands shook uncontrollably. She gave the blade a strong pull sideways. A warm substance flooded into her mouth, and everything before her eyes reddened, in a vision of spouting blood. She gathered her strength and plunged the point of the blade deep into her throat.

LEVELS OF READING

Summary:

Pay attention to the **literal** meaning of the text. Briefly describe the narrative of Yukio Mishima's "Patriotism." Who tells the story? What happens? Is the conclusion to the story foreshadowed in any way? Concentrate on the highlights; avoid too much detail when summarizing. Again, drawing a simple outline of the main points of the text will help you better analyze the text at other levels of interpretation.

Analysis:

Find what you believe is **symbolic** in the text. For instance, why are Reiko's beauty and the enthusiastic lovemaking of this couple significant in terms of the story's outcome? In what ways is the lieutenant's patriotism symbolized? Find any other symbols you think are important in the story and explain the meaning of these symbols. With the help of the background material provided about Yukio Mishima and his world, make an argument about this text, and include the mention of the more **figurative** aspects of the text when making points in defense of your argument.

Application:

Apply Plato's theory of the governor to "Patriotism." Outline an argument you wish to make about this literary text using Plato's theory to help you explain what some part of the story may mean. The "part" of the text you choose to analyze may include any of the following: a character, a setting, a symbol or symbols, an important change, a motivation, a goal, a result. Consider the following as possibilities, but explore other original interpretations too:

- Plato's dialogue is especially helpful in trying to explain the idea of human enlightenment and the role of that enlightenment in government. Would you describe the lieutenant as an enlightened governor? If so, what characteristics indicate his enlightenment? If not, what characteristics interfere with his enlightenment?
- Are there any parallels between Socrates' death by poison and the lieutenant's ritual suicide? To what extent and in what ways are the deaths of these two men culturally determined?
- Can the story of the lieutenant's suicide be in any way construed as an **allegory** of Japanese politics? Consider information in Mishima's biographical sketch when looking at his story in this way.
- Is the lieutenant's vision **clear** in the Platonic sense? In your view, is he inside or outside of the cave?

UNIT 6

MICHEL DE MONTAIGNE

Michel de Montaigne (1533–1592) was born in his father's chateau thirty miles east of Bordeaux, France. His father was a prosperous French merchant in fish and wine; his mother's family was of Spanish Jewish origin and equally well-to-do. The children of the family were brought up in the Catholic faith. Though the era was one of religious controversy, sharpened by a religious civil war that lasted most of Montaigne's life, the family was tolerant. Five of the children, including Michel, remained Catholic for life, while three others followed the Protestant faith.

Until he was six years old, Montaigne was schooled by a tutor who spoke Latin but no French. When he was sent to the Collège de Guyenne in Bordeaux to complete his education, it was said that his Latin was better than his teachers'.

In 1565 Montaigne married Françoise de la Chassaigne. The couple had six children together; however, only one survived beyond infancy.

Montaigne served as a member of the French Parliament for many years in addition to handling the considerable responsibility of running his family's vast estate and business interests. Exhausted at thirty-eight, he retired to his estate and began to write. In 1580 the first two books of Essays *were published in Bordeaux. The first three-book edition of his essays was published in Paris in 1588. Until the end of his life, at sixty, Montaigne continued to revise the 1588 edition of his essays, adding another quarter in length to the volume in the form of marginalia.*

WE TASTE NOTHING PURE
Michel de Montaigne

1 ^AThe weakness of our condition makes it impossible for things to come into our experience in their natural simplicity and purity. The elements that we enjoy are corrupted, and the metals likewise; and gold must be debased by some other material to fit it for our service.

^CNeither virtue thus in its simple form, which Aristo and Pyrrho and also the Stoics made the end of life, nor the sensual pleasure of the Cyrenaics and Aristippus could be serviceable to life without admixture.

^AOf the pleasures and good things that we have, there is not one exempt from some mixture of pain and discomfort:

^BRight from the fount of these delights of ours
A bitter something rises, which chokes us 'mid the flowers.
LUCRETIUS

Our utmost sensual pleasure has an air of groaning and lament about it. Wouldn't you say that it is dying of anguish? Indeed, when we forge a picture of it at its highest point, we deck it with sickly and painful epithets and qualities: languor, softness, weakness, faintness, *morbidezza*: a great testimony to their consanguinity and consubstantiality.

5 ^CProfound joy has more seriousness than gaiety about it; extreme and full contentment, more soberness than sprightliness. *Even felicity, unless it tempers itself, overwhelms* [Seneca]. Happiness racks us.

^AThat is what an old Greek verse says, in this sense: "The gods sell us all the good things they give us." That is to say, they give us none pure and perfect, none that we do not buy at the price of some evil.

^CToil and pleasure, very unlike in nature, are nevertheless joined by I know not what natural association. Socrates says that some god tried to lump together and confuse pain and pleasure, but that, not being able to come out successful, he decided to couple them, at least by the tail.

^BMetrodorus used to say that in sadness there is some alloy of pleasure. I do not know whether he meant something else, but for my part I indeed imagine that there is design, consent, and pleasure in feeding one's melancholy; I mean beyond the ambition that can also be involved. There is some shadow of daintiness and luxury that smiles on us and flatters us in the very lap of melancholy. Are there not some natures that feed on it?

> A certain kind of pleasure 'tis to weep.
> OVID

^CAnd one Attalus, in Seneca, says that the memory of our lost friends is agreeable to us like the bitterness in a wine that is too old—

> Boy, that serve old Falernian wine,
> Pour me a bitterer cup for mine
> CATULLUS

—and like apples sweetly tart.

10   ^BNature reveals this confusion to us; painters hold that the movements and wrinkles of the face that serve for weeping serve also for laughing. In truth, before one or the other is completely expressed, watch the progress of the painting: you are in doubt toward which one it is going. And the extremity of laughter is mingled with tears. ^C*There is no evil without its compensation* [Seneca].

When I imagine man besieged by desirable delights—let us put the case that all his members should be forever seized with a pleasure like that of generation at its most excessive point—I feel him sink under the weight of his delight, and I see him wholly incapable of supporting a pleasure so pure, so constant, and so universal. In truth, he flees it when he is in it, and naturally hastens to escape it, as from a place where he cannot stand firm, where he is afraid of sinking.

^BWhen I confess myself religiously to myself, I find that the best goodness I have has some tincture of vice. And I fear that Plato in his most verdant virtue (I who am as sincere and loyal an admirer of it, and of virtues of similar stamp, as a man can be), if he had listened to it closely—and he did listen to it closely—would have sensed in it some false note of human admixture, but an obscure note, perceptible only to himself. Man, in all things and throughout, is but patchwork and motley.

^AThe very laws of justice cannot subsist without some mixture of injustice. And Plato says that those men are undertaking to cut off the Hydra's head who

aspire to remove all drawbacks and disadvantages from the laws. *Every exemplary punishment has in it some injustice against individuals, which is compensated by public utility,* says Tacitus.

^BIt is likewise true that for the uses of life and for the service of public business there may be excess in the purity and perspicacity of our minds. That penetrating clarity has too much subtlety and curiosity in it. These must be weighted and blunted to make them more obedient to example and practice, and thickened and obscured to relate them to this shadowy and earthy life. Therefore common and less high-strung minds are found to be more fit and more successful for conducting affairs. And the lofty and exquisite ideas of philosophy are found to be inept in practice. That acute vivacity of mind, that supple and restless versatility, disturbs our negotiations. Human enterprises must be handled more roughly and superficially, and a good and great part of them left for the rights of fortune. There is no need to light up affairs so deeply and so subtly. You get lost considering so many contrasting aspects and diverse shapes: ^C*in revolving mutually contradictory things, their minds had become stupefied* [Livy].

15 This is what the ancients say of Simonides: because his imagination presented him—on the question that King Hiero had put to him, to answer which he had had many days to meditate—with diverse acute and subtle considerations, being in doubt which was the most probable, he totally despaired of the truth.

^BHe who seeks and embraces all the circumstances and consequences impedes his choice. An average intelligence conducts equally well, and suffices to carry out, things of great or little weight. Note that the best managers are those who least know how to tell us how they are so, and that the self-satisfied storytellers most often do nothing worth while. I know one great talker and very excellent portrayer of every sort of managing, who has very pitifully let the revenue of a hundred thousand francs slip through his hands. I know another who speaks and gives advice better than any man in his council, and there is no better show of mind and competence in the world; however, in practice, his servants find him quite different; I mean without taking bad luck into account.

LEVELS OF READING

Summary:

Find the main idea of Montaigne's essay, "We Taste Nothing Pure." Do the examples he gives help to substantiate his argument? Why or why not? What conclusions, if any, does Montaigne draw as a result of his argument?

Analysis:

Find what you believe is **inferred** in this essay. Montaigne, like Dr. Martin Luther King, Jr., in "Letter from Birmingham City Jail" cites many classical Greek and Latin sources as examples to lend support to his thoughts. Is there any relationship between Montaigne's use of these antique sources and King's? What effect does the use of these sources lend to the overall argument?

Application:

Apply Plato's theory of enlightenment to "We Taste Nothing Pure." Outline an argument you wish to make about Montaigne's essay using Plato's ideas to help you explain what some part of the essay may mean. The "part" of the text you choose to analyze may include any of the following: a source, a reference, an example, an inference. Consider the following as possibilities, but explore other original interpretations too:

- Sense perception is pertinent to both Plato's allegory (vision) and Montaigne's title (taste). Is "tasting nothing pure" akin to seeing shadows in a cave?
- Montaigne, like Plato, derives a **conclusion** from his **premises**. In what ways to the premises and conclusions of these writers relate to one another?
- Is Montaigne enlightened in the Platonic sense?
- Montaigne has two direct references to Plato in this essay. Is there any indication in "The Allegory of the Cave" that Plato is aware of the vice admixed with his virtue?

Start Your Own Argument:

At the conclusion of "The Allegory of the Cave," in paragraph 61, Socrates says that "the State in which the rulers are the most reluctant to govern is always the best and most quietly governed, and the state in which they are the most eager, the worst." Montaigne has similar thoughts on this topic. Can you think of any present-day states that fit the bill as examples of "the best" and "the worst" States (i.e., nations) according to Socrates and Montaigne?

ARGUMENT OFFERING A HYPOTHETICAL EXAMPLE AS EVIDENCE/COMPARISON AND CONTRAST (WOOLF) AND ARGUMENT DIRECTLY ENGAGING THE ARGUMENT OF ANOTHER WRITER/CITATION (WALKER)

Chapter 1 of Virginia Woolf's *A Room of One's Own*, offers the hypothetical examples of "Oxbridge" and "Fernham" as a means of both making her point and exposing an injustice. Most of the body of this essay records her visits to these colleges and the stark contrast between them. What conclusions do these visits help her—and us—to reach?

VIRGINIA WOOLF

Born Virginia Stephen, Virginia Woolf (1882–1941) was one of four children in a well-to-do London family, whose ancestors included generations of writers. Her mother was Julia Jackson Duckworth, a member of a noted publishing family, and her father was Leslie Stephen, a literary critic. Woolf was educated at home by her father. She was a precocious child and, despite the lack of the formal education allowed her brothers, began to write as early as age six. To educate herself, she made ample use of the family library and closely followed the educations of her brothers.

Her mother died when Woolf was in her early teens. She was sexually abused by her half brother, Gerald Duckworth. In 1904, her father died after a long battle with cancer. Following her father's death, Woolf moved with her two brothers and sister to a house in Bloomsbury, which became central to the activities of what was to become known as the Bloomsbury Group. But when her brother Toby died in 1906, Woolf suffered a prolonged mental breakdown.

On August 10, 1912, Virginia Stephen married Leonard Woolf at St. Pancras Registry Office in London. A series of "nervous ailments" followed, sending Leonard Woolf to seek the opinions of medical experts. Though Woolf's psychological ailments persisted, she wrote prolifically, producing an array of novels and essays, and growing fame.

When she was relatively well, Woolf and her husband were very much a part of the Bloomsbury circle, a clique of authors and artists all experimenting with the new "modernism" flourishing after the First World War. Extremely upset by the carnage of this war and its political aftermath, Woolf lived most of her life in dire fear of a second world war, which she (correctly) viewed as an inevitable consequence of the peace forged after the first war. These fears, and her deep sense of pacifism, coupled with a feeling that men were making most of the decisions so detrimental to world peace, stirred Woolf's nascent feminism and informed most of her writing.

Nevertheless, the depression, headaches, and other psychological ailments continued, with only brief respites. Though she kept working, her sense of gloom persisted, and on March 8, 1941, Virginia Woolf committed suicide by walking into the river Ouse. As added insurance, she had weighted the pockets of her coat with stones.

A prolific writer of novels and essays, her work was all published by the Hogarth Press, which she founded with her husband. The Hogarth Press also published T.S. Eliot's The Waste Land *(1922), and the complete twenty-four-volume English translation of the works of Sigmund Freud.*

In the following essay, Virginia Woolf's use of two devices is particularly striking. First, she is one of the foremost innovators in what is now called "stream of consciousness" narration. With this technique, a writer follows the true path of the narrator's mind, the thoughts of which are nowhere near as linear as most fictional narration would have us believe. Though digressive, the thoughts are all related, even if, as Freud had shown, they seem accidental. The second important device Woolf employs in this essay is an extended compare/contrast example. Using the comparison/contrast between Oxbridge and Fernham, Woolf makes an important point about educational institutions in England in the 1920s. That point blossoms into branches concerning the relationship between money and education, between education and the sexes, between the sexes and writing. Beyond all of the above, Woolf is a powerfully descriptive writer, as this chapter from *A Room of One's Own* demonstrates. Pay special attention to her use of adjectives and adverbs.

Coming to Terms with the Reading:

Before reading/rereading Virginia Woolf's *A Room of One's Own,* it is best to have a firm grasp on the meanings of the following terms:

1. Oxbridge
2. Fernham
3. beadle
4. fellows/scholars
5. androgynous

CHAPTER ONE FROM *A ROOM OF ONE'S OWN*
Virginia Woolf

1 But, you may say, we asked you to speak about women and fiction—what has that got to do with a room of one's own? I will try to explain. When you asked me to speak about women and fiction I sat down on the banks of a river and began to wonder what the words meant. They might mean simply a few remarks about Fanny Burney; a few more about Jane Austen; a tribute to the Brontës and a sketch of Haworth Parsonage under snow; some witticisms if possible about Miss Mitford; a respectful allusion to George Eliot; a reference to Mrs. Gaskell and one would have done. But at second sight the words seemed not so simple. The title women and fiction might mean, and you may have meant it to mean, women and what they are like; or it might mean women and the fiction that they write; or it might mean women and the fiction that is written about them; or it might mean that somehow all three are inextricably mixed together and you want me to consider them in that light. But when I began to consider the subject in this last way, which seemed the most interesting, I soon saw that it had one fatal drawback. I should never be able to come to a conclusion. I should never be able to fulfil what is, I understand, the first duty of a lecturer—to hand you after an hour's discourse a nugget of pure truth to wrap up between the pages of your notebooks and keep on the mantel-piece for ever. All I could do was to offer you an opinion upon one minor point—a woman must have money and a room of her own if she is to write fiction; and that, as you will see, leaves the great problem of the true nature of woman and the true nature of fiction unsolved. I have shirked the duty of coming to a conclusion upon these two questions—women and fiction remain, so far as I am concerned, unsolved problems. But in order to make some amends I am going to do what I can to show you how I arrived at this opinion about the room and the money. I am going to develop in your presence as fully and freely as I can the train of thought which led me to think this. Perhaps if I lay bare the ideas, the prejudices, that lie behind this statement you will find that they have some bearing upon women and some upon fiction. At any rate, when a subject is highly

controversial—and any question about sex is that—one cannot hope to tell the truth. One can only show how one came to hold whatever opinion one does hold. One can only give one's audience the chance of drawing their own conclusions as they observe the limitations, the prejudices, the idiosyncrasies of the speaker. Fiction here is likely to contain more truth than fact. Therefore I propose, making use of all the liberties and licences of a novelist, to tell you the story of the two days that preceded my coming here—how, bowed down by the weight of the subject which you have laid upon my shoulders, I pondered it, and made it work in and out of my daily life. I need not say that what I am about to describe has no existence; Oxbridge is an invention; so is Fernham; "I" is only a convenient term for somebody who has no real being. Lies will flow from my lips, but there may perhaps be some truth mixed up with them; it is for you to seek out this truth and to decide whether any part of it is worth keeping. If not, you will of course throw the whole of it into the wastepaper basket and forget all about it.

Here then was I (call me Mary Beton, Mary Seton, Mary Carmichael or by any name you please—it is not a matter of any importance) sitting on the banks of a river a week or two ago in fine October weather, lost in thought. That collar I have spoken of, women and fiction, the need of coming to some conclusion on a subject that raises all sorts of prejudices and passions, bowed my head to the ground. To the right and left bushes of some sort, golden and crimson, glowed with the colour, even it seemed burnt with the heat, of fire. On the further bank the willows wept in perpetual lamentation, their hair about their shoulders. The river reflected whatever it chose of sky and bridge and burning tree, and when the undergraduate had oared his boat through the reflections they closed again, completely, as if he had never been. There one might have sat the clock round lost in thought. Thought— to call it by a prouder name than it deserved—had let its line down into the stream. It swayed, minute after minute, hither and thither among the reflections and the weeds, letting the water lift it and sink it, until—you know the little tug—the sudden conglomeration of an idea at the end of one's line: and then the cautious hauling of it in, and the careful laying of it out? Alas, laid on the grass how small, how insignificant this thought of mine looked; the sort of fish that a good fisherman puts back into the water so that it may grow fatter and be one day worth cooking and eating. I will not trouble you with that thought now, though if you look carefully you may find it for yourselves in the course of what I am going to say.

But however small it was, it had, nevertheless, the mysterious property of its kind—put back into the mind, it became at once very exciting, and important; and as it darted and sank, and flashed hither and thither, set up such a wash and tumult of ideas that it was impossible to sit still. It was thus that I found myself walking with extreme rapidity across a grass plot. Instantly a man's figure rose to intercept me. Nor did I at first understand that the gesticulations of a curious-looking object, in a cut-away coat and evening shirt, were aimed at me. His face expressed horror and indignation. Instinct rather than reason came to my help; he was a Beadle; I was a woman. This was the turf; there was the path. Only the Fellows and Scholars are allowed here; the gravel is the place for me. Such thoughts were the work of a moment. As I regained the path the arms of the Beadle sank, his face assumed its usual repose, and though turf is better walking than gravel, no very great harm was done. The only charge I could bring against the Fellows and Scholars of whatever the college might happen to be was that in protection of their turf, which has been rolled for 300 years in succession, they had sent my little fish into hiding.

What idea it had been that had sent me so audaciously trespassing I could not now remember. The spirit of peace descended like a cloud from heaven, for if the spirit of peace dwells anywhere, it is in the courts and quadrangles of Oxbridge on a fine October morning. Strolling through those colleges past those ancient halls the roughness of the present seemed smoothed away; the body seemed contained in a miraculous glass cabinet through which no sound could penetrate, and the mind, freed from any contact with facts (unless one trespassed on the turf again), was at liberty to settle down upon whatever meditation was in harmony with the moment. As chance would have it, some stray memory of some old essay about revisiting Oxbridge in the long vacation brought Charles Lamb to mind—Saint Charles, said Thackeray, putting a letter of Lamb's to his forehead. Indeed, among all the dead (I give you my thoughts as they came to me), Lamb is one of the most congenial; one to whom one would have liked to say, Tell me then how you wrote your essays? For his essays are superior even to Max Beerbohm's, I thought, with all their perfection, because of that wild flash of imagination, that lightning crack of genius in the middle of them which leaves them flawed and imperfect, but starred with poetry. Lamb then came to Oxbridge perhaps a hundred years ago. Certainly he wrote an essay—the name escapes me—about the manuscript of one of Milton's poems which he saw here. It was *Lycidas* perhaps, and Lamb wrote how it shocked him to think it possible that any word in *Lycidas* could have been different from what it is. To think of Milton changing the words in that poem seemed to him a sort of sacrilege. This led me to remember what I could of *Lycidas* and to amuse myself with guessing which word it could have been that Milton had altered, and why. It then occurred to me that the very manuscript itself which Lamb had looked at was only a few hundred yards away, so that one could follow Lamb's footsteps across the quadrangle to that famous library where the treasure is kept. Moreover, I recollected, as I put this plan into execution, it is in this famous library that the manuscript of Thackeray's *Esmond* is also preserved. The critics often say that *Esmond* is Thackeray's most perfect novel. But the affectation of the style, with its imitation of the eighteenth century, hampers one, so far as I remember; unless indeed the eighteenth-century style was natural to Thackeray—a fact that one might prove by looking at the manuscript and seeing whether the alterations were for the benefit of the style or of the sense. But then one would have to decide what is style and what is meaning, a question which—but here I was actually at the door which leads into the library itself. I must have opened it, for instantly there issued, like a guardian angel barring the way with a flutter of black gown instead of white wings, a deprecating, silvery, kindly gentleman, who regretted in a low voice as he waved me back that ladies are only admitted to the library if accompanied by a Fellow of the College or furnished with a letter of introduction.

5   That a famous library has been cursed by a woman is a matter of complete indifference to a famous library. Venerable and calm, with all its treasures safe locked within its breast, it sleeps complacently and will, so far as I am concerned, so sleep for ever. Never will I wake those echoes, never will I ask for that hospitality again, I vowed as I descended the steps in anger. Still an hour remained before luncheon, and what was one to do? Stroll on the meadows? sit by the river? Certainly it was a lovely autumn morning; the leaves were fluttering red to the ground; there was no great hardship in doing either. But the sound of music reached my ear. Some service or celebration was going forward. The organ complained magnificently as I passed the chapel door. Even the sorrow of Christianity sounded in that serene air more like the recollection of sorrow than sorrow itself; even the groanings of the ancient organ seemed lapped in peace. I had no wish to enter had I the right, and this time the verger might have stopped me, demanding perhaps my baptismal certificate, or a letter of introduction from the Dean. But the outside of these magnificent buildings is often as beautiful as the inside. Moreover, it was amusing enough to watch the congregation assembling, coming in and going out again, busying themselves at the door of the chapel like bees at the mouth of a hive. Many were in cap and gown; some had tufts of fur on their shoulders; others were wheeled in bath-chairs; others, though not past middle age, seemed creased and crushed into shapes so singular that one was reminded of those giant crabs and crayfish who heave with difficulty across the sand of an aquarium. As I leant against the wall the University indeed seemed a sanctuary in which are preserved rare types which would soon be obsolete if left to fight for existence on the pavement of the Strand. Old stories of old deans and old dons came back to mind, but before I had summoned up courage

to whistle—it used to be said that at the sound of a whistle old Professor———instantly broke into a gallop—the venerable congregation had gone inside. The outside of the chapel remained. As you know, its high domes and pinnacles can be seen, like a sailing-ship always voyaging never arriving, lit up at night and visible for miles, far away across the hills. Once, presumably, this quadrangle with its smooth lawns, its massive buildings, and the chapel itself was marsh too, where the grasses waved and the swine rooted. Teams of horses and oxen, I thought, must have hauled the stone in wagons from far countries, and then with infinite labour the grey blocks in whose shade I was now standing were poised in order one on top of another, and then the painters brought their glass for the windows, and the masons were busy for centuries up on that roof with putty and cement, spade and trowel. Every Saturday somebody must have poured gold and silver out of a leathern purse into their ancient fists, for they had their beer and skittles presumably of an evening. An unending stream of gold and silver, I thought, must have flowed into this court perpetually to keep the stones coming and the masons working; to level, to ditch, to dig and to drain. But it was then the age of faith, and money was poured liberally to set these stones on a deep foundation, and when the stones were raised, still more money was poured in from the coffers of kings and queens and great nobles to ensure that hymns should be sung here and scholars taught. Lands were granted; tithes were paid. And when the age of faith was over and the age of reason had come, still the same flow of gold and silver went on; fellowships were founded; lectureships endowed; only the gold and silver flowed now, not from the coffers of the king, but from the chests of merchants and manufacturers, from the purses of men who had made, say, a fortune from industry, and returned, in their wills, a bounteous share of it to endow more chairs, more lectureships, more fellowships in the university where they had learnt their craft. Hence the libraries and laboratories; the observatories; the splendid equipment of costly and delicate instruments which now stands on glass shelves, where centuries ago the grasses waved and the swine rooted. Certainly, as I strolled round the court, the foundation of gold and silver seemed deep enough; the pavement laid solidly over the wild grasses. Men with trays on their heads went busily from staircase to staircase. Gaudy blossoms flowered in window-boxes. The strains of the gramophone blared out from the rooms within. It was impossible not to reflect—the reflection whatever it may have been was cut short. The clock struck. It was time to find one's way to luncheon.

It is a curious fact that novelists have a way of making us believe that luncheon parties are invariably memorable for something very witty that was said, or for something very wise that was done. But they seldom spare a word for what was eaten. It is part of the novelist's convention not to mention soup and salmon and ducklings, as if soup and salmon and ducklings were of no importance whatsoever, as if nobody ever smoked a cigar or drank a glass of wine. Here, however, I shall take the liberty to defy that convention and to tell you that the lunch on this occasion began with soles, sunk in a deep dish, over which the college cook had spread a counterpane of the whitest cream, save that it was branded here and there with brown spots like the spots on the flanks of a doe. After that came the partridges, but if this suggests a couple of bald, brown birds on a plate you are mistaken. The partridges, many and various, came with all their retinue of sauces and salads, the sharp and the sweet, each in its order; their potatoes, thin as coins but not so hard; their sprouts, foliated as rosebuds but more succulent. And no sooner had the roast and its retinue been done with than the silent serving-man, the Beadle himself perhaps in a milder manifestation, set before us, wreathed in napkins, a confection which rose all sugar from the waves. To call it pudding and so relate it to rice and tapioca would be an insult. Meanwhile the wineglasses had flushed yellow and flushed crimson; had been emptied; had been filled. And thus by degrees was lit, halfway down the spine, which is the seat of the soul, not that hard little electric light which we call brilliance, as it pops in and out upon our lips, but the more profound, subtle and subterranean glow, which is the rich yellow flame of rational intercourse. No need to hurry. No need to sparkle. No need to be anybody but oneself. We are all going to heaven and Vandyck is of the company—in other words, how good life seemed, how sweet its rewards, how trivial this grudge or that grievance, how admirable friendship and the society of one's kind, as, lighting a good cigarette, one sunk among the cushions in the window-seat.

If by good luck there had been an ash-tray handy, if one had not knocked the ash out of the window in default, if things had been a little different from what they were, one would not have seen, presumably, a cat without a tail. The sight of that abrupt and truncated animal padding softly across the quadrangle changed by some fluke of the subconscious intelligence the emotional light for me. It was as if some one had let fall a shade. Perhaps the excellent hock was relinquishing its hold. Certainly, as I watched the Manx cat pause in the middle of the lawn as if it too questioned the universe, something seemed lacking, something seemed different. But what was lacking, what was different, I asked myself, listening to the talk. And to answer that question I had to think myself out of the room, back into the past, before the war indeed, and to set before my eyes the model of another luncheon party held in rooms not very far distant from these; but different. Everything was different. Meanwhile the talk went on among the guests, who were many and young, some of this sex, some of that; it went on swimmingly, it went on agreeably, freely, amusingly. And as it went on I set it against the background of that other talk, and as I matched the two together I had no doubt that one was the descendant, the legitimate heir of the other. Nothing was changed; nothing was different save only—here I listened with all my ears not entirely to what was being said, but to the murmur or current behind it. Yes, that was it— the change was there. Before the war at a luncheon party like this people would have said precisely the same things but they would have sounded different, because in those days they were accompanied by a sort of humming noise, not articulate, but musical, exciting, which changed the value of the words themselves. Could one set that humming noise to words? Perhaps with the help of the poets one could. A book lay beside me and, opening it, I turned casually enough to Tennyson. And here I found Tennyson was singing:

> There has fallen a splendid tear
>   From the passion-flower at the gate.
> She is coming, my dove, my dear;
>   She is coming, my life, my fate;
> The red rose cries, "She is near, she is near;"
>   And the white rose weeps, "She is late;"
> The larkspur listens, "I hear, I hear;"
>   And the lily whispers, "I wait."

Was that what men hummed at luncheon parties before the war? And the women?

> My heart is like a singing bird
>   Whose nest is in a water'd shoot;
> My heart is like an apple tree
>   Whose boughs are bent with thick-set fruit;
> My heart is like a rainbow shell
>   That paddles in a halcyon sea;
> My heart is gladder than all these
>   Because my love is come to me.

Was that what women hummed at luncheon parties before the war?

10   There was something so ludicrous in thinking of people humming such things even under their breath at luncheon parties before the war that I burst out laughing, and had to explain my laughter by pointing at the Manx cat, who did look a little absurd, poor beast, without a tail, in the middle of the lawn. Was he

really born so, or had he lost his tail in an accident? The tail-less cat, though some are said to exist in the Isle of Man, is rarer than one thinks. It is a queer animal, quaint rather than beautiful. It is strange what a difference a tail makes—you know the sort of things one says as a lunch party breaks up and people are finding their coats and hats.

This one, thanks to the hospitality of the host, had lasted far into the afternoon. The beautiful October day was fading and the leaves were falling from the trees in the avenue as I walked through it. Gate after gate seemed to close with gentle finality behind me. Innumerable beadles were fitting innumerable keys into well-oiled locks; the treasure-house was being made secure for another night. After the avenue one comes out upon a road—I forget its name—which leads you, if you take the right turning, along to Fernham. But there was plenty of time. Dinner was not till half-past seven. One could almost do without dinner after such a luncheon. It is strange how a scrap of poetry works in the mind and makes the legs move in time to it along the road. Those words—

> There has fallen a splendid tear
>   From the passion-flower at the gate.
> She is coming, my dove, my dear—

sang in my blood as I stepped quickly along towards Headingley. And then, switching off into the other measure, I sang, where the waters are churned up by the weir:

> My heart is like a singing bird
>   Whose nest is in a water'd shoot;
> My heart is like an apple tree . . .

What poets, I cried aloud, as one does in the dusk, what poets they were!

In a sort of jealousy, I suppose, for our own age, silly and absurd though these comparisons are, I went on to wonder if honestly one could name two living poets now as great as Tennyson and Christina Rossetti were then. Obviously it is impossible, I thought, looking into those foaming waters, to compare them. The very reason why the poetry excites one to such abandonment, such rapture, is that it celebrates some feeling that one used to have (at luncheon parties before the war perhaps), so that one responds easily, familiarly, without troubling to check the feeling, or to compare it with any that one has now. But the living poets express a feeling that is actually being made and torn out of us at the moment. One does not recognize it in the first place; often for some reason one fears it;

one watches it with keenness and compares it jealously and suspiciously with
the old feeling that one knew. Hence the difficulty of modern poetry; and it is
because of this difficulty that one cannot remember more than two consecutive
lines of any good modern poet. For this reason—that my memory failed me—
the argument flagged for want of material. But why, I continued, moving on
towards Headingley, have we stopped humming under our breath at luncheon
parties? Why has Alfred ceased to sing

> She is coming, my dove, my dear?

Why has Christina ceased to respond

> My heart is gladder than all these
> Because my love is come to me?

Shall we lay the blame on the war? When the guns fired in August 1914, did the
faces of men and women show so plain in each other's eyes that romance was
killed? Certainly it was a shock to women in particular with their illusions about
education, and so on to see the faces of our rulers in the light of the shell-fire.
So ugly they looked—German, English, French—so stupid. But lay the blame
where one will, on whom one will, the illusion which inspired Tennyson and
Christina Rossetti to sing so passionately about the coming of their loves is far
rarer now than then. One has only to read, to look, to listen, to remember. But
why say "blame?" Why, if it was an illusion, not praise the catastrophe, whatever
it was, that destroyed illusion and put truth in its place? For truth . . . those dots
mark the spot where, in search of truth, I missed the turning up to Fernham. Yes
indeed, which was truth and which was illusion, I asked myself. What was the
truth about these houses, for example, dim and festive now with their red windows in the dusk, but raw and red and squalid, with their sweets and their boot-
laces, at nine o'clock in the morning? And the willows and the river and the
gardens that run down to the river, vague now with the mist stealing over them,
but gold and red in the sunlight—which was the truth, which was the illusion
about them? I spare you the twists and turns of my cogitations, for no conclusion was found on the road to Headingley, and I ask you to suppose that I soon
found out my mistake about the turning and retraced my steps to Fernham.

As I have said already that it was an October day, I dare not forfeit your
respect and imperil the fair name of fiction by changing the season and describing lilacs hanging over garden walls, crocuses, tulips and other flowers of spring.

Fiction must stick to facts, and the truer the facts the better the fiction—so we are told. Therefore it was still autumn and the leaves were still yellow and falling, if anything, a little faster than before, because it was now evening (seven twenty-three to be precise) and a breeze (from the southwest to be exact) had risen, But for all that there was something odd at work:

> My heart is like a singing bird
>> Whose nest is in a water'd shoot;
> My heart is like an apple tree
>> Whose boughs are bent with thick-set fruit—

perhaps the words of Christina Rossetti were partly responsible for the folly of the fancy—it was nothing of course but a fancy—that the lilac was shaking its flowers over the garden walls, and the brimstone butterflies were scudding hither and thither, and the dust of the pollen was in the air. A wind blew, from what quarter I know not, but it lifted the half-grown leaves so that there was a flash of silver grey in the air. It was the time between the lights when colours undergo their intensification and purples and golds burn in window-panes like the beat of an excitable heart; when for some reason the beauty of the world revealed and yet soon to perish (here I pushed into the garden, for, unwisely, the door was left open and no beadles seemed about), the beauty of the world which is so soon to perish, has two edges, one of laughter, one of anguish, cutting the heart asunder. The gardens of Fernham lay before me in the spring twilight, wild and open, and in the long grass, sprinkled and carelessly flung, were daffodils and bluebells, not orderly perhaps at the best of times, and now wind-blown and waving as they tugged at their roots. The windows of the building, curved like ships' windows among generous waves of red brick, changed from lemon to silver under the flight of the quick spring clouds. Somebody was in a hammock, somebody, but in this light they were phantoms only, half guessed, half seen, raced across the grass—would no one stop her?—and then on the terrace, as if popping out to breathe the air, to glance at the garden, came a bent figure, formidable yet humble, with her great forehead and her shabby dress—could it be the famous scholar, could it be J———H———herself? All was dim, yet intense too, as if the scarf which the dusk had flung over the garden were torn asunder by star or sword—the flash of some terrible reality leaping, as its way is, out of the heart of the spring. For youth———

Here was my soup. Dinner was being served in the great dining-hall. Far from being spring it was in fact an evening in October. Everybody was assem-

UNIT 7

bled in the big dining-room. Dinner was ready. Here was the soup. It was a plain gravy soup. There was nothing to stir the fancy in that. One could have seen through the transparent liquid any pattern that there might have been on the plate itself. But there was no pattern. The plate was plain. Next came beef with its attendant greens and potatoes—a homely trinity, suggesting the rumps of cattle in a muddy market, and sprouts curled and yellowed at the edge, and bargaining and cheapening, and women with string bags on Monday morning. There was no reason to complain of human nature's daily food, seeing that the supply was sufficient and coal-miners doubtless were sitting down to less. Prunes and custard followed. And if any one complains that prunes, even when mitigated by custard, are an uncharitable vegetable (fruit they are not), stringy as a miser's heart and exuding a fluid such as might run in misers' veins who have denied themselves wine and warmth for eighty years and yet not given to the poor, he should reflect that there are people whose charity embraces even the prune. Biscuits and cheese came next, and here the water-jug was liberally passed round, for it is the nature of biscuits to be dry, and these were biscuits to the core. That was all. The meal was over. Everybody scraped their chairs back; the swing-doors swung violently to and fro; soon the hall was emptied of every sign of food and made ready no doubt for breakfast next morning. Down corridors and up staircases the youth of England went banging and singing. And was it for a guest, a stranger (for I had no more right here in Fernham than in Trinity or Somerville or Girton or Newnham or Christchurch), to say, "The dinner was not good," or to say (we were now, Mary Seton and I, in her sitting-room), "Could we not have dined up here alone?" for if I had said anything of the kind I should have been prying and searching into the secret economies of a house which to the stranger wears so fine a front of gaiety and courage. No, one could say nothing of the sort. Indeed, conversation for a moment flagged. The human frame being what it is, heart, body and brain all mixed together, and not contained in separate compartments as they will be no doubt in another million years, a good dinner is of great importance to good talk. One cannot think well, love well, sleep well, if one has not dined well. The lamp in the spine does not light on beef and prunes. We are all *probably* going to heaven, and Vandyck is, we *hope*, to meet us round the next corner—that is the dubious and qualifying state of mind that beef and prunes at the end of the day's work breed between them. Happily my friend, who taught science, had a cupboard where there was a squat bottle and little glasses—(but there should have been sole and partridge to begin with)—so that we were able to draw up to the fire and repair some of the damages of the day's living. In a minute or so we were slipping freely in and out among all those

objects of curiosity and interest which form in the mind in the absence of a particular person, and are naturally to be discussed on coming together again—
how somebody has married, another has not; one thinks this, another that; one
has improved out of all knowledge, the other most amazingly gone to the bad—
with all those speculations upon human nature and the character of the amazing world we live in which spring naturally from such beginnings. While these
things were being said, however, I became shamefacedly aware of a current setting in of its own accord and carrying everything forward to an end of its own.
One might be talking of Spain or Portugal, of book or racehorse, but the real
interest of whatever was said was none of those things, but a scene of masons on
a high roof some five centuries ago. Kings and nobles brought treasure in huge
sacks and poured it under the earth. This scene was for ever coming alive in my
mind and placing itself by another of lean cows and a muddy market and withered greens and the stringy hearts of old men—these two pictures, disjointed
and disconnected and nonsensical as they were, were for ever coming together
and combating each other and had me entirely at their mercy. The best course,
unless the whole talk was to be distorted, was to expose what was in my mind
to the air, when with good luck it would fade and crumble like the head of the
dead king when they opened the coffin at Windsor. Briefly, then, I told Miss
Seton about the masons who had been all those years on the roof of the chapel,
and about the kings and queens and nobles bearing sacks of gold and silver on
their shoulders, which they shovelled into the earth; and then how the great
financial magnates of our own time came and laid cheques and bonds, I suppose,
where the others had laid ingots and rough lumps of gold. All that lies beneath
the colleges down there, I said; but this college, where we are now sitting, what
lies beneath its gallant red brick and the wild unkempt grasses of the garden?
What force is behind the plain china off which we dined, and (here it popped
out of my mouth before I could stop it) the beef, the custard and the prunes?

15   Well, said Mary Seton, about the year 1860—Oh, but you know the story,
she said, bored, I suppose, by the recital. And she told me—rooms were hired.
Committees met. Envelopes were addressed. Circulars were drawn up. Meetings were held; letters were read out; so-and-so has promised so much; on the
contrary, Mr.———won't give a penny. The *Saturday Review* has been very rude.
How can we raise a fund to pay for offices? Shall we hold a bazaar? Can't we find
a pretty girl to sit in the front row? Let us look up what John Stuart Mill said on
the subject. Can any one persuade the editor of the———to print a letter? Can
we get Lady———to sign it? Lady———is out of town. That was the way it
was done, presumably, sixty years ago, and it was a prodigious effort, and a great

deal of time was spent on it. And it was only after a long struggle and with the utmost difficulty that they got thirty thousand pounds together. So obviously we cannot have wine and partridges and servants carrying tin dishes on their heads, she said. We cannot have sofas and separate rooms. "The amenities," she said, quoting from some book or other, "will have to wait."

At the thought of all those women working year after year and finding it hard to get two thousand pounds together, and as much as they could do to get thirty thousand pounds, we burst out in scorn at the reprehensible poverty of our sex. What had our mothers been doing then that they had no wealth to leave us? Powdering their noses? Looking in at shop windows? Flaunting in the sun at Monte Carlo? There were some photographs on the mantel-piece. Mary's mother—if that was her picture—may have been a wastrel in her spare time (she had thirteen children by a minister of the church), but if so her gay and dissipated life had left too few traces of its pleasures on her face. She was a homely body; an old lady in a plaid shawl which was fastened by a large cameo; and she sat in a basket-chair, encouraging a spaniel to look at the camera, with the amused, yet strained expression of one who is sure that the dog will move directly the bulb is pressed. Now if she had gone into business; had become a manufacturer of artificial silk or a magnate on the Stock Exchange; if she had left two or three hundred thousand pounds to Fernham, we could have been sitting at our ease tonight and the subject of our talk might have been archaeology, botany, anthropology, physics, the nature of the atom, mathematics, astronomy, relativity, geography. If only Mrs. Seton and her mother and her mother before her had learnt the great art of making money and had left their money, like their fathers and their grandfathers before them, to found fellowships and lectureships and prizes and scholarships appropriated to the use of their own sex, we might have dined very tolerably up here alone off a bird and a bottle of wine; we might have looked forward without undue confidence to a pleasant and honourable lifetime spent in the shelter of one of the liberally endowed professions. We might have been exploring or writing; mooning about the venerable places of the earth; sitting contemplative on the steps of the Parthenon, or going at ten to an office and coming home comfortably at half-past four to write a little poetry. Only, if Mrs. Seton and her like had gone into business at the age of fifteen, there would have been—that was the snag in the argument—no Mary. What, I asked, did Mary think of that? There between the curtains was the October night, calm and lovely, with a star or two caught in the yellowing trees. Was she ready to resign her share of it and her memories (for they had been a happy family, though a large one) of games and quarrels up in Scotland, which she is never tired of praising for the fineness of its air and the quality of its cakes, in order that Fernham might have been endowed with fifty thousand pounds or so by a stroke of the pen? For, to endow a college would necessitate the suppression of families altogether. Making a fortune and bearing thirteen children—no human being could stand it. Consider the facts, we said. First there are nine months before the baby is born. Then the baby is born. Then there are three or four months spent in feeding the baby. After the baby is fed there are certainly five years spent in playing with the baby. You cannot, it seems, let children run about the streets. People who have seen them running wild in Russia say that the sight is not a pleasant one. People say, too, that human nature takes its shape in the years between one and five. If Mrs. Seton, I said, had been making money, what sort of memories would you have had of games and quarrels? What would you have known of Scotland, and its fine air and cakes and all the rest of it? But it is useless to ask these questions, because you would never have come into existence at all. Moreover, it is equally useless to ask what might have happened if Mrs. Seton and her mother and her mother before her had amassed great wealth and laid it under the foundations of college and library, because, in the first place, to earn money was impossible for them, and in the second, had it been possible, the law denied them the right to possess what money they earned. It is only for the last forty-eight years that Mrs. Seton has had a penny of her own. For all the centuries before that it would have been her husband's property—a thought which, perhaps, may have had its share in keeping Mrs. Seton and her mothers off the Stock Exchange. Every penny I earn, they may have said, will be taken from me and disposed of according to my husband's wisdom—perhaps to found a scholarship or to endow a fellowship in Balliol or Kings, so that to earn money, even if I could earn money, is not a matter that interests me very greatly. I had better leave it to my husband.

At any rate, whether or not the blame rested on the old lady who was looking at the spaniel, there could be no doubt that for some reason or other our mothers had mismanaged their affairs very gravely. Not a penny could be spared for "amenities;" for partridges and wine, beadles and turf, books and cigars, libraries and leisure. To raise bare walls out of the bare earth was the utmost they could do.

So we talked standing at the window and looking, as so many thousands look every night, down on the domes and towers of the famous city beneath us. It was very beautiful, very mysterious in the autumn moonlight. The old stone looked very white and venerable. One thought of all the books that were assembled down there; of the pictures of old prelates and worthies hanging in the panelled rooms; of the painted windows that would be throwing strange globes and crescents on the pavement; of the tablets and memorials and inscriptions; of the fountains and the grass; of the quiet rooms looking across the quiet quadrangles. And (pardon me the thought) I thought, too, of the admirable smoke and drink and the deep armchairs and the pleasant carpets: of the urbanity the geniality, the dignity which are the offspring of luxury and privacy and space. Certainly our mothers had not provided us with anything comparable to all this—our mothers who found it difficult to scrape together thirty thousand pounds, our mothers who bore thirteen children to ministers of religion at St. Andrews.

19   So I went back to my inn, and as I walked through the dark streets I pondered this and that, as one does at the end of the day's work. I pondered why it was that Mrs. Seton had no money to leave us; and what effect poverty has on the mind; and what effect wealth has on the mind; and I thought of the queer old gentlemen I had seen that morning with tufts of fur upon their shoulders; and I remembered how if one whistled one of them ran; and I thought of the organ booming in the chapel and of the shut doors of the library; and I thought how unpleasant it is to be locked out; and I thought how it is worse perhaps to be locked in; and, thinking of the safety and prosperity of the one sex and of the poverty and insecurity of the other and of the effect of tradition and of the lack of tradition upon the mind of a writer, I thought at last that it was time to roll up the crumpled skin of the day, with its arguments and its impressions and its anger and its laughter, and cast it into the hedge. A thousand stars were flashing across the blue wastes of the sky. One seemed alone with an inscrutable society. All human beings were laid asleep—prone, horizontal, dumb. Nobody seemed stirring in the streets of Oxbridge. Even the door of the hotel sprang open at the touch of an invisible hand—not a boots was sitting up to light me to bed, it was so late.

READING/WRITING ASSISTS

Thesis (and its counterargument):

Readers often expect to find a clear statement of the writer's argument in a **thesis statement**, usually found in a sentence or two at the end of the first or, at the latest, second paragraph of an argumentative essay. In this essay, Virginia Woolf expresses her argument in the form of an "opinion" in the first paragraph. Are opinions weaker than outright "arguments?" Why would Woolf state her argument in the form of opinion?

Many who write arguments state their views in opposition to the argument of a particular person (Freud, Jung) or persons (Dr. King) or school of thought (Marx, Darwin). Virginia Woolf seems to posit her argument against society as a whole. What is it about English society, circa 1928, that Woolf's argument opposes?

The Shape of the Argument:

"Mapping" the structure of an argument can help us better understand the argument itself, while also showing us new models for shaping our own arguments in essay form. Notice that though Woolf's argument appears very *digressive*, in that she often seems to move away from the main point of her essay, each digression circles back to the main idea and adds another dimension to the larger situation she wishes to expose and change through her argument. To better understand Woolf's argument, it is best to start by outlining her essay, paragraph by paragraph:

Paragraph 1:	Woolf **frames** her argument around her quandary over her subject for a speaking engagement, "Women and Fiction." Thinking about what this topic might mean, and what she might say about it leads Woolf to form an "opinion," her argument. What is Woolf's opinion?
Paragraphs 2, 3, 4, 5:	Woolf devotes several long paragraphs to the **setting** at Oxbridge, and her thoughts and experiences as she moves in that setting. In paragraph 3, she is literally chased off the "turf." In paragraph 4, she is not admitted to the library. These experiences, and her observations in the chapel, in paragraph 5, lead to some important conclusions. What are these conclusions?
Paragraph 6:	The luncheon. What are Woolf's reasons for describing this luncheon in such detail?
Paragraphs 7, 8, 9, 10:	Paragraphs 7 and 10 appear to be a digression about life and art before the war. Paragraphs 8 and 9 return to Woolf's immediate experience at Oxbridge. What connection, if any, is there between these paragraphs?

Paragraphs 11 and 12:   The Fernham experience. Fernham's gates, unlike
                         Oxbridge's, are not locked. And once again, a meal
                         is described in some detail. What comparisons/
                         contrasts can be made between the two schools?
                         What about this comparison/contrast is significant
                         to Woolf's argument?

Paragraphs 13, 14,
15, 16, 17, and 18:   Women, money and education. In what ways,
                         according to Woolf, are these connected?

Paragraph 19:   What conclusion/s does Woolf reach about women,
                         education, and money?

Rhetorical Moves:

Woolf's essay is characterized by her **stream of consciousness** narrative. In the
early paragraphs of Chapter One, for instance, Woolf's thoughts, likened to a fish
swimming about, move from the writer Charles Lamb, to John Milton and his
poem, "Lycidas," to Thackery and his novel *Esmond,* to manuscripts, to the library.
She is abruptly pulled away from her thoughts by the guard's "present" refusal to
admit her to the library. Are Woolf's digressions effective? Does the inclusion of
her stream of consciousness contribute to or detract from her argument?

Also, Woolf's essay makes use of an extended comparison/contrast to further her argument. What is compared/contrasted, and is the comparison/contrast
an effective rhetorical strategy?

ARGUMENT OFFERING A HYPOTHETICAL EXAMPLE AS EVIDENCE/COMPARISON AND CONTRAST (WOOLF) AND ARGUMENT DIRECTLY ENGAGING THE ARGUMENT OF ANOTHER WRITER/CITATION (WALKER)

Alice Walker's argument in "In Search of Our Mothers' Gardens" is, in many respects, a direct response to the argument found in Virginia Woolf's essay "A Room of One's Own." In her essay, Walker quotes Woolf, pointing out the short-comings of Woolf's argument by citing her exact words, a common technique when making a point counter to another's.

ALICE WALKER

The eighth and last child of Willie Lee and Minnie Low Grant Walker, share-croppers, Alice Walker (1944–) was born in Eatonton, Georgia. She earned a B.A. at Sarah Lawrence in 1965.

From the mid-sixties until the mid-seventies, she lived in Tougaloo, Missis-sippi, where she was active in the civil rights movement of the 1960s and other social movements of the 1970s. She remains a political activist to this day. She currently resides in northern California.

In 1983, she won a Pulitzer Prize for her novel, The Color Purple.

Walker's essay, "In Search of Our Mothers' Gardens," is an active engagement with the argument of Virginia Woolf in her essay, "A Room of One's Own." Walker often quotes Woolf's essay when making her counterargument. Perhaps even more important for Walker's argumentative purposes, she uses a passage from Jean Toomer's *Cane,* an early twentieth-century African American mixed-genre novel, as her epigram; she tells us a good deal about the life and work of the early African American poet Phillis Wheatley; and she refers to a poem written by the African poet Okot p'Bitek, "Song of Lawino." Citation is especially necessary in Walker's essay, given its argument, and each citation is carefully chosen and skillfully deployed. Pay close attention to Walker's choice and placement of citations in the course of her essay.

Coming to Terms with the Reading:

Before reading/rereading Alice Walker's, "In Search of Our Mothers' Gardens," it is best to have a firm grasp on the meanings of the following terms:

1. Saints
2. contrary instincts
3. matriarch

IN SEARCH OF OUR MOTHERS' GARDENS
Alice Walker

*I described her own nature and temperament. Told how they needed a larger life for
their expression . . . I pointed out that in lieu of proper channels, her emotions had overflowed into paths that dissipated them. I talked, beautifully I thought, about an art
that would be born, an art that would open the way for women the likes of her. I asked
her to hope, and build up an inner life against the coming of that day . . . I sang,
with a strange quiver in my voice, a promise song.*

—Jean Toomer, "Avey,"
CANE

1   The poet speaking to a prostitute who falls asleep while he's talking—When
the poet Jean Toomer walked through the South in the early twenties, he
discovered a curious thing: black women whose spirituality was so intense, so
deep, so *unconscious,* that they were themselves unaware of the richness they
held. They stumbled blindly through their lives: creatures so abused and mutilated in body, so dimmed and confused by pain, that they considered themselves
unworthy even of hope. In the selfless abstractions their bodies became to the men
who used them, they became more than "sexual objects," more even than mere
women: they became "Saints." Instead of being perceived as whole persons, their
bodies became shrines: what was thought to be their minds became temples suitable for worship. These crazy Saints stared out at the world, wildly, like lunatics—
or quietly, like suicides; and the "God" that was in their gaze was as mute as a
great stone.

Who were these Saints? These crazy, loony, pitiful women?

Some of them, without a doubt, were our mothers and grandmothers.

In the still heat of the post-Reconstruction South, this is how they seemed
to Jean Toomer: exquisite butterflies trapped in an evil honey, toiling away their

lives in an era, a century, that did not acknowledge them, except as "the *mule* of the world." They dreamed dreams that no one knew—not even themselves, in any coherent fashion—and saw visions no one could understand. They wandered or sat about the countryside crooning lullabies to ghosts, and drawing the mother of Christ in charcoal on courthouse walls.

5   They forced their minds to desert their bodies and their striving spirits sought to rise, like frail whirlwinds from the hard red clay. And when those frail whirlwinds fell, in scattered particles, upon the ground, no one mourned. Instead, men lit candles to celebrate the emptiness that remained, as people do who enter a beautiful but vacant space to resurrect a God.

Our mothers and grandmothers, some of them: moving to music not yet written. And they waited.

They waited for a day when the unknown thing that was in them would be made known; but guessed, somehow in their darkness, that on the day of their revelation they would be long dead. Therefore to Toomer they walked, and even ran, in slow motion. For they were going nowhere immediate, and the future was not yet within their grasp. And men took our mothers and grandmothers, "but got no pleasure from it." So complex was their passion and their calm.

To Toomer, they lay vacant and fallow as autumn fields, with harvest time never in sight: and he saw them enter loveless marriages, without joy; and become prostitutes, without resistance; and become mothers of children, without fulfillment.

For these grandmothers and mothers of ours were not Saints, but Artists; driven to a numb and bleeding madness by the springs of creativity in them for which there was no release. They were Creators, who lived lives of spiritual waste, because they were so rich in spirituality—which is the basis of Art—that the strain of enduring their unused and unwanted talent drove them insane. Throwing away this spirituality was their pathetic attempt to lighten the soul to a weight their work-worn, sexually abused bodies could bear.

10   What did it mean for a black woman to be an artist in our grandmothers' time? In our great-grandmothers' day? It is a question with an answer cruel enough to stop the blood.

Did you have a genius of a great-great-grandmother who died under some ignorant and depraved white overseer's lash? Or was she required to bake biscuits for a lazy backwater tramp, when she cried out in her soul to paint watercolors of sunsets, or the rain falling on the green and peaceful pasturelands? Or was her body broken and forced to bear children (who were more often than not sold away from her)—eight, ten, fifteen, twenty children—when her one joy was the thought of modeling heroic figures of rebellion, in stone or clay?

How was the creativity of the black woman kept alive, year after year and century after century, when for most of the years black people have been in America, it was a punishable crime for a black person to read or write? And the freedom to paint, to sculpt, to expand the mind with action did not exist. Consider, if you can bear to imagine it, what might have been the result if singing, too, had been forbidden by law. Listen to the voices of Bessie Smith, Billie Holiday, Nina Simone, Roberta Flack, and Aretha Franklin, among others, and imagine those voices muzzled for life. Then you may begin to comprehend the lives of our "crazy," "Sainted" mothers and grandmothers. The agony of the lives of women who might have been Poets, Novelists, Essayists, and Short-Story Writers (over a period of centuries), who died with their real gifts stifled within them.

And, if this were the end of the story, we would have cause to cry out in my paraphrase of Okot p'Bitek's great poem:

> O, my clanswomen
> Let us all cry together!
> Come,
> Let us mourn the death of our mother,
> The death of a Queen
> The ash that was produced
> By a great fire!
> O, this homestead is utterly dead
> Close the gates
> With *lacari* thorns,
> For our mother
> The creator of the Stool is lost!
> And all the young women
> Have perished in the wilderness!

But this is not the end of the story, for all the young women—our mothers and grandmothers, *ourselves*—have not perished in the wilderness. And if we ask ourselves why, and search for and find the answer, we will know beyond all efforts to erase it from our minds, just exactly who, and of what, we black American women are.

15   One example, perhaps the most pathetic, most misunderstood one, can provide a backdrop for our mothers' work: Phillis Wheatley, a slave in the 1700s.

Virginia Woolf, in her book *A Room of One's Own,* wrote that in order for a woman to write fiction she must have two things, certainly: a room of her own (with key and lock) and enough money to support herself.

What then are we to make of Phillis Wheatley, a slave, who owned not even herself? This sickly, frail black girl who required a servant of her own at times—her health was so precarious—and who, had she been white, would have been easily considered the intellectual superior of all the women and most of the men in the society of her day.

Virginia Woolf wrote further, speaking of course not of our Phillis, that "any woman born with a great gift in the sixteenth century [insert "eighteenth century," insert "black woman," insert "born or made a slave"] would certainly have gone crazed, shot herself, or ended her days in some lonely cottage outside the village, half witch, half wizard [insert "Saint"], feared and mocked at. For it needs little skill and psychology to be sure that a highly gifted girl who had tried to use her gift for poetry would have been so thwarted and hindered by contrary instincts [add "chains, guns, the lash, the ownership of one's body by someone else, submission to an alien religion"], that she must have lost her health and sanity to a certainty."

The key words, as they relate to Phillis, are "contrary instincts." For when we read the poetry of Phillis Wheatley—as when we read the novels of Nella Larsen or the oddly false-sounding autobiography of that freest of all black women writers, Zora Hurston—evidence of "contrary instincts" is everywhere. Her loyalties were completely divided, as was, without question, her mind.

20   But how could this be otherwise? Captured at seven, a slave of wealthy, doting whites who instilled in her the "savagery" of the Africa they "rescued" her from . . . one wonders if she was even able to remember her homeland as she had known it, or as it really was.

Yet, because she did try to use her gift for poetry in a world that made her a slave, she was "so thwarted and hindered by . . . contrary instincts, that she . . . lost her health. . . ." In the last years of her brief life, burdened not only with the need to express her gift but also with a penniless, friendless "freedom" and several small children for whom she was forced to do strenuous work to feed, she lost her health, certainly. Suffering from malnutrition and neglect and who knows what mental agonies, Phillis Wheatley died.

So torn by "contrary instincts" was black, kidnapped, enslaved Phillis that her description of "the Goddess"—as she poetically called the Liberty she did not have—is ironically, cruelly humorous. And, in fact, has held Phillis up to ridicule for more than a century. It is usually read prior to hanging Phillis's memory as that of a fool. She wrote:

The Goddess comes, she moves divinely fair,
Olive and laurel binds her *golden* hair.
Wherever shines this native of the skies,
Unnumber'd charms and recent graces rise. [My italics]

It is obvious that Phillis, the slave, combed the "Goddess's" hair every morning; prior, perhaps, to bringing in the milk, or fixing her mistress's lunch. She took her imagery from the one thing she saw elevated above all others.

With the benefit of hindsight we ask, "How could she?"

25   But at last, Phillis, we understand. No more snickering when your stiff, struggling, ambivalent lines are forced on us. We know now that you were not an idiot or a traitor; only a sickly little black girl, snatched from your home and country and made a slave; a woman who still struggled to sing the song that was your gift, although in a land of barbarians who praised you for your bewildered tongue. It is not so much what you sang, as that you kept alive, in so many of our ancestors, *the notion of song.*

Black women are called, in the folklore that so aptly identifies one's status in society, "the *mule* of the world," because we have been handed the burdens that everyone else—*everyone* else—refused to carry. We have also been called "Matriarchs," "Superwomen," and "Mean and Evil Bitches." Not to mention "Castraters" and "Sapphire's Mama." When we have pleaded for understanding, our character has been distorted; when we have asked for simple caring, we have been handed empty inspirational appellations, then stuck in the farthest corner. When we have asked for love, we have been given children. In short, even our plainer gifts, our labors of fidelity and love, have been knocked down our throats. To be an artist and a black woman, even today, lowers our status in many respects, rather than raises it: and yet, artists we will be.

Therefore we must fearlessly pull out of ourselves and look at and identify with our lives the living creativity some of our great-grandmothers were not allowed to know. I stress *some* of them because it is well known that the majority of our great-grandmothers knew, even without "knowing" it, the reality of their spirituality, even if they didn't recognize it beyond what happened in the singing at church—and they never had any intention of giving it up.

How they did it—those millions of black women who were not Phillis Wheatley, or Lucy Terry or Frances Harper or Zora Hurston or Nella Larsen or Bessie Smith; or Elizabeth Catlett, or Katherine Dunham, either—brings me to the title of this essay, "In Search of Our Mothers' Gardens," which is a personal account that is yet shared, in its theme and its meaning, by all of us. I found, while thinking about the far-reaching world of the creative black woman, that often the truest answer to a question that really matters can be found very close.

In the late 1920s my mother ran away from home to marry my father. Marriage, if not running away, was expected of seventeen-year-old girls. By the time she was twenty, she had two children and was pregnant with a third. Five children later, I was born. And this is how I came to know my mother: she seemed a large, soft, loving-eyed woman who was rarely impatient in our home. Her quick, violent temper was on view only a few times a year, when she battled with the white landlord who had the misfortune to suggest to her that her children did not need to go to school.

30   She made all the clothes we wore, even my brothers' overalls. She made all the towels and sheets we used. She spent the summers canning vegetables and fruits. She spent the winter evenings making quilts enough to cover all our beds.

During the "working" day, she labored beside—not behind—my father in the fields. Her day began before sunup, and did not end until late at night. There was never a moment for her to sit down, undisturbed, to unravel her own private thoughts; never a time free from interruption—by work or the noisy inquiries of her many children. And yet, it is to my mother—and all our mothers who were not famous—that I went in search of the secret of what has fed that muzzled and often mutilated, but vibrant, creative spirit that the black woman has inherited, and that pops out in wild and unlikely places to this day.

But when, you will ask, did my overworked mother have time to know or care about feeding the creative spirit?

The answer is so simple that many of us have spent years discovering it. We have constantly looked high, when we should have looked high—and low.

For example: in the Smithsonian Institution in Washington, D.C., there hangs a quilt unlike any other in the world. In fanciful, inspired, and yet simple and identifiable figures, it portrays the story of the Crucifixion. It is considered rare, beyond price. Though it follows no known pattern of quilt-making, and though it is made of bits and pieces of worthless rags, it is obviously the work of a person of powerful imagination and deep spiritual feeling. Below this quilt I saw a note that says it was made by "an anonymous Black woman in Alabama, a hundred years ago."

35   If we could locate this "anonymous" black woman from Alabama, she would turn out to be one of our grandmothers—an artist who left her mark in the only

materials she could afford, and in the only medium her position in society allowed her to use.

As Virginia Woolf wrote further, in *A Room of One's Own*:

> Yet genius of a sort must have existed among women as it must have existed among the working class. [Change this to "slaves" and "the wives and daughters of sharecroppers."] Now and again an Emily Brontë or a Robert Burns [change this to "a Zora Hurston or a Richard Wright"] blazes out and proves its presence. But certainly it never got itself on to paper. When, however, one reads of a witch being ducked, of a woman possessed by devils [or "Sainthood"], of a wise woman selling herbs [our root workers], or even a very remarkable man who had a mother, then I think we are on the track of a lost novelist, a suppressed poet, of some mute and inglorious Jane Austen . . . Indeed, I would venture to guess that Anon, who wrote so many poems without signing them, was often a woman . . . .

And so our mothers and grandmothers have, more often than not anonymously, handed on the creative spark, the seed of the flower they themselves never hoped to see: or like a sealed letter they could not plainly read.

And so it is, certainly, with my own mother. Unlike "Ma" Rainey's songs, which retained their creator's name even while blasting forth from Bessie Smith's mouth, no song or poem will bear my mother's name. Yet so many of the stories that I write, that we all write, are my mother's stories. Only recently did I fully realize this: that through years of listening to my mother's stories of her life, I have absorbed not only the stories themselves, but something of the manner in which she spoke, something of the urgency that involves the knowledge that her stories—like her life—must be recorded. It is probably for this reason that so much of what I have written is about characters whose counterparts in real life are so much older than I am.

But the telling of these stories, which came from my mother's lips as naturally as breathing, was not the only way my mother showed herself as an artist. For stories, too, were subject to being distracted, to dying without conclusion. Dinners must be started, and cotton must be gathered before the big rains. The artist that was and is my mother showed itself to me only after many years. This is what I finally noticed:

40   Like Mem, a character in *The Third Life of Grange Copeland,* my mother adorned with flowers whatever shabby house we were forced to live in. And not just your typical straggly country stand of zinnias, either. She planted ambitious

gardens—and still does—with over fifty different varieties of plants that bloom profusely from early March until late November. Before she left home for the fields, she watered her flowers, chopped up the grass, and laid out new beds. When she returned from the fields she might divide clumps of bulbs, dig a cold pit, uproot and replant roses, or prune branches from her taller bushes or trees— until night came and it was too dark to see.

Whatever she planted grew as if by magic, and her fame as a grower of flowers spread over three counties. Because of her creativity with her flowers, even my memories of poverty are seen through a screen of blooms—sunflowers, petunias, roses, dahlias, forsythia, spirea, delphiniums, verbena . . . and on and on.

And I remember people coming to my mother's yard to be given cuttings from her flowers; I hear again the praise showered on her because whatever rocky soil she landed on, she turned into a garden. A garden so brilliant with colors, so original in its design, so magnificent with life and creativity, that to this day people drive by our house in Georgia—perfect strangers and imperfect strangers—and ask to stand or walk among my mother's art.

I notice that it is only when my mother is working in her flowers that she is radiant, almost to the point of being invisible—except as Creator: hand and eye. She is involved in work her soul must have. Ordering the universe in the image of her personal conception of Beauty.

Her face, as she prepares the Art that is her gift, is a legacy of respect she leaves to me, for all that illuminates and cherishes life. She has handed down respect for the possibilities—and the will to grasp them.

45   For her, so hindered and intruded upon in so many ways, being an artist has still been a daily part of her life. This ability to hold on, even in very simple ways, is work black women have done for a very long time.

This poem is not enough, but it is something, for the woman who literally covered the holes in our walls with sunflowers:

> They were women then
> My mama's generation
> Husky of voice—Stout of
> Step
> With fists as well as
> Hands
> How they battered down
> Doors
> And ironed

Starched white
Shirts
How they led
Armies
Headragged Generals
Across mined
Fields
Booby-trapped
Kitchens
To discover books
Desks
A place for us
How they knew what we
Must know
Without knowing a page
Of it
Themselves.

Guided by my heritage of a love of beauty and a respect for strength—in search of my mother's garden, I found my own.

And perhaps in Africa over two hundred years ago, there was just such a mother; perhaps she painted vivid and daring decorations in oranges and yellows and greens on the walls of her hut; perhaps she sang—in a voice like Roberta Flack's—*sweetly* over the compounds of her village; perhaps she wove the most stunning mats or told the most ingenious stories of all the village storytellers. Perhaps she was herself a poet—though only her daughter's name is signed to the poems that we know.

Perhaps Phillis Wheatley's mother was also an artist.

50   Perhaps in more than Phillis Wheatley's biological life is her mother's signature made clear.

1974

UNIT 7

READING/WRITING ASSISTS

Thesis (and its counterargument):

Walker does not clearly elaborate her **thesis** until paragraph nine, and its **counterargument** is not mentioned until paragraph sixteen. Rather than jump right into her argument in the first paragraph—or even the first sentence, as is sometimes the case in essays—Walker's main idea slowly unfolds, like the quilt she uses as a metaphor for the anonymous artistry of many black women before her. Is it a good idea for Walker to wait so long to let her reader know her argument and its counterargument?

The Shape of the Argument:

"Mapping" the structure of an argument can help us better understand the argument itself, while also showing us new models for shaping our own arguments in essay form. Walker's argument, while eventually very direct, begins in circumspection—and introspection. By way of introduction, she looks back to the early twentieth-century South of author Jean Toomer (himself a Northerner) in order to first elaborate her idea of the Saint, and the reasons for her "sainthood." This phenomenon will become pivotal in her argument later, when she turns to the stand taken by Virginia Woolf, an early twentieth-century British feminist and author, in her essay, "A Room of One's Own." To better understand Walker's argument, it is best to start by outlining the entire essay, paragraph by paragraph:

Epigraph:

Alice Walker begins her essay with an **epigraph**, a quotation from another source. Referring to other texts, also known as **citation**, is an important element of Walker's essay overall. In the margins, keep a list of all those cited in the course of Walker's argument.

Paragraphs 1–8:	How does Walker describe the Saints? Do you find her description of them powerful? Why? Underline **descriptive words** you think lend particular authority and vivacity to her description of these women.
Paragraph 9:	Walker's **thesis statement**. Restate Walker's thesis in your own words.
Paragraph 10:	Walker asks two questions. Are these **rhetorical questions**? Why or why not?
Paragraphs 11–15:	Walker answers her own questions and provides some historical evidence and examples in her answers. Much of Walker's essay leans her own argument against **historical**

	research. Does Walker's historical research provide adequate support for her argument?
Paragraph 16:	**Counterargument**. Walker brings Woolf an early British feminist into her argument. After reading Woolf's, "A Room of One's Own," what reasons could be offered for seeing Woolf's feminist argument as somewhat antithetical to Walker's?
Paragraphs 17–25:	**Extended example.** Once again, an essay writer offers an extended example in defense of a position. Does Walker's reference to Wheatley help her argument? What about Wheatley helps Walker to advance her argument with Woolf?
Paragraphs 26–36:	More historical background, and another extended example. What does Walker argue about her mother and legions of women like her? Is Walker's argument about these women valid?
Paragraphs 37:	Return to **antithesis**.
Paragraphs 38–46:	Return to examples. Is there a "call and response" character to the prose here, in Walker's back-and-forth between her argument with Woolf, and her examples? How do the cited Woolf and Walker's other examples "call" and "respond" to one another?
Paragraphs 47–50:	**Conclusions**

Rhetorical Moves:

Walker packs her essay with examples of historical black women. Some of these examples are described in detail; others are just mentioned. But all are appropriate. When writing persuasive essays, a wealth of examples and some detail give life to the essay, but always make sure that examples are appropriate, and research as needed.

Walker's essay also makes liberal use of **citation**, the quotation of other writers' words. In fact, her essay begins with a citation from Jean Toomer's *Cane*. She gives only a one-sentence context for this quotation from "Avey," however, and her contextualization of this quote is hardly exhaustive. Might the effectiveness of this quotation change if the reader knew the whole context? Similarly, Walker **paraphrases** a poem by the Ugandan poet, Okot p'Bitek. (**Paraphrase** (par'e-

UNIT 7

fraz') *n.* **1.** A restatement of a text or passage in another form or in other words, often to clarify meaning.) The original wording of p'Bitek's poem is as follows:

> O, my clansmen
> Let us all cry together!
> Come,
> Let us mourn the death of my husband,
> The death of a Prince
> The Ash that was produced
> By a great fire!
> O, this homestead is utterly dead
> Close the gates
> With *lacari* thorns,
> For the Prince
> The heir to the Stool is lost!
> And all the young men
> Have perished in the wilderness!

The poem, in its original, is sung by a woman, Lawino, whose husband, Ocol, is not dead, but rather, has just taken another wife. Though this is not unexpected in a polygamous culture, the facts that his new wife is not younger, but older (almost the age of his mother) and Westernized (she wears make-up and speaks English) are what provoked Lawino's outcry. Lawino's cry is to the men in her clan; she is hoping they will force Ocol to mend his ways and preserve African tradition. Do these changes in the words and context of this poem advance or undermine Walker's argument?

AMA ATA AIDOO

Born in Abeadzi Kyiakor, Gold Coast (now Ghana), Ama Ata Aidoo (1942–) was the daughter of the chief of Abeadzi Kyiakor; therefore, she grew up in a royal household. Though it was a household with a clear sense of African tradition, Ama Ata Aidoo received a Western education, graduating from the University of Ghana in 1964. She was already writing fiction, drama, and poetry.

The most prevalent theme in Ama Ata Aidoo's corpus is the conflict between traditional African culture and Western values. Her protagonists, mainly female, often are caught between encroaching Westernization and an African tribal culture not particularly generous to women.

Ama Ata Aidoo has taught for many years in Africa and in the United States. For years, she was a professor at the University of Ghana. She has also lived in Zimbabwe.

Playwright, poet, novelist, and short-story writer, Ama Ata Aidoo has emerged as one of Africa's most renowned voices, speaking out on such issues as the legacy of colonialism, clashes in value systems, and the place of women in Africa's post-colonial societies.

NO SWEETNESS HERE
Ama Ata Aidoo

1 He was beautiful, but that was not important. Beauty does not play such a vital role in a man's life as it does in a woman's, especially if that man is a Fanti. If a man's beauty is so ill-mannered as to be noticeable, people discreetly ignore its existence. Only an immodest girl like me would dare comment on a boy's beauty. "Kwesi is so handsome," I was always telling his mother. "If ever I am transferred from this place, I will kidnap him." I enjoyed teasing the dear woman and she enjoyed being teased about him. She would look scandalised, pleased and alarmed all in one fleeting moment.

"Ei, Chicha." She called me the Fanticised version of "teacher." "You should not say such things. The boy is not very handsome really." But she knew she was lying. "Besides, Chicha, who cares whether a boy is handsome or not?" Again she knew that at least she cared, for, after all, didn't the boy's wonderful personality throw a warm light on the mother's lively though already waning beauty? Then gingerly, but in a remarkably matter-of-fact tone, she would voice out her gnawing fear "Please Chicha, I always know you are just making fun of me, but please, promise me you won't take Kwesi away with you." Almost at once her tiny mouth would quiver and she would hide her eyes in her cloth as if ashamed of her great love and her fears. But I understood. "O, Maami, don't cry, you know I don't mean it.

"Chicha I am sorry, and I trust you. Only I can't help fearing, can I? What will I do, Chicha, what would I do, should something happen to my child?" She would raise her pretty eyes, glistening with unshed tears.

"Nothing will happen to him," I would assure her. "He is a good boy. He does not fight and therefore there is no chance of anyone beating him. He is not dull, at least not too dull which means he does not get more cane-lashes than the rest of his mates. . . ."

Reprinted from *No Sweetness Here and Other Stories* (1971), The Feminist Press.

5   "Chicha, I shall willingly submit to your canes if he gets his sums wrong," she would hastily intervene.

"Don't be funny. A little warming-up on a cold morning wouldn't do him any harm. But if you say so, I won't object to hitting that soft flesh of yours." At this, the tension would break and both of us begin laughing. Yet I always went away with the image of her quivering mouth and unshed tears in my mind.

Maami Ama loved her son; and this is a statement silly, as silly as saying Maami Ama is a woman. Which mother would not? At the time of this story, he had just turned ten years old. He was in Primary Class Four and quite tall for his age. His skin was as smooth as shea-butter and as dark as charcoal. His black hair was as soft as his mother's. His eyes were of the kind that always remind one of a long dream on a hot afternoon. It is indecent to dwell on a boy's physical appearance, but then Kwesi's beauty was indecent.

The evening was not yet come. My watch read 4.15 P.M., that ambiguous time of the day, which the Fantis, despite their great ancient astronomic knowledge, have always failed to identify. For the very young and very old, it is certainly evening for they've stayed at home all day and they begin to persuade themselves that the day is ending. Bored with their own company, they sprawl in the marketplace or by their own walls. The children begin to whimper for their mothers, for they are tired with playing "house." Fancying themselves starving, they go back to what was left of their lunch, but really they only pray that mother will come home from the farm soon. The very old certainly do not go back on lunch remains but they do bite back at old conversational topics which were fresh at ten o'clock.

"I say, Kwame, as I was saying this morning, my first wife was a most beautiful woman," old Kofi would say.

10   "Oh! yes, yes, she was an unusually beautiful girl. I remember her." Old Kwame would nod his head but the truth was he was tired of the story and he was sleepy. "It's high time the young people came back from the farm."

But I was a teacher, and I went the white man's way. School was over. Maami Ama's hut was at one end of the village and the school was at the other. Nevertheless it was not a long walk from the school to her place because Bamso is not really a big village. I had left my books to little Grace Ason to take home for me; so I had only my little clock in my hand and I was walking in a leisurely way. As I passed the old people, they shouted their greetings. Here too it was always the Fanticised form of the English.

"Kudiimin-o, Chicha." Then I would answer, "Kudiimin, Nana." When I greeted first, the response was "Tanchiw," that is "Thank you."

"Chicha, how are you?"

"Nana, I am well."

15 "And how are the children?"

"Nana, they are well."

"*Yoo,* that is good." When an old man felt inclined to be talkative, especially if he had more than me for audience, he would compliment me on the work I was doing. Then he would go on to the assets of education, especially female education, ending up with quoting Dr. Aggrey.

So this evening too, I was delayed: but it was as well, for when I arrived at the hut, Maami Ama had just arrived from the farm. The door opened, facing the village, and so I could see her. Oh, that picture is still vivid in my mind. She was sitting on a low stool with her load before her. Like all the loads the other women would bring from the farms into their homes, it was colourful with miscellaneous articles. At the very bottom of the wide wooden tray were the cassava and yam tubers, rich muddy brown, the colour of the earth. Next were the plantain, of the green colour of the woods from which they came. Then there were the gay vegetables, the scarlet pepper, garden eggs, golden pawpaw and crimson tomatoes. Over this riot of colours the little woman's eyes were fixed, absorbed, while the tiny hands delicately picked the pepper. I made a scratchy noise at the door. She looked up and smiled. Her smile was a wonderful flashing whiteness.

"Oh Chicha, I have just arrived."

20 "So I see. *Ayekoo.*"

"*Yaa,* my own. And how are you, my child?"

"Very well, Mother."

"And you?"

"Tanchiw. Do sit down, there's a stool in that corner. Sit down. Mmmm . . . Life is a battle. What can we do? We are just trying, my daughter."

25 "Why were you longer at the farm today?"

"After weeding that plot I told you about last week, I thought I would go for one or two yams."

"Ah!" I cried.

"You know tomorrow is Ahobaa. Even if one does not feel happy, one must have some yam for old Ahor."

"Yes. So I understand. The old saviour deserves it. After all it is not often that a man offers himself a sacrifice to the gods to save his people from a pestilence."

30 "No, Chicha, we Fantis were so lucky."

"But Maami Ama, why do you look so sad? After all, the yams are quite big." She gave me a small grin, looking at the yams she had now packed at the corner.

"Do you think so? Well, they are the best of the lot. My daughter, when life fails you, it fails you totally. One's yams reflect the total sum of one's life. And mine look wretched enough."

"O, Maami, why are you always speaking in this way? Look at Kwesi, how many mothers can boast of such a son? Even though he is only one, consider those who have none at all. Perhaps some woman is sitting at some corner envying you."

She chuckled. "What an unhappy woman she must be who would envy Ama! But thank you, I should be grateful for Kwesi."

35 After that we were quiet for a while. I always loved to see her moving quietly about her work. Having finished unpacking, she knocked the dirt out of the tray and started making fire to prepare the evening meal. She started humming a religious lyric. She was a Methodist.

We are fighting
We are fighting
We are fighting for Canaan, the Heavenly Kingdom above.

I watched her and my eyes became misty, she looked so much like my own mother. Presently, the fire began to smoke. She turned round. "Chicha."

"Maami Ama."

"Do you know that tomorrow I am going to have a formal divorce?"

"Oh!" And I could not help the dismay in my voice.

40 I had heard, soon after my arrival in the village, that the parents of that most beautiful boy were as good as divorced. I had hoped they would come to a respectful understanding for the boy's sake. Later on when I got to know his mother, I had wished for this, for her own sweet self's sake. But as time went on I had realised this could not be or was not even desirable. Kodjo Fi was a selfish and bullying man, whom no decent woman ought to have married. He got on marvellously with his two other wives but they were three of a feather. Yet I was sorry to hear Maami was going to have a final breach with him.

"Yes, I am," she went on. "I should. What am I going on like this for? What is man struggling after? Seven years is a long time to bear ill-usage from a man coupled with contempt and insults from his wives. What have I done to deserve the abuse of his sisters? And his mother!"

"Does she insult you too?" I exclaimed.

"Why not? Don't you think she would? Considering that I don't buy her the most expensive cloths on the market and I don't give her the best fish from my soup, like her daughters-in-law do."

I laughed. "The mean old witch!"

45   "Chicha, don't laugh. I am quite sure she wanted to eat Kwesi but I baptised him and she couldn't."

"Oh, don't say that Maami. I am quite sure they all like you, only you don't know."

"My child, they don't. They hate me."

"But what happened?" I asked the question I had wanted to ask for so long.

"You would ask, Chicha! I don't know. They suddenly began hating me when Kwesi was barely two. Kodjo Fi reduced my housekeeping money and sometimes he refused to give me anything at all. He wouldn't eat my food. At first, I used to ask him why. He always replied, "It is nothing." If I had not been such an unlucky woman, his mother and sisters might have taken my side, but for me there was no one. That planting time, although I was his first wife, he allotted to me the smallest, thorniest plot."

50   "Ei, what did you say about it?"

"What could I say? At that time my mother was alive, though my father was already dead. When I complained to her about the treatment I was getting from my husband, she told me that in marriage, a woman must sometimes be a fool. But I have been a fool for far too long a time."

"Oh!" I frowned.

"Mother has died and left me and I was an only child too. My aunts are very busy looking after the affairs of their own daughters. I've told my uncles several times but they never take me seriously. They feel I am only a discontented woman."

"You?" I asked in surprise.

55   "Perhaps you would not think so. But there are several who do feel like that in this village."

She paused for a while, while she stared at the floor.

"You don't know, but I've been the topic of gossip for many years. Now, I only want to live on my own looking after my child. I don't think I will ever get any more children. Chicha, our people say a bad marriage kills the soul. Mine is fit for burial."

"Maami, don't grieve."

"My daughter, my mother and father who brought me to this world have left me alone and I've stopped grieving for them. When death summoned them, they were glad to lay down their tools and go to their parents. Yes, they loved me all right but even they had to leave me. Why should I make myself unhappy about a man for whom I ceased to exist a long time ago?"

60   She went to the big basket, took out some cassava and plantain, and sitting down began peeling them. Remembering she had forgotten the wooden bowl into which she would put the food, she got up to go for it. She looked like an orphan indeed.

"In this case," I continued the conversation, "what will happen to Kwesi?"

"What will happen to him?" she asked in surprise. "This is no problem. They may tell me to give him to his father."

"And would you?"

"No, I wouldn't."

65   "And would you succeed in keeping him if his father insisted?"

"Well, I would struggle, for my son is his father's child but he belongs to my family."

I sat there listening to these references to the age-old customs of my people of which I had been ignorant. I was surprised. She washed the food, now cut into lumps and arranged it in the cooking-pot. She added water and put it on the fire. She blew at it and it burst into flames.

"Maami Ama, has not your husband got a right to take Kwesi from you?" I asked her.

"He has, I suppose, but not entirely. Anyway, if the elders who would make the divorce settlement ask me to let him go and stay with his father, I would refuse."

70   "You are a brave woman."

"Life has taught me to be brave," she said, looking at me and smiling, "By the way, what is the time?"

I told her, "It is six minutes to six o'clock."

"And Kwesi has not yet come home?" she exclaimed.

"Mama, here I am," a piping voice announced.

75   "My husband, my brother, my father, my all-in-all, where are you?" And there he was. All at once, for the care-worn village woman, the sun might well have been rising from the east instead of setting behind the coconut palms. Her eyes shone. Kwesi saluted me and then his mother. He was a little shy of me and he ran away to the inner chamber. There was a thud which meant he had thrown his books down.

"Kwesi," his mother called out to him. "I have always told you to put your books down gently. I did not buy them with sand, and you ought to be careful with them."

He returned to where we were. I looked at him. He was very dirty. There was sand in his hair, ears and eyes. His uniform was smeared with mud, crayon and berry-juice. His braces were hanging down on one side. His mother gave an affectionate frown. "Kwesi, you are very dirty, just look at yourself. You are a disgrace to me. Anyone would think your mother does not look after you well." I was very much amused, for I knew she meant this for my ears. Kwesi just stood there, without a care in the world.

"Can't you play without putting sand in your hair?" his mother persisted.

"I am hungry," he announced. I laughed.

80   "Shame, shame, and your chicha is here. Chicha, you see? He does not fetch me water. He does not fetch me firewood. He does not weed my farm on Saturdays as other schoolboys do for their mothers. He only eats and eats." I looked at him; he fled again into the inner chamber for shame. We both started laughing at him. After a time I got up to go.

"Chicha, I would have liked you to eat before you went away; that's why I am hurrying up with the food." Maami tried to detain me.

"Oh, it does not matter. You know I eat here when I come, but today I must go away. I have the children's books to mark."

"Then I must not keep you away from your work."

"Tomorrow I will come to see you," I promised.

85   "*Yoo,* thank you."

"Sleep well, Maami."

"Sleep well, my daughter." I stepped into the open air. The sun was far receding. I walked slowly away. Just before I was out of earshot, Maami shouted after me, "And remember, if Kwesi gets his sums wrong, I will come to school to receive his lashes, if only you would tell me."

"*Yoo,*" I shouted back. Then I went away.

The next day was Ahobaada. It was a day of rejoicing for everyone. In the morning, old family quarrels were being patched up. In Maami Ama's family all became peaceful. Her aunts had—or thought they had—reconciled themselves to the fact that, when Maami Ama's mother was dying, she had instructed her sisters, much to their chagrin, to give all her jewels to her only child. This had been one of the reasons why the aunts and cousins had left Ama so much to her own devices. "After all, she has her mother's goods, what else does she need?" they were often saying. However, today, aunts, cousins and nieces have come to a better understanding. Ahobaa is a season of goodwill! Nevertheless, Ama is going to have a formal divorce today . . .

90   It had not been laid down anywhere in the Education Ordinance that school-children were to be given holidays during local festivals. And so no matter how much I sympathised with the kids, I could not give them a holiday, although Ahobaa was such an important occasion for them they naturally felt it a grievance to be forced to go to school while their friends at home were eating too much yam and meat. But they had their revenge on me. They fidgeted the whole day. What was worse, the schoolroom was actually just one big shed. When I left the Class One chicks to look at the older ones, they chattered; when I turned to them, Class Two and Class Three began shouting. Oh, it was a fine situation. In the afternoon, after having gone home to taste the festive dishes, they nearly drove me mad. So I was relieved when it was three o'clock. Feeling no sense of guilt, I turned them all out to play. They rushed out to the field. I packed my books on the table for little Grace to take home. My intention was to go and see the divorce proceedings which had begun at one o'clock and then come back at four to dismiss them. These divorce cases took hours to settle, and I hoped I would hear some of it.

As I walked down between the rows of desks, I hit my leg against one. The books on it tumbled down. As I picked them up I saw they belonged to Kwesi. It was the desk he shared with a little girl. I began thinking about him and the unhappy connection he had with what was going on at that moment down in the village. I remembered every word of the conversation I had had with his mother the previous evening. I became sad at the prospect of a possible separation from the mother who loved him so much and whom he loved. From his infancy they had known only each other, a lonely mother and a lonely son. Through the hot sun, she had carried him on her back as she weeded her corn-field. How could she dare to put him down under a tree in the shade when there was no one to look after him? Other women had their own younger sisters or

UNIT 7

those of their husbands to help with the baby; but she had had no one. The only face the little one had known was his mother's. And now . . .

"But," I told myself, "I am sure it will be all right with him."

"Will it?" I asked myself.

"Why not? He is a happy child."

95   "Does that solve the problem?"

"Not all together, but . . ."

"No buts; one should think of the house into which he would be taken now. He may not be a favourite there."

But my other voice told me that a child need not be a favourite to be happy.

I had to bring the one-man argument to an end. I had to hurry. Passing by the field, I saw some of the boys playing football. At the goal at the further end was a headful of hair shining in the afternoon sun. I knew the body to which it belonged. A goalkeeper is a dubious character in infant soccer. He is either a good goalkeeper and that is why he is at the goal, which is usually difficult to know in a child or he is a bad player. If he is a bad player, he might as well be in the goal as anywhere else. Kwesi loved football, that was certain, and he was always the goalkeeper. Whether he was good or not I had never been able to see. Just as I passed, he caught a ball and his team clapped. I heard him give the little squeaky noise that passed for his laugh. No doubt he was a happy child.

100   Now I really ran into the village. I immediately made my way to Nana Kum's house for the case was going on there. There was a great crowd in front of the house. Why were there so many people about? Then I remembered that it being a holiday, everyone was at home. And of course, after the eating and the drinking of palm-wine in the morning and midday, divorce proceedings certainly provide an agreeable diversion, especially when other people are involved and not ourselves.

The courtyard was a long one and as I jostled to where Maami Ama was sitting, pieces of comments floated into my ears. "The elders certainly have settled the case fairly," someone was saying. "But it seemed as if Kodjo Fi had no strong proofs for his arguments," another was saying. "Well, they both have been sensitive. If one feels one can't live with a woman, one might as well divorce her. And I hate a woman who cringes to a man," a third said. Finally I reached her side, around her were her family, her two aunts, Esi and Ama, her two cousins and the two uncles. To the right were the elders who were judging the case; opposite were Kodjo Fi and his family.

"I have come, Maami Ama," I announced myself.

She looked at me. "You ought to have been here earlier, the case has been settled already."

"And how are things?" I inquired.

105   "I am a divorced woman."

"What were his grounds for wanting to divorce you?"

"He said I had done nothing, he only wanted to . . ."

"Eh! Only the two of you know what went wrong," the younger aunt cried out, reproachfully. "If after his saying that, you had refused to be divorced, he would have had to pay the Ejecting Fee, but now he has got the better of you."

"But aunt," Maami protested, "how could I refuse to be divorced?"

110   "It's up to you. I know it's your own affair, only I wouldn't like your mother's ghost to think that we haven't looked after you well."

"I agree with you," the elder aunt said.

"Maami Ama, what was your debt?" I asked her.

"It is quite a big sum."

"I hope you too had something to reckon against him?"

115   "I did. He reckoned the dowry, the ten cloths he gave me, the Knocking Fee. . . ."

All this had been heard by Kodjo Fi and his family and soon they made us aware of it.

"Kodjo," his youngest sister burst out, "you forgot to reckon the Knife Fee."

"No. Yaa, I did not forget," Kodjo Fi told her. "She had no brothers to whom I would give the fee."

"It's all right then," his second sister added.

120   But the rest of his womenfolk took this to be a signal for more free comments.

"She is a bad woman and I think you are well rid of her," one aunt screamed.

"I think she is a witch," the youngest sister said.

"Oh, that she is. Anyway, only witches have no brothers or sisters. They eat them in the mother's womb long before they are born."

Ama's aunts and cousins had said nothing so far. They were inclined to believe Ama was a witch too. But Maami sat still. When the comments had gone down a bit, she resumed the conversation with me.

125   "As I was saying, Chicha, he also reckoned the price of the trunk he had given me and all the cost of the medicine he gave me to make me have more children. There was only the Cooking Cost for me to reckon against his."

"Have you got money to pay the debt?" I asked her.

UNIT 7

"No, but I am not going to pay it. My uncles will pay it out of the family fund and put the debt down against my name."

"Oh!"

"But you are a fool," Maami Ama's eldest aunt shouted at her.

130   "I say you are a fool," she insisted.

"But aunt . . ." Maami Ama began to protest.

"Yes! And I hope you are not going to answer back. I was born before your mother and now that she is dead, I'm your mother! Besides, when she was alive I could scold her when she went wrong, and now I say you are a fool. For seven years you have struggled to look after a child. Whether he ate or not was your affair alone. Whether he had any cloth or not did not concern any other person. When Kwesi was a child he had no father. When he nearly died of measles, no grandmother looked in. As for aunts, he began getting them when he started going to school. And now you are allowing them to take him away from you. Now that he is grown enough to be counted among the living, a father knows he has got a son."

"So, so!" Kodjo Fi's mother sneered at her. "What did you think? That Kodjo would give his son as a present to you, eh? The boy belongs to his family, but he must be of some service to his father too."

"Have I called your name?" Ama's aunt asked the old woman.

135   "You have not called her name but you were speaking against her son." This again was from Kodjo Fi's youngest sister.

"And who are you to answer my mother back?" Ama's two cousins demanded of her.

"Go away. But who are you people?"

"Go away, too, you greedy lot."

"It is you who are greedy, witches."

140   "You are always calling other people witches. Only a witch can know a witch."

Soon everyone was shouting at everyone else. The people who have come started going home, and only the most curious ones stood by to listen. Maami Ama was murmuring something under her breath which I could not hear. I persuaded her to come with me. All that time no word had passed between her and her ex-husband. As we turned to go, Kodjo Fi's mother shouted at her, "You are hurt. But that is what you deserve. We will get the child. We will! What did you want to do with him?"

Maami Ama turned round to look at her. "What are you putting yourself to so much trouble for? When Nana Kum said the boy ought to go and stay with his father, did I make any objection? He is at the school. Go and fetch him. Tomorrow, you can send your carriers to come and fetch his belongings from my hut." These words were said quietly.

Then I remembered suddenly that I had to hurry to school to dismiss the children. I told Maami Ama to go home but that I would try to see her before night.

This time I did not go by the main street. I took the back door through back streets and lanes. It was past four already. As I hurried along, I heard a loud roaring sound which I took to be echoes of the quarrel, so I went my way. When I reached the school, I did not like what I saw. There was not a single childish soul anywhere. But everyone's books were there. The shed was as untidy as ever. Little Grace had left my books too. Of course I was more than puzzled. "How naughty these children are. How did they dare to disobey me when I had told them to wait there until I came to dismiss them?" It was no use looking around the place. They were not there. "They need discipline," I threatened to the empty shed. I picked up my books and clock. Then I noticed that Kwesi's desk was clean of all his books. Nothing need be queer about this; he had probably taken his home. As I was descending the hill the second time that afternoon, I saw that the whole school was at the other end of the main street. What were the children doing so near Maami Ama's place? I ran towards them.

145   I was not prepared for what I saw. As if intentionally, the children had formed a circle. When some of them saw me, they all began to tell me what had happened. But I did not hear a word. In the middle of the circle, Kwesi was lying flat on his back. His shirt was off. His right arm was swollen to the size of his head. I simply stood there with my mouth open. From the back yard, Maami Ama screamed, "I am drowning, people of Bamso, come and save me!" Soon the whole village was there.

What is the matter? What has happened? Kwesi has been bitten by a snake. Where? When? At school. He was playing football. Where? What has happened? Bitten by a snake, a snake, a snake.

Questions and answers were tossed from mouth to mouth in the shocked evening air. Meanwhile, those who knew about snake-bites were giving the names of different cures. Kwesi's father was looking anxiously at his son. That strong powerful man was almost stupid with shock and alarm. Dose upon dose was forced down the reluctant throat but nothing seemed to have any effect. Women paced up and down around the hut, totally oblivious of the fact that had left their festive meals half prepared. Each one was trying to imagine how she would have

felt if Kwesi had been her child, and in imagination they suffered more that the
suffering mother. "The gods and spirits of our fathers protect us from calamity!"

After what seemed an unbearably long time, the messenger who had been earlier sent to Surdo, the village next to Bamso, to summon the chief medicine man
arrived, followed by the eminent doctor himself. He was renowned for his cure
of snake-bites. When he appeared, everyone gave a sigh of relief. They all remembered someone, perhaps a father, brother or husband, he had snatched from the
jaws of death. When he gave his potion to the boy, he would be violently sick
and then of course, he would be out of danger. The potion was given. Thirty
minutes; an hour; two hours; three, four hours. He had not retched. Before midnight he was dead. No grown-up in Bamso village slept that night. Kwesi was the
first boy to have died since the school was inaugurated some six years previously.
"And he was his mother's only child. She has no one now. We do not understand it. Life is not sweet!" This was their verdict.

The morning was very beautiful. It seemed as if every natural object in and
around the village had kept vigil too. So they too were tired. I was tired too. I
had gone to bed at about five o'clock in the morning and since it was a Saturday I could have a long sleep. At ten o'clock, I was suddenly roused from sleep
by shouting. I opened my window but I could not see the speakers. Presently
Kweku Sam, one of the young men in the village, came past my window. "Good
morning Chicha." He shouted his greeting to me.

150   "Good morning, Kweku," I responded. "What is the shouting about?"

"They are quarrelling."

"And what are they quarrelling about now?"

"Each is accusing the other of having been responsible for the boy's death."

"How?"

155   "Chicha, I don't know. Only women make too much trouble for themselves
It seems as if they are never content to sit quiet but they must always hurl abuse
at each other. What has happened is too serious to be a subject for quarrels. Perhaps the village has displeased the gods in some unknown way and that is why
they have taken away this boy." He sighed. I could not say anything to that. I could
not explain it myself, and if the villagers believed there was something more in
Kwesi's death than the ordinary human mind could explain, who was I to argue?

"Is Maami Ama herself there?"

"No, I have not seen her there."

He was quiet and I was quiet.

"Chicha, I think I should go away now. I have just heard that my sister has given birth to a girl."

160   "So," I smiled to myself. "Give her my congratulations and tell her I will come to see her tomorrow."

"*Yoo.*"

He walked away to greet his new niece. I stood for a long time at the window staring at nothing, while I heard snatches of words and phrases from the quarrel. And these were mingled with weeping. Then I turned from the window. Looking into the little mirror on the wall, I was not surprised to see my whole face bathed in unconscious tears. I did not feel like going to bed. I did not feel like doing anything at all. I toyed with the idea of going to see Maami Ama and then finally decided against it. I could not bear to face her; at least, not yet. So I sat down thinking about him. I went over the most presumptuous daydreams I had indulged in on his account. "I would have taken him away with me in spite of his mother's protests." She was just being absurd. "The child is a boy, and sooner or later, she must learn to live without him. The highest class here is Primary Six and when I am going away, I will take him. I will give him a secondary education. Perhaps, who knows, one day he may win a scholarship to the university." In my daydreams, I had never determined what career he would have followed, but he would be famous, that was certain. Devastatingly handsome, he would be the idol of women and the envy of every man. He would visit Britain, America and all these countries we have heard so much about. He would see all the seven wonders of the world. "Maami shall be happy in the end," I had told myself. "People will flock to see the mother of such an illustrious man. Although she has not had many children, she will be surrounded by her grandchildren. Of course, away from the village." In all these reveries his father never had a place, but there was I, and there was Maami Ama, and there was his father, and he, that bone of contention, was host to all three. I saw the highest castles I had built for him come tumbling down, noiselessly and swiftly.

He was buried at four o'clock. I had taken the schoolchildren to where he lay in state. When his different relatives saw the little uniformed figure they all forgot their differences and burst into loud lamentations. "Chicha, O Chicha, what shall I do now that Kwesi is dead?" His grandmother addressed me. "Kwesi, my Beauty, Kwesi my Master, Kwesi-my-own-Kwesi," one aunt was chanting, "Father Death has done me an ill turn."

"Chicha," the grandmother continued, "my washing days are over, for who will give me water? My eating days are over, for who will give me food?" I stood there, saying nothing. I had let the children sing "Saviour Blessed Saviour." And we had gone to the cemetery with him.

165   After the funeral, I went to the House of Mourning as one should do after a burial. No one was supposed to weep again for the rest of the day. I sat there listening to visitors who had come from the neighbouring villages.

"This is certainly sad, and it is most strange. School has become like business, those who found it earlier for their children are eating more than the children themselves. To have a schoolboy snatched away like this is unbearable indeed," one woman said.

"Ah, do not speak," his father's youngest sister broke in. "We have lost a treasure."

"My daughter," said the grandmother again, "Kwesi is gone, gone for ever to our forefathers. And what can we do?"

"What can we do indeed? When flour is scattered in the sand, who can sift it? But this is the saddest I've heard, that he was his mother's only one."

170   "Is that so?" another visitor cried. "I always thought she had other children. What does one do, when one's only water-pot breaks?" she whispered. The question was left hanging in the air. No one dared say anything more.

I went out. I never knew how I got there, but I saw myself approaching Maami Ama's hut. As usual, the door was open. I entered the outer room. She was not there. Only sheep and goats from the village were busy munching at the cassava and the yams. I looked into the inner chamber. She was there. Still clad in the cloth she had worn to the divorce proceedings, she was not sitting, standing or lying down. She was kneeling, and like one drowning who catches at a straw, she was clutching Kwesi's books and school uniform to her breast. "Maami Ama, Maami Ama," I called out to her. She did not move. I left her alone. Having driven the sheep and goats away, I went out, shutting the door behind me. "I must go home now," I spoke to myself once more. The sun was sinking behind the coconut palm. I looked at my watch. It was six o'clock; but this time, I did not run.

LEVELS OF READING

Summary:

Pay attention to the **literal** meaning of the text. Briefly describe the narrative of Ama Ata Aidoo's, "No Sweetness Here." Repeat the story of the text in your own words. Who tells the story? In what situations do the women in "No Sweetness Here" find themselves? Do they have any control over their own destinies? Who controls their futures? How does Maami Ama react to her situation? Concentrate on the highlights; avoid too much detail when summarizing. Again, drawing a simple outline of the main points of the text will help you better analyze the text at other levels of interpretation.

Analysis:

Find what you believe is **symbolic** in the text. For example, what is so significant about the impending divorce proceeding in "No Sweetness Here"? What do yams signify in this culture? Why might Kwesi himself be a symbolic figure in this story? Find any other symbols you think are important in this story and explain the meaning of these symbols. With the help of the background material provided about Ama Ata Aidoo, make an argument about this text, and include mention of the more **figurative** aspects of the text when making points in defense of your argument.

Application:

Apply what you have learned about women, education and authorship (even of a life) from Virginia Woolf's *A Room of One's Own* and Alice Walker's *In Search of Our Mothers' Gardens* to help you make an argument about Aidoo's short story. The "part" of the story you choose to analyze may include any of the following: a character, a setting, a symbol or symbols, an important change, a motivation, a goal, a result. Consider the following as possibilities, but explore other original interpretations too:

- Note the dates of Woolf's and Walker's essays. Do any of the points Woolf makes about women, education and money obtain for Maami Ama? Can you use the later insights of Walker to gain any additional grasp on the situation this woman finds herself in? Does she make an attempt to author her own life's story?

· Woolf's emphasis is on **writing** as a creative outlet for women. Is there any evidence of other "outlets" of creativity—as described by Walker—for the women in Aidoo's story?

· How much agency do the women in this story have? Are they residing in what is called a **patriarchal** society? How much control do men have over these women's lives? Does Maami Ama have any control over her own life?

· Do women need, as Woolf argues, an education, a private income and a room of one's own—with key and lock—to realize creative potential? Or to fashion a self?

Start Your Own Argument:

What important point does Walker think Woolf overlooked in her argument about women and writing? Might the dates of composition of these two essays have a bearing on both Woolf's oversight and Walker's insight? What does Walker's essay contribute to Woolf's earlier feminism? Also, when comparing and contrasting Woolf's argument and Walker's counterargument, would what Marx has to say about class conflict be useful? Does Freud's theory of repression apply to either or both of these arguments? How so?

EIGHT

ARGUMENT TRACING AND REVISING:
A HISTORICAL PERSPECTIVE

THOMAS KUHN

Thomas Kuhn (1922–1996) was born in Cincinnati, Ohio. He received his B.A., M.A., and Ph.D. degrees in physics from Harvard University, where he also briefly served as an assistant professor in the history of science, before joining the faculty of the University of California at Berkeley, where he was named a full professor of the history of science in 1961. From 1964 until 1979, he was a professor at Princeton; in 1979 he joined the faculty at MIT.

Professor Kuhn's groundbreaking book, The Structure of Scientific Revolutions, *published in 1962, was begun while Dr. Kuhn was still a graduate student in physics. It has now sold well over a million copies and has been translated into sixteen languages. It remains to this day required reading in many basic courses in the history and philosophy of science.*

Since Dr. Kuhn pointed out the similarities between revolutions in science and politics, his book also has enjoyed some influence in cultural studies. That interest in Dr. Kuhn's thesis has grown beyond scientific circles is not at all surprising, since it is remarkably adaptable in other disciplines, including the humanities.

Dr. Kuhn's argument is ingenious in its simplicity, yet at the time of its publication, and continuing to the present, it still provokes strong reactions in the philosophic and scientific communities in particular. In his book, Dr. Kuhn argues that most of what science does in research is conservative, designed to provide further proof for "paradigms," or scientific models already in place and accepted by the scientific community—and the general public, to an extent—as "true," i.e., verifiable. This is what Kuhn calls "normal science." When in the course of their research, scientists bump up against phenomena that do not "fit" into the paradigm or model, they either try to make the data fit, explain it away, or ignore it altogether. Only when the bits of ill-fitting, rationalized, and/or ignored materials

*add up to a critical mass does a "paradigm shift" occur. Paradigm shifts represent
what Kuhn calls "scientific revolutions."*

*The most common example given to buttress Kuhn's argument is the transition
from the Copernican model of the universe to the model proposed by Galileo. For
centuries, backed up by the Catholic Church, science worked hard to prove that
the earth was the center of the solar system, forcing uncooperative data into that
model, or ignoring what seemed to contradict it. It took years for Galileo's data to
force a paradigm shift in the scientific community, and even longer for the Church
to capitulate and accept the replacement of its theologically preferable paradigm.
Only in the late twentieth century did the Church finally vindicate Galileo, reversing his excommunication on the grounds of heresy.*

*According to Kuhn's theory, though, scientists are now busy doing nothing
more than "normal science," working overtime to find data to confirm the long-
held theory that the sun is the center of our universe. Perhaps another paradigm
shift will occur in the future.*

As is the case with Virginia Woolf's *A Room of One's Own* and Karl Marx's
Manifesto, to name but two examples, Thomas Kuhn's essays, taken from his
controversial book, *The Structure of Scientific Revolutions,* traces a history.
Woolf imagines a hypothetical situation to "create" her history; Marx examines
real past historical patterns. Both Woolf and Marx, however, trace history in
order to call for societal change in their present. Thomas Kuhn, while tracing
important points in the history of science, wants to overturn what he calls the
"concept of development-by-accumulation," i.e. the development of science
through history. Before Kuhn, scientists thought any new knowledge generated
must build on what is already known, a theory similar to that of Woolf and
Marx. After Kuhn, scientists had to question the validity of the historical
knowledge of all scientific theory. In other words, Woolf and Marx seem to say,
This history helps to explain the problems we encounter in the present. But,
Kuhn says, This history has nothing to do with where we are today.

Coming to Terms with the Reading:

Before reading/rereading Thomas Kuhn's "The Nature of Normal Science," and "The Nature and Necessity of Scientific Revolutions," it is best to have a firm grasp on the meanings of the following terms:

1. paradigm
2. normal science
3. the box
4. empirical observation
5. scientific revolutions
6. circular argument/tautology
7. anomaly
8. cumulative
9. paradigm shift

THE NATURE OF NORMAL SCIENCE
Thomas Kuhn

1   What then is the nature of the more professional and esoteric research that a group's reception of a single paradigm permits? If the paradigm represents work that has been done once and for all, what further problems does it leave the united group to resolve? Those questions will seem even more urgent if we now note one respect in which the terms used so far may be misleading. In its established usage, a paradigm is an accepted model or pattern, and that aspect of its meaning has enabled me, lacking a better word, to appropriate 'paradigm' here. But it will shortly be clear that the sense of 'model' and 'pattern' that permits the appropriation is not quite the one usual in defining 'paradigm.' In grammar, for example, '*amo, amas, amat*' is a paradigm because it displays the pattern to be used in conjugating a large number of other Latin verbs, e.g., in producing '*laudo, laudas, laudat.*' In this standard application, the paradigm functions by permitting the replication of examples any one of which could in principle serve to replace it. In a science, on the other hand, a paradigm is rarely an object for replication. Instead, like an accepted judicial decision in the common law, it is an object for further articulation and specification under new or more stringent conditions.

To see how this can be so, we must recognize how very limited in both scope and precision a paradigm can be at the time of its first appearance. Paradigms gain their status because they are more successful than their competitors in solving a few problems that the group of practitioners has come to recognize as acute. To be more successful is not, however, to be either completely successful with a single problem or notably successful with any large number. The success of a paradigm—whether Aristotle's analysis of motion, Ptolemy's computations of planetary position, Lavoisier's application of the balance, or Maxwell's mathematization of the electromagnetic field—is at the start largely a promise of success discoverable in selected and still incomplete examples. Normal science consists in the actualization of that promise, an actualization achieved by extending the knowledge of those facts that the paradigm displays as particularly reveal-

Reprinted from *The Structure of Scientific Revolutions,* (1996), by permission of University of Chicago Press.

ing, by increasing the extent of the match between those facts and the paradigm's predictions, and by further articulation of the paradigm itself.

Few people who are not actually practitioners of a mature science realize how much mop-up work of this sort a paradigm leaves to be done or quite how fascinating such work can prove in the execution. And these points need to be understood. Mopping-up operations are what engage most scientists throughout their careers. They constitute what I am here calling normal science. Closely examined, whether historically or in the contemporary laboratory, that enterprise seems an attempt to force nature into the preformed and relatively inflexible box that the paradigm supplies. No part of the aim of normal science is to call forth new sorts of phenomena; indeed those that will not fit the box are often not seen at all. Nor do scientists normally aim to invent new theories, and they are often intolerant of those invented by others.[1] Instead, normal-scientific research is directed to the articulation of those phenomena and theories that the paradigm already supplies.

Perhaps these are defects. The areas investigated by normal science are, of course, minuscule; the enterprise now under discussion has drastically restricted vision. But those restrictions, born from confidence in a paradigm, turn out to be essential to the development of science. By focusing attention upon a small range of relatively esoteric problems, the paradigm forces scientists to investigate some part of nature in a detail and depth that would otherwise be unimaginable. And normal science possesses a built-in mechanism that ensures the relaxation of the restrictions that bound research whenever the paradigm from which they derive ceases to function effectively. At that point scientists begin to behave differently, and the nature of their research problems changes. In the interim, however, during the period when the paradigm is successful, the profession will have solved problems that its members could scarcely have imagined and would never have undertaken without commitment to the paradigm. And at least part of that achievement always proves to be permanent.

5   To display more clearly what is meant by normal or paradigm-based research, let me now attempt to classify and illustrate the problems of which normal science principally consists. For convenience I postpone theoretical activity and begin with fact-gathering, that is, with the experiments and observations described in the technical journals through which scientists inform their professional colleagues of the results of their continuing research. On what aspects of nature do scientists ordinarily report? What determines their choice? And,

---

[1] Bernard Barber, "Resistance by Scientists to Scientific Discovery," *Science,* CXXXIV (1961), 596–602.

since most scientific observation consumes much time, equipment, and money, what motivates the scientist to pursue that choice to a conclusion?

There are, I think, only three normal foci for factual scientific investigation, and they are neither always nor permanently distinct. First is that class of facts that the paradigm has shown to be particularly revealing of the nature of things. By employing them in solving problems, the paradigm has made them worth determining both with more precision and in a larger variety of situations. At one time or another, these significant factual determinations have included: in astronomy—stellar position and magnitude, the periods of eclipsing binaries and of planets; in physics—the specific gravities and compressibilities of materials, wave lengths and spectral intensities, electrical conductivities and contact potentials; and in chemistry—composition and combining weights, boiling points and acidity of solutions, structural formulas and optical activities. Attempts to increase the accuracy and scope with which facts like these are known occupy a significant fraction of the literature of experimental and observational science. Again and again complex special apparatus has been designed for such purposes, and the invention, construction, and deployment of that apparatus have demanded first-rate talent, much time, and considerable financial backing. Synchrotrons and radiotelescopes are only the most recent examples of the lengths to which research workers will go if a paradigm assures them that the facts they seek are important. From Tycho Brahe to E. O. Lawrence, some scientists have acquired great reputations, not from any novelty of their discoveries, but from the precision, reliability, and scope of the methods they developed for the redetermination of a previously known sort of fact.

A second usual but smaller class of factual determinations is directed to those facts that, though often without much intrinsic interest, can be compared directly with predictions from the paradigm theory. As we shall see shortly, when I turn from the experimental to the theoretical problems of normal science, there are seldom many areas in which a scientific theory, particularly if it is cast in a predominantly mathematical form, can be directly compared with nature. No more than three such areas are even yet accessible to Einstein's general theory of relativity.[2] Furthermore,

---

[2]The only long-standing check point still generally recognized is the precession of Mercury's perihelion. The red shift in the spectrum of light from distant stars can be derived from considerations more elementary than general relativity, and the same may be possible for the bending of light around the sun, a point now in some dispute. In any case, measurements of the latter phenomenon remain equivocal. One additional check point may have been established very recently: the gravitational shift of Mossbauer radiation. Perhaps there will soon be others in this now active but long dormant field. For an up-to-date capsule account of the problem, see L. I. Schiff, "A Report on the NASA Conference on Experimental Tests of Theories of Relativity," *Physics Today,* XIV (1961), 42–48.

even in those areas where application is possible, it often demands theoretical and instrumental approximations that severely limit the agreement to be expected. Improving that agreement or finding new areas in which agreement can be demonstrated at all presents a constant challenge to the skill and imagination of the experimentalist and observer. Special telescopes to demonstrate the Copernican prediction of annual parallax; Atwood's machine, first invented almost a century after the *Principia,* to give the first unequivocal demonstration of Newton's second law; Foucault's apparatus to show that the speed of light is greater in air than in water; or the gigantic scintillation counter designed to demonstrate the existence of the neutrino—these pieces of special apparatus and many others like them illustrate the immense effort and ingenuity that have been required to bring nature and theory into closer and closer agreement.[3] That attempt to demonstrate agreement is a second type of normal experimental work, and it is even more obviously dependent than the first upon a paradigm. The existence of the paradigm sets the problem to be solved; often the paradigm theory is implicated directly in the design of apparatus able to solve the problem. Without the *Principia,* for example, measurements made with the Atwood machine would have meant nothing at all.

A third class of experiments and observations exhausts, I think, the fact-gathering activities of normal science. It consists of empirical work undertaken to articulate the paradigm theory, resolving some of its residual ambiguities and permitting the solution of problems to which it had previously only drawn attention. This class proves to be the most important of all, and its description demands its subdivision. In the more mathematical sciences, some of the experiments aimed at articulation are directed to the determination of physical constants. Newton's work, for example, indicated that the force between two unit masses at unit distance would be the same for all types of matter at all positions in the universe. But his own problems could be solved without even estimating the size of this attraction, the universal gravitational constant; and no one else devised apparatus able to determine it for a century after the *Principia* appeared. Nor was Cavendish's famous determination in the 1790's the last. Because of its

UNIT 8

---

[3]For two of the parallax telescopes, see Abraham Wolf, *A History of Science, Technology, and Philosophy in the Eighteenth Century* (2d ed.; London, 1952), pp. 103–5. For the Atwood machine, see N. R. Hanson, *Patterns of Discovery* (Cambridge, 1958), pp. 100–102, 207–8. For the last two pieces of special apparatus, see M. L. Foucault, "Méthode générale pour mesurer la vitesse de la lumière dans l'air et les milieux transparents. Vitesses relatives de la lumière dans l'air et dans l'eau . . . ," *Comptes rendus . . . de l'Académie des sciences,* XXX (1850), 551–60; and C. L. Cowan, Jr., *et al.,* "Detection of the Free Neutrino: A Confirmation," *Science,* CXXIV (1956), 103–4.

central position in physical theory, improved values of the gravitational constant
have been the object of repeated efforts ever since by a number of outstanding
experimentalists.[4] Other examples of the same sort of continuing work would
include determinations of the astronomical unit, Avogadro's number, Joule's
coefficient, the electronic charge, and so on. Few of these elaborate efforts would
have been conceived and none would have been carried out without a paradigm
theory to define the problem and to guarantee the existence of a stable solution.

Efforts to articulate a paradigm are not, however, restricted to the determination of universal constants. They may, for example, also aim at quantitative
laws: Boyle's Law relating gas pressure to volume, Coulomb's Law of electrical
attraction, and Joule's formula relating heat generated to electrical resistance and
current are all in this category. Perhaps it is not apparent that a paradigm is prerequisite to the discovery of laws like these. We often hear that they are found
by examining measurements undertaken for their own sake and without theoretical commitment. But history offers no support for so excessively Baconian a
method. Boyle's experiments were not conceivable (and if conceived would have
received another interpretation or none at all) until air was recognized as an elas-
tic fluid to which all the elaborate concepts of hydrostatics could be applied.[5]
Coulomb's success depended upon his constructing special apparatus to measure the force between point charges. (Those who had previously measured electrical forces using ordinary pan balances, etc., had found no consistent or simple
regularity at all.) But that design, in turn, depended upon the previous recognition that every particle of electric fluid acts upon every other at a distance. It was
for the force between such particles—the only force which might safely be
assumed a simple function of distance—that Coulomb was looking.[6] Joule's
experiments could also be used to illustrate how quantitative laws emerge through
paradigm articulation. In fact, so general and close is the relation between qualitative paradigm and quantitative law that, since Galileo, such laws have often

---

[4]J. H. P[oynting] reviews some two dozen measurements of the gravitational constant between
1741 and 1901 in "Gravitation Constant and Mean Density of the Earth," *Encyclopaedia Bri-
tannica* (11th ed.; Cambridge, 1910–11), XII, 385–89.

[5]For the full transplantation of hydrostatic concepts into pneumatics, see *The Physical Treatises
of Pascal,* trans. I. H. B. Spiers and A. G. H. Spiers, with an introduction and notes by F. Barry
(New York, 1937). Torricelli's original introduction of the parallelism ("We live submerged at
the bottom of an ocean of the element air") occurs on p. 164. Its rapid development is displayed
by the two main treatises.

[6]Duane Roller and Duane H. D. Roller, *The Development of the Concept of Electric Charge: Electricity from the Greeks to Coulomb* ("Harvard Case Histories in Experimental Science," Case 8;
Cambridge, Mass., 1954), pp. 66–80.

been correctly guessed with the aid of a paradigm years before apparatus could be designed for their experimental determination.[7]

10   Finally, there is a third sort of experiment which aims to articulate a paradigm. More than the others this one can resemble exploration, and it is particularly prevalent in those periods and sciences that deal more with the qualitative than with the quantitative aspects of nature's regularity. Often a paradigm developed for one set of phenomena is ambiguous in its application to other closely related ones. Then experiments are necessary to choose among the alternative ways of applying the paradigm to the new area of interest. For example, the paradigm applications of the caloric theory were to heating and cooling by mixtures and by change of state. But heat could be released or absorbed in many other ways— e.g., by chemical combination, by friction, and by compression or absorption of a gas—and to each of these other phenomena the theory could be applied in several ways. If the vacuum had a heat capacity, for example, heating by compression could be explained as the result of mixing gas with void. Or it might be due to a change in the specific heat of gases with changing pressure. And there were several other explanations besides. Many experiments were undertaken to elaborate these various possibilities and to distinguish between them; all these experiments arose from the caloric theory as paradigm, and all exploited it in the design of experiments and in the interpretation of results.[8] Once the phenomenon of heating by compression had been established, all further experiments in the area were paradigm-dependent in this way. Given the phenomenon, how else could an experiment to elucidate it have been chosen?

Turn now to the theoretical problems of normal science, which fall into very nearly the same classes as the experimental and observational. A part of normal theoretical work, though only a small part, consists simply in the use of existing theory to predict factual information of intrinsic value. The manufacture of astronomical ephemerides, the computation of lens characteristics, and the production of radio propagation curves are examples of problems of this sort. Scientists, however, generally regard them as hack work to be relegated to engineers or technicians. At no time do very many of them appear in significant scientific journals. But these journals do contain a great many theoretical discussions of problems that, to the nonscientist, must seem almost identical. These are the manipulations of theory undertaken, not because the predictions in which they

---

[7]For examples, see T. S. Kuhn, "The Function of Measurement in Modern Physical Science," *Isis,* LII (1961), 161–93.
[8]T. S. Kuhn, "The Caloric Theory of Adiabatic Compression," *Isis,* XLIX (1958), 132-40.

result are intrinsically valuable, but because they can be confronted directly with experiment. Their purpose is to display a new application of the paradigm or to increase the precision of an application that has already been made.

The need for work of this sort arises from the immense difficulties often encountered in developing points of contact between a theory and nature. These difficulties can be briefly illustrated by an examination of the history of dynamics after Newton. By the early eighteenth century those scientists who found a paradigm in the *Principia* took the generality of its conclusions for granted, and they had every reason to do so. No other work known to the history of science has simultaneously permitted so large an increase in both the scope and precision of research. For the heavens Newton had derived Kepler's Laws of planetary motion and also explained certain of the observed respects in which the moon failed to obey them. For the earth he had derived the results of some scattered observations on pendulums and the tides. With the aid of additional but *ad hoc* assumptions, he had also been able to derive Boyle's Law and an important formula for the speed of sound in air. Given the state of science at the time, the success of the demonstrations was extremely impressive. Yet given the presumptive generality of Newton's Laws, the number of these applications was not great, and Newton developed almost no others. Furthermore, compared with what any graduate student of physics can achieve with those same laws today, Newton's few applications were not even developed with precision. Finally, the *Principia* had been designed for application chiefly to problems of celestial mechanics. How to adapt it for terrestrial applications, particularly for those of motion under constraint, was by no means clear. Terrestrial problems were, in any case, already being attacked with great success by a quite different set of techniques developed originally by Galileo and Huyghens and extended on the Continent during the eighteenth century by the Bernoullis, d'Alembert, and many others. Presumably their techniques and those of the *Principia* could be shown to be special cases of a more general formulation, but for some time no one saw quite how.[9]

Restrict attention for the moment to the problem of precision. We have already illustrated its empirical aspect. Special equipment—like Cavendish's apparatus, the Atwood machine, or improved telescopes—was required in order

---

[9]C. Truesdell, "A Program toward Rediscovering the Rational Mechanics of the Age of Reason," *Archive for History of the Exact Sciences,* I (1960), 3–36, and "Reactions of Late Baroque Mechanics to Success, Conjecture, Error, and Failure in Newton's *Principia*," *Texas Quarterly,* X (1967), 281–97. T. L. Hankins, "The Reception of Newton's Second Law of Motion in the Eighteenth Century." *Archives internationales d'histoire des sciences,* XX (1967), 42–65.

to provide the special data that the concrete applications of Newton's paradigm demanded. Similar difficulties in obtaining agreement existed on the side of theory. In applying his laws to pendulums, for example, Newton was forced to treat the bob as a mass point in order to provide a unique definition of pendulum length. Most of his theorems, the few exceptions being hypothetical and preliminary, also ignored the effect of air resistance. These were sound physical approximations. Nevertheless, as approximations they restricted the agreement to be expected between Newton's predictions and actual experiments. The same difficulties appear even more clearly in the application of Newton's theory to the heavens. Simple quantitative telescopic observations indicate that the planets do not quite obey Kepler's Laws, and Newton's theory indicates that they should not. To derive those laws, Newton had been forced to neglect all gravitational attraction except that between individual planets and the sun. Since the planets also attract each other, only approximate agreement between the applied theory and telescopic observation could be expected.[10]

The agreement obtained was, of course, more than satisfactory to those who obtained it. Excepting for some terrestrial problems, no other theory could do nearly so well. None of those who questioned the validity of Newton's work did so because of its limited agreement with experiment and observation. Nevertheless, these limitations of agreement left many fascinating theoretical problems for Newton's successors. Theoretical techniques were, for example, required for treating the motions of more than two simultaneously attracting bodies and for investigating the stability of perturbed orbits. Problems like these occupied many of Europe's best mathematicians during the eighteenth and early nineteenth century. Euler, Lagrange, Laplace, and Gauss all did some of their most brilliant work on problems aimed to improve the match between Newton's paradigm and observation of the heavens. Many of these figures worked simultaneously to develop the mathematics required for applications that neither Newton nor the contemporary Continental school of mechanics had even attempted. They produced, for example, an immense literature and some very powerful mathematical techniques for hydrodynamics and for the problem of vibrating strings. These problems of application account for what is probably the most brilliant and consuming scientific work of the eighteenth century. Other examples could be discovered by an examination of the post-paradigm period in the

---

[10]Wolf, *op, cit.,* pp. 75–81, 96–101; and William Whewell, *History of the Inductive Sciences* (rev. ed.; London, 1847), II, 213–71.

development of thermodynamics, the wave theory of light, electromagnetic theory, or any other branch of science whose fundamental laws are fully quantitative. At least in the more mathematical sciences, most theoretical work is of this sort.

But it is not all of this sort. Even in the mathematical sciences there are also theoretical problems of paradigm articulation; and during periods when scientific development is predominantly qualitative, these problems dominate. Some of the problems, in both the more quantitative and more qualitative sciences, aim simply at clarification by reformulation. The *Principia,* for example, did not always prove an easy work to apply, partly because it retained some of the clumsiness inevitable in a first venture and partly because so much of its meaning was only implicit in its applications. For many terrestrial applications, in any case, an apparently unrelated set of Continental techniques seemed vastly more powerful. Therefore, from Euler and Lagrange in the eighteenth century to Hamilton, Jacobi, and Hertz in the nineteenth, many of Europe's most brilliant mathematical physicists repeatedly endeavored to reformulate mechanical theory in an equivalent but logically and aesthetically more satisfying form. They wished, that is, to exhibit the explicit and implicit lessons of the *Principia* and of Continental mechanics in a logically more coherent version, one that would be at once more uniform and less equivocal in its application to the newly elaborated problems of mechanics.[11]

Similar reformulations of a paradigm have occurred repeatedly in all of the sciences, but most of them have produced more substantial changes in the paradigm than the reformulations of the *Principia* cited above. Such changes result from the empirical work previously described as aimed at paradigm articulation. Indeed, to classify that sort of work as empirical was arbitrary. More than any other sort of normal research, the problems of paradigm articulation are simultaneously theoretical and experimental; the examples given previously will serve equally well here. Before he could construct his equipment and make measurements with it, Coulomb had to employ electrical theory to determine how his equipment should be built. The consequence of his measurements was a refinement in that theory. Or again, the men who designed the experiments that were to distinguish between the various theories of heating by compression were generally the same men who had made up the versions being compared. They were working both with fact and with theory, and their work produced not simply new

---

[11]René Dugas, *Histoire de la mécanique* (Neuchatel, 1950), Books IV–V.

information but a more precise paradigm, obtained by the elimination of ambiguities that the original from which they worked had retained. In many sciences, most normal work is of this sort.

These three classes of problems—determination of significant fact, matching of facts with theory, and articulation of theory—exhaust, I think, the literature of normal science, both empirical and theoretical. They do not, of course, quite exhaust the entire literature of science. These are also extraordinary problems, and it may well be their resolution that makes the scientific enterprise as a whole so particularly worthwhile. But extraordinary problems are not to be had for the asking. They emerge only on special occasions prepared by the advance of normal research. Inevitably, therefore, the overwhelming majority of the problems undertaken by even the very best scientists usually fall into one of the three categories outlined above. Work under the paradigm can be conducted in no other way, and to desert the paradigm is to cease practicing the science it defines. We shall shortly discover that such desertions do occur. They are the pivots about which scientific revolutions turn. But before beginning the study of such revolutions, we require a more panoramic view of the normal-scientific pursuits that prepare the way.

THE NATURE AND NECESSITY OF SCIENTIFIC REVOLUTIONS
Thomas Kuhn

1   These remarks permit us at last to consider the problems that provide this
essay with its title. What are scientific revolutions, and what is their function in scientific development? Much of the answer to these questions has been
anticipated in earlier sections. In particular, the preceding discussion has indicated that scientific revolutions are here taken to be those non-cumulative developmental episodes in which an older paradigm is replaced in whole or in part
by an incompatible new one. There is more to be said, however, and an essential part of it can be introduced by asking one further question. Why should a
change of paradigm be called a revolution? In the face of the vast and essential
differences between political and scientific development, what parallelism can justify the metaphor that finds revolutions in both?

One aspect of the parallelism must already be apparent. Political revolutions
are inaugurated by a growing sense, often restricted to a segment of the political community, that existing institutions have ceased adequately to meet the
problems posed by an environment that they have in part created. In much the
same way, scientific revolutions are inaugurated by a growing sense, again often
restricted to a narrow subdivision of the scientific community, that an existing
paradigm has ceased to function adequately in the exploration of an aspect of
nature to which that paradigm itself had previously led the way. In both political and scientific development the sense of malfunction that can lead to crisis is
prerequisite to revolution. Furthermore, though it admittedly strains the
metaphor, that parallelism holds not only for the major paradigm changes, like
those attributable to Copernicus and Lavoisier, but also for the far smaller ones
associated with the assimilation of a new sort of phenomenon, like oxygen or
X-rays. Scientific revolutions, as we noted at the end of Section V, need seem revolutionary only to those whose paradigms are affected by them. To outsiders
they may, like the Balkan revolutions of the early twentieth century, seem normal parts of the developmental process. Astronomers, for example, could accept

---

Reprinted from *The Structure of Scientific Revolutions,* (1996), by permission of University of
Chicago Press.

X-rays as a mere addition to knowledge, for their paradigms were unaffected by the existence of the new radiation. But for men like Kelvin, Crookes, and Roentgen, whose research dealt with radiation theory or with cathode ray tubes, the emergence of X-rays necessarily violated one paradigm as it created another. That is why these rays could be discovered only through something's first going wrong with normal research.

This genetic aspect of the parallel between political and scientific development should no longer be open to doubt. The parallel has, however, a second and more profound aspect upon which the significance of the first depends. Political revolutions aim to change political institutions in ways that those institutions themselves prohibit. Their success therefore necessitates the partial relinquishment of one set of institutions in favor of another, and in the interim, society is not fully governed by institutions at all. Initially it is crisis alone that attenuates the role of political institutions as we have already seen it attenuate the role of paradigms. In increasing numbers individuals become increasingly estranged from political life and behave more and more eccentrically within it. Then, as the crisis deepens, many of these individuals commit themselves to some concrete proposal for the reconstruction of society in a new institutional framework. At that point the society is divided into competing camps or parties, one seeking to defend the old institutional constellation, the others seeking to institute some new one. And, once that polarization has occurred, *political recourse fails.* Because they differ about the institutional matrix within which political change is to be achieved and evaluated, because they acknowledge no supra-institutional framework for the adjudication of revolutionary difference, the parties to a revolutionary conflict must finally resort to the techniques of mass persuasion, often including force. Though revolutions have had a vital role in the evolution of political institutions, that role depends upon their being partially extrapolitical or extrainstitutional events.

The remainder of this essay aims to demonstrate that the historical study of paradigm change reveals very similar characteristics in the evolution of the sciences. Like the choice between competing political institutions, that between competing paradigms proves to be a choice between incompatible modes of community life. Because it has that character, the choice is not and cannot be determined merely by the evaluative procedures characteristic of normal science, for these depend in part upon a particular paradigm, and that paradigm is at issue. When paradigms enter, as they must, into a debate about paradigm choice, their role is necessarily circular. Each group uses its own paradigm to argue in that paradigm's defense.

UNIT 8

5   The resulting circularity does not, of course, make the arguments wrong or even ineffectual. The man who premises a paradigm when arguing in its defense can nonetheless provide a clear exhibit of what scientific practice will be like for those who adopt the new view of nature. That exhibit can be immensely persuasive, often compellingly so. Yet, whatever its force, the status of the circular argument is only that of persuasion. It cannot be made logically or even probabilistically compelling for those who refuse to step into the circle. The premises and values shared by the two parties to a debate over paradigms are not sufficiently extensive for that. As in political revolutions, so in paradigm choice—there is no standard higher than the assent of the relevant community. To discover how scientific revolutions are effected, we shall therefore have to examine not only the impact of nature and of logic, but also the techniques of persuasive argumentation effective within the quite special groups that constitute the community of scientists.

To discover why this issue of paradigm choice can never be unequivocally settled by logic and experiment alone, we must shortly examine the nature of the differences that separate the proponents of a traditional paradigm from their revolutionary successors. That examination is the principal object of this section and the next. We have, however, already noted numerous examples of such differences, and no one will doubt that history can supply many others. What is more likely to be doubted than their existence—and what must therefore be considered first—is that such examples provide essential information about the nature of science. Granting that paradigm rejection has been a historic fact, does it illuminate more than human credulity and confusion? Are there intrinsic reasons why the assimilation of either a new sort of phenomenon or a new scientific theory must demand the rejection of an older paradigm?

First notice that if there are such reasons, they do not derive from the logical structure of scientific knowledge. In principle, a new phenomenon might emerge without reflecting destructively upon any part of past scientific practice. Though discovering life on the moon would today be destructive of existing paradigms (these tell us things about the moon that seem incompatible with life's existence there), discovering life in some less well-known part of the galaxy would not. By the same token, a new theory does not have to conflict with any of its predecessors. It might deal exclusively with phenomena not previously known, as the quantum theory deals (but, significantly, not exclusively) with subatomic phenomena unknown before the twentieth century. Or again, the new theory might be simply a higher level theory than those known before, one that linked together a whole group of lower level theories without substantially changing any. Today, the theory of energy conservation provides just such links between dynamics, chemistry, electricity, optics, thermal theory, and so on. Still other compatible relationships between old and new theories can be conceived. Any and all of them might be exemplified by the historical process through which science has developed. If they were, scientific development would be genuinely cumulative. New sorts of phenomena would simply disclose order in an aspect of nature where none had been seen before. In the evolution of science new knowledge would replace ignorance rather than replace knowledge of another and incompatible sort.

Of course, science (or some other enterprise, perhaps less effective) might have developed in that fully cumulative manner. Many people have believed that it did so, and most still seem to suppose that cumulation is at least the ideal that historical development would display if only it had not so often been distorted by human idiosyncrasy. There are important reasons for that belief. In Section X we shall discover how closely the view of science-as-cumulation is entangled with a dominant epistemology that takes knowledge to be a construction placed directly upon raw sense data by the mind. And in Section XI we shall examine the strong support provided to the same historiographic schema by the techniques of effective science pedagogy. Nevertheless, despite the immense plausibility of that ideal image, there is increasing reason to wonder whether it can possibly be an image of *science*. After the pre-paradigm period the assimilation of all new theories and of almost all new sorts of phenomena has in fact demanded the destruction of a prior paradigm and a consequent conflict between competing schools of scientific thought. Cumulative acquisition of unanticipated novelties proves to be an almost non-existent exception to the rule of scientific development. The man who takes historic fact seriously must suspect that science does not tend toward the ideal that our image of its cumulativeness has suggested. Perhaps it is another sort of enterprise.

If, however, resistant facts can carry us that far, then a second look at the ground we have already covered may suggest that cumulative acquisition of novelty is not only rare in fact but improbable in principle. Normal research, which *is* cumulative, owes its success to the ability of scientists regularly to select problems that can be solved with conceptual and instrumental techniques close to those already in existence. (That is why an excessive concern with useful problems, regardless of their relation to existing knowledge and technique, can so easily inhibit scientific development.) The man who is striving to solve a problem defined by existing knowledge and technique is not, however, just looking around. He knows what he wants to achieve, and he designs his instruments and directs his thoughts accordingly. Unanticipated novelty, the new discovery, can emerge only to the extent that his anticipations about nature and his instruments prove wrong. Often the importance of the resulting discovery will itself be proportional to the extent and stubbornness of the anomaly that foreshadowed it. Obviously, then, there must be a conflict between the paradigm that discloses anomaly and the one that later renders the anomaly lawlike. The examples of discovery through paradigm destruction examined in Section VI did not confront us with mere historical accident. There is no other effective way in which discoveries might be generated.

10   The same argument applies even more clearly to the invention of new theories. There are, in principle, only three types of phenomena about which a new theory might be developed. The first consists of phenomena already well explained by existing paradigms, and these seldom provide either motive or point of departure for theory construction. When they do, as with the three famous anticipations discussed at the end of Section VII, the theories that result are seldom accepted, because nature provides no ground for discrimination. A second class of phenomena consists of those whose nature is indicated by existing paradigms but whose details can be understood only through further theory articulation. These are the phenomena to which scientists direct their research much of the time, but that research aims at the articulation of existing paradigms rather than at the invention of new ones. Only when these attempts at articulation fail do scientists encounter the third type of phenomena, the recognized anomalies whose characteristic feature is their stubborn refusal to be assimilated to existing paradigms. This type alone gives rise to new theories. Paradigms provide all phenomena except anomalies with a theory-determined place in the scientist's field of vision.

But if new theories are called forth to resolve anomalies in the relation of an existing theory to nature, then the successful new theory must somewhere permit predictions that are different from those derived from its predecessor. That difference could not occur if the two were logically compatible. In the process of being assimilated, the second must displace the first. Even a theory like energy conservation, which today seems a logical superstructure that relates to nature only through independently established theories, did not develop historically without paradigm destruction. Instead, it emerged from a crisis in which an essential ingredient was the incompatibility between Newtonian dynamics and some recently formulated consequences of the caloric theory of heat. Only after the caloric theory had been rejected could energy conservation become part of science.[1] And only after it had been part of science for some time could it come to seem a theory of a logically higher type, one not in conflict with its predecessors. It is hard to see how new theories could arise without these destructive changes in beliefs about nature. Though logical inclusiveness remains a permissible view of the relation between successive scientific theories, it is a historical implausibility.

A century ago it would, I think, have been possible to let the case for the necessity of revolutions rest at this point. But today, unfortunately, that cannot be done because the view of the subject developed above cannot be maintained if the most prevalent contemporary interpretation of the nature and function of scientific theory is accepted. That interpretation, closely associated with early logical positivism and not categorically rejected by its successors, would restrict the range and meaning of an accepted theory so that it could not possibly conflict with any later theory that made predictions about some of the same natural phenomena. The best-known and the strongest case for this restricted conception of a scientific theory emerges in discussions of the relation between contemporary Einsteinian dynamics and the older dynamical equations that descend from Newton's *Principia*. From the viewpoint of this essay these two theories are fundamentally incompatible in the sense illustrated by the relation of Copernican to Ptolemaic astronomy: Einstein's theory can be accepted only with the recognition that Newton's was wrong. Today this remains a minority view.[2] We must therefore examine the most prevalent objections to it.

The gist of these objections can be developed as follows. Relativistic dynamics cannot have shown Newtonian dynamics to be wrong, for Newtonian dynamics is still used with great success by most engineers and, in selected applications, by many physicists. Furthermore, the propriety of this use of the older theory can be proved from the very theory that has, in other applications, replaced it. Einstein's theory can be used to show that predictions from Newton's equations will be as good as our measuring instruments in all applications that satisfy a small number of restrictive conditions. For example, if Newtonian theory is to provide a good approximate solution, the relative velocities of the bodies considered must be small compared with the velocity of light. Subject to this condition and a few others, Newtonian theory seems to be derivable from Einsteinian, of which it is therefore a special case.

[1] Silvanus P. Thompson, *Life of William Thomson Baron Kelvin of Largs* (London, 1910), I, 266–81.
[2] See, for example, the remarks by P. P. Wiener in *Philosophy of Science*, XXV (1958), 298.

But, the objection continues, no theory can possibly conflict with one of its special cases. If Einsteinian science seems to make Newtonian dynamics wrong, that is only because some Newtonians were so incautious as to claim that Newtonian theory yielded entirely precise results or that it was valid at very high relative velocities. Since they could not have had any evidence for such claims, they betrayed the standards of science when they made them. In so far as Newtonian theory was ever a truly scientific theory supported by valid evidence, it still is. Only extravagant claims for the theory—claims that were never properly parts of science—can have been seen shown by Einstein to be wrong. Purged of these merely human extravagances, Newtonian theory has never been challenged and cannot be.

15   Some variant of this argument is quite sufficient to make any theory ever used by a significant group of competent scientists immune to attack. The much-maligned phlogiston theory, for example, gave order to a large number of physical and chemical phenomena. It explained why bodies burned—they were rich in phlogiston—and why metals had so many more properties in common than did their ores. The metals were all compounded from different elementary earths combined with phlogiston, and the latter, common to all metals, produced common properties. In addition, the phlogiston theory accounted for a number of reactions in which acids were formed by the combustion of substances like carbon and sulphur. Also, it explained the decrease of volume when combustion occurs in a confined volume of air—the phlogiston released by combustion "spoils" the elasticity of the air that absorbed it, just as fire "spoils" the elasticity of a steel spring.[3] If these were the only phenomena that the phlogiston theorists had claimed for their theory, that theory could never have been challenged. A similar argument will suffice for any theory that has ever been successfully applied to any range of phenomena at all.

But to save theories in this way, their range of application must be restricted to those phenomena and to that precision of observation with which the experimental evidence in hand already deals.[4] Carried just a step further (and the step can scarcely be avoided once the first is taken), such a limitation prohibits the scientist from claiming to speak "scientifically" about any phenomenon not

---

[3]James B. Conant, *Overthrow of the Phlogiston Theory* (Cambridge, 1950), pp. 13–16; and J. R. Partington, *A Short History of Chemistry* (2d ed.; London, 1951), pp. 85–88. The fullest and most sympathetic account of the phlogiston theory's achievements is by H. Metzger, *Newton, Stahl, Boerhaave et la doctrine chimique* (Paris, 1930), Part II.

[4]Compare the conclusions reached through a very different sort of analysis by R. B. Braithwaite, *Scientific Explanation* (Cambridge, 1953), pp. 50–87, esp. p. 76.

already observed. Even in its present form the restriction forbids the scientist to rely upon a theory in his own research whenever that research enters an area or seeks a degree of precision for which past practice with the theory offers no precedent. These prohibitions are logically unexceptionable. But the result of accepting them would be the end of the research through which science may develop further.

By now that point too is virtually a tautology. Without commitment to a paradigm there could be no normal science. Furthermore, that commitment must extend to areas and to degrees of precision for which there is no full precedent. If it did not, the paradigm could provide no puzzles that had not already been solved. Besides, it is not only normal science that depends upon commitment to a paradigm. If existing theory binds the scientist only with respect to existing applications, then there can be no surprises, anomalies, or crises. But these are just the signposts that point the way to extraordinary science. If positivistic restrictions on the range of a theory's legitimate applicability are taken literally, the mechanism that tells the scientific community what problems may lead to fundamental change must cease to function. And when that occurs, the community will inevitably return to something much like its pre-paradigm state, a condition in which all members practice science but in which their gross product scarcely resembles science at all. Is it really any wonder that the price of significant scientific advance is a commitment that runs the risk of being wrong?

More important, there is a revealing logical lacuna in the positivist's argument, one that will reintroduce us immediately to the nature of revolutionary change. Can Newtonian dynamics really be *derived* from relativistic dynamics? What would such a derivation look like? Imagine a set of statements, $E_1, E_2, \ldots,$ E_n, which together embody the laws of relativity theory. These statements contain variables and parameters representing spatial position, time, rest mass, etc. From them, together with the apparatus of logic and mathematics, is deducible a whole set of further statements including some that can be checked by observation. To prove the adequacy of Newtonian dynamics as a special case, we must add to the E_1's additional statements, like $(v/c)^2 \ll 1$, restricting the range of the parameters and variables. This enlarged set of statements is then manipulated to yield a new set, $N_1, N_2, \ldots, N_m$, which is identical in form with Newton's laws of motion, the law of gravity, and so on. Apparently Newtonian dynamics has been derived from Einsteinian, subject to a few limiting conditions.

Yet the derivation is spurious, at least to this point. Though the N_1's are a special case of the laws of relativistic mechanics, they are not Newton's Laws. Or at least they are not unless those laws are reinterpreted in a way that would have been impossible until after Einstein's work. The variables and parameters that in the Einsteinian E_1's represented spatial position, time, mass, etc., still occur in the N_1's; and they there still represent Einsteinian space, time, and mass. But the physical referents of these Einsteinian concepts are by no means identical with those of the Newtonian concepts that bear the same name. (Newtonian mass is conserved; Einsteinian is convertible with energy. Only at low relative velocities may the two be measured in the same way, and even then they must not be conceived to be the same.) Unless we change the definitions of the variables in the N_1's, the statements we have derived are not Newtonian. If we do change them, we cannot properly be said to have *derived* Newton's Laws, at least not in any sense of "derive" now generally recognized. Our argument has, of course, explained why Newton's Laws ever seemed to work. In doing so it has justified, say, an automobile driver in acting as though he lived in a Newtonian universe. An argument of the same type is used to justify teaching earth-centered astronomy to surveyors. But the argument has still not done what it purported to do. It has not, that is, shown Newton's Laws to be a limiting case of Einstein's. For in the passage to the limit it is not only the forms of the laws that have changed. Simultaneously we have had to alter the fundamental structural elements of which the universe to which they apply is composed.

20   This need to change the meaning of established and familiar concepts is central to the revolutionary impact of Einstein's theory. Though subtler than the changes from geocentrism to heliocentrism, from phlogiston to oxygen, or from corpuscles to waves, the resulting conceptual transformation is no less decisively destructive of a previously established paradigm. We may even come to see it as a prototype for revolutionary reorientations in the sciences. Just because it did not involve the introduction of additional objects or concepts, the transition from Newtonian to Einsteinian mechanics illustrates with particular clarity the scientific revolution as a displacement of the conceptual network through which scientists view the world.

These remarks should suffice to show what might, in another philosophical climate, have been taken for granted. At least for scientists, most of the apparent differences between a discarded scientific theory and its successor are real. Though an out-of-date theory can always be viewed as a special case of its up-to-date successor, it must be transformed for the purpose. And the transformation is one that can be undertaken only with the advantages of hindsight, the explicit guidance of the more recent theory. Furthermore, even if that transformation were a legitimate device to employ in interpreting the older theory, the result of its application would be a theory so restricted that it could only restate what was already known. Because of its economy, that restatement would have utility, but it could not suffice for the guidance of research.

Let us, therefore, now take it for granted that the differences between successive paradigms are both necessary and irreconcilable. Can we then say more explicitly what sorts of differences these are? The most apparent type has already been illustrated repeatedly. Successive paradigms tell us different things about the population of the universe and about that population's behavior. They differ, that is, about such questions as the existence of subatomic particles, the materiality of light, and the conservation of heat or of energy. These are the substantive differences between successive paradigms, and they require no further illustration. But paradigms differ in more than substance, for they are directed not only to nature but also back upon the science that produced them. They are the source of the methods, problem-field, and standards of solution accepted by any mature scientific community at any given time. As a result, the reception of a new paradigm often necessitates a redefinition of the corresponding science. Some old problems may be relegated to another science or declared entirely "unscientific." Others that were previously non-existent or trivial may, with a new paradigm, become the very archetypes of significant scientific achievement. And as the problems change, so, often, does the standard that distinguishes a real scientific solution from a mere metaphysical speculation, word game, or mathematical play. The normal-scientific tradition that emerges from a scientific revolution is not only incompatible but often actually incommensurable with that which has gone before.

The impact of Newton's work upon the normal seventeenth-century tradition of scientific practice provides a striking example of these subtler effects of paradigm shift. Before Newton was born the "new science" of the century had at last succeeded in rejecting Aristotelian and scholastic explanations expressed in terms of the essences of material bodies. To say that a stone fell because its "nature" drove it toward the center of the universe had been made to look a mere tautological word-play, something it had not previously been. Henceforth the entire flux of sensory appearances, including color, taste, and even weight, was to be explained in terms of the size, shape, position, and motion of the elementary corpuscles of base matter. The attribution of other qualities to the elementary atoms was a resort to the occult and therefore out of bounds for science. Molière caught the new spirit precisely when he ridiculed the doctor who explained opium's efficacy as a soporific by attributing to it a dormitive potency.

UNIT 8

During the last half of the seventeenth century many scientists preferred to say that the round shape of the opium particles enabled them to sooth the nerves about which they moved.[5]

In an earlier period explanations in terms of occult qualities had been an integral part of productive scientific work. Nevertheless, the seventeenth century's new commitment to mechanico-corpuscular explanation proved immensely fruitful for a number of sciences, ridding them of problems that had defied generally accepted solution and suggesting others to replace them. In dynamics, for example, Newton's three laws of motion are less a product of novel experiments than of the attempt to reinterpret well-known observations in terms of the motions and interactions of primary neutral corpuscles. Consider just one concrete illustration. Since neutral corpuscles could act on each other only by contact, the mechanico-corpuscular view of nature directed scientific attention to a brand-new subject of study, the alternation of particulate motions by collisions. Descartes announced the problem and provided its first putative solution. Huyghens, Wren, and Wallis carried it still further, partly by experimenting with colliding pendulum bobs, but mostly by applying previously well-known characteristics of motion to the new problem. And Newton embedded their results in his laws of motion. The equal "action" and "reaction" of the third law are the changes in quantity of motion experienced by the two parties to a collision. The same change of motion supplies the definition of dynamical force implicit in the second law. In this case, as in many others during the seventeenth century, the corpuscular paradigm bred both a new problem and a large part of that problem's solution.[6]

25   Yet, though much of Newton's work was directed to problems and embodied standards derived from the mechanico-corpuscular world view, the effect of the paradigm that resulted from his work was a further and partially destructive change in the problems and standards legitimate for science. Gravity, interpreted as an innate attraction between every pair of particles of matter, was an occult quality in the same sense as the scholastics' "tendency to fall" had been. Therefore, while the standards of corpuscularism remained in effect, the search for a mechanical explanation of gravity was one of the most challenging problems for those who accepted the *Principia* as paradigm. Newton devoted much attention to it and so did many of his eighteenth-century successors. The only apparent

---

[5]For corpuscularism in general, see Marie Boas, "The Establishment of the Mechanical Philosophy," *Osiris,* X (1952), 412–541. For the effect of particle-shape on taste, see *ibid.*, p. 483.
[6]R. Dugas, *La mécanique au XVIIᵉ siècle* (Neuchatel, 1954), pp. 177–85, 284–98, 345–56.

option was to reject Newton's theory for its failure to explain gravity, and that alternative, too, was widely adopted. Yet neither of these views ultimately triumphed. Unable either to practice science without the *Principia* or to make that work conform to the corpuscular standards of the seventeenth century, scientists gradually accepted the view that gravity was indeed innate. By the mid-eighteenth century that interpretation had been almost universally accepted, and the result was a genuine reversion (which is not the same as a retrogression) to a scholastic standard. Innate attractions and repulsions joined size, shape, position, and motion as physically irreducible primary properties of matter.[7]

The resulting change in the standards and problem-field of physical science was once again consequential. By the 1740's, for example, electricians could speak of the attractive "virtue" of the electric fluid without thereby inviting the ridicule that had greeted Molière's doctor a century before. As they did so, electrical phenomena increasingly displayed an order different from the one they had shown when viewed as the effects of a mechanical effluvium that could act only by contact. In particular, when electrical action-at-a-distance became a subject for study in its own right, the phenomenon we now call charging by induction could be recognized as one of its effects. Previously, when seen at all, it had been attributed to the direct action of electrical "atmospheres" or to the leakages inevitable in any electrical laboratory. The new view of inductive effects was, in turn, the key to Franklin's analysis of the Leyden jar and thus to the emergence of a new and Newtonian paradigm for electricity. Nor were dynamics and electricity the only scientific fields affected by the legitimization of the search for forces innate to matter. The large body of eighteenth-century literature on chemical affinities and replacement series also derives from this supramechanical aspect of Newtonianism. Chemists who believed in these differential attractions between the various chemical species set up previously unimagined experiments and searched for new sorts of reactions. Without the data and the chemical concepts developed in that process, the later work of Lavoisier and, more particularly, of Dalton would be incomprehensible.[8] Changes in the standards governing permissible problems, concepts, and explanations can transform a science. In the next section I shall even suggest a sense in which they transform the world.

Other examples of these nonsubstantive differences between successive paradigms can be retrieved from the history of any science in almost any period of

---

[7]I. B. Cohen, *Franklin and Newton: An Inquiry into Speculative Newtonian Experimental Science and Franklin's Work in Electricity as an Example Thereof* (Philadelphia, 1956), chaps. vi–vii.
[8]For electricity, see *ibid*, chaps. viii–ix. For chemistry, see Metzger, *op. cit.*, Part I.

its development. For the moment let us be content with just two other and far briefer illustrations. Before the chemical revolution, one of the acknowledged tasks of chemistry was to account for the qualities of chemical substances and for the changes these qualities underwent during chemical reactions. With the aid of a small number of elementary "principles"—of which phlogiston was one— the chemist was to explain why some substances are acidic, others metalline, combustible, and so forth. Some success in this direction had been achieved. We have already noted that phlogiston explained why the metals were so much alike, and we could have developed a similar argument for the acids. Lavoisier's reform, however, ultimately did away with chemical "principles," and thus ended by depriving chemistry of some actual and much potential explanatory power. To compensate for this loss, a change in standards was required. During much of the nineteenth century failure to explain the qualities of compounds was no indictment of a chemical theory.[9]

Or again, Clerk Maxwell shared with other nineteenth-century proponents of the wave theory of light the conviction that light waves must be propagated through a material ether. Designing a mechanical medium to support such waves was a standard problem for many of his ablest contemporaries. His own theory, however, the electromagnetic theory of light, gave no account at all of a medium able to support light waves, and it clearly made such an account harder to provide than it had seemed before. Initially, Maxwell's theory was widely rejected for those reasons. But, like Newton's theory, Maxwell's proved difficult to dispense with, and as it achieved the status of a paradigm, the community's attitude toward it changed. In the early decades of the twentieth century Maxwell's insistence upon the existence of a mechanical ether looked more and more like lip service, which it emphatically had not been, and the attempts to design such an ethereal medium were abandoned. Scientists no longer thought it unscientific to speak of an electrical "displacement" without specifying what was being displaced. The result, again, was a new set of problems and standards, one which, in the event, had much to do with the emergence of relativity theory.[10]

These characteristic shifts in the scientific community's conception of its legitimate problems and standards would have less significance to this essay's thesis if one could suppose that they always occurred from some methodologically lower to some higher type. In that case their effects, too, would seem cumulative. No wonder that some historians have argued that the history of science

---

[9]E. Meyerson, *Identity and Reality* (New York, 1930), chap. x.
[10]E. T. Whittaker, *A History of the Theories of Aether and Electricity,* II (London, 1953), 28–30.

records a continuing increase in the maturity and refinement of man's conception of the nature of science.[11] Yet the case for cumulative development of science's problems and standards is even harder to make than the case for cumulation of theories. The attempt to explain gravity, though fruitfully abandoned by most eighteenth-century scientists, was not directed to an intrinsically illegitimate problem; the objections to innate forces were neither inherently unscientific nor metaphysical in some pejorative sense. There are no external standards to permit a judgment of that sort. What occurred was neither a decline nor a raising of standards, but simply a change demanded by the adoption of a new paradigm. Furthermore, that change has since been reversed and could be again. In the twentieth century Einstein succeeded in explaining gravitational attractions, and that explanation has returned science to a set of canons and problems that are, in this particular respect, more like those of Newton's predecessors than of his successors. Or again, the development of quantum mechanics has reversed the methodological prohibition that originated in the chemical revolution. Chemists now attempt, and with great success, to explain the color, state of aggregation, and other qualities of the substances used and produced in their laboratories. A similar reversal may even be underway in electromagnetic theory. Space, in contemporary physics, is not the inert and homogenous substratum employed in both Newton's and Maxwell's theories; some of its new properties are not unlike those once attributed to the ether; we may someday come to know what an electric displacement is.

30   By shifting emphasis from the cognitive to the normative functions of paradigms, the preceding examples enlarge our understanding of the ways in which paradigms give form to the scientific life. Previously, we had principally examined the paradigm's role as a vehicle for scientific theory. In that role it functions by telling the scientist about the entities that nature does and does not contain and about the ways in which those entities behave. That information provides a map whose details are elucidated by mature scientific research. And since nature is too complex and varied to be explored at random, that map is as essential as observation and experiment to science's continuing development. Through the theories they embody, paradigms prove to be constitutive of the research activity. They are also, however, constitutive of science in other respects, and that is now the point. In particular, our most recent examples show that paradigms

[11]For a brilliant and entirely up-to-date attempt to fit scientific development into this Procrustean bed, see C. C. Gillispie, *The Edge of Objectivity: An Essay in the History of Scientific Ideas* (Princeton, 1960).

provide scientists not only with a map but also with some of the directions essential for map-making. In learning a paradigm the scientist acquires theory, methods, and standards together, usually in an inextricable mixture. Therefore, when paradigms change, there are usually significant shifts in the criteria determining the legitimacy both of problems and of proposed solutions.

That observation returns us to the point from which this section began, for it provides our first explicit indication of why the choice between competing paradigms regularly raises questions that cannot be resolved by the criteria of normal science. To the extent, as significant as it is incomplete, that two scientific schools disagree about what is a problem and what a solution, they will inevitably talk through each other when debating the relative merits of their respective paradigms. In the partially circular arguments that regularly result, each paradigm will be shown to satisfy more or less the criteria that it dictates for itself and to fall short of a few of those dictated by its opponent. There are other reasons, too, for the incompleteness of logical contact that consistently characterizes paradigm debates. For example, since no paradigm ever solves all the problems it defines and since no two paradigms leave all the same problems unsolved, paradigm debates always involve the question: Which problems is it more significant to have solved? Like the issue of competing standards, that question of values can be answered only in terms of criteria that lie outside of normal science altogether, and it is that recourse to external criteria that most obviously makes paradigm debates revolutionary. Something even more fundamental than standards and values is, however, also at stake. I have so far argued only that paradigms are constitutive of science. Now I wish to display a sense in which they are constitutive of nature as well.

READING/WRITING ASSISTS

Thesis (and its counterargument):

The first of Kuhn's essays presented here, "The Nature of Normal Science," is primarily definitional, designed to explain the nature and operation of paradigms in what he calls "normal science." The second, "The Nature and Necessity of Scientific Revolutions," while also offering a definition of a scientific revolution, more importantly offers Kuhn's **thesis statement**, and the **counterargument** against which he presents his idea. Both are clearly stated, however late in the readings.

The Shape of the Argument:

"Mapping" the structure of an argument can help us better understand the argument itself, while also showing us new models for shaping our own arguments in essay form. In order to understand Kuhn's main point about the nature and necessity of scientific revolutions, it is essential to first understand the nature of "normal science" and the importance of paradigms for that venture. To better understand Kuhn's argumentative structure, it is best to outline the entire essay, paragraph by paragraph:

"The Nature of Normal Science":

Paragraph 1:	Definition of a paradigm. What is the difference between other paradigms and a scientific paradigm?
Paragraph 2:	With regard to paradigms, Kuhn says normal science consists mainly of three activities. List these three activities: 1._____ 2._____ 3._____
Paragraphs 3, 4, and 5:	In these paragraphs, Kuhn mentions some of the strengths and weaknesses of normal science. What are these strengths and weaknesses? Also significant in paragraph 3, is that Kuhn introduces the idea of scientists working inside a "box." Most people are familiar with the phrase "thinking outside the box" but lack a clear understanding of the origin of the phrase. What might Thomas Kuhn mean if he congratulated someone for "thinking outside the box"?
Paragraphs 6, 7, 8, 9, and 10:	Return to paragraph 2. Here Kuhn further explains the three activities of normal scientific research. As an example, he includes some experiments designed to articulate a paradigm. It is important to have a clear idea of these scientific activities.

UNIT 8

| Paragraphs 11, 12, and 13: | What do scientists using existing theories to do? Why is there a need for this kind of work in science? Is theory without concrete examples useful to science? |
| Paragraphs 14, 15, and 16: | What happens when scientists encounter problems with the paradigm? According to Kuhn, what is the ultimate goal of normal science? |

"The Nature and Necessity of Scientific Revolutions":

Paragraph 1:	What are scientific revolutions? What is their function in science? Why call a change in paradigm a "revolution"?
Paragraphs 2 and 3:	In paragraphs 1, 2, and 3, Kuhn uses an extended parallel between scientific revolutions and political revolutions as a basis of comparison and contrast. In what ways are these kinds of revolutions similar? In what ways do they differ? Why is this parallel useful to Kuhn?
Paragraphs 4 and 5:	What is the nature of a "circular argument"?
Paragraph 6:	Given the nature of circular arguments, does the acceptance of a new paradigm require rejection of the old?
Paragraphs 7 and 8:	**The counterargument**. Kuhn establishes the theory of scientific development in the history of science prior to his own idea. What is this theory?
Paragraph 9:	According to Kuhn, what are scientists working in laboratories looking to accomplish?
Paragraph 10:	What does Kuhn believe are the three types of phenomena about which a new theory may be developed?
Paragraph 11:	What then is Kuhn's **thesis**? Notice that Kuhn relates the statement of his argument to the question asked in paragraph 6.
Paragraphs 12, 13, and 14:	Kuhn returns to the **counterargument**.
Paragraphs 15, 16, 17, 18, 19, and 20:	Kuhn offers proof for his **thesis**.

Paragraph 21:	What does Kuhn say is especially important about the differences between succeeding paradigms?
Paragraphs 22, 23, 24, 25, and 26:	According to the example offered with regard to Newton's theory, what sorts of differences in paradigms define a scientific revolution?
Paragraphs 27 and 28:	Kuhn offers yet more examples. Why?
Paragraph 29:	What is Kuhn's case against cumulative science?
Paragraphs 30 and 31:	Kuhn returns to his own argument. What conclusion does he draw?

Rhetorical Moves:

In Charles Darwin's essay, "Natural Selection," he uses **rhetorical questions** to great effect. Thomas Kuhn, in the course of his argument, also poses many questions. Unlike Darwin's questions, however, Kuhn's questions seem more "genuine," in that he asks them not to confirm an expected answer but rather in the hope of generating new knowledge. Interestingly, both writers are scientists, but the way they employ the use of questions in their essays is very different. For what reason or reasons does Kuhn offer so many questions in the course of making his argument?

Throughout these essays, and the book from which they are taken, *The Structure of Scientific Revolutions,* Kuhn uses only masculine pronouns when describing hypothetical scientists doing research. His book was published in 1962. Since then, grammatical rules for the use of personal pronouns in essay writing have changed. (It could be useful to consult a recent grammar handbook with regard to pronoun use.) Why did Kuhn address his argument to a male audience? Does doing so make his argument any more or less persuasive?

UNIT 8

GABRIEL GARCÍA MÁRQUEZ

Gabriel García Márquez was born in 1928 in the small Columbian town of Ara-cataca. There he was raised by his grandparents, who, Márquez has said, often told him stories. García Márquez attended law school but dropped out to write full-time.

His first career was as a journalist, mainly for El Espectador *and other Columbian newspapers. His left-wing politics angered the Columbian government, especially the dictator Laureano Gomez and his successor, General Gustavo Rojas Pinilla. Due to his support of Fidel Castro, and the government in Cuba, García Márquez was denied access to the United States, and so, when he had to seek asylum outside Columbia, he moved to Europe, Mexico, and Venezuela. In the early 1980s, García Márquez was finally welcomed back to Columbia, where he resides to this day. Until recently, he continued to submit editorials to newspapers all over the world, including those in the United States. He is now finishing his long-awaited autobiography,* Living to Tell the Tale, *the first part of which has already been published in Spanish and English.*

While living in Mexico, García Márquez published what is considered to be his masterpiece novel, One Hundred Years of Solitude *in 1967. Other major literary works include* Chronicle of a Death Foretold *(1981),* Love in the Time of Cholera *(1988), and* The General and His Labyrinth *(1990), as well as numerous short stories and nonfiction essays and books.*

García Márquez is known for writing novels in the genre known as "magical realism," which blends realistic narrative with the fantastic. Critics have suggested that there is a political dimension to both the realistic and the fantastic in García Márquez' fiction and he has never denied that this is so. His novels and stories are often read as allegories of Latin American politics, but perhaps equally important, they offer his readers an artful escape to imaginary worlds inhabited by very human individuals.

A VERY OLD MAN WITH ENORMOUS WINGS
Gabriel García Márquez

A TALE FOR CHILDREN

1   On the third day of rain they had killed so many crabs inside the house that
Pelayo had to cross his drenched courtyard and throw them into the sea,
because the newborn child had a temperature all night and they thought it was
due to the stench. The world had been sad since Tuesday. Sea and sky were a single ash-gray thing and the sands of the beach, which on March nights glim-
mered like powdered light, had become a stew of mud and rotten shellfish. The
light was so weak at noon that when Pelayo was coming back to the house after
throwing away the crabs, it was hard for him to see what it was that was moving and groaning in the rear of the courtyard. He had to go very close to see
that it was an old man, a very old man, lying face down in the mud, who, in spite
of his tremendous efforts, couldn't get up, impeded by his enormous wings.

Frightened by that nightmare, Pelayo ran to get Elisenda, his wife, who was
putting compresses on the sick child, and he took her to the rear of the courtyard. They both looked at the fallen body with mute stupor. He was dressed like
a ragpicker. There was only a few faded hairs left on his bald skull and very few
teeth in his mouth, and his pitiful condition of a drenched great-grandfather
had taken away any sense of grandeur he might have had. His huge buzzard
wings, dirty and half-plucked, were forever entangled in the mud. They looked
at him so long and so closely that Pelayo and Elisenda very soon overcame their
surprise and in the end found him familiar. Then they dared speak to him, and
he answered in an incomprehensible dialect with a strong sailor's voice. That
was how they skipped over the inconvenience of the wings and quite intelli-
gently concluded that he was a lonely castaway from some foreign ship wrecked
by the storm. And yet, they called in a neighbor woman who knew everything
about life and death to see him, and all she needed was one look to show them
their mistake.

"A Very Old Man with Enormous Wings," by Gabriel Garcia Marquez, reprinted from *Leaf
Storm* (1990), HarperCollins Publishers Inc.

UNIT 8

"He's an angel," she told them. "He must have been coming for the child, but the poor fellow is so old that the rain knocked him down."

On the following day everyone knew that a flesh-and-blood angel was held captive in Pelayo's house. Against the judgment of the wise neighbor woman, for whom angels in those times were the fugitive survivors of a celestial conspiracy, they did not have the heart to club him to death. Pelayo watched over him all afternoon from the kitchen, armed with his bailiff's club, and before going to bed he dragged him out of the mud and locked him up with the hens in the wire chicken coop. In the middle of the night, when the rain stopped, Pelayo and Elisenda were still killing crabs. A short time afterward the child woke up without a fever and with a desire to eat. Then they felt magnanimous and decided to put the angel on a raft with fresh water and provisions for three days and leave him to his fate on the high seas. But when they went out into the courtyard with the first light of dawn, they found the whole neighborhood in front of the chicken coop having fun with the angel, without the slightest reverence, tossing him things to eat through the openings in the wire as if he weren't a supernatural creature but a circus animal.

5   Father Gonzaga arrived before seven o'clock, alarmed at the strange news. By that time onlookers less frivolous than those at dawn had already arrived and they were making all kinds of conjectures concerning the captive's future. The simplest among them thought that he should be named mayor of the world. Others of sterner mind felt that he should be promoted to the rank of five-star general in order to win all wars. Some visionaries hoped that he could be put to stud in order to implant on earth a race of winged wise men who could take charge of the universe. But Father Gonzaga, before becoming a priest, had been a robust woodcutter. Standing by the wire, he reviewed his catechism in an instant and asked them to open the door so that he could take a close look at that pitiful man who looked more like a huge decrepit hen among the fascinated chickens. He was lying in a corner drying his open wings in the sunlight among the fruit peels and breakfast leftovers that the early risers had thrown him. Alien to the impertinences of the world, he only lifted his antiquarian eyes and murmured something in his dialect when Father Gonzaga went into the chicken coop and said good morning to him in Latin. The parish priest had his first suspicion of an impostor when he saw that he did not understand the language of God or know how to greet His ministers. Then he noticed that seen close up he was much too human: he had an unbearable smell of the outdoors, the back side of his wings was strewn with parasites and his main feathers had been mistreated by terrestrial winds, and nothing about him measured up to the proud

dignity of angels. Then he came out of the chicken coop and in a brief sermon warned the curious against the risks of being ingenuous. He reminded them that the devil had the bad habit of making use of carnival tricks in order to confuse the unwary. He argued that if wings were not the essential element in determining the difference between a hawk and an airplane, they were even less so in the recognition of angels. Nevertheless, he promised to write a letter to his bishop so that the latter would write to his primate so that the latter would write to the Supreme Pontiff in order to get the final verdict from the highest courts.

His prudence fell on sterile hearts. The news of the captive angel spread with such rapidity that after a few hours the courtyard had the bustle of a marketplace and they had to call in troops with fixed bayonets to disperse the mob that was about to knock the house down. Elisenda, her spine all twisted from sweeping up so much marketplace trash, then got the idea of fencing in the yard and charging five cents admission to see the angel.

The curious came from far away. A traveling carnival arrived with a flying acrobat who buzzed over the crowd several times, but no one paid any attention to him because his wings were not those of an angel but, rather, those of a sidereal bat. The most unfortunate invalids on earth came in search of health: a poor woman who since childhood had been counting her heartbeats and had run out of numbers; a Portuguese man who couldn't sleep because the noise of the stars disturbed him; a sleepwalker who got up at night to undo the things he had done while awake; and many others with less serious ailments. In the midst of that shipwreck disorder that made the earth tremble, Pelayo and Elisenda were happy with fatigue, for in less than a week they had crammed their rooms with money and the line of pilgrims waiting their turn to enter still reached beyond the horizon.

The angel was the only one who took no part in his own act. He spent his time trying to get comfortable in his borrowed nest, befuddled by the hellish heat of the oil lamps and sacramental candles that had been placed along the wire. At first they tried to make him eat some mothballs, which, according to the wisdom of the wise neighbor woman, were the food prescribed for angels. But he turned them down, just as he turned down the papal lunches that the penitents brought him, and they never found out whether it was because he was an angel or because he was an old man that in the end he ate nothing but eggplant mush. His only supernatural virtue seemed to be patience. Especially during the first days, when the hens pecked at him, searching for the stellar parasites that proliferated in his wings, and the cripples pulled out feathers to touch their defective parts with, and even the most merciful threw stones at him, trying to get him to rise so they could see him standing. The only time they succeeded in arousing him was when they burned his side with an iron for branding steers, for he had been motionless for so many hours that they thought he was dead. He awoke with a start, ranting in his hermetic language and with tears in his eyes, and he flapped his wings a couple of times, which brought on a whirlwind of chicken dung and lunar dust and a gale of panic that did not seem to be of this world. Although many thought that his reaction had been one not of rage but of pain, from then on they were careful not to annoy him, because the majority understood that his passivity was not that of a hero taking his ease but that of a cataclysm in repose.

Father Gonzaga held back the crowd's frivolity with formulas of maidservant inspiration while awaiting the arrival of a final judgment on the nature of the captive. But the mail from Rome showed no sense of urgency. They spent their time finding out if the prisoner had a navel, if his dialect had any connection with Aramaic, how many times he could fit on the head of a pin, or whether he wasn't just a Norwegian with wings. Those meager letters might have come and gone until the end of time if a providential event had not put an end to the priest's tribulations.

10   It so happened that during those days, among so many other carnival attractions, there arrived in town the traveling show of the woman who had been changed into a spider for having disobeyed her parents. The admission to see her was not only less than the admission to see the angel, but people were permitted to ask her all manner of questions about her absurd state and to examine her up and down so that no one would ever doubt the truth of her horror. She was a frightful tarantula the size of a ram and with the head of a sad maiden. What was most heartrending, however, was not her outlandish shape but the sincere affliction with which she recounted the details of her misfortune. While still practically a child she had sneaked out of her parents' house to go to a dance, and while she was coming back through the woods after having danced all night without permission, a fearful thunderclap rent the sky in two and through the crack came the lightning bolt of brimstone that changed her into a spider. Her only nourishment came from the meatballs that charitable souls chose to toss into her mouth. A spectacle like that, full of so much human truth and with such a fearful lesson, was bound to defeat without even trying that of a haughty angel who scarcely deigned to look at mortals. Besides, the few miracles attributed to the angel showed a certain mental disorder, like the blind man who didn't recover his sight but grew three new teeth, or the paralytic who didn't get to walk but almost won the lottery, and the leper whose sores sprouted sunflowers. Those consolation miracles, which were more like mocking fun, had already ruined the

angel's reputation when the woman who had been changed into a spider finally crushed him completely. That was how Father Gonzaga was cured forever of his insomnia and Pelayo's courtyard went back to being as empty as during the time it had rained for three days and crabs walked through the bedrooms.

The owners of the house had no reason to lament. With the money they saved they built a two-story mansion with balconies and gardens and high netting so that crabs wouldn't get in during the winter, and with iron bars on the windows so that angels wouldn't get in. Pelayo also set up a rabbit warren close to town and gave up his job as bailiff for good, and Elisenda bought some satin pumps with high heels and many dresses of iridescent silk, the kind worn on Sunday by the most desirable women in those times. The chicken coop was the only thing that didn't receive any attention. If they washed it down with creolin and burned tears of myrrh inside it every so often, it was not in homage to the angel but to drive away the dungheap stench that still hung everywhere like a ghost and was turning the new house into an old one. At first, when the child learned to walk, they were careful that he not get too close to the chicken coop. But then they began to lose their fears and got used to the smell, and before the child got his second teeth he'd gone inside the chicken coop to play, where the wires were falling apart. The angel was no less standoffish with him than with other mortals, but he tolerated the most ingenious infamies with the patience of a dog who had no illusions. They both came down with chicken pox at the same time. The doctor who took care of the child couldn't resist the temptation to listen to the angel's heart, and he found so much whistling in the heart and so many sounds in his kidneys that it seemed impossible for him to be alive. What surprised him most, however, was the logic of his wings. They seemed so natural on that completely human organism that he couldn't understand why other men didn't have them too.

When the child began school it had been some time since the sun and rain had caused the collapse of the chicken coop. The angel went dragging himself about here and there like a stray dying man. They would drive him out of the bedroom with a broom and a moment later find him in the kitchen. He seemed to be in so many places at the same time that they grew to think that he'd been duplicated, that he was reproducing himself all through the house, and the exasperated and unhinged Elisenda shouted that it was awful living in that hell full of angels. He could scarcely eat and his antiquarian eyes had also become so foggy that he went about bumping into posts. All he had left were the bare cannulae of his last feathers. Pelayo threw a blanket over him and extended him the charity of letting him sleep in the shed, and only then did they notice that he had a temperature at night, and was delirious with the tongue twisters of an old Norwegian. That was one of the few times they become alarmed, for they thought he was going to die and not even the wise neighbor woman had been able to tell them what to do with dead angels.

And yet he not only survived his worst winter, but seemed improved with the first sunny days. He remained motionless for several days in the farthest corner of the courtyard, where no one would see him, and at the beginning of December some large, stiff feathers began to grow on his wings, the feathers of a scarecrow, which looked more like another misfortune of decrepitude. But he must have known the reason for those changes, for he was quite careful that no one should notice them, that no one should hear the sea chanteys that he sometimes sang under the stars. One morning Elisenda was cutting some bunches of onions for lunch when a wind that seemed to come from the high seas blew into the kitchen. Then she went to the window and caught the angel in his first attempts at flight. They were so clumsy that his fingernails opened a furrow in the vegetable patch and he was on the point of knocking the shed down with the ungainly flapping that slipped on the light and couldn't get a grip on the air. But he did manage to gain altitude. Elisenda let out a sigh of relief, for herself and for him, when she saw him pass over the last houses, holding himself up in some way with the risky flapping of a senile vulture. She kept watching him even when she was through cutting the onions and she kept on watching until it was no longer possible for her to see him, because then he was no longer an annoyance in her life but an imaginary dot on the horizon of the sea.

LEVELS OF READING

Summary:

Pay attention to the **literal** meaning of the text. Briefly describe the narrative of Gabriel García Márquez' story, "A Very Old Man with Enormous Wings." Who tells the story? Where is the story set and why is this particular setting important to the idea that García Márquez is trying to convey? Describe some of this village's inhabitants. Do any of them resemble people you know? Concentrate on the highlights; avoid too much detail when summarizing. Again, drawing a simple outline of the main points of the text will help you better analyze the text at other levels of interpretation.

Analysis:

Find what you believe is **symbolic** in the text. The inhabitants of García Márquez' Columbian village immediately generate potential symbolic interpretations for the very old man with enormous wings, but they are conventional. In what ways does their culture limit their symbolic interpretations? What is symbolically relevant about the uses to which Pelayo and Elisenda put the very old man and what they acquire as a result? What is the symbolic significance of the "pilgrims" who came to see the old man? How is his abandonment significant? Find any other symbols you think are important in the story and explain the meaning of these symbols. With the help of the background material provided about Gabriel García Márquez, make an argument about this text, and include the mention of the more **figurative** aspects of the text when making points in defense of your argument.

Application:

Apply what you have learned about paradigms, normal science, and scientific revolution to García Márquez' story. Outline an argument you wish to make about this literary text using Kuhn's theory to help you explain what some part of "A Very Old Man with Enormous Wings" may mean. The "part" of the story you choose to analyze may include any of the following: a character, a setting, a symbol or symbols, an important change, a motivation, a goal, a result. Consider the following as possibilities, but explore other original interpretations too:

- What role does **empirical observation** play in this story? Are the villagers' empirical observations reliable?
- Do the inhabitants of this village engage in "**normal science**"? How so?
- Does the very old man with enormous wings fit the **paradigm** in their normal-scientific approach? What do villagers do with data that fails to fit the paradigm?
- Is there any character within the story capable of thinking outside the box?
- In what ways is the science these villagers practice cumulative? In other words, what influence does history have on their theories about the nature and origin of the very old man with enormous wings?
- Does a **scientific revolution** of sorts occur in this Columbian village? What informs the nature and necessity of this revolution? Does it bear any resemblance to the nature and necessity of the scientific revolutions Kuhn describes in his argument?

SANTHA RAMA RAU

Santha Rama Rau (1923–) was born in Madras, India, and spent the early years of her life in the household of her Hindu grandmother. When she was six, her father, a diplomat, was sent to England, where she then lived for many years. She was sent to college in the United States and published her early essays in The New Yorker.

Her autobiography, Gifts of Passage, *was published in 1961. She also wrote an account of her return to India after many years abroad,* Home to India. *"By Any Other Name" is an episode in Rau's life story. At the time of this event in her life—her introduction to the British colonial schools then dominating the Indian education system—she had rarely been outside the confines of her own family's home, and rarely exposed to people outside the family circle. Nevertheless, Rau's detailed recollection underscores once again (as do the autobiographical narratives of childhood told by Nisa and Dexter Jeffries) the ability of children to size up situations, people, and events having profound effects on their short lives.*

BY ANY OTHER NAME
Santha Rama Rau

1   At the Anglo-Indian day school in Zorinabad to which my sister and I were sent when she was eight and I was five and a half, they changed our names. On the first day of school, a hot, windless morning of a north Indian September, we stood in the headmistress's study and she said, "Now you're the *new* girls. What are your names?"

My sister answered for us. "I am Premila, and she"—nodding in my direction—"is Santha."

The headmistress had been in India, I suppose, fifteen years or so, but she still smiled her helpless inability to cope with Indian names. Her rimless half-glasses glittered, and the precarious bun on the top of her head trembled as she shook her head. "Oh, my dears, those are much too hard for me. Suppose we give you pretty English names. Wouldn't that be more jolly? Let's see, now—Pamela for you, I think." She shrugged in a baffled way at my sister. "That's as close as I can get. And for *you,*" she said to me, "how about Cynthia? Isn't that nice?"

My sister was always less easily intimidated than I was, and while she kept a stubborn silence, I said, "Thank you," in a very tiny voice.

5   We had been sent to that school because my father, among his responsibilities as an officer of the civil service, had a tour of duty to perform in the villages around that steamy little provincial town, where he had his headquarters at that time. He used to make his shorter inspection tours on horseback, and a week before, in the stale heat of a typically postmonsoon day, we had waved good-by to him and a little procession—an assistant, a secretary, two bearers, and the man to look after the bedding rolls and luggage. They rode away through our large garden, still bright green from the rains, and we turned back into the twilight of the house and the sound of fans whispering in every room.

Up to then, my mother had refused to send Premila to school in the British-run establishments of that time, because, she used to say, "you can bury a dog's tail for seven years and it still comes out curly, and you can take a Britisher away

"By Any Other Name," by Santha Rama Rau, reprinted from *Gifts of Passage* (1961), William Morris Agency.

from his home for a lifetime and he still remains insular." The examinations and degrees from entirely Indian schools were not, in those days, considered valid. In my case, the question had never come up, and probably never would have come up if Mother's extraordinary good health had not broken down. For the first time in my life, she was not able to continue the lessons she had been giving us every morning. So our Hindi books were put away, the stories of the Lord Krishna as a little boy were left in mid-air, and we were sent to the Anglo-Indian school.

That first day at school is still, when I think of it, a remarkable one. At that age, if one's name is changed, one develops a curious form of dual personality. I remember having a certain detached and disbelieving concern in the actions of "Cynthia," but certainly no responsibility. Accordingly, I followed the thin, erect back of the headmistress down the veranda to my classroom feeling, at most, a passing interest in what was going to happen to me in this strange, new atmosphere of School.

The building was Indian in design, with wide verandas opening onto a central courtyard, but Indian verandas are usually whitewashed, with stone floors. These, in the tradition of British schools, were painted dark brown and had matting on the floors. It gave a feeling of extra intensity to the heat.

I suppose there were about a dozen Indian children in the school—which contained perhaps forty children in all—and four of them were in my class. They were all sitting at the back of the room, and I went to join them. I sat next to a small, solemn girl who didn't smile at me. She had long, glossy-black braids and wore a cotton dress, but she still kept on her Indian jewelry—a gold chain around her neck, thin gold bracelets, and tiny ruby studs in her ears. Like most Indian children, she had a rim of black kohl around her eyes. The cotton dress should have looked strange, but all I could think of was that I should ask my mother if I couldn't wear a dress to school, too, instead of my Indian clothes.

10   I can't remember too much about the proceedings in class that day, except for the beginning. The teacher pointed to me and asked me to stand up. "Now, dear, tell the class your name."

I said nothing.

"Come along," she said, frowning slightly. "What's your name, dear?"

"I don't know," I said, finally.

The English children in the front of the class—there were about eight or ten of them—giggled and twisted around in their chairs to look at me. I sat down quickly and opened my eyes very wide, hoping in that way to dry them off. The little girl with the braids put out her hand and very lightly touched my arm. She still didn't smile.

15   Most of that morning I was rather bored. I looked briefly at the children's drawings pinned to the wall, and then concentrated on a lizard clinging to the ledge of the high, barred window behind the teacher's head. Occasionally it would shoot out its long yellow tongue for a fly, and then it would rest, with its eyes closed and its belly palpitating, as though it were swallowing several times quickly. The lessons were mostly concerned with reading and writing and simple numbers—things that my mother had already taught me—and I paid very little attention. The teacher wrote on the easel blackboard words like "bat" and "cat," which seemed babyish to me; only "apple" was new and incomprehensible.

When it was time for the lunch recess, I followed the girl with braids out onto the veranda. There the children from the other classes were assembled. I saw Premila at once and ran over to her, as she had charge of our lunchbox. The children were all opening packages and sitting down to eat sandwiches. Premila and I were the only ones who had Indian food—thin wheat chapatties, some vegetable curry, and a bottle of buttermilk. Premila thrust half of it into my hand and whispered fiercely that I should go and sit with my class, because that was what the others seemed to be doing.

The enormous black eyes of the little Indian girl from my class looked at my food longingly, so I offered her some. But she only shook her head and plowed her way solemnly through her sandwiches.

I was very sleepy after lunch, because at home we always took a siesta. It was usually a pleasant time of day, with the bedroom darkened against the harsh afternoon sun, the drifting off into sleep with the sound of Mother's voice reading a story in one's mind, and, finally, the shrill, fussy voice of the ayah waking one for tea.

At school, we rested for a short time on low, folding cots on the veranda, and then we were expected to play games. During the hot part of the afternoon we played indoors, and after the shadows had begun to lengthen and the slight breeze of the evening had come up we moved outside to the wide courtyard.

20   I had never really grasped the system of competitive games. At home, whenever we played tag or guessing games, I was always allowed to "win"—"because," Mother used to tell Premila, "she is the youngest, and we have to allow for that." I had often heard her say it, and it seemed quite reasonable to me, but the result was that I had no clear idea of what "winning" meant.

When we played twos-and-threes that afternoon at school, in accordance with my training, I let one of the small English boys catch me, but was naturally rather puzzled when the other children did not return the courtesy. I ran about for what seemed like hours without ever catching anyone, until it was time for school to close. Much later I learned that my attitude was called "not being a good sport," and I stopped allowing myself to be caught, but it was not for years that I really learned the spirit of the thing.

When I saw our car come up to the school gate, I broke away from my class-mates and rushed toward it yelling, "Ayah! Ayah!" It seemed like an eternity since I had seen her that morning—a wizened, affectionate figure in her white cotton sari, giving me dozens of urgent and useless instructions on how to be a good girl at school. Premila followed more sedately, and she told me on the way home never to do that again in front of the other children.

When we got home we went straight to Mother's high, white room to have tea with her, and I immediately climbed onto the bed and bounced gently up and down on the springs. Mother asked how we had liked our first day in school. I was so pleased to be home and to have left that peculiar Cynthia behind that I had nothing whatever to say about school, except to ask what "apple" meant. But Premila told Mother about the classes, and added that in her class they had weekly tests to see if they had learned their lessons well.

I asked, "What's a test?"

25   Premila said, "You're too small to have them. You won't have them in your class for donkey's years." She had learned the expression that day and was using it for the first time. We all laughed enormously at her wit. She also told Mother, in an aside, that we should take sandwiches to school the next day. Not, she said, that *she* minded. But they would be simpler for me to handle.

That whole lovely evening I didn't think about school at all. I sprinted bare-foot across the lawns with my favorite playmate, the cook's son, to the stream at the end of the garden. We quarreled in our usual way, waded in the tepid water under the lime trees, and waited for the night to bring out the smell of the jas-mine. I listened with fascination to his stories of ghosts and demons, until I was too frightened to cross the garden alone in the semidarkness. The ayah found me, shouted at the cook's son, scolded me, hurried me in to supper—it was an entirely usual, wonderful evening.

It was a week later, the day of Premila's first test, that our lives changed rather abruptly. I was sitting at the back of my class, in my usual inattentive way, only half listening to the teacher. I had started a rather guarded friendship with the girl with the braids, whose name turned out to be Nalini (Nancy, in school). The three other Indian children were already fast friends. Even at that age it was apparent to all of us that friendship with the English or Anglo-Indian children was out of the question. Occasionally, during the class, my new friend and I would draw pictures and show them to each other secretly.

The door opened sharply and Premila marched in. At first, the teacher smiled at her in a kindly and encouraging way and said, "Now, you're little Cynthia's sister?"

Premila didn't even look at her. She stood with her feet planted firmly apart and her shoulders rigid, and addressed herself directly to me. "Get up," she said. "We're going home."

30   I didn't know what had happened, but I was aware that it was a crisis of some sort. I rose obediently and started to walk toward my sister.

"Bring your pencils and your notebook," she said.

I went back for them, and together we left the room. The teacher started to say something just as Premila closed the door, but we didn't wait to hear what it was.

In complete silence we left the school grounds and started to walk home. Then I asked Premila what the matter was. All she would say was "We're going home for good."

It was a very tiring walk for a child of five and a half, and I dragged along behind Premila with my pencils growing sticky in my hand. I can still remember looking at the dusty hedges, and the tangles of thorns in the ditches by the side of the road, smelling the faint fragrance from the eucalyptus trees and wondering whether we would ever reach home. Occasionally a horse-drawn tonga passed us, and the women, in their pink or green silks, stared at Premila and me trudging along on the side of the road. A few coolies and a line of women carrying baskets of vegetables on their heads smiled at us. But it was nearing the hottest time of day, and the road was almost deserted. I walked more and more slowly, and shouted to Premila, from time to time, "Wait for me!" with increasing peevishness. She spoke to me only once, and that was to tell me to carry my notebook on my head, because of the sun.

35   When we got to our house the ayah was just taking a tray of lunch into Mother's room. She immediately started a long, worried questioning about what are you children doing back here at this hour of the day.

Mother looked very startled and very concerned, and asked Premila what had happened.

Premila said, "We had our test today, and She made me and the other Indians sit at the back of the room, with a desk between each one."

Mother said, "Why was that, darling?"

"She said it was because Indians cheat," Premila added. "So I don't think we should go back to that school."

40   Mother looked very distant, and was silent a long time. At last she said, "Of course not, darling." She sounded displeased.

We all shared the curry she was having for lunch, and afterward I was sent off to the beautifully familiar bedroom for my siesta. I could hear Mother and Premila talking through the open door.

Mother said, "Do you suppose she understood all that?"

Premila said, "I shouldn't think so. She's a baby."

Mother said, "Well, I hope it won't bother her."

45   Of course, they were both wrong. I understood it perfectly, and I remember it all very clearly. But I put it happily away, because it had all happened to a girl called Cynthia, and I never was really particularly interested in her.

LEVELS OF READING

Summary:

Pay attention to the **literal** meaning of the text. Briefly describe the sequence of events in "By Any Other Name." Who tells the story? Where is the story set and why is this particular setting important to the idea that Santha Rama Rau is trying to convey? Concentrate on the highlights; avoid too much detail when summarizing. Again, drawing a simple outline of the main points of the text will help you better analyze the text at other levels of interpretation.

Analysis:

Find what you believe is **implicit** or **symbolic** in the text. Why is Rau's detailed description of her teacher significant? What does that description tell us about her? What is significant about Rau's change of school and consequent change of name? At the school, what is implicitly conveyed concerning Indian food and Indian dress? Find other examples of deeper meaning in the descriptions of people, places, and events in Rau's autobiography and make an argument about this text, including mention of the more suggestive aspects of the text.

Application:

Apply what you have learned about paradigms, normal science, and scientific revolution to Santha Rama Rau's personal story. Outline an argument you wish to make about her story using Kuhn's theory to help you explain what some part of "By Any Other Name" may mean. The "part" of the story you choose to analyze may include any of the following: a character, a setting, a symbol or symbols, an important change, a motivation, a goal, a result. Consider the following as possibilities, but explore other original interpretations too:

- Even though she is only five and a half when sent to the British school, Santha is adept at **empirical observation**. Consider both the reliability of the empirical data she collects and her interpretation of that data.
- What function does Kuhn's idea of **anomaly** serve in this story?
- The British education Santha Rama Rau temporarily experiences forces her to undergo several **paradigm shifts** in a short space of time. What is the nature of those shifts? What is "**normal science**" and where is the "**revolution**" in thinking in terms of colonizer and colonized? Does the paradigm shift occur if the colonized refuse its imposition?

Start Your Own Argument:

Following from the above consider whether the villagers in García Márquez' story, little Santha Rama Rau, and even Kuhn himself are able to "think outside the box." For instance, isn't Kuhn the grammarian guilty of what he accuses scientists of, i.e., an inability to "think outside the box"? What "box" was he unable to free himself from? How might historical circumstances and/or grammatical conventions (also, to an extent, historically contingent) have helped to inform his choice of pronouns? What other writers you have read "think outside the box"?

CAUSE AND EFFECT

GEORG SIMMEL

Georg Simmel (1858–1918) was born in Berlin, Germany, the youngest of seven children. His father, a man of Jewish origins who had converted to Christianity, died when Simmel was still young; his relationship with his mother was at best distant. Fortunately, a guardian left Simmel a private fortune, so Simmel was able to study history and philosophy at the University of Berlin, earning a doctorate in philosophy in 1881. His interests, however, remained eclectic, including social science, psychology, and history. Simmel's wife, Gertrude, also became a philosopher of some accomplishment.

Unable to secure a full-time academic position, Simmel remained at the University of Berlin as a privadozent (an unpaid lecturer dependent upon student fees). In 1901, after sixteen years and when Simmel was forty-three years old, the University finally gave him an honorary title but refused to allow him participation in university governance. Though he was at this point the author of six books translated into five languages, his applications for more permanent academic positions were always unsuccessful.

In 1914, Simmel was finally granted a professorship at the University of Strasbourg on the border between France and Germany, far from his beloved Berlin. The timing could not have been worse. Only months after arriving there, all university activities were interrupted by the First World War, and the lecture halls of the University were converted into military hospitals.

Simmel's essay, "The Metropolis and Mental Life" traces a cause-and-effect relationship, though it may be more precise to say effect-and-cause relationship. In this case, the usual cause-and-effect structure is turned on its head since Simmel often tells us the "effects" of urban life before determining what he believes are the "causes" of those effects. Nevertheless, his essay presents ideas regarding urban life still current today—the "blasé attitude," for instance—ideas that one could argue have been exported beyond the boundaries of cities, at least to an extent.

The "cause and effect" essay generally explains the reasons for certain outcomes. In Georg Simmel's "The Metropolis and Mental Life" the effect is often given before the cause is explained. This reversed structure may be appropriate because (like Marx, among others) Simmel is inventing terms new to his readers, such as "cosmopolitanism" and "depersonalization." And so, Simmel first names the term, defines it, and then explains its origins in modern metropolitan life.

Coming to Terms with the Reading:

Before reading/rereading Georg Simmel's "The Metropolis and Mental Life," it is best to have a firm grasp of the meaning of the following terms:

1. intellectualism
2. modern life
3. money economy
4. reserve
5. blasé attitude
6. cosmopolitanism
7. specialization
8. depersonalization

THE METROPOLIS AND MENTAL LIFE
Georg Simmel

1   The deepest problems of modern life flow from the attempt of the individual to maintain the independence and individuality of his existence against the sovereign powers of society, against the weight of the historical heritage and the external culture and technique of life. This antagonism represents the most modern form of the conflict which primitive man must carry on with nature for his own bodily existence. The eighteenth century may have called for liberation from all the ties which grew up historically in politics, in religion, in morality and in economics in order to permit the original natural virtue of man, which is equal in everyone, to develop without inhibition; the nineteenth century may have sought to promote, in addition to man's freedom, his individuality (which is connected with the division of labor) and his achievements which make him unique and indispensable but which at the same time make him so much the more dependent on the complementary activity of others; Nietzsche may have seen the relentless struggle of the individual as the prerequisite for his full development, while Socialism found the same thing in the suppression of all competition—but in each of these the same fundamental motive was at work, namely the resistance of the individual to being levelled, swallowed up in the social-technological mechanism. When one inquires about the products of the specifically modern aspects of contemporary life with reference to their inner meaning—when, so to speak, one examines the body of culture with reference to the soul, as I am to do concerning the metropolis today—the answer will require the investigation of the relationship which such a social structure promotes between the individual aspects of life and those which transcend the existence of single individuals. It will require the investigation of the adaptations made by the personality in its adjustment to the forces that lie outside of it.

    The psychological foundation, upon which the metropolitan individuality is erected, is the intensification of emotional life due to the swift and continuous shift

Reprinted from *Georg Simmel on Individuality and Social Forms*, (University of Chicago, 1948). Translated by Edward A. Shils. Originally published as "Die Grosstadt und das Geistesleben," in *Die Grosstadt. Jahrbuch der Gehe-Stiftung* 9 (1903).

of external and internal stimuli. Man is a creature whose existence is dependent on differences, i.e., his mind is stimulated by the difference between present impressions and those which have preceded. Lasting impressions, the slightness in their differences, the habituated regularity of their course and contrasts between them, consume, so to speak, less mental energy than the rapid telescoping of changing images, pronounced differences within what is grasped at a single glance, and the unexpectedness of violent stimuli. To the extent that the metropolis creates these psychological conditions—with every crossing of the street, with the tempo and multiplicity of economic, occupational and social life—it creates in the sensory foundations of mental life, and in the degree of awareness necessitated by our organization as creatures dependent on differences, a deep contrast with the slower, more habitual, more smoothly flowing rhythm of the sensory-mental phase of small town and rural existence. Thereby the essentially intellectualistic character of the mental life of the metropolis becomes intelligible as over against that of the small town which rests more on feelings and emotional relationships. These latter are rooted in the unconscious levels of the mind and develop most readily in the steady equilibrium of unbroken customs. The locus of reason, on the other hand, is in the lucid, conscious upper strata of the mind and it is the most adaptable of our inner forces. In order to adjust itself to the shifts and contradictions in events, it does not require the disturbances and inner upheavals which are the only means whereby more conservative personalities are able to adapt themselves to the same rhythm of events. Thus the metropolitan type— which naturally takes on a thousand individual modifications—creates a protective organ for itself against the profound disruption with which the fluctuations and discontinuities of the external milieu threaten it. Instead of reacting emotionally, the metropolitan type reacts primarily in a rational manner, thus creating a mental predominance through the intensification of consciousness, which in turn is caused by it. Thus the reaction of the metropolitan person to those events is moved to a sphere of mental activity which is least sensitive and which is furthest removed from the depths of the personality.

This intellectualistic quality which is thus recognized as a protection of the inner life against the domination of the metropolis, becomes ramified into numerous specific phenomena. The metropolis has always been the seat of money economy because the many-sidedness and concentration of commercial activity have given the medium of exchange an importance which it could not have acquired in the commercial aspects of rural life. But money economy and the domination of the intellect stand in the closest relationship to one another. They have in common a purely matter-of-fact attitude in the treatment of persons and things in which a formal justice is often combined with an unrelenting hardness. The purely intellectualistic person is indifferent to all things personal because, out of them, relationships and reactions develop which are not to be completely understood by purely rational methods—just as the unique element in events never enters into the principle of money. Money is concerned only with what is common to all, i.e., with the exchange value which reduces all quality and individuality to a purely quantitative level. All emotional relationships between persons rest on their individuality, whereas intellectual relationships deal with persons as with numbers, that is, as with elements which, in themselves, are indifferent, but which are of interest only insofar as they offer something objectively perceivable. It is in this very manner that the inhabitant of the metropolis reckons with his merchant, his customer, and with his servant, and frequently with the persons with whom he is thrown into obligatory association. These relationships stand in distinct contrast with the nature of the smaller circle in which the inevitable knowledge of individual characteristics produces, with an equal inevitability, an emotional tone in conduct, a sphere which is beyond the mere objective weighting of tasks performed and payments made. What is essential here as regards the economic-psychological aspect of the problem is that in less advanced cultures production was for the customer who ordered the product so that the producer and the purchaser knew one another. The modern city, however, is supplied almost exclusively by production for the market, that is, for entirely unknown purchasers who never appear in the actual field of vision of the producers themselves. Thereby, the interests of each party acquire a relentless matter-of-factness, and its rationally calculated economic egoism need not fear any divergence from its set path because of the imponderability of personal relationships. This is all the more the case in the money economy which dominates the metropolis in which the last remnants of domestic production and direct barter of goods have been eradicated and in which the amount of production on direct personal order is reduced daily. Furthermore, this psychological intellectualistic attitude and the money economy are in such close integration that no one is able to say whether it was the former that effected the latter or *vice versa*. What is certain is only that the form of life in the metropolis is the soil which nourishes this interaction most fruitfully, a point which I shall attempt to demonstrate only with the statement of the most outstanding English constitutional historian to the effect that through the entire course of English history London has never acted as the heart of England but often as its intellect and always as its money bag.

In certain apparently insignificant characters or traits of the most external aspects of life are to be found a number of characteristic mental tendencies. The modern mind has become more and more a calculating one. The calculating exactness of practical life which has resulted from a money economy corresponds to the ideal of natural science, namely that of transforming the world into an arithmetical problem and of fixing every one of its parts in a mathematical formula. It has been money economy which has thus filled the daily life of so many people with weighing, calculating, enumerating and the reduction of qualitative values to quantitative terms. Because of the character of calculability which money has there has come into the relationships of the elements of life a precision and a degree of certainty in the definition of the equalities and inequalities and an unambiguousness in agreements and arrangements, just as externally this precision has been brought about through the general diffusion of pocket watches. It is, however, the conditions of the metropolis which are cause as well as effect for this essential characteristic. The relationships and concerns of the typical metropolitan resident are so manifold and complex that, especially as a result of the agglomeration of so many persons with such differentiated interests, their relationships and activities intertwine with one another into a many-membered organism. In view of this fact, the lack of the most exact punctuality in promises and performances would cause the whole to break down into an inextricable chaos. If all the watches in Berlin suddenly went wrong in different ways even only as much as an hour, its entire economic and commercial life would be derailed for some time. Even though this may seem more superficial in its significance, it transpires that the magnitude of distances results in making all waiting and the breaking of appointments an ill-afforded waste of time. For this reason the technique of metropolitan life in general is not conceivable without all of its activities and reciprocal relationships being organized and coordinated in the most punctual way into a firmly fixed framework of time which transcends all subjective elements. But here too there emerge those conclusions which are in general the whole task of this discussion, namely, that every event, however restricted to this superficial level it may appear, comes immediately into contact with the depths of the soul, and that the most banal externalities are, in the last analysis, bound up with the final decisions concerning the meaning and the style of life. Punctuality, calculability, and exactness, which are required by the complications and extensiveness of metropolitan life are not only most intimately connected with its capitalistic and intellectualistic character but also color the content of life and are conducive to the exclusion of those irrational, instinctive, sovereign human traits and impulses which originally seek to determine the form of life from within instead of receiving it from the outside in a general, schematically precise form. Even though those lives which are autonomous and characterised by these vital impulses are not entirely impossible in the city, they are, none the less, opposed to it *in abstracto*. It is in the light of this that we can explain the passionate hatred of personalities like Ruskin and Nietzsche for the metropolis—personalities who found the value of life only in unschematized individual expressions which cannot be reduced to exact equivalents and in whom, on that account, there flowed from the same source as did that hatred, the hatred of the money economy and of the intellectualism of existence.

5   The same factors which, in the exactness and the minute precision of the form of life, have coalesced into a structure of the highest impersonality, have, on the other hand, an influence in a highly personal direction. There is perhaps no psychic phenomenon which is so unconditionally reserved to the city as the blasé outlook. It is at first the consequence of those rapidly shifting stimulations of the nerves which are thrown together in all their contrasts and from which it seems to us the intensification of metropolitan intellectuality seems to be derived. On that account it is not likely that stupid persons who have been hitherto intellectually dead will be blasé. Just as an immoderately sensuous life makes one blasé because it stimulates the nerves to their utmost reactivity until they finally can no longer produce any reaction at all, so, less harmful stimuli, through the rapidity and the contradictoriness of their shifts, force the nerves to make such violent responses, tear them about so brutally that they exhaust their last reserves of strength and, remaining in the same milieu, do not have time for new reserves to form. This incapacity to react to new stimulations with the required amount of energy constitutes in fact that blasé attitude which every child of a large city evinces when compared with the products of the more peaceful and more stable milieu.

Combined with this physiological source of the blasé metropolitan attitude there is another which derives from a money economy. The essence of the blasé attitude is an indifference toward the distinctions between things. Not in the sense that they are not perceived, as is the case of mental dullness, but rather that the meaning and the value of the distinctions between things, and therewith of the things themselves, are experienced as meaningless. They appear to the blasé person in a homogeneous, flat and gray color with no one of them worthy of being preferred to another. This psychic mood is the correct subjective reflection of a complete money economy to the extent that money takes the place of all the manifoldness of things and expresses all qualitative distinctions between them in the distinction of "how much." To the extent that money, with its colorlessness and its indifferent quality, can become a common denominator of all values it becomes the frightful leveler—it hollows out the core of things, their peculiarities, their specific values and their uniqueness and incomparability in a way which is beyond repair. They all float with the same specific gravity in the

UNIT 9

constantly moving stream of money. They all rest on the same level and are distinguished only by their amounts. In individual cases this coloring, or rather this de-coloring of things, through their equation with money, may be imperceptibly small. In the relationship, however, which the wealthy person has to objects which can be bought for money, perhaps indeed in the total character which, for this reason, public opinion now recognizes in these objects, it takes on very considerable proportions. This is why the metropolis is the seat of commerce and it is in it that the purchasability of things appears in quite a different aspect than in simpler economies. It is also the peculiar seat of the blasé attitude. In it is brought to a peak, in a certain way, that achievement in the concentration of purchasable things which stimulates the individual to the highest degree of nervous energy. Through the mere quantitative intensification of the same conditions this achievement is transformed into its opposite, into this peculiar adaptive phenomenon—the blasé attitude—in which the nerves reveal their final possibility of adjusting themselves to the content and the form of metropolitan life by renouncing the response to them. We see that the self-preservation of certain types of personalities is obtained at the cost of devaluing the entire objective world, ending inevitably in dragging the personality downward into a feeling of its own valuelessness.

Whereas the subject of this form of existence must come to terms with it for himself, his self-preservation in the face of the great city requires of him a no less negative type of social conduct. The mental attitude of the people of the metropolis to one another may be designated formally as one of reserve. If the unceasing external contact of numbers of persons in the city should be met by the same number of inner reactions as in the small town, in which one knows almost every person he meets and to each of whom he has a positive relationship, one would be completely atomized internally and would fall into an unthinkable mental condition. Partly this psychological circumstance and partly the privilege of suspicion which we have in the face of the elements of metropolitan life (which are constantly touching one another in fleeting contact) necessitates in us that reserve, in consequence of which we do not know by sight neighbors of years standing and which permits us to appear to small-town folk so often as cold and uncongenial. Indeed, if I am not mistaken, the inner side of this external reserve is not only indifference but more frequently than we believe, it is a slight aversion, a mutual strangeness and repulsion which, in a close contact which has arisen any way whatever, can break out into hatred and conflict. The entire inner organization of such a type of extended commercial life rests on an extremely varied structure of sympathies, indifferences and aversions of the briefest as well as of the most enduring sort. This sphere of indifference is, for this reason, not as great as it seems superficially. Our minds respond, with some definite feeling, to almost every impression emanating from another person. The unconsciousness, the transitoriness and the shift of these feelings seem to raise them only into indifference. Actually this latter would be as unnatural to us as immersion into a chaos of unwished-for suggestions would be unbearable. From these two typical dangers of metropolitan life we are saved by antipathy which is the latent adumbration of actual antagonism since it brings about the sort of distanciation and deflection without which this type of life could not be carried on at all. Its extent and its mixture, the rhythm of its emergence and disappearance, the forms in which it is adequate—these constitute, with the simplified motives (in the narrower sense) an inseparable totality of the form of metropolitan life. What appears here directly as dissociation is in reality only one of the elementary forms of socialization.

This reserve with its overtone of concealed aversion appears once more, however, as the form or the wrappings of a much more general psychic trait of the metropolis. It assures the individual of a type and degree of personal freedom to which there is no analogy in other circumstances. It has its roots in one of the great developmental tendencies of social life as a whole; in one of the few for which an approximately exhaustive formula can be discovered. The most elementary stage of social organization which is to be found historically, as well as in the present, is this: a relatively small circle almost entirely closed against neighboring foreign or otherwise antagonistic groups but which has however within itself such a narrow cohesion that the individual member has only a very slight area for the development of his own qualities and for free activity for which he himself is responsible. Political and familial groups began in this way as do political and religious communities; the self-preservation of very young associations requires a rigorous setting of boundaries and a centripetal unity and for that reason it cannot give room to freedom and the peculiarities of inner and external development of the individual. From this stage social evolution proceeds simultaneously in two divergent but none the less corresponding directions. In the measure that the group grows numerically, spatially, and in the meaningful content of life, its immediate inner unity and the definiteness of its original demarcation against others are weakened and rendered mild by reciprocal interactions and interconnections. And at the same time the individual gains a freedom of movement far beyond the first jealous delimitation, and gains also a peculiarity and individuality to which the division of labor in groups, which have become larger, gives both occasion and necessity. However much the particular conditions and

UNIT 9

forces of the individual situation might modify the general scheme, the state and Christianity, guilds and political parties and innumerable other groups have developed in accord with this formula. This tendency seems, to me, however to be quite clearly recognizable also in the development of individuality within the framework of city life. Small town life in antiquity as well as in the Middle Ages imposed such limits upon the movements of the individual in his relationships with the outside world and on his inner independence and differentiation that the modern person could not even breathe under such conditions. Even today the city dweller who is placed in a small town feels a type of narrowness which is very similar. The smaller the circle which forms our environment and the more limited the relationships which have the possibility of transcending the boundaries, the more anxiously the narrow community watches over the deeds, the conduct of life and the attitudes of the individual and the more will a quantitative and qualitative individuality tend to pass beyond the boundaries of such a community.

The ancient *polis* seems in this regard to have had a character of a small town. The incessant threat against its existence by enemies from near and far brought about that stern cohesion in political and military matters, that supervision of the citizen by other citizens, and that jealousy of the whole toward the individual whose own private life was repressed to such an extent that he could compensate himself only by acting as a despot in his own household. The tremendous agitation and excitement, and the unique colorfulness of Athenian life is perhaps explained by the fact that a people of incomparably individualized personalities were in constant struggle against the incessant inner and external oppression of a de-individualizing small town. This created an atmosphere of tension in which the weaker were held down and the stronger were impelled to the most passionate type of self-protection. And with this there blossomed in Athens, what, without being able to define it exactly, must be designated as "the general human character" in the intellectual development of our species. For the correlation, the factual as well as the historical validity of which we are here maintaining, is that the broadest and the most general contents and forms of life are intimately bound up with the most individual ones. Both have a common prehistory and also common enemies in the narrow formations and groupings, whose striving for self-preservation set them in conflict with the broad and general on the outside, as well as the freely mobile and individual on the inside. Just as in feudal times the "free" man was he who stood under the law of the land, that is, under the law of the largest social unit, but he was unfree who derived his legal rights only from the narrow circle of a feudal community—so today in an intellectualized and refined sense the citizen of the metropolis is "free" in contrast with the trivialities and prejudices which bind the small town person. The mutual reserve and indifference, and the intellectual conditions of life in large social units are never more sharply appreciated in their significance for the independence of the individual than in the dense crowds of the metropolis because the bodily closeness and lack of space make intellectual distance really perceivable for the first time. It is obviously only the obverse of this freedom that, under certain circumstances, one never feels as lonely and as deserted as in this metropolitan crush of persons. For here, as elsewhere, it is by no means necessary that the freedom of man reflect itself in his emotional life only as a pleasant experience.

10   It is not only the immediate size of the area and population which, on the basis of world-historical correlation between the increase in the size of the social unit and the degree of personal inner and outer freedom, makes the metropolis the locus of this condition. It is rather in transcending this purely tangible extensiveness that the metropolis also becomes the seat of cosmopolitanism. Comparable with the form of the development of wealth—(beyond a certain point property increases in ever more rapid progression as out of its own inner being)—the individual's horizon is enlarged. In the same way, economic, personal and intellectual relations in the city (which are its ideal reflection), grow in a geometrical progression as soon as, for the first time, a certain limit has been passed. Every dynamic extension becomes a preparation not only for a similar extension but rather for a larger one and from every thread which is spun out of it there continue, growing as out of themselves, an endless number of others. This may be illustrated by the fact that within the city the "unearned increment" of ground rent, through a mere increase in traffic, brings to the owner profits which are self-generating. At this point the quantitative aspects of life are transformed qualitatively. The sphere of life of the small town is, in the main, enclosed within itself. For the metropolis it is decisive that its inner life is extended in a wave-like motion over a broader national or international area. Weimar was no exception because its significance was dependent upon individual personalities and died with them, whereas the metropolis is characterised by its essential independence even of the most significant individual personalities; this is rather its antithesis and it is the price of independence which the individual living in it enjoys. The most significant aspect of the metropolis lies in this functional magnitude beyond its actual physical boundaries and this effectiveness reacts upon the latter and gives to it life, weight, importance and responsibility. A person does not end with limits of his physical body or with the area to which his physical activity is immediately confined but embraces, rather, the totality of meaningful effects which

emanates from him temporally and spatially. In the same way the city exists only in the totality of the effects which transcend their immediate sphere. These really are the actual extent in which their existence is expressed. This is already expressed in the fact that individual freedom, which is the logical historical complement of such extension, is not only to be understood in the negative sense as mere freedom of movement and emancipation from prejudices and philistinism. Its essential characteristic is rather to be found in the fact that the particularity and incomparability which ultimately every person possesses in some way is actually expressed, giving form to life. That we follow the laws of our inner nature—and this is what freedom is—becomes perceptible and convincing to us and to others only when the expressions of this nature distinguish themselves from others; it is our irreplaceability by others which shows that our mode of existence is not imposed upon us from the outside.

Cities are above all the seat of the most advanced economic division of labor. They produce such extreme phenomena as the lucrative vocation of the *quatorzieme* in Paris. These are persons who may be recognized by shields on their houses and who hold themselves ready at the dinner hour in appropriate costumes so they can be called upon on short notice in case thirteen persons find themselves at the table. Exactly in the measure of its extension the city offers to an increasing degree the determining conditions for the division of labor. It is a unit which, because of its large size, is receptive to a highly diversified plurality of achievements while at the same time the agglomeration of individuals and their struggle for the customer forces the individual to a type of specialized accomplishment in which he cannot be so easily exterminated by the other. The decisive fact here is that in the life of a city, struggle with nature for the means of life is transformed into a conflict with human beings and the gain which is fought for is granted, not by nature, but by man. For here we find not only the previously mentioned source of specialization but rather the deeper one in which the seller must seek to produce in the person to whom he wishes to sell ever new and unique needs. The necessity to specialize one's product in order to find a source of income which is not yet exhausted and also to specialize a function which cannot be easily supplanted is conducive to differentiation, refinement and enrichment of the needs of the public which obviously must lead to increasing personal variation within this public.

All this leads to the narrower type of intellectual individuation of mental qualities to which the city gives rise in proportion to its size. There is a whole series of causes for this. First of all there is the difficulty of giving one's own personality a certain status within the framework of metropolitan life. Where quantitative increase of value and energy has reached its limits, one seizes on qualitative distinctions, so that, through taking advantage of the existing sensitivity to differences, the attention of the social world can, in some way, be won for oneself. This leads ultimately to the strangest eccentricities, to specifically metropolitan extravagances of self-distanciation, of caprice, of fastidiousness, the meaning of which is no longer to be found in the content of such activity itself but rather in its being a form of "being different"—of making oneself noticeable. For many types of persons these are still the only means of saving for oneself, through the attention gained from others, some sort of self-esteem and the sense of filling a position. In the same sense there operates an apparently insignificant factor which in its effects however is perceptibly cumulative, namely, the brevity and rarity of meetings which are allotted to each individual as compared with social intercourse in a small city. For here we find the attempt to appear to-the-point, clear-cut and individual with extraordinarily greater frequency than where frequent and long association assures to each person an unambiguous conception of the other's personality.

This appears to me to be the most profound cause of the fact that the metropolis places emphasis on striving for the most individual forms of personal existence—regardless of whether it is always correct or always successful. The development of modern culture is characterised by the predominance of what one can call the objective spirit over the subjective; that is, in language as well as in law, in the technique of production as well as in art, in science as well as in the objects of domestic environment, there is embodied a sort of spirit [*Geist*], the daily growth of which is followed only imperfectly and with an even greater lag by the intellectual development of the individual. If we survey for instance the vast culture which during the last century has been embodied in things and in knowledge, in institutions and comforts, and if we compare them with the cultural progress of the individual during the same period—at least in the upper classes—we would see a frightful difference in rate of growth between the two which represents, in many points, rather a regression of the culture of the individual with reference to spirituality, delicacy and idealism. This discrepancy is in essence the result of the success of the growing division of labor. For it is this which requires from the individual an ever more one-sided type of achievement which, at its highest point, often permits his personality as a whole to fall into neglect. In any case this overgrowth of objective culture has been less and less satisfactory for the individual. Perhaps less conscious than in practical activity and in the obscure complex of feelings which flow from him, he is reduced to a negligible quantity. He becomes a single cog as over against the vast overwhelming organization of things and forces which gradually take out of his hands everything connected with progress, spirituality and value. The operation of these forces results in the transformation of the latter from a subjective form into one of purely objective existence. It need only be pointed out that the metropolis is the proper arena for this type of culture which has outgrown every personal element. Here in buildings and in educational institutions, in the wonders and comforts of space-conquering technique, in the formations of social life and in the concrete institutions of the State is to be found such a tremendous richness of crystallizing, depersonalized cultural accomplishments that the personality can, so to speak, scarcely maintain itself in the face of it. From one angle life is made infinitely more easy in the sense that stimulations, interests, and the taking up of time and attention, present themselves from all sides and carry it in a stream which scarcely requires any individual efforts for its ongoing. But from another angle, life is composed more and more of these impersonal cultural elements and existing goods and values which seek to suppress peculiar personal interests and incomparabilities. As a result, in order that this most personal element be saved, extremities and peculiarities and individualizations must be produced and they must be over-exaggerated merely to be brought into the awareness even of the individual himself. The atrophy of individual culture through the hypertrophy of objective culture lies at the root of the bitter hatred which the preachers of the most extreme individualism, in the footsteps of Nietzsche, directed against the metropolis. But it is also the explanation of why indeed they are so passionately loved in the metropolis and indeed appear to its residents as the saviors of their unsatisfied yearnings.

When both of these forms of individualism which are nourished by the quantitative relationships of the metropolis, i.e., individual independence and the elaboration of personal peculiarities, are examined with reference to their historical position, the metropolis attains an entirely new value and meaning in the world history of the spirit. The eighteenth century found the individual in the grip of powerful bonds which had become meaningless—bonds of a political, agrarian, guild and religious nature—delimitations which imposed upon the human being at the same time an unnatural form and for a long time an unjust inequality. In this situation arose the cry for freedom and equality—the belief in the full freedom of movement of the individual in all his social and intellectual relationships which would then permit the same noble essence to emerge equally from all individuals as Nature had placed it in them and as it had been distorted by social life and historical development. Alongside of this liberalistic ideal there grew up in the nineteenth century from Goethe and the Romantics, on the one hand, and from the economic division of labor on the other, the further tendency, namely, that individuals who had been liberated from their historical bonds sought now to distinguish themselves from one another. No longer was it the "general human quality" in every individual but rather his qualitative uniqueness and irreplaceability that now became the criteria of his value. In the conflict and shifting interpretations of these two ways of defining the position of the individual within the totality is to be found the external as well as the internal history of our time. It is the function of the metropolis to make a place for the conflict and for the attempts at unification of both of these in the sense that its own peculiar conditions have been revealed to us as the occasion and the stimulus for the development of both. Thereby they attain a quite unique place, fruitful with an inexhaustible richness of meaning in the development of the mental life. They reveal themselves as one of those great historical structures in which conflicting life-embracing currents find themselves with equal legitimacy. Because of this, however, regardless of whether we are sympathetic or antipathetic with their individual expressions, they transcend the sphere in which a judge-like attitude on our part is appropriate. To the extent that such forces have been integrated, with the fleeting existence of a single cell, into the root as well as the crown of the totality of historical life to which we belong—it is our task not to complain or to condone but only to understand.

READING/WRITING ASSISTS

Thesis (and its counterargument):

Readers often expect to find a clear statement of the writer's argument in a **thesis statement**, usually found in a sentence or two at the end of the first or, at the latest, second paragraph of an argumentative essay. Simmel's thesis is posited not so much in response to a **counterargument**, but rather as a means to explore historical difference and changes in the psychological make-up of the individual in his or her relationship to society, especially within the "modern" city. Pay special attention to the ways in which Simmel suggests the individual personality was regarded during the eighteenth and nineteenth centuries. What signal relationship does Simmel plan to explore in his effort to better explain the "body of culture with reference to the soul"?

The Shape of the Argument:

"Mapping" the structure of an argument can help us better understand the argument itself, while also showing us new models for shaping our own arguments in essay form. Reading Nietzsche's "Good and Evil" may help make Simmel's argument more clear, since he refers to Nietzsche's philosophy more than once. Reading Freud's "Second Lecture" and Marx's *Manifesto* also may help clarify Simmel's thoughts. But Simmel's essay mainly builds on key terms that he claims are in relationship to one another in modern culture and that, in tandem, have profound consequences to personality development in the modern metropolis. To better understand Simmel's definitions of these terms, and their relationships to one another, it is best to start by outlining the entire essay paragraph by paragraph:

Paragraph 1:   In the first long paragraph of this essay, Simmel outlines a historical past with regard to the idea of individualism within a larger society. Trace that outline and try to understand what Simmel argues has changed. Note that Simmel's **thesis** is clearly stated in terms of what he plans "to do" in this essay.

Paragraph 2:   Simmel's essay concerns individuality, but a specific individuality—the metropolitan. In what respects, according to Simmel, does the foundation of metropolitan mental life differ from that of rural mental life?

Paragraph 3:   Connection between **intellectualism** and money. What is this connection? What is different about urban producers and consumers?

Paragraph 4:   How does Simmel connect **intellectualism, capitalism,** and **time**?

Paragraph 5:   What is the "**blasé attitude**" and why are modern city dwellers particularly prone to it?

Paragraph 6:   What is the connection between the blasé attitude and money?

Paragraph 7:   **Reserve**: What is it? How does it operate psychologically?

Paragraph 8:   What is reserve's connection to personal freedom? Is this freedom physical, psychological, or a bit of both? How does personal freedom evolve in groups?

Paragraph 9:   Here Simmel gives another example of a close-knit community impairing individual freedom. But what does he say are some consequences of the liberating forces of metropolitan life?

Paragraph 10:   What is **cosmopolitanism**? What cities in the world have this quality?

Paragraph 11:   Think of some examples of the kind of economic **specialization** Simmel finds in an urban environment.

Paragraph 12:   Extreme example of individualism in cities. Is this kind of extreme individualism still found in/confined to cities today?

Paragraph 13:   What is the connection between objectification and depersonalization?

Paragraph 14:   By way of conclusion, Simmel returns to his characterization of eighteenth- and nineteenth-century individualism and its difference from that of the "modern city." What is this important difference?

Rhetorical Moves:

Like Jung, Simmel relies on key terms to make his argument. Though Jung's argument is dependent on the tracing of one term, transference, through his patient's analysis, Simmel's essay is accretive, in that he continues to add terms, while showing their connection to one another and to the urban dweller's mental life. Do Simmel's terms add up to a convincing argument regarding changes in mental life in the modern city?

Rhetorically, Simmel's essay is based on a cause and effect relationship. His argument is mainly about the **effects** of urban life on the individual psyche, but in order to "prove" those effects, he must show the **causes** of them in the body of his essay. To test the rhetorical and logical validity of Simmel's argument, it may help to consider the following: Any effect can have more than one possible cause. Does Simmel ever narrow his argument to *one* probable cause? Does he need to do so? If the cause can be said to be responsible for the effect, it must be capable of producing the effect claimed. Are Simmel's causes capable of producing the effects he claims? Are the conditions of modern urban life such that the causes of the mental effects Simmel claims can exist? Do the causes of the changes in mental urban life always produce the same effects Simmel claims?

SAUL BELLOW

Saul Bellow (1915–2005) was born in Lachine, Quebec, three years after his parents emigrated from Russia in 1913. The family moved to Chicago in 1924. In 1924, Bellow earned a B.A. from Northwestern University in anthropology and sociology. He was discouraged from studying English literature by a professor who told him that "Jews have difficulty understanding English." After finishing his B.A., Bellow completed some graduate work at the University of Wisconsin. He left to join the Merchant Marine during World War II.

Bellow taught at several colleges, including Bard College, Princeton, and the University of Minnesota. In 1962, he became a professor on the Committee for Social Thought at the University of Chicago.

Bellow has published numerous novels: Dangling Man *(1944),* The Victim *(1947),* The Adventures of Augie March *(National Book Award 1954),* Herzog *(International Literary Prize 1964), and* Humboldt's Gift *(Pulitzer Prize 1975). He won a Nobel Prize for Literature in 1976.*

LOOKING FOR MR. GREEN
Saul Bellow

Whatsoever thy hand findeth to do, do it with thy might. . . .

1   Hard work? No, it wasn't really so hard. He wasn't used to walking and stair-climbing, but the physical difficulty of his new job was not what George Grebe felt most. He was delivering relief checks in the Negro district, and although he was a native Chicagoan this was not a part of the city he knew much about—it needed a depression to introduce him to it. No, it wasn't literally hard work, not as reckoned in foot-pounds, but yet he was beginning to feel the strain of it, to grow aware of its peculiar difficulty. He could find the streets and numbers, but the clients were not where they were supposed to be, and he felt like a hunter inexperienced in the camouflage of his game. It was an unfavorable day, too—fall, and cold, dark weather, windy. But, anyway, instead of shells in his deep trench-coat pocket he had the cardboard of checks, punctured for the spindles of the file, the holes reminding him of the holes in player-piano paper. And he didn't look much like a hunter, either; his was a city figure entirely, belted up in this Irish conspirator's coat. He was slender without being tall, stiff in the back, his legs looking shabby in a pair of old tweed pants gone through and fringy at the cuffs. With this stiffness, he kept his head forward, so that his face was red from the sharpness of the weather; and it was an indoors sort of face with gray eyes that persisted in some kind of thought and yet seemed to avoid definiteness of conclusion. He wore sideburns that surprised you somewhat by the tough curl of the blond hair and the effect of assertion in their length. He was not so mild as he looked, nor so youthful; and nevertheless there was no effort on his part to seem what he was not. He was an educated man; he was a bachelor; he was in some ways simple; without lushing, he liked a drink; his luck had not been good. Nothing was deliberately hidden.

He felt that his luck was better than usual today. When he had reported for work that morning he had expected to be shut up in the relief office at a clerk's

"Looking for Mr. Green," by Saul Bellow, reprinted from *Mosby's Memoirs and Other Stories* (1951), by permission of Viking Penguin, a division of Penguin Group (USA) Inc. Copyright © 1951 and renewed 1979 by Saul Bellow.

job, for he had been hired downtown as a clerk, and he was glad to have, instead, the freedom of the streets and welcomed, at least at first, the vigor of the cold and even the blowing of the hard wind. But on the other hand he was not getting on with the distribution of the checks. It was true that it was a city job; nobody expected you to push too hard at a city job. His supervisor, that young Mr. Raynor, had practically told him that. Still, he wanted to do well at it. For one thing, when he knew how quickly he could deliver a batch of checks, he would know also how much time he could expect to clip for himself. And then, too, the clients would be waiting for their money. That was not the most important consideration, though it certainly mattered to him. No, but he wanted to do well, simply for doing-well's sake, to acquit himself decently of a job because he so rarely had a job to do that required just this sort of energy. Of this peculiar energy he now had a superabundance; once it had started to flow, it flowed all too heavily. And, for the time being anyway, he was balked. He could not find Mr. Green.

So he stood in his big-skirted trench coat with a large envelope in his hand and papers showing from his pocket, wondering why people should be so hard to locate who were too feeble or sick to come to the station to collect their own checks. But Raynor had told him that tracking them down was not easy at first and had offered him some advice on how to proceed. "If you can see the postman, he's your first man to ask, and your best bet. If you can't connect with him, try the stores and tradespeople around. Then the janitor and the neighbors. But you'll find the closer you come to your man the less people will tell you. They don't want to tell you anything."

"Because I'm a stranger."

5 "Because you're white. We ought to have a Negro doing this, but we don't at the moment, and of course you've got to eat, too, and this is public employment. Jobs have to be made. Oh, that holds for me too. Mind you, I'm not letting myself out. I've got three years of seniority on you, that's all. And a law degree. Otherwise, you might be back of the desk and I might be going out into the field this cold day. The same dough pays us both and for the same, exact, identical reason. What's my law degree got to do with it? But you have to pass out these checks, Mr. Grebe, and it'll help if you're stubborn, so I hope you are."

"Yes, I'm fairly stubborn."

Raynor sketched hard with an eraser in the old dirt of his desk, left-handed, and said, "Sure, what else can you answer to such a question. Anyhow, the trouble you're going to have is that they don't like to give information about anybody. They think you're a plainclothes dick or an installment collector, or summons-server or something like that. Till you've been seen around the neighborhood for a few months and people know you're only from the relief."

It was dark, ground-freezing, pre-Thanksgiving weather; the wind played hob with the smoke, rushing it down, and Grebe missed his gloves, which he had left in Raynor's office. And no one would admit knowing Green. It was past three o'clock and the postman had made his last delivery. The nearest grocer, himself a Negro, had never heard the name Tulliver Green, or said he hadn't. Grebe was inclined to think that it was true, that he had in the end convinced the man that he wanted only to deliver a check. But he wasn't sure. He needed experience in interpreting looks and signs and, even more, the will not to be put off or denied and even the force to bully if need be. If the grocer did know, he had got rid of him easily. But since most of his trade was with reliefers, why should he prevent the delivery of a check? Maybe Green, or Mrs. Green, if there was a Mrs. Green, patronized another grocer. And was there a Mrs. Green? It was one of Grebe's great handicaps that he hadn't looked at any of the case records. Raynor should have let him read files for a few hours. But he apparently saw no need for that, probably considering the job unimportant. Why prepare systematically to deliver a few checks?

But now it was time to look for the janitor. Grebe took in the building in the wind and gloom of the late November day—trampled, frost-hardened lots on one side; on the other, an automobile junk yard and then the infinite work of Elevated frames, weak-looking, gaping with rubbish fires; two sets of leaning brick porches three stories high and a flight of cement stairs to the cellar. Descending, he entered the underground passage, where he tried the doors until one opened and he found himself in the furnace room. There someone rose toward him and approached, scraping on the coal grit and bending under the canvas-jacketed pipes.

10   "Are you the janitor?"

"What do you want?"

"I'm looking for a man who's supposed to be living here. Green."

"What Green?"

"Oh, you maybe have more than one Green?" said Grebe with new, pleasant hope. "This is Tulliver Green."

15   "I don't think I c'n help you, mister. I don't know any."

"A crippled man."

The janitor stood bent before him. Could it be that he was crippled? Oh, God! what if he was. Grebe's gray eyes sought with excited difficulty to see. But no, he was only very short and stooped. A head awakened from meditation, a strong-haired beard, low, wide shoulders. A staleness of sweat and coal rose from his black shirt and the burlap sack he wore as an apron.

"Crippled how?"

Grebe thought and then answered with the light voice of unmixed candor, "I don't know. I've never seen him." This was damaging, but his only other choice was to make a lying guess, and he was not up to it. "I'm delivering checks for the relief to shut-in cases. If he weren't crippled he'd come to collect himself. That's why I said crippled. Bedridden, chair-ridden—is there anybody like that?"

20   This sort of frankness was one of Grebe's oldest talents, going back to child-hood. But it gained him nothing here.

"No suh. I've got four buildin's same as this that I take care of. I don' know all the tenants, leave alone the tenants' tenants. The rooms turn over so fast, people movin' in and out every day. I can't tell you."

The janitor opened his grimy lips, but Grebe did not hear him in the piping of the valves and the consuming pull of air to flame in the body of the furnace. He knew, however, what he had said.

"Well, all the same, thanks. Sorry I bothered you. I'll prowl around upstairs again and see if I can turn up someone who knows him."

Once more in the cold air and early darkness he made the short circle from the cellarway to the entrance crowded between the brickwork pillars and began to climb to the third floor. Pieces of plaster ground under his feet; strips of brass tape from which the carpeting had been torn away marked old boundaries at the sides. In the passage, the cold reached him worse than in the street; it touched him to the bone. The hall toilets ran like springs. He thought grimly as he heard the wind burning around the building with a sound like that of the furnace, that this was a great piece of constructed shelter. Then he struck a match in the gloom and searched for names and numbers among the writings and scribbles on the walls. He saw WHOODY-DOODY GO TO JESUS, and zigzags, caricatures, sexual scrawls, and curses. So the sealed rooms of pyramids were also decorated, and the caves of human dawn.

25   The information on his card was, TULLIVER GREEN—APT 3D. There were no names, however, and no numbers. His shoulders drawn up, tears of cold in his eyes, breathing vapor, he went the length of the corridor and told himself that if he had been lucky enough to have the temperament for it he would bang on one of the doors and bawl out "Tulliver Green!" until he got results. But it wasn't in him to make an uproar and he continued to burn matches, passing the light over the walls. At the rear, in a corner off the hall, he discovered a door he had

not seen before and he thought it best to investigate. It sounded empty when he knocked, but a young Negress answered, hardly more than a girl. She opened only a bit, to guard the warmth of the room.

"Yes suh?"

"I'm from the district relief station on Prairie Avenue. I'm looking for a man named Tulliver Green to give him his check. Do you know him?"

No, she didn't; but he thought she had not understood anything of what he had said. She had a dream-bound, dream-blind face, very soft and black, shut off. She wore a man's jacket and pulled the ends together at her throat. Her hair was parted in three directions, at the sides and transversely, standing up at the front in a dull puff.

"Is there somebody around here who might know?"

30   "I jus' taken this room las' week."

He observed that she shivered, but even her shiver was somnambulistic and there was no sharp consciousness of cold in the big smooth eyes of her handsome face.

"All right, miss, thank you. Thanks," he said, and went to try another place.

Here he was admitted. He was grateful, for the room was warm. It was full of people, and they were silent as he entered—ten people, or a dozen, perhaps more, sitting on benches like a parliament. There was no light, properly speaking, but a tempered darkness that the window gave, and everyone seemed to him enormous, the men padded out in heavy work clothes and winter coats, and the women huge, too, in their sweaters, hats, and old furs. And, besides, bed and bedding, a black cooking range, a piano piled towering to the ceiling with papers, a dining-room table of the old style of prosperous Chicago. Among these people Grebe, with his cold-heightened fresh color and his smaller stature, entered like a schoolboy. Even though he was met with smiles and goodwill, he knew, before a single word was spoken, that all the currents ran against him and that he would make no headway. Nevertheless he began. "Does anybody here know how I can deliver a check to Mr. Tulliver Green?"

"Green?" It was the man that had let him in who answered. He was in short sleeves, in a checkered shirt, and had a queer, high head, profusely overgrown and long as a shako; the veins entered it strongly from his forehead. "I never heard mention of him. Is this where he live?"

35   "This is the address they gave me at the station. He's a sick man, and he'll need his check. Can't anybody tell me where to find him?"

He stood his ground and waited for a reply, his crimson wool scarf wound about his neck and drooping outside his trench coat, pockets weighted with the block of checks and official forms. They must have realized that he was not a college boy employed afternoons by a bill collector, trying foxily to pass for a relief clerk, recognized that he was an older man who knew himself what need was, who had had more than an average seasoning in hardship. It was evident enough if you looked at the marks under his eyes and at the sides of his mouth.

"Anybody know this sick man?"

"No suh." On all sides he saw heads shaken and smiles of denial. No one knew. And maybe it was true, he considered, standing silent in the earthen, musky human gloom of the place as the rumble continued. But he could never really be sure.

"What's the matter with this man?" said shako-head.

40   "I've never seen him. All I can tell you is that he can't come in person for his money. It's my first day in this district."

"Maybe they given you the wrong number?"

"I don't believe so. But where else can I ask about him?" He felt that this persistence amused them deeply, and in a way he shared their amusement that he should stand up so tenaciously to them. Though smaller, though slight, he was his own man, he retracted nothing about himself, and he looked back at them, gray-eyed, with amusement and also with a sort of courage. On the bench some man spoke in his throat, the words impossible to catch, and a woman answered with a wild, shrieking laugh, which was quickly cut off.

"Well, so nobody will tell me?"

"Ain't nobody who knows."

45   "At least, if he lives here, he pays rent to someone. Who manages the building?"

"Greatham Company. That's on Thirty-ninth Street."

Grebe wrote it in his pad. But, in the street again, a sheet of wind-driven paper clinging to his leg while he deliberated what direction to take next, it seemed a feeble lead to follow. Probably this Green didn't rent a flat, but a room. Sometimes there were as many as twenty people in an apartment; the real-estate agent would know only the lessee. And not even the agent could tell you who the renters were. In some places the beds were even used in shifts, watchmen or jitney drivers or short-order cooks in night joints turning out after a day's sleep and surrendering their beds to a sister, a nephew, or perhaps a stranger, just off the bus. There were large numbers of newcomers in this terrific, blight-bitten portion of the city between Cottage Grove and Ashland, wandering from house to house and room to room. When you saw them, how could you know them? They didn't carry bundles on their backs or look picturesque. You only saw a man, a Negro, walking in the street or riding in the car, like everyone else, with his thumb closed on a transfer. And therefore how were you supposed to tell? Grebe thought the Greatham agent would only laugh at his question.

But how much it would have simplified the job to be able to say that Green was old, or blind, or consumptive. An hour in the files, taking a few notes, and he needn't have been at such a disadvantage. When Raynor gave him the block of checks Grebe asked, "How much should I know about these people?" Then Raynor had looked as though Grebe were preparing to accuse him of trying to make the job more important than it was. Grebe smiled, because by then they were on fine terms, but nevertheless he had been getting ready to say something like that when the confusion began in the station over Staika and her children.

Grebe had waited a long time for this job. It came to him through the pull of an old schoolmate in the Corporation Counsel's office, never a close friend, but suddenly sympathetic and interested—pleased to show, moreover, how well he had done, how strongly he was coming on even in these miserable times. Well, he was coming through strongly, along with the Democratic administration itself. Grebe had gone to see him in City Hall, and they had had a counter lunch or beers at least once a month for a year, and finally it had been possible to swing the job. He didn't mind being assigned the lowest clerical grade, nor even being a messenger, though Raynor thought he did.

50   This Raynor was an original sort of guy and Grebe had taken to him immediately. As was proper on the first day, Grebe had come early, but he waited long, for Raynor was late. At last he darted into his cubicle of an office as though he had just jumped from one of those hurtling huge red Indian Avenue cars. His thin, rough face was wind-stung and he was grinning and saying something breathlessly to himself. In his hat, a small fedora, and his coat, the velvet collar a neat fit about his neck, and his silk muffler that set off the nervous twist of his chin, he swayed and turned himself in his swivel chair, feet leaving the ground, so that he pranced a little as he sat. Meanwhile he took Grebe's measure out of his eyes, eyes of an unusual vertical length and slightly sardonic. So the two men sat for a while, saying nothing, while the supervisor raised his hat from his miscombed hair and put it in his lap. His cold-darkened hands were not clean. A steel beam passed through the little makeshift room, from which machine belts once had hung. The building was an old factory.

"I'm younger than you; I hope you won't find it hard taking orders from me," said Raynor. "But I don't make them up, either. You're how old, about?"

"Thirty-five."

"And you thought you'd be inside doing paperwork. But it so happens I have to send you out."

"I don't mind."

55 "And it's mostly a Negro load we have in this district."

"So I thought it would be."

"Fine. You'll get along. *C'est un bon boulot.* Do you know French?"

"Some."

"I thought you'd be a university man."

60 "Have you been in France?" said Grebe.

"No, that's the French of the Berlitz School. I've been at it for more than a year, just as I'm sure people have been, all over the world, office boys in China and braves in Tanganyika. In fact, I damn well know it. Such is the attractive power of civilization. It's overrated, but what do you want? *Que voulez-vous?* I get *Le Rire* and all the spicy papers, just like in Tanganyika. It must be mystifying, out there. But my reason is that I'm aiming at the diplomatic service. I have a cousin who's a courier, and the way he describes it is awfully attractive. He rides in the *wagon-lits* and reads books. While we—What did you do before?"

"I sold."

"Where?"

"Canned meat at Stop and Shop. In the basement."

65 "And before that?"

"Window shades, at Goldblatt's."

"Steady work?"

"No, Thursdays and Saturdays. I also sold shoes."

"You've been a shoe-dog too. Well. And prior to that? Here it is in your folder." He opened the record. "Saint Olaf's College, instructor in classical languages. Fellow, University of Chicago, 1926–27. I've had Latin, too. Let's trade quotations—'*Dum spiro spero.*'"

70 "'*De dextram misero.*'"

"'*Alea jacta est.*'"

"'*Excelsior.*'"

Raynor shouted with laughter, and other workers came to look at him over the partition. Grebe also laughed, feeling pleased and easy. The luxury of fun on a nervous morning.

When they were done and no one was watching or listening, Raynor said rather seriously, "What made you study Latin in the first place? Was it for the priesthood?"

75 "No."

"Just for the hell of it? For the culture? Oh, the things people think they can pull!" He made his cry hilarious and tragic. "I ran my pants off so I could study for the bar, and I've passed the bar, so I get twelve dollars a week more than you as a bonus for having seen life straight and whole. I'll tell you, as a man of culture, that even though nothing looks to be real, and everything stands for something else, and that thing for another thing, and that thing for a still further one—there ain't any comparison between twenty-five and thirty-seven dollars a week, regardless of the last reality. Don't you think that was clear to your Greeks? They were a thoughtful people, but they didn't part with their slaves."

This was a great deal more than Grebe had looked for in his first interview with his supervisor. He was too shy to show all the astonishment he felt. He laughed a little, aroused, and brushed at the sunbeam that covered his head with its dust. "Do you think my mistake was so terrible?"

"Damn right it was terrible, and you know it now that you've had the whip of hard times laid on your back. You should have been preparing yourself for trouble. Your people must have been well-off to send you to the university. Stop me, if I'm stepping on your toes. Did your mother pamper you? Did your father give in to you? Were you brought up tenderly, with permission to go and find out what were the last things that everything else stands for while everybody else labored in the fallen world of appearances?"

"Well, no, it wasn't exactly like that." Grebe smiled. *The fallen world of appearances!* no less. But now it was his turn to deliver a surprise. "We weren't rich. My father was the last genuine English butler in Chicago—"

80 "Are you kidding?"

"Why should I be?"

"In a livery?"

"In livery. Up on the Gold Coast."

"And he wanted you to be educated like a gentleman?"

85 "He did not. He sent me to the Armour Institute to study chemical engineering. But when he died I changed schools."

He stopped himself, and considered how quickly Raynor had reached him. In no time he had your valise on the table and all your stuff unpacked. And afterward, in the streets, he was still reviewing how far he might have gone, and how much he might have been led to tell if they had not been interrupted by Mrs. Staika's great noise.

But just then a young woman, one of Raynor's workers, ran into the cubicle exclaiming, "Haven't you heard all the fuss?"

"We haven't heard anything."

"It's Staika, giving out with all her might. The reporters are coming. She said she phoned the papers, and you know she did."

90   "But what is she up to?" said Raynor.

"She brought her wash and she's ironing it here, with our current, because the relief won't pay her electric bill. She has her ironing board set up by the admitting desk, and her kids are with her, all six. They never are in school more than once a week. She's always dragging them around with her because of her reputation."

"I don't want to miss any of this," said Raynor, jumping up. Grebe, as he followed with the secretary, said, "Who is this Staika?"

"They call her the 'Blood Mother of Federal Street.' She's a professional donor at the hospitals. I think they pay ten dollars a pint. Of course it's no joke, but she makes a very big thing out of it and she and the kids are in the papers all the time."

A small crowd, staff and clients divided by a plywood barrier, stood in the narrow space of the entrance, and Staika was shouting in a gruff, mannish voice, plunging the iron on the board and slamming it on the metal rest.

95   "My father and mother came in a steerage, and I was born in our house, Robey by Huron. I'm no dirty immigrant. I'm a U.S. citizen. My husband is a gassed veteran from France with lungs weaker'n paper, that hardly can he go to the toilet by himself. These six children of mine, I have to buy the shoes for their feet with my own blood. Even a lousy little white Communion necktie, that's a couple of drops of blood; a little piece of mosquito veil for my Vadja so she won't be ashamed in church for the other girls, they take my blood for it by Goldblatt. That's how I keep goin'. A fine thing if I had to depend on the relief. And there's plenty of people on the rolls—fakes! There's nothin' *they* can't get, that can go and wrap bacon at Swift and Armour anytime. They're lookin' for them by the Yards. They never have to be out of work. Only they rather lay in their lousy beds and eat the public's money." She was not afraid, in a predominantly Negro station, to shout this way about Negroes.

Grebe and Raynor worked themselves forward to get a closer view of the woman. She was flaming with anger and with pleasure at herself, broad and huge, a golden-headed woman who wore a cotton cap laced with pink ribbon. She was barelegged and had on black gym shoes, her Hoover apron was open and her great breasts, not much restrained by a man's undershirt, hampered her arms as she worked at the kid's dress on the ironing board. And the children, silent and white, with a kind of locked obstinacy, in sheepskins and lumber-jackets, stood behind her. She had captured the station, and the pleasure this gave her was enormous. Yet her grievances were true grievances. She was telling the truth. But she behaved like a liar. The look of her small eyes was hidden, and while she raged she also seemed to be spinning and planning.

"They send me out college caseworkers in silk pants to talk me out of what I got comin'. Are they better'n me? Who told them? Fire them. Let 'em go and get married, and they you won't have to cut electric from people's budget."

The chief supervisor, Mr. Ewing, couldn't silence her and he stood with folded arms at the head of his staff, bald—bald-headed, saying to his subordinates like the ex-school principal he was, "Pretty soon she'll be tired and go."

95 "No she won't," said Raynor to Grebe. "She'll get what she wants. She knows more about the relief even than Ewing. She's been on the rolls for years, and she always gets what she wants because she puts on a noisy show. Ewing knows it. He'll give in soon. He's only saving face. If he gets bad publicity, the commissioner'll have him on the carpet, downtown. She's got him submerged; she'll submerge everybody in time, and that includes nations and governments."

100 Grebe replied with his characteristic smile, disagreeing completely. Who would take Staika's orders, and what changes could her yelling ever bring about?

No, what Grebe saw in her, the power that made people listen, was that her cry expressed the war of flesh and blood, perhaps turned a little crazy and certainly ugly, on this place and this condition. And at first, when he went out, the spirit of Staika somehow presided over the whole district for him, and it took color from her; he saw her color, in the spotty curb fires, and the fires under the El, the straight alley of flamey gloom. Later, too, when he went into a tavern for a shot of rye, the sweat of beer, association with West Side Polish streets, made him think of her again.

He wiped the corners of his mouth with his muffler, his handkerchief being inconvenient to reach for, and went out again to get on with the delivery of his checks. The air bit cold and hard and a few flakes of snow formed near him. A train struck by and left a quiver in the frames and a bristling icy hiss over the rails.

Crossing the street, he descended a flight of board steps into a basement grocery, setting off a little bell. It was a dark, long store and it caught you with its stinks of smoked meat, soap, dried peaches, and fish. There was a fire wrinkling and flapping in the little stove, and the proprietor was waiting, an Italian with a long, hollow face and stubborn bristles. He kept his hands warm under his apron.

No, he didn't know Green. You knew people but not names. The same man might not have the same name twice. The police didn't know, either, and mostly didn't care. When somebody was shot or knifed they took the body away and didn't look for the murderer. In the first place, nobody would tell them anything. So they made up a name for the coroner and called it quits. And in the second place, they didn't give a goddamn anyhow. But they couldn't get to the bottom of a thing even if they wanted to. Nobody would get to know even a tenth of what went on among these people. They stabbed and stole, they did every crime and abomination you ever heard of, men and men, women and women, parents and children, worse than the animals. They carried on their own way, and the horrors passed off like a smoke. There was never anything like it in the history of the whole world.

105   It was a long speech, deepening with every word in its fantasy and passion and becoming increasingly senseless and terrible: a swarm amassed by suggestion and invention, a huge, hugging, despairing knot, a human wheel of heads, legs, bellies, arms, rolling through his shop.

Grebe felt that he must interrupt him. He said sharply, "What are you talking about! All I asked was whether you knew this man."

"That isn't even the half of it. I been here six years. You probably don't want to believe this. But suppose it's true?"

"All the same," said Grebe, "there must be a way to find a person."

The Italian's close-spaced eyes had been queerly concentrated, as were his muscles, while he leaned across the counter trying to convince Grebe. Now he gave up the effort and sat down on his stool. "Oh—I suppose. Once in a while. But I been telling you, even the cops don't get anywhere."

110   "They're always after somebody. It's not the same thing."

"Well, keep trying if you want. I can't help you."

But he didn't keep trying. He had no more time to spend on Green. He slipped Green's check to the back of the block. The next name on the list was FIELD, WINSTON.

He found the backyard bungalow without the least trouble; it shared a lot with another house, a few feet of yard between. Grebe knew these two-shack arrangements. They had been built in vast numbers in the days before the swamps were filled and the streets raised, and they were all the same—a boardwalk along the fence, well under street level, three or four ball-headed posts for clotheslines, greening wood, dead shingles, and a long, long flight of stairs to the rear door.

A twelve-year-old boy let him into the kitchen, and there the old man was, sitting by the table in a wheelchair.

115   "Oh, it's d'Government man," he said to the boy when Grebe drew out his checks. "Go bring me my box of papers." He cleared a space on the table.

"Oh, you don't have to go to all that trouble," said Grebe. But Field laid out his papers: Social Security card, relief certification, letters from the state hospital in Manteno, and a naval discharge dated San Diego, 1920.

"That's plenty," Grebe said. "Just sign."

"You got to know who I am," the old man said. "You're from the Government. It's not your check, it's a Government check and you got no business to hand it over till everything is proved."

He loved the ceremony of it, and Grebe made no more objections. Field emptied his box and finished out the circle of cards and letters.

120   "There's everything I done and been. Just the death certificate and they can close book on me." He said this with a certain happy pride and magnificence. Still he did not sign; he merely held the little pen upright on the golden-green corduroy of his thigh. Grebe did not hurry him. He felt the old man's hunger for conversation.

"I got to get better coal," he said. "I send my little gran'son to the yard with my order and they fill his wagon with screening. The stove ain't made for it. It fall through the grate. The order says Franklin County egg-size coal."

"I'll report it and see what can be done."

"Nothing can be done, I expect. You know and I know. There ain't no little ways to make things better, and the only big thing is money. That's the only sunbeams, money. Nothing is black where it shines, and the only place you see black is where it ain't shining. What we colored have to have is our own rich. There ain't no other way."

Grebe sat, his reddened forehead bridged levelly by his close-cut hair and his cheeks lowered in the wings of his collar—the caked fire shone hard within the isinglass-and-iron frames but the room was not comfortable—sat and listened while the old man unfolded his scheme. This was to create one Negro millionaire a month by subscription. One clever, good-hearted young fellow elected every month would sign a contract to use the money to start a business employing Negroes. This would be advertised by chain letters and word of mouth, and every Negro wage earner would contribute a dollar a month. Within five years there would be sixty millionaires.

125   "That'll fetch respect," he said with a throat-stopped sound that came out like a foreign syllable. "You got to take and organize all the money that gets thrown away on the policy wheel and horse race. As long as they can take it away from you, they got no respect for you. Money, that's d' sun of humankind!" Field was a Negro of mixed blood, perhaps Cherokee, or Natchez; his skin was reddish. And he sounded, speaking about a golden sun in this dark room, and looked—shaggy and slab-headed—with the mingled blood of his face and broad lips, and with the little pen still upright in his hand, like one of the underground kings of mythology, old judge Minos himself.

And now he accepted the check and signed. Not to soil the slip, he held it down with his knuckles. The table budged and creaked, the center of the gloomy, heathen midden of the kitchen covered with bread, meat, and cans, and the scramble of papers.

"Don't you think my scheme'd work?"

"It's worth thinking about. Something ought to be done, I agree."

"It'll work if people will do it. That's all. That's the only thing, anytime. When they understand it in the same way, all of them."

130   "That's true," said Grebe, rising. His glance met the old man's.

"I know you got to go," he said. "Well, God bless you, boy, you ain't been sly with me. I can tell it in a minute."

He went back through the buried yard. Someone nursed a candle in a shed, where a man unloaded kindling wood from a sprawl-wheeled baby buggy and two voices carried on a high conversation. As he came up the sheltered passage he heard the hard boost of the wind in the branches and against the house fronts, and then, reaching the sidewalk, he saw the needle-eye red of cable towers in the open icy height hundreds of feet above the river and the factories—those keen points. From here, his view was obstructed all the way to the South Branch and its timber banks, and the cranes beside the water. Rebuilt after the Great Fire, this part of the city was, not fifty years later, in ruins again, factories boarded up, buildings deserted or fallen, gaps of prairie between. But it wasn't desolation that this made you feel, but rather a faltering of organization that set free a huge energy, an escaped, unattached, unregulated power from the giant raw place. Not only must people feel it but, it seemed to Grebe, they were compelled to match it. In their very bodies. He no less than others, he realized. Say that his parents had been servants in their time, whereas he was supposed not to be one. He thought that they had never done any service like this, which no one visible asked for, and probably flesh and blood could not even perform. Nor could anyone show why it should be performed; or see where the performance would lead. That did not mean that he wanted to be released from it, he realized with a grimly pensive face. On the contrary. He had something to do. To be compelled to feel this energy and yet have no task to do—that was horrible; that was suffering; he knew what that was. It was now quitting time. Six o'clock. He could go home if he liked, to his room, that is, to wash in hot water, to pour a drink, lie down on his quilt, read the paper, eat some liver paste on crackers before going out to dinner. But to think of this actually made him feel a little sick, as though he had swallowed hard air. He had six checks left, and he was determined to deliver at least one of these: Mr. Green's check.

So he started again. He had four or five dark blocks to go, past open lots, condemned houses, old foundations, closed schools, black churches, mounds, and
he reflected that there must be many people alive who had once seen the neighborhood rebuilt and new. Now there was a second layer of ruins; centuries of history accomplished through human massing. Numbers had given the place forced
growth; enormous numbers had also broken it down. Objects once so new, so
concrete that it could never have occurred to anyone they stood for other things,
had crumbled. Therefore, reflected Grebe, the secret of them was out. It was
that they stood for themselves by agreement, and were natural and not unnatural by agreement, and when the things themselves collapsed the agreement
became visible. What was it, otherwise, that kept cities from looking peculiar?
Rome, that was almost permanent, did not give rise to thoughts like these. And
was it abidingly real? But in Chicago, where the cycles were so fast and the familiar died out, and again rose changed, and died again in thirty years, you saw the
common agreement or covenant, and you were forced to think about appearances
and realities. (He remembered Raynor and he smiled. Raynor was a clever boy.)
Once you had grasped this, a great many things became intelligible. For instance,
why Mr. Field should conceive such a scheme. Of course, if people were to agree
to create a millionaire, a real millionaire would come into existence. And if you
wanted to know how Mr. Field was inspired to think of this, why, he had within
sight of his kitchen window the chart, the very bones of a successful scheme—
the El with its blue and green confetti of signals. People consented to pay dimes
and ride the crash-box cars, and so it was a success. Yet how absurd it looked; how
little reality there was to start with. And yet Yerkes, the great financier who built
it, had known that he could get people to agree to do it. Viewed as itself, what
a scheme of a scheme it seemed, how close to an appearance. Then why wonder
at Mr. Field's idea? He had grasped a principle. And then Grebe remembered, too,
that Mr. Yerkes had established the Yerkes Observatory and endowed it with
millions. Now how did the notion come to him in his New York museum of a
palace or his Aegean-bound yacht to give money to astronomers? Was he awed
by the success of his bizarre enterprise and therefore ready to spend money to find
out where in the universe being and seeming were identical? Yes, he wanted to
know what abides; and whether flesh is Bible grass; and he offered money to be
burned in the fire of suns. Okay, then, Grebe thought further, these things exist
because people consent to exist with them—we have got so far—and also there
is a reality which doesn't depend on consent but within which consent is a game.
But what about need, the need that keeps so many vast thousands in position?

UNIT 9

You tell me that, you *private* little gentleman and *decent* soul—he used these words against himself scornfully. Why is the consent given to misery? And why so painfully ugly? Because there is *something* that is dismal and permanently ugly? Here he sighed and gave it up, and thought it was enough for the present moment that he had a real check in his pocket for a Mr. Green who must be real beyond question. If only his neighbors didn't think they had to conceal him.

This time he stopped at the second floor. He struck a match and found a door. Presently a man answered his knock and Grebe had the check ready and showed it even before he began. "Does Tulliver Green live here? I'm from the relief."

140   The man narrowed the opening and spoke to someone at his back.

"Does he live here?"

"Uh-uh. No."

"Or anywhere in this building? He's a sick man and he can't come for his dough." He exhibited the check in the light, which was smoky—the air smelled of charred lard—and the man held off the brim of his cap to study it.

"Uh-uh. Never seen the name."

145   "There's nobody around here that uses crutches?"

He seemed to think, but it was Grebe's impression that he was simply waiting for a decent interval to pass.

"No, suh. Nobody I ever see."

"I've been looking for this man all afternoon"—Grebe spoke out with sudden force—"and I'm going to have to carry this check back to the station. It seems strange not to be able to find a person to *give* him something when you're looking for him for a good reason. I suppose if I had bad news for him I'd find him quick enough."

There was a responsive motion in the other man's face. "That's right, I reckon."

150   "It almost doesn't do any good to have a name if you can't be found by it. It doesn't stand for anything. He might as well not have any," he went on, smiling. It was as much of a concession as he could make to his desire to laugh.

"Well, now, there's a little old knot-back man I see once in a while. He might be the one you lookin' for. Downstairs."

"Where? Right side or left? Which door?"

"I don't know which. Thin-face little knot-back with a stick."

But no one answered at any of the doors on the first floor. He went to the end of the corridor, searching by matchlight, and found only a stairless exit to the yard, a drop of about six feet. But there was a bungalow near the alley, an old house like Mr. Field's. To jump was unsafe. He ran from the front door, through the underground passage into the yard. The place was occupied. There was a light through the curtains, upstairs. The name on the ticket under the broken, scoop-shaped mailbox was Green! He exultantly rang the bell and pressed against the locked door. Then the lock clicked faintly and a long staircase opened before him. Someone was slowly coming down—a woman. He had the impression in the weak light that she was shaping her hair as she came, making herself presentable, for he saw her arms raised. But it was for support that they were raised; she was feeling her way downward, down the wall, stumbling. Next he wondered about the pressure of her feet on the treads; she did not seem to be wearing shoes. And it was a freezing stairway. His ring had got her out of bed, perhaps, and she had forgotten to put them on. And then he saw that she was not only shoeless but naked; she was entirely naked, climbing down while she talked to herself, a heavy woman, naked and drunk. She blundered into him. The contact of her breasts, though they touched only his coat, made him go back against the door with a blind shock. See what he had tracked down, in his hunting game!

155 The woman was saying to herself, furious with insult, "So I cain't fuck, huh? I'll show that son of a bitch kin I, cain't I."

What should he do now? Grebe asked himself. Why, he should go. He should turn away and go. He couldn't talk to this woman. He couldn't keep her standing naked in the cold. But when he tried he found himself unable to turn away.

He said, "Is this where Mr. Green lives?"

But she was still talking to herself and did not hear him.

"Is this Mr. Green's house?"

160 At last she turned her furious drunken glance on him. "What do you want?" Again her eyes wandered from him; there was a dot of blood in their enraged brilliance. He wondered why she didn't feel the cold.

"I'm from the relief."

"Awright, what?"

"I've got check for Tulliver Green."

This time she heard him and put out her hand.

165 "No, no, for *Mr.* Green. He's got to sign," he said. How was he going to get Green's signature tonight!

"I'll take it. He cain't."

He desperately shook his head, thinking of Mr. Field's precautions about identification. "I can't let you have it. It's for him. Are you Mrs. Green?"

"Maybe I is, and maybe I ain't. Who want to know?"

"Is he upstairs?"

170 "Awright. Take it up yourself, you goddamn fool."

Sure, he was a goddamn fool. Of course he could not go up because Green would probably be drunk and naked, too. And perhaps he would appear on the landing soon. He looked eagerly upward. Under the light was a high narrow brown wall. Empty! It remained empty!

"Hell with you, then!" he heard her cry. To deliver a check for coal and clothes, he was keeping her in the cold. She did not feel it, but his face was burning with frost and self-ridicule. He backed away from her.

"I'll come tomorrow, tell him."

"Ah, hell with you. Don't never come. What you doin' here in the nighttime? Don' come back." She yelled so that he saw the breadth of her tongue. She stood astride in the long cold box of the hall and held on to the banister and the wall. The bungalow itself was shaped something like a box, a clumsy, high box pointing into the freezing air with its sharp, wintry lights.

175   "If you are Mrs. Green, I'll give you the check," he said, changing his mind.

"Give here, then." She took it, took the pen offered with it in her left hand and tried to sign the receipt on the wall. He looked around, almost as though to see whether his madness was being observed, and came near to believing that someone was standing on a mountain of used tires in the auto-junking shop next door.

"But are you Mrs. Green?" he now thought to ask. But she was already climbing the stairs with the check, and it was too late, if he had made an error, if he was now in trouble, to undo the thing. But he wasn't going to worry about it. Though she might not be Mrs. Green, he was convinced that Mr. Green was upstairs. Whoever she was, the woman stood for Green, whom he was not to see this time. Well, you silly bastard, he said to himself, so you think you found him. So what? Maybe you really did find him—what of it? But it was important that there was a real Mr. Green whom they could not keep him from reaching because he seemed to come as an emissary from hostile appearances. And though the self-ridicule was slow to diminish, and his face still blazed with it, he had, nevertheless, a feeling of elation, too. "For after all," he said, "he *could* be found!"

LEVELS OF READING

Summary:

Pay attention to the **literal** meaning of the text. Briefly describe the narrative of Saul Bellow's "Looking for Mr. Green." Who tells the story? Where is the story set? Why is the setting especially important? Concentrate on the highlights;

avoid too much detail when summarizing. Again, drawing a simple outline of the main points of the text will help you better analyze the text at other levels of interpretation.

Analysis:

Find what you believe is **symbolic** in this text. What is symbolic about the name "Mr. Green"? Why are the apartments in the buildings Grebe visits unmarked? What is significant about Grebe's inability to find Mr. Green? Why is it important that he is delivering "relief checks"? Why does Grebe need help "interpreting looks and signs" to do his job well? With the help of the background material provided about Saul Bellow and his world, make an argument about this story, and include the mention of the more **figurative** aspects of the text when making points in defense of your argument.

Application:

Apply Georg Simmel's theory concerning the metropolis and mental life to this story. Outline an argument you wish to make about this literary text using Simmel's theory to help you explain what some part of the story may mean. The "part" of the text you choose to analyze may include any of the following: a character, a setting, a symbol or symbols, an important change, a motivation, a goal, a result. Consider the following as possibilities, but explore other original interpretations too:

- Since Simmel connects "**intellectualism**" and money, is it significant that Grebe has a college degree? In what ways does he tend to "intellectualize" his job of distributing money to those in need?
- Who has the "**blasé attitude**" in this story? Does it have any connection to money or the lack of money?
- Explain how Simmel's idea of "**reserve**" works in this story. Who maintains a reserve, and how is this reserve used to keep others at a distance?
- Have the "**liberating forces**" Simmel claims work in urban life given any special freedom to anyone in this story?
- Are there any signs of the **cosmopolitanism** Simmel suggests in Bellow's Chicago?
- How do Simmel's ideas about **objectification** and **depersonalization** work in Bellow's narrative?

UNIT 9

MICHAEL GOLD

Michael Gold (1894–1967), was born Yitzhak Granich in New York City to Jewish immigrants. The oldest of three sons, Gold went to work at twelve, when his father's health and business failed and he was no longer able to support the family. Until adulthood, he lived on the Lower East Side of Manhattan. At about the same time he moved to New York's Greenwich Village, he adopted the name Michael Gold, taken in memory of a Jewish soldier who had "fought to free the slaves" in the American Civil War.

In 1914, when Gold was 21, he was knocked down by police at a demonstration in Union Square. This experience led to the epiphany described at the end of Jews Without Money. *Gold then left manual labor and became a full-time writer, contributing to socialist publications such as* The Masses *and* The New Masses. *In 1917, after the United States entered the First World War, Gold went to live in Mexico, mainly to avoid the draft. He returned to the United States in 1920 and became associate editor of* The Liberator.

A lifelong member of the Communist Party, Gold published three novels as well as a daily column for The Daily Worker, *where he became a staff writer in 1933.* Jews Without Money *was published in 1930.*

It is easy to read Gold's Jews Without Money *as though it were a novel: The vivacity of the setting and the hardships encountered seem almost too intensely colorful to be true. Nevertheless, his story is autobiographical, and the two chapters here, each telling of an important episode in young Yitzhak's early life in lower Manhattan still contain a ring of truth for many more-recent immigrants to this country.*

FIFTY CENTS A NIGHT
Michael Gold

1

I can never forget the East Side street where I lived as a boy.

It was a block from the notorious Bowery, a tenement canyon hung with fire-escapes, bed-clothing, and faces.

Always these faces at the tenement windows. The street never failed them. It was an immense excitement. It never slept. It roared like a sea. It exploded like fireworks.

People pushed and wrangled in the street. There were armies of howling pushcart peddlers. Women screamed, dogs barked and copulated. Babies cried.

5   A parrot cursed. Ragged kids played under truck-horses. Fat housewives fought from stoop to stoop. A beggar sang.

At the livery stable coach drivers lounged on a bench. They hee-hawed with laughter, they guzzled cans of beer.

Pimps, gamblers and red-nosed bums; peanut politicians, pugilists in sweaters; tinhorn sports and tall longshoremen in overalls. An endless pageant of East Side life passed through the wicker doors of Jake Wolf's saloon.

The saloon goat lay on the sidewalk, and dreamily consumed a *Police Gazette.*

East Side mothers with heroic bosoms pushed their baby carriages, gossiping. Horse cars jingled by. A tinker hammered at brass. Junkbells clanged.

10   Whirlwinds of dust and newspaper. The prostitutes laughed shrilly. A prophet passed, an old-clothes Jew with a white beard. Kids were dancing around the hurdy-gurdy. Two bums slugged each other.

Excitement, dirt, fighting, chaos! The sound of my street lifted like the blast of a great carnival or catastrophe. The noise was always in my ears. Even in sleep I could hear it; I can hear it now.

2

The East Side of New York was then the city's red light district, a vast 606 playground under the business management of Tammany Hall.

Reprinted from *Jews without Money*, (1996), Carroll & Graf Publishers, Inc.

UNIT 9

The Jews had fled from the European pogroms; with prayer, thanksgiving and solemn faith from a new Egypt into a new Promised Land.

They found awaiting them the sweatshops, the bawdy houses and Tammany Hall.

15   There were hundreds of prostitutes on my street. They occupied vacant stores, they crowded into flats and apartments in all the tenements. The pious Jews hated the traffic. But they were pauper strangers here; they could do nothing. They shrugged their shoulders, and murmured: "This is America." They tried to live.

They tried to shut their eyes. We children did not shut our eyes. We saw and knew.

On sunshiny days the whores sat on chairs along the sidewalks. They sprawled indolently, their legs taking up half the pavements. People stumbled over a gauntlet of whores' meaty legs.

The girls gossiped and chirped like a jungle of parrots. Some knitted shawls and stockings. Others hummed. Others chewed Russian sunflower seeds and monotonously spat out the shells.

The girls winked and jeered, made lascivious gestures at passing males. They pulled at coat-tails and cajoled men with fake honeyed words. They called their wares like pushcart peddlers. At five years I knew what it was they sold.

20   The girls were naked under flowery kimonos. Chunks of breast and belly occasionally flashed. Slippers hung from their feet; they were always ready for "business."

Earth's trees, grass, flowers could not grow on my street; but the rose of syphilis bloomed by night and by day.

3

It was a spring morning. I had joined, as on other mornings, my gang of little Yids gathered on the sidewalk. There were six or seven of us.

Spring excited us. The sky was blue over our ghetto. The sidewalks sparkled, the air was fresh. Everything seemed hopeful. In winter the streets were vacant, now people sprang up by magic.

Parades of Jews had appeared in these first soft days, to walk, to talk. To curse, to bargain, to smoke pipes, to sniff like hibernating bears at the spring.

25   Pushcarts appeared. Pale bearded peddlers crawled from their winter cellars, again shouted in the street. Oranges blazed on the carts; calico was for sale,

clocks, sweet potatoes, herrings, potted geraniums and goloshes. Spring ushered in a huge, ragged fair.

We spun tops on the sidewalks. We chased street cars and trucks and stole dangerous rides. Nigger, our leader, taught us how to steal apples from a pushcart. We threw a dead cat into the store of the Chinese laundryman. He came out, a yellow madman, a hot flat-iron in his hand. We ran away.

Nigger then suggested a new game: that we tease the prostitutes.

We began with Rosie. She lounged in a tenement hallway, a homely little woman in a red shawl. Ready, go. We spurted before her in short dashes, our hearts beating with danger and joy.

We screamed at her, making obscene gestures:

30   "Fifty cents a night! That's what your charge; fifty cents a night! Yah, yah, yah!"

Rosie started. A look came into her sleepy eyes. But she made no answer. She drew her shawl about her. We were disappointed. We had hoped she would rave and curse.

"Fifty cents a night! Fifty cents a night!"

Rosie bit her lip. Spots appeared on her sallow face. That was all; she wouldn't talk. The game didn't work. We tried again. This time she turned on her heel and walked into the gloomy hallway. We looked for another victim.

4

A fat, haughty prostitute sat on a chair two tenements away. She wore a red kimono decorated with Japanese cherry trees, mountains, waterfalls and old philosophers. Her black hair was fastened by a diamond brooch. At least a million dollars' worth of paste diamonds glittered from her fat fingers.

35   She was eating an apple. She munched it slowly with the dignity of a whole Chamber of Commerce at its annual banquet. Her lap spread before her like a table.

We scampered around her in a monkey gang. We yelled those words whose terrible meaning we could not fully guess:

"Fifty cents a night!"

Aha. This time the plans of our leader worked. The game was a good one. The fat prostitute purpled with rage. Her eyes bulged with loathing. Sweat appeared on her painted cheeks. She flung her apple at us, and screamed: "Thieves! American bummers! Loafers! Let me catch you! I'll rip you in half!"

She spat like a poisoned cat. She shook her fist. It was fun. The whole street was amused.

UNIT 9

40   "Fifty cents a night! Yah, yah, yah!"

Then I heard my mother's voice calling me from the tenement window. I hated to leave the fun, just when it was good. But my mother called me again and again. So up I went.

I entered blinking from the sunlight. I was surprised to find Rosie sitting in our kitchen. She was crying. My mother pounced upon me and slapped my face.

"Murderer!" she said, "why did you make Rosie cry?"

"Did I make her cry?" I asked stupidly.

45   My mother grabbed me, and laid me across her knee. She beat me with the cat-o'-nine-tails. I howled and wriggled, but she gave me a good licking. Rosie stood there pleading for me. The poor girl was sorry she had gotten me this licking. My mother was in a rage.

"This will teach you not to play with that Nigger! This will teach you not to learn all those bad, nasty things in the street!"

Vain beating; the East Side street could not be banished with a leather strap. It was my world; it was my mother's world, too. We *had* to live in it, and learn what it chose to teach us.

5

I will always remember that licking, not because it humiliated me, or taught me anything, but because the next day was my fifth birthday.

My father was young then. He loved good times. He took the day off from work and insisted that I be given a birthday party. He bought me a velvet suit with lace collar and cuffs, and patent leather shoes. In the morning he insisted that we all go to be photographed. He made my mother wear her black plush gown. He made her dress my sister in the Scotch plaid. Himself he arrayed in his black suit that made him look like a lawyer.

50   My mother groaned as we walked through the street. She hated new shoes, new clothes, all fuss or feathers. I was miserable, too. My gang saw me, and snickered at my velvet suit.

But my father was happy, and so was my sister, Esther. They chattered like two children.

It was solemn at the photographer's. My father sat stiffly in a dark carved throne. My mother stood upright beside him, with one hand on his shoulder, to show her wedding ring. My sister rested against my father's knee. I stood on the other side of the throne, holding a basket of artificial flowers.

The bald, eager little photographer disappeared behind a curtain. He snapped his fingers before us, and said, "Watch the birdie." I watched, my neck hurting me because of the clamp. Something clicked; the picture was taken. We went home, exhausted but triumphant.

In the evening the birthday party was held. Many tenement neighbors came with their children. Brandy was drunk, sponge cake and herring eaten, songs were sung. Every one pinched my cheek and praised me. They prophesied I would be a "great man."

55   Then there was talk. Reb Samuel the umbrella maker was a pious and learned Jew. Whenever he was in a group the talk turned to holy things.

"I have read in the paper," said my father, "that a Dybbuk has entered a girl on Hester Street. But I don't believe it. Are there Dybbuks in America, too?"

"Of course," said Reb Samuel quietly.

Mendel Bum laughed a raucous brandy laugh. He had eaten of everything; the sponge cake, the herring, the quince jam, the apples, *kraut knishes,* fried fish and cheese *blintzes.* He had drunk from every bottle, the fiery Polish *slivovitz,* the *wishniak,* the plum brandy, the Roumanian wine. Now his true nature appeared.

"I don't believe in Dybbuks!" he laughed. "It is all a grandmother story!"

60   My father banged on the table and leaped to his feet. "Silence, atheist!" he shouted, "in my house we want no wisdom from you!"

Mendel shrugged his shoulders.

"Well," said Reb Samuel quietly, "in the synagogue at Korbin, a girl was once brought. Her lips did not move. From her belly came shrieks and groans of a Dybbuk. He had entered her body while she was in the forest. She was dying with agony.

"The Rabbi studied the matter. Then he instructed two men to take her in a wagon back into that forest. They were told to nail her hair to a tree, drive away with her, and cut off her hair with a scissors.

"This they did. They whipped the horses, and drove and drove. The girl screamed, she raved of fire and water. But when they reached home she was cured. The Dybbuk had left her. All this, my friends, I saw myself."

65   "Once," said my mother shyly, "I myself saw a Dybbuk that had entered a dog. It was in Hungary. The dog lay under the table and talked in a human voice. Then he gave a long howl and died. So it must be true about the Dybbuks."

6

Some one broke into song. Others marked time with feet and chairs, or beat glasses on the table. When the chorus came, there was a glorious volume of sound. Every one sang, from the venerable Reb Samuel to the smallest child.

My father, that marvelous story-teller, told about a Roumanian ne'er-do-well, who married a grave-digger's daughter that he might succeed to her father's job, and bury all the people who had despised him.

Mottke the vest-maker attacked Jews who changed their names in this country.

"If his name is Garlic in the old country, here he thinks it refined to call himself Mr. Onions," said Mottke.

70 The mothers talked about their babies. A shy little banana peddler described a Russian pogrom.

"It started at both bazaars, just before the Passover," he said. "Some one gave vodka to the peasants, and told them we Jews had killed some Christian children to use the blood. Ach, friends, what one saw then; the yelling, the murder, the flames! I myself saw a peasant cut off my uncle's head with an ax."

At the other end of the table Fyfka the Miser was gobbling all the roast chicken he could grab, and drinking glass after glass of beer. It was a free meal, so he was stuffing himself.

Some one told of a pregnant mother in Russia who had been frightened by a Cossack, and had borne a child with a pig's head.

Leichner the housepainter drank some wine. He told of a Jew in his native village who had been troubled by devils. They were colored red and green and blue. They rattled at the windows every night until the man could get no sleep. He went to a Rabbi and bought six magic words which he repeated until the devils retreated.

75 The hum of talk, tinkle of glasses, all the hot, happy excitement of the crowded room made me sleepy. I climbed on my mother's lap and began to fall asleep.

"What, too tired even for your own party?" said my mother affectionately.

I heard Reb Samuel talking again in his slow kind voice.

Bang, bang! Two pistol shots rang out in the backyard! I jumped to my feet, with the others. We rushed to the windows. We saw two men with pistols standing in the moonlit yard. Bang, bang! They fired again at each other. One man fell.

The other ran through the hall. A girl screamed in the bawdy house. The clothesline pole creaked. In the moonlight a cat crawled on its belly. It sniffed at the sudden corpse.

80 "Two gamblers fighting, maybe," said my father.

"Ach, America," Reb Samuel sighed.

All of us left the windows and went back to the singing, and story-telling. It was commonplace, this shooting. The American police would take care of it. It was discussed for some minutes, then forgotten by the birthday party.

But I have never forgotten it, for it burned into my mind the memory of my fifth birthday.

BANANAS
Michael Gold

1

1   Esther was dead. My mother had borne everything in life, but this she could not bear. It frightened one to see how quiet she became. She was no longer active, cheerful, quarrelsome. She sat by the window all day, and read her prayer book. As she mumbled the endless Hebrew prayers, tears flowed silently down her face. She did not speak, but we knew why she was crying. Esther was dead.

For months she was sunk in this stupor. She forgot to cook or sweep. My father and I had to do things. She was afraid, too, that I might be killed by a truck, and would not let me go out peddling the newspapers. She clung fiercely to my little brother and me and devoured us with kisses, and kept us beside her for hours. My father watched her anxiously during her long, gloomy apathies by the window.

"Katie, what is wrong?" he implored. "Katie, of what are you thinking?"

"Nothing," she said drearily. "I am only watching the children at play in the street."

5   "But you mustn't!" my father cried. "It reminds you of Esther! You will make yourself sick, Katie!"

"Let me be sick," she said. "Let me go out of this world. One loves a child for years, then a truck kills it."

My father shook his head mournfully. What could he say to comfort her? Esther was dead. Words were futile. It is twenty years since Esther was killed, but my mother is still unconsoled. She visits the cemetery once a month and scatters flowers over Esther's grave. She still weeps for her child. It is as if Esther had died yesterday; my mother will never be consoled.

2

With my mother so helpless, my father had to crawl off his sickbed to hunt for work. But he found nothing. He asked here and there in a faint-hearted way. It did no good. He was sick, discouraged, and could speak no English. He was

Reprinted from *Jews without Money*, (1996), Carroll & Graf Publishers, Inc.

unskilled at any trade but house painting, and his obsessive fear of climbing on a scaffold shut him out of this work. There was little else he could do. He walked the streets gloomily.

It is hard to say how we lived during the next year. Out of every ten Americans one is a pauper, who applies for help to organized charity. There is another pauper tenth that is too proud for such begging. We were in the latter tenth.

10   I can't describe how we managed to live. Does the survivor remember everything from the time when the ship founders until he is washed up on the beach? All I know is we went on living.

The neighbors helped us. They brought in portions of their suppers, and paper bags containing sugar, coffee, beans, flour. Jake Wolf the saloonkeeper quietly paid our rent for months. Other people were kind. Once Rosie the prostitute placed a crumpled five-dollar bill in my hand.

"Give this to your mother," she said. "Tell her you found it in the street."

I tried to relay this lie to my mother, but broke down under questioning. My mother sighed.

"Give Rosie my heartfelt thanks," she said. "Say we will pay it back some day. But don't tell your poppa; he is too proud."

15   Big Tim Sullivan the Tammany Hall leader sent us a basket on Thanksgiving Day, stuffed with nuts, candies, cranberries, celery, and a huge, blue-skinned turkey.

"What kind of a holiday is it, this Thanksgiving?" my mother asked.

I, the scholar of the family, told her it was the day the Pilgrims had given thanks to God for America.

"So it's an American holiday," my mother said, "and not for Jews."

The turkey was a fine fat bird, but unfortunately of heathen origin. It was not *kosher,* and therefore forbidden to us. We eyed it with longing, but my father sold the turkey to one of the Irish bartenders in Jake's saloon.

3

20   "I must do something! I must find some work! We are starving!" my father would cry, beating his breast with both fists in despair.

The neighbors tried to help us, but they themselves were poor. Some well-meaning neighbor secretly mailed a post card to the Charity society, telling of our plight.

One day a stranger called. He was a slim fair-haired, young Christian with a brisk hurry-up manner and a stylish collar and necktie. He placed his umbrella against the wall, and shuffled through a bunch of index cards. He had a bad cold, and was forever blowing the most startling bugle-calls with his nose.

"Does Herman Gold live here?" he asked, sniffling irritably.

"Yes, sir," said my mother.

25 She was very respectful, for this was evidently one of the brusque young men who came from the Board of Health, or the Public School, or the Christian missions, or the settlement houses. They asked many questions, and one must answer them or go to jail.

"I am from the United Charities," said this young man, "and some one wrote us about you. We will help you if you will answer some questions. How many children have you?"

"Two," said my mother.

"How old?"

"One is six, the other ten."

30 "Husband sick?"

"Yes, sir."

"Private doctor or free clinic?"

"Private."

"Where do you get the money to pay him?"

35 "We, we—" my mother began.

The young investigator was making rapid notations on an index card. His eyes swept the room as he talked, as if he were tabulating every pot, pan, dishcloth and stick of furniture in our home. He interrupted my mother in her long explanation of our relations with Dr. Solow.

"And so your husband is out of work? Is he kind to you? Does he drink? What salary does he receive while working? Does he smoke? Has he tried to find a job recently? Does he ever beat you? How much of his salary does he give you when he is working? What rent do you pay? How much do your groceries cost per week?"

My mother was flustered by this Niagara of questions. She resented the brisk stranger who came into her home and asked personal questions with such an air of authority. But he was an official. She cleared her throat, and was about to give him his answers, when my father stalked in.

He had been resting in the bedroom, and was half-undressed. His face was pale, he trembled with rage. He glared at the young blond question-asker, and shouted:

40 "Get out of this house, mister! You have no business here. It is true we are poor, but that does not give you the right to insult us."

"I am not insulting you," said the young investigator, blowing his nose and shuffling his index cards nervously, "I ask these questions in about fifty homes a day. It is just the regular form."

My father drew himself up proudly.

"I spit on your regular form," he said. "We don't want any charity; we can live without it, mister."

"Very well," said the young man, gathering up his umbrella, his overcoat, his index cards, and making briskly for the door. "I'll report what you just said." He paused a moment to scratch a few more notes; then, blowing a last bugle-call on his damp nose, scurried down the hall. What he reported on his cards we never knew, but we were spared the indignity of any further visits by Organized Charity. Every one on the East Side hated and feared that cruel machine that helped no one without first systematically degrading him and robbing him of all human status. One's neighbors were kinder. Tammany Hall was kinder. Starvation was kinder. There were thousands of families like ours that would rather have died than be bullied, shamed and finger-printed like criminals by the callous policemen of Organized Charity.

4

45   The neighbors were talking about us. They were worrying. In the tenement each woman knew what was cooking for supper in her neighbor's pot. Each knew the cares, too, that darkened a neighbor's heart.

One night a neighbor called. He kissed the *mezzuzah* over the door, and wiped his feet on the burlap rags. Then he timidly entered our kitchen like an intruder.

"Good evening, Mr. Lipzin," said my mother. "Please sit down."

"Good evening," he stammered, seating himself. "It was raining to-day, and I did not sell many bananas, so I brought you some. Maybe your children like bananas."

He handed my mother a bunch of bananas, and she took them, saying: "Thanks, Mr. Lipzin."

50   The pot-bellied little peddler shyly fingered his beard. He had come for a purpose, but was too embarrassed to speak. Sweat appeared on his red, fat, honest face, which wind and sun had tanned. He scratched his head, and stared at us in a painful silence. Minutes passed.

"How is your health, Mr. Lipzin?" my mother asked.

"I am stronger, thanks be to God," he said bashfully. "It was only the rheumatism again."

"That is good. And how is your new baby, Mr. Lipzin?"

"God be thanked, she is strong like a tiger," he said.

55 He fell dumb again. He tapped his knees with his fingers, and his shoulders twitched. He was known as a silent man in the tenement; in the ten years we lived there this was the first time he had called on us.

My father fidgeted uneasily. He was about to say something to break the spell cast by the tongue-tied peddler, when Mr. Lipzin became articulate. "Excuse me, but my wife nagged me into coming here," he stammered. "She is worrying about you. Excuse me, but they say you have been out of work a long time and can find nothing to do, Mr. Gold."

"Yes, Mr. Lipzin, why should one conceal it?" said my father. "Life is dark for us now."

"*Nu,*" said the little peddler, as he wiped his forehead, "so that is why my wife nagged me to see you. If there is nothing else, one can at least make a kind of living with bananas. I have peddled them, with God's help, for many years. It is a hard life, but one manages to live.

"Yes," he went on, in a mournful, hesitant sing-song, "for a few dollars one buys a stock of bananas from the wholesalers on Attorney Street. Then one rents a push-cart for ten cents a day from the pushcart stables on Orchard Street. Then one finds a street corner and stands there and the people come and buy the bananas."

60 "So well?" my father demanded, a hostile glare in his eyes.

The little peddler saw this, and was frightened again into incoherence.

"Excuse me, one makes a living, with God's help," he managed to say.

My father stood up and folded his arms haughtily.

"And you are suggesting, Mr. Lipzin, that I, too, should go out peddling bananas?" he asked.

65 The peddler sweated like a runner with embarrassment. He stood up and edged toward the door to make his escape.

"No, no, God forbid," he stammered. "Excuse me, it was my wife who nagged me to come here. No, no, Mr. Gold! Good evening to you all; may God be with you!"

He went out, mopping his fiery face with a bandanna. My father stared after him, his arms still folded in that fierce, defiant attitude.

"What a gall! What meddling neighbors we have! To come and tell me that I ought to peddle these accursed bananas! After my fifteen years in America, as if I were a greenhorn! I, who once owned a suspender shop, and was a foreman of house painters! What do you think of such gall, Katie?"

"I don't know," said my mother quietly. "It is not disgraceful to make an honest living by peddling."

70   "You agree with him?" my father cried.

"No," said my mother, "but Mr. Lipzin is a good man. He came here to help you, and you insulted him."

"So you do agree with him!" my father stormed. He stamped indignantly into the bedroom, where he flung himself on the bed and smoked his pipe viciously. My mother sighed, then she and my brother and I ate some of the bananas.

5

My proud father. He raved, cursed, worried, he held long passionate conversations with my mother.

"Must I peddle bananas, Katie? I can't do it; the disgrace would kill me!"

75   "Don't do it," my mother would say gently. "We can live without it."

"But where will I find work?" he would cry. "The city is locked against me! I am a man in a trap!"

"Something will happen. God has not forgotten us," said my mother.

"I will kill myself! I can't stand it! I will take the gas pipe to my nose! I refuse to be a peddler!"

"Hush, the children will hear you," said my mother.

80   I could hear them thrashing it out at night in the bedroom. They talked about it at the supper table, or sat by the stove in the gloomy winter afternoons, talking, talking. My father was obsessed with the thought of bananas. They became a symbol to him of defeat, of utter hopelessness. And when my mother assured him he need not become a peddler, he would turn on her and argue that it was the one way out. He was in a curious fever of mixed emotions.

Two weeks after Mr. Lipzin's visit he was in the street with a pushcart, peddling the accursed bananas.

He came back the first night, and gave my mother a dollar bill and some silver. His face was gray; he looked older by ten years; a man who had touched bottom. My mother tried to comfort him, but for days he was silent as one who has been crushed by a calamity. Hope died in him; months passed, a year passed; he was still peddling bananas.

I remember meeting him one evening with his pushcart. I had managed to sell all my papers and was coming home in the snow. It was that strange, portentous hour in downtown New York when the workers are pouring homeward in the twilight. I marched among thousands of tired men and women whom the factory whistles had unyoked. They flowed in rivers through the clothing factory districts, then down along the avenues to the East Side.

I met my father near Cooper Union. I recognized him, a hunched, frozen figure in an old overcoat standing by a banana cart. He looked so lonely, the tears came to my eyes. Then he saw me, and his face lit with his sad, beautiful smile—Charlie Chaplin's smile.

85 "Ach, it's Mikey," he said. "So you have sold your papers! Come and eat a banana."

He offered me one. I refused it. I was eleven years old, but poisoned with a morbid proletarian sense of responsibility. I felt it crucial that my father *sell* his bananas, not give them away. He thought I was shy, and coaxed and joked with me, and made me eat the banana. It smelled of wet straw and snow.

"You haven't sold many bananas to-day, pop," I said anxiously.

He shrugged his shoulders.

"What can I do? No one seems to want them."

90 It was true. The work crowds pushed home morosely over the pavements. The rusty sky darkened over New York buildings, the tall street lamps were lit, innumerable trucks, street cars and elevated trains clattered by. Nobody and nothing in the great city stopped for my father's bananas.

"I ought to yell," said my father dolefully. "I ought to make a big noise like other peddlers, but it makes my throat sore. Anyway, I'm ashamed of yelling, it makes me feel like a fool."

I had eaten one of his bananas. My sick conscience told me that I ought to pay for it somehow. I must remain here and help my father.

"I'll yell for you, pop," I volunteered.

"Ach, no," he said, "go home; you have worked enough to-day. Just tell momma I'll be late."

95 But I yelled and yelled. My father, standing by, spoke occasional words of praise, and said I was a wonderful yeller. Nobody else paid attention. The workers drifted past us wearily, endlessly; a defeated army wrapped in dreams of home. Elevated trains crashed; the Cooper Union clock burned above us; the sky grew black, the wind poured, the slush burned through our shoes. There were thousands of strange, silent figures pouring over the sidewalks in snow. None of them stopped to buy bananas. I yelled and yelled, nobody listened.

My father tried to stop me at last. "*Nu*," he said smiling to console me, "that was wonderful yelling, Mikey. But it's plain we are unlucky to-day! Let's go home."

I was frantic, and almost in tears. I insisted on keeping up my desperate yells. But at last my father persuaded me to leave with him. It was after nightfall. We covered the bananas with an oilcloth and started for the pushcart stable. Down Second Avenue we plodded side by side. For many blocks my father was thoughtful. Then he shook his head and sighed:

"So you see how it is, Mikey. Even at banana peddling I am a failure. What can be wrong? The bananas are good, your yelling was good, the prices are good. Yes, it is plain; I am a man without luck."

He paused to light his pipe, while I pushed the cart for him. Then he took the handles again and continued his meditations.

100   "Look at me," he said. "Twenty years in America, and poorer than when I came. A suspender shop I had, and it was stolen from me by a villain. A house painter foreman I became, and fell off a scaffold. Now bananas I sell, and even at that I am a failure. It is all luck." He sighed and puffed at his pipe.

"Ach, Gott, what a rich country America is! What an easy place to make one's fortune! Look at all the rich Jews! Why has it been so easy for them, so hard for me? I am just a poor little Jew without money."

"Poppa, lots of Jews have no money," I said to comfort him.

"I know it, my son," he said, "but don't be one of them. It's better to be dead in this country than not to have money. Promise me you'll be rich when you grow up, Mikey!"

"Yes, poppa."

105   "Ach," he said fondly, "this is my one hope now! This is all that makes me happy! I am a greenhorn, but you are an American! You will have it easier than I; you will have luck in America!"

"Yes, poppa," I said, trying to smile with him. But I felt older than he; I could not share his naïve optimism; my heart sank as I remembered the past and thought of the future.

LEVELS OF READING

Summary:

Pay attention to the **literal** meaning of these texts. Briefly describe the narrative of Michael Gold's "Fifty Cents a Night" and "Bananas." Who tells the story? Where is the story set? Why is the setting especially important? Concentrate on the highlights; avoid too much detail when summarizing. Again, drawing a simple outline of the main points of the text will help you better analyze the text at other levels of interpretation.

Analysis:

Find what you believe is **implicit** or symbolic in these texts. Why is it important that the women in Gold's first story cost "fifty cents a night"? How do the crowding, noise, and dirt all figure symbolically in these stories? Why is it symbolically significant that the women in "Fifty Cents a Night" live right beside families in these tenements? What is important about the fact that the father in "Bananas" must resort to selling bananas? With the help of the background material provided about Michael Gold and his world, make an argument about this story, and include a deeper analysis of what is implied, rather than stated in the text.

Application:

Apply Georg Simmel's theory concerning the metropolis and mental life to these stories. Outline an argument you wish to make about these literary texts using Simmel's theory to help you explain what some part of the story may mean. The "part" of the text you choose to analyze may include any of the following: a character, a setting, a symbol or symbols, an important change, a motivation, a goal, a result. Consider the following as possibilities, but explore other original interpretations too:

- In either "Fifty Cents a Night" or "Bananas" is there any sign of the **intellectualism** Simmel claims is part of mental life in urban cultures?
- Are there any signs of the "close-knit community" impairing individual freedoms in either of these stories? How does the existence of this close-knit community on the Lower East Side of Manhattan complicate Simmel's ideas about urban life? How does this compare with the way the "close-knit community" works in Bellow's "Looking for Mr. Green"?
- In either "Fifty Cents a Night" or "Bananas" is there any sign of the **blasé attitude**?
- Is Simmel's notion of "**reserve**" anywhere apparent in these stories?
- Have any of the **liberating forces** Simmel claims work in urban life given any special freedom to any character in these stories?

UNIT 9

· How do Simmel's ideas of **objectification** and **depersonalization** work in Gold's stories? Do Gold's and Bellow's stories show that objectification and depersonalization happen in the same way in all communities? Do objectification and depersonalization differ within small communities as opposed to larger ones?

Start Your Own Argument:

A century after Simmel proposed his thesis, is his argument still valid? Are any of his ideas apparent in non-urban settings?

TEN

ARGUMENT IN FRAGMENTS, ARGUMENTS WITHIN THE ARGUMENT

FRIEDRICH NIETZSCHE

Friedrich Nietzsche (1844–1900) was born in Rochen, Prussia. His father, Ludwig, a Lutheran minister, died of head injuries sustained in a fall a year earlier when Nietzsche was only five. He was then raised by his mother, in a household that also included his grandmother, two maiden aunts, and a sister, Elisabeth.

From 1858 until 1864, Nietzsche attended the competitive Schulpforta school. He then went to the University of Bonn, where he studied theology and philology. He left there one year later when he transferred to the University of Leipzig and committed himself to the study of classical philology only. It was during this time that Nietzsche began to be plagued with the migraine headaches that were to continue for the rest of his life.

In 1869, prior to the completion of his Ph.D., and at the remarkable age of 24, Nietzsche was appointed a professor of philology at the University of Basel, Switzerland. Ill health from which he was not expected to recover forced him to resign in 1879. Despite the prognosis, Nietzsche did recover; he never, however, returned to teaching. In 1889, Nietzsche suffered a mental breakdown in Turin, Italy. Speculation as to the cause of the breakdown continues, but it is known that by this time Nietzsche suffered from an advanced case of syphilis.

He spent the rest of his years living with his sister in Weimar, Germany, where he died on August 25, 1900. His sister, Elisabeth, continued to edit his notes and form them into books—with an amount of input of her own still in dispute. Though her brother died in 1900, for example, his Will to Power *was published by his sister one year later, in 1901.*

The following essay is taken from The Genealogy of Morals, *published in 1887 and translated into English in 1966. Nietzsche's idea of the* ubermensch, *usually translated as the "superman," but more literally translated as the "overman," taken from* The Will to Power, *and his concept of "noble morality," taken from* The Genealogy of Morals, *have often been interpreted as postulating, if not endorsing, a master/slave society and have been identified with totalitarian philosophies, particularly Nazism. According to Nietzsche, the "masses" conform to tradition, while the "overman" is secure, independent, and highly individualistic. "Slave morality" is created by weak, resentful individuals who encourage such behavior as gentleness and kindness because the behavior serves their interests. Reviewing Plato's idea of "the governor" in "The Allegory of the Cave" and/or Dr. Martin Luther King's idea of "unjust laws" should provide interesting counterpoints to Nietzsche's philosophy of power relations.*

As the title of this essay indicates, Nietzsche's argument depends heavily on the revision of a value system imposed by binary oppositions in language. In the course of making his argument, Nietzsche repeatedly takes a pair of opposed terms, for example "good" and "evil," and questions both their definitions and their assigned sociocultural values. Though one would assume that "good" is a term that should be valued above its opposite, "bad," Nietzsche shows, by careful analysis of the customary definitions of both, that bad can be good and good, bad. In order to fully appreciate and understand Nietzsche's lengthy and complex argument in this essay, it is necessary to follow his often paradoxical train of thought when re-visioning received ideas of value and privilege embedded in everyday language.

———

Nietzsche's argument is made in the space of seventeen short sections, some of which appear discrete and/or digressive until stitched to the argument as a whole. Many of these sections (as well as his title) are based on a binary opposition of two ostensibly contradictory terms with a built-in value system. In making an argument about the nature of "good" and "evil" then, Nietzsche incorporates other arguments about other polarities, in effect building around the smaller arguments a larger one: a critique of the limitations built in to everyday language. Though the apparent structure of Nietzsche's essay differs substantially from Dr. Martin Luther King's five-part essays within his five-part essay, the "nesting" effect is the same.

Coming to Terms with the Reading:

Before reading/rereading Friedrich Nietzsche's, "'Good and Evil,' 'Good and Bad,'" it is best to have a firm grasp of the meaning of the following terms:

1. hypothesis
2. etymology
3. genealogy
4. egoistic/unegoistic
5. conceptual transformation
6. conjecture
7. *ressentiment*/resentment
8. blond beast

GOOD AND EVIL
Friedrich Nietzsche

1

These English psychologists, whom one has also to thank for the only attempts hitherto to arrive at a history of the origin of morality—they themselves are no easy riddle; I confess that, as living riddles, they even possess one essential advantage over their books—*they are interesting!* These English psychologists—what do they really want? One always discovers them voluntarily or involuntarily at the same task, namely at dragging the *partie honteuse*[1] of our inner world into the foreground and seeking the truly effective and directing agent, that which has been decisive in its evolution, in just that place where the intellectual pride of man would least *desire* to find it (in the *vis inertiae*[2] of habit, for example, or in forgetfulness, or in a blind and chance mechanistic hooking-together of ideas, or in something purely passive, automatic, reflexive, molecular, and thoroughly stupid)—what is it really that always drives these psychologists in just *this* direction? Is it a secret, malicious, vulgar, perhaps self-deceiving instinct for belittling man? Or possibly a pessimistic suspicion, the mistrustfulness of disappointed idealists grown spiteful and gloomy? Or a petty subterranean hostility and rancor toward Christianity (and Plato) that has perhaps not even crossed the threshold of consciousness? Or even a lascivious taste for the grotesque, the painfully paradoxical, the questionable and absurd in existence? Or finally—something of each of them, a little vulgarity, a little gloominess, a little anti-Christianity, a little itching and need for spice?

But I am told they are simply old, cold, and tedious frogs, creeping around men and into men as if in their own proper element, that is, in a *swamp*. I rebel at that idea; more, I do not believe it; and if one may be allowed to hope where

[1] Shame.
[2] Inertia.

one does not know, then I hope from my heart they may be the reverse of this—
that these investigators and microscopists of the soul may be fundamentally
brave, proud, and magnanimous animals, who know how to keep their hearts
as well as their sufferings in bounds and have trained themselves to sacrifice all
desirability to truth, *every* truth, even plain, harsh, ugly, repellent, unchristian,
immoral truth.—For such truths do exist.—

2

All respect then for the good spirits that may rule in these historians of morality! But it is, unhappily, certain that the *historical spirit* itself is lacking in them,
that precisely all the good spirits of history itself have left them in the lurch! As
is the hallowed custom with philosophers, the thinking of all of them is *by nature*
unhistorical; there is no doubt about that. The way they have bungled their
moral genealogy comes to light at the very beginning, where the task is to investigate the origin of the concept and judgment "good." "Originally"—so they
decree—"one approved unegoistic actions and called them good from the point
of view of those to whom they were done, that is to say, those to whom they were
useful; later one *forgot* how this approval originated and, simply because unegoistic actions were always *habitually* praised as good, one also felt them to be
good—as if they were something good in themselves." One sees straightaway
that this primary derivation already contains all the typical traits of the idiosyncrasy of the English psychologists—we have "utility," "forgetting," "habit," and
finally "error," all as the basis of an evaluation of which the higher man has hitherto been proud as though it were a kind of prerogative of man as such. This pride
has to be humbled, this evaluation disvalued: has that end been achieved?

   Now it is plain to me, first of all, that in this theory the source of the concept "good" has been sought and established in the wrong place: the judgment
"good" did *not* originate with those to whom "goodness" was shown! Rather it
was "the good" themselves, that is to say, the noble, powerful, high-stationed
and high-minded, who felt and established themselves and their actions as good,
that is, of the first rank, in contradistinction to all the low, low-minded, common and plebeian. It was out of this *pathos of distance*[1] that they first seized the
right to create values and to coin names for values: what had they to do with utility! The viewpoint of utility is as remote and inappropriate as it possibly could

---

[1]Cf. *Beyond Good and Evil,* section 257.

be in face of such a burning eruption of the highest rank-ordering, rank-defining value judgments: for here feeling has attained the antithesis of that low degree of warmth which any calculating prudence, any calculus of utility, presupposes—and not for once only, not for an exceptional hour, but for good. The pathos of nobility and distance, as aforesaid, the protracted and domineering fundamental total feeling on the part of a higher ruling order in relation to a lower order, to a "below"—*that* is the origin of the antithesis "good" and "bad." (The lordly right of giving names extends so far that one should allow oneself to conceive the origin of language itself as an expression of power on the part of the rulers: they say "this *is* this and this," they seal every thing and event with a sound and, as it were, take possession of it.) It follows from this origin that the word "good" was definitely *not* linked from the first and by necessity to "unegoistic" actions, as the superstition of these genealogists of morality would have it. Rather it was only when aristocratic value judgments *declined* that the whole antithesis "egoistic" "unegoistic" obtruded itself more and more on the human conscience—it is, to speak in my own language, the *herd instinct* that through this antithesis at last gets its word (and its *words*) in. And even then it was a long time before that instinct attained such dominion that moral evaluation was actually stuck and halted at this antithesis (as, for example, is the case in contemporary Europe: the prejudice that takes "moral," "unegoistic," "*désintéressé*" as concepts of equivalent value already rules today with the force of a "fixed idea" and brain-sickness).

3

In the second place, however: quite apart from the historical untenability of this hypothesis regarding the origin of the value judgment "good," it suffers from an inherent psychological absurdity. The utility of the unegoistic action is supposed to be the source of the approval accorded it, and this source is supposed to have been *forgotten*—but how is this forgetting *possible*? Has the utility of such actions come to an end at some time or other? The opposite is the case: this utility has rather been an everyday experience at all times, therefore something that has been underlined again and again: consequently, instead of fading from consciousness, instead of becoming easily forgotten, it must have been impressed on the consciousness more and more clearly. How much more reasonable is that opposing theory (it is not for that reason more true—) which Herbert Spencer,[1]

---

[1] Herbert Spencer (1820–1903) was probably the most widely read English philosopher of his time. He applied the principle of evolution to many fields, including sociology and ethics.

for example, espoused: that the concept "good" is essentially identical with the concept "useful," "practical," so that in the judgments "good" and "bad" mankind has summed up and sanctioned precisely its *unforgotten* and *unforgettable* experiences regarding what is useful-practical and what is harmful-impractical. According to this theory, that which has always proved itself useful is good: therefore it may claim to be "valuable in the highest degree," "valuable in itself." This road to an explanation is, as aforesaid, also a wrong one, but at least the explanation is in itself reasonable and psychologically tenable.

4

The signpost to the *right* road was for me the question: what was the real etymological significance of the designations for "good" coined in the various languages? I found they all led back to the *same conceptual transformation*—that everywhere "noble," "aristocratic" in the social sense, is the basic concept from which "good" in the sense of "with aristocratic soul," "noble," "with a soul of a high order," "with a privileged soul" necessarily developed: a development which always runs parallel with that other in which "common," "plebeian," "low" are finally transformed into the concept "bad." The most convincing example of the latter is the German word *schlecht* [bad] itself: which is identical with *schlicht* [plain, simple]—compare *schlechtweg* [plainly], *schlechterdings* [simply]—and orginally designated the plain, the common man, as yet with no inculpatory implication and simply in contradistinction to the nobility. About the time of the Thirty Years' War, late enough therefore, this meaning changed into the one now customary.[1]

    With regard to a moral genealogy this seems to me a *fundamental* insight; that it has been arrived at so late is the fault of the retarding influence exercised by the democratic prejudice in the modern world toward all questions of origin. And this is so even in the apparently quite objective domain of natural science and physiology, as I shall merely hint here. But what mischief this prejudice is capable of doing, especially to morality and history, once it has been unbridled to the point of hatred is shown by the notorious case of Buckle;[2] here the *plebeianism* of the modern spirit, which is of English origin, erupted once again on its native

---

[1]Cf. *Dawn,* section 231, included in the present volume.
[2]Henry Thomas Buckle (1821–1862), English historian, is known chiefly for his *History of Civilization* (1857ff.). The suggestion in the text is developed more fully in section 876 of *The Will to Power.*

soil, as violently as a mud volcano and with that salty, noisy, vulgar eloquence
with which all volcanos have spoken hitherto.—

5

With regard to *our* problem, which may on good grounds be called a *quiet* problem and one which fastidiously directs itself to few ears, it is of no small interest to ascertain that through those words and roots which designate "good" there
frequently still shines the most important nuance by virtue of which the noble
felt themselves to be men of a higher rank. Granted that, in the majority of cases,
they designate themselves simply by their superiority in power (as "the powerful," "the masters," "the commanders") or by the most clearly visible signs of
this superiority, for example, as "the rich," "the possessors" (this is the meaning
of *arya;* and of corresponding words in Iranian and Slavic). But they also do it
by a *typical character trait:* and this is the case that concerns us here. They call
themselves, for instance, "the truthful"; this is so above all of the Greek nobility, whose mouthpiece is the Megarian poet Theognis.[1] The root of the word
coined for this, *esthlos,*[2] signifies one who *is,* who possesses reality, who is actual,

---

[1] Nietzsche's first publication, in 1867 when he was still a student at the University of Leipzig, was
an article in a leading classical journal, *Rheinisches Museum,* on the history of the collection of the
maxims of Theognis ("Zur Geschichte der Theognideischen Spruchsammlung"). Theognis of
Megara lived in the sixth century B.C.

[2] Greek: good, brave. Readers who are not classical philologists may wonder as they read this section how well taken Nietzsche's points about the Greeks are. In this connection one could obviously cite a vast literature, but in this brief commentary it will be sufficient to quote Professor
Gerald F. Else's monumental study *Aristotle's Poetics: The Argument* (Cambridge, Mass., Harvard
University Press, 1957), a work equally notable for its patient and thorough scholarship and its
spirited defense of some controversial interpretations. On the points at issue here, Else's comments
are not, I think, controversial; and that is the reason for citing them here.

"The dichotomy is mostly taken for granted in Homer: there are not many occasions when
the heaven-wide gulf between heroes and commoners even has to be mentioned.[30] [[30] Still, one
finds 'good' (*esthloi*) and 'bad' (*kakoi*) explicitly contrasted a fair number of times: B366, Z489,
I319, . . .] In the . . . seventh and sixth centuries, on the other hand, the antithesis grows common. In Theognis it amounts to an obsession . . . Greek thinking begins with and for a long time
holds to the proposition that mankind is divided into 'good' and 'bad,' and these terms are quite
as much social, political, and economic as they are moral. . . . The dichotomy is absolute and
exclusive for a simple reason: it began as the aristocrats' view of society and reflects their idea of
the gulf between themselves and the 'others.' In the minds of a comparatively small and close-
knit group like the Greek aristocracy there are only two kinds of people, 'we' and 'they'; and of
course 'we' are the good people, the proper, decent, good-looking, right-thinking ones, while
'they' are the rascals, the poltroons, the good-for-nothings . . . Aristotle knew and sympathized
with this older aristocratic, 'practical' ideal, not as superior to the contemplative, but at least as
next best to it" (p. 75).

who is the true; then, with a subjective turn, the true as the truthful: in this phase of conceptual transformation it becomes a slogan and catchword of the nobility and passes over entirely into the sense of "noble," as distinct from the *lying* common man, which is what Theognis takes him to be and how he describes him—until finally, after the decline of the nobility, the word is left to designate nobility of soul and becomes as it were ripe and sweet. In the word *kakos,*[3] as in *deilos*[4] (the plebeian in contradistinction to the *agathos*[5]), cowardice is emphasized: this perhaps gives an indication in which direction one should seek the etymological origin of *agathos,* which is susceptible of several interpretations. The Latin *malus*[6] (beside which I set *melas*[7]) may designate the common man as the dark-colored, above all as the black-haired man *("hic niger est*[8]—"),* as the pre-Aryan occupant of the soil of Italy who was distinguished most obviously from the blond, that is Aryan, conqueror race by his color; Gaelic, at any rate, offers us a precisely similar case—*fin* (for example in the name *Fin-Gal*), the distinguishing word for nobility, finally for the good, noble, pure, orginally meant the blond-headed, in contradistinction to the dark, black-haired aboriginal inhabitants.

The Celts, by the way, were definitely a blond race; it is wrong to associate traces of an essentially dark-haired people which appear on the more careful ethnographical maps of Germany with any sort of Celtic origin or blood-mixture, as Virchow[9] still does: it is rather the *pre-Aryan* people of Germany who emerge in these places. (The same is true of virtually all Europe: the suppressed race has gradually recovered the upper hand again, in coloring, shortness of skull, perhaps even in the intellectual and social instincts: who can say whether modern democracy, even more modern anarchism and especially that inclination for *"commune,"* for the most primitive form of society, which is now shared by all the socialists of Europe, does not signify in the main a tremendous *counterattack*—

---

[3]Greek: bad, ugly, ill-born, mean, craven.
[4]Greek: cowardly, worthless, vile, wretched.
[5]Greek: good, well-born, gentle, brave, capable.
[6]Bad.
[7]Greek: black, dark.
[8]Quoted from Horace's *Satires,* I.4, line 85: "He that backbites an absent friend . . . and cannot keep secrets, is black, O Roman, beware!" *Niger,* originally "black," also came to mean unlucky and, as in this quotation, wicked. Conversely, *candidus* means white, bright, beautiful, pure, guileless, candid, honest, happy, fortunate. And in *Satires,* I.5, 41, Horace speaks of "the whitest souls earth ever bore" (*animae qualis neque candidiores terra tulit*).
[9]Rudolf Virchow (1821–1902) was one of the greatest German pathologists, as well as a liberal politician, a member of the German Reichstag (parliament), and an opponent of Bismarck.

and that the conqueror and *master race,*[9] the Aryan, is not succumbing physiologically, too?

I believe I may venture to interpret Latin *bonus*[10] as "the warrior," provided I
am right in tracing *bonus* back to an earlier *duonus*[11] (compare *bellum = duellum = duen-lum,* which seems to me to contain *duonus*). Therefore *bonus* as the
man of strife, of dissention (*duo*), as the man of war: one sees what constituted
the "goodness" of a man in ancient Rome. Our German *gut* [good] even: does
it is not signify "the godlike," the man of "godlike race"? And is it not identical
with the popular (originally noble) name of the Goths? The grounds for this
conjecture cannot be dealt with here.—

6

To this rule that a concept denoting political superiority always resolves itself
into a concept denoting superiority of soul it is not necessarily an exception
(although it provides occasions for exceptions) when the highest caste is at the
same time the *priestly* caste and therefore emphasizes in its total description of
itself a predicate that calls to mind its priestly function. It is then, for example,
that "pure" and "impure" confront one another for the first time as designations
of station; and here too there evolves a "good" and a "bad" in a sense no longer
referring to station. One should be warned, moreover, against taking these concepts "pure" and "impure" too ponderously or broadly, not to say symbolically:
all the concepts of ancient man were rather at first incredibly uncouth, coarse,
external, narrow, straightforward, and altogether *unsymbolical* in meaning to a
degree that we can scarcely conceive. The "pure one" is from the beginning
merely a man who washes himself, who forbids himself certain foods that produce skin ailments, who does not sleep with the dirty women of the lower strata,
who has an aversion to blood—no more, hardly more! On the other hand, to be
sure, it is clear from the whole nature of an essentially priestly aristocracy why
antithetical valuations could in precisely this instance soon become dangerously
deepened, sharpened, and internalized; and indeed they finally tore chasms
between man and man that a very Achilles of a free spirit would not venture to
leap without a shudder. There is from the first something *unhealthy* in such

---

[9] For a detailed discussion both of this concept and of Nietzsche's attitude toward the Jews and
anti-Semitism, see Kaufmann's *Nietzsche,* Chapter 10: "The Master-Race."
[10] Good.
[11] Listed in Harper's Latin Dictionary as the old form of *bonus,* with the comment: "for *duonus,*
cf. *bellum.*" And *duellum* is identified as an early and poetic form of *bellum* (war).

priestly aristocracies and in the habits ruling in them which turn them away from action and alternate between brooding and emotional explosions, habits which seem to have as their almost invariable consequence that intestinal morbidity and neurasthenia which has afflicted priests at all times; but as to that which they themselves devised as a remedy for this morbidity—must one not assert that it has ultimately proved itself a hundred times more dangerous in its effects than the sickness it was supposed to cure? Mankind itself is still ill with the effects of this priestly naïveté in medicine! Think, for example, of certain forms of diet (abstinence from meat), of fasting, of sexual continence, of flight "into the wilderness" (the Weir Mitchell isolation cure[1]—without, to be sure, the subsequent fattening and over-feeding which constitute the most effective remedy for the hysteria induced by the ascetic ideal): add to these the entire antisensualistic metaphysic of the priests that makes men indolent and overrefined, their autohypnosis in the manner of fakirs and Brahmins—Brahma used in the shape of a glass knob and a fixed idea—and finally the only-too-comprehensible satiety with all this, together with the radical cure for it, *nothingness* (or God— the desire for a *unio mystica* with God is the desire of the Buddhist for nothingness, Nirvana—and no more!). For with the priests *everything* becomes more dangerous, not only cures and remedies, but also arrogance, revenge, acuteness, profligacy, love, lust to rule, virtue, disease—but it is only fair to add that it was on the soil of this *essentially dangerous* form of human existence, the priestly form, that man first became *an interesting animal,* that only here did the human soul in a higher sense acquire *depth* and become *evil*—and these are the two basic respects in which man has hitherto been superior to other beasts!

7

One will have divined already how easily the priestly mode of valuation can branch off from the knightly-aristocratic and then develop into its opposite; this is particularly likely when the priestly caste and the warrior caste are in jealous opposition to one another and are unwilling to come to terms. The knightly-aristocratic value judgments presupposed a powerful physicality, a flourishing, abundant, even overflowing health, together with that which serves to preserve it: war, adventure, hunting, dancing, war games, and in general all that involves vigorous, free, joyful activity. The priestly-noble mode of valuation presupposes,

UNIT 10

---

[1]The cure developed by Dr. Silas Weir Mitchell (1829–1914, American) consisted primarily in isolation, confinement to bed, dieting, and massage.

as we have seen, other things: it is disadvantageous for it when it comes to war! As is well known, the priests are the *most evil enemies*—but why? Because they are the most impotent. It is because of their impotence that in them hatred grows to monstrous and uncanny proportions, to the most spiritual and poisonous kind of hatred. The truly great haters in world history have always been priests; likewise the most ingenious[1] haters: other kinds of spirit[2] hardly come into consideration when compared with the spirit of priestly vengefulness. Human history would be altogether too stupid a thing without the spirit that the impotent have introduced into it—let us take at once the most notable example. All that has been done on earth against "the noble," "the powerful," "the masters," "the rulers," fades into nothing compared with what *Jews* have done against them; the Jews, that priestly people, who in opposing their enemies and conquerors were ultimately satisfied with nothing less than a radical revaluation of their enemies' values, that is to say, an act of the *most spiritual revenge.* For this alone was appropriate to a priestly people, the people embodying the most deeply repressed[3] priestly vengefulness. It was the Jews who, with awe-inspiring consistency, dared to invert the aristocratic value-equation (good = noble = powerful = beautiful = happy = beloved of God) and to hang on to this inversion with their teeth, the teeth of the most abysmal hatred (the hatred of impotence), saying "the wretched alone are the good; the poor, impotent, lowly alone are the good; the suffering, deprived, sick, ugly alone are pious, alone are blessed by God, blessedness is for them alone—and you, the powerful and noble, are on the contrary the evil, the cruel, the lustful, the insatiable, the godless to all eternity; and you shall be in all eternity the unblessed, accursed, and damned!" . . . One knows *who* inherited this Jewish revaluation . . . In connection with the tremendous and immeasurably fateful initiative provided by the Jews through this most fundamental of all declarations of war, I recall the proposition I arrived at on a previous occasion (*Beyond Good and Evil,* section 195)[4]—that with the Jews there begins *the slave revolt in morality:* that revolt which has a history of two thousand years behind it and which we no longer see because it—has been victorious.

---

[1] *Geistreich.*

[2] *Geist.*

[3] *Zurückgetretensten.*

[4] See my commentary on that section in *Beyond Good and Evil* (New York, Vintage Books, 1966), section 195, note 11.

8

But you do not comprehend this? You are incapable of seeing something that required two thousand years to achieve victory?—There is nothing to wonder at in that: all *protracted* things are hard to see, to see whole. *That,* however, is what has happened: from the trunk of that tree of vengefulness and hatred, Jewish hatred—the profoundest and sublimest kind of hatred, capable of creating ideals and reversing values, the like of which has never existed on earth before—there grew something equally incomparable, a *new love,* the profoundest and sublimest kind of love—and from what other trunk could it have grown?

One should not imagine it grew up as the denial of that thirst for revenge, as the opposite of Jewish hatred! No, the reverse is true! That love grew out of it as its crown, as its triumphant crown spreading itself farther and farther into the purest brightness and sunlight, driven as it were into the domain of light and the heights in pursuit of the goals of that hatred—victory, spoil, and seduction—by the same impulse that drove the roots of that hatred deeper and deeper and more and more covetously into all that was profound and evil. This Jesus of Nazareth, the incarnate gospel of love, this "Redeemer" who brought blessedness and victory to the poor, the sick, and the sinners—was he not this seduction in its most uncanny and irresistible form, a seduction and bypath to precisely those *Jewish* values and new ideals? Did Israel not attain the ultimate goal of its sublime vengefulness precisely through the bypath of this "Redeemer," this ostensible opponent and disintegrator of Israel? Was it not part of the secret black art of truly *grand* politics of revenge, of a farseeing, subterranean, slowly advancing, and premeditated revenge, that Israel must itself deny the real instrument of its revenge before all the world as a mortal enemy and nail it to the cross, so that "all the world," namely all the opponents of Israel, could unhesitatingly swallow just this bait? And could spiritual subtlety imagine any *more dangerous* bait than this? Anything to equal the enticing, intoxicating, overwhelming, and undermining power of that symbol of the "holy cross," that ghastly paradox of a "God on the cross," that mystery of an unimaginable ultimate cruelty and self-crucifixion of God *for the salvation of man?*

What is certain, at least, is that *sub hoc signo*[1] Israel, with its vengefulness and revaluation of all values, has hitherto triumphed again and again over all other ideals, over all *nobler* ideals.—

---

[1] Under this sign.

9

"But why are you talking about *nobler* ideals! Let us stick to the facts: the people have won—or 'the slaves' or 'the mob' or 'the herd' or whatever you like to call them—if this has happened through the Jews, very well! in that case no people ever had a more world-historic mission. 'The masters' have been disposed of; the morality of the common man has won. One may conceive of this victory as at the same time a blood-poisoning (it has mixed the races together)—I shan't contradict; but this in-toxication has undoubtedly been *successful*. The 'redemption' of the human race (from 'the masters,' that is) is going forward; everything is visibly becoming Judaized, Christianized, mob-ized (what do the words matter!). The progress of this poison through the entire body of mankind seems irresistible, its pace and tempo may from now on even grow slower, subtler, less audible, more cautious—there is plenty of time.—To this end, does the church today still have any *necessary* role to play? Does it still have the right to exist? Or could one do without it? *Quaeritur.*[1] It seems to hinder rather than hasten this progress. But perhaps that is its usefulness.—Certainly it has, over the years, become something crude and boorish, something repellent to a more delicate intellect, to a truly modern taste. Ought it not to become at least a little more refined?—Today it alienates rather than seduces.—Which of us would be a free spirit if the church did not exist? It is the church, and not its poison, that repels us.— Apart from the church, we, too, love the poison.—"

This is the epilogue of a "free spirit" to my speech; an honest animal, as he has abundantly revealed, and a democrat, moreover; he had been listening to me till then and could not endure to listen to my silence. For at this point I have much to be silent about.

10

The slave revolt in morality begins when *ressentiment*[1] itself becomes creative and gives birth to values: the *ressentiment* of natures that are denied the true reaction, that of deeds, and compensate themselves with an imaginary revenge. While every noble morality develops from a triumphant affirmation of itself, slave morality from the outset says No to what is "outside," what is "different," what

---

[1] One asks.
[1] Resentment. The term is discussed above, in section 3 of the Introduction.

is "not itself"; and *this* No is its creative deed. This inversion of the value-positing eye—this *need* to direct one's view outward instead of back to oneself—is of the essence of *ressentiment:* in order to exist, slave morality always first needs a hostile external world; it needs, physiologically speaking, external stimuli in order to act at all—its action is fundamentally reaction.

The reverse is the case with the noble mode of valuation: it acts and grows spontaneously, it seeks its opposite only so as to affirm itself more gratefully and triumphantly—its negative concept "low," "common," "bad" is only a subsequently-invented pale, contrasting image in relation to its positive basic concept—filled with life and passion through and through—"we noble ones, we good, beautiful, happy ones!" When the noble mode of valuation blunders and sins against reality, it does so in respect to the sphere with which it is *not* sufficiently familiar, against a real knowledge of which is has indeed inflexibly guarded itself: in some circumstances it misunderstands the sphere it despises, that of the common man, of the lower orders; on the other hand, one should remember that, even supposing that the affect of contempt, of looking down from a superior height, *falsifies* the image of that which it despises, it will at any rate still be a much less serious falsification than that perpetrated on its opponent—*in effigie* of course—by the submerged hatred, the vengefulness of the impotent. There is indeed too much carelessness, too much talking lightly, too much looking away and impatience involved in contempt, even too much joyfulness, for it to be able to transform its object into a real caricature and monster.

One should not overlook the almost benevolent nuances that the Greek nobility, for example, bestows on all the words it employs to distinguish the lower orders from itself; how they are continuously mingled and sweetened with a kind of pity, consideration, and forbearance, so that finally almost all the words referring to the common man have remained as expressions signifying "unhappy," "pitiable" (campore *deilos,*[2] *deilaios,*[3] *pon ēros,*[4] *mochthēros,*[5] the last two of which properly designate the common man as workslave and beast of burden)—and how on the other hand "bad," "low," "unhappy" have never ceased to sound to the Greek ear as one note with a tone-color in which "unhappy" preponderates: this as an inheritance from the ancient nobler aristocratic mode of evaluation,

---

[2]All of the footnoted words in this section are Greek. The first four mean *wretched,* but each has a separate note to suggest some of its other connotations. *Deilos:* cowardly, worthless, vile.
[3]Paltry.
[4]Oppressed by toils, good for nothing, worthless, knavish, base, cowardly.
[5]Suffering hardship, knavish.

which does not belie itself even in its contempt (—philologists should recall the sense in which *oïzyros,*[6] *anolbos,*[7] *tlēmōn,*[8] *dystychein,*[9] *xymphora*[10] are employed). The "well-born" *felt* themselves to be the "happy"; they did not have to establish their happiness artificially by examining their enemies, or to persuade themselves, *deceive* themselves, that they were happy (as all men of *ressentiment* are in the habit of doing); and they likewise knew, as rounded men replete with energy and therefore *necessarily* active, that happiness should not be sundered from action—being active was with them necessarily a part of happiness (whence *eu prattein*[11] takes its origin)—all very much the opposite of "happiness" at the level of the impotent, the oppressed, and those in whom poisonous and inimical feelings are festering, with whom it appears as essentially narcotic, drug, rest, peace, "sabbath," slackening of tension and relaxing of limbs, in short *passively.*

While the noble man lives in trust and openness with himself (*gennaios*[12] "of noble descent" underlines the nuance "upright" and probably also "naïve"), the man of *ressentiment* is neither upright nor naïve nor honest and straightforward with himself. His soul *squints*: his spirit loves hiding places, secret paths and back doors, everything covert entices him as *his* world, *his* security, *his* refreshment: he understands how to keep silent, how not to forget, how to wait, how to be provisionally self-deprecating and humble. A race of such men of *ressentiment* is bound to become eventually *cleverer* than any noble race; it will also honor cleverness to a far greater degree: namely, as a condition of existence of the first importance; while with noble men cleverness can easily acquire a subtle flavor of luxury and subtlety—for here it is far less essential than the perfect functioning of the regulating *unconscious* instincts or even than a certain imprudence, perhaps a bold recklessness whether in the face of danger or of the enemy, or that enthusiastic impulsiveness in anger, love, reverence, gratitude, and revenge by which noble souls have at all times recognized one another. *Ressentiment* itself, if it should appear in the noble man, consummates and exhausts itself in an immediate reaction, and therefore does not *poison:* on the other hand, it fails to appear at all on countless occasions on which it inevitably appears in the weak and impotent.

---

[6]Woeful, miserable, toilsome; wretch.
[7]Unblest, wretched, luckless, poor.
[8]Wretched, miserable.
[9]To be unlucky, unfortunate.
[10]Misfortune.
[11]To do well in the sense of faring well.
[12]High-born, noble, high-minded.

5   To be incapable of taking one's enemies, one's accidents, even one's misdeeds seriously for very long—that is the sign of strong, full natures in whom there is an excess of the power to form, to mold, to recuperate and to forget (a good example of this in modern times is Mirabeau,[13] who had no memory for insults and vile actions done him and was unable to forgive simply because he—forgot). Such a man shakes off with a *single* shrug many vermin that eat deep into others; here alone genuine "love of one's enemies" is possible—supposing it to be possible at all on earth. How much reverence has a noble man for his enemies!—and such reverence is a bridge to love.—For he desires his enemy for himself, as his mark of distinction; he can endure no other enemy than one in whom there is nothing to despise and *very much* to honor! In contrast to this, picture "the enemy" as the man of *ressentiment* conceives him—and here precisely is his deed, his creation: he has conceived "the evil enemy," "*the Evil One,*" and this in fact is his basic concept, from which he then evolves, as an afterthought and pendant, a "good one"—himself!

<h2 style="text-align:center">11</h2>

This, then, is quite the contrary of what the noble man does, who conceives the basic concept "good" in advance and spontaneously out of himself and only then creates for himself an idea of "bad"! This "bad" of noble origin and that "evil" out of the cauldron of unsatisfied hatred—the former an after-production, a side issue, a contrasting shade, the latter on the contrary the original thing, the beginning, the distinctive *deed* in the conception of a slave morality—how different these words "bad" and "evil" are, although they are both apparently the opposite of the same concept "good." But it is *not* the same concept "good": one should ask rather precisely *who* is "evil" in the sense of the morality of *ressentiment.* The answer, in all strictness, is: *precisely* the "good man" of the other morality, precisely the noble, powerful man, the ruler, but dyed in another color, interpreted in another fashion, seen in another way by the venomous eye of *ressentiment.*

Here there is one thing we shall be the last to deny: he who knows these "good men" only as enemies knows only *evil enemies,* and the same men who are held so sternly in check *inter pares*[1] by custom, respect, usage, gratitude, and

---

[13]Honoré Gabriel Riqueti, Comte de Mirabeau (1749–1791), was a celebrated French Revolutionary statesman and writer.
[1]Among equals.

even more by mutual suspicion and jealousy, and who on the other hand in their relations with one another show themselves so resourceful in consideration, self-control, delicacy, loyalty, pride, and friendship—once they go outside, where the strange, the *stranger* is found, they are not much better than uncaged beasts of prey. There they savor a freedom from all social constraints, they compensate themselves in the wilderness for the tension engendered by protracted confinement and enclosure within the peace of society, they go *back* to the innocent conscience of the beast of prey, as triumphant monsters who perhaps emerge from a disgusting[2] procession of murder, arson, rape, and torture, exhilarated and undisturbed of soul, as if it were no more than a students' prank, convinced they have provided the poets with a lot more material for song and praise. One cannot fail to see at the bottom of all these noble races the beast of prey, the splendid *blond beast*[3] prowling about avidly in search of spoil and victory; this hidden core needs to erupt from time to time, the animal has to get out again and go back to the wilderness: the Roman, Arabian, Germanic, Japanese nobility, the Homeric heroes, the Scandinavian Vikings—they all shared this need.

---

[2] *Scheusslichen.*

[3] This is the first appearance in Nietzsche's writings of the notorious "blond beast." It is encountered twice more in the present section; a variant appears in section 17 of the second essay; and then the *blonde Bestie* appears once more in *Twilight,* "The 'Improvers' of Mankind," section 2 (*Portable Niezsche,* p. 502). That is all. For a detailed discussion of these passages see Kaufmann's *Nietzsche,* Chapter 7, section III: " . . . The 'blond beast' is not a racial concept and does not refer to the 'Nordic race' of which the Nazis later made so much. Nietzsche specifically refers to Arabs and Japanese . . . —and the 'blondness' presumably refers to the beast, the lion."

Francis Golffing, in his free translation of the *Genealogy,* deletes the blond beast three times out of four; only where it appears the second time in the original text, he has "the blond Teutonic beast." This helps to corroborate the myth that the blondness refers to the Teutons. Without the image of the lion, however, we lose not only some of Nietzsche's poetry as well as any chance to understand one of his best known coinages; we also lose an echo of the crucial first chapter of *Zarathustra,* where the lion represents the second stage in "The Three Metamorphoses" of the spirit—above the obedient camel but below the creative child (*Portable Nietzsche,* pp. 138f.).

Arthur Danto has suggested that if lions were black and Nietzsche had written "Black Beast," the expression would "provide support for African instead of German nationalists" (*Nietzsche as Philosopher,* New York, Macmillan, 1965, p. 170). Panthers *are* black and magnificent animals, but anyone calling Negroes black beasts and associating them with "a disgusting procession of murder, arson, rape, and torture," adding that "the animal has to get out again and go back to the wilderness," and then going on to speak of "their hair-raising cheerfulness and profound joy in all destruction," would scarcely be taken to "provide support for . . . nationalists." On the contrary, he would be taken for a highly prejudiced critic of the Negro.

No other German writer of comparable stature has been a more extreme critic of German nationalism than Nietzsche. For all that, it is plain that in this section he sought to describe the behavior of the ancient Greeks and Romans, the Goths and the Vandals, not that of nineteenth-century Germans.

It is the noble races that have left behind them the concept "barbarian" wherever they have gone; even their highest culture betrays a consciousness of it and even a pride in it (for example, when Pericles says to his Athenians in his famous funeral oration "our boldness has gained access to every land and sea, everywhere raising imperishable monuments to its goodness *and wickedness*"). This "boldness" of noble races, mad, absurd, and sudden in its expression, the incalculability, even incredibility of their undertakings—Pericles specially commends the *rhathymia*[4] of the Athenians—their indifference to and contempt for security, body, life, comfort, their hair-raising[5] cheerfulness and profound joy in all destruction, in all the voluptuousness of victory and cruelty—all this came together, in the minds of those who suffered from it, in the image of the "barbarian," the "evil enemy," perhaps as the "Goths," the "Vandals." The deep and icy mistrust the German still arouses today whenever he gets into a position of power is an echo of that inextinguishable horror with which Europe observed for centuries that raging of the blond Germanic beast (although between the old Germanic tribes and us Germans there exists hardly a conceptual relationship, let alone one of blood).

I once drew attention to the dilemma in which Hesiod found himself when he concocted his succession of cultural epochs and sought to express them in terms of gold, silver, and bronze: he knew no way of handling the contradiction presented by the glorious but at the same time terrible and violent world of Homer except by dividing one epoch into two epochs, which he then placed one behind the other—first the epoch of the heroes and demigods of Troy and Thebes, the form in which that world had survived in the memory of the noble races who were those heroes' true descendants; then the bronze epoch, the form in which that same world appeared to the descendants of the downtrodden, pillaged, mistreated, abducted, enslaved: an epoch of bronze, as aforesaid, hard, cold, cruel, devoid of feeling or conscience, destructive and bloody.

Supposing that what is at any rate believed to be the "truth" really is true, and the *meaning of all culture* is the reduction of the beast of prey "man" to a tame and civilized animal, a *domestic animal,* then one would undoubtedly have to regard all those instincts of reaction and *ressentiment* through whose aid the noble races and

---

[4]Thucydides, 2.39. In *A Historical Commentary on Thucydides,* vol. II (Oxford, Clarendon Press, 1956; corrected imprint of 1966), p. 118, A. W. Gomme comments on this word: "in its original sense, 'ease of mind,' 'without anxiety' . . . But ease of mind can in certain circumstances become carelessness, remissness, frivolity: Demosthenes often accused the Athenians of *rhathymia . . .* "

[5]*Entsetzliche.*

their ideals were finally confounded and overthrown as the actual *instruments of culture;* which is not to say that the *bearers* of these instincts themselves represent culture. Rather is the reverse not merely probable—no! today it is *palpable!* These bearers of the oppressive instincts that thirst for reprisal, the descendants of every kind of European and non-European slavery, and especially of the entire pre-Aryan populace—they represent the *regression* of mankind! These "instruments of culture" are a disgrace to man and rather an accusation and counterargument against "culture" in general! One may be quite justified in continuing to fear the blond beast at the core of all noble races and in being on one's guard against it: but who would not a hundred times sooner fear where one can also admire than *not* fear but be permanently condemned to the repellent sight of the ill-constituted, dwarfed, atrophied, and poisoned?[6] And is that not *our* fate? What today constitutes *our* antipathy to "man"?—for we *suffer* from man, beyond doubt.

Not fear; rather that we no longer have anything left to fear in man; that the maggot[7] "man" is swarming in the foreground; that the "tame man," the hopelessly mediocre and insipid[8] man, has already learned to feel himself as the goal and zenith, as the meaning of history, as "higher man"—that he has indeed a certain right to feel thus, insofar as he feels himself elevated above the surfeit of ill-constituted, sickly, weary and exhaused people of which Europe is beginning to stink today, as something at least relatively well-constituted, at least still capable of living, at least affirming life.

12

At this point I cannot suppress a sigh and a last hope. What is it that I especially find utterly unendurable? That I cannot cope with, that makes me choke and faint? Bad air! Bad air! The approach of some ill-constituted thing; that I have to smell the entrails of some ill-constituted soul!

How much one is able to endure: distress, want, bad weather, sickness, toil, solitude. Fundamentally one can cope with everything else, born as one is to a

---

[6]If the present section is not clear enough to any reader, he might turn to *Zarathustra*'s contrast of the *overman* and the *last man* (Prologue, sections 3–5) and, for good measure, read also the first chapter or two of Part One. Then he will surely see how Aldous Huxley's *Brave New World* and George Orwell's *1984*—but especially the former—are developments of Nietzsche's theme. Huxley, in his novel, uses Shakespeare as a foil; Nietzsche, in the passage above, Homer.

[7]*Gewürm* suggests wormlike animals; *wimmelt* can mean swarm or crawl but is particularly associated with maggots—in a cheese, for example.

[8]*Unerquicklich.*

subterranean life of struggle; one emerges again and again into the light, one experiences again and again one's golden hour of victory—and then one stands forth as one was born, unbreakable, tensed, ready for new, even harder, remoter things, like a bow that distress only serves to draw tauter.

But grant me from time to time—if there are divine goddesses in the realm beyond good and evil—grant me the sight, but *one* glance of something perfect, wholly achieved, happy, mighty, triumphant, something still capable of arousing fear! Of a man who justifies *man,* of a complementary and redeeming lucky hit on the part of man for the sake of which one may still *believe in man*!

For this is how things are: the diminution and leveling of European man constitutes *our* greatest danger, for the sight of him makes us weary.—We can see nothing today that wants to grow greater, we suspect that things will continue to go down, down, to become thinner, more good-natured, more prudent, more comfortable, more mediocre, more indifferent, more Chinese, more Christian—there is no doubt that man is getting "better" all the time.

Here precisely is what has become a fatality for Europe—together with the fear of man we have also lost our love of him, our reverence for him, our hopes for him, even the will to him. The sight of man now makes us weary—what is nihilism today if it is not *that*?—We are weary *of man.*

13

But let us return: the problem of the *other* origin of the "good," of the good as conceived by the man *ressentiment,* demands its solution.

That lambs dislike great birds of prey does not seem strange: only it gives no ground for reproaching these birds of prey for bearing off little lambs. And if the lambs say among themselves: "these birds of prey are evil; and whoever is least like a bird of prey, but rather its opposite, a lamb—would he not be good?" there is no reason to find fault with this institution of an ideal, except perhaps that the birds of prey might view it a little ironically and say: "*we* don't dislike them at all, these good little lambs; we even love them: nothing is more tasty than a tender lamb."

To demand of strength that it should *not* express itself as strength, that it should *not* be a desire to overcome, a desire to throw down, a desire to become master, a thirst for enemies and resistances and triumphs, is just as absurd as to demand of weakness that it should express itself as strength. A quantum of force is equivalent to a quantum of drive, will, effect—more, it is nothing other than precisely this very driving, willing, effecting, and only owing to the seduction of language (and of the fundamental errors of reason that are petrified in it) which conceives and misconceives all effects as conditioned by something that causes effects, by a "subject," can it appear otherwise. For just as the popular mind separates the lightning from its flash and takes the latter for an *action*, for the operation of a subject called lightning, so popular morality also separates strength from expressions of strength, as if there were a neutral substratum behind the strong man, which was *free* to express strength or not to do so. But there is no such substratum; there is no "being" behind doing, effecting, becoming; "the doer" is merely a fiction added to the deed—the deed is everything. The popular mind in fact doubles the deed; when it sees the lightning flash, it is the deed of a deed: it posits the same event first as cause and then a second time as its effect. Scientists do no better when they say "force moves," "force causes," and the like—all its coolness, its freedom from emotion notwithstanding, our entire science still lies under the misleading influence of language and has not disposed of that little changeling, the "subject" (the atom, for example is such a changeling, as is the Kantian "thing-in-itself"); no wonder if the submerged, darkly glowering emotions of vengefulness and hatred exploit this belief for their own ends and in fact maintain no belief more ardently than the belief that *the strong man is free* to be weak and the bird of prey to be a lamb—for thus they gain the right to make the bird of prey *accountable* for being a bird of prey.

When the oppressed, downtrodden, outraged exhort one another with the vengeful cunning of impotence: "let us be different from the evil, namely good! And he is good who does not outrage, who harms nobody, who does not attack, who does not requite, who leaves revenge to God, who keeps himself hidden as we do, who avoids evil and desires little from life, like us, the patient, humble, and just"—this, listened to calmly and without previous bias, really amounts to no more than: "we weak ones are, after all, weak; it would be good if we did nothing *for which we are not strong enough*"; but this dry matter of fact, this prudence of the lowest order which even insects possess (posing as dead, when in great danger, so as not to do "too much"), has, thanks to the counterfeit and self-deception of impotence, clad itself in the ostentatious garb of the virtue of quiet, calm resignation, just as if the weakness of the weak—that is to say, their *essence,* their effects, their sole ineluctable, irremovable reality—were a voluntary achievement, willed, chosen, a *deed,* a *meritorious* act. This type of man *needs* to believe in a neutral independent "subject," prompted by an instinct for self-preservation and self-affirmation in which every lie is sanctified. The subject (or, to use a more popular expression, the *soul*) has perhaps been believed in hitherto more firmly than anything else on earth because it makes possible to the majority of mortals, the weak and oppressed of every kind, the sublime self-deception that interprets weakness as freedom, and their being thus-and-thus as a *merit*.

14

Would anyone like to take a look into the secret of how *ideals are made on earth*? Who has the courage?—Very well! Here is a point we can see through into this dark workshop. But wait a moment or two, Mr. Rash and Curious: your eyes must first get used to this false iridescent light.—All right! Now speak! What is going on down there? Say what you see, man of the most perilous kind of inquisitiveness—now I am the one who is listening.—

—"I see nothing, but I hear the more. There is a soft, wary, malignant muttering and whispering coming from all the comers and nooks. It seems to me one is lying; a saccharine sweetness clings to every sound. Weakness is being lied into something *meritorious*, not doubt of it—so it is just as you said"—

—Go on!

—"and impotence which does not requite into 'goodness of heart' anxious lowliness into 'humility'; subjection to those one hates into 'obedience' (that is, to one of whom they say he commands this subjection—they call him God). The inoffensiveness of the weak man, even the cowardice of which he has so much, his lingering at the door, his being ineluctably compelled to wait, here acquire flattering names, such as 'patience,' and are even called virtue itself; his inability for revenge is called unwillingness to revenge, perhaps even forgiveness ('for *they* know not what they do—we alone known what *they* do!'). They also speak of 'loving one's enemies'—and sweat as they do so,"

—Go on!

—"They are miserable, no doubt of of it, all these mutterers and nook counterfeiters, although they crouch warmly together—but they tell me their misery is a sign of being chosen by God; one beats the dogs one likes best; perhaps this misery is also a preparation; a testing, a schooling, perhaps it is even more—something that will one day be made good and recompensed with interest; with huge payments of gold, no! of happiness. This they call 'bliss.'"

—Go on!

—"Now they give me to understand that they are not merely better than the mighty, the lords of the earth whose spittle they have to lick (*not* from fear, not at

all from fear, but because God has commanded them to obey this authorities)[1]—
that they are not merely better but are also 'better off' or at least will be better off
someday. But enough! enough! I can't take any more. Bad air! Bad air! This workshop where *ideals are manufactured*—it seems to me it stinks of so many lies."

—No! Wait a moment! You have said nothing yet of the masterpiece of these
black magicians, who make whiteness, milk, and innocence of every blackness—
haven't you noticed their perfection or refinement, their boldest, subtlest, most
ingenious, most mendacious artistic stroke? Attend to them! These cellar rodents
full of vengefulness and hatred—what have they made of revenge and hatred?
Have you heard these words uttered? If you trusted simpy to their words, would
you suspect you were among men of *ressentiment?* . . .

—"I understand; I'll open my ears again (oh! oh! oh! and *close* my nose).
Now I can really hear what they have been saying all along: 'We good men—*we
are the just*'—what they desire they call, not retaliation, but 'the triumph of *justice*'; what they hate is not their enemy, no! they hate 'injustice,' they hate 'god-
lessness'; what they believe in and hope for is not the hope of revenge, the
intoxication of sweet revenge (—'sweeter than honey' Homer called it), but the
victory of God, of the *just* God, over the godless; what there is left for them to
love on earth is not their brothers in hatred but their 'brothers in love,' as they
put it, all the good and just on earth."

—And what do they call that which serves to console them for all the suffering
of life—their phantasmagoria of anticipated future bliss?

—"What? Do I hear aright? They call that 'the Last Judgment,' the coming
of their kingdom, of the 'Kingdom of God'—meanwhile, however, they live 'in
faith,' 'in love,' 'in hope.' "

—Enough! Enough!

15

In faith in what? In love of what? In hope of what?—These weak people—some
day or other *they* too intend to be the strong, there is no doubt of that, some day
their "kingdom" too shall come—they term it "the kingdom of God," of course,
as aforesaid: for one is so very humble in all things! To experience *that* one needs
to live a long time, beyond death—indeed one needs eternal life, so as to be
eternally indemnified in the "kingdom of God" for this earthly life "in faith, in
love, in hope." Indemnified for what? How indemnified?

---

[1]Allusion to Romans 13:1-2

Dante, I think, committed a crude blunder when, with a terror-inspiring ingenuity, he placed above the gateway of his hell the inscription "I too was created by eternal love"—at any rate, there would be more justification for placing above the gateway to the Christian Paradise and its "eternal bliss" the inscription "I too was created by eternal *hate*"—provided a truth may be placed above the gateway to a lie! For *what* is it that constitutes the bliss of this Paradise?

We might even guess, but it is better to have it expressly described for us by an authority not to be underestimated in such matters, Thomas Aquinas, the great teacher and saint. "*Beati in regno coelesti,*" he says, meek as a lamb, "*videbunt poenas damnatorum,* **ut beatitudo illis magis complaceat.**"[1] Or if one would like to hear it in a stronger key, perhaps from the mouth of a triumphant Church Father, adjuring his Christians to avoid the cruel pleasures of the public games—but why? "For the faith offers us much more"—he says, *De Spectaculis,* chs. 29f.—"*something much stronger;* thanks to the Redemption, quite other joys are at our command; in place of athletes we have our martyrs; if we crave blood, we have the blood of Christ . . . But think of what awaits us on the day of his return, the day of his triumph!"—and then he goes on, the enraptured visionary.[2] "*At enim supersunt alia spectacula, ille ultimus et perpetuus judicii dies, ille nationibus insperatus, ille derisus, cum tanta saeculi vetustas et tot ejus nativitates uno igne haurientur. Quae tunc spectaculi latitudo!* **Quid admirer! Quid rideam! Ubi**

---

[1]The blessed in the kingdom of heaven will see the punishments of the damned, *in order that their bliss be more delightful for them.*—To be precise, what we find in *Summa Theologiae,* III, *Supplementum,* Q. 94, Art. 1, is this: "In order that the bliss of the saints may be more delightful for them and that they may render more copious thanks to God for it, it is given to them to see perfectly the punishment of the damned." *Ut beatitudo sanctorum eis magis complaceat, et de ea uberiores gratias Deo agant, datur eis ut poenam impiorum perfecte intueantur.*

[2]Nietzsche quotes Tertullian in the original Latin. This footnote offers, first, an English translation, and then some discussion.

"Yes, and there are other sights: that last day of judgment, with its everlasting issues; that day unlooked for by the nations, the theme of their derision, when the world hoary with age, and all its many products, shall be consumed in one great flame! How vast a spectacle then bursts upon the eye! *What there excites my admiration? what my derision? Which sight gives me joy? which rouses me to exultation?*—as I see so many illustrious monarchs, whose reception into the heavens was publicly announced, groaning now in the lowest darkness with great Jove himself, and those, too, who bore witness of their exultation; governors of provinces, too, who persecuted the Christian name, in fires more fierce than those with which in the days of their pride they raged against the followers of Christ. What world's wise men besides, the very philosophers, in fact, who taught their followers that God had no concern in aught that is sublunary, and were wont to assure them that either they had no souls, or that they would never return to the bodies which at death they had left, now covered with shame before the poor deluded ones, as one fire consumes them! Poets also, trembling not before the judgment-seat of Rhadamanthus or Minos, but of the unexpected Christ! I shall have a better opportunity then of hearing the tragedians, louder-voiced in

(*continued*)

gaudeam! Ubi exultem, *spectans tot et tantos* **reges,** *qui in coelum recepti nuntia-bantur, cum ipso Jove et ipsis suis testibus in imis tenebris congemescentes! Item prae-sides"* (the provincial governors) *"persecutores dominici nominis saevioribus quam ipsi flammis saevierunt insultantibus contra Christianos liquescentes! Quos praeterea sapientes illos philosophos coram discipulis suis una conflagrantibus erubescentes, quibus nihil ad deum pertinere suadebant, quibus animas aut nullas aut non in pristina corpora redituras affirmabant! Etiam poëtas non ad Rhadamanti nec ad Minois, sed ad inopinati Christi tribunal palpitantes! Tunc magis tragoedi audiendi, magis scil-icet vocales"* (in better voice, yet worse screamers) *"in sua propria calamitate; tunc histriones cognoscendi, solutiores multo per ignem; tunc, spectandus auriga in flam-mea rota totus rubens, tunc xystici contemplandi non in gymnasiis, sed in igne jacu-lati, nisi quod ne tunc quidem illos velim vivos, ut qui malim ad eos potius conspectum* **insatiabilem** *conferre, qui in dominum desaevierunt. 'Hic est ille,' dicam, 'fabri aut quaestuariae filius'"* (what follows, and especially this term for the mother of Jesus, which is found in the Talmud, shows that from here on Tertullian is referring to the Jews), *"'sabbati destructor, Samarites et daemonium habens. Hic est, quem a Juda redemistis, hic est ille arundine et colaphis diver-beratus, sputamentis dedecora-*

---

their own calamity; of viewing the play-actors, much more 'dissolute' [another translation has "much lither of limb"] in the dissolving flame; of looking upon the charioteer, all glowing in his chariot of fire; of beholding the wrestlers, not in their gymnasia, but tossing in the fiery billows; unless even then I shall not care to attend to such ministers of sin, in my eager wish rather to fix a gaze *insatiable* on those whose fury vented itself against the Lord. 'This,' I shall say, 'this is that carpenter's or hireling's son, that Sabbath-breaker, that Samaritan and devil-possessed! This is He whom you purchased from Judas! [*Quaestuaria* means prostitute, not carpenter: see Nietzsche's parenthesis above.] This is He whom you struck with reed and fist, whom you contemptuously spat upon, to whom you gave gall and vinegar to drink! This is He whom His disciples secretly stole away, that it might be said He had risen again, or the gardener abstracted, that his lettuces might come to no harm from the crowds of visitants!' What quaestor or priest in his munifi-cence will bestow on you the favour of seeing and *exulting in such things as these*? And yet even now we in a measure have them *by faith* in the picturings of imagination. But what are the things which eye has not seen, ear has not heard, and which have not so much as dimly dawned upon the human heart? Whatever they are, they are nobler, I believe, than circus, and both theatres, and every race-course." [Translation by the Rev. S. Thelwall.] There are two standard transla-tions of Tertullian's *De Spectaculis.* One is by the Rev. S. Thelwall in *The Ante-Nicene Fathers: Trans-lations of The Writings of the Fathers down to A.D. 325,* edited by the Rev. Alexander Roberts, D.D. and James Donaldson, LL.D., in volume III: *Latin Christianity: Its Founder, Tertullian* (American Reprint of the Edinburgh Edition, Grand Rapids, Mich., Wm. B. Eerdmans Pub-lishing Company, 1957). The other translation is by Rudolph Arbesmann, O.S.A., Ph.D., Ford-ham University, in *The Fathers of the Church: A New Translation,* in the volume entitled *Tertullian: Disciplinary, Moral and Ascetical Works* (New York, Fathers of the Church, Inc., 1959, Impri-matur Francis Cardinal Spellman).

In the former edition we are told in a footnote to the title that although there has been some dispute as to whether the work was written before or after Tertullian's "lapse" from orthodoxy to

tus, felle et aceto potatus. Hic est, quem clam discentes subripuerunt, ut resurrexisse dicatur vel hortulanus detraxit, ne lactucae suae frequentia commeantium laederentur.' Ut talia spectes, **ut talibus exultes,** *quis tibi praetor aut consul aut guaestor aut sacerdos de sua liberalitate praestabit? Et tamen haec jam habemus quodammodo* **per fidem** *spiritu imaginante repraesentata. Ceterum qualia illa sunt, quae nec oculus vidit nec auris audivit nec in cor hominis ascenderunt?"* (1 Cor. 2,9.) *"Credo circo et utraque cavea"* (first and fourth rank or, according to others, the comic and tragic stage) *"et omni stadio gratiora."*—**Perfidem:** thus is it written.

16

Let us conclude. The two *opposing* values "good and bad," "good and evil" have been engaged in a fearful struggle on earth for thousands of years; and though the latter value has certainly been on top for a long time, there are still places where the struggle is as yet undecided. One might even say that it has risen ever higher and thus become more and more profound and spiritual: so that today there is perhaps no more decisive mark of a *"higher nature,"* a more spiritual

---

Montanism, "a work so colourless that doctors can disagree about even its shading, must be regarded as practically orthodox. Exaggerated expressions are but the characteristics of the author's genius. We find the like in all writers of strongly marked individuality. Neander dates this treatise *circa* A.D. 197." And in a footnote to the last sentence quoted by Nietzsche, which concludes the last chapter of the treatise, we read: "This concluding chapter, which Gibbon delights to censure, because its fervid rhetoric so fearfully depicts the punishments of Christ's enemies, 'appears to Dr. Neander to contain a beautiful specimen of lively faith and Christian confidence.'"

In the latter edition we are informed that *"De Spectaculis* is one of Tertullian's most interesting and original works" (p. 38). And chapter 30, which Nietzsche quotes almost in its entirety, omitting only the first four lines, is introduced by a footnote that begins (and it continues in the same vein): "Tertullian gives here a colorful description of the millennium, picturing the feverish expectation of an early return of Christ . . ."

It is noteworthy that the Protestant edition finds the work "so colourless," while the Roman Catholic edition considers it "colorful"—and neither of them evinces any sensitivity to what outraged Nietzsche or Gibbon.

Edward Gibbon's comments are found in Chapter XV of *The History of The Decline and Fall of the Roman Empire:* "The condemnation of the wisest and most virtuous of the Pagans, on account of their ignorance or disbelief of the divine truth, seems to offend the reason and the humanity of the present age. But the primitive church, whose faith was of a much firmer consistence, delivered over, without hesitation, to eternal torture the far greater part of the human species. . . . These rigid sentiments, which had been unknown to the ancient world, appear to have infused a spirit of bitterness into a system of love and harmony. . . . The Christians, who, in this world, found themselves oppressed by the power of the Pagans, were sometimes seduced by resentment and spiritual pride to delight in the prospect of their future triumph. 'You are fond of spectacles,' exclaims the stern Tertullian; 'except the greatest of all spectacles, the last and eternal judgment of the universe. How shall I admire, how laugh . . .'"

nature, than that of being divided in this sense and a genuine battleground of these opposed values.[1]

The symbol of this struggle, inscribed in letters legible across all human history, is "Rome against Judea, Judea against Rome":—there has hitherto been no greater event than *this* struggle, *this* question, *this* deadly contradiction. Rome felt the Jew to be something like anti-nature itself, its antipodal monstrosity as it were: in Rome the Jew stood "*convicted* of hatred for the whole humam race"; and rightly, provided one has a right to link the salvation and future of the human race with the unconditional dominance of aristocratic values, Roman values.

How, on the other hand, did the Jews feel about Rome? A thousand signs tell us; but it suffices to recall the Apocalypse of John, the most wanton of all literary outbursts that vengefulness has on its conscience. (One should not underestimate the profound consistency of the Christian instinct when it signed this book of hate with the name of the disciple of love, the same disciple to whom it attributed that amorous-enthusiastic Gospel: there is a piece of truth in this, however much literary counterfeiting might have been required to produce it.) For the Romans were the strong and noble, and nobody stronger and nobler has yet existed on earth or even been dreamed of: every remnant of them, every inscription gives delight, if only one divines *what* it was that was there at work. The Jews, on the contrary, were the priestly nation of *ressentiment par excellence,* in whom there dwelt an unequaled popular-moral genius: one only has to compare similarly gifted nations—the Chinese or the Germans, for instance—with the Jews, to sense which is of the first and which of the fifth rank.[2]

Which of them has won *for the present,* Rome or Judea? But there can be no doubt: consider to whom one bows down in Rome itself today, as if they were the epitome of all the highest values—and not only in Rome but over almost half the earth, everywhere that man has become tame or desires to become tame: *three Jews,* as is known, and *one Jewess* (Jesus of Nazareth, the fisherman Peter, the rug weaver Paul, and the mother of the aforementioned Jesus, named Mary). This is very remarkable: Rome has been defeated beyond all doubt.

---

[1] This remark, which recalls *Beyond Good and Evil,* section 200, is entirely in keeping with the way in which the contrast of master and slave morality is introduced in *Beyond Good and Evil,* section 260; and it ought not to be overlooked. It sheds a good deal of light not only on this contrast but also on Nietzsche's *amor fati,* his love of fate. Those who ignore all this material are to misunderstand Nietzsche's moral philosophy.

[2] Having said things that can easily be misconstrued as grist to the mill of the German anti-Semites, Nietzsche goes out of his way, as usual, to express his admiration for the Jews and his disdain for the Germans.

5   There was, to be sure, in the Renaissance an uncanny and glittering reawak-
ening of the classical ideal, of the noble mode of evaluating all things; Rome
itself, oppressed by the new superimposed Judaized Rome that presented the
aspect of an ecumenical synagogue and was called the "church," stirred like one
awakened from seeming death: but Judea immediately triumphed again, thanks
to that thoroughly plebeian (German and English) *ressentiment* movement called
the Reformation, and to that which was bound to arise from it, the restoration
of the church—the restoration too of the ancient sepulchral repose of classical
Rome.

With the French Revolution, Judea once again triumphed over the classical
ideal, and this time in an even more profound and decisive sense: the last political noblesse in Europe, that of the *French* seventeenth and eighteenth century,
collapsed beneath the popular instincts of *ressentiment*—greater rejoicing, more
uproarious enthusiasm had never been heard on earth! To be sure, in the midst
of it there occurred the most tremendous, the most unexpected thing: the ideal
of antiquity itself stepped *incarnate* and in unheard-of splendor before the eyes
and conscience of mankind—and once again, in opposition to the mendacious
slogan of *ressentiment,* "supreme rights of the majority," in opposition to the will
to the lowering, the abasement, the leveling and the decline and twilight of
mankind, there sounded stronger, simpler, and more insistently than ever the
terrible and rapturous counterslogan "supreme rights of the few"! Like a last
signpost to the *other* path, Napoleon appeared, the most isolated and late-born
man there has ever been, and in him the problem of the *noble ideal as such* made
flesh—one might well ponder *what* kind of problem it is: Napoleon, this synthesis of the *inhuman* and *superhuman.*

17

Was that the end of it? Had that greatest of all conflicts of ideals been placed *ad
acta*[1] for all time? Or only adjourned, indefinitely adjourned?

Must the ancient fire not some day flare up much more terribly, after much
longer preparation? More: must one not desire it with all one's might? even will
it? even promote it?

Whoever begins at this point, like my readers, to reflect and pursue his train

---

[1]Disposed of.

of thought will not soon come to the end of it—reason enough for me to come to an end, assuming it has long since been abundantly clear what my *aim* is, what the aim of that dangerous slogan is that is inscribed at the head of my last book *Beyond Good and Evil.*—At least this does *not* mean "Beyond Good and Bad."—

Note.[2] I take the opportunity provided by this treatise to express publicly and formally a desire I have previously voiced only in occasional conversation with scholars; namely, that some philosophical faculty might advance *historical* studies *of morality* through a series of academic prize-essays—perhaps this present book will serve to provide a powerful impetus in this direction. In case this idea should be implemented, I suggest the following question: It deserves the attention of philologists and historians as well as that of professional philosophers:

"*What light does linguistics, and especially the study of etymology, throw on the history of the evolution of moral concepts?*"

On the other hand, it is equally necessary to engage the interest of physiologists and doctors in these problems (of the *value* of existing evaluations); it may be left to academic philosophers to act as advocates and mediators in this matter too, after they have on the whole succeeded in the past in transforming the originally so reserved and mistrustful relations between philosophy, physiology, and medicine into the most amicable and fruitful exchange. Indeed, every table of values, every "thou shalt" known to history or ethnology, requires first a *physiological* investigation and interpretation, rather than a psychological one; and every one of them needs a critique on the part of medical science. The question: what is the *value* of this or that table of values and "morals"? should be viewed from the most divers perspectives; for the problem "value *for what?*" cannot be examined too subtly. Something, for example, that possessed obvious value in relation to the longest possible survival of a race (or to the enhancement of its power of adaptation to a particular climate or to the preservation of the greatest number) would by no means possess the same value if it were a question, for instance, of producing a stronger type. The well-being of the majority and the well-being of the few are opposite viewpoints of value: to consider the former *a priori* of higher value may be left to the naïveté of English biologists.—*All* the sciences have from now on to prepare the way for the future task of the philosophers: this task understood as the solution of the *problem of value,* the determination of the *order of rank among values.*

---

[2]*Anmerkung.*

READING/WRITING ASSISTS

Thesis (and its counterargument):

Readers often expect to find a clear statement of the writer's argument in a **thesis statement**, usually found in a sentence or two at the end of the first or, at the latest, second paragraph of an argumentative essay. Nietzsche's thesis, stated obliquely at the beginning of his essay, is in response to the argument of "British psychologists" (and later, philosophers) at odds with his own idea about the origins and nature of "good" and "evil." In the case of this essay, the **counterargument** may be more clear at the beginning of the essay than the argument itself. Nevertheless, once the counterargument is clarified, it is possible to state, though perhaps only in its most basic form, Nietzsche's viewpoint. Try to do so.

The Shape of the Argument:

"Mapping" the structure of an argument can help us better understand the argument itself, while also showing us new models for shaping our own arguments in essay form. Nietzsche's essay is divided into seventeen sections of varying lengths. As is the case in other essays constructed in this manner, carefully reading and analyzing the point of each section leads to an understanding of his larger argument, however complex and seemingly obscure. Such careful scrutiny helps to expose a number of contradictions and/or deliberate ambiguities in Nietzsche's line of thought. To better understand Nietzsche's main points about the origin and nature of the terms "good" and "evil"—and their relationship to "good" and "bad," it is best to start by outlining the entire essay, section by section, paragraph by paragraph:

Section 1:

Paragraph 1:   Nietzsche begins by accusing psychologists of dragging the "inner world" of human beings, i.e., shame, into the outer. What is it that pushes psychologists in this direction?

Paragraph 2:   What does Nietzsche hope for in those investigating the inner world (morality) of humans?

Section 2:

Paragraph 1:   What should be the task of moral philosophers/psychologists? Why is history so important to this task? How is the historical theory of these experts unhistorical?

Paragraph 2:   Nietzsche begins an explication of his quote from English psychologists in the paragraph above. Here is an excellent example of closely reading the words of others to refute their claims. The first part of the quotation deals with "unegoistic" actions and their relation to the good. What does Nietzsche conclude about the rationality of this claim? The next idea Nietzsche examines has to do with the difference between those who **do** good and those who **receive** good. How does Nietzsche's analysis of this relationship differ from his predecessors?

Section 3:

Paragraph 1:   Continuation of the explication of above quotation. Here Nietzsche analyzes the word "forgot." What does Nietzsche conclude about the "forgotten" utility of the unegoistic action?

Section 4:

Paragraph 1:   Ever the philologist, Nietzsche now delves into the etymological sources of the words "good" and "bad." Is there any point in doing so?

Paragraph 2:   What does Nietzsche claim is the democratic prejudice toward all questions of origin?

Section 5:

Paragraph 1:   Outline the example of "conceptual transformation" Nietzsche gives here. In the latter half of this paragraph, is Nietzsche himself guilty of a conceptual transformation?

Paragraph 2:   What additional conclusions about race and power does Nietzsche reach in this paragraph?

Paragraph 3:   **"Conjecture"**: What is the difference between conjecture and hypothesis?

Section 6:

Paragraph 1:   Another turn in terms, becoming typical in this essay: One mode of valuation develops into its opposite. How does this turn operate in Nietzsche's example of the priests? Notice also in this paragraph Nietzsche's mention of the **"Weir Mitchell cure."** Virginia Woolf underwent this treatment for her "depression."

Section 7:

Paragraph 1:   In trying to explain the competition between the "priestly caste" and the "warrior caste" to position themselves as the ultimate "good," what does Nietzsche argue about potency and impotency? Here Nietzsche sees all Jews as members of the "priestly caste." (Later, given his explanation regarding the origins of Christianity, one would assume practicing Christians should be included in the "priestly caste" as well.) Nietzsche is the thinker most often cited as the origin of the theories adopted by the Nazis to rationalize the Final Solution. In reading the remainder of this essay, form an opinion as to whether his theories could have been/were used as the basis for totalitarian (mis)rule.

Section 8:

Paragraph 1:   Out of "Jewish hatred" grew love?

Paragraph 2:   Christianity envisioned as a "Jewish plot." How does this plot work, exactly? Convincing hypothesis, or conjecture?

Paragraph 3:   Conclusion: Christianity as a "Jewish triumph." And then . . . silence.

Section 9:

Paragraph 1:   Interlocutor breaks in; notice quotation marks around this
                 passage. Here Nietzsche fabricates an imagined dialogue with
                 an imaginary listener. What is meant by "race" in this para-
                 graph? Does this definition differ in any way from current
                 definition/s?

Paragraph 2:   Nietzsche answers his respondent with silence. Why?

Section 10:

Paragraph 1:   Define Nietzsche's idea of *ressentiment*/resentment. Sound right?

Paragraph 2:   Resentment vs. the "noble" mode of valuation; "contempt."

Paragraph 3:   Further explanation of above.

Paragraph 4:   Further explanation of resentment.

Paragraph 5:   Psychological effects of forgetting/remembering—what is this
                 passage designed to do in service of the argument?

Section 11:

Paragraph 1:   How "noble morality" constructs "good"; how "slave moral-
                 ity" constructs "good."

Paragraph 2:   Nietzsche's famous "blond beast" is introduced. To whom is
                 Nietzsche referring here, and how do these people become the
                 "blond beast," the "ruler dyed in another color"?

Paragraph 3:   What, according to Nietzsche, is the connection between
                 what he calls the "noble race" and the "barbarian"?

Paragraph 4:   Here Nietzsche gives an example of the significance of subjec-
                 tive perception, the epochs.

Paragraph 5:   Must the "blond beast" be subdued by culture? Who repre-
                 sents the "blond beast" and who represents culture in this
                 paragraph?

Paragraph 6:   Why have we no longer anything to fear in humankind?

Section 12:

Paragraphs 1,   Bad air! What smells so rank to Nietzsche?
2, 3, 4, and 5:

Section 13:

Paragraph 1:   Return to original problem of definition.
Paragraphs 2   Parable of lambs to express a point regarding strength's
and 3:   expression of itself. Is it possible for the strong to be weak? Is
                  it ever desirable? Are the strong still strong without an expres-
                  sion of strength?
Paragraph 4:   Weakness expressed as a merit. Can the weak by definition be
                  strong?

Section 14:

This entire section seems to be almost a burlesque adaptation of Plato's "Allegory of
the Cave." It is a dialogue between Nietzsche and Mr. Rash and Curious. What is the
lesson or message Nietzsche hopes this allegorical dialogue will convey?

Section 15:

In this long section, Nietzsche quotes Aquinas and Tertullian with regard to the Last
Judgment. Do these examples strengthen or weaken his argument?

Section 16:

Paragraph 1:   Conclusions drawn about opposing values "good" and "bad."
Paragraph 2:   Nietzsche's "answer" to the question is posited in terms of
                  another opposition: "Rome against Judea," "Judea against
                  Rome." He claims the French Revolution—and by extension,
                  the American Revolution—are founded on the same ideals.
                  What sort of "triumph" of ideals does Nietzsche claim here?
                  Are his claims valid?

UNIT 10

Section 17:

Twilight of the Idols: It is the heading of his last book, *Beyond Good and Evil,* that Nietzsche refers to here, followed by the explanation: "That is, the old truth is approaching its end." What is the difference between "good" and "evil" and "good" and "bad"? Has Nietzsche's argument made the difference between these two binaries any more clear?

Rhetorical Moves:

(1) Section 11 contains perhaps the most major crux in all of Nietzsche's writing. Exactly whom is the "blond beast" supposed to represent? Proponents of the argument that Nietzsche's philosophy is based on extreme anti-Semitism read in this passage a direct correlation between the "blond beast" and the "blond Aryan" conqueror. Others, such as the notable Nietzsche scholar Walter Kaufmann, argue that "[t]he 'blond beast' is not a racial concept and does not refer to the 'Nordic race' of which the Nazis later made so much . . . the 'blondness' presumably refers to the beast, the lion" (*Nietzsche,* Chapter 7, section III).

To better understand the confusion here, refer to the end of **Section 11**, paragraph 1. As Nietzsche transitions from the first paragraph of this section to the second, it seems clear that he is referring to those who ascribe to the morality of resentment. The pronoun *they* in this paragraph seems to consistently refer to "men" of resentment. It is *they* who turn into beasts of prey, i.e., the "blond beast."

But in the final sentence of the second paragraph of this section, it is the members of the "noble races" who become the beast of prey, the "splendid blond beast." Paragraph 3 continues in this vein. Notably, the "noble races" Nietzsche lists at the end of this paragraph include the Scandinavian and the Germanic "races."

The interpretation of these two important transitions can lead to two completely different interpretations of his main idea. If the "blond beast" refers to those who value the morality of resentment, what effect on Nietzsche's larger argument would that conclusion bring with it? If the "blond beast" refers to Aryans and other "barbarian" (and the quotation marks are Nietzsche's) conquerors, what effect on Nietzsche's larger argument would that conclusion bring with it?

Considering other racial references earlier in the essay, and the overall conclusions reached at the end of this essay, which interpretation seems more plausible in context?

(2) Nietzsche's essay is riddled with binary oppositions. Here is just a sample:

good/evil
good/bad
egoistic/unegoistic
light/dark
noble/plebian
noble/slave
pure/impure
superiority/inferiority
inward/outward
action/reaction
active/passive
strong/weak

In the first sentence of **Section 7**, Nietzsche writes of "one mode of valuation developing into its opposite." Given that **each** of the terms above has a "valuation," does not this phrase describe Nietzsche's rhetorical *modus operandi* throughout this essay? It could be said that the argument, from a rhetorical standpoint, is based entirely on Nietzsche's ability to demonstrate the dynamics of "one mode of valuation developing into its opposite." Nietzsche repeatedly takes a pair of terms, assigns each a "mode of valuation" and then turns each term in the pair into its opposite. But what does this rhetorical wizardry do to/for Nietzsche's larger claims?

FLANNERY O'CONNOR

Mary Flannery O'Connor (1925–1964) was born on March 25, 1925, in Savannah, Georgia, the only child in a Catholic family. When she was only sixteen years old, her father died at 41 of lupus, the disease that would also prove fatal to O'Connor at 39.

A talented graphic artist, O'Connor graduated in 1945 from Georgia State College for Women, earning an A.B. degree in English. Two years later, in 1947, O'Connor finished her MFA in Creative Writing at the University of Iowa. She then moved to New York and Connecticut for a time, until her diagnosis forced her to return to her mother's farm in Milledgeville, Georgia, where she wrote for two hours each day and raised peacocks until her death. Fiercely private, little is known of her brief life.

O'Connor's first novel, Wise Blood, *was published in 1952. "Everything That Rises Must Converge" first appeared in her second short-story collection, published in 1965.*

EVERYTHING THAT RISES MUST CONVERGE
Flannery O'Connor

Her doctor had told Julian's mother that she must lose twenty pounds on account of her blood pressure, so on Wednesday nights Julian had to take her downtown on the bus for a reducing class at the Y. The reducing class was designed for working girls over fifty, who weighed from 165 to 200 pounds. His mother was one of the slimmer ones, but she said ladies did not tell their age or weight. She would not ride the buses by herself at night since they had been integrated, and because the reducing class was one of her few pleasures, necessary for her health, and *free,* she said Julian could at least put himself out to take her, considering all she did for him. Julian did not like to consider all she did for him, but every Wednesday night he braced himself and took her.

She was almost ready to go, standing before the hall mirror, putting on her hat, while he, his hands behind him, appeared pinned to the door frame, waiting like Saint Sebastian[1] for the arrows to begin piercing him. The hat was new and had cost her seven dollars and a half. She kept saying, "Maybe I shouldn't have paid that for it. No, I shouldn't have. I'll take it off and return it tomorrow. I shouldn't have bought it."

Julian raised his eyes to heaven. "Yes, you should have bought it," he said. "Put it on and let's go." It was a hideous hat. A purple velvet flap came down on one side of it and stood up on the other; the rest of it was green and looked like a cushion with the stuffing out. He decided it was less comical than jaunty and pathetic. Everything that gave her pleasure was small and depressed him.

She lifted the hat one more time and set it down slowly on top of her head. Two wings of gray hair protruded on either side of her florid face, but her eyes, sky-blue, were as innocent and untouched by experience as they must have been when she was ten. Were it not that she was a widow who had struggled fiercely to feed and clothe and put him through school and who was supporting him still, "until he got on his feet," she might have been a little girl that he had to take to town.

Excerpt from *Everything That Rises Must Converge*, by Flannery O'Connor (1965), Farrar, Straus & Giroux.

UNIT 10

449

5   "It's all right, it's all right," he said. "Let's go." He opened the door himself and
started down the walk to get her going. The sky was a dying violet and the houses
stood out darkly against it, bulbous liver-colored monstrosities of a uniform ugliness though no two were alike. Since this had been a fashionable neighborhood
forty years ago, his mother persisted in thinking they did well to have an apartment in it. Each house had a narrow collar of dirt around it in which sat, usually,
a grubby child. Julian walked with his hands in his pockets, his head down and
thrust forward and his eyes glazed with the determination to make himself completely numb during the time he would be sacrificed to her pleasure.

The door closed and he turned to find the dumpy figure, surmounted by the
atrocious hat, coming toward him. "Well," she said, "you only live once and
paying a little more for it, I at least won't meet myself coming and going."

"Some day I'll start making money," Julian said gloomily—he knew he never
would—"and you can have one of those jokes whenever you take the fit." But
first they would move. He visualized a place where the nearest neighbors would
be three miles away on either side.

"I think your're doing fine," she said, drawing on her gloves. "You've only been
out of school a year. Rome wasn't built in a day."

She was one of the few members of the Y reducing class who arrived in hat
and gloves and who had a son who had been to college. "It takes time," she said,
"and the world is in such a mess. This hat looked better on me than any of the
others, though when she brought it out I said, 'Take that thing back. I wouldn't
have it on my head,' and she said, 'Now wait till you see it on,' and when she
put it on me, I said, 'We-ull,' and she said, 'If you ask me, that hat does something for you and you do something for the hat, and besides,' she said, 'with
that hat, you won't meet yourself coming and going.'"

10   Julian thought he could have stood his lot better if she had been selfish, if she
had been an old hag who drank and screamed at him. He walked along, saturated
in depression, as if in the midst of his martyrdom he had lost his faith. Catching
sight of his long, hopeless, irritated face, she stopped suddenly with a grief-stricken
look, and pulled back on his arm. "Wait on me," she said. "I'm going to return
it. I was out of my head. I can pay the gas bill with the seven-fifty."

He caught her arm in a vicious grip. "You are not going to take it back," he
said. "I like it."

"Well," she said, "I don't think I ought . . ."

"Shut up and enjoy it," he muttered, more depressed than ever.

"With the world in the mess it's in," she said, "it's a wonder we can enjoy anything. I tell you, the bottom rail is on the top."

15   Julian sighed.

"Of course," she said, "if you know who you are, you can go anywhere." She said this every time he took her to the reducing class. "Most of them in it are not our kind of people," she said, "but I can be gracious to anybody. I know who I am."

"They don't give a damn for your graciousness," Julian said savagely. "Knowing who you are is good for one generation only. You haven't the foggiest idea where you stand now or who you are."

She stopped and allowed her eyes to flash at him. "I most certainly do know who I am," she said, "and if you don't know who you are, I'm ashamed of you."

"Oh hell," Julian said.

20   "Your great-grandfather was a former governor of this state," she said. "Your grandfather was a prosperous landowner. Your grandmother was a Godhigh."

"Will you look around you," he said tensely, "and see where you are now?" and he swept his arm jerkily out to indicate the neighborhood, which the growing darkness at least made less dingy.

"You remain what you are," she said. "Your great-grandfather had a plantation and two hundred slaves."

"There are no more slaves," he said irritably.

"They were better off when they were," she said. He groaned to see that she was off on that topic. She rolled onto it every few days like a train on an open track. He knew every stop, every junction, every swamp along the way, and knew the exact point at which her conclusion would roll majestically into the station: "It's ridiculous. It's simply not realistic. They should rise, yes, but on their own side of the fence."

25   "Let's skip it," Julian said.

"The ones I feel sorry for," she said, "are the ones that are half white. They're tragic."

"Will you skip it?"

"Suppose we were half white. We would certainly have mixed feelings."

"I have mixed feelings now," he groaned.

30   "Well let's talk about something pleasant," she said. "I remember going to Grandpa's when I was a little girl. Then the house had double stairways that went up to what was really the second floor—all the cooking was done on the first. I used to like to stay down in the kitchen on account of the way the walls smelled. I would sit with my nose pressed against the plaster and take deep breaths. Actually the place belonged to the Godhighs but your grandfather Chestny paid the mortgage and saved it for them. They were in reduced circumstances." she said, "but reduced or not, they never forgot who they were."

"Doubtless that decayed mansion reminded them," Julian muttered. He never spoke of it without contempt or thought of it without longing. He had seen it once when he was a child before it had been sold. The double stairways had rotted and been torn down. Negroes were living in it. But it remained in his mind as his mother had known it. It appeared in his dreams regularly. He would stand on the wide porch, listening to the rustle of oak leaves, then wander through the high-ceilinged hall into the parlor that opened onto it and gaze at the worn rugs and faded draperies. It occurred to him that it was he, not she, who could have appreciated it. He preferred its threadbare elegance to anything he could name and it was because of it that all the neighborhoods they had lived in had been a torment to him—whereas she had hardly known the difference. She called her insensitivity "being adjustable."

"And I remember the old darky who was my nurse, Caroline. There was no better person in the world. I've always had a great respect for my colored friends," she said. "I'd do anything in the world for them and they'd . . ."

"Will you for God's sake get off that subject?" Julian said. When he got on a bus by himself, he made it a point to sit down beside a Negro, in reparation as it were for his mother's sins.

"You're mighty touchy tonight," she said. "Do you feel all right?"

35   "Yes I feel all right," he said. "Now lay off."

She pursed her lips. "Well, you certainly are in a vile humor," she observed. "I just won't speak to you at all."

They had reached the bus stop. There was no bus in sight and Julian, his hands still jammed in his pockets and his head thrust forward, scowled down the empty street. The frustration of having to wait on the bus as well as ride on it began to creep up his neck like a hot hand. The presence of his mother was borne in upon him as she gave a pained sigh. He looked at her bleakly. She was holding herself very erect under the preposterous hat, wearing it like a banner of her imaginary dignity. There was in him an evil urge to break her spirit. He suddenly unloosened his tie and pulled it off and put it in his pocket.

She stiffened. "Why must you look like *that* when you take me to town?" she said. "Why must you deliberately embarrass me?"

"If you'll never learn where you are," he said, "you can at least learn where I am."

40   "You look like a—thug," she said.

"Then I must be one," he murmured.

"I'll just go home," she said. "I will not bother you. If you can't do a little thing like that for me . . ."

Rolling his eyes upward, he put his tie back on. "Restored to my class," he muttered. He thrust his face toward her and hissed, "True culture is in the mind, the *mind*," he said, and tapped his head, "the mind."

"It's in the heart," she said, "and in how you do things and how you do things is because of who you *are*."

45   "Nobody in the damn bus cares who you are."

"I care who I am," she said icily.

The lighted bus appeared on top of the next hill and as it approached, they moved out into the street to meet it. He put his hand under her elbow and hoisted her up on the creaking step. She entered with a little smile, as if she were going into a drawing room where everyone had been waiting for her. While he put in the tokens, she sat down on one of the broad front seats for three which faced the aisle. A thin woman with protruding teeth and long yellow hair was sitting on the end of it. His mother moved up beside her and left the room for Julian beside herself. He sat down and looked at the floor across the aisle where a pair of thin feet in red and white canvas sandals were planted.

His mother immediately began a general conversation meant to attract any-one who felt like talking. "Can it get any hotter?" she said and removed from her purse a folding fan, black with a Japanese scene on it, which she began to flutter before her.

"I reckon it might could," the woman with the protruding teeth said, "but I know for a fact my apartment couldn't get no hotter."

50   "It must get the afternoon sun," his mother said. She sat forward and looked up and down the bus. It was half filled. Everybody was white. "I see we have the bus to ourselves," she said. Julian cringed.

"For a change," said the woman across the aisle, the owner of the red and white canvas sandals. "I come on one the other day and they were thick as fleas— up front and all through."

"The world is in a mess everywhere," his mother said, "I don't know how we've let it get in this fix."

"What gets my goat is all those boys from good families stealing automobile tires," the woman with the protruding teeth said. "I told my boy, I said you may not be rich but you been raised right and if I ever catch you in any such mess, they can send you on to the reformatory. Be exactly where you belong."

"Training tells," his mother said. "Is your boy in high school?"

55   "Ninth grade," the woman said.

"My son just finished college last year. He wants to write but he's selling type-writers until he gets started," his mother said.

The woman leaned forward and peered at Julian. He threw her such a malevolent look that she subsided against the seat. On the floor across the aisle there was an abandoned newspaper. He got up and got it and opened it out in front of him. His mother discreetly continued the conversation in a lower tone but the woman across the aisle said in a loud voice, "Well that's nice. Selling typewriters is close to writing. He can go right from one to the other."

"I tell him," his mother said, "that Rome wasn't built in a day."

Behind the newspaper Julian was withdrawing into the inner compartment of his mind where he spent most of his time. This was a kind of mental bubble in which he established himself when he could not bear to be a part of what was going on around him. From it he could see out and judge but in it he was safe from any kind of penetration from without. It was the only place where he felt free of the general idiocy of his fellows. His mother had never entered it but from it he could see her with absolute clarity.

60   The old lady was clever enough and he thought that if she had started from any of the right premises, more might have been expected of her. She lived according to the laws of her own fantasy world, outside of which he had never seen her set foot. The law of it was to sacrifice herself for him after she had first created the necessity to do so by making a mess of things. If he had permitted her sacrifices, it was only because her lack of foresight had made them necessary. All of her life had been a struggle to act like a Chestny without the Chestny goods, and to give him everything she thought a Chestny ought to have; but since, said she, it was fun to struggle, why complain? And when you had won, as she had won, what fun to look back on the hard times! He could not forgive her that she had enjoyed the struggle and that she thought *she* had won.

What she meant when she said she had won was that she had brought him up successfully and had sent him to college and that he had turned out so well— good looking (her teeth had gone unfilled so that his could be straightened), intelligent (he realized he was too intelligent to be a success), and with a future ahead of him (there was of course no future ahead of him). She excused his gloominess on the grounds that he was still growing up and his radical ideas on his lack of practical experience. She said he didn't yet know a thing about "life," that he hadn't even entered the real world—when already he was as disenchanted with it as a man of fifty.

The further irony of all this was that in spite of her, he had turned out so well. In spite of going to only a third-rate college, he had, on his own initiative, come out with a first-rate education; in spite of growing up dominated by a small mind, he had ended up with a large one; in spite of all her foolish views, he was free of prejudice and unafraid to face facts. Most miraculous of all, instead of being blinded by love for her as she was for him, he had cut himself emotionally free of her and could see her with complete objectivity. He was not dominated by his mother.

The bus stopped with a sudden jerk and shook him from his meditation. A woman from the back lurched forward with little steps and barely escaped falling in his newspaper as she righted herself. She got off and a large Negro got on. Julian kept his paper lowered to watch. It gave him a certain satisfaction to see injustice in daily operation. It confirmed his view that with a few exceptions there was no one worth knowing within a radius of three hundred miles. The Negro was well dressed and carried a briefcase. He looked around and then sat down on the other end of the seat where the woman with the red and white canvas sandals was sitting. He immediately unfolded a newspaper and obscured himself behind it. Julian's mother's elbow at once prodded insistently into his ribs. "Now you see why I won't ride on these buses by myself," she whispered.

The woman with the red and white canvas sandals had risen at the same time the Negro sat down and had gone further back in the bus and taken the seat of the woman who had got off. His mother leaned forward and cast her an approving look.

65   Julian rose, crossed the aisle, and sat down in the place of the woman with the canvas sandals. From this position, he looked serenely across at his mother. Her face had turned an angry red. He stared at her, making his eyes the eyes of a stranger. He felt his tension suddenly lift as if he had openly declared war on her.

He would have liked to get in conversation with the Negro and to talk with him about art or politics or any subject that would be above the comprehension of those around them, but the man remained entrenched behind his paper. He was either ignoring the change of seating or had never noticed it. There was no way for Julian to convey his sympathy.

His mother kept her eyes fixed reproachfully on his face. The woman with the protruding teeth was looking at him avidly as if he were a type of monster new to her.

"Do you have a light?" he asked the Negro.

Without looking away from his paper, the man reached in his pocket and handed him a packet of matches.

70   "Thanks," Julian said. For a moment he held the matches foolishly. A NO SMOKING sign looked down upon him from over the door. This alone would not have deterred him; he had no cigarettes. He had quit smoking some months

before because he could not afford it. "Sorry," he muttered and handed back the matches. The Negro lowered the paper and gave him an annoyed look. He took the matches and raised the paper again.

His mother continued to gaze at him but she did not take advantage of his momentary discomfort. Her eyes retained their battered look. Her face seemed to be unnaturally red, as if her blood pressure had risen. Julian allowed no glimmer of sympathy to show on his face. Having got the advantage, he wanted desperately to keep it and carry it through. He would have liked to teach her a lesson that would last her a while, but there seemed no way to continue the point. The Negro refused to come out from behind his paper.

Julian folded his arms and looked stolidly before him, facing her but as if he did not see her, as if he had ceased to recognize her existence. He visualized a scene in which, the bus having reached their stop, he would remain in his seat and when she said, "Aren't you going to get off?" he would look at her as at a stranger who had rashly addressed him. The corner they got off on was usually deserted, but it was well lighted and it would not hurt her to walk by herself the four blocks to the Y. He decided to wait until the time came and then decide whether or not he would let her get off by herself. He would have to be at the Y at ten to bring her back, but he could leave her wondering if he was going to show up. There was no reason for her to think she could always depend on him.

He retired again into the high-ceilinged room sparsely settled with large pieces of antique furniture. His soul expanded momentarily but then he became aware of his mother across from him and the vision shriveled. He studied her coldly. Her feet in little pumps dangled like a child's and did not quite reach the floor. She was training on him an exaggerated look of reproach. He felt completely detached from her. At that moment he could with pleasure have slapped her as he would have slapped a particularly obnoxious child in his charge.

He began to imagine various unlikely ways by which he could teach her a lesson. He might make friends with some distinguished Negro professor or lawyer and bring him home to spend the evening. He would be entirely justified but her blood pressure would rise to 300. He could not push her to the extent of making her have a stroke, and moreover, he had never been successful at making any Negro friends. He had tried to strike up an acquaintance on the bus with some of the better types, with ones that looked like professors or ministers or lawyers. One morning he had sat down next to a distinguished-looking dark brown man who had answered his questions with a sonorous solemnity but who had turned out to be an undertaker. Another day he had sat down beside a cigar-smoking

Negro with a diamond ring on his finger, but after a few stilted pleasantries, the Negro had rung the buzzer and risen, slipping two lottery tickets into Julian's hand as he climbed over him to leave.

75   He imagined his mother lying desperately ill and his being able to secure only a Negro doctor for her. He toyed with that idea for a few minutes and then dropped it for a momentary vision of himself participating as a sympathizer in a sit-in demonstration. This was possible but he did not linger with it. Instead, he approached the ultimate horror. He brought home a beautiful suspiciously Negroid women. Prepare yourself, he said. There is nothing you can do about it. This is the woman I've chosen. She's intelligent, dignified, even good, and she's suffered and she hasn't thought it *fun*. Now persecute us, go ahead and persecute us. Drive her out of here, but remember, you're driving me too. His eyes were narrowed and through the indignation he had generated, he saw his mother across the aisle, purple-faced, shrunken to the dwarflike proportions of her moral nature, sitting like a mummy beneath the ridiculous banner of her hat.

He was tilted out of his fantasy again as the bus stopped. The door opened with a sucking hiss and out of the dark a large, gaily dressed, sullen-looking colored women got on with a little boy. The child, who might have been four, had on a short plaid suit and a Tyrolean hat with a blue feather in it. Julian hoped that he would sit down beside him and that the woman would push in beside his mother. He could think of no better arrangement.

As she waited for her tokens, the woman was surveying the seating possibilities—he hoped with the idea of sitting where she was least wanted. There was something familiar-looking about her but Julian could not place what it was. She was a giant of a woman. Her face set not only to meet opposition but to seek it out. The downward tilt of her larger lower lip was like a warning sign: DON'T TAMPER WITH ME. Her bulging figure was encased in a green crepe dress and her feet overflowed in red shoes. She had on a hideous hat. A purple velvet flap came down on one side of it and stood up on the other; the rest of it was green and looked like a cushion with the stuffing out. She carried a mammoth red pocketbook that bulged throughout as if it were stuffed with rocks.

To Julian's disappointment, the little boy climbed up on the empty seat beside his mother. His mother lumped all children, black and white, into the common category, "cute," and she thought little Negroes were on the whole cuter than little white children. She smiled at the little boy as he climbed on the seat.

Meanwhile the woman was bearing down upon the empty seat beside Julian. To his annoyance, she squeezed herself into it. He saw his mother's face change as the woman settled herself next to him and he realized with satisfaction that this was more objectionable to her than it was to him. Her face seemed almost gray and there was a look of dull recognition in her eyes, as if suddenly she had sickened at some awful confrontation. Julian saw that it was because she and the woman had, in a sense, swapped sons. Though his mother would not realize the symbolic significance of this, she would feel it. His amusement showed plainly on his face.

80   The woman next to him muttered something unintelligible to herself. He was conscious of a kind of bristling next to him, muted growling like that of an angry cat. He could not see anything but the red pocketbook upright on the bulging green thighs. He visualized the woman as she had stood waiting for her tokens— the ponderous figure, rising from the red shoes upward over the solid hips, the mammoth bosom, the haughty face, to the green and purple hat.

His eyes widened.

The vision of the two hats, identical, broke upon him with the radiance of a brilliant sunrise. His face was suddenly lit with joy. He could not believe that Fate had thrust upon his mother such a lesson. He gave a loud chuckle so that she would look at him and see that he saw. She turned her eyes on him slowly. The blue in them seemed to have turned a bruised purple. For a moment he had an uncomfortable sense of her innocence, but it lasted only a second before principle rescued him. Justice entitled him to laugh. His grin hardened until it said to her as plainly as if he were saying aloud: Your punishment exactly fits your pettiness. This should teach you a permanent lesson.

Her eyes shifted to the woman. She seemed unable to bear looking at him and to find the woman preferable. He became conscious again of the bristling presence at his side. The woman was rumbling like a volcano about to become active. His mother's mouth began to twitch slightly at one corner. With a sinking heart, he saw incipient signs of recovery on her face and realized that this was going to strike her suddenly as funny and was going to be no lesson at all. She kept her eyes on the woman and an amused smile came over her face as if the woman were a monkey that had stolen her hat. The little Negro was looking up at her with large fascinated eyes. He had been trying to attract her attention for some time.

"Carver!" the woman said suddenly. "Come heah!"

85   When he saw that the spotlight was on him at last, Carver drew his feet up and turned himself toward Julian's mother and giggled.

"Carver!" the woman said. "You heah me? Come heah!"

Carver slid down from the seat but remained squatting with his back against the base of it, his head turned slyly around toward Julian's mother, who was smiling at him. The woman reached a hand across the aisle and snatched him to her. He righted himself and hung backwards on her knees, grinning at Julian's mother. "Isn't he cute?" Julian's mother said to the woman with the protruding teeth.

"I reckon he is," the woman said without conviction.

The Negress yanked him upright but he eased out of her grip and shot across the aisle and scrambled, giggling wildly, onto the seat beside his love.

90 "I think he likes me," Julian's mother said, and smiled at the woman. It was the smile she used when she was being particularly gracious to an inferior. Julian saw everything lost. The lesson had rolled off her like rain on a roof.

The woman stood up and yanked the little boy off the seat as if she were snatching him from contagion. Julian could feel the rage in her at having no weapon like his mother's smile. She gave the child a sharp slap across his leg. He howled once and then thrust his head into her stomach and kicked his feet against her shins. "Behave," she said vehemently.

The bus stopped and the Negro who had been reading the newspaper got off. The woman moved over and set the little boy down with a thump between herself and Julian. She held him firmly by the knee. In a moment he put his hands in front of his face and peeped at Julian's mother through his fingers.

"I see yoooooooo!" she said and put her hand in front of her face and peeped at him.

The woman slapped his hand down. "Quit yo' foolishness," she said, "before I knock the living Jesus out of you!"

95 Julian was thankful that the next stop was theirs. He reached up and pulled the cord. The woman reached up and pulled it at the same time. Oh my God, he thought. He had the terrible intuition that when they got off the bus together, his mother would open her purse and give the little boy a nickel. The gesture would be as natural to her as breathing. The bus stopped and the woman got up and lunged to the front, dragging the child, who wished to stay on, after her. Julian and his mother got up and followed. As they neared the door, Julian tried to relieve her of her pocketbook.

"No," she murmured, "I want to give the little boy a nickel."

"No!" Julian hissed. "No!"

She smiled down at the child and opened her bag. The bus door opened and the woman picked him up by the arm and descended with him, hanging at her hip. Once in the street she set him down and shook him.

Julian's mother had to close her purse while she got down the bus step but as soon as her feet were on the ground, she opened it again and began to rummage inside. "I can't find but a penny," she whispered, "but it looks like a new one."

100   "Don't do it!" Julian said fiercely between his teeth. There was a streetlight on the corner and she hurried to get under it so that she could better see into her pocketbook. The woman was heading off rapidly down the street with the child still hanging backward on her hand.

"Oh little boy!" Julian's mother called and took a few quick steps and caught up with them just beyond the lamppost. "Here's a bright new penny for you," and she held out the coin, which shone bronze in the dim light.

The huge woman turned and for a moment stood, her shoulders lifted and her face frozen with frustrated rage, and stared at Julian's mother. Then all at once she seemed to explode like a piece of machinery that had been given one ounce of pressure too much. Julian saw the black fist swing out with the red pocketbook. He shut his eyes and cringed as he heard the woman shout. "He don't take nobody's pennies!" When he opened his eyes, the woman was disappearing down the street with the little boy staring wide-eyed over her shoulder. Julian's mother was sitting on the sidewalk.

"I told you not to do that," Julian said angrily. " I told you not to do that!"

He stood over her for a minute, gritting his teeth. Her legs were stretched out in front of her and her hat was on her lap. He squatted down and looked her in the face. It was totally expressionless. "You got exactly what you deserved," he said. "Now get up."

105   He picked up her pocketbook and put what had fallen out back in it. He picked the hat up off her lap. The penny caught his eye on the sidewalk and he picked that up and let it drop before her eyes into the purse. Then he stood up and leaned over and held his hands out to pull her up. She remained immobile. He sighed. Rising above them on either side were black apartment buildings, marked with irregular rectangles of light. At the end of the block a man came out of a door and walked off in the opposite direction. "All right," he said, "suppose somebody happens by and wants to know why you're sitting on the sidewalk?"

She took the hand and, breathing hard, pulled heavily up on it and then stood for a moment, swaying slightly as if the spots of light in the darkness were circling around her. Her eyes, shadowed and confused, finally settled on his face. He did not try to conceal his irritation. "I hope this teaches you a lesson," he said. She leaned forward and her eyes raked his face. She seemed trying to determine his identity. Then, as if she found nothing familiar about him, she started off with a headlong movement in the wrong direction.

"Aren't you going on to the Y?" he asked.

"Home," she muttered.

"Well, are we walking?"

110   For answer she kept going. Julian followed along, his hands behind him. He saw no reason to let the lesson she had had go without backing it up with an explanation of its meaning. She might as well be made to understand what had happened to her. "Don't think that was just an uppity Negro woman," he said. "That was the whole colored race which will no longer take your condescending pennies. That was your black double. She can wear the same hat as you, and to be sure," he added gratuitously (because he thought it was funny), "it looked better on her than it did on you. What all this means," he said, "is that the old world is gone. The old manners are obsolete and your graciousness is not worth a damn." He thought bitterly of the house that had been lost for him. "You aren't who you think you are," he said.

She continued to plow ahead, paying no attention to him. Her hair had come undone on one side. She dropped her pocketbook and took no notice. He stooped and picked it up and handed it to her but she did not take it.

"You needn't act as if the world had come to an end," he said, "because it hasn't. From now on you've got to live in a new world and face a few realities for a change. Buck up," he said, "it won't kill you."

She was breathing fast.

"Let's wait on the bus," he said.

115   "Home," she said thickly.

"I hate to see you behave like this," he said. "Just like a child. I should be able to expect more of you." He decided to stop where he was and make her stop and wait for a bus. "I'm not going any farther," he said, stopping. "We're going on the bus."

She continued to go on as if she had not heard him. He took a few steps and caught her arm and stopped her. He looked into her face and caught his breath. He was looking into a face he had never seen before. "Tell Grandpa to come get me," she said.

He stared, stricken.

"Tell Caroline to come get me," she said.

120   Stunned, he let her go and she lurched forward again, walking as if one leg were shorter than the other. A tide of darkness seemed to be sweeping her from him. "Mother!" he cried. "Darling, sweetheart, wait!" Crumpling, she fell to the pavement. He dashed forward and fell at her side, crying, "Mamma, Mamma!" He turned her over. Her face was fiercely distorted. One eye, large and staring,

UNIT 10

moved slightly to the left as if it had become unmoored. The other remained fixed on him, raked his face again, found nothing, and closed.

"Wait here, wait here!" he cried and jumped up and began to run for help toward a cluster of lights he saw in the distance ahead of him. "Help, help!" he shouted, but his voice was thin, scarcely a thread of sound. The lights drifted farther away the faster he ran and his feet moved numbly as if they carried him nowhere. The tide of darkness seemed to sweep him back to her, postponing from moment to moment his entry into the world of guilt and sorrow.

LEVELS OF READING

Summary:

Pay attention to the **literal** meaning of the text. Briefly describe the narrative of Flannery O'Connor's "Everything That Rises Must Converge." Repeat the story of the text in your own words. Who tells this story? Who are the players in this little drama? State in a few sentences the "persona" of each of the characters in this story. What happens to each of them? Concentrate on the highlights; avoid too much detail when summarizing. Again, drawing a simple outline of the main points of the text will help you better analyze the text at other levels of interpretation.

Analysis:

Find what you believe is **symbolic** in the text. What is the significance of Julian's mother attending a "reducing class"? What does her hat symbolize? Why is it important that Julian has been to college? Why is Julian's mother's tracing of her—and his—lineage important to the symbolism of this story? What is the significance of the penny Julian's mother offers? Find any other symbols you think are important in the story and explain the meaning of these symbols. With the help of the background material provided about Flannery O'Connor and her world, make an argument about this text, and include the mention of the more **figurative** aspects of the text when making points in defense of your argument.

Application:

Apply Nietzsche's theory of "good" and "evil" to "Everything that Rises Must Converge." Outline an argument you wish to make about this literary text using

Nietzsche's theory to help you explain what some part of the story may mean. The "part" of the text you choose to analyze may include any of the following: a character, a setting, a symbol or symbols, an important change, a motivation, a goal, a result. Consider the following as possibilities, but explore other original interpretations too:

- Are Nietzsche's notions of "good" and "evil" important here or are his ideas about "good" and "bad" more useful in analyzing O'Connor's story?
- Are Nietzsche's ideas about the connections between "race" and "power" useful in understanding O'Connor's characters?
- Does Julian's mother engage in a "slave morality" or a "noble morality" or a bit of both?
- Relate Nietzsche's idea of **resentment** to Julian, his mother, the mother of the child on the bus, or all involved.
- Is it possible to equate Nietzsche's **blond beast** with the character of any of these characters?
- According to Nietzsche, what might be the effects of Julian's mother "remembering" so much of her past? Is Julian's mother guilty of the "democratic prejudice" regarding "all notions of origin"?
- Has Julian's education helped him gain "conceptual transformation"? How so?

Start Your Own Argument:

Should Nietzsche's argument be blamed for the excesses of totalitarianism?

UNIT 10

NICCOLÓ MACHIAVELLI

Niccoló Machiavelli (1469–1527) was born to a wealthy Florentine lawyer. In 1498, he began his career as a politician in the independent city-state of Florence. He was sent on diplomatic missions to Germany and France, as well as other city-states within what is now Italy. When the republic collapsed ten years later, he was driven into exile, where he spent his retirement writing. All of his books, including his most famous, The Prince *(1513), were published after his death.*

The main question of The Prince *is whether or not a prince can maintain his glory while serving the public interest. Machiavelli also wonders if practical political success can be achieved only at the expense of traditional moral values. Must the prince be ruthless, deceptive, and selfish to be successful? Machiavelli's answers to these questions have made his name into an adjective often used to describe those who maintain power through cunning: "Machiavellian."*

ON THOSE WHO HAVE BECOME PRINCES THROUGH WICKEDNESS
Niccoló Machiavelli

But because there are yet two more ways one can from an ordinary citizen become prince, which cannot completely be attributed to either Fortune or skill, I believe they should not be left unmentioned, although one of them will be discussed at greater length in a treatise on republics. These two are: when one becomes prince through some wicked and nefarious means or when a private citizen becomes prince of his native city through the favor of his fellow citizens. And in discussing the first way, I shall cite two examples, one from classical times and the other from recent days, without otherwise entering into the merits of this method, since I consider them sufficient for anyone forced to imitate them.

Agathocles the Sicilian, not only from being an ordinary citizen but from being of low and abject status, became King of Syracuse. This man, a potter's son, lived a wicked life at every stage of his career; yet he joined to his wickedness such strength of mind and of body that, when he entered upon a military career, he rose through the ranks to become commander of Syracuse. Once placed in such a position, having considered becoming prince and holding with violence and without any obligations to others what had been granted to him by universal consent, and having made an agreement with Hamilcar the Carthaginian, who was waging war with his armies in Sicily, he called together one morning the people and the senate of Syracuse as if he were going to discuss things concerning the state; and with a prearranged signal, he had his troops kill all the senators and the richest members of the populace; and when they were dead, he seized and held the rule of the city without any opposition from the citizenry. And although he was twice defeated by the Carthaginians and eventually besieged, not only was he able to defend his city but, leaving part of his troops for the defense of the siege, with his other men he attacked Africa, and in a short time he freed Syracuse from the siege and forced the Carthaginians into dire straits: they were obliged to make peace with him and to be content with possession of Africa and to leave Sicily to Agathocles.

Excerpts from *The Prince,* by Niccoló Machiavelli, reprinted from *The Portable Machiavelli,* edited and translated by Peter Bondanella and Mark Musa (1979), by permission of Viking Penguin, a division of Penguin Group (USA) Inc. Copyright © 1979 by Viking Penguin, Inc.

Anyone, therefore, who examines the deeds and the life of this man will observe nothing or very little that can be attributed to Fortune; since, as was said earlier, not with the aid of others but by rising through the ranks, which involved a thousand hardships and dangers, did he come to rule the principality which he then maintained by many brave and dangerous efforts. Still, it cannot be called skill to kill one's fellow citizens, to betray friends, to be without faith, without mercy, without religion; by these means one can acquire power but not glory. For if one were to consider Agathocles's ability in getting into and out of dangers, and his greatness of spirit in supporting and in overcoming adversities, one can see no reason why he should be judged inferior to any most excellent commander; nevertheless, his vicious cruelty and inhumanity, along with numerous wicked deeds, do not permit us to honor him among the most excellent of men. One cannot, therefore, attribute to either Fortune or skill what he accomplished without either the one or the other.

In our own days, during the reign of Alexander VI, Oliverotto of Fermo, who many years before had been left as a child without a father, was brought up by his maternal uncle, Giovanni Fogliani. In the early days of his youth he was sent to serve as a soldier under Paulo Vitelli so that, once he was versed in that skill, he might attain some outstanding military position. Then, after Paulo died, he served under his brother, Vitellozzo; and in a very brief time, because of his intelligence and his vigorous body and mind, he became the commander of his troops. But since he felt it was servile to work for others, he decided to seize Fermo with the aid of some citizens of Fermo who preferred servitude to the liberty of their native city, and with the assistance of the followers of Vitellozzo; and he wrote to Giovanni Fogliani about how, having been away many years from home, he wished to come to see him and his city and to inspect his inheritance; and since he had exerted himself for no other reason than to acquire glory, he wanted to arrive in honorable fashion, accompanied by an escort of a hundred horsemen from among his friends and servants so that his fellow citizens might see that he had not spent his time in vain; and he begged his uncle to arrange for an honorable reception from the people of Fermo, one which might bring honor not only to Giovanni but also to himself, being his pupil. Giovanni, therefore, in no way failed in his duty toward his nephew: he had him received in honorable fashion by the people of Fermo, and he gave him rooms in his own house. Oliverotto, after a few days had passed and he had secretly made the preparations necessary for his forthcoming wickedness, gave a magnificent banquet to which he invited Giovanni Fogliani and all of the first citizens of Fermo. And when the meal and all the other entertainment customary at such banquets were completed, Oliverotto, according to plan, began to discuss serious matters, speaking of the greatness of Pope Alexander and his son, Cesare, and of their undertakings. After Giovanni and the others had replied to his comments, he suddenly rose up, announcing that these were matters to be discussed in a more secluded place; and he retired into another room, followed by Giovanni and all the other citizens. No sooner were they seated than from secret places in the room out came soldiers who killed Giovanni and all the others. After this murder, Oliverotto mounted his horse, paraded through the town, and besieged the chief officials in the government palace; so that out of fear they were forced to obey him and to constitute a government of which he made himself prince. And when all those were killed who, if they had been discontent, might have threatened him, he strengthened himself by instituting new civil and military laws; so that, in the space of the year that he held the principality, not only was he secure in the city of Fermo, but he had become feared by all its neighbors. His expulsion would have been as difficult as that of Agathocles if he had not permitted himself to be tricked by Cesare Borgia, when at Sinigaglia, as was noted above, the Duke captured the Orsini and the Vitelli; there he, too, was captured, a year after he committed the parricide, and together with Vitellozzo, who had been his teacher in ingenuity and wickedness, he was strangled.

5   One might wonder how Agathocles and others like him, after so many betrayals and cruelties, could live for such a long time secure in their cities and defend themselves from outside enemies without being plotted against by their own citizens; many others, using cruel means, were unable even in peaceful times to hold on to their state, not to speak of the uncertain times of war. I believe that this depends on whether cruelty be well or badly used. Well used are those cruelties (if it is permitted to speak well of evil) that are carried out in a single stroke, done out of necessity to protect oneself, and are not continued but are instead converted into the greatest possible benefits for the subjects. Badly used are those cruelties which, although being few at the outset, grow with the passing of time instead of disappearing. Those who follow the first method can remedy their condition with God and with men as Agathocles did; the others cannot possibly survive.

Wherefore it is to be noted that in taking a state its conqueror should weigh all the harmful things he must do and do them all at once so as not to have to repeat them every day, and in not repeating them to be able to make men feel secure and to win them over with the benefits he bestows upon them. Anyone who does otherwise, either out of timidity or because of poor advice, is always obliged to keep his knife in his hand; nor can he ever count upon his subjects, who, because of their fresh and continual injuries, cannot feel secure with him. Injuries, therefore, should be inflicted all at the same time, for the less they are tasted, the less they offend; and benefits should be distributed a bit at a time in order that they may be savored fully. And a prince should, above all, live with his subjects in such a way that no unforeseen event, either good or bad, may make him alter his course; for when emergencies arise in adverse conditions, you are not in time to resort to cruelty, and that good you do will help you little, since it will be judged a forced measure and you will earn from it no thanks whatsoever.

ON CRUELTY AND MERCY AND WHETHER IT IS BETTER TO BE LOVED THAN TO BE FEARED OR THE CONTRARY
Niccoló Machiavelli

Proceeding to the other qualities mentioned above, I say that every prince must desire to be considered merciful and not cruel; nevertheless, he must take care not to misuse this mercy. Cesare Borgia was considered cruel; nonetheless, his cruelty had brought order to Romagna, united it, restored it to peace and obedience. If we examine this carefully, we shall see that he was more merciful than the Florentine people, who, in order to avoid being considered cruel, allowed the destruction of Pistoia. Therefore, a prince must not worry about the reproach of cruelty when it is a matter of keeping his subjects united and loyal; for with a very few examples of cruelty he will be more compassionate than those who, out of excessive mercy, permit disorders to continue, from which arise murders and plundering; for these usually harm the community at large, while the executions that come from the prince harm one individual in particular. And the new prince, above all other princes, cannot escape the reputation of being called cruel, since new states are full of dangers. And Virgil, through Dido, states: "My difficult condition and the newness of my rule make me act in such a manner, and to set guards over my land on all sides."

Nevertheless, a prince must be cautious in believing and in acting, nor should he be afraid of his own shadow; and he should proceed in such a manner, tempered by prudence and humanity, so that too much trust may not render him imprudent nor too much distrust render him intolerable.

From this arises an argument: whether it is better to be loved than to be feared, or the contrary. I reply that one should like to be both one and the other; but since it is difficult to join them together, it is much safer to be feared than to be loved when one of the two must be lacking. For one can generally say this about men: that they are ungrateful, fickle, simulators and deceivers, avoiders of danger, greedy for gain; and while you work for their good they are completely yours, offering

UNIT 10

you their blood, their property, their lives, and their sons, as I said earlier, when danger is far away; but when it comes nearer to you they turn away. And that prince who bases his power entirely on their words, finding himself stripped of other preparations, comes to ruin; for friendships that are acquired by a price and not by greatness and nobility of character are purchased but are not owned, and at the proper moment they cannot be spent. And men are less hesitant about harming someone who makes himself loved than one who makes himself feared because love is held together by a chain of obligation which, since men are a sorry lot, is broken on every occasion in which their own self-interest is concerned; but fear is held together by a dread of punishment which will never abandon you.

A prince must nevertheless make himself feared in such a manner that he will avoid hatred, even if he does not acquire love; since to be feared and not to be hated can very well be combined; and this will always be so when he keeps his hands off the property and the women of his citizens and his subjects. And if he must take someone's life, he should do so when there is proper justification and manifest cause; but, above all, he should avoid the property of others; for men forget more quickly the death of their father than the loss of their patrimony. Moreover, the reasons for seizing their property are never lacking; and he who begins to live by stealing always finds a reason for taking what belongs to others; on the contrary, reasons for taking a life are rarer and disappear sooner.

5   But when the prince is with his armies and has under his command a multitude of troops, then it is absolutely necessary that he not worry about being considered cruel; for without that reputation he will never keep an army united or prepared for any combat. Among the praiseworthy deeds of Hannibal is counted this: that, having a very large army, made up of all kinds of men, which he commanded in foreign lands, there never arose the slightest dissention, neither among themselves nor against their prince, both during his good and his bad fortune. This could not have arisen from anything other than his inhuman cruelty, which, along with his many other abilities, made him always respected and terrifying in the eyes of his soldiers; and without that, to attain the same effect, his other abilities would not have sufficed. And the writers of history, having considered this matter very little, on the one hand admire these deeds of his and on the other condemn the main cause of them.

And that it be true that his other abilities would not have been sufficient can be seen from the example of Scipio, a most extraordinary man not only in his time but in all recorded history, whose armies in Spain rebelled against him; this came about from nothing other than his excessive compassion, which gave to his soldiers more liberty than military discipline allowed. For this he was censured in the senate by Fabius Maximus, who called him the corruptor of the Roman militia. The Locrians, having been ruined by one of Scipio's officers, were not avenged by him, nor was the arrogance of that officer corrected, all because of his tolerant nature; so that someone in the senate who tried to apologize for him said that there were many men who knew how not to err better than they knew how to correct errors. Such a nature would have, in time, damaged Scipio's fame and glory if he had maintained it during the empire; but, living under the control of the senate, this harmful characteristic of his not only concealed itself but brought him fame.

I conclude, therefore, returning to the problem of being feared and loved, that since men love at their own pleasure and fear at the pleasure of the prince, a wise prince should build his foundation upon that which belongs to him, not upon that which belongs to others: he must strive only to avoid hatred, as has been said.

LEVELS OF READING

Summary:

Pay attention to the **literal** meaning of the text. Briefly describe Machiavelli's examples of those who have become princes through wickedness and his argument and conclusions concerning whether it is better for a prince to be merciful rather than cruel. In what ways other than "Fortune" or "skill" does one become a prince? Concentrate on the highlights; avoid too much detail when summarizing. Again, drawing a simple outline of the main points of the text will help you better analyze the text at other levels of interpretation.

Analysis:

Find what you believe is **implicit** in the text. In what way does Machiavelli's classical example of one who became a prince relate to his other example from "recent days"? What does Machiavelli mean when he says, "[M]en forget more quickly the death of their father than the loss of their patrimony"? With the help of the background material provided about Machiavelli and his world, make an argument about these texts, and include the mention of the more **implicit** aspects of Machiavelli's arguments.

UNIT 10

Application:

Apply Nietzsche's theory of "good" and "evil" to these two chapters of Machiavelli's *The Prince*. Outline an argument you wish to make about these chapters using Nietzsche's theory to help you explain what some part of them may mean. The "part" of the text you choose to analyze may include any of the following: a character, a setting, an important change, a motivation, a goal, a result. Consider the following as possibilities, but explore other original interpretations too:

- Are Nietzsche's notions of "good" and "evil' important here or are his ideas about "good" and "bad" more useful in analyzing Machiavelli's chapters?
- Do the princes Machiavelli describes engage in a "slave morality" or a "noble morality" or a bit of both?
- Relate Nietzsche's idea of **resentment** to the princes or those they govern, or both.
- Is it possible to correlate Nietzsche's **blond beast** with the actions described in these two chapters?
- Relate Machiavelli's ideas concerning fear and love to Nietzsche's ideas on the same.
- Does anyone described in Machiavelli's chapters achieve a "conceptual transformation"? How so?

Start Your Own Argument:

Should Nietzsche's argument be blamed for the excesses of totalitarianism?

ELEVEN

ARGUMENT BY MEANS OF PARADOX, PREMISES AND CONCLUSIONS

HANNAH ARENDT

Hannah Arendt (1906–1975) was born in Hanover, Germany, the only child of Paul and Martha (Cohn) Arendt, secular Jews. Her father died of syphilitic insanity when Arendt was only seven years old. Her mother later remarried Martin Beerwald, bringing two stepsisters into Arendt's family. An avid reader from early childhood, Arendt claimed that she had read "everything" by the time she was sixteen years old.

Arendt studied at the University of Marburg with Martin Heidegger, later to become known as one of the "fathers" of the philosophical school of existentialism. Though married and a father, and seventeen years older than his student, Heidegger began a brief but passionate affair with Arendt in 1925. The affair ended when she left Marburg to study with Karl Jaspers at the University of Heidelburg. There she earned her Ph.D. in philosophy, writing her dissertation on love in the writings of St. Augustine.

In September 1929, the same year she completed her Ph.D., Arendt married Gunther Stern. Beginning in 1937, she worked for Zionist causes inside Nazi Germany. She was eventually arrested in Berlin for this work. Released almost by oversight, Arendt escaped to Paris, where she met Heimlich Blucher. After their divorces, he became her second husband in 1940. When Germany invaded France six months later, the couple became separated in the south of France, where they were both interned as "stateless" Germans. In May 1941, both managed to escape to the United States and they were reunited in New York City. Arendt became a United States citizen in 1951.

Arendt held several teaching posts at notable universities in the United States, including the University of California at Berkeley and the University of Chicago. She was the first woman to become a full professor (of politics) at Princeton. In 1967, she accepted a professorship at what is now called New School University in New York City, where she remained until she died in 1975.

The Origins of Totalitarianism *(1951), from which this chapter is taken, was Arendt's first major philosophical work. Many books followed, including her famous study of the trial of Nazi war criminal Adolph Eichmann,* Eichmann in Jerusalem: A Report on the Banality of Evil *(1963), which began as a series of articles covering the trial for* The New Yorker.

Arendt, who was schooled in philosophy, which includes the study of logic, composed an essay riddled with complex examples of logical statements worded in ways that can seem illogical to the uninitiated. The argument made is simple enough: Totalitarianism differs from other forms of political oppression, namely despotism and tyranny. In proving her case, and in the process of explaining the ways in which totalitarianism differs from tyranny and despotic rule, Arendt challenges totalitarianism's strict, often illogical, adherence to logic. Many of her sentences offer difficult-to-understand paradoxes to make a point. She also makes abundant use of the "If . . . then . . ." construction. These statements may at first be taken for statements of truth, until one notices that the "if" clause of the sentences is patently false. In logic, if the "if" clause—known as the premise—is false, then the "then" clause—known as the conclusion—is automatically false. (Note: The if . . . then . . . statement above is logically true.) Therefore, upon closer examination, one notices that Arendt is using this logical construction both to make her case and to call into question the logic of totalitarianism. Between logically false statements disguised as seeming truth claims and paradoxical twists and turns, understanding Arendt's argument can be difficult at times. But by the end of the essay, when she more explicitly explains to the reader the logic of illogic, it becomes apparent that Arendt has accomplished the difficult and dazzling: writing in language that actually enacts *her rhetorical goals.*

———

Like Plato, Hannah Arendt leads the reader through a maze of premises and conclusions; since the premises are false the conclusions drawn also are false. In addition, Arendt relies on a number of paradoxes to make her point about the differences between totalitarianism and other forms of political oppression.

Coming to Terms with the Reading:

Before reading/rereading Hannah Arendt's "Ideology and Terror: A Novel Form of Government," it is best to have a firm grasp of the meaning of the following terms:

1. totalitarian
2. ideology
3. one-party system
4. despotism/dictatorship
5. *consensus iuris*
6. *lumen naturale*
7. *ius naturale*
8. *Weltanschauugen*

IDEOLOGY AND TERROR:
A NOVEL FORM OF GOVERNMENT
Hannah Arendt

In the preceding chapters we emphasized repeatedly that the means of total domination are not only more drastic but that totalitarianism differs essentially from other forms of political oppression known to us such as despotism, tyranny and dictatorship. Wherever it rose to power, it developed entirely new political institutions and destroyed all social, legal and political traditions of the country. No matter what the specifically national tradition or the particular spiritual source of its ideology, totalitarian government always transformed classes into masses, supplanted the party system, not by one-party dictatorships, but by a mass movement, shifted the center of power from the army to the police, and established a foreign policy openly directed toward world domination. Present totalitarian governments have developed from one-party systems; whenever these became truly totalitarian, they started to operate according to a system of values so radically different from all others, that none of our traditional legal, moral, or common sense utilitarian categories could any longer help us to come to terms with, or judge, or predict their course of action.

If it is true that the elements of totalitarianism can be found by retracing the history and analyzing the political implications of what we usually call the crisis of our century, then the conclusion is unavoidable that this crisis is no mere threat from the outside, no mere result of some aggressive foreign policy of either Germany or Russia, and that it will no more disappear with the death of Stalin than it disappeared with the fall of Nazi Germany. It may even be that the true predicaments of our time will assume their authentic form—though not necessarily the cruelest—only when totalitarianism has become a thing of the past.

It is in the line of such reflections to raise the question whether totalitarian government, born of this crisis and at the same time its clearest and only unequivocal symptom, is merely a makeshift arrangement, which borrows its methods of intimidation, its means of organization and its instruments of violence from the well-known political arsenal of tyranny, despotism and dictatorships, and owes its existence only to the deplorable, but perhaps accidental failure of the traditional political forces—liberal or conservative, national or socialist, republican or monarchist, authoritarian or democratic. Or whether, on the contrary, there is such a thing as the *nature* of totalitarian government, whether it has its own essence and can be compared with and defined like other forms of government such as Western thought has known and recognized since the times of ancient philosophy. If this is true, then the entirely new and unprecedented forms of totalitarian organization and course of action must rest on one of the few basic experiences which men can have whenever they live together, and are concerned with public affairs. If there is a basic experience which finds its political expression in totalitarian domination, then, in view of the novelty of the totalitarian form of government, this must be an experience which, for whatever reason, has never before served as the foundation of a body politic and whose general mood—although it may be familiar in every other respect—never before has pervaded, and directed the handling of, public affairs.

If we consider this in terms of the history of ideas, it seems extremely unlikely. For the forms of government under which men live have been very few; they were discovered early, classified by the Greeks and have proved extraordinarily long-lived. If we apply these findings, whose fundamental idea, despite many variations, did not change in the two and a half thousand years that separate Plato from Kant, we are tempted at once to interpret totalitarianism as some modern form of tyranny, that is a lawless government where power is wielded by one man. Arbitrary power, unrestricted by law, wielded in the interest of the ruler and hostile to the interests of the governed, on one hand, fear as the principle of action, namely fear of the people by the ruler and fear of the ruler by the people, on the other—these have been the hallmarks of tyranny throughout our tradition.

5   Instead of saying that totalitarian government is unprecedented, we could also say that it has exploded the very alternative on which all definitions of the essence of governments have been based in political philosophy, that is the alternative between lawful and lawless government, between arbitrary and legitimate power. That lawful government and legitimate power, on one side, lawlessness and arbitrary power on the other, belonged together and were inseparable has never been questioned. Yet, totalitarian rule confronts us with a totally different kind of government. It defies, it is true, all positive laws, even to the extreme of defying those which it has itself established (as in the case of the Soviet Constitution of 1936, to quote only the most outstanding example) or which it did not care

to abolish (as in the case of the Weimar Constitution which the Nazi government never revoked). But it operates neither without guidance of law nor is it arbitrary, for it claims to obey strictly and unequivocally those laws of Nature or of History from which all positive laws always have been supposed to spring.

It is the monstrous, yet seemingly unanswerable claim of totalitarian rule that, far from being "lawless," it goes to the sources of authority from which positive laws received their ultimate legitimation, that far from being arbitrary it is more obedient to these suprahuman forces than any government ever was before, and that far from wielding its power in the interest of one man, it is quite prepared to sacrifice everybody's vital immediate interests to the execution of what it assumes to be the law of History or the law of Nature. Its defiance of positive laws claims to be a higher form of legitimacy which, since it is inspired by the sources themselves, can do away with petty legality. Totalitarian lawfulness pretends to have found a way to establish the rule of justice on earth—something which the legality of positive law admittedly could never attain. The discrepancy between legality and justice could never be bridged because the standards of right and wrong into which positive law translates its own source of authority—"natural law" governing the whole universe, or divine law revealed in human history, or customs and traditions expressing the law common to the sentiments of all men—are necessarily general and must be valid for a countless and unpredictable number of cases, so that each concrete individual case with its unrepeatable set of circumstances somehow escapes it.

Totalitarian lawfulness, defying legality and pretending to establish the direct reign of justice on earth, executes the law of History or of Nature without translating it into standards of right and wrong for individual behavior. It applies the law directly to mankind without bothering with the behavior of men. The law of Nature or the law of History, if properly executed, is expected to produce mankind as its end product; and this expectation lies behind the claim to global rule of all totalitarian governments. Totalitarian policy claims to transform the human species into an active unfailing carrier of a law to which human beings otherwise would only passively and reluctantly be subjected. If it is true that the link between totalitarian countries and the civilized world was broken through the monstrous crimes of totalitarian regimes, it is also true that this criminality was not due to simple aggressiveness, ruthlessness, warfare and treachery, but to a conscious break of that *consensus iuris* which, according to Cicero, constitutes a "people," and which, as international law, in modern times has constituted the civilized world insofar as it remains the foundation-stone of international relations even under the conditions of war. Both moral judgment and legal punishment presuppose this basic consent; the criminal can be judged justly only because he takes part in the *consensus iuris,* and even the revealed law of God can function among men only when they listen and consent to it.

At this point the fundamental difference between the totalitarian and all other concepts of law comes to light. Totalitarian policy does not replace one set of laws with another, does not establish its own *consensus iuris,* does not create, by one revolution, a new form of legality. Its defiance of all, even its own positive laws implies that it believes it can do without any *consensus iuris* whatever, and still not resign itself to the tyrannical state of lawlessness, arbitrariness and fear. It can do without the *consensus iuris* because it promises to release the fulfillment of law from all action and will of man; and it promises justice on earth because it claims to make mankind itself the embodiment of the law.

This identification of man and law, which seems to cancel the discrepancy between legality and justice that has plagued legal thought since ancient times, has nothing in common with the *lumen naturale* or the voice of conscience, by which Nature or Divinity as the sources of authority for the *ius naturale* or the historically revealed commands of God, are supposed to announce their authority in man himself. This never made man a walking embodiment of the law, but on the contrary remained distinct from him as the authority which demanded consent and obedience. Nature or Divinity as the source of authority for positive laws were thought of as permanent and eternal; positive laws were changing and changeable according to circumstances, but they possessed a relative permanence as compared with the much more rapidly changing actions of men; and they derived this permanence from the eternal presence of their source of authority. Positive laws, therefore, are primarily designed to function as stabilizing factors for the ever changing movements of men.

10   In the interpretation of totalitarianism, all laws have become laws of movement. When the Nazis talked about the law of nature or when the Bolsheviks talk about the law of history, neither nature nor history is any longer the stabilizing source of authority for the actions of mortal men; they are movements in themselves. Underlying the Nazis' belief in race laws as the expression of the law of nature in man, is Darwin's idea of man as the product of a natural development which does not necessarily stop with the present species of human beings, just as under the Bolsheviks' belief in class struggle as the expression of the law of history lies Marx's notion of society as the product of a gigantic historical movement which races according to its own law of motion to the end of historical times when it will abolish itself.

UNIT 11

The difference between Marx's historical and Darwin's naturalistic approach has frequently been pointed out, usually and rightly in favor of Marx. This has led us to forget the great and positive interest Marx took in Darwin's theories; Engels could not think of a greater compliment to Marx's scholarly achievements than to call him the "Darwin of history." If one considers, not the actual achievement, but the basic philosophies of both men, it turns out that ultimately the movement of history and the movement of nature are one and the same. Darwin's introduction of the concept of development into nature, his insistence that, at least in the field of biology, natural movement is not circular but unilinear, moving in an infinitely progressing direction, means in fact that nature is, as it were, being swept into history, that natural life is considered to be historical. The "natural" law of the survival of the fittest is just as much a historical law and could be used as such by racism as Marx's law of the survival of the most progressive class. Marx's class struggle, on the other hand, as the driving force of history is only the outward expression of the development of productive forces which in turn have their origin in the "labor-power" of men. Labor, according to Marx, is not a historical but a natural-biological force—released through man's "metabolism with nature" by which he conserves his individual life and reproduces the species. Engels saw the affinity between the basic convictions of the two men very clearly because he understood the decisive role which the concept of development played in both theories. The tremendous intellectual change which took place in the middle of the last [nineteenth] century consisted in the refusal to view or accept anything "as it is" and in the consistent interpretation of everything as being only a stage of some further development. Whether the driving force of this development was called nature or history is relatively secondary. In these ideologies, the term "law" itself changed its meaning: from expressing the framework of stability within which human actions and motions can take place, it became the expression of the motion itself.

Totalitarian politics which proceeded to follow the recipes of ideologies has unmasked the true nature of these movements insofar as it clearly showed that there could be no end to this process. If it is the law of nature to eliminate everything that is harmful and unfit to live, it would mean the end of nature itself if new categories of the harmful and unfit-to-live could not be found; if it is the law of history that in a class struggle certain classes "wither away," it would mean the end of human history itself if rudimentary new classes did not form, so that they in turn could "wither away" under the hands of totalitarian rulers. In other words, the law of killing by which totalitarian movements seize and exercise power would remain a law of the movement even if they ever succeeded in making all of humanity subject to their rule.

By lawful government we understand a body politic in which positive laws are needed to translate and realize the immutable *ius naturale* or the eternal commandments of God into standards of right and wrong. Only in these standards, in the body of positive laws of each country, do the *ius naturale* or the Commandments of God achieve their political reality. In the body politic of totalitarian government, this place of positive laws is taken by total terror, which is designed to translate into reality the law of movement of history or nature. Just as positive laws, though they define transgressions, are independent of them—the absense of crimes in any society does not render laws superfluous but, on the contrary, signifies their most perfect rule—so terror in totalitarian government has ceased to be a mere means for the suppression of opposition, though it is also used for such purposes. Terror becomes total when it becomes independent of all opposition; it rules supreme when nobody any longer stands in its way. If lawfulness is the essence of nontyrannical government and lawlessness is the essence of tyranny, then terror is the essence of totalitarian domination.

Terror is the realization of the law of movement; its chief aim is to make it possible for the force of nature or of history to race freely through mankind, unhindered by any spontaneous human action. As such, terror seeks to "stabilize" men in order to liberate the forces of nature or history. It is this movement which singles out the foes of mankind against whom terror is let loose, and no free action of either opposition or sympathy can be permitted to interfere with the elimination of the "objective enemy" of History or Nature, of the class or the race. Guilt and innocence become senseless notions; "guilty" is he who stands in the way of the natural or historical process which has passed judgment over "inferior races," over individuals "unfit to live," over "dying classes and decadent peoples." Terror executes these judgments, and before its court, all concerned are subjectively innocent: the murdered because they did nothing against the system, and the murderers because they do not really murder but execute a death sentence pronounced by some higher tribunal. The rulers themselves do not claim to be just or wise, but only to execute historical or natural laws; they do not apply laws, but execute a movement in accordance with its inherent law. Terror is lawfulness, if law is the law of the movement of some suprahuman force, Nature or History.

15   Terror as the execution of a law of movement whose ultimate goal is not the welfare of men or the interest of one man but the fabrication of mankind, eliminates individuals for the sake of the species, sacrifices the "parts" for the sake of

the "whole." The suprahuman force of Nature or History has its own beginning and its own end, so that it can be hindered only by the new beginning and the individual end which the life of each man actually is.

Positive laws in constitutional government are designed to erect boundaries and establish channels of communication between men whose community is continually endangered by the new men born into it. With each new birth, a new beginning is born into the world, a new world has potentially come into being. The stability of the laws corresponds to the constant motion of all human affairs, a motion which can never end as long as men are born and die. The laws hedge in each new beginning and at the same time assure its freedom of movement, the potentiality of something entirely new and unpredictable; the boundaries of positive laws are for the political existence of man what memory is for his historical existence: they guarantee the pre-existence of a common world, the reality of some continuity which transcends the individual life span of each generation, absorbs all new origins and is nourished by them.

Total terror is so easily mistaken for a symptom of tyrannical government because totalitarian government in its initial stages must behave like a tyranny and raze the boundaries of man-made law. But total terror leaves no arbitrary lawlessness behind it and does not rage for the sake of some arbitrary will or for the sake of despotic power of one man against all, least of all for the sake of a war of all against all. It substitutes for the boundaries and channels of communication between individual men a band of iron which holds them so tightly together that it is as though their plurality had disappeared into One Man of gigantic dimensions. To abolish the fences of laws between men—as tyranny does—means to take away man's liberties and destroy freedom as a living political reality; for the space between men as it is hedged in by laws, is the living space of freedom. Total terror uses this old instrument of tyranny but destroys at the same time also the lawless, fenceless wilderness of fear and suspicion which tyranny leaves behind. This desert, to be sure, is no longer a living space of freedom, but it still provides some room for the fear-guided movements and suspicion-ridden actions of its inhabitants.

By pressing men against each other, total terror destroys the space between them; compared to the condition within its iron band, even the desert of tyranny, insofar as it is still some kind of space, appears like a guarantee of freedom. Totalitarian government does not just curtail liberties or abolish essential freedoms; nor does it, at least to our limited knowledge, succeed in eradicating the love for freedom from the hearts of man. It destroys the one essential prerequisite of all freedom which is simply the capacity of motion which cannot exist without space.

Total terror, the essence of totalitarian government, exists neither for nor against men. It is supposed to provide the forces of nature or history with an incomparable instrument to accelerate their movement. This movement, proceeding according to its own law, cannot in the long run be hindered; eventually its force will always prove more powerful than the most powerful forces engendered by the actions and the will of men. But it can be slowed down and is slowed down almost inevitably by the freedom of man, which even totalitarian rulers cannot deny, for this freedom—irrelevant and arbitrary as they may deem it—is identical with the fact that men are being born and that therefore each of them *is* a new beginning, begins, in a sense, the world anew. From the totalitarian point of view, the fact that men are born and die can be only regarded as an annoying interference with higher forces. Terror, therefore, as the obedient servant of natural or historical movement has to eliminate from the process not only freedom in any specific sense, but the very source of freedom which is given with the fact of the birth of man and resides in his capacity to make a new beginning. In the iron band of terror, which destroys the plurality of men and makes out of many the One who unfailingly will act as though he himself were part of the course of history or nature, a device has been found not only to liberate the historical and natural forces, but to accelerate them to a speed they never would reach if left to themselves. Practically speaking, this means that terror executes on the spot the death sentences which Nature is supposed to have pronounced on races or individuals who are "unfit to live," or History on "dying classes," without waiting for the slower and less efficient processes of nature or history themselves.

20   In this concept, where the essence of government itself has become motion, a very old problem of political thought seems to have found a solution similar to the one already noted for the discrepancy between legality and justice. If the essence of government is defined as lawfulness, and if it is understood that laws are the stabilizing forces in the public affairs of men (as indeed it always has been since Plato invoked Zeus, the god of the boundaries, in his *Laws*), then the problem of movement of the body politic and the actions of its citizens arises. Lawfulness sets limitations to actions, but does not inspire them; the greatness, but also the perplexity of laws in free societies is that they only tell what one should not, but never what one should do. The necessary movement of a body politic can never be found in its essence if only because this essence —again since Plato—has always been defined with a view to its permanence. Duration seemed one of the surest yardsticks for the goodness of a government. It is still for Montesquieu the supreme proof for the badness of tyranny that only tyrannies are liable to be destroyed from within, to decline by themselves, whereas all

other governments are destroyed through exterior circumstances. Therefore what the definition of governments always needed was what Montesquieu called a "principle of action" which, different in each form of government, would inspire government and citizens alike in their public activity and serve as a criterion, beyond the merely negative yardstick of lawfulness, for judging all action in public affairs. Such guiding principles and criteria of action are, according to Montesquieu, honor in a monarchy, virtue in a republic and fear in a tyranny.

In a perfect totalitarian government, where all men have become One Man, where all action aims at the acceleration of the movement of nature or history, where every single act is the execution of a death sentence which Nature or History has already pronounced, that is, under conditions where terror can be completely relied upon to keep the movement in constant motion, no principle of action separate from its essence would be needed at all. Yet as long as totalitarian rule has not conquered the earth and with the iron band of terror made each single man a part of one mankind, terror in its double function as essence of government and principle, not of action, but of motion, cannot be fully realized. Just as lawfulness in constitutional government is insufficient to inspire and guide men's actions, so terror in totalitarian government is not sufficient to inspire and guide human behavior.

While under present conditions totalitarian domination still shares with other forms of government the need for a guide for the behavior of its citizens in public affairs, it does not need and could not even use a principle of action strictly speaking, since it will eliminate precisely the capacity of man to act. Under conditions of total terror not even fear can any longer serve as an advisor of how to behave, because terror chooses its victims without reference to individual actions or thoughts, exclusively in accordance with the objective necessity of the natural or historical process. Under totalitarian conditions, fear probably is more widespread than ever before; but fear has lost its practical usefulness when actions guided by it can no longer help to avoid the dangers man fears. The same is true for sympathy or support of the regime; for total terror not only selects its victims according to objective standards; it chooses it executioners with as complete a disregard as possible for the candidate's conviction and sympathies. The consistent elimination of conviction as a motive for action has become a matter of record since the great purges in Soviet Russia and the satellite countries. The aim of totalitarian education has never been to instill convictions but to destroy the capacity to form any. The introduction of purely objective criteria into the selective system of the SS troops was Himmler's great organizational invention; he selected the candidates from photographs according to purely racial criteria. Nature itself decided, not only who was to be eliminated, but also who was to be trained as an executioner.

No guiding principle of behavior, taken itself from the realm of human action, such as virtue, honor, fear, is necessary or can be useful to set into motion a body politic which no longer uses terror as a means of intimidation, but whose essence is terror. In its stead, it has introduced an entirely new principle into public affairs that dispenses with human will to action altogether and appeals to the craving need for some insight into the law of movement according to which the terror functions and upon which, therefore, all private destinies depend.

The inhabitants of a totalitarian country are thrown into and caught in the process of nature or history for the sake of accelerating its movement; as such, they can only be executioners or victims of its inherent law. The process may decide that those who today eliminate races and individuals or the members of dying classes and decadent peoples are tomorrow those who must be sacrificed. What totalitarian rule needs to guide the behavior of its subjects is a preparation to fit each of them equally well for the role of executioner and the role of victim. This two-sided preparation, the substitute for a principle of action, is the ideology.

25   Ideologies—isms which to the satisfaction of their adherents can explain everything and every occurrence by deducing it from a single premise—are a very recent phenomenon and, for many decades, played a negligible role in political life. Only with the wisdom of hindsight can we discover in them certain elements which have made them so disturbingly useful for totalitarian rule. Not before Hitler and Stalin were the great political potentialities of the ideologies discovered.

Ideologies are known for their scientific character: they combine the scientific approach with results of philosophical relevance and pretend to be scientific philosophy. The word "ideology" seems to imply that an idea can become the subject matter of a science just as animals are the subject matter of zoology, and that the suffix -*logy* in ideology, as in zoology, indicates nothing but the *logoi*, the scientific statements made on it. If this were true, an ideology would indeed be a pseudo-science and a pseudo-philosophy, transgressing at the same time the limitations of science and the limitations of philosophy. Deism, for example, would then be the ideology which treats the idea of God, with which philosophy is concerned, in the scientific manner of theology for which God is a revealed reality. (A theology which is not based on revelation as a given reality but treats God as an idea would be as mad as a zoology which is no longer sure of the physical, tangible existence of animals.) Yet we know that this is only part of the truth.

Deism, though it denies divine revelation, does not simply make "scientific" statements on a God which is only an "idea," but uses the idea of God in order to explain the course of the world. The "ideas" of isms—race in racism, God in deism, etc.—never form the subject matter of the ideologies and the suffix -*logy* never indicates simply a body of "scientific" statements.

An ideology is quite literally what its name indicates: it is the logic of an idea. Its subject matter is history, to which the "idea" is applied; the result of this application is not a body of statements about something that is, but the unfolding of a process which is in constant change. The ideology treats the course of events as though it followed the same "law" as the logical exposition of its "idea." Ideologies pretend to know the mysteries of the whole historical process—the secrets of the past, the intricacies of the present, the uncertainties of the future—because of the logic inherent in their respective ideas.

Ideologies are never interested in the miracle of being. They are historical, concerned with becoming and perishing, with the rise and fall of cultures, even if they try to explain history by some "law of nature." The word "race" in racism does not signify any genuine curiosity about the human races as a field for scientific exploration, but is the "idea" by which the movement of history is explained as one consistent process.

The "idea" of an ideology is neither Plato's eternal essence grasped by the eyes of the mind nor Kant's regulative principle of reason but has become an instrument of explanation. To an ideology, history does not appear in the light of an idea (which would imply that history is seen *sub specie* of some ideal eternity which itself is beyond historical motion) but as something which can be calculated by it. What fits the "idea" into this new role is its own "logic," that is a movement which is the consequence of the "idea" itself and needs no outside factor to set it into motion. Racism is the belief that there is a motion inherent in the very idea of race, just as deism is the belief that a motion is inherent in the very notion of God.

30　　The movement of history and the logical process of this notion are supposed to correspond to each other, so that whatever happens, happens according to the logic of one "idea." However, the only possible movement in the realm of logic is the process of deduction from a premise. Dialectical logic, with its process from thesis through antithesis to synthesis which in turn becomes the thesis of the next dialectical movement, is not different in principle, once an ideology gets hold of it; the first thesis becomes the premise and its advantage for ideological explanation is that this dialectical device can explain away factual contradictions as stages of one identical, consistent movement.

As soon as logic as a movement of thought—and not as a necessary control of thinking—is applied to an idea, this idea is transformed into a premise. Ideological world explanations performed this operation long before it became so eminently fruitful for totalitarian reasoning. The purely negative coercion of logic, the prohibition of contradictions, became "productive" so that a whole line of thought could be initiated, and forced upon the mind, by drawing conclusions in the manner of mere argumentation. This argumentative process could be interrupted neither by a new idea (which would have been another premise with a different set of consequences) nor by a new experience. Ideologies always assume that one idea is sufficient to explain everything in the development from the premise, and that no experience can teach anything because everything is comprehended in this consistent process of logical deduction. The danger in exchanging the necessary insecurity of philosophical thought for the total explanation of an ideology and its *Weltanschauung,* is not even so much the risk of falling for some usually vulgar, always uncritical assumption as of exchanging the freedom inherent in man's capacity to think for the strait jacket of logic with which man can force himself almost as violently as he is forced by some outside power.

The *Weltanschauungen* and ideologies of the nineteenth century are not in themselves totalitarian, and although racism and communism have become the decisive ideologies of the twentieth century they were not, in principle, any "more totalitarian" than the others; it happened because the elements of experience on which they were orginally based—the struggle between the races for world domination, and the struggle between the classes for political power in the respective countries— turned out to be politically more important than those of other ideologies. In this sense the ideological victory of racism and communism over all other isms was decided before the totalitarian movements took hold of precisely these ideologies. On the other hand, all ideologies contain totalitarian elements, but these are fully developed only by totalitarian movements, and this creates the deceptive impression that only racism and communism are totalitarian in character. The truth is, rather, that the real nature of all ideologies was revealed only in the role that the ideology plays in the apparatus of totalitarian domination. Seen from this aspect, there appear three specifically totalitarian elements that are peculiar to all ideological thinking.

First, in their claim to total explanation, ideologies have the tendency to explain not what is, but what becomes, what is born and passes away. They are in all cases concerned solely with the element of motion, that is, with history in the customary sense of the word. Ideologies are always oriented toward history, even when, as in the case of racism, they seemingly proceed from the premise of nature; here, nature serves merely to explain historical matters and reduce them to matters of nature. The claim to total explanation promises to explain all historical happenings, the total explanation of the past, the total knowledge of the present, and the reliable prediction of the future. Secondly, in this capacity ideological thinking becomes independent of all experience from which it cannot learn anything new even if it is a question of something that has just come to pass. Hence ideological thinking becomes emancipated from the reality that we perceive with our five senses, and insists on a "truer" reality concealed behind all perceptible things, dominating them from this place of concealment and requiring a sixth sense that enables us to become aware of it. The sixth sense is provided by precisely the ideology, that particular ideological indoctrination which is taught by the educational institutions, established exclusively for this purpose, to train the "political soldiers" in the *Ordensburgen* of the Nazis or the schools of the Comintern and the Cominform. The propaganda of the totalitarian movement also serves to emancipate thought from experience and reality; it always strives to inject a secret meaning into every public, tangible event and to suspect a secret intent behind every public political act. Once the movements have come to power, they proceed to change reality in accordance with their ideological claims. The concept of enmity is replaced by that of conspiracy, and this produces a mentality in which reality—real enmity or real friendship—is no longer experienced and understood in its own terms but is automatically assumed to signify something else.

Thirdly, since the ideologies have no power to transform reality, they achieve this emancipation of thought from experience through certain methods of demonstration. Ideological thinking orders facts into an absolutely logical procedure which starts from an axiomatically accepted premise, deducing everything else from it; that is, it proceeds with a consistency that exists nowhere in the realm of reality. The deducing may proceed logically or dialectically; in either case it involves a consistent process of argumentation which, because it thinks in terms of a process, is supposed to be able to comprehend the movement of the suprahuman, natural or historical processes. Comprehension is achieved by the mind's imitating, either logically or dialectically, the law of "scientifically" established movements with which through the process of imitation it becomes integrated. Ideological argumentation, always a kind of logical deduction, corresponds to the two aforementioned elements of the ideologies—the element of movement and of emancipation from reality and experience—first, because its thought movement does not spring from experience but is self-generated, and, secondly, because it transforms the one and only point that is taken and accepted from experienced reality into an axiomatic premise, leaving from then on the subsequent argumentation process completely untouched from any further experience. Once it has established its premise, its point of departure, experiences no longer interfere with ideological thinking, nor can it be taught by reality.

35   The device both totalitarian rulers used to transform their respective ideologies into weapons with which each of their subjects could force himself into step with the terror movement was deceptively simple and inconspicuous: they took them dead seriously, took pride the one in his supreme gift for "ice cold reasoning" (Hitler) and the other in the "mercilessness of his dialectics," and proceeded to drive ideological implications into extremes of logical consistency which, to the onlooker, looked preposterously "primitive" and absurd: a "dying class" consisted of people condemned to death; races that are "unfit to live" were to be exterminated. Whoever agreed that there are such things as "dying classes" and did not draw the consequence of killing their members, or that the right to live had something to do with race and did not draw the consequence of killing "unfit races," was plainly either stupid or a coward. This stringent logicality as a guide to action permeates the whole structure of totalitarian movements and governments. It is exclusively the work of Hitler and Stalin, who, although they did not add a single new thought to the ideas and propaganda slogans of their movements, for this reason alone must be considered ideologists of the greatest importance.

READING/WRITING ASSISTS

Thesis (and its counterargument):

Readers often expect to find a clear statement of the writer's argument in a **thesis statement**, usually found in a sentence or two at the end of the first or, at the latest, second paragraph of an argumentative essay. Arendt's thesis, "emphasized repeatedly" in "previous chapters" of the book from which this essay was taken, is stated in the first sentence of this essay. Her **counterargument**, then, derives from others who have insisted that totalitarianism is the same as other forms of political oppression, namely despotism, tyranny, and dictatorship. Given that Arendt's essay follows hard on the heels of World War II and its aftermath, what might have suggested to Arendt that totalitarianism is a "novel" form of government, in need of definition? As you read Arendt's highly logical and tightly structured essay, decide whether she proves her case: If totalitarianism is indeed a novel form of government, what, according to Arendt, makes it so?

The Shape of the Argument:

"Mapping" the structure of an argument can help us better understand the argument itself, while also showing us new models for shaping our own arguments in essay form. As fascinating as Arendt's argument itself is, the structuring of her argument, and her use of the most basic tenets of logic in making it, are perhaps even more so. Though dense and full of paradox, Arendt's argument is often legalistic. Though charged with emotion, Arendt's argument is precise in its structure and content, often relying on classical sources. It helps to first read Darwin's "Natural Selection," and Marx's *Manifesto,* since Arendt's own argument is informed by her reading of Darwin's "law of nature" and Marx's "law of history." To better understand Arendt's main points about totalitarianism, ideology, and terror, it is best to start by outlining the entire essay, paragraph by paragraph:

Section I:

Paragraph 1:   Arendt's **thesis** framed around its **counterargument**. Simply put, what is the thesis of this essay, and what argument does Arendt pose it against?

Paragraph 2:   Arendt uses **paradox** (see **Rhetorical Moves**, p.492) to make a point about totalitarianism. What is that point?

Paragraph 3:   According to Arendt, does totalitarianism borrow from other forms of government to combat what is perceived as a crisis in the 20th century? Is there a basic human experience on which totalitarianism rests? What seems to be Arendt's answers to these questions?

Paragraph 4:   Totalitarian governments **might** be _____, but in fact_____.

Paragraph 5:   Totalitarian governments **might** be _____, but in fact_____.

Paragraphs 6, 7,   The **paradox** of totalitarian "lawfulness." What is this
8, 9, and 10:   paradox?

Paragraphs 11 and 12:	Arendt continues her reflection on the philosophies of Marx and Darwin, as reflected by the Bolsheviks and the Nazis. Both Marx and Darwin changed the meaning of the word "law," but in what way? According to Arendt, what is the significance of the conflict between stability and motion in their scheme of thought? Notice the repeated use of the **if . . . then . . .** structure in paragraph 11. To better understand Arendt's reason for using this structure, see **Rhetorical Moves**, below.
Paragraphs 13, 14, 15:	As proposed in these three paragraphs, what is the place of terror in totalitarian governments?
Paragraph 16:	**Interruption**: What is the role of positive laws in constitutional governments?
Paragraphs 17, 18, 19:	Return to an outlining of the place of terror in totalitarian governments. For what purpose does Arendt interrupt her six-paragraph summation of the role of terror in totalitarian governments with the **interruption** above? Does the interruption serve her rhetorical purpose?
Paragraphs 20, 21, 22, 23, and 24:	Here Arendt returns to the conflict between motion and stability, first mentioned in paragraph 11. Here too, Arendt proposes a paradox: that there is motion but no action in totalitarian regimes. How can this be so? With what recourse does this phenomenon leave the individual citizen?

Section II:

Paragraph 25:	Arendt now takes up the second half of her totalitarian equation: ideology. What are ideologies? Do you agree with Arendt's contention that ideologies are a "very recent phenomenon" (second half of the 20th century)?
Paragraph 26:	Are *logoi* and -isms scientific? Why or why not?
Paragraphs 27, 28, and 29:	Now Arendt defines ideology again. What, according to her, is the "pretense" of ideology? In telling us what ideology **isn't**, does Arendt tell us what it **is**?
Paragraph 30:	Logic as a movement of thought. What characterizes this motion? Is it the same as or different from the idea of motion expressed earlier in this essay?

UNIT 11

Paragraphs 31   What is the importance of premises in logic? How has Arendt
and 32:   underscored this importance throughout her essay?

Paragraphs 33   Outline the three "specifically totalitarian elements peculiar to
and 34:   all ideological thinking," according to Arendt:

1. _____

2. _____

3. _____

Paragraph 35:   What is the importance of logic in ideology?

Rhetorical Moves:

Even though Arendt's essay is divided into two parts, in reality it is a tripartite essay, one that reflects the elements in her title: ideology, terror, and a "novel form of government." In the essay itself, Arendt reverses her terms, first addressing the "novel" form of government, totalitarianism, before turning to "terror," and finally to "ideology." Is the reversal of terms necessary to Arendt's argument? Why not title the essay "A Novel Form of Government: Terror and Ideology"?

In addition, Arendt makes extensive use of two rhetorical devices in her essay, paradox and *modus ponens*.

Par-a-dox\'par-e-daks\ *n* **1**: a tenet contrary to received opinion **2 a**: a statement that is seemingly contrary or opposed to common sense and yet is perhaps true **b**: a self-contradictory statement that at first seems true **c**: an argument that apparently derives self-contradictory conclusions by valid deduction from acceptable premises **3**: something (as a person, condition, or act) with seemingly contradictory qualities or phases

Arendt seems to argue that totalitarian governments are based in definition **1c**. Find one section of her argument that provides an example of this kind of paradox.

Modus ponens: The **if . . . then . . .** statement. Formal logic dictates that if the **premise** (the "**if**" clause of the sentence) is false, then the **conclusion** following (the "**then**" clause of the sentence) is also false, no matter how true it may seem. Paragraph 11, for example, makes extensive use of this device. Scrutinized carefully, Arendt's essay is found to have a number of sentences that at first appear to convey a truth, only to negate that "truth" once the validity of the premise is denied. In fact, this construction underscores the false logic of the totalitarian project Arendt describes at the end of her essay. As such, her essay is a brilliant example of words enacting what they describe.

TADEUSZ BOROWSKI

Born in Zytomierz, a Polish city then in the Soviet Ukraine, Tadeusz Borowski (1922–1951) was the son of a laborer and a seamstress. Often separated from his parents in his early life, he was sent to a boarding school for children of indigent parents. He then secretly attended the University of Warsaw, studying literature, though the Nazis forbade Polish citizens from attending university.

The publication of his first book of poems, Wherever the Earth, *in 1942, resulted in the arrest of Borowski and his fiancée, Maria Rundo. In 1943, both were sent to Auschwitz, fortunately just weeks after the Germans had stopped gassing "Aryans." He also spent time in Dachau, from which he was liberated by invading Allied forces in 1945. After the liberation, he was separated from his fiancée, who made her way to Sweden and did not want to return to Poland. Borowski eventually persuaded her, and they were married shortly after they were reunited at the barbed wire of the Polish border.*

Once free from the Nazis, the Polish government convinced Borowski that a Communist revolution would prevent any more horrors such as Auschwitz occurring on Polish soil. But soon after, political purges and the existence of Soviet prison camps were revealed. Appalled by the direction of Polish politics and his participation in the Communist regime, Borowski took his own life—ironically, by gassing himself—only three days after the birth of his first child, a daughter. He was only 29 years old.

THIS WAY FOR THE GAS, LADIES AND GENTLEMEN
Tadeusz Borowski

All of us walk around naked. The delousing is finally over, and our striped suits are back from the tanks of Cyclone B solution, an efficient killer of lice in clothing and of men in gas chambers. Only the inmates in the blocks cut off from ours by the "Spanish goats" still have nothing to wear. But all the same, all of us walk around naked: the heat is unbearable. The camp has been sealed off tight. Not a single prisoner, not one solitary louse, can sneak through the gate. The labor Kommandos have stopped working. All day, thousands of naked men shuffle up and down the roads, cluster around the squares, or lie against the walls and on top of the roofs. We have been sleeping on plain boards, since our mattresses and blankets are still being disinfected. From the rear blockhouses we have a view of the F.K.L.—*Frauen Konzentration Lager;* there too the delousing is in full swing. Twenty-eight thousand women have been stripped naked and driven out of the barracks. Now they swarm around the large yard between the blockhouses.

The heat rises, the hours are endless. We are without even our usual diversion: the wide roads leading to the crematoria are empty. For several days now, no new transports have come in. Part of "Canada" has been liquidated and detailed to a labor Kommando—one of the very toughest—at Harmenz. For there exists in the camp a special brand of justice based on envy: when the rich and mighty fall, their friends see to it that they fall to the very bottom. And Canada, our Canada, which smells not of maple forests but of French perfume, has amassed great fortunes in diamonds and currency from all over Europe.

Several of us sit on the top bunk, our legs dangling over the edge. We slice the neat loaves of crisp, crunchy bread. It is a bit coarse to the taste, the kind that stays fresh for days. Sent all the way from Warsaw—only a week ago my mother held this white loaf in her hands . . . dear Lord, dear Lord . . .

We unwrap the bacon, the onion, we open a can of evaporated milk. Henri, the fat Frenchman, dreams aloud of the French wine brought by the transports from Strasbourg, Paris, Marseille. . . . Sweat streams down his body.

5   "Listen, *mon ami,* next time we go up on the loading ramp, I'll bring you real champagne. You haven't tried it before, eh?"

"No. But you'll never be able to smuggle it through the gate, so stop teasing. Why not try and 'organize' some shoes for me instead—you know, the perforated kind, with a double sole, and what about that shirt you promised me long ago?"

"*Patience, patience.* When the new transports come, I'll bring all you want. We'll be going on the ramp again!"

"And what if there aren't any more 'cremo' transports?" I say spitefully. "Can't you see how much easier life is becoming around here: no limit on packages, no more beatings? You even write letters home. . . . One hears all kind of talk, and, dammit, they'll run out of people!"

"Stop talking nonsense." Henri's serious fat face moves rhythmically, his mouth is full of sardines. We have been friends for a long time, but I do not even know his last name. "Stop talking nonsense," he repeats, swallowing with effort. "They can't run out of people, or we'll starve to death in this blasted camp. All of us live on what they bring."

10   "All? We have our packages . . ."

"Sure, you and your friend, and ten other friends of yours. Some of you Poles get packages. But what about us, and the Jews, and the Russkis? And what if we had no food, no 'organization' from the transports, do you think you'd be eating those packages of yours in peace? We wouldn't let you!"

"You would, you'd starve to death like the Greeks. Around here, whoever has grub, has power."

"Anyway, you have enough, we have enough, so why argue?"

Right, why argue? They have enough, I have enough, we eat together and we sleep on the same bunks. Henri slices the bread, he makes a tomato salad. It tastes good with the commissary mustard.

15   Below us, naked sweat-drenched men crowd the narrow barracks aisles or lie packed in eights and tens in the lower bunks. Their nude, withered bodies stink of sweat and excrement; their cheeks are hollow. Directly beneath me, in the bottom bunk, lies a rabbi. He has covered his head with a piece of rag torn off a blanket and reads from a Hebrew prayer book (there is no shortage of this type of literature at the camp), wailing loudly, monotonously.

"Can't somebody shut him up? He's been raving as if he'd caught God himself by the feet."

"I don't feel like moving. Let him rave. They'll take him to the oven that much sooner."

"Religion is the opium of the people," Henri, who is a Communist and a *rentier,* says sententiously. "If they didn't believe in God and eternal life, they'd have smashed the crematoria long ago."

"Why haven't you done it then?"

20 The question is rhetorical; the Frenchman ignores it.

"Idiot," he says simply, and stuffs a tomato in his mouth.

Just as we finish our snack, there is a sudden commotion at the door. The Muslims scurry in fright to the safety of their bunks, a messenger runs into the Block Elder's shack. The Elder, his face solemn, steps out at once.

"Canada! *Antreten!* But fast! There's a transport coming!"

"Great God!" yells Henri, jumping off the bunk. He swallows the rest of his tomato, snatches his coat, screams *"Raus"* at the men below, and in a flash is at the door. We can hear a scramble in the other bunks. Canada is leaving for the ramp.

25 "Henri, the shoes!" I call after him.

"Keine Angst!" he shouts back, already outside.

I proceed to put away the food. I tie a piece of rope around the suitcase where the onions and the tomatoes from my father's garden in Warsaw mingle with Portuguese sardines, bacon from Lublin (that's from my brother), and authentic sweetmeats from Salonica. I tie it all up, pull on my trousers, and slide off the bunk.

"Platz!" I yell, pushing my way through the Greeks. They step aside. At the door I bump into Henri.

"Was ist los?"

30 "Want to come with us on the ramp?"

"Sure, why not?"

"Come along then, grab your coat! We're short a few men. I've already told the Kapo," and he shoves me out of the barracks door.

We line up. Someone has marked down our numbers, someone up ahead yells, "March, march," and now we are running towards the gate, accompanied by the shouts of a multilingual throng that is already being pushed back to the barracks. Not everybody is lucky enough to be going on the ramp. . . . We have almost reached the gate. *Links, zwei, drei, vier! Mützen ab!* Erect, arms stretched stiffly along our hips, we march past the gate briskly, smartly, almost gracefully. A sleepy S.S. man with a large pad in his hand checks us off, waving us ahead in groups of five.

"Hundert!" he calls after we have all passed.

35 *"Stimmt!"* comes a hoarse answer from out front.

We march fast, almost at a run. There are guards all around, young men with automatics. We pass camp II B, then some deserted barracks and a clump of unfamiliar green—apple and pear trees. We cross the circle of watchtowers and, running, burst on to the highway. We have arrived. Just a few more yards. There, surrounded by trees, is the ramp.

A cheerful little station, very much like any other provincial railway stop: a small square framed by tall chestnuts and paved with yellow gravel. Not far off, beside the road, squats a tiny wooden shed, uglier and more flimsy than the ugliest and flimsiest railway shack; farther along lie stacks of old rails, heaps of wooden beams, barracks parts, bricks, paving stones. This is where they load freight for Birkenau: supplies for the construction of the camp, and people for the gas chambers. Trucks drive around, load up lumber, cement, people—a regular daily routine.

And now the guards are being posted along the rails, across the beams, in the green shade of the Silesian chestnuts, to form a tight circle around the ramp. They wipe the sweat from their faces and sip out of their canteens. It is unbearably hot; the sun stands motionless at its zenith.

"Fall out!"

40   We sit down in the narrow streaks of shade along the stacked rails. The hungry Greeks (several of them managed to come along, God only knows how) rummage underneath the rails. One of them finds some pieces of mildewed bread, another a few half-rotten sardines. They eat.

"Schweinedreck," spits a young, tall guard with corn-colored hair and dreamy blue eyes. "For God's sake, any minute you'll have so much food to stuff down your guts, you'll bust!" He adjusts his gun, wipes his face with a handkerchief.

"Hey you, fatso!" His boot lightly touches Henri's shoulder. *"Pass mal auf,* want a drink?"

"Sure, but I haven't got any marks," replies the Frenchman with a professional air.

"Schade, too bad."

45   "Come, come, Herr Posten, isn't my word good enough any more? Haven't we done business before? How much?"

"One hundred. *Gemacht?"*

"Gemacht."

We drink the water, lukewarm and tasteless. It will be paid for by the people who have not yet arrived.

"Now you be careful," says Henri, turning to me. He tosses away the empty bottle. It strikes the rails and bursts into tiny fragments. "Don't take any money, they might be checking. Anyway, who the hell needs money? You've got enough to eat. Don't take suits, either, or they'll think you're planning to escape. Just get a shirt, silk only, with a collar. And a vest. And if you find something to drink, don't bother calling me. I know how to shift for myself, but you watch your step or they'll let you have it."

50   "Do they beat you up here?"

"Naturally. You've got to have eyes in your ass. *Arschaugen*."

Around us sit the Greeks, their jaws working greedily, like huge human insects. They munch on stale lumps of bread. They are restless, wondering what will happen next. The sight of the large beams and the stacks of rails has them worried. They dislike carrying heavy loads.

"*Was wir arbeiten?*" . . . they ask.

"*Niks. Transport kommen, alles Krematorium, compris?*"

55   "*Alles verstehen,*" they answer in crematorium Esperanto. All is well—they will not have to move the heavy rails or carry the beams.

In the meantime, the ramp has become increasingly alive with activity, increasingly noisy. The crews are being divided into those who will open and unload the arriving cattle cars and those who will be posted by the wooden steps. They receive instructions on how to proceed most efficiently. Motorcycles drive up, delivering S.S. officers, bemedalled, glittering with brass, beefy men with highly polished boots and shiny, brutal faces. Some have brought their briefcases, others hold thin, flexible whips. This gives them an air of military readiness and agility. They walk in and out of the commissary—for the miserable little shack by the road serves as their commissary, where in the summertime they drink mineral water, *Studentenquelle,* and where in winter they can warm up with a glass of hot wine. They greet each other in the state-approved way, raising an arm Roman fashion, then shake hands cordially, exchange warm smiles, discuss mail from home, their children, their families. Some stroll majestically on the ramp. The silver squares on their collars glitter, the gravel crunches under their boots, their bamboo whips snap impatiently.

We lie against the rails in the narrow streaks of shade, breathe unevenly, occasionally exchange a few words in our various tongues, and gaze listlessly at the majestic men in green uniforms, at the green trees, and at the church steeple of a distant village.

"The transport is coming," somebody says. We spring to our feet, all eyes turn in one direction. Around the bend, one after another, the cattle cars begin rolling in. The train backs into the station, a conductor leans out, waves his hand, blows a whistle. The locomotive whistles back with a shrieking noise, puffs, the train rolls slowly alongside the ramp. In the tiny barred windows appear pale, wilted, exhausted human faces, terror-stricken women with tangled hair, unshaven men. They gaze at the station in silence. And then, suddenly, there is a stir inside the cars and a pounding against the wooden boards.

"Water! Air!"—weary, desperate cries.

60   Heads push through the windows, mouths gasp frantically for air. They draw a few breaths, then disappear; others come in their place, then also disappear. The cries and moans grow louder.

A man in a green uniform covered with more glitter than any of the others jerks his head impatiently, his lips twist in annoyance. He inhales deeply, then with a rapid gesture throws his cigarette away and signals to the guard. The guard removes the automatic from his shoulder, aims, sends a series of shots along the train. All is quiet now. Meanwhile, the trucks have arrived, steps are being drawn up, and the Canada men stand ready at their posts by the train doors. The S.S. officer with the briefcase raises his hand.

"Whoever takes gold, or anything at all besides food, will be shot for stealing Reich property. Understand? *Verstanden?*"

"*Jawohl!*" we answer eagerly.

"*Also los!* Begin!"

65   The bolts crack, the doors fall open. A wave of fresh air rushes inside the train. People . . . inhumanly crammed, buried under incredible heaps of luggage, suitcases, trunks, packages, crates, bundles of every description (everything that had been their past and was to start their future). Monstrously squeezed together, they have fainted from heat, suffocated, crushed one another. Now they push towards the opened doors, breathing like fish cast out on the sand.

"Attention! Out, and take your luggage with you! Take out everything. Pile all your stuff near the exits. Yes, your coats too. It is summer. March to the left. Understand?"

"Sir, what's going to happen to us?" They jump from the train on to the gravel, anxious, worn-out.

"Where are you people from?"

"Sosnowiec-Będzin. Sir, what's going to happen to us?" They repeat the question stubbornly, gazing into our tired eyes.

70   "I don't know. I don't understand Polish."

It is the camp law: people going to their death must be deceived to the very end. This is the only permissible form of charity. The heat is tremendous. The sun hangs directly over our heads, the white, hot sky quivers, the air vibrates, an occasional breeze feels like a sizzling blast from a furnace. Our lips are parched, the mouth fills with the salty taste of blood, the body is weak and heavy from lying in the sun. Water!

A huge, multicoloured wave of people loaded down with luggage pours from the train like a blind, mad river trying to find a new bed. But before they have a chance to recover, before they can draw a breath of fresh air and look at the sky, bundles are snatched from their hands, coats ripped off their backs, their purses and umbrellas taken away.

"But please, sir, it's for the sun, I cannot . . ."

"*Verboten!*" one of us barks through clenched teeth. There is an S.S. man standing behind your back, calm, efficient, watchful.

75   "*Meine Herrschaften,* this way, ladies and gentlemen, try not to throw your things around, please. Show some goodwill," he says courteously, his restless hands playing with the slender whip.

"Of course, of course," they answer as they pass, and now they walk alongside the train somewhat more cheerfully. A woman reaches down quickly to pick up her handbag. The whip flies, the woman screams, stumbles, and falls under the feet of the surging crowd. Behind her, a child cries in a thin little voice "Mamele!"—a very small girl with tangled black curls.

The heaps grow. Suitcases, bundles, blankets, coats, handbags that open as they fall, spilling coins, gold, watches; mountains of bread pile up at the exits, heaps of marmalade, jams, masses of meat, sausages; sugar spills on the gravel. Trucks, loaded with people, start up with a deafening roar and drive off amidst the wailing and screaming of the women separated from their children, and the stupefied silence of the men left behind. They are the ones who had been ordered to step to the right—the healthy and the young who will go to the camp. In the end, they too will not escape death, but first they must work.

Trucks leave and return, without interruption, as on a monstrous conveyor belt. A Red Cross van drives back and forth, back and forth, incessantly: it transports the gas that will kill these people. The enormous cross on the hood, red as blood, seems to dissolve in the sun.

The Canada men at the trucks cannot stop for a single moment, even to catch their breath. They shove the people up the steps, pack them in tightly, sixty per truck, more or less. Near by stands a young, cleanshaven "gentleman," as S.S. officer with a notebook in his hand. For each departing truck he enters a mark; sixteen gone means one thousand people, more or less. The gentleman is calm, precise. No truck can leave without a signal from him, or a mark in his notebook: *Ordnung muss sein.* The marks swell into thousands, the thousands into whole transports, which afterwards we shall simply call "from Salonica," "from Strasbourg," "from Rotterdam." This one will be called "Sosnowiec-Będzin." The new prisoners from Sosnowiec-Będzin will receive serial numbers 131–2—thousand, of course, though afterwards we shall simply say 131–2, for short.

80   The transports swell into weeks, months, years. When the war is over, they will count up the marks in their notebooks—all four and a half million of them. The bloodiest battle of the war, the greatest victory of the strong, united Germany. *Ein Reich, ein Volk, ein Führer*—and four crematoria.

The train has been emptied. A thin, pock-marked S.S. man peers inside, shakes his head in disgust, and motions to our group, pointing his finger at the door.

"*Rein.* Clean it up!"

We climb inside. In the corners amid human excrement and abandoned wrist-watches lie squashed, trampled infants, naked little monsters with enormous heads and bloated bellies. We carry them out like chickens, holding several in each hand.

"Don't take them to the trucks, pass them on to the women," says the S.S. man, lighting a cigarette. His cigarette lighter is not working properly; he examines it carefully.

85   "Take them, for God's sake!" I explode as the women run from me in horror, covering their eyes.

The name of God sounds strangely pointless, since the women and the infants will go on the trucks, every one of them, without exception. We all know what this means, and we look at each other with hate and horror.

"What, you don't want to take them?" asks the pock-marked S.S. man with a note of surprise and reproach in his voice, and reaches for his revolver.

"You mustn't shoot, I'll carry them." A tall, grey-haired woman takes the little corpses out of my hands and for an instant gazes straight into my eyes.

"My poor boy," she whispers and smiles at me. Then she walks away, staggering along the path. I lean against the side of the train. I am terribly tired. Someone pulls at my sleeve.

90   "*En avant,* to the rails, come on!"

I look up, but the face swims before my eyes, dissolves, huge and transparent, melts into the motionless trees and the sea of people . . . I blink rapidly: Henri.

"Listen, Henri, are we good people?"

"That's stupid. Why do you ask?"

"You see, my friend, you see, I don't know why, but I am furious, simply furious with these people—furious because I must be here because of them. I feel no pity. I am not sorry they're going to the gas chamber. Damn them all! I could throw myself at them, beat them with my fists. It must be pathological, I just can't understand . . ."

95   "Ah, on the contrary, it is natural, predictable, calculated. The ramp exhausts you, you rebel—and the easiest way to relieve your hate is to turn against some-one weaker. Why, I'd even call it healthy. It's simple logic, *compris?*" He props him-self up comfortably against the heap of rails. "Look at the Greeks, they know how to make the best of it! They stuff their bellies with anything they find. One of them has just devoured a full jar of marmalade."

"Pigs! Tomorrow half of them will die of the shits."

"Pigs? You've been hungry."

"Pigs!" I repeat furiously. I close my eyes. The air is filled with ghastly cries, the earth trembles beneath me, I can feel sticky moisture on my eyelids. My throat is completely dry.

The morbid procession streams on and on—trucks growl like mad dogs. I shut my eyes tight, but I can still see corpses dragged from the train, trampled infants, cripples piled on top of the dead, wave after wave . . . freight cars roll in, the heaps of clothing, suitcases, and bundles grow, people climb out, look at the sun, take a few breaths, beg for water, get into the trucks, drive away. And again freight cars roll in, again people. . . . The scenes become confused in my mind— I am not sure if all of this is actually happening, or if I am dreaming. There is a humming inside my head; I feel that I must vomit.

100   Henri tugs at my arm.

"Don't sleep, we're off to load up the loot."

All the people are gone. In the distance, the last few trucks roll along the road in clouds of dust, the train has left, several S.S. officers promenade up and down the ramp. The silver glitters on their collars. Their boots shine, their red, beefy faces shine. Among them there is a woman—only now I realize she has been here all along—withered, flat-chested, bony, her thin, colourless hair pulled back and tied in a "Nordic" knot; her hands are in the pockets of her wide skirt. With a rat-like, resolute smile glued on her thin lips she sniffs around the corners of the ramp. She detests feminine beauty with the hatred of a woman who is her-self repulsive, and knows it. Yes, I have seen her many times before and I know her well: she is the commandant of the F.K.L. She has come to look over the new crop of women, for some of them, instead of going on the trucks, will go on foot—to the concentration camp. There our boys, the barbers from Zauna, will shave their heads and will have a good laugh at their "outside world" modesty.

We proceed to load the loot. We lift huge trunks, heave them on to the trucks. There they are arranged in stacks, packed tightly. Occasionally somebody slashes one open with a knife, for pleasure or in search of vodka and perfume. One of the crates falls open; suits, shirts, books drop out on the ground. . . . I pick up a small, heavy package. I unwrap it—gold, about two handfuls, bracelets, rings, brooches, diamonds. . . .

"Gib hier," an S.S. man says calmly, holding up his briefcase already full of gold and colorful foreign currency. He locks the case, hands it to an officer, takes another, an empty one, and stands by the next truck, waiting. The gold will go to the Reich.

105   It is hot, terribly hot. Our throats are dry, each word hurts. Anything for a sip of water! Faster, faster, so that it is over, so that we may rest. At last we are done, all the trucks have gone. Now we swiftly clean up the remaining dirt: there must be "no trace left of the *Schweinerei*." But just as the last truck disappears behind the trees and we walk, finally, to rest in the shade, a shrill whistle sounds around the bend. Slowly, terribly slowly, a train rolls in, the engine whistles back with a deafening shriek. Again weary, pale faces at the windows, flat as though cut out of paper, with huge, feverishly burning eyes. Already trucks are pulling up, already the composed gentleman with the notebook is at his post, and the S.S. men emerge from the commissary carrying briefcases for the gold and money. We unseal the train doors.

It is impossible to control oneself any longer. Brutally we tear suitcases from their hands, impatiently pull off their coats. Go on, go on, vanish! They go, they vanish. Men, women, children. Some of them know.

Here is a woman—she walks quickly, but tries to appear calm. A small child with a pink cherub's face runs after her and, unable to keep up, stretches out his little arms and cries: "Mama! Mama!"

"Pick up your child, woman!"

"It's not mine, sir, not mine!" she shouts hysterically and runs on, covering her face with her hands. She wants to hide, she wants to reach those who will not ride the trucks, those who will go on foot, those who will stay alive. She is young, healthy, good-looking, she wants to live.

110   But the child runs after her, wailing loudly: "Mama, mama, don't leave me!"

"It's not mine, not mine, no!"

Andrei, a sailor from Sevastopol, grabs hold of her. His eyes are glassy from vodka and the heat. With one powerful blow he knocks her off her feet, then, as she falls, takes her by the hair and pulls her up again. His face twitches with rage.

"Ah, you bloody Jewess! So you're running from your own child! I'll show you, you whore!" His huge hand chokes her, he lifts her in the air and heaves her on to the truck like a heavy sack of grain.

"Here! And take this with you, bitch!" and he throws the child at her feet.

115   "*Gut gemacht,* good work. That's the way to deal with degenerate mothers," says the S.S. man standing at the foot of the truck. *"Gut, gut, Russki."*

"Shut your mouth," growls Andrei through clenched teeth, and walks away. From under a pile of rags he pulls out a canteen, unscrews the cork, takes a few deep swallows, passes it to me. The strong vodka burns the throat. My head swims, my legs are shaky, again I feel like throwing up.

And suddenly, above the teeming crowd pushing forward like a river driven by an unseen power, a girl appears. She descends lightly from the train, hops on to the gravel, looks around inquiringly, as if somewhat surprised. Her soft, blonde hair has fallen on her shoulders in a torrent, she throws it back impatiently. With a natural gesture she runs her hands down her blouse, casually straightens her skirt. She stands like this for an instant, gazing at the crowd, then turns and with a gliding look examines our faces, as though searching for someone. Unknowingly, I continue to stare at her, until our eyes meet.

"Listen, tell me, where are they taking us?"

I look at her without saying a word. Here, standing before me, is a girl, a girl with enchanting blonde hair, with beautiful breasts, wearing a little cotton blouse, a girl with a wise, mature look in her eyes. Here she stands, gazing straight into my face, waiting. And over there is the gas chamber: communal death, disgusting and ugly. And over in the other direction is the concentration camp: the shaved head, the heavy Soviet trousers in sweltering heat, the sickening, stale odour of dirty, damp female bodies, the animal hunger, the inhuman labor, and later the same gas chamber, only an even more hideous, more terrible death. . . .

120   Why did she bring it? I think to myself, noticing a lovely gold watch on her delicate wrist. They'll take it away from her anyway.

"Listen, tell me," she repeats.

I remain silent. Her lips tighten.

"I know," she says with a shade of proud contempt in her voice, tossing her head. She walks off resolutely in the direction of the trucks. Someone tries to stop her; she boldly pushes him aside and runs up the steps. In the distance I can only catch a glimpse of her blonde hair flying in the breeze.

I go back inside the train; I carry out dead infants; I unload luggage. I touch corpses, but I cannot overcome the mounting, uncontrollable terror. I try to escape from the corpses, but they are everywhere: lined up on the gravel, on the cement edge of the ramp, inside the cattle cars. Babies, hideous naked women, men twisted by convulsions. I run off as far as I can go, but immediately a whip slashes across my back. Out of the corner of my eye I see an S.S. man, swearing profusely. I stagger forward and run, lose myself in the Canada group. Now, at last, I can once more rest against the stack of rails. The sun has leaned low over the horizon and illuminates the ramp with a reddish glow; the shadows of the trees have become elongated, ghostlike. In the silence that settles over nature at this time of day, the human cries seem to rise all the way to the sky.

125   Only from this distance does one have a full view of the inferno on the teeming ramp. I see a pair of human beings who have fallen to the ground locked in a last desperate embrace. The man has dug his fingers into the woman's flesh and has caught her clothing with his teeth. She screams hysterically, swears, cries, until at last a large boot comes down over her throat and she is silent. They are pulled apart and dragged like cattle to the truck. I see four Canada men lugging a corpse: a huge, swollen female corpse. Cursing, dripping wet from the strain, they kick out of their way some stray children who have been running all over the ramp, howling like dogs. The men pick them up by the collars, heads, arms, and toss them inside the trucks, on top of the heaps. The four men have trouble lifting the fat corpse on to the car, they call others for help, and all together they hoist up the mound of meat. Big, swollen, puffed-up corpses are being collected from all over the ramp; on top of them are piled the invalids, the smothered, the sick, the unconscious. The heap seethes, howls, groans. The driver starts the motor, the truck begins rolling.

"Halt! Halt!" an S.S. man yells after them. "Stop, damn you!"

They are dragging to the truck an old man wearing tails and a band around his arm. His head knocks against the gravel and pavement; he moans and wails in an uninterrupted monotone: *"Ich will mit dem Herrn Kommandanten sprechen*—I wish to speak with the commandant . . ."* With senile stubbornness he keeps repeating these words all the way. Thrown on the truck, trampled by others, choked, he still wails: *"Ich will mit dem . . ."*

"Look here, old man!" a young S.S. man calls, laughing jovially. "In half an hour you'll be talking with the top commandant! Only don't forget to greet him with a *Heil Hitler!*"

Several other men are carrying a small girl with only one leg. They hold her by the arms and the one leg. Tears are running down her face and she whispers faintly: "Sir, it hurts, it hurts . . ." They throw her on the truck on top of the corpses. She will burn alive along with them.

130   The evening has come, cool and clear. The stars are out. We lie against the rails. It is incredibly quiet. Anaemic bulbs hang from the top of the high lamp-posts; beyond the circle of light stretches an impenetrable darkness. Just one step, and a man could vanish for ever. But the guards are watching, their automatics ready.

"Did you get the shoes?" asks Henri.

"No."

"Why?"

"My God, man, I am finished, absolutely finished!"

135   "So soon? After only two transports? Just look at me, I . . . since Christmas, at least a million people have passed through my hands. The worst of all are the transports from around Paris—one is always bumping into friends."

"And what do you say to them?"

"That first they will have a bath, and later we'll meet at the camp. What would you say?"

I do not answer. We drink coffee with vodka; somebody opens a tin of cocoa and mixes it with sugar. We scoop it up by the handful, the cocoa sticks to the lips. Again coffee, again vodka.

"Henri, what are we waiting for?"

140   "There'll be another transport."

"I'm not going to unload it! I can't take any more."

"So, it's got you down? Canada is nice, eh?" Henri grins indulgently and disappears into the darkness. In a moment he is back again.

"All right. Just sit here quietly and don't let an S.S. man see you. I'll try to find you your shoes."

"Just leave me alone. Never mind the shoes." I want to sleep. It is very late.

145   Another whistle, another transport. Freight cars emerge out of the darkness, pass under the lamp-posts, and again vanish in the night. The ramp is small, but the circle of lights is smaller. The unloading will have to be done gradually. Somewhere the trucks are growling. They back up against the steps, black, ghost-like, their searchlights flash across the trees. *Wasser! Luft!* The same all over again, like a late showing of the same film: a volley of shots, the train falls silent. Only this time a little girl pushes herself halfway through the small window and, losing her balance, falls out on to the gravel. Stunned, she lies still for a moment,

then stands up and begins walking around in a circle, faster and faster, waving her rigid arms in the air, breathing loudly and spasmodically, whining in a faint voice. Her mind has given way in the inferno inside the train. The whining is hard on the nerves: an S.S. man approaches calmly, his heavy boot strikes between her shoulders. She falls. Holding her down with his foot, he draws his revolver, fires once, then again. She remains face down, kicking the gravel with her feet, until she stiffens. They proceed to unseal the train.

I am back on the ramp, standing by the doors. A warm, sickening smell gushes from inside. The mountain of people filling the car almost halfway up to the ceiling is motionless, horribly tangled, but still steaming.

"Ausladen!" comes the command. An S.S. man steps out from the darkness. Across his chest hangs a portable searchlight. He throws a stream of light inside.

"Why are you standing about like sheep? Start unloading!" His whip flies and falls across our backs. I seize a corpse by the hand; the fingers close tightly around mine. I pull back with a shriek and stagger away. My heart pounds, jumps up to my throat. I can no longer control the nausea. Hunched under the train I begin to vomit. Then, like a drunk, I weave over to the stack of rails.

I lie against the cool, kind metal and dream about returning to the camp, about my bunk, on which there is no mattress, about sleep among comrades who are not going to the gas tonight. Suddenly I see the camp as a haven of peace. It is true, others may be dying, but one is somehow still alive, one has enough food, enough strength to work. . . .

150   The lights on the ramp flicker with a spectral glow, the wave of people—feverish, agitated, stupefied people—flows on and on, endlessly. They think that now they will have to face a new life in the camp, and they prepare themselves emotionally for the hard struggle ahead. They do not know that in just a few moments they will die, that the gold, money, and diamonds which they have so prudently hidden in their clothing and on their bodies are now useless to them. Experienced professionals will probe into every recess of their flesh, will pull the gold from under the tongue and the diamonds from the uterus and the colon. They will rip out gold teeth. In tightly sealed crates they will ship them to Berlin.

The S.S. men's black figures move about, dignified, businesslike. The gentleman with the notebook puts down his final marks, rounds out the figures: fifteen thousand.

Many, very many, trucks have been driven to the crematoria today.

It is almost over. The dead are being cleared off the ramp and piled into the last truck. The Canada men, weighed down under a load of bread, marmalade, and sugar, and smelling of perfume and fresh linen, line up to go. For several days the entire camp will live off this transport. For several days the entire camp will talk about "Sosnowiec-Będzin." "Sosnowiec-Będzin" was a good, rich transport.

The stars are already beginning to pale as we walk back to the camp. The sky grows translucent and opens high above our heads—it is getting light.

155   Great columns of smoke rise from the crematoria and merge up above into a huge black river which very slowly floats across the sky over Birkenau and disappears beyond the forests in the direction of Trzebinia. The "Sosnowiec-Będzin" transport is already burning.

We pass a heavily armed S.S. detachment on its way to change guard. The men march briskly, in step, shoulder to shoulder, one mass, one will.

"Und morgen die ganze Welt . . ." they sing at the top of their lungs.

"Rechts ran! To the right march!" snaps a command from up front. We move out of their way.

LEVELS OF READING

Summary:

Pay attention to the **literal** meaning of the text. Briefly describe the narrative of Tadeusz Borowski's "This Way for the Gas, Ladies and Gentlemen." Who tells the story? Where is the story set? Why is the setting especially important? Concentrate on the highlights; avoid too much detail when summarizing. Again, drawing a simple outline of the main points of the text will help you better analyze the text at other levels of interpretation.

Analysis:

Find what you believe is **symbolic** in this text. What is the symbolic significance of the delousing at the beginning of the story? Why is the safest part of the camp named Canada? Explain the symbolic significance of the SS men, "bemedalled, glittering with brass, beefy men with highly polished boots and shiny, brutal faces." With the help of the background material provided about Tadeusz Borowski and his world, make an argument about this story, and include the mention of the more **figurative** aspects of the text when making points in defense of your argument.

Und . . . Welt: "And tomorrow the whole world . . ."

Application:

Apply Hannah Arendt's theory concerning totalitarianism to this story. Outline an argument you wish to make about this literary text using Arendt's theory to help you explain what some part of the story may mean. The "part" of the text you choose to analyze may include any of the following: a character, a setting, a symbol or symbols, an important change, a motivation, a goal, a result. Consider the following as possibilities, but explore other original interpretations too:

- Think about the ways in which Arendt describes **terror** and its uses in totalitarian governments. Find examples of "terror" as Arendt describes it, in Borowski's story. Does terror function at Birkenau the way Arendt claims it does?
- Think about the ways in which **motion** and **action**, in Arendt's sense, function in the totalitarian government at Birkenau. Does terror prevent motion? Does it prevent action? How do motion and action differ?
- What **ideology** is behind the creation of Birkenau? What false premise stated by Arendt in her essay are Birkenau's "conclusions" based upon?
- Is the "government" of Birkenau "**totalitarian**" in Arendt's sense of the word? If so, how so? Find examples from the story to support your theory.
- Do you see any examples of totalitarian "lawfulness" in Borowski's story? Where? What significance has this "lawfulness" for the inmates of Birkenau?
- What –ism forms the basis for the construction of Birkenau? Is there anything "scientific" about it? Is there anything "scientific" in what follows from the –ism?
- Can you find any or all of the three "specifically totalitarian elements peculiar to all ideological thinking" in "This Way for the Gas, Ladies and Gentlemen"?

Start Your Own Argument:

Arendt's essay, as stated earlier, is at least partly an emotional—though logically constructed—response to the aftermath of World War II. Is her warning still to be heeded today? Has the threat of totalitarian government been eclipsed by yet other "novel" forms of government?

MARK LEVINE

Mark Levine (1919–) was born into a family of six children and grew up in Deblin, Poland. As an adult, he spent a period in Warsaw but fled to Russia during World War II. At the end of the war, he settled for a time in a Displaced Persons camp for Jewish survivors of the Holocaust in Landsberg, Germany. He eventually emigrated to Palestine in 1948. After ten years in Israel, he and his family moved to the United States, where he worked as a claims examiner for the International Ladies Garment Workers Union and graduated from Queens College, CUNY.

He currently lives and writes in Queens, New York.

The following autobiographical essay is a reminiscence of childhood. In it, the author looks back at one episode in his life, which occurred in a small Polish village in 1924 or '25, when he was five or six years old.

LOST ON A SATURDAY
Mark Levine

There was a little town, or call it a village, or even better, call it a "shtetl." You couldn't find it on any map, but it really did exist near the junction of two rivers, lazily floating from the Carpathian Mountains down to the Baltic Sea.

On one of those Saturday afternoons when everything and everybody was enveloped in a kind of blissful quietness, Moyshele was bored. . . . There was nothing to do. He couldn't go out to play with the "other" boys. He couldn't run barefoot, whistle, play marbles, or do anything a boy likes to do. It was "shabbos." Nobody told him not to do all those things, but he knew that he was not supposed to do what the other kids did. He really did not understand why, but he knew it.

Then father came to the rescue. After his traditional afternoon nap on Saturdays, dressed in his Saturday best, he said to Moyshele, "Let's go," and they took off to the "shtible." This was one place where the boy liked to go.

The shtible was a place where adult males went to pray. But it was also a place where one met his neighbors or friends and listened to the latest news about what was happening in the wide world or just anything that people liked to talk about—such as who married off another daughter, or who became a father of a fifth or sixth child, or who got sick and subsequently recuperated without seeing the only doctor in town. They believed that if God wanted you to get well, you didn't need a doctor's help.

5   The shtible was on the upper floor of an old, dilapidated building, though the room where all the fathers and the other men assembled to pray was neat and clean. The walls were painted many years ago by an unknown artist, depicting biblical characters and all kinds of exotic animals and trees. In Moyshele's imagination, the scenery on the walls looked like a big garden where Moses lived before he led his people through the desert on their way to the "Promised Land."

To reach that prayer room one had to climb one flight of stairs that creaked and swayed sideways, creating fear that the steps may collapse any minute. But holding on to his father's strong arm, Moyshele was in good spirits and well protected.

Reprinted by permission of Mark Levine

There were other fathers with little boys. While the adults were busy greeting and talking to each other, the kids were playing a game of telling stories. Each of them, when it came his turn, had to tell his story about something that happened to him.

As young and little as these boys were, their imaginations carried them way beyond their age. There was always one who managed to tell something that was absolutely unbelievable. So the rest would call him a big liar, but they really didn't mind because it was a good story. Moyshele's turn to tell the story he had in his mind did not come, so he lost interest and disappointedly sat down on those creaking stairs, where he eventually fell asleep.

Rays of the setting sun on the horizon added beautifully to the approaching end of the late Sabbath afternoon. It was getting darker by the minute, and the fathers with their boys, one by one, were leaving for home.

10 Moyshele was left behind unnoticed by the adults and by his own father, who was sure that his little boy went home by himself. They all left. Soon father arrived home, where Moyshele's mother was setting the table for the traditional meal to celebrate the end of the last week and arrival of the new one. But suddenly the whole family realized that Moyshele was missing. . . . Everybody in the house was asking the same question: "Where is Moyshele; where is Moyshele?" It seemed that the only words they could utter were: "Where is Moyshele?" It was like the whole world was coming to an end. In no time word spread in the shtetl that the boy had got lost.

By now it was already pitch dark outside. The whole community was in an uproar over what had happened to that child. Who knows, he could have lost his way winding up in a neighboring village or, God forbid, kidnapped by gypsies or fallen into a ravine . . . or something even worse than that. . . .

The more courageous younger men decided not to waste time, but to go and search for the boy. Those carrying lanterns were leading the way. They looked everywhere possible, hoping to find him: in narrow alleys, abandoned old houses, places where kids would usually play, but to no avail.

In the meantime, Moyshele was sound asleep on the creaking stairs. He may have been dreaming of playing with other kids on the green meadow not far from the flour mill, or sitting on one of those two riverbanks with a fishing rod, hoping to catch something. . . . There were so many nice dreams to dream. He could have dreamed about being in heaven with good angels. Who knows? Under the roof of a prayer house, one could dream about the most pleasant and desirable things.

The volunteers of the search party almost ran out of ideas where to look for the boy. Then one wised up and asked: "Why don't we go to the shtible where he was last with his father?" And suddenly, all those good Samaritans at once agreed and were yelling, "Yeah, Yankel is right, let's go to the shtible." It is interesting to note that in that shtetl everybody thought that Yankel was not the smartest guy. While they were approaching the shtible Moyshele was not asleep anymore. At first he did not realize where he was. But gradually, he started to sort out the events of that extraordinary day in his life. It didn't cross his mind that he was lost, especially in a house of prayer. In a house of prayer you are under a constant watch of the Ruler of the whole world, so nothing bad can happen to you. He even considered a short prayer in his present situation; he had been told that praying hard when wishing for something helps a lot. He was very skeptical about that because there were many times he was praying for something he really, really wanted, but he never got it. It is very easy to lose faith when wishful thinking does not come true. Meanwhile, the good Samaritans came closer and closer to where Moyshele was "philosophizing" about the power of prayer. Then he heard some noise coming from the courtyard that sounded like human voices.

15   Suddenly, a faint light in the darkness pierced through the chinks in the wooden wall of the staircase. Moyshele's heart started to pound faster and faster. When those good people came very close, Moyshele, with his clenched little fists, started to bang on the wall, screaming, "I am here; it's me, Moyshele! I am not lost; I am here!" Then he heard the sweetest sound—his father's voice—saying loudly, "Moyshele, you're not lost; you are not lost anymore. We found you."

While the good Samaritans were congratulating each other with the great success of the search, Yankel ran to the beadle of the shtible for the key to open the door down the stairs. Finally in the arms of his Papa, Moyshele heard someone saying: "Now the boy is safe, and saving one little boy is like saving all little boys in the world. . . ."

LEVELS OF READING

Summary:

Pay attention to the **literal** meaning of the text. Briefly describe the narrative of Mark Levine's "Lost on a Saturday." Who tells the story? Where is the story set? Why is the setting especially important? Concentrate on the highlights; avoid too much detail when summarizing. Again, drawing a simple outline of the main points of the text will help you better analyze the text at other levels of interpretation.

Analysis:

Find what you believe is **symbolic** in this text. What is the difference between a "little town" and a "shtetl"? Why is that difference significant? What do the pictures painted on the walls of the shtible symbolize? Why is storytelling so important to this group? With the help of the background material provided about Mark Levine and his world, make an argument about this story, and include the mention of the more **figurative** aspects of the text when making points in defense of your argument.

Application:

Apply Hannah Arendt's theory concerning totalitarianism to this autobiographical story. Outline an argument you wish to make about this literary text using Arendt's theory to help you explain what some part of the story may mean. The "part" of the text you choose to analyze may include any of the following: a character, a setting, a symbol or symbols, an important change, a motivation, a goal, a result. Consider the following as possibilities, but explore other original interpretations too:

- In the shtetl of 1924, at "the junction of two rivers, lazily flowing from the Carpathian Mountains," is there any sign of what is to come for Moyshele and his family? What **ideology** frames Moyshele's future?
- Is the shtible only a place to pray? Is there anything "political" about it?
- Can the "dilapidation" of the shtible be related in any way to the political climate in Poland in 1924?
- Find Deblin and Birkenau on a map. What is significant about their locations?

- What does the final line of Mark Levine's narrative foreshadow? How do the coming events underscore again Hannah Arendt's assumed relationship between **ideology** and **terror**?

Start Your Own Argument:

Arendt's essay, as stated above, is at least partly an emotional—though logically constructed—response to the aftermath of World War II. Is her warning still to be heeded today? Has the threat of totalitarian government been eclipsed by yet other "novel" forms of government?